MULTIWAY CONTINGENCY TABLES ANALYSIS
for the
SOCIAL SCIENCES

THOMAS D. WICKENS

University of California, Los Angeles

LAWRENCE ERLBAUM ASSOCIATES, PUBLISHERS
1989   Hillsdale, New Jersey   Hove and London

Lawrence Erlbaum Associates, Inc., Publishers
365 Broadway
Hillsdale, New Jersey 07642

Library of Congress Cataloging-in-Publication Data

Wickens, Thomas D.
   Multiway contingency tables analysis for the social sciences / Thomas D. Wickens.
      p.   cm.
   Bibliography: p.
   Includes indexes.
   ISBN 0-8058-0377-7 : $24.95. — ISBN 0-8058-0378-5 (pbk.)
   1. Social sciences—Statistical methods. 2. Contingency tables.
3. Mathematical statistics. I. Title.
HA29.W5134   1989
300'.01'51—dc20   89-34824
                                                              CIP

Printed in the United States of America
10 9 8 7 6 5 4 3 2

To Lucia

Contents

Preface

The analysis of frequency data—those that come from counting things—is a topic that is often shorted in conventional statistics courses. These data are usually examined with a conventional chi-square test of contingency in a two-way table. Since this test does not require the assumption of a normal distribution, it is often viewed as a "nonparametric" procedure, which has given the impression that it is somehow inferior to "parametric" procedures such as the analysis of variance. This impression is incorrect. Counted data cannot be deemed superior or inferior on statistical grounds. If one has counted things, then counts are what one must analyze. One needs statistical procedures that are appropriate to their characteristics.

Counted data are very common in the social sciences. An observation provides a classification, not a numerical score. Examples of such data abound: the response of a person to a survey question is a classification, as is the correctness or incorrectness of the solution to a problem or the recall or nonrecall of a word. One should not force these data into the incorrect structure of a continuous variable.

The impression that the frequency-table methods are weak has developed in part because procedures that accommodate elaborate designs have not been readily available. In this respect, the simplicity of the commonly used procedures has compared poorly to the richness of the analysis of variance or of multiple regression. This situation has changed in the past two decades, however. A great many new procedures have been developed, both for two-way frequency tables and for multi-dimensional classifications. These provide the same degree of richness that has long been available to the treatment of continuous data. Many of the new procedures are computationally expensive; their development, and certainly their application, has waited for the availability of cheap computing power.

The present book introduces the frequency-table methods to researchers in psychology and the social sciences. It is designed for use both by researchers as a handbook of the techniques and as a text for students at the upper undergraduate and graduate levels. It does not presuppose an extensive background in statistics, although I do assume that the reader is familiar with the basic concepts of data analysis and hypothesis testing, such as are provided by a good introductory course. Of course, statistics is very much a domain in which the more one knows, the more one can take from study. The reader who comes to this material with an understanding of the linear models of multiple regression and the analysis of variance will find many stimulating parallels. In any case, a mathematical background beyond college algebra is unnecessary. I have drawn on concepts from calculus in a few places where they simplify explanation, but those developments can be skimmed without loss to the larger understanding.

Throughout this book, I have used mathematical formalism to display relationships as equations. Readers who find a formula to be an obstacle should recognize that they are used in three ways, which should be approached somewhat differently. The most important equations are those that show, in compact symbolic form, the relationship between important conceptual entities. The various log-linear models for data are the most prominent examples here (e.g., the series of models in Equations 3.7, 3.14, 3.18, 3.19, and 3.22). The reader should try to understand what these equations represent and to translate their formal structure into an understanding of the relationships that they describe. After some practice, these equations are the most compact and convenient way to represent the relationships. The second class of equations are those that tell how a particular quantity is calculated. The equations that give the standard errors of the association coefficients in Chapter 9 are good examples of this type (e.g., Equation 9.50). Frequently there is little point in worrying about the exact form of these equations: the most important thing is to know that they exist and that they can be called upon if needed. Finally, equations are often used to show the steps in a longer derivation (e.g., the sequence leading from Equation 2.25 to Equation 2.26). Here the intermediate steps per se are frequently unimportant; what is important is the flow of the argument. One should avoid bogging down in the details, particularly on a first reading. Start by trying to understand where the derivation is going and what it will show.

I have developed this book over several years of teaching this material to graduate students at UCLA. If my treatment is helpful, it owes much to the help of these students. They have asked me for methods to analyze complicated sets of real data, have forced me to make clear explanations of concepts that I discovered I did not understand as well as I thought I did, and have pointed out many errors in the earlier drafts of this book. To these students, and to my other colleagues who have helped me, my thanks. If I do not include personal acknowledgments, it is because such a list would be too long. Many of you will recognize your contributions. Unfortunately, an informal multiple-recapture analysis (see Section 10.5) of the number of errors, typographical and otherwise, that have already been found and corrected tells me with certainty that there are others yet unobserved. These are only my responsibility. Naturally, I would value any further suggestions and thoughts from my readers.

A final note: I was introduced to the analysis of multivariate frequency tables through reading the book by Bishop, Fienberg, and Holland (1975) during the break between fall and winter quarters several years ago. I remember clearly my growing enthusiasm as I realized that these techniques could answer some statistical problems that I had previously been unable to solve and could bring to the analysis of frequency tables the type of elegance I had thought applied only to the analysis of variance. I hope that this book is able to convey this range of possibilities to my readers and that some of you will share my excitement and feeling of discovery.

Thomas D. Wickens

1 Introduction

The data collected in psychological or other social-science investigations often take the form of classifications. An animal learns to solve a problem or fails to learn it; a person is male or is female, does or does not buy a particular product, votes for one or another group of candidates; a dim light is seen or is not noticed; a word that has been studied is or is not recalled on a later test, that word is confused with one or another different word; and so on. In these examples the particular item of interest—the animal, the person, or the word—is assigned to exactly one of a set of alternatives. This book considers ways in which the resulting data are analyzed.

1.1. THE ANALYSIS OF CATEGORICAL DATA

The essential characteristic of these examples is that a collection of entities are classified, each placed into exactly one of a small set of classes. Most generally, these classes are unordered. For example, there is no intrinsic reason, except perhaps lexicographic order, to list the category female either before or after the category male. In the nomenclature of measurement theory, the categories form a nominal scale, rather than any of the higher types of scale such as ordinal, interval, or ratio. Ordered categories are possible, of course; families, say, could be classified as having zero, one, two, or more than 2 children, creating an ordered set of four categories. Throughout most of this book—Chapter 13 is the exception—ordering of this type, while permissible, is not essential. The procedures to be discussed apply to both ordered and unordered categories. The fundamental variable is the classification scheme and the fundamental data are the numbers of observations classified into each category.

If the items are classified by a single system of categories, a complicated analysis is unnecessary. At most, one can ask whether some categories are more likely than others and by how much, or whether the pattern approximates some particular distribution. But any interesting entity can be classified in several ways simultaneously. The result is a multidimensional table. For example, one might classify people who are polled in an opinion survey both as to where they live and as to their opinion. If a region is divided into 4 areas and there are 3 possible answers to the opinion question, then each respondent falls into one of 12 cells, conceptually structured as a 4×3 table. Frequencies in this table constitute the data from that part of the poll.

With a two-way classification of this sort, one can ask whether there is an association between the two classification schemes and whether certain cells are unusually rare or unusually frequent. One might ask, for example, whether respondents from a particular region are more than usually likely to hold a particular opinion. In introductory statistics, one learns to analyze data of this type using a procedure probably called a "chi-square test" for independence or for homogeneity. This test is an appropriate choice, and is the starting point for the methods in this book.

Just as one can look at two classifications simultaneously in a two-way table, one can extend the analysis to more than two classifications. The respondents in the poll can be classified by sex as well as region and opinion, to make a $4 \times 2 \times 3$ table. Analyzing this multiway table allows more complicated relationships to be revealed.

At first glance, it seems easy to reduce a multiway table to several two-way tables. The three-way region-by-sex-by-opinion table can be collapsed into three two-way tables relating region to sex, region to opinion, and sex to opinion. This strategy seems to obviate the need for any higher-order analysis scheme. However, this simple procedure is not satisfactory. For one thing, where many attributes are involved, the two-way tables proliferate unmercifully. With data classified along 3 attributes, only 3 tables are needed, but with 7 classification dimensions—not an unreasonable number—there are 21 two-way tables involving all the data, along with thousands of others that are obtained by holding some of the variables constant. Making sense of so many separate results is difficult.

Collapsing to two-way tables creates more serious problems. Many important hypotheses cannot be expressed using two-way tables alone. With continuous data, hypotheses that concern interactions of variables must be tested by a multiway analysis of variance rather than by a set of t-tests. Similarly, with frequency tables, many hypotheses involve the interaction of classifications. Because they ignore these higher-order associations, two-factor tests can be deceptive, misleading, or simply wrong. Interesting multifactor associations just cannot be expressed in two-factor form. Even when the data can ultimately be collapsed to a two-way test, the pattern of associations should be considered in its fuller form first.

All this is enough to demand a set of higher-order analysis techniques and an organized set of procedures to employ them.

Some parallels between the classification analysis methods and other common statistical procedures may be helpful. Most statistical tests concern the detection and measurement of associations among variables. For example, with t-tests or the analysis of variance, a set of classifications (the groups) is related to an ordered numerical dependent variable; in tests of correlation, two continuous variables are related to each other. If the data take the form of ranks, one can use one of several tests designed for the purpose: the so-called "nonparametric" tests such as the Mann-Whitney U-test, the Wilcoxon test, the rank correlation methods, and so on. These tests are the counterparts of the tests for independence in a two-way table. As more variables are added, the continuous-variable procedures are readily extended: the tests of differences among means becoming multifactor analyses of variance, while simple regression and correlation extend to multiple regression and correlation and to other forms of multivariate analysis. Multivariate versions of the nonparametric tests also exist, although they are less thoroughly developed. Much of this book concerns the analogous extension for frequency data.

It is tempting to adapt the continuous variable methods to the analysis of frequency data. One's first thought is to let numerical variables stand for categories, that is, to use some form of dummy coding. For example, one could code female subjects by 1 and males by 2, then analyze the data as if this two-level variable were truly continuous. With more than two levels, several such dummy variables can be used. As long as the categorically-classified variables are used as predictors of one or more continuous variables, this procedure is satisfactory. One obtains the analysis of variance in the guise of a regression model.† When all variables are discrete, however, these procedures do not work. One might still use the discrete variables as the dependent variable in something like a t-test, but this is not the proper analysis—it leads neither to the best nor to the most powerful tests. Both the analysis of variance and the comparable nonparametric tests are based on the assumption of a continuous distribution for the dependent variable. The two-level coding does not even approximate this continuity. Where there are three or more levels to the classification, coding by a single numerical

---

†For details, see any books about multiple regression and the analysis of variance. In the domain of psychology, Cohen & Cohen (1975) or Pedhazur (1982) are good sources for multiple regression and the connection to the analysis of variance; for standard analysis of variance theory, see Keppel (1982), Kirk (1982), Myers (1979) or Winer (1971). A good coverage of basic statistics can be found in Hays (1988), while Harris (1985) and Tatsuoka (1988) are useful for multivariate concepts. The reader may have other favorites. In what follows, these general references are not duplicated unless specific sections are cited.

variable breaks down altogether, for a numerical variable intrinsically orders its levels, while a categorical classification need not be ordered. A set of methods specifically directed at frequencies is needed.

Incidentally, it is inappropriate to think of the frequency-table methods as less powerful, but more robust, nonparametric alternatives to the analysis of variance or to multiple regression and correlation. As the next four chapters attempt to show, the character of frequency data demands its own set of hypotheses and procedures, which are different from those appropriate to continuous data. It is a matter of picking the right technique for the situation, not of stronger or weaker alternatives.

1.2. SOME PRINCIPLES OF DATA ANALYSIS

Because the study of statistics is a branch of probability theory, hence of mathematics, it is tempting to think of it as a completely exact discipline. Although this may be nearly the case for the mathematical branch of statistics, it is far from true for the analysis of real data. The decisions and choices that must be made transcend the purely mathematical aspects of the theory (or perhaps fall beneath them!). Much of the practical study of statistics is devoted to these non-mathematical aspects, a distribution reflected in this book. Indeed, were only computation important, a couple of chapters would suffice. The greatest difficulties lie in deciding how to use the methods and in making an appropriate choice among the many potential analysis strategies. In one way or another, most of this book concerns these choices. Hence, a discussion of some noncomputational principles of data analysis is a good place to start.

First, a fundamental principle: one cannot analyze a set of data without knowing what the data mean. Mathematical and statistical principles alone cannot create a meaningful analysis. For one thing, sensible questions come only from an understanding of what is being investigated. More deeply, the interpretation of any set of data depends on many nonstatistical decisions as well as on statistical ones. Some of these concern the precursors to the analysis, such as whether the observations satisfy the assumptions on which a statistical technique is based. Others concern the nature of the conclusions that can be drawn.

A nearly trivial example illustrates this point. Consider a table of numbers:

28	13
9	35

Without knowing anything more, one cannot analyze this table. Perhaps the numbers are only nominal designations (the numbers on the backs of athletic players are a favorite example), in which case they cannot be numerically compared at all. If the ordinal character of the numbers is meaningful (big numbers are more of something than small ones) and if the square layout of the table reflects a crossing of classifications, then one observes an association between the numbers in the rows and those in the columns: the larger numbers are in the upper left and in the lower right. Given the further information that these are frequencies and that they come from independent observations (something one may believe, but usually cannot test), then a statistical analysis (using the chi-square test) tells one that this association is large enough that it is unlikely to be accidental. However, there again one is stopped.

Now suppose that the table is the classification of 85 students from an experiment using two textbooks to teach a course, say one by Jones and one by Smith:

Final Examination Score

	Low	High
Jones	28	13
Smith	9	35

With this information, stronger conclusions are possible. The proportion of high-scoring students is greater for those who used Smith than for those who used Jones. One might now assert that the textbooks were causal in determining the performance, and so select Smith's text the next time the course is given. However, even this conclusion is based on information not contained in the numbers. If the students were randomly assigned to the textbook conditions, then such a conclusion may be warranted, but if the assignment was not random, it may be wrong. Suppose that the students were free to chose between the two texts, both on sale at the bookstore. Perhaps Smith's book is more attractive to the best students than Jones'. If so, no implication can be drawn concerning the best book for the entire class.

There is nothing special about this books-and-examination example; any other situation is the same. Two fundamental principles stand out:

• A meaningful statistical analysis cannot be performed without nonstatistical information.

• The more nonstatistical information that is available, the stronger the conclusions that can be drawn.

Put so baldly, these principles are obvious, but it is surprising how often they are overlooked.

A rough distinction can be made between two types of statistical analysis. Sometimes one comes to an investigation with a set of questions already prepared. The purpose of data analysis is to answer these questions. An analysis of this sort is called a *confirmatory analysis*. It is driven by the questions and, ideally, is very precise. In contrast, an *exploratory analysis* is directed by patterns in the data, without specific questions. Its progress is dictated by the data, rather than by a question; indeed, the expressions *data driven* and *question driven* can be used instead of *exploratory* and *confirmatory*. Without the planned questions of a confirmatory analysis, the results of an exploratory analysis are much weaker. A principal goal of statistical analysis is to separate real phenomena from accidental occurrences. Because one examines a much wider range of potential results in an exploratory analysis, one guards against accidents by asking that the evidence for each result be stronger than in a confirmatory analysis. Thus, it is not uncommon to find that a confirmatory analysis can answer a question but that an exploratory analysis can only raise that question for further study.

This idea is expressed by a third principle:

• A confirmatory analysis yields conclusions that are both stronger and more precise than those of an exploratory analysis.

This statement is really a corollary of the second principle, since the questions are a form of extrastatistical information that directs one's attention to certain aspects of the data. Many experiments have both confirmatory and exploratory phases, and it is usually advisable to separate the two parts in discussing the results.

When one has a particular question to answer, one is usually directed to an equally particular statistical technique to answer it. This directness is expressed in the final principle:

• A precisely formulated question gives rise to a specific statistical analysis. Weak questions give little direction.

Although these four principles do not dictate any particular statistical procedure, they permeate the broader choices that direct the overall analysis. As such, they are essential to the ideas discussed in any statistical text.

1.3. SOME STATISTICAL THEORY

The basic techniques of statistical analysis are probably familiar to the reader from introductory statistics courses. Nevertheless, a brief review may be valuable, if only to standardize terminology.

Real data usually show considerable variability. Responses differ, even under apparently identical conditions. The theory of inferential statistics formalizes this element of uncertainty. There is a *population* of entities—the subjects, observations, material, or whatever—that one wishes to investigate. The ultimate goal of the analysis is to draw conclusions about this population. If it were possible to observe all members of a population, one could directly measure what one wanted and there would be no need for statistical inference at all. However, exhaustive observation of a population is usually conceptually and practically impossible. Instead, one observes a subset of the population, known as a *sample*, and makes inferences based on its contents. Because the sample does not contain all members of the population, its properties differ somewhat from those of the population, and because different samples do not contain exactly the same members, their properties vary.

The distinction between population and sample quantities is important. The former are not directly observable, but are what one would like to know about; the latter can readily be seen, but are of less interest except inasmuch as they mirror the population. To portray this distinction here, Greek letters† stand for population parameters and Latin letters for sample quantities. There is one exception to this rule: when sample values are used explicitly to estimate a population value, the result is indicated by using the population symbol and placing a ˆ over it. For example, a population mean is denoted by the Greek letter μ (mu) and the sample mean that estimates μ is indicated by $\hat{\mu}$ (read "mu hat").

To make a link between the population and a sample, the nature of the population and of the sampling procedure must be described formally. To do so, one postulates a *statistical model* for the entities in the population. Typically, this model is a probability distribution that characterizes the variation among individuals. This distribution, together with some quantities known as *parameters* on which the distribution depends, describes the population. In classical statistics, the distribution is taken to be normal and the parameters are means, variances, correlation coefficients, and regression coefficients. For frequency models, the parameters are either probabilities or quantities closely related to them. Questions about a population are phrased in terms of its parameters.

The problem of inference now becomes one of finding out about the parameters of the model, based on the sample. Numerical quantities analogous to the parameters can be calculated in the sample and are known as *statistics*. Frequently a statistic is used to approximate a parameter; in this role it is called an *estimator* of that parameter. It is these estimators that are denoted by the hats. For example, the probability that a person can answer a particular question correctly is a parameter, potentially applying to some large population of people, while the proportion of a sample of people who answer it correctly is a statistic and is an estimate of that probability.

Because of the sample-to-sample variation, statistics (unlike parameters) are random variables. Their distribution is known as a *sampling distribution*. In real experiments, one does not collect many samples and empirically construct the sampling distribution of a statistic. Only a single sample is obtained. The form of

---

†To help get their names straight, a copy of the Greek alphabet is given in the table in Appendix A6.

the sampling distribution is inferred from the statistical model for the population and from the properties of the sampling operation. Except in a few specialized procedures, the sampling distributions are theoretical, not empirical, entities.

Consider some familiar examples. For real number scores, one often adopts the model of a normal distribution, which has two parameters, the mean μ and the variance σ^2. If a sample of N observations is drawn and its mean calculated, that sample mean is a statistic having a sampling distribution. As most elementary statistics books show, that distribution is itself normal with mean μ and variance σ^2/N. More to the point here is a population of two-valued events. Such events are known as *Bernoulli events*, and their two possible outcomes are often referred to as "success" and "failure." They are the simplest nontrivial probabilistic entity. The statistical model for a Bernoulli event has one parameter, π, that gives the probability of a success, essentially treating the event as if it were the flip of a biased coin. In a sample of N Bernoulli events, the total number of successes has a distribution over the integers from 0 to N. When the events are independent and have the same value of π, the total count has the well-known *binomial distribution*:

$$P(x \text{ successes}) = \frac{N!}{x!(N-x)!} \, \pi^x (1-\pi)^{N-x}$$

If x successes are observed in a sample, then π is estimated by the sample proportion, $\hat{\pi} = x/N$.

From here, two somewhat different approaches can be distinguished. The more direct is *model fitting*. To find out about the population, one seeks an adequate way to describe it. This description takes the form of a mathematical statement or *model* of the relevant aspects of the population. The relationships embodied in this model and the estimates of its parameters characterize the population. The other approach is *hypothesis testing*. If a specific question can be expressed as a hypothesis about a particular parameter, one constructs a statistical test directed at that parameter. Many of the tests covered in elementary statistics are of this form, and it is common for elementary texts to adopt a hypothesis-testing point of view almost exclusively.

For example, consider two groups of numerical scores. A model-fitting approach to these data would be to postulate a probabilistic model for the scores and to estimate its parameters. For a model, one might choose a normal distribution with means μ_1 and μ_2 for the two groups and common variance σ^2. One then estimates these three parameters using sample means and variances. From a pure model-fitting point of view, one would stop here. Hypothesis testing goes a bit further. One might consider the hypothesis that $\mu_1 = \mu_2$ and develop a test (the t-test would do) to determine whether the data are inconsistent with this hypothesis. The result is a decision to keep or to reject the hypothesis that $\mu_1 = \mu_2$.

Fitting a model and estimating its parameters are positive operations and are conceptually straightforward. One finds the model, records how well it fits, and considers its meaning. Hypothesis testing is more convoluted. Its fundamental logic is negative: to show that something is necessary, show that one is in trouble without it. The next section discusses this logic and its implementation in a statistical test.

Model fitting and hypothesis testing are not exclusive operations, but complement each other. When fitting a model, one often tests hypotheses based on it, while the process of hypothesis testing can be viewed as the comparison of two models. At times concern is with the meaning of a model that fits, at times with the interpretation of a tested hypothesis. When the emphasis is on the presence or absence of a particular effect, a hypothesis-testing mode of operation is called for; when one is trying to picture the collection of relationships in a set of data, model fitting is more appropriate. Particularly as one turns to more intricate sets of data, both procedures have their place and the best work needs them both.

1.4. HYPOTHESIS-TESTING LOGIC

At first glance, the way that one goes about hypothesis testing seems backwards, although its basis is actually quite sensible. Suppose that one wishes to show the presence of some property of the data, such as an association between two variables or a difference between two means. Rather than looking for this effect, one starts with a hypothesis that the effect is absent. This hypothesis is known as the *null hypothesis* and is symbolized by H_0. Typically, H_0 fixes the values of some parameters. From H_0 one constructs a theoretical description of the population, known as the *null-hypothesis model* (or *null model*). This null model is fit to the data. If it fits successfully, nothing has been lost by omitting the effect. If it fails to fit, then something about the missing part must have been necessary. One concludes that H_0 is false and that the effect of interest is essential.

A more complete description of the hypothesis-testing operation requires two models. The first is the null model just mentioned. The second is based on an *alternative hypothesis*, H_1, which expresses the presence of the effect one is studying. Thus, the *alternative-hypothesis model* (or *alternative model*) is just like the null model except that it allows an additional effect. The test compares how well these two models fit.

With two groups of numbers, one commonly tests for equality of means with a *t*-test. The null model here is a description of the scores as normally distributed, the two groups having identical means μ and variances σ^2. Under the alternative-hypothesis model, the means differ, group 1 being composed of normal scores with parameters μ_1 and σ^2; group 2 being similar, except for a potentially different mean μ_2. The parameters μ and σ^2 of the null model and μ_1, μ_2, and σ^2 of the alternative model are estimated and the fit of the two models is compared. If the alternative model agrees with the data much more closely than does the null model, then H_0 can be rejected. If both are reasonably satisfactory, the null model is retained, being the simpler of the two.

One must be careful in applying this procedure, for it only makes sense if the more general alternative is in reasonable agreement with the data. When both models are absurd, the difference in fit between them is of no help in making decisions about their parameters. Thus, in the test of means, if the assumption of normal distributions is badly violated, the test is contaminated. In this particular case, different pairs of null and alternative models exist in the realm of non-parametric statistics that allow related hypotheses about the center of the distribution to be tested.

To discriminate between H_0 and H_1, one calculates a numerical quantity that tends to have different values under the different hypotheses. Because it is calculated from a sample, this quantity is a statistic and has a sampling distribution. As an indication of its role in choosing between the hypotheses, it is known as a *test statistic*. With normal scores, the t-statistic, which directly depends on the difference between sample means, is used.

An effective test statistic has different sampling distributions under the null and alternative models. The top panel of Figure 1.1 shows such a distribution when H_0 is true; the bottom panel shows one of the many possibilities when it is false. Unless the evidence provided by the sample is so conclusive that statistical analysis is unnecessary, these distributions overlap and for certain values of the statistic there is uncertainty about which model is true. To decide between the two models, one constructs a *decision rule* that rejects the simpler null-hypothesis model whenever the observed data are improbable given that model. To create this rule, one first chooses a probability criterion or *significance level*, which determines what one deems an improbable result. This probability is denoted α and most commonly equals 0.05 (or 5%). From here there are two slightly different ways to proceed.

One procedure translates α into a *critical value* of the test statistic. This is a value C_α such that when H_0 is true there is a probability of α of obtaining a result that deviates as much or more than C_α in the direction in which H_1 lies. In Figure 1.1, the point C_α is chosen so that the area under the shaded part of the null distribution amounts to 5% of the total area. The decision rule follows from this value: if the test statistic exceeds C_α, then H_0 is rejected; if it is below C_α, then H_0 is retained.

The other approach to hypothesis testing leaves the decision rule in terms of the tail probabilities. The exact probability of a result at least as extreme as the observed result is calculated. If this value, known as the *descriptive level*, is less than α, then H_0 is rejected. The net effect of either method is the same; the difference mainly lies in where the comparison is made. In the first case the test statistic is compared to C_α, in the second the descriptive level is compared to α. The big practical difficulty with the descriptive-level method is that it requires the evaluation of areas in tails of distributions. Calculation of these probabilities

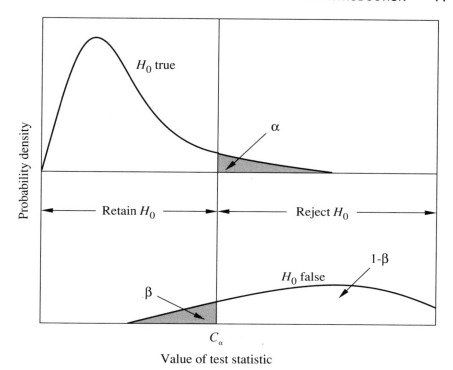

FIGURE 1.1.   Sampling distributions of a test statistic under the null hypothesis and under an alternative

is often laborious, so for hand work large tables are necessary. With the advent of computers, calculation is not an obstacle, and descriptive levels are often reported as part of a program's output and are readily compared with α. One should distinguish between these descriptive levels and the significance level on which the decision rule is based. The former refers to the data, the latter to the investigators standard of evidence. If one's computer program prints out "$p = 0.0113$" next to a result, one should not report this value as the "significance level" of the result. That quantity remains at the value adopted for the analysis, perhaps 0.05.

Figure 1.1 shows a test constructed in one tail of the distribution, known as a *one-tailed test*. Where alternative values lie on both sides of the null distribution, a *two-tailed test* is appropriate. In this test, a proportion $\alpha/2$ of the deviant results is excluded from each tail. The *t*-test of means is a typical example of a two-tailed test. The critical values are set at the $\alpha/2$ point of the distribution and single-tail descriptive levels are doubled to obtain their two-tailed values. In constructing the tests, one must distinguish between the number of tails used to examine the test statistic and the *directionality* of H_1, since a nondirectional H_1 sometimes leads to a one-tailed test. Most of the tests in this book are based on statistics' that measure goodness of fit. Small values of these statistics indicate agreement with H_0 and large values indicate disagreement. Thus, the tests are one-tailed, even though H_1 is omnidirectional and allows deviations of any type. A violation of H_0 in any direction leads to a bad fit and a to a big test-statistic value. The F-test in the analysis of variance is another example of a statistic that is tested in one tail of its sampling distribution, yet is responsive to discrepancies of any sort.

The significance criterion α is the conditional probability of one type of error, that of rejecting H_0 given that it is true. Such an error is called a *Type-I error*. A second way to make an error is to fail to reject H_0 when it is wrong. The conditional probability of this *Type-II error* is conventionally denoted by β, and is represented in the lower portion of Figure 1.1 by the shaded portion of the alternative distribution. A more optimistic measure of test performance than the error rate is the *power* of the test, defined as the conditional probability of rejecting H_0 given that a particular alternative is true. The power is the complement of the type-II error probability and equals $1 - \beta$. Finding β or the power requires specifying the particular form of the alternative distribution, which entails some assumptions beyond those needed to construct the test of H_0. A particular alternative parameter value is required. For example, for the t-test of normal scores, calculation of β involves postulating a particular difference $\mu_1 - \mu_2$, even when H_1 is the more general assertion that $\mu_1 \neq \mu_2$. The power is different for different values of $\mu_1 - \mu_2$: it is small when the difference is near 0 and near 1.0 when $|\mu_1 - \mu_2|$ is large. Note that α, β, and $1 - \beta$ are conditional probabilities that depend on the true state of the population. They cannot be interpreted as unconditional probabilities that a correct or an incorrect decision is made.

The decision procedure just described fixes the Type I error rate for a single test, or *testwise error rate*, to α. Most investigations involve more than a single test. For example, with four conditions one may want to look at the six comparisons between pairs of groups. Running multiple tests raises the problem of *simultaneous inference*. The difficulty is that when several tests are run, the probability of at least one error is generally greater than the error probability for any one test. The probability of one or more Type-I errors in a family of tests, given all the null hypotheses are true, is known as the *familywise error rate* and is denoted by α_F. It almost always exceeds the testwise rate, α. To prevent α_F from becoming too large, one sometimes decides to fix it instead of α. Since $\alpha \leq \alpha_F$, one must set a more stringent standard for the individual tests. Control of familywise error rates is not a serious problem when one is running a few tests of specific hypotheses, but is essential when many similar tests are run. It is more important in exploratory analysis than confirmatory analysis. One reason why the conclusions from an exploratory analysis are weaker than those from a confirmatory analysis is that the family of tests under consideration is much larger and forces the adoption of a more stringent criterion for significance.

There are many ways to control familywise error (Miller, 1981). Many are specific to particular testing situations. One procedure, based on a relationship known as the *Bonferroni inequality*, is both simple and widely applicable. Suppose that a family of K tests is run with Type-I error probabilities of $\alpha_1, \alpha_2, \ldots,$ and α_K. The Bonferroni inequality states that

$$\alpha_F \leq \alpha_1 + \alpha_2 + \ldots + \alpha_K \tag{1.1}$$

Using this inequality, one can ensure that the familywise error is no greater than some value α_C by picking the individual tests so that their Type-I error rates sum to no more than α_C. Usually the division is into equal parts, with the individual error set to $\alpha = \alpha_C/K$. For example, if 6 tests are to be run and one wishes to hold α_F to less than $\alpha_C = 0.1$, then one can run each test at the $\alpha = 0.1/6 = 0.0167$ level. Because the Bonferroni relationship is an inequality rather than an exact equation, the true α_F is somewhat less than the nominal α_C. The table Appendix A.2 shows a more extensive example of the consequences of a Bonferroni correction. This table gives Bonferroni-corrected critical values of the χ^2 (chi-squared) distribution, which is used for most tests in this book. For example, with $\alpha_F = 0.05$ and 2 degrees of freedom (a parameter of the χ^2 distribution), the uncorrected critical value ($K = 1$) is 5.99, the value corrected for $K = 2$ tests is 7.38, with $K = 5$ it is 9.21, and so forth.

Three limits to the conclusions drawn from a hypothesis test should be noted. First, there are usually forms of the alternative model that differ only infinitesimally from the null model. Since the differences among these hypotheses fall within the range of sampling uncertainty, it is impossible to prove H_0 true. For example, one can never establish that two means are exactly equal; they might differ by an amount that is too small to detect. In fact, it is virtually certain that some small deviation from H_0 is present in the population. Reflecting this, one speaks of *retaining H_0*, but not of *accepting* it. When one asserts that H_0 is true, one goes beyond a pure hypothesis test. Usually, one wants to say that if any important deviation from H_0 has been present, it would have been found. Ideally, this conclusion is buttressed by showing that the test has sufficient power to detect the smallest interesting effect.

The second limit arises because the decision criterion is based on the sampling distribution under H_0, not on that under H_1. Rejection of H_0 does not prove that H_1 is true. Both models could fit badly. As noted above, such an occurrence renders the whole hypothesis testing framework questionable. For similar reasons, retaining a model does not mean that there are no simpler models that provide equally satisfactory fits.

Finally, note that the distribution under H_0 depends on both H_0 and other untested characteristics of the sampling model. For example, most tests require that the members of the sample be independent of each other, but this assumption is not part of what differentiates H_0 from H_1. The test cannot be run without making these assumptions (here comes the first principle from Section 1.2), and retention or rejection of H_0 must be interpreted in light of how well the assumptions are satisfied. The character of the fit may be more closely related to the untested aspects of a model than to parts that are under test. Very often further testing is necessary.

By hypothesis-testing standards, the model-fitting approach is weak. If one fits a model to a set of data and stops there, one is put in the position of accepting a null hypothesis. Yet any specific model is surely wrong in some detail, so the acceptable model is merely one whose flaws are not substantial enough to be detected with the available data. It is hardly the truth. However, when one is interested in the model as an adequate approximation to the data, minor discrepancies are not serious. A simple model that describes a set of data well, albeit not perfectly, is likely to be more helpful to a researcher than an elaborate explanation or a complicated model that defies interpretation. When approaching analysis from this model-fitting point of view, one frequently ignores small but statistically significant effects (by hypothesis-testing criteria) in favor of a more comprehensible model that is consistent with the preponderance of the data. Such a procedure is particularly valuable when the number of observations is very large and hypothesis tests have a great deal of power to identify tiny effects.

1.5. A NOTE ON COMPUTER PROGRAMS

Except for the simplest situations, the analyses described in this book must be done on a computer. There is too much computation to make hand calculation practical. Fortunately, canned programs are available for most techniques. The major statistical packages include routines for multifactor frequency analysis; for example, the program BMDP4F from the BMDP package (Dixon, 1983), the LOGLINEAR procedure in SPSSx (SPSS, Inc., 1983), and PROC CATMOD in SAS (SAS Institute, 1985). Most of the analyses in this book can be done using one or more of these packages. There are also several specialized programs that are more or less widely distributed.

Each of these programs has it strengths and its weaknesses, and although the basic models can be fit by any of them, they are not entirely equivalent. Of the three packages, the BMDP program is the most compatible with most of this book—the material in Chapters 2 to 10, at least. It is particularly well adapted to the fitting and testing of sequences of hierarchical log-linear models, such as those that express hypotheses of independence and quasi-independence. It uses a notation similar to the bracket form described in Chapter 3. The other packages can also fit these hierarchical log-linear models and some others as well. They use a linear-models representation that is not always as simple. This formulation of the models emphasizes the parallels—both proper and deceptive—to regression analysis and the analysis of variance. The linear models approach is most strongly felt in the CATMOD procedure in the SAS package. This program uses the weighted least-squares estimation scheme described in Chapter 12. Thus, SAS is the most compatible with that chapter. It can fit a larger collection of models, but requires a deeper knowledge of statistics to use it efficiently.

Many statistical programs, including versions of the three packages just mentioned, are starting to become available on personal computers. Certainly these "small" machines now have more than enough computational power to analyze large data sets and to run very sophisticated analyses.† As more powerful personal machines appear on the market and more inclusive statistical packages become available for them, they will be used for a larger portion of routine statistical work.

Notwithstanding the importance of the computer to frequency-table analysis, this book does not include instructions or control sequences for any specific programs, nor does it treat the interpretation of particular output. There are three reasons for this apparent omission. First, the optimum choice of a program depends more on personal preference than might be expected. My choice of a program, among several that do the job, may be different from yours. It is always easiest to use a program (or a packaged system) that one knows well, for familiarity easily overcomes differences in the complexity of a program. Too much space and too many alternatives are entailed in a useful treatment of the major practical alternatives. Second, even if one or two packages were selected, presentation would still be risky since their form is not stable. Most techniques discussed in this book have been developed or popularized within the past two decades, some much more recently. Future development is inevitable, and will lead to changes in statistical theory and practice. Without too long a lag, the programs evolve to accommodate these changes. The migration to personal machines should accelerate these changes. Several times I have prepared material about the use of a program, only to find, when reusing it a year or so later, that the programs had changed just sufficiently to make the examples misleading. There is much that is frustrating in using computers, but obsolete documentation can be avoided. Finally, using the computer is not really the hard part of analyzing data. The most difficult tasks are deciding what analysis to run and interpreting the results. These tasks are much easier if one has a good understanding of the statistical principles, and these principles are easiest to acquire before one gets tangled in technical minutia. When one knows what one is doing, one can usually figure out the programs, and when they do something other than what one had intended, one has a good chance of recognizing the mistake.

---

†All the analyses in this book were originally run on an early IBM personal computer (with a numerical coprocessor chip), using programs written for the purpose. Only for the descending stepwise analysis in Section 8.3 was the speed of the machine an inconvenience.

Of course, the correct use of a packaged program does not always come easily, as any user knows. Several attempts are always necessary. A helpful strategy when starting out with an unfamiliar program or package is to first run an example to which one knows the answer, either through hand calculation or by picking it from a book. Only when one can reproduce these results should one move to data where the results are unknown. The manuals for all the packages contain several examples, and it is usually easier to adapt one of them to one's problem than to construct a novel procedure from scratch using the general reference section. Modification of the procedures to a novel use can come after something is running. Even when one understands how to use the program, it is a good idea to examine one's output carefully for inconsistencies or improbable results.

2 Two-way Tables

After one has learned them, the numerical procedures in this book are not complicated. Most are used in the analysis of a two-way contingency table. Many will be familiar (although perhaps not in depth) from elementary statistics, under a title such as *Chi-square tests*. The present chapter introduces frequency-table analysis in this context, with a discussion of the two-way table—familiar material perhaps, but foreshadowing advanced topics to follow.

2.1. THE BASIC TEST OF UNRELATEDNESS

Suppose that one has data on the way in which 481 subjects solve a problem in elementary statistics. In particular, suppose that every subject is classified in two ways:

- By background, as having taken one statistics class or more than one
- By whether the solution to the problem is correct or in error

These two classifications cross to form the fourfold table of *observed frequencies* in the top panel of Table 2.1. The sums of the rows and columns are appended to this table.

The first classification divides the population of subjects into two subpopulations: those with one course and those with more than one. Clearly, an important question concerns the proportion of correct solutions in each subpopulation. This proportion is $80/331 = 0.24$ for the subpopulation of subjects who took one class and $84/150 = 0.56$ for the multiple-class subpopulation. These proportions

17

TABLE 2.1
A Test for the Homogeneity of Two Populations of Students

Original Data (Observed Frequencies)

| | | Solution Accuracy | | Total |
		Correct	Error	
Number of	One	80	251	331
classes	Multiple	84	66	150
	Total	164	317	481

Expected Frequencies

$$\text{Expected frequency} = \frac{\text{(row total)(column total)}}{\text{total number of observations}}$$

| | | Solution Accuracy | | Total |
		Correct	Error	
Number of	One	112.9	218.1	331
classes	Multiple	51.1	98.9	150
	Total	164	317	481

Calculation of the Test Statistic

$$X^2 = \sum_{\text{cells}} \frac{(\text{observed} - \text{expected})^2}{\text{expected}}$$

$$= \frac{(80 - 112.9)^2}{112.9} + \ldots + \frac{(66 - 98.9)^2}{98.9} = 46.54$$

Degrees of freedom = (rows − 1)(columns − 1)

$$= (2 - 1)(2 - 1) = 1$$

appear to differ, but one needs a statistical test to distinguish true effects from accidents of sampling. This test compares the two hypotheses

H_0: probability of a correct solution for one-class subjects
= probability of a correct solution for multiple-class subjects

(2.1)

H_1: probability of a correct solution for one-class subjects
≠ probability of a correct solution for multiple-class subjects

The test itself is simple and is shown in the balance of Table 2.1. Its rationale is discussed later; for the moment concentrate on how it works. First a set of *expected frequencies* is constructed that are consistent with the row and column marginal sums and for which the null hypothesis holds. These are created by multiplying row sums by column sums and dividing each result by the total number of observations. These numbers correspond to the frequencies that would occur if the marginal frequencies were the same as those observed (notice that the marginals of the two tables agree) and if the conditional proportion of correct solutions were the same in both rows. These "expected frequencies" are not, of course, what one would actually expect the data to look like if the two conditional proportions were equal. For one thing, their values are not integers; for another, real data show statistical fluctuation. The expected frequencies are, however, the mathematical average, or estimated *expected value*, around which the observed data fluctuate if H_0 is true.

The observed frequencies should be close to the expected frequencies if the null hypothesis is true. To check this, the two sets of numbers are compared by calculating a measure of discrepancy, known as the *Pearson goodness-of-fit statistic* (Pearson, 1900), denoted X^2 and shown in the final section of Table 2.1.† In essence, X^2 is an adjusted sum of the squared differences between observed and expected frequencies. Large values indicate big discrepancies between the two sets of frequencies, and small values indicate a close fit. Exact agreement of observed and expected frequencies is unlikely, but chance effects should not be too large, so one can set a limit beyond which X^2 is unlikely to go. Thus, X^2 is a test statistic that discriminates between the two hypotheses of Equations 2.1.

The sampling distribution to which values of the Pearson test statistic are referred (in the manner of Figure 1.1) is the theoretical chi-square distribution. This distribution is denoted by the Greek symbol χ^2 to distinguish it from the observed statistic X^2, for which a Latin letter is used. There are actually a family of χ^2 distributions, which differ in the value of a positive integer known as the *degrees of freedom*. For the two-way test here, this number is the product of the number of rows and the number of columns, each reduced by 1. Critical values of the χ^2 distribution are provided in the table in Appendix A.1. With one degree of freedom, the critical value at the 5% level is 3.84. The observed value of X^2 is much greater than this criterion, meaning that there is much more discrepancy between the observed and the expected frequencies than can be attributed to chance. The null hypothesis is rejected in favor of its alternative.

The alternative hypothesis is nondirectional, in that violations of the null hypothesis of any sort lead to large values of X^2. If the null hypothesis is rejected, one can usually go further toward identifying the specific relationships present. In this example, one asks which subpopulation has the larger proportion

---

†Throughout this book, the number of decimal places in numerical results is chosen to make the presentation clear and to avoid giving an impression of spurious precision. However, greater accuracy is used in the calculations leading to these results. Hence, if one checks the calculations using intermediate results as presented, minor differences may be observed. Using the single-decimal expected frequencies in Table 2.1, for example, one obtains $X^2 = 46.68$, not 46.54 as shown there. The latter figure is based on more accurate expected frequencies and is correct.

of correct solutions. Since the test shows that the two subpopulations differ in the frequency of errors, the one-class subpopulation makes fewer correct answers (24%) then the multiple-class subpopulation (56%).

The remainder of this chapter amplifies the discussion of this basic test, expanding and justifying its steps.

2.2. SOME NOTATION

The informal notation used in the last section is not ultimately satisfactory. A more systematic notation is necessary if the testing procedures are to be generalized. Here, as in many quantitative fields, the notation must strike a balance between being too simple, and thus inexact, and being too exhaustive, and thus confusing. A reasonably complete and consistent notation is best, with allowance for simplification where practical.

Consider a two-way table with a rows and b columns formed from two classification schemes. Index the rows and columns by the letters i and j, respectively. Use the Greek letter π to denote a theoretical population probability. Subscript it appropriately, so that $\pi_{j|i}$ denotes the conditional probability of an observation in column j of the table given that it is in row i. With this notation, the two hypotheses that were tested in the last section (Equations 2.1) are

$$H_0: \pi_{j|i} = \pi_{j|k} \text{ for all } i,k = 1,2,\ldots,a \text{ and } j = 1,2,\ldots,b$$
$$H_1: \pi_{j|i} \neq \pi_{j|k} \text{ for some } i,j,k \tag{2.2}$$

It is frequently useful to think of the indices i, j, and k as taking values from *index sets*, $\mathscr{A}$ and $\mathscr{B}$ rather than just being integers. In this notation, the range $i = 1, 2, \ldots, a$ becomes $i \in \mathscr{A}$, where $\mathscr{A}$ is the set $\{1, 2, \ldots, a\}$. For numerical values, the set notation is no advance, but one can now let the index sets contain entities other than integers. Thus, in the example above, one can let $\mathscr{A} = \{o,m\}$ (for "one class" and "multiple classes") and $\mathscr{B} = \{c,e\}$ (for "correct" and "error"). It is much easier to remember what $\pi_{c|m}$ means than $\pi_{1|2}$. This type of mnemonic notation is especially valuable in a large problem.

For data sampled from a single population, the conditional probabilities, $\pi_{j|i}$ are less useful than the probabilities that an observation falls in a particular cell. These are denoted simply by π_{ij}.

Denote the observed data by the subscripted variable x, here with two subscripts, x_{ij}. So in Table 2.1, using the letter subscripts, $x_{oc} = 80$ and $x_{oe} = 251$. There is no need to indicate conditionalization (as was done with $\pi_{j|i}$), for these values are frequencies not probabilities. To speak of proportions instead of probabilities, the letter p is used instead of x. So the simple proportion in cell i,j is

$$p_{ij} = \frac{x_{ij}}{\text{total frequency in table}}$$

The conditional proportion in column j given row i is

$$p_{j|i} = \frac{x_{ij}}{\text{frequency in row } i}$$

The next need is for a way to write sums. Sums can occur either over a range of integers or over the members of an index set. Most commonly here, sums are over the entire range for which the subscript is defined. In these cases, the explicit limits are dropped, and a single letter is used to designate the subscript in question. Thus, there are several equivalent ways to write the sum of x_{ij} over all the rows:

$$\sum_{i=1}^{a} x_{ij} = \sum_{i \in \mathcal{A}} x_{ij} = \sum_{i} x_{ij}$$

The simpler designation is particularly useful for multiple sums, because it allows several sums to be combined in a single summation symbol:

$$\sum_{i,j} x_{ij} = \sum_{i \in \mathcal{A}} \sum_{j \in \mathcal{B}} x_{ij}$$

Where the sum is over every cell in the table, the word *cells* is used instead of listing the separate indices. So in a two-way table, the sums just given are also written as

$$\sum_{\text{cells}} x_{ij}$$

This notation is very useful for formulae that stay the same regardless of the number of dimensions in the table.

In formulae that contain many sums, the Σ notation is cumbersome. A single symbol in lieu of a sum is tidier. In a two-way table, one can readily assign symbols to represent the row and column sums needed to get the expected frequencies; for example, one might use r_i for row sums and c_j for column sums. However, in tables with more than two dimensions, this type of ad hoc notation proliferates and becomes difficult to remember. A more systematic notation indicates summation over an index by replacing that index with a plus sign. For example,

$$x_{+j} = \sum_{i} x_{ij} \quad \text{and} \quad x_{i+} = \sum_{j} x_{ij}$$

$$x_{++} = \sum_{i} x_{i+} = \sum_{j} x_{+j} = \sum_{i,j} x_{ij}$$

Again using Table 2.1, $x_{o+} = 331$, $x_{+e} = 317$, and $x_{++} = 481$. Some authors use a dot here, instead of a plus.

For the expected frequencies, write $\hat{\mu}_{ij}$. The hat on this symbol indicates that it is an estimate of a population quantity, as will be discussed in Section 2.3. With this definition, enough notation is available to rewrite the formulae used in Table 2.1:

$$\hat{\mu}_{ij} = \frac{x_{i+}x_{+j}}{x_{++}} \tag{2.3}$$

$$X^2 = \sum_{\text{cells}} \frac{(x_{ij} - \hat{\mu}_{ij})^2}{\hat{\mu}_{ij}} \tag{2.4}$$

and

$$\text{degrees of freedom} = (a-1)(b-1) \tag{2.5}$$

Finally, a way to associate the degrees of freedom with a test statistic is useful. This is done here by placing the number of degrees of freedom in parentheses following the test statistic. For the results in Section 2.1, write $X^2(1) = 48.54$ and refer it to a $\chi^2(1)$ distribution. Some authors put the degree of freedom in a subscript, writing χ_1^2 for the distribution and X_1^2 for the statistic.

2.3.   THREE DESCRIPTIONS OF TWO-WAY DATA

The test performed in Section 2.1 compared the distribution of responses in two populations. The null hypothesis stated that these distributions were the same. This hypothesis of identical distribution is appropriate to this example, but would not apply to all sets of data. In fact, there are three different experimental procedures that generate two-way tables of frequencies. These lead to different constraints on the data, to different null hypotheses, and to different probability models for the population of scores, although the actual tests are the same. The three null hypotheses are referred to here as hypotheses of *homogeneity*, of *independence*, and of *unrelated classification*.

In two-dimensional tables, where comprehensible hypotheses are easy to construct, the differences among these hypotheses are not great. Either the rows and columns are related or they are not. However, with more classification dimensions the differences among the models are more important and affect both the underlying sampling theory and the conclusions that are drawn. In multi-dimensional tables, many forms of partial association exist, and a test that is valuable for one sampling model may be meaningless for another. Thus, it pays to get the models straight from the beginning. This section describes the models in terms of the design of the investigation. A more formal probabilistic character-ization of the sampling models appears in Section 4.2.

One way to distinguish among the three descriptions is to look at the roles of the marginal frequency distributions (Barnard, 1947; Pearson, 1947). For some designs, these distributions are determined before any of the data are collected, or at least belong to factors unrelated to the questions one is investigating. In others, they are free. In a two-way table, sometimes one marginal distribution is fixed, sometimes neither, and sometimes both.

Homogeneity. The first type of procedure compares the effects in several different populations. Consider the experiment of Section 2.1. There are two populations of subjects, those who took one course and those who took more than one. The characteristics of these populations are embodied in two sets of conditional probabilities, one for each population. Clearly, the observed distribution of solvers and nonsolvers in a sample from each population reflects these distributions. In contrast, the sizes of the samples of o and m subjects are determined by such things as the way that the subjects are obtained or the frequency with which advanced courses have been given. These are properties of the investigation, not of the subjects. A different study could pick different proportions of subjects of the two types without affecting either the underlying populations or the conclusion that one would expect to draw.

The null hypothesis tested here is that the distributions of the responses in the two populations are the same, as stated in Equations 2.1. Thus, one speaks of this as a test of the *homogeneity* of the two populations. More abstractly, the probabilistic structure underlying these data is a pair of binomial distributions, which can be laid out as

$$
\begin{array}{c|cc|c}
 & j = c & j = e & \\
\hline
i = o & \pi_{c|o} & \pi_{e|o} & 1.0 \\
i = m & \pi_{c|m} & \pi_{e|m} & 1.0 \\
\end{array}
\tag{2.6}
$$

Each row is a complete probability distribution, whose probabilities sum to unity. The test of homogeneity compares the rows to each other, testing the null hypothesis that corresponding probabilities are the same, that is, that $\pi_{j|o} = \pi_{j|m}$, $j \in \{c,e\}$.

Independence. In the second type of model, both classifications are sampled simultaneously from a single population. Consider another type of data that could be obtained from the example experiment. Suppose that all 331 of the one-class subjects are classified by which of two approaches (a or b) they use to attack the problem and by whether their solution is correct (Table 2.2). Although this table is superficially similar to Table 2.1, the underlying sampling situation is different and a different pair of hypotheses is tested. Only a single population of subjects is involved, so both classifications are sampled and the fourfold table is drawn from a single probability distribution rather than two separate distribu-

TABLE 2.2
Observed Frequencies of the Correct Solution as Classified by
the Approach to the Problem for the One-class Subjects from Table 2.1

| | | Solution Accuracy | | Total |
		Correct	Error	
Approach	a	26	115	141
chosen	b	54	136	190
	Total	80	251	331

tions. The fundamental parameters of this distribution are unconditional probabilities π_{ij}, giving a table that can be schematized as

$$
\begin{array}{c|cc}
 & j = c & j = e \\
\hline
i = a & \pi_{ac} & \pi_{ae} \\
i = b & \pi_{bc} & \pi_{be}
\end{array}
\qquad (2.7)
$$

The four probabilities form a single four-level distribution—they sum to 1.0—
rather than the two separate binomials of Display 2.6.

In Display 2.7, the null hypothesis of no association is defined by the probabilistic *independence* of the classifications, rather than by the homogeneity of the
distribution. The appropriate hypotheses in this situation are

H_0: row classification is independent of column classification,
H_1: row and column classifications are dependent.   (2.8)

In probability theory, independence occurs whenever a joint event is the product
of the simple event probabilities, without any conditionalization,

$$P(\text{row}_i \text{ and } \text{column}_j) = P(\text{row}_i)P(\text{column}_j)$$

The probability in row i is the sum of all the probabilities in that row, or π_{i+}
(remember that the + subscript indicates summation over that index). Similarly,
the probability in column j is π_{+j}. Then the assertion of independence is

$$\pi_{ij} = \pi_{i+}\pi_{+j} \qquad (2.9)$$

In other words, the hypothesis of independence is equivalent to the statement that
the joint probability in a cell is the product of the marginal probabilities.

The emphasis on the marginal probabilities points up another difference between the homogeneity and independence models. Only in the latter case do both
these distributions reflect the subjects' behavior. One can meaningfully speak of
the probability that a one-class subject solves the problem correctly or that a
subject adopts solution method a, and one can extract estimates of these values
from the marginal frequencies in Table 2.2. However, for the mixed collection of

subjects in Table 2.1, the proportion of correct responses depends both on the solution rate for each subpopulation and on the relative sizes of the two samples. It is not a pure measure of any subject's behavior.

The difference between the homogeneity and independence models is similar to the difference between the regression and correlation models in regression theory. In the former, several different populations are sampled; in the latter, a single population with several attributes is sampled. As here, the tests used with the two models are similar, although the conclusions that one draws are different.

Unrelated Classification.   The third type of situation is the least common. In the test of independence, the experimental design constrains only the total sample size. In the test of homogeneity, the marginal frequencies of observations from the two populations are treated as fixed. One can also construct designs in which both sets of marginal frequencies are fixed. Suppose, for example, that 40 solutions are drawn from the one-class population, half solutions by female students and half by male. These are given to a judge who, knowing the original distribution but not the individual assignments, sorts them into two groups of 20, trying to identify the sex of the solver (Table 2.3). By design, both the rows and columns sum to 20. One wishes to know whether the judge's classification is related to the true sex of the solvers.

The sampling description underlying this design is different from either of the two just discussed, reflecting the different marginal constraints. The null hypothesis tested here is similar to that of the homogeneity situation, although the column constraints make the conditionalization different. It can be described as a hypothesis of *unrelated classification.* This model gives rise to a hypergeometric sampling distribution, which is used as the basis of a specialized testing procedure in Section 2.11.

The unrelated classification description also applies when the entire population of interest has been examined or where the sample is so restricted as to constitute a population in its own right. In either of these cases both row and column totals are fixed, even though one can still ask questions about the presence or absence of an association between them. Such a case could occur, for

TABLE 2.3
Classification of the Solutions of 40 Subjects from
the One-class Group by Sex of Solver and by a Judge

| | | Classification by Judge | | |
		Female	Male	Total
True classification of solver	Female	12	8	20
	Male	8	12	20
	Total	20	20	

example, if one were studying a collection of patients who had been in accidents that created one of several types of lesion in a particular brain structure. The patients are then classified by their ability to perform a certain task, and one asks whether the lesion type is related to performance. Because the investigation is limited to this group and because another group of patients is likely to be quite different (the accidents and the actual lesions will be different), it makes sense to treat the group by itself and adopt the fixed-marginals model.

2.4. THE EXPECTED FREQUENCIES

Tests of either independence or homogeneity are conducted by first estimating the expected value of the cell frequencies under the null hypothesis, then comparing these values to the observed frequencies. The result is the statistic X^2. The formula for the expected frequencies was asserted in Section 2.1 without explanation. This section shows how that formula follows from basic principles.

Consider the independence model. Subjects are sampled, then tallied, each falling into one of the ab cells, according to the probability distribution of the π_{ij}. Out of a sample of size N, an average of $N\pi_{ij}$ observations appear in cell i,j. More formally, the number of observations has a multinomial distribution, and the expected value (or mean) of this distribution is

$$\mu_{ij} = N\pi_{ij}$$

The Greek letters indicate that population quantities are in question, except for the total sample size.

If the null hypothesis of independence holds, then π_{ij} equals the product of the row and column marginals (Equation 2.9). Using this result, one finds that

$$\mu_{ij} = N\pi_{i+}\pi_{+j} \tag{2.10}$$

If the marginal probabilities were known, this equation would give a value to compare to the x_{ij}. However, as population characteristics they are unknown. They are estimated by the observed marginal proportions

$$p_{i+} = \frac{x_{i+}}{x_{++}} \quad \text{and} \quad p_{+j} = \frac{x_{+j}}{x_{++}}$$

The sample size N is the same thing as x_{++}, so the expected frequencies are estimated as

$$\hat{\mu}_{ij} = Np_{i+}p_{+j} = x_{++}\left(\frac{x_{i+}}{x_{++}}\right)\left(\frac{x_{+j}}{x_{++}}\right) = \frac{x_{i+}x_{+j}}{x_{++}} \tag{2.11}$$

The homogeneity model leads to a similar result. There are a distributions, each with b members, determined by the conditional probabilities $\pi_{j|i}$ (recall

Display 2.6). Suppose that n_i observations are made from population i. The row distributions are multinomial, so the expected values of the cell frequencies are

$$\mu_{ij} = n_i \pi_{j|i}$$

Under the null hypothesis $\pi_{j|i}$ is the same for all i, so it can be replaced by the common symbol $\bar{\pi}_j$ to give

$$\mu_{ij} = n_i \bar{\pi}_j \tag{2.12}$$

An estimate of $\bar{\pi}_j$ is obtained from the marginal proportions as $\hat{\bar{\pi}}_j = x_{j+}/x_{++}$. The fixed row frequencies n_i are x_{i+}, so that

$$\hat{\mu}_{ij} = n_i \hat{\bar{\pi}}_j = x_{i+} \left(\frac{x_{j+}}{x_{++}} \right) = \frac{x_{i+}x_{+j}}{x_{++}} \tag{2.13}$$

An argument similar to that for the homogeneity hypothesis applies to the unrelated classification description, except that $\bar{\pi}_j$ is now a fixed proportion rather than an unknown parameter. The result is the same as Equation 2.13.

The values of the expected frequencies are the same for all three situations (Equations 2.11 and 2.13). Thus, the value of X^2 calculated in all three cases is the same. It is not the statistical tests that distinguish the types of hypothesis, but their interpretation.

2.5. ASSUMPTIONS OF THE CHI-SQUARE TEST

An essential part of a statistical test based on X^2 is the comparison to a χ^2 distribution. The correspondence between the sampling distribution of X^2 and the theoretical χ^2 distribution is not automatic, however. It depends on several assumptions that the X^2 statistic does not test. As part of any application, these assumptions must be examined.† They can be divided into three parts, relating to the independence of the observations, the similarity of their distribution, and the sample size.

The first consideration is most important:

• Separate observations are probabilistically independent.

If independence fails, the whole structure of the analysis falls apart. One expects each additional observation to provide more information, but when they are not

---

†Although not completely consistent with this book, the discussion of Lewis & Burke (1949), who attack the misuse of χ^2 tests in psychological research, remains valuable. See also Delucchi (1983).

independent, this information is contaminated. A myriad of interobservation relationships potentially alter and bias the conclusions.

In practice, the assumption of independence is usually reduced to the principle that each observation comes from a different subject. Generally, this is a wise rule to follow, since different subjects usually behave independently. This principle should not be followed without thought, however. On one hand, separate subjects may not be independent if they are run simultaneously or otherwise linked. On the other hand, a series of trials from a single subject sometimes can be treated as independent events. Psychophysical data, where many similar observations are collected from one subject, are an example of a situation where the independence of repeated observations is plausible. Without separate subjects, risks are greater, however, and one should approach any such analysis with caution.

As it is often stated, the separate-subject rule is coupled with a second clause stating that no subject should be omitted from the table. This principle ensures that no bias is created by the systematic exclusion of some part of the population. This condition has a different status from the separate-subject rule, since it affects the generality of the inference, not whether an inference can be made at all. There are cases where one properly wishes to extract subpopulations of the subjects for separate analysis. In analyzing a political poll, for example, one might want to look at only those subjects who have expressed a definite opinion or those who claim affiliation with one particular political party. Of course, the conclusions that derive from a subsample apply only to the subpopulation from which it is drawn—avowed Democrats, say, or those persons who state an opinion. What one cannot do with any degree of statistical support is to extend the conclusions to wider populations—to Republicans, or to voters in general. When such extensions are made, their bases must lie outside the particular body of data.

The best way to deal with a serious failure of independence is to recast the analysis to include the dependencies. Sometimes dependency can be eliminated by organizing the data in a higher-dimension table. Examples of this modification appear in various places below. If the dependencies cannot be accommodated, one can only fall back on approximate tests or start over again. Fortunately, there are limits to the amount of damage done by a restricted failure of independence. In a common type of dependence, the observations are collected in groups of G, and the members of these groups are not independent. If one uses X^2/G as a test statistic instead of X^2, comparing it with the usual χ^2 distribution with $(a-1)(b-1)$ degrees of freedom, one obtains a test with a type I error probability that does not exceed the nominal level (Altham, 1976; Cohen, 1976; Rao & Scott, 1981). The test is conservative, possibly very much so, but it is safe. Thus, if the data from Table 2.1 were contaminated by being collected in pairs, one could use $X^2/2 = 23.27$ as a test statistic instead of 46.54. With this value, the conclusion stands, in spite of the dependence. Another type of dependence occurs when the observations are a time series in which any observation is positively associated with the previous K observations. This situation easily arises if a series of classifications of a subject's behavior is taken at fixed intervals that are sufficiently short that the subject is sometimes engaged in the same activity for more than one consecutive observation. For binary observations of this type, $X^2/(2K+1)$ is a safe statistic, although a conservative one (Altham, 1979).

The second fundamental assumption concerns the heterogeneity of the population:

• All observations are identically distributed.

This condition ensures that all the data are similar and that all speak to the same effects. If this assumption fails, the aggregation of data of several dissimilar types produces an ensemble that is not representative of either type. What the amalgam shows is unclear. The pooling can also destroy the χ^2 approximation of the sampling distribution by giving X^2 larger values than for a homogeneous sample and biasing the test toward rejection of H_0 (Brier, 1980; Fellegi, 1980; Fienberg, 1979). Potentially inhomogeneous collections of data are common, so one must always be wary of improper aggregates. Fortunately, there are ways to analyze data that come from several different sources. Indeed, part of the reason for moving to multidimensional tables is to find ways to treat them.

The third assumption differs from the other two, in that it is not related to the information embodied in the data, but to the accuracy of the χ^2 approximation to the Pearson X^2 statistic.

• The number of observations is large.

By their nature, frequencies are discrete; thus, any statistic calculated from a particular sample takes one of a finite set of values. The continuous χ^2 distribution is used to approximate its distribution. Strictly, this approximation is accurate only in the limit as the sample size tends to infinity, hence, one says that X^2 is *asymptotically distributed as* χ^2. In large samples, the jumps in the sampling distribution of X^2 are insignificant and a χ^2 distribution can be used for testing, but for small samples, the χ^2 approximation is inaccurate.

How large need a sample be? Because the small frequencies create the inaccuracies, the criteria can be expressed in terms of the smallest expected frequencies (note: not the smallest observed frequencies). Different authors have proposed different rules, demanding minimum frequencies between 1 and 10. What standard one adopts depends to some extent on how cautious one wishes to be. Recent evidence (Berry & Mielke, 1988; Bradley, Bradley, McGrath, & Cutcomb, 1979; Camilli & Hopkins, 1978; Hutchinson, 1979; Koehler, 1986; Koehler & Larntz, 1980; Larntz, 1978; Milligan, 1980) suggests that one can get by with somewhat fewer observations than recommended by earlier writers. The following minimum conditions apply to two-way tables:

1. For tests with 1 degree of freedom, all the $\hat{\mu}_{ij}$ should exceed 2 or 3.
2. With more degrees of freedom, $\hat{\mu}_{ij} \approx 1$ in a few cells is tolerable.
3. In large tables up to 20% of the cells can have $\hat{\mu}_{ij}$ appreciably less than 1.
4. The total sample should be at least 4 or 5 times the number of cells.
5. Samples should be appreciably larger when the marginal categories are not equally likely.

If any of these principles are violated, one should abandon the test. Certainly, one is safer, particularly near the borderline of statistical significance, with larger samples. Another rule of thumb warns one to distrust any conclusion that changes if a single observation is shifted from one cell to another.

There is less information available concerning the effect of small frequencies on the multidimensional tests discussed in the later chapters of this book. What information there is (Koehler, 1986; Larntz, 1978; Milligan, 1980) suggests that similar rules to those of the two-way case should apply when the goodness of fit of a model to a complete table is being tested. Tests based on the difference in fit between two models (to be discussed in Chapters 3, 4, and 5) are somewhat more robust. Their large-sample properties depend more nearly on the frequency per degree of freedom than on the minimum expected cell size (Haberman, 1977).

When faced with small frequencies in a 2×2 table, one can sometimes avoid the χ^2 approximation by using the exact methods described in Section 2.11. With larger tables, there may be little to do other than to demand, for safety, a more stringent level of significance or to try to obtain more data. If the low frequencies are a consequence of a single rare row or column in a large table, it may be best to drop that category with a corresponding restriction in the generality of one's conclusion. Before becoming too concerned with small cells, however, one should note that in small tables with few observations, the power to detect anything other than mammoth effects is negligible (Overall, 1980). It is often more profitable to collect additional data than to fret about statistical details.

In any discussion of assumptions, one should keep in mind that the statistical descriptions underlying any test are phrased as abstract mathematical principles and so cannot be perfectly fulfilled. The assumption of identical distribution, for example, is often vulnerable. Accordingly, neither a slavish demand that the assumptions be perfectly satisfied nor a promiscuous disregard of their importance leads to a satisfactory analysis. One must select the level at which one is satisfied with the assumptions, based on the seriousness of the potential violations, on their magnitude, and on the uses to which the results will be put. The example of psychophysical data just mentioned (discussed further in Chapter 6) is a case where it may be worth tolerating minor violations of some assumptions to give access to more powerful analytical machinery. Further examples appear throughout the book or can be drawn from any sensible application of these methods.

2.6. THE ODDS RATIO

Beyond a test of significance, one often wants a way to measure how much association is present. A single number is needed that expresses the magnitude of an effect, that can be interpreted, and that is comparable from one table to another. It is a common error to use a test statistic such as X^2 for an effect-size measure. Big values of X^2 seem to indicate more severe violations of the null hypothesis than do small values. However, this need not be so. Test statistics indicate to what extent the data provide evidence inconsistent with the null hypothesis and may be large either because the deviation is large or because the quality of the evidence is good—here because the sample is large. If the definition of X^2 is rewritten in terms of the observed and expected proportions instead of frequencies, then using p_{ij} and writing $\hat{\pi}_{ij} = \hat{\mu}_{ij}/N$ for the expected probabilities under the model, one finds that

$$X^2 = N \sum_{\text{cells}} \frac{(p_{ij} - \hat{\pi}_{ij})^2}{\hat{\pi}_{ij}} \tag{2.14}$$

This result shows that if the sample size (N) is doubled, then X^2 also doubles, even though the discrepancy, as measured by the probabilities, is unchanged. Such behavior is appropriate in a measure of evidence but is unsatisfactory in an effect-size measure. A measure affected by sample size is especially unsuitable when one wishes to compare results across different experiments or from one subgroup of subjects to another.

Many measures of effect size do not depend on the sample size. Several coefficients, valuable for different tasks, are treated in Chapter 9. Although a full discussion of these measures in this chapter would be an unwarranted digression, one measure, the *odds ratio* or *cross-product ratio*, is tied so closely to the test procedures that it is helpful to introduce it here. This statistic gives an easy way to summarize association in a 2 × 2 table.

The odds ratio begins with a different way to talk about the probability of an event, known as the *odds*. The odds of any event are calculated by taking the ratio of the probability that the event occurs to the probability that it does not. Consider the example of Section 2.1 again. For the one-class subjects (group *o*) the odds of a correct solution equal the probability of a correct solution divided by the probability that it is not correct:

$$odds_{c|o} = \frac{\pi_{c|o}}{1 - \pi_{c|o}} = \frac{\pi_{c|o}}{\pi_{e|o}} \tag{2.15}$$

Similarly, for the multiple-class population of subjects, $odds_{c|m} = \pi_{c|m}/\pi_{e|m}$. These ratios are large when a correct solution is likely and small when it is unlikely. The odds can be interpreted as the number of times that the event occurs for each time that it does not. For example, were the probability of a correct solution equal to $2/3$ for the one-class subjects, then 2 subjects would make correct responses for each subject that made an error, and $odds_{c|o} = 2$.

Now consider what it means for two populations to be different. The presence of a population effect implies that the odds in the two populations are not the same. The extent to which the odds differ is summarized by their ratio, known (naturally enough) as the *odds ratio* and denoted by α. For the problem-solving data, the odds ratio is

$$\alpha = \frac{odds_{c|m}}{odds_{c|o}} = \frac{\pi_{c|m}\pi_{e|o}}{\pi_{e|m}\pi_{c|o}} \tag{2.16}$$

When the populations are homogeneous, the odds are the same and $\alpha = 1$. The more that the populations differ, the farther α is from 1. If a correct solution is more likely from the multiple-class subjects, then $\alpha > 1$, but if c is more likely in population o, then $\alpha < 1$. The smallest value α can take is 0, when c is impossible in population m. If c is impossible for o, then α is arbitrarily large, in effect infinite. Since the odds ratio does not depend on the sample size and is responsive only to the difference in the populations, it is a good effect-size measure.

As just defined, the odds ratio is a population quantity. For any real set of data, it must be estimated. The natural estimate of $\pi_{j|i}$ is the corresponding sample proportion x_{ij}/x_{i+}. Substituting this estimate into the definition of α in Equation 2.16 gives

$$\hat{\alpha} = \frac{(x_{mc}/x_{m+})(x_{oe}/x_{o+})}{(x_{me}/x_{m+})(x_{oc}/x_{o+})}$$

$$= \frac{x_{mc}x_{oe}}{x_{me}x_{oc}} \tag{2.17}$$

This ratio is the product of elements on one diagonal of the data matrix divided by the product of those on the other. This structure gives rise to another name for the odds ratio: the *cross-product ratio*. Other estimates of the odds ratio are discussed in Section 9.1.

For the example of Section 2.1, the ratio of frequencies (from Table 2.1) is

$$\hat{\alpha} = \frac{251 \times 84}{80 \times 66} = 3.99$$

In this example the minor diagonal (251 and 84) has been placed over the major to conform with the subscripts in Equation 2.17. This orientation is natural here: one expects the multiple-class subpopulation to give more correct answers, and it is convenient to assign this state of things to large values of α. Without such a reason, one usually puts the major diagonal (upper left to lower right) over the minor diagonal (upper right to lower left). Organizing the numbers in this way gives $\hat{\alpha} = 0.25$.

The odds ratio has one serious problem: it is not additively symmetric. An odds ratio that is greater than 1 by a given amount does not correspond to as substantial an effect as an odds ratio that is smaller than 1 by the same amount. Positive associations have odds ratios that are spread out from 1 to ∞, while negative associations have odds ratios that are squeezed between 0 and 1. However, the ratio is multiplicatively symmetric. Effects with $\alpha = K$ and $\alpha = 1/K$ are of comparable magnitude but opposite direction. To turn this multiplicative symmetry into additive symmetry, one takes the natural logarithm† of α. This quantity varies from $-\infty$ to ∞, with $\log \alpha = 0$ when there is no effect. It has the nice property that positive and negative numbers of the same absolute value represent associations of the same strength. Although the introduction of the logarithm makes the measure less intuitive, its symmetry is especially useful when one is comparing several effects, some of which are associated in one direction and some in the other. For the example, $\log \hat{\alpha} = 1.38$.

2.7. THE LOG-LINEAR MODEL

Three interpretations of the null hypothesis are discussed in Section 2.3: homogeneity of conditional probabilities, probabilistic independence, and unrelated classification. All imply a relationship among the expected frequencies that allows the null hypothesis to be rewritten as a model for the frequencies. This model provides one means to extend the analysis of two-way tables to tables in more dimensions. In particular, all three hypotheses imply that the logarithm of the expected frequencies is the sum of row and column terms:

$$\log \mu_{ij} = \text{constant} + (\text{row term}) + (\text{column term}) \qquad (2.18)$$

Because the logarithm of μ_{ij} is a linear combination of parameters, this model and others like it are commonly called *log-linear models*.

---

†The natural logarithm, or logarithm to the base $e = 2.71828$, is not the same as the common logarithm, which uses the base 10. Common logarithms are useful for calculation (although they have been rendered less important by inexpensive hand calculators) or for scaling data, but have less theoretical value. The symbol "ln" is often used for the natural logarithm, particularly in engineering applications or on calculators. In the mathematical and statistical literature, including most of the primary sources for this book, the natural logarithm is denoted by "log". The latter convention is followed here. Common logarithms are converted to natural logarithms by multiplying by $\log_e 10 = 2.302585$ or dividing by $\log_{10} e = 0.4342945$. The usual properties of logarithms, such as the change of products to sums and of powers to products, apply to any base.

The log-linear Model 2.18 may not be obvious at first glance but follows readily from any of the null-hypothesis models. First consider a hypothesis of independence. As described in Section 2.4 (Equation 2.10), the expected cell frequency under this hypothesis is a product of the marginal probabilities, or $\mu_{ij} = N\pi_{i+}\pi_{+j}$. Taking logarithms turns this product into a sum that has the form of Equation 2.18:

$$\log \mu_{ij} = \log N + \log \pi_{i+} + \log \pi_{+j} \qquad (2.19)$$

A similar argument applies to the hypothesis of homogeneity or of unrelated classification. There the expected cell frequencies are $\mu_{ij} = n_i \bar{\pi}_j$ (Equation 2.12). Again taking logarithms gives a sum:

$$\log \mu_{ij} = \log n_i + \log \bar{\pi}_j \qquad (2.20)$$

Although Equations 2.19 and 2.20 are forms of Equation 2.18, they are superficially different. It is convenient to have a single form for both. Henceforth the linear model for $\log \mu_{ij}$ in a two-way table with unrelated rows and columns is written as

$$\log \mu_{ij} = \lambda + \lambda_{A(i)} + \lambda_{B(j)} \qquad (2.21)$$

To avoid a proliferation of symbols, the same letter λ is used for all three terms, with two-part subscripts to distinguish them.† The first part of the subscript indicates the dimension of the table to which the term applies—here A indicates the rows and B the columns. The second part, placed in parentheses, is the index for that term. When a set of parameters is discussed collectively, the latter portion of the subscript is dropped, so that one speaks of λ_A instead of $\lambda_{A(i)}$.

There are many ways to assign numbers to the λ parameters in Equation 2.21—for example, both Equations 2.19 and 2.20 give different assignments for the same original frequencies. One can always add something to one term and take it away from another to get the same sum. To make the values unique, two constraints are necessary. The most common convention, and the one used in this book, makes the subscripted parameters sum to 0:

$$\sum_i \lambda_{A(i)} = 0 \quad \text{and} \quad \sum_j \lambda_{B(j)} = 0 \qquad (2.22)$$

---

†The notation for log-linear models varies from one author to another. The present notation combines that used by Goodman (1970, 1971) or Haberman (1978, 1979) with that used by Bishop, Fienberg, & Holland (1975). Goodman writes λ_i^A, λ_j^B, etc., while Bishop Fienberg, and Holland write $u_{1(i)}$, $u_{2(j)}$, etc. (the numbers indicate the ordinal position of the subscript in the sequence of factors). However, the superscript tends to be read as an exponent until one is quite familiar with the notation and to produce a disturbingly dense typography, while the use of the Latin letter u blurs the distinction between population and sample, and the number is less mnemonic than a letter. The present notation avoids these problems.

Another approach fixes the value of one of the $\lambda_{A(i)}$ and one of the $\lambda_{B(j)}$. Often the last category is fixed by assigning $\lambda_{A(a)} = \lambda_{B(b)} = 0$.

Although the numerical evaluation of Equation 2.21 is not central to this chapter, an example may help to show how the log-linear model works. In the top panel of Table 2.4 is a table of frequencies that are perfectly consonant with the null hypothesis of independence, homogeneity, or unrelated classification. Logarithms of these frequencies appear in the second panel. The third section shows a set of parameters that fit this table (their extraction from the table is explained in Section 5.3). Notice that they have been chosen to satisfy the sums of Equations 2.22. The combination of these parameters is demonstrated in the final panel: these sums agree with the logarithms to within rounding error. The original frequencies can be recovered from the logarithms by exponentiating their values, using the fact that $e^{(\log x)} = x$.

Suppose now that the null hypothesis is false. How does this change Model

TABLE 2.4
Frequencies Under Independence and their Log-linear Representation

Original Frequencies, μ_{ij}

6	14	10	30
9	21	15	45
15	35	25	75

Logarithms of Frequencies, $\log \mu_{ij}$

1.792	2.639	2.302
2.197	3.044	2.708

Parameters of the Log-linear Model

$$\lambda = 2.447$$

$$\lambda_{A(1)} = -0.203 \qquad \lambda_{A(2)} = 0.203$$

$$\lambda_{B(1)} = -0.453 \qquad \lambda_{B(2)} = 0.394 \qquad \lambda_{B(3)} = 0.058$$

Reconstruction of the Table of Logarithms

$$\log \mu_{ij} = \lambda + \lambda_{A(i)} + \lambda_{B(j)}$$

2.447 − 0.203 − 0.453 = 1.791	2.447 − 0.203 + 0.394 = 2.638	2.447 − 0.203 + 0.058 = 2.302
2.447 + 0.203 − 0.453 = 2.197	2.447 + 0.203 + 0.394 = 3.044	2.447 + 0.203 + 0.058 = 2.708

2.21? To allow for an association between the rows and columns, a term is added that depends on both the row and the column:

$$\log \mu_{ij} = \text{constant} + (\text{row term}) + (\text{column term}) + (\text{association})$$

In the standard notation, the association parameter is denoted $\lambda_{AB(ij)}$, and the model is

$$\log \mu_{ij} = \lambda + \lambda_{A(i)} + \lambda_{B(j)} + \lambda_{AB(ij)} \qquad (2.23)$$

The double subscript on λ_{AB} indicates joint dependence on both the rows and columns.

Observe the relationship between the model that includes association and the model that excludes it. The simpler model (Equation 2.21) is a special case of the more general version (Equation 2.23), differing from it in that $\lambda_{AB(ij)} = 0$. This result connects the tests of unrelatedness to the parameter-testing scheme discussed in Section 1.4. In those terms, the hypotheses of homogeneity, independence, or unrelated classification are reexpressed as

$$H_0: \lambda_{AB(ij)} = 0 \qquad \text{for all } i \in \mathcal{A}, j \in \mathcal{B},$$
$$H_1: \lambda_{AB(ij)} \neq 0 \qquad \text{for some } i \in \mathcal{A}, j \in \mathcal{B} \qquad (2.24)$$

The connection between the parameters of the log-linear models and the hypothesis of unrelatedness is central to the analysis throughout this book.

2.8.   THE LIKELIHOOD-RATIO TEST STATISTIC

The test in Section 2.1 used the Pearson statistic to measure deviations from the null hypothesis. Other measures of discrepancy can be used. There are several other statistics that also have large-sample χ^2 distributions under the null hypothesis. Only one among these is important here. The *likelihood-ratio statistic*, which is conventionally denoted G^2 (some authors use L^2) to distinguish it from the Pearson X^2, is defined as

$$G^2 = 2 \sum_{\text{cells}} (\text{observed}) \log \left(\frac{\text{observed}}{\text{expected}} \right)$$
$$= 2 \sum_{\text{cells}} x_{ij} \log \left(\frac{x_{ij}}{\hat{\mu}_{ij}} \right) \qquad (2.25)$$

If any of the $x_{ij} = 0$, then the corresponding terms of the sum are zero. Note the multiplier 2, the omission of which is a frequent computational error. The number of degrees of freedom for this test is the same as that for the Pearson statistic. The motivation for this statistic is discussed in Chapter 4.

Once again, take the data in Table 2.1 as an example. The observed and expected frequencies are not changed by the new test statistic. Evaluation of Equation 2.25 gives

$$G^2(1) = 2 \left(80 \log\frac{80}{112.9} + 251 \log\frac{251}{218.1} + 84 \log\frac{84}{51.1} \right.$$
$$\left. + 66 \log\frac{66}{98.9} \right) = 45.40$$

The conclusion to reject homogeneity is the same as when the Pearson statistic is used—recall that $X^2(1) = 46.54$ for these data.

Some computational simplicity is gained when the formula for the expected frequencies is incorporated into that for G^2. Substituting $x_{i+}x_{+j}/x_{++}$ for $\hat{\mu}_{ij}$ in Equation 2.25, and using the fact that the logarithm of a product is the sum of the logarithms, give

$$G^2 = 2 \sum_{\text{cells}} x_{ij} \log \frac{x_{ij}x_{++}}{x_{i+}x_{+j}}$$

$$= 2 \sum_{\text{cells}} x_{ij} [\log x_{ij} - \log x_{i+} - \log x_{+j} + \log x_{++}]$$

$$= 2 \left(\sum_{\text{cells}} x_{ij} \log x_{ij} - \sum_{\text{cells}} x_{ij} \log x_{i+} - \sum_{\text{cells}} x_{ij} \log x_{+j} \right.$$
$$\left. + \sum_{\text{cells}} x_{ij} \log x_{++} \right)$$

All sums are over both i and j. However, in the last three terms, the logarithmic part of the expression does not depend on one or both of these indices, and so it can be extracted from that part of the sum. For example, the second term is

$$\sum_{\text{cells}} x_{ij} \log x_{i+} = \sum_i \sum_j x_{ij} \log x_{i+}$$

$$= \sum_i \left[\left(\sum_j x_{ij} \right) \log x_{i+} \right]$$

$$= \sum_i x_{i+} \log x_{i+}$$

Making analogous simplifications in the other terms gives

$$G^2 = 2 \left(\sum_{i,j} x_{ij} \log x_{ij} - \sum_i x_{i+} \log x_{i+} - \sum_j x_{+j} \log x_{+j} \right.$$
$$\left. + x_{++} \log x_{++} \right) \qquad (2.26)$$

This formula is a sum of terms, each of which has the form $x \log x$, where x is an integer from the contingency table or from its marginals. To calculate G^2 in this way the expected frequencies are not needed. This result, combined with the fact that many pocket calculators can calculate $x \log x$ easily, means that G^2 can be found without writing down any intermediate steps.

Equation 2.26 applied to the example data is

$$
\begin{aligned}
G^2 &= 2(80 \log + 251 \log 251 + 84 \log 84 + 66 \log 66 \\
&\quad - 331 \log 331 - 150 \log 150 \\
&\quad - 164 \log 164 - 317 \log 317 \\
&\quad + 481 \log 481) \\
&= 2(350.56 + 1386.89 + 372.19 + 276.52 \\
&\quad - 1920.50 - 751.60 \\
&\quad - 836.38 - 1825.57 \\
&\quad + 2970.59) \\
&= 45.40
\end{aligned}
$$

Of course, the same result was obtained from Equation 2.25. In using Equation 2.26, one must be careful to carry a sufficient number of intermediate places, so that the final result is accurate. When calculating G^2 on a computer, where the precision is fixed, the original definition, Equation 2.25, is preferable to Equation 2.26.

In most respects, the properties of the Pearson and the likelihood-ratio statistics are similar. Both test the same null hypothesis. Both are referred to a χ^2 distribution with the same number of degrees of freedom, so both have the same critical value and the same probabilistic interpretation. Although they are not equally powerful against exactly the same alternatives, their power functions are nearly the same. Under most circumstances a particular null hypothesis is retained or rejected by both statistics alike.

Which of these two statistics should one choose? As neither measure is uniformly superior to the other, the choice is largely a matter of convenience and personal preference. The following points aid in a decision, but do not force it:

- The formula for the Pearson statistic is intuitively more transparent than the formula for the likelihood-ratio statistic. It is more familiar to many readers.
- The likelihood-ratio statistic derives more directly from the principles of statistical testing than the Pearson statistic (see Chapters 4 and 5). It is more closely connected to similar tests in other branches of statistics.
- The approximation of the Pearson statistic by the theoretical chi-square distribution is somewhat more robust for small samples than is the approximation of the likelihood-ratio statistic (see Fienberg, 1979, 1980, Appendix IV; Koehler, 1986; Koehler & Larntz, 1980; Larntz, 1978).
- The likelihood-ratio statistic provides a consistent sequence of additive test statistics when it is applied to a sequence of hierarchically ordered models (see

Sections 3.8 and 5.6) or to the decomposition of a complex model (see Sections 6.5 and 9.1). The Pearson statistic may show inconsistencies, although these are confusing only when the difference between models is small and so present no practical problems.

- When the expected frequencies can be bypassed, the likelihood-ratio statistic is more rapidly calculated. However, it needs a source of logarithms.

Notwithstanding these points, the similarities of the statistics dominate their differences; for most purposes, one may choose either. In the examples in this book, sometimes one is used, sometimes the other, and sometimes both. Of course, in a research report one selects a single test statistic and uses it consistently.

2.9. POWER CALCULATIONS

As described in Section 1.3, a statistical test is characterized by two conditional probabilities. One, which must always be supplied, is the type I error probability, α. The second can be specified in two ways: either as the probability of failing to reject a false null hypothesis (a type II error, denoted by β) or as the probability of correctly rejecting this false null-hypothesis (known as the *power*, $1 - \beta$). The value of β or $1 - \beta$ is not needed to run a test. Nevertheless, it gives useful information about the quality of the test and the number of observations that one needs to make.

The usefulness of power calculations is limited by the need to know the specific true alternative hypothesis to which the power applies. One knows one's null hypothesis, but in a typical research setting what is really true is unknown. Sometimes there are ways to approximate the alternative based on a theoretical analysis or on the results of prior research, although generally these give only rough values. Fortunately, one is usually interested only in approximate answers, and either rough estimates based on earlier work or guesses at the smallest interesting effect are satisfactory. One wants to know whether the power of a test is 80% or 30%, but does not care about the difference between 80% and 85%. Similarly, it makes little difference whether sample-size calculations say that 90 or 110 subjects are required to attain a given power; what one needs to know is that a sample of 20 subjects is unsatisfactory and that one of 500 is unnecessary.

Figure 1.1 illustrates the basis for the power analysis. First, the null hypothesis is used to construct the decision rule. Then, this criterion is applied to the distribution of the test statistic under the alternative hypothesis to find the power. For tests based on the χ^2 distribution, the alternative distribution is known as the *noncentral chi-square distribution* (for properties of which see Johnson & Kotz, 1970, Chapter 28). This distribution depends on the same degrees-of-freedom value as the central chi-square test and on a *noncentrality parameter*, here

TABLE 2.5
Power Calculation in a 2 × 3 Table

Alternative Hypothesis Probabilities $\pi_{ij}^{(1)}$

0.2	0.1	0.1
0.3	0.1	0.2

Alternative Hypothesis Frequencies $\mu_{ij}^{(1)}$

20	10	10
30	10	20

Frequencies Derived from $\mu_{ij}^{(1)}$ *under* H_0, $\mu_{ij}^{(0)}$

20	8	12
30	12	18

Power Calculation

$$\omega = \sum_{\text{cells}} \frac{(\mu_{ij}^{(1)} - \mu_{ij}^{(0)})^2}{\mu_{ij}^{(0)}} = 1.39$$

With $\nu = 2$ degrees of freedom, the figure in Appendix A.3 gives $1 - \beta = 0.17$.

denoted by ω, that measures the discrepancy between the null and the alternative models.†

For a particular alternative hypothesis, the noncentrality parameter is readily found: it is the value of X^2 or G^2 calculated by using the expected frequencies under the alternative hypothesis as if they were data. Table 2.5 shows an example. Suppose one wishes to detect dependence in a 2 × 3 table in which the true probabilities are those given as $\pi_{ij}^{(1)}$ at the top of the table. These probabilities are a specific alternative to the null hypothesis of independence; the superscript "(1)" indicates their affiliation to the alternative hypothesis. The test of independence in this situation is based on 2 degrees of freedom, so that the critical value for the test is 5.99. This value gives the decision rule. Suppose that $N = 100$ observations are to be made. The expected value of the frequencies equal N times the probabilities, denoted $\mu_{ij}^{(1)}$ in the second part of the table. Now treat this table as data. The expected frequencies under the null hypothesis of independence—call them $\pi_{ij}^{(0)}$—are obtained as usual, and the Pearson statistic formula is applied to them. The result is the noncentrality parameter $\omega = 1.39$. The power of the test equals the probability that an observation from a noncentral χ^2 distribution with

---

†The letter λ is often used for the noncentrality parameter, but λ is used for so many other things in this book that a different choice is warranted.

$\nu = 2$ degrees of freedom and noncentrality $\omega = 1.39$ exceeds the critical value of 5.99.

There is no simple formula for the cumulative distribution function of the noncentral χ^2, so one needs a set of tables to find the power. Such tables exist, indexed by ν, ω, and the criterion value (e.g., Cohen, 1977, Chapter 7; Haynam, Govindarajulu, Leone, and Siefert, 1982-3), but for most practical uses, less cumbersome materials suffice. In Appendix A.3 is a plot of the probability that a noncentral χ^2 variate exceeds the upper-tail 5% critical value of the central $\chi^2(\nu)$ distribution, with different lines for different values of ν. The power for a 5% test is read directly from this figure, without further calculation. To keep the size of the figure within bounds, the abscissa is plotted as $\sqrt{\omega}$, and a logarithmic scale is used on the ordinate. For the example above $\sqrt{\omega} = 1.18$, so by starting with this value on the abscissa and using the 2 degrees-of-freedom line, the power is read from the ordinate as $1 - \beta = 0.17$, indicating only about one chance in 6 that the test would yield a significant result. Almost certainly, this power is unsatisfactory. It suggests that either more observations should be obtained or the investigation should be redesigned.

In Appendix A.3, points up to $\nu = 100$ are plotted. In the rare cases where larger values of ν occur, the noncentral χ^2 distribution is roughly normal. To get percentage points for a particular value x, the distribution is converted to a standard cumulative normal distribution by

$$z = \frac{x - \nu - \omega + 1}{\sqrt{2\nu + 4\omega}} \tag{2.27}$$

Normal-distribution tables then apply (e.g., the table in Appendix A.4). This approximation is not accurate unless ν is large.

The noncentrality parameter can be written with cell probabilities instead of frequencies. Let $\pi_{ij}^{(0)}$ and $\pi_{ij}^{(1)}$ be the probabilities of cell i,j under the null and alternative hypotheses, respectively. For the test of independence in a two-way table, these probabilities are related by

$$\pi_{ij}^{(0)} = \pi_{i+}^{(1)}\, \pi_{+j}^{(1)} \tag{2.28}$$

For a sample of size N, the frequencies are $\mu_{ij} = N\pi_{ij}$ and the Pearson statistic is

$$\omega = N \sum_{\text{cells}} \frac{(\pi_{ij}^{(1)} - \pi_{ij}^{(0)})^2}{\pi_{ij}^{(0)}} \tag{2.29}$$

(cf. Equation 2.14). Similarly, the likelihood-ratio statistic is

$$\omega = 2N \sum_{\text{cells}} \pi_{ij}^{(1)} \log \frac{\pi_{ij}^{(1)}}{\pi_{ij}^{(0)}} \tag{2.30}$$

As a second example of a problem for which the noncentral χ^2 is necessary, consider how one estimates the size of the sample needed to attain a particular power. Suppose that one plans to test for the homogeneity of 3 populations on a 4-level categorization using the likelihood-ratio test statistic at $\alpha = 0.05$ and that one wants a power of 0.8. To start, one needs to know what one is trying to detect. Rough estimates of the distributions—they can be very rough—might be obtained from pilot work, from a theoretical analysis, or as the smallest interesting deviation from homogeneity. Say that the distributions at the top of Table 2.6 are selected. These three distributions are now combined into a single distribution over the complete table. When variabilities are equal, statistical tests that compare populations are most efficient when the samples are of equal size. If subject cost or availability does not prevent it, one should put one-third of the observations in each row of the table. Dividing each population's probabilities by 3 gives the alternative probabilities $\pi_{ij}^{(1)}$, shown in the second panel of Table 2.6. The corresponding probabilities under the null hypothesis, $\pi_{ij}^{(0)}$, are calculated from Equation 2.28. Applying Equation 2.30 to these two sets of probabilities

TABLE 2.6
Sample-size Calculation for a Test of Homogeneity in Three Populations

Original Probability Distributions

Population 1	0.13	0.46	0.31	0.10
Population 2	0.15	0.52	0.26	0.07
Population 3	0.05	0.35	0.44	0.16

Alternative Hypothesis Probabilities $\pi_{ij}^{(1)}$

0.0433	0.1533	0.1033	0.0333
0.0500	0.1733	0.0867	0.0233
0.0167	0.1167	0.1467	0.0533

Probabilities Derived from $\pi_{ij}^{(1)}$ *under* H_o, $\pi_{ij}^{(0)}$

0.0367	0.1478	0.1122	0.0367
0.0367	0.1478	0.1122	0.0367
0.0367	0.1478	0.1122	0.0367

Sample Size Calculation

$$\omega = 2N \sum_{\text{cells}} \pi_{ij}^{(1)} \log \frac{\pi_{ij}^{(1)}}{\pi_{ij}^{(0)}} = 0.060N$$

From Appendix A.3 with $\nu = 6$ and $1 - \beta = 0.8$, $\omega = 13.7$.

$0.060N = 13.7$

$N = 228$

gives $\omega = 0.060N$. Another value of ω is obtained from Appendix A.3: the test is on 6 degrees of freedom with a desired power of $1 - \beta = 0.8$, hence, reading across the 0.8 horizontal to the $\nu = 6$ line and then dropping down to the abscissa, $\sqrt{\omega} \approx 3.7$ or $\omega \approx 13.7$. The sample size is chosen to make these values of ω the same, that is, so that $13.7 = 0.060N$. Then $N \approx 228$. This is the total sample size: about 76 observations should be made from each of the three populations.

2.10. THE CORRECTION FOR CONTINUITY

As noted in Section 2.5, the sampling distribution of the observations in a contingency table is discrete and is only approximated by the continuous χ^2 distribution. Regardless of the sample size, some degree of mismatch between these distributions is inevitable. To adjust for this mismatch, a correction for the Pearson statistic has been proposed, known as *Yates' correction for continuity* (Yates, 1934). This correction applies to single degree-of-freedom tests, such as that in a 2×2 table. The correction is analogous to the correction for continuity applied when a normal distribution is used to approximate the discrete binomial distribution (as described in most introductory statistics books). For the χ^2 test, $1/2$ is subtracted from the absolute differences between observed and expected frequencies before each difference is squared:

$$X_c^2 = \sum_{\text{cells}} \frac{(|x_{ij} - \hat{\mu}_{ij}| - 1/2)^2}{\hat{\mu}_{ij}} \qquad (2.31)$$

The balance of the test is unchanged. Because the squared terms are smaller, $X_c^2 < X^2$ and a significant result slightly harder to obtain. For example, Yates' correction applied to the data in Section 2.1 gives $X_c^2 = 45.14$, rather than $X^2 = 46.54$.

The appropriateness of Yates' correction is a somewhat controversial matter. Each of the sampling schemes described in Section 2.3 leads to different implications and to different corrections. Where one or two of the marginals are treated as free parameters, Yates' correction is somewhat conservative (Camili & Hopkins, 1978; Conover, 1974; Grizzle, 1967). The consequent loss of power argues against its use (although see Berkson, 1978-9; Mantel & Greenhouse, 1968 for other points of view). In the less common hypothesis of unrelated classification, where both marginals are fixed, it is more appropriate. If a correction is desired, several other statistics are less conservative and may be better choices (Overall, Rhoades, & Starbuck, 1987, describe 8 test statistics for a 2×2 table; Upton, 1982, considers 22 of them).

Fortunately, the uncorrected X^2 statistic does not serve badly. One does not go wrong by using it. Accordingly, since Yates' correction does not extend readily to larger tables or to multidimensional problems, it is not used in this book.

2.11. EXACT TESTS

When one worries about the quality of the χ^2 approximation, one may ignore that approximation and work directly with the sampling distribution of the discrete statistic. The essential procedure is simple: one looks at all possible ways the data might have come out and calculates the probability of a result at least as deviant from the null hypothesis as that observed. This probability is the descriptive level of the result. Obviously, this approach makes most sense when the number of observations is small, since for those cases the χ^2 approximation is worst and there are fewer configurations to examine.

An example is shown in Table 2.7. The first portion shows the original 2×2 table to be tested. There is an excess of frequency on the minor diagonal of this table (the 6 and the 9). There are 3 other tables with the same marginal frequencies that are more unbalanced than the original table. These configurations, along with the original data, appear in the second part of Table 2.7. The directional (one-sided) descriptive level is the probability of obtaining one of these four outcomes from among all tables with the same marginal frequencies. If this sum is less than 0.05, the result is significant at the 5% level by a one-sided criterion.

To calculate the probabilities of the tables, a sampling model is needed. The homogeneity and independence models are hard to use here because they depend

TABLE 2.7
Fisher's Exact Test

Original Data

4	9	13
6	3	9
10	12	22

Tested Tables and Probability Calculation

4	9	$\dfrac{13!\ 9!\ 10!\ 12!}{4!\ 9!\ 6!\ 3!\ 22!} = 0.09288$
6	3	

3	10	$\dfrac{13!\ 9!\ 10!\ 12!}{3!\ 10!\ 7!\ 2!\ 22!} = 0.01592$
7	2	

2	11	$\dfrac{13!\ 9!\ 10!\ 12!}{2!\ 11!\ 8!\ 1!\ 22!} = 0.00109$
8	1	

1	12	$\dfrac{13!\ 9!\ 10!\ 12!}{1!\ 12!\ 9!\ 0!\ 22!} = 0.00002$
9	0	

One-sided descriptive level = 0.10991

on the unknown marginal distributions (the various π's in Equations 2.10 and 2.12). A more tractable choice is the unrelated-classification model where both sets of marginals are viewed as fixed. This model leads to what is known as *Fisher's exact test* (Fisher, 1935, Section 2.1.02; Yates, 1934). Consider a general 2 × 2 table and let the letters A, B, C, D, and N stand for the fixed marginal frequencies:

$$
\begin{array}{cc|c}
x_{11} & x_{12} & A \\
x_{21} & x_{22} & B \\
\hline
C & D & N
\end{array}
\qquad (2.32)
$$

Obtaining this configuration is tantamount to solving a sampling problem. Suppose that a population of size N consists of A objects of one type and B objects of another. From this population a sample of size C is drawn without replacement (hence leaving D objects unchosen), which is found to contain x_{11} objects of the first type and x_{21} of the second. The probability of this result is given by the *hypergeometric distribution*:†

$$
P(\text{Display } 2.32) = \frac{\binom{A}{x_{11}}\binom{B}{x_{21}}}{\binom{N}{C}} = \frac{A!\, B!\, C!\, D!}{x_{11}!\, x_{12}!\, x_{21}!\, x_{22}!\, N!} \qquad (2.33)
$$

The probabilities of the 4 outcomes, based on this formula, are shown in Table 2.7. Their sum is 0.110, which is the one-sided descriptive level of the result. Had this value been less than 0.05, the null hypothesis of independence or of no association could have been rejected at the 5% level (one-sided) in favor of the directional alternative that excess frequency lies on the minor diagonal.

Tests in a bidirectional (two-sided) sense are more complicated, owing to the difficulty of deciding what represents a "more deviant" result. Several solutions are possible, depending on whether one measures the effect by the rarity of the outcome or by some effect-size index (Krüger, Lehmacher, & Wall, 1981). The easiest way is to divide the type I probability in half and put $\alpha/2$ in each tail. If the sum of the probabilities in Table 2.7 is less than 0.025, one rejects the null hypothesis at the 5% level, two tailed. To determine a two-tailed descriptive level, one cannot just double the one-tailed level, however, but should consider alternatives that are extreme in the opposite direction (Freeman & Halton, 1951).

These calculations are impractical when the frequencies are much larger than

---

†Equation 2.33 follows from a counting-rule argument. There are $\binom{N}{C}$ samples of size C that can be chosen from N objects, which gives the denominator of Equation 2.33. This sample is composed of x_{11} objects chosen from A possibilities and x_{21} chosen from B possibilities. The numerator is the product of the number of ways of making each of these choices.

those in the example. Many different configurations are consistent with the observed marginals, so that the amount of computation is excessive. Consider, for example, the difficulties that would attend using this test on the data in Section 2.1, for which 67 separate tables with values of x_{22} from 0 to 66 need to be evaluated, each involving factorials of numbers as large as 481. Fortunately, in such tables the χ^2 approximation is more than satisfactory. For smaller values of N, where one might want to use exact procedures, tables have been calculated that, for a given combination of N, A, and C, allow one to look up a value of x_{11} that is just sufficient to reject the hypothesis of unrelated distributions (up to $N = 25$ by Finney, 1948 and Latscha, 1953; reprinted in some books of tables, such as Beyer, 1968, Pearson & Hartley, 1954; up to $N = 50$ by Krüger, et al., 1981). With these tables, exact tests are rapid. They are particularly handy when many 2×2 tables must be examined.

When the discrete probability models are used in a hypothesis-testing procedure, the critical values are chosen to be the nearest exact value that does not exceed the nominal significance level. Thus, the actual level of the test is always somewhat less than the level as represented and the tests are conservative. Difficulties also arise from the assumption of fixed marginal distributions when the test should be of independence or homogeneity. The use of Fisher's exact test has been criticized on these grounds (e.g., Garside & Mack, 1976; Overall, et al., 1987; Upton, 1982). As with the closely related problem of the correction for continuity, the issues here are complicated (see Berkson, 1978-9, and the discussion of that article, particularly Kempthorne, 1979, and the references cited there).

In principle, Fisher's exact procedure can be extended to tables larger than 2×2 and to tables with more than two dimensions. However, in these situations the number of more deviant tables is so large that the labor required to calculate and tabulate them is prohibitive. Computer algorithms have been developed that help somewhat (Freeman & Halton, 1951; Mehta & Patel, 1983; Pagano & Halvorsen, 1981), but even with a computer the computation rapidly exceeds practical bounds. The appropriateness of the fixed-marginals assumption is also more questionable in these tables.

2.12. OTHER MODELS FOR A TWO-WAY TABLE

Thus far in this chapter, expected frequencies of only one type have been considered. Even though three different sets of constraints and interpretations are described in Section 2.3, all three led to the same formula for $\hat{\mu}_{ij}$. Other models for expected frequencies can be developed, however. These can be divided into two classes: those that are simpler than the independence model and those that posit a more complex structure.

The simpler models are straightforward. Essentially, they postulate that one or another set of marginals follows a distribution, usually uniform, that is given by hypothesis rather than being determined by the data. For example, one might surmise that the two approaches in the problem-solving example are equally likely (the data, reproduced in Table 2.8, are from Table 2.2). With this constraint, one-half the correct responses and one-half the errors should fall in each class, converting the observed frequencies to the expected frequencies in Table 2.8. Note that while the column marginals in these tables agree, the row marginals in the expected table divide the total frequency evenly. These expected frequencies are more constrained than they would be for a test of independence, which is reflected in their poorer fit. There are $(a - 1)b$ degrees of freedom for a test of this hypothesis (as found by the methods described in Section 3.11). With 2 degrees of freedom, the null hypothesis can be rejected.

Tests in which the row distribution is given a fixed nonuniform shape are conducted in an analogous manner, as are tests in which the column distribution or both distributions are specified.

The hypotheses tested here are compound. The null hypothesis is rejected if the marginal distribution is uneven, if the classifications are associated, or if both are true. This compounding makes the tests both more difficult to interpret and less useful than the tests of association alone. In practice, these compound models do not often express meaningful research questions. Accordingly, their discussion is limited to these remarks and to some comments in Section 3.7. In any case, when they are necessary, they are easy enough to run.

TABLE 2.8
Testing an Independence Model with Equal Row Frequencies

Observed Frequencies

		Solution Accuracy correct	error	
Approach	a	26	115	141
Chosen	b	54	136	190
		80	251	331

Expected Frequencies $\hat{\mu}_{ij} = \frac{x_{+j}}{a}$

		Solution Accuracy correct	error	
Approach	a	40.0	125.5	165.5
Chosen	b	40.0	125.5	165.5
		80	251	331

$X^2(2) = 11.56$
$G^2(2) = 11.77$

The other class of two-way models involves the description of dependence within the table. Such models can fit even when association is present. These models are very useful, for they give a way to say something about the nature of the dependence when some form of association is present. Many such models can be constructed (see Goodman, 1972a, 1985 for a large selection). For example, one may wish to postulate that different relationships hold for cells on the diagonal of a square table than for cells off it, or to treat the order in which the categories are listed as significant. The analysis of these models depends on techniques that are developed in Chapters 11 and 13.

PROBLEMS

2.1. For the following situations, decide whether the appropriate null hypothesis is of independence, homogeneity, or unrelated classification.

a. During the course of an experiment, each subject waits for 5 minutes in a room where another person is working. The next day, the subject is asked to identify this person from a set of 5 photographs. Twenty subjects are tested in the same room in which they waited, 20 in a different room. The data are

	Identification	
	Correct	Incorrect
Same room	13	7
Different room	11	9

b. Both members of 35 pairs of siblings are asked to solve a puzzle that requires the disassembly of two bent wires. The solutions are classified by whether they were completed within 1 minute:

		Elder sibling	
		< 1 min	≥ 1 min
Younger sibling	< 1 min	13	5
	≥ 1 min	7	10

c. A flock of 30 birds is introduced into a large cage. One-half are of species s_1, the other half are of species s_2. There are 30 nesting sites in the cage, half near to the ground and half high up. Each bird takes possession of one site. The number of birds of each species in each location is

	Location	
	Low	High
Species s_1	16	4
Species s_2	4	16

2.2. Test for unrelatedness in the three experiments of Problem 2.1. State your conclusions in a form appropriate to the design.

2.3. You are discussing the results of an informal sidewalk poll conducted by a friend in which two questions were asked. The results are

| | | Question 1 | | |
		a_1	a_2	a_3
Question 2	Yes	31	16	15
	No	21	18	20

a. Test these data for unrelatedness, using the likelihood-ratio statistic.
b. Upon further discussion, you discover that when two people walking together were encountered, both were questioned. What problems does this introduce? Taking this fact into account, what can you say about the results?

2.4. You have made two categorical measurements on the same subject each day for 60 days. These form the table

4	1	18
1	12	1
12	4	6

You wish to test for an association between the two factors, but you worry that the observations are not independent.
a. Explain how you could test to see whether the classification of factor A (say) is related to the classification for the previous day. Note: the actual test requires data that are not in the table above, so do not try to run it.
b. Suppose that your analysis shows that each response is associated with the response on the previous two days. What are you able to conclude about the relationship?

2.5. Two raters listen to tape recordings of five-minute interviews with three-member families (father, mother, and child) and rate the interaction according to which of the three dominates the interview. Twenty families are rated. Concern is raised as to whether the two raters are making the classifications in the same way. To test whether their ratings are comparable, the distribution of scores for each rater is tabulated and the two distributions compared:

	F	M	C
Rater A	10	8	2
Rater B	7	12	1

$$X^2(2) = 1.66$$

Since the test statistic is not sufficient to reject the hypothesis of homogeneity, the two raters are judged to be using the categories in the same way. There are several problems with this analysis. Identify them. Note: the proper way to run this analysis is covered in Section 9.5.

2.6. A second experiment replicating the design of Problem 2.1b with 88 subjects gives the results

| | | Elder sibling | |
		< 1 min	≥ 1 min
Younger sibling	< 1 min	24	11
	≥ 1 min	22	31

Which of the two studies shows the larger association between siblings? Remember that the size of an effect is not the same thing as its statistical descriptive level.

2.7. You wish to replicate the experiment in Problem 2.1a. Using those data as a guide to the size of a potential effect, how many subjects would you need to run to have a 95% chance of successfully detecting an effect of the test room?

2.8. Demonstrate that the parameter estimates $\hat{\lambda} = 2.1583$, $\hat{\lambda}_{E(1)} = 0.1438$, and $\hat{\lambda}_{Y(1)} = 0.0286$ give expected frequencies for the unrelatedness model for the data in Problem 2.1b.

2.9. Calculate the continuity-corrected test statistics for the data in Problem 2.1b and c.

2.10. Suppose that an experiment similar to that in Problem 2.1c is run that uses only 8 birds, 3 of the first species and 5 of the other. There are 4 nest locations at each height. Two birds of the first species are observed in higher nest sites. What is the descriptive level of this result (in a two-sided sense)? Are the location and the species associated?

3

Models for Three-way Tables

Most real entities can be classified with respect to more than two attributes and placed in tables with more than two dimensions. These tables demand extensions of the procedures described in Chapter 2. The present chapter treats the analysis of three-way tables. The ideas introduced here are developed further in later chapters: the sampling models more fully in Chapter 4, the estimation and testing procedures in Chapter 5, and the interpretation of the models and tests in Chapters 6 to 8.

3.1. THE THREE-WAY TABLE

Three-way frequency tables arise from many types of designs. Consider a three examples:

1. A questionnaire is administered to 200 student volunteers. This questionnaire involves, among other things, three yes-no questions concerning dating habits. This categorization places each student in one cell of a $2 \times 2 \times 2$ table.
2. Three groups of 30 children are assembled, of ages 4, 6, and 8 years. Each child is given two problems to solve. Each problem is scored as correct or incorrect, giving each child a 2×2 classification. With the age factor, each child falls into one cell of a $3 \times 2 \times 2$ table.
3. In a study of the acquisition of a skilled task, six equal-size groups of subjects are run, determined by combinations of two sets of instructions and three levels of practice. The 180 subjects are randomly assigned to the 6 condi-

tions. The following day, each subject is given a retention test that produces a rating of low, moderate, or high skill in the task. Including the group assignment, each subject falls in one cell of a $2 \times 3 \times 3$ table.

Although all three examples generate three-way tables, the designs of the studies are different. In the first no marginal distribution is constrained by the design, in the second the age frequencies are fixed, and in the third both grouping factors are determined by the experimenter. Just as with two-way tables, these design characteristics are reflected in different null hypotheses of no effect, similar to the hypotheses of independence and homogeneity described in Section 2.3. Unlike in the two-way case, these differences influence the choice of an appropriate model for the expected frequencies.

In a two-way table there is only one way to describe unrelatedness: either the rows and columns of the table are associated or they are not. A three-way table offers more possibilities. Several hypotheses of partial association or partial independence can be constructed. The next five sections describe a series of models of increasing complexity. All but two of these models build directly on the idea of independence or unrelatedness in a two-way configuration, extending it to three dimensions. One model, discussed in Section 3.5, goes beyond the assertion of unrelatedness to describe a specific form of association. The series of models is summarized in Figure 3.1. This figure embodies much of the information in the five sections and should be consulted as that material is read.

As these models are presented, it is instructive to apply them to a single table of numbers. The $2 \times 2 \times 3$ table of frequencies in Table 3.1 is used as an example throughout. The three dimensions of the table, or *factors*, are denoted by uppercase letters, here A, B, and C. Their particular levels are indicated by subscripted lowercase letters, for example, the levels of A are a_1 and a_2. Where convenient, a more mnemonic choice of letters is used. Thus, in the third example above, one might let I stand for the instruction category, P for practice, and R for the result of the retention test. Regardless of the letters used to designate the factors, they are indexed by the subscripts i, j, and k. Thus, an individual observation from Table 3.1 is denoted x_{ijk}. The matching of the index letter to the factor names is usually obvious. In particular, where the generic factor names A, B, and C, are used, they are indexed by i, j, and k, respectively. The number of levels of a factor is indicated by the lower-case form of its name: there are a levels of factor A, b levels of factor B, etc.

The emphasis on unrelatedness and independence as interpretative concepts makes it helpful to have a shorthand notation for the presence or absence of an association between factors. In what is called here the *independence notation*, the symbol $\perp\!\!\!\perp$ is used, standing between letters that represent unrelated factors. Thus, the lack of an association between factors A and B in a two-way table is indicated by $A \perp\!\!\!\perp B$. This symbol is used regardless of whether the lack of association corresponds to independence, homogeneity, or unrelated classifica-

Model	Graph	Fitted marginals
Complete independence $[A][B][C]$ $A \perp\!\!\!\perp B \perp\!\!\!\perp C$ $df = abc - a - b - c + 2$	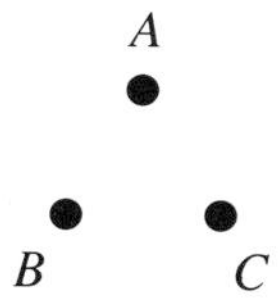	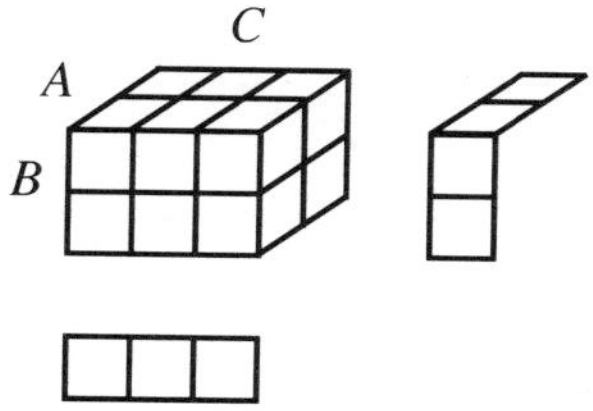
One-factor independence (3 similar models) $[AB][C]$ $AB \perp\!\!\!\perp C$ $df = (ab-1)(c-1)$	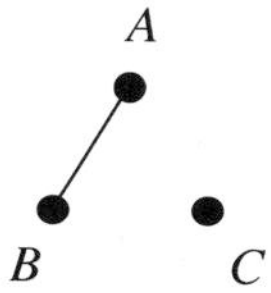	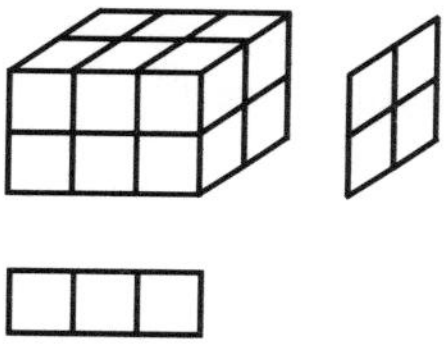
Conditional independence (3 similar models) $[AB][BC]$ $A \perp\!\!\!\perp C \mid B$ $df = (a-1)\, b\, (c-1)$	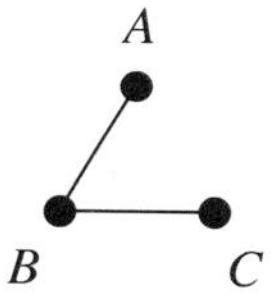	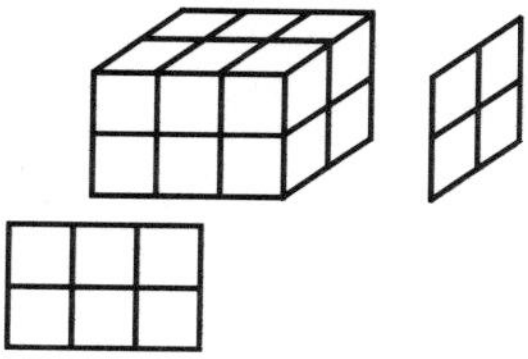
Homogeneous associations $[AB][AC][BC]$ $df = (a-1)(b-1)(c-1)$	NO GRAPH	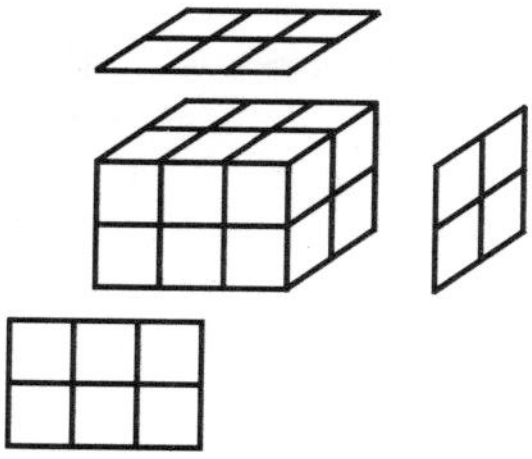
Three-way associations (saturated model) $[ABC]$ $df = 0$	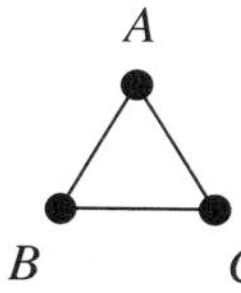	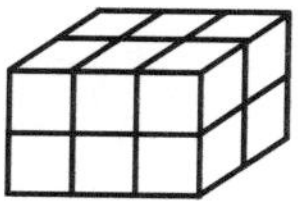

FIGURE 3.1. Models for a three-way table

TABLE 3.1
A Three-way Table of Frequencies

| | a_1 | | | a_2 | | |
	c_1	c_2	c_3	c_1	c_2	c_3
b_1	7	5	3	15	20	2
b_2	22	49	140	4	3	5

tion as distinguished in Section 2.3 above. When an association is present, the unrelatedness symbol is canceled by writing $A \not\perp\!\!\!\perp B$.

In a two-way table with $A \perp\!\!\!\perp B$, the marginal frequency distributions (x_{i+} and x_{+j}) determine the expected frequencies. The marginal distributions play a similar role with multiway tables. With three factors, there are several marginal distributions: three sets of two-way marginals, formed by summing over one of the subscripts (x_{ij+}, x_{i+k}, and x_{+jk}), three sets of one-way marginals, formed by summing over two subscripts, (x_{i++}, x_{+j+}, and x_{++k}), and one overall sum (x_{+++}). Visualization of these marginal tables as collapsed forms of the block of data is helpful (Figure 3.2). Note that the higher-order marginal tables (such as x_{i++}) are themselves marginals of the lower-order marginals (such as x_{ij+}).

3.2. COMPLETE INDEPENDENCE

The most direct expression of independence in a three-factor design is the assertion that the factors are completely dissociated. Under this model, known as *complete independence* or *complete unrelatedness*, the classification of any factor has no influence on the classification of any other factor or combination of factors. When complete independence holds, factor A is unrelated to factor B, to factor C, and to the combinations of B and C, using the same definition of

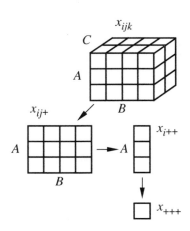

FIGURE 3.2. Extracting the marginal tables from a three-way table of frequencies

pplies to the two-factor case. Moreover, B is unrelated to A and C (or their combination) and C is unrelated to A and B. Note that unrelatedness at the level of the combinations is necessary—it is not sufficient for the two-way marginals to show independence for this model to hold (see Problem 3.4).

Complete independence is a very strong condition for any set of data to obey. Just as the model of independence serves as a null hypothesis for a two-way table, complete independence is most useful as a null model against which to contrast various forms of association. If complete independence is rejected, then some form of association is present. Thus, in the first study described in the last section (the 3-item dating questionnaire), one determines whether there is any association among the three questions by testing for their complete independence. Rejection of this hypothesis implies some relationship among the questions.

Several notation schemes have been developed to symbolically represent multifactor models. An obvious choice is the independence notation. In this notation, the complete independence of three factors is indicated by $A \perp\!\!\!\perp B \perp\!\!\!\perp C$. A second representation, closely related to this one, is graphical. The factors are represented by points and their associations by lines between them, in a figure technically known as a *graph*. The three completely independent factors are pictured as three distinct points,

The graphical notation is particularly useful tables with more than three factors, and is discussed further in Section 6.3.

The independence notation emphasizes the factors that are unrelated to each other. Sometimes a model is easier to understand if one concentrates on the presence of associations. A third notational scheme emphasizes this aspect of the models. The *association notation* (or *bracket notation*) describes a model by listing within sets of brackets the interassociated combinations of factors. The representation of the complete independence model in this way is almost trivial. There are no associations, so the model is described by isolating the three factors in separate pairs of brackets, as $[A][B][C]$. The bracket notation is more general than the independence notation, in that it can describe many models that cannot be expressed in terms of unrelatedness.†

---

†Similar notation schemes are used by other authors. Several denote unrelateness as $[A \otimes B]$ rather than $A \perp\!\!\!\perp B$; the latter symbol derives from Dawid (1979). The association notation is much more variable: the model $[AB][C]$ in the next section is variously denoted by (AB, C) (Agresti, 1984), $C_{12}C_3$ (Bishop, Fienberg, & Holland, 1975), $[12][3]$ (Fienberg, 1980), $\{AB\}, \{C\}$ (Goodman, 1970, 1971, etc.), AB, C (Haberman, 1978, 1979), and AB/C (Upton, 1978). Undoubtedly, other forms occur.

The expected frequencies under complete independence are easy to find. As with the two-factor model of independence, the joint probability of a cell, π_{ijk}, is the product of the probabilities of the three classifications considered separately. These probabilities, in turn, are given by the marginal probabilities π_{i++}, π_{+j+}, and π_{++k}. Thus, if complete independence holds, then the cell probabilities obey the relationship

$$\pi_{ijk} = \pi_{i++}\pi_{+j+}\pi_{++k} \tag{3.1}$$

The natural estimates of the marginal probabilities are the corresponding proportions. Substituting these estimates into Equation 3.1 gives the expected frequencies:

$$\hat{\mu}_{ijk} = x_{+++}\hat{\pi}_{ijk}$$
$$= x_{+++}p_{i++}p_{+j+}p_{++k}$$
$$= x_{+++}\left(\frac{x_{i++}}{x_{+++}}\right)\left(\frac{x_{+j+}}{x_{+++}}\right)\left(\frac{x_{++k}}{x_{+++}}\right)$$
$$= \frac{x_{i++}x_{+j+}x_{++k}}{x_{+++}^2} \tag{3.2}$$

This procedure for constructing the expected frequencies makes their marginal sums agree with their counterparts in the data. For factor A this equivalence is

$$\sum_{j,k}\hat{\mu}_{ijk} = x_{i++}$$

Similar equations apply to factors B and C. These indentities give another way to interpret the complete independence model. Fitting the model amounts to selecting a set of expected frequencies that (1) have no association among the factors and (2) make the one-way marginals agree. These fitted marginal distributions are illustrated in Figure 3.1.

For the sample data, Equation 3.2 yields the expected frequencies

	a_1			a_2		
	c_1	c_2	c_3	c_1	c_2	c_3
b_1	7.5	12.0	23.3	1.6	2.6	5.1
b_2	32.0	51.3	100.0	6.9	11.1	21.7

$$\tag{3.3}$$

The hypothesis that this pattern accurately reflects the data is tested with the same test statistics that apply to a two-way table, either

$$X^2 = \sum_{\text{cells}}\frac{(x_{ijk} - \hat{\mu}_{ijk})^2}{\hat{\mu}_{ijk}} = 290.41 \tag{3.4}$$

or

$$G^2 = 2 \sum_{\text{cells}} x_{ijk} \log \frac{x_{ijk}}{\hat{\mu}_{ijk}} = 169.28 \qquad (3.5)$$

For reasons discussed in detail in Section 3.11, the χ^2 approximation for these statistics has $abc - a - b - c + 2$ degrees of freedom, which for this table is 7. Complete independence is solidly rejected; one concludes that some interfactor association is present.

The size of the difference between X^2 and G^2 in this example may be discon-certing at first glance. Is one statistic that much more powerful than the other? In fact, neither is very accurate, due to the presence of small expected frequencies. Differences between test statistics of this magnitude occasionally appear when a model fails catastrophically in its rare cells. This sensitivity is illustrated here by the fact that 79% of the value of X^2 comes from the two cells with the smallest values of $\hat{\mu}$. Actually, the discrepancy has no practical consequence: both X^2 and G^2 are so far in the tail of a $\chi^2(7)$ distribution that the model is rejected by any conceivable criterion. The difference between the statistics is much diminished for the better-fitting model in the next section.

As in the two-dimensional case, the expected-frequency formula (Equation 3.2) and the definition of G^2 (Equation 3.5) can be combined into a single formula,

$$
\begin{aligned}
G^2 &= 2 \sum_{\text{cells}} x_{ijk} \log \frac{x_{ijk} x_{+++}^2}{x_{i++} x_{+j+} x_{++k}} \\
&= 2 \Big(\sum_{i,j,k} x_{ijk} \log x_{ijk} - \sum_i x_{i++} \log x_{i++} - \sum_j x_{+j+} \log x_{+j+} \\
&\quad - \sum_k x_{++k} \log x_{++k} + 2 x_{+++} \log x_{+++} \Big)
\end{aligned}
\qquad (3.6)
$$

This formula results from expansion of the logarithm and simplification of the sum, as in Equation 2.26. Equation 3.6 lets one bypass the expected frequencies when calculating G^2.

The three-factor model of complete independence has a log-linear form. Start-ing from the multiplicative model of Equation 3.1, one takes logarithms to turn products to sums. Each term depends on a single subscript, and the model in the λ-notation is

$$\log \mu_{ijk} = \lambda + \lambda_{A(i)} + \lambda_{B(j)} + \lambda_{C(k)} \qquad (3.7)$$

Expected frequencies constructed according to Equation 3.2 fit this model.

As with the two-factor log-linear model, the parameters of Equation 3.7 are underdetermined. To obtain unique estimates, one constraint must be placed on the values of each set of parameters, λ_A, λ_B, and λ_C. One can fix the value of any single parameter or can constrain any function of them. The most common solution is to set the sum of each parameter type to zero,

$$\sum_i \lambda_{A(i)} = \sum_j \lambda_{B(j)} = \sum_k \lambda_{C(k)} = 0 \qquad (3.8)$$

With these constraints the parameters are estimated by averages of log $\hat{\mu}_{ijk}$ (as shown in Section 5.3):

$$\hat{\lambda} = \frac{\sum\limits_{\text{cells}} \log \hat{\mu}_{ijk}}{abc} \qquad (3.9)$$

$$\hat{\lambda}_{A(i)} = \frac{\sum\limits_{j,k} \log \hat{\mu}_{ijk}}{bc} - \hat{\lambda} \qquad (3.10)$$

and so forth. Applying these formulae to the expected frequencies in Display 3.3 gives $\hat{\lambda} = 2.51$, $\hat{\lambda}_A = 0.76$ and -0.76, $\hat{\lambda}_B = -0.73$ and 0.73, and $\hat{\lambda}_C = -0.54$, -0.06, and 0.60. In the present case, these estimates do not help one to understand Table 3.1, since the failure of the model to fit the data makes them meaningless.

3.3.   INDEPENDENCE OF ONE FACTOR

Models for a three-way table other than complete independence permit some form of association among the factors. The next two types of models allow certain factors to covary, while denying other relationships. The simpler of these partial-association models is *single-factor independence*, which asserts that one factor is unrelated to the other two. This model is readily explicable in terms of two-factor independence. Suppose that factor C is jointly unrelated to factors A and B and that the joint AB relationship is unknown. This assertion implies that the ab-level factor created from the combinations of A and B is unrelated to C in the two-way sense. Using the independence notation, this model is denoted $AB \perp\!\!\!\perp C$. It is consistent with any pattern of association or lack of association between A and B.

The single-factor independence model can be represented in several ways. Graphically, the model $AB \perp\!\!\!\perp C$ is pictured by connecting two points standing for A and B, leaving point C detached:

In the bracket notation, an allowance for AB relationships is provided, so the model is symbolized $[AB][C]$. Viewed in terms of its constraints on the marginal distributions of the expected frequencies, the model forces these distributions to agree with the data for any combination of A and B as well as for the simple C marginal

$$\sum_k \hat{\mu}_{ijk} = x_{ij+} \quad \text{and} \quad \sum_{i,j} \hat{\mu}_{ijk} = x_{++k} \tag{3.11}$$

It is unnecessary to specify that the A and B marginals of $\hat{\mu}_{ij}$ sum to x_{i++} and x_{+j+}, respectively. Their agreement follows from the fitting of the AB marginals: if $\hat{\mu}_{ijk}$ and x_{ijk} agree exactly when summed over k, then any subtables produced by further summing also agree.

In a three-way table, there are three version of the single-factor independence model, depending on which of the three factors is deemed unrelated to the other two. These three models are $A \perp\!\!\!\perp BC$, $AC \perp\!\!\!\perp B$, and $AB \perp\!\!\!\perp C$. Only $AB \perp\!\!\!\perp C$ is discussed in detail here; the others are comparable.

Expected frequencies for the model $AB \perp\!\!\!\perp C$ follow directly from the two-factor formulation. The relationship between A and B is unspecified, so they can be rewritten as a single classification. For Table 3.1 this reorganization gives the two-way table

	c_1	c_2	c_3
a_1b_1	7	5	3
a_1b_2	22	49	140
a_2b_1	15	20	2
a_2b_2	4	3	5

Applying the formula for two-factor independence to this table (whose marginals are x_{ij+} and x_{++k}) gives the expected-frequency formula

$$\hat{\mu}_{ijk} = \frac{x_{ij+}\, x_{++k}}{x_{+++}} \tag{3.12}$$

The expected frequencies for Table 3.1 are

	a_1			a_2		
	c_1	c_2	c_3	c_1	c_2	c_3
b_1	2.6	4.2	8.2	6.5	10.4	20.2
b_2	36.8	59.1	115.1	2.1	3.4	6.5

To test the hypothesis $AB \perp\!\!\!\perp C$, these frequencies are compared to the data using either of the standard test statistics. The degrees of freedom for this test follow from recasting the three-way table in two dimensions, equaling $(ab - 1)(c - 1)$.

For Table 3.1, the test statistics are $X^2(6) = 62.63$ and $G^2(6) = 67.49$, indicating that the hypothesis is rejected and that some additional association is present.

Incorporating the expected frequencies into G^2 (as in Equations 2.26 and 3.6) gives

$$G^2 = 2 \left(\sum_{i,j,k} x_{ijk} \log x_{ijk} - \sum_{i,j} x_{ij+} \log x_{ij+} - \sum_k x_{++k} \log x_{++k} \right.$$
$$\left. + x_{+++} \log x_{+++} \right) \tag{3.13}$$

Single-factor independence is the simplest model that can meaningfully be fitted to data from a design in which the frequencies of two factors are determined by the investigator. Whenever a pattern of frequencies is preassigned, it must be part of all models that are fitted to the data. Thus, in the third study in Section 3.1, the frequencies of the instruction-by-practice combinations were chosen in advance. Hence, every model should include IP terms. A complete independence model $I \perp\!\!\!\perp P \perp\!\!\!\perp R$ should not be used here; the simplest valid model is $IP \perp\!\!\!\perp R$. The issue is one of design, not of empirical fit. A good experimenter will choose the group sizes to be equal, which means that a model without the IP term fits the data about as well as a model with it. Nevertheless, the IP relationship concerns the experimenter's behavior, not that of the subjects, and should be present in any valid model.

The single-factor independence model is useful as a null hypothesis in a test for relationships between two factors and a third. Again looking at the instruction and practice example, the hypothesis $IP \perp\!\!\!\perp R$ is used to test whether the experimental groups influence the retention scores. If this hypothesis is rejected, then R is related to the IP combinations.

Beginning users of frequency models sometimes make the mistake of interpreting the fit of the model $[AB][C]$ as a test for the presence of an AB association. Actually, the model $[AB][C]$ is noncommittal about how A and B are related. It is a more flexible model than the complete-independence model $[A][B][C]$ and fits whenever that model is satisfied. The test for AB effects in a three-way table should be based on the hypothesis $A \perp\!\!\!\perp B|C$, which is described in the next section.

The log-linear version of the model $[AB][C]$ looks like that of the complete independence model, with the addition of a term $\lambda_{AB(ij)}$ to express any joint relationship between A and B:

$$\log \mu_{ijk} = \lambda + \lambda_{A(i)} + \lambda_{B(j)} + \lambda_{C(k)} + \lambda_{AB(ij)} \tag{3.14}$$

Again, constraints are needed to give these parameters unique values: they sum to 0 over any available subscript,

$$\sum_i \lambda_{A(i)} = \sum_j \lambda_{B(j)} = \sum_k \lambda_{C(k)} = \sum_i \lambda_{AB(ij)} = \sum_j \lambda_{AB(ij)} = 0 \tag{3.15}$$

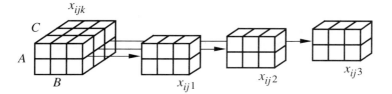

FIGURE 3.3.   Slicing a three-way table into K two-way tables

3.4.   CONDITIONAL INDEPENDENCE

The third type of model for a three-way table is built on two-factor independence in a more subtle way. One can reduce a three-factor table to a series of two-way tables by fixing the level of one of the factors—in effect by slicing the table into a series of sections (Figure 3.3). By slicing the table at the jth level of B, for example, one obtains an AC table. The association in this table is known as the *conditional association* of A and C given b_j. If A and C are unrelated in this table, they are said to be *conditionally independent given b_j*, an assertion that is denoted by $A \perp\!\!\!\perp C|b_j$. This hypothesis is easily tested using the test of unrelatedness for a two-way table.

The model of *conditional independence* for the full table asserts that two factors are conditionally unrelated at all levels of the third. If A is conditionally unrelated to C given B, written $A \perp\!\!\!\perp C|B$, then the relationship $A \perp\!\!\!\perp C|b_j$ holds for all b_j. This model allows association between A and B and between B and C; what it denies is a direct link between A and C. In the bracket notation, this conditional independence model is $[AB][BC]$, while as a graph it is represented by connecting two points to the third,

Once again, there are three versions of this model, $A \perp\!\!\!\perp B|C$, $A \perp\!\!\!\perp C|B$, and $B \perp\!\!\!\perp C|A$, depending on which pair of factors are unassociated—that is, across which factor the table is sliced.

The conditional independence model is more complicated than the two models discussed so far. The effects that it represents depend on the relationships among all three factors and are hard to picture accurately using two-way tables. Indeed, this three-dimensional character creates some surprises for one who thinks of the data only by means of two-way tables. Although factors A and C have no direct association in the model $A \perp\!\!\!\perp C|B$, they are linked through B and may show an association when considered by themselves. Their common association with B may induce an association between them, so that $A \perp\!\!\!\perp C$ may fail. Whether this two-factor association is meaningful or not depends on the interpretation of the factors.

Expected frequencies for the model $A \perp\!\!\!\perp C|B$ follow readily from its interpretation as a series of two-factor assertions. At each level b_j, fit the two-way model $A \perp\!\!\!\perp C$ to give the expected frequencies

$$\hat{\mu}_{ijk} = \frac{x_{ij+} \; x_{+jk}}{x_{+j+}} \tag{3.16}$$

These estimates constrain the expected frequencies to equal the observed frequencies in both the AB and the BC marginals. The fitted marginals appear in the numerator of this formula and the single-factor marginal that is common to them appears in the denominator. Within each slice, a test of the hypothesis that $A \perp\!\!\!\perp C|b_j$ has $(a - 1)(c - 1)$ degrees of freedom, so a test of the hypothesis $A \perp\!\!\!\perp C|B$ has $(a - 1)b(c - 1)$ degrees of freedom. An equation for G^2 can also be derived (see Problem 3.2).

For the example data, Equation 3.16 gives the expected frequencies:

	a_1			a_2			
	c_1	c_2	c_3	c_1	c_2	c_3	
b_1	6.3	7.2	1.4	15.7	17.8	3.6	
b_2	24.6	49.2	137.2	1.4	2.8	6.2	(3.17)

A nearly satisfactory fit is obtained ($X^2(4) = 9.60$ and $G^2(4) = 7.92$). By the likelihood-ratio criterion, the model cannot be rejected, while the Pearson statistic barely exceeds the 5% critical value of 9.49.

An important use of the conditional-independence model is to test for the presence of an association between a pair of factors that is not mediated by a third factor. For example, in the second study of Section 3.1, two problems (factors P and Q) are given to three groups of children of differing ages (factor A). Suppose that one wishes to see whether there is an association between the scores on the two problems. One can test for the interproblem association directly, using the null hypothesis $P \perp\!\!\!\perp Q$ in a two-way table. However, this test does not take into account the association with age. A PQ association may appear simply because young subjects do poorly on both problems and older subjects do better. If one is not interested in this aspect of the association, it can be excluded from the test by working with a model that includes AP and AQ associations, testing the hypothesis $P \perp\!\!\!\perp Q|A$. Rejection of this model establishes the necessity of PQ terms. Note that the data may show both a two-way association, $P \not\!\perp\!\!\!\perp Q$, and conditional independence given age, $P \perp\!\!\!\perp Q|A$.

As the last paragraph may suggest, the interpretation of conditional independence can be tricky and contain traps for the unwary. It is discussed further in Sections 3.12 and 3.13, and in more generality in the rules for collapsing tables in Section 5.10.

In log-linear form, the model [AB][BC] adds the term $\lambda_{BC(jk)}$ to the one factor independence model (Equation 3.14), giving

$$\log \mu_{ijk} = \lambda + \lambda_{A(i)} + \lambda_{B(j)} + \lambda_{C(k)} + \lambda_{AB(ij)} + \lambda_{BC(jk)} \tag{3.18}$$

As always, the parameters sum to zero over any subscript.

3.5. HOMOGENEOUS ASSOCIATION

As one moves from complete independence, $A \perp\!\!\!\perp B \perp\!\!\!\perp C$, to one-factor independence, $AB \perp\!\!\!\perp C$, to conditional independence, $A \perp\!\!\!\perp C|B$, one adds the terms $\lambda_{AB(ij)}$ and $\lambda_{BC(jk)}$ to the log-linear model. The obvious next step is to add the last two-factor association term, $\lambda_{AC(ik)}$, to Equation 3.18. The result is the *homogeneous-association model*, denoted by [AB][AC][BC], which has the log-linear representation

$$\log \mu_{ijk} = \lambda + \lambda_{A(i)} + \lambda_{B(j)} + \lambda_{C(k)} + \lambda_{AB(ij)} + \lambda_{AC(ik)} + \lambda_{BC(jk)} \tag{3.19}$$

This model implies a fundamental association between each pair of factors. Unlike the other models for a three-factor table, it has no expression as a lack of association, so cannot be described with the independence notation. For a similar reason the model lacks a graphical picture. The logical candidate for a graph—a triangle—is better used for the saturated model discussed in the next section.

To understand what the homogeneous-association model implies, return to the sliced three-way table in Figure 3.3. Suppose that $A \perp\!\!\!\perp C|B$ does not fit, but that Equation 3.19 is satisfactory. Then there is a conditional association of A and C given b_j whose form is determined by the parameters $\lambda_{AC(ik)}$. These parameters are the same at every level of b_j. Thus, under the model [AB][AC][BC] the association between A and C does not interact with B (Bartlett, 1935). If this model fails to fit, then the association parameters change with j and the AC association *interacts* with B. As the form [AB][AC][BC] suggests, this description is symmetrical: one could slice the table across any of the three factors and obtain the same interpretation.

When working with an experiment in which two factors have been manipulated by the experimenter and a third classification measured, another view of the homogeneous-association model is helpful. Consider again the third example from Section 3.1—the acquisition of the skilled task. In discussing this design, it is natural to express the probability of a particular retention performance as a function of the experimental group (the combination of instruction and practice). For instruction type i and practice level j, denote the conditional probability of retention level k by $\pi_{k|ij}$. If the homogeneous-association model fits (but no simpler model), then both instruction and practice influence the skill, but these influences are distinct. Under this model, one can write

$$\pi_{k|ij} = \text{(term depending on } i \text{ and } k) \text{ (term depending on } j \text{ and } k)$$

Taking the logarithm gives, for appropriate parameters α_{ik} and β_{jk},

$$\log \pi_{k|ij} = \alpha_{ik} + \beta_{jk} \tag{3.20}$$

This equation is an *additive model* for the influence of instruction and practice. Their effects are a sum of separate, noninteracting terms. Except that the model is logarithmic, Equation 3.20 is like the model for a two-factor analysis of variance in which two main effects are present but no interaction occurs. This parallel is treated more fully in Section 3.10, and descriptions like Equation 3.20 (but with a more systematic choice of parameters and notation) are the topic of Chapter 7.

Estimation of the expected frequencies is more difficult for this model than for any of the other three-way models. The model requires that all the two-factor marginals of the observed and expected frequencies agree. Although the expected frequencies depend only on these two-way marginals, there is no closed formula for $\hat{\mu}_{ijk}$. Estimation of μ_{ijk} uses one of several iterative procedures in which a set of tentative estimates is repeatedly adjusted until the $\hat{\mu}_{ijk}$ are determined to whatever accuracy one wishes. Manual calculation is impractical; a computer is essential. The procedure is described in Section 5.2.

When applied to the sample data, the iterative procedures give the expected frequencies

	a_1			a_2		
	c_1	c_2	c_3	c_1	c_2	c_3
b_1	5.6	6.8	2.7	16.4	18.2	2.3
b_2	23.4	47.2	140.3	2.6	14.8	4.7

$$\tag{3.21}$$

The model has $(a - 1)(b - 1)(c - 1) = 2$ degrees of freedom and both X^2 and G^2 are 2.83. The agreement between observed and expected frequencies is close enough that the model cannot be rejected, a result that is not surprising since the simpler model $[AB][BC]$ almost fit.

3.6. THE SATURATED MODEL

The final three-factor model removes all the restrictions that determined the simpler models. It introduces a term that depends on all three factors into the log-linear model. With this term, any pattern of association among the factors can be described. The model is comparable to the complete dependence model in the two-way case. The generality of this model lets the expected frequencies mirror their observed counterparts exactly. In effect, the full ABC table plays the role of the marginal table by which this model is fitted to data. As the use of this table suggests, the model is denoted [ABC]. Its log-linear representation is

$$\log \mu_{ijk} = \lambda + \lambda_{A(i)} + \lambda_{B(j)} + \lambda_{C(k)} + \lambda_{AB(ij)} + \lambda_{AC(ik)}$$
$$+ \lambda_{BC(jk)} + \lambda_{ABC(ijk)} \quad (3.22)$$

The model is fully parameterized, with exactly as many free parameters as there are data points (after the usual summation constraints). For this reason, it is called the *saturated model*. Since $\hat{\mu}_{ijk} = x_{ijk}$, the fit is perfect and, for any set of data, $X^2(0) = G^2(0) = 0$. Obviously, these numbers do not test anything.

The graph of the model [ABC] is a triangle. This triangular graph is interpreted as implying both two- and three-way association. This convention links the graphical representations to the concept of conditional independence, which is particularly useful when one gets to higher-order tables (see Sections 6.3 and 6.5; also Edwards & Kreiner, 1983).

The importance of the untestable saturated model is twofold. First, it is the logical endpoint of the series of models that has been developed in the last four sections. As such, it is the most general alternative hypothesis against which other models are tested and is the resort when these partial-association models fail. Second, the saturated model can sometimes be used to reexpress a set of data in a more intelligible way. Although the model has as many parameters as there are data points, these parameters express the table in a new way. For example, the single-factor parameters λ_A, λ_B, and λ_C, capture the marginal distributions in a way that none of the raw x_{ijk} can do. These parameters can be estimated in the saturated model without raising questions about the adequacy of fit.

An idea of the nature of the saturated model is obtained by looking at how it differs from the homogeneous-association model. In the table sliced along factor B (Figure 3.3), not only is $A \not\perp C | b_j$ for at least some slices, but differences in the extent or pattern of the association parameters across these slices are allowed. When the probabilities of one factor are conditioned on the other two classifications, they are no longer logarithmically additive. A term that depends on both subscripts must be added to Equation 3.20, giving

$$\log \pi_{k|ij} = \alpha_{ik} + \beta_{jk} + \gamma_{ijk}$$

These effects—the variation in *AC* association and the parameters γ_{ijk}—constitute an interaction in the sense of the analysis of variance.

3.7. CONSTANT-FREQUENCY MODELS

The five varieties of model for the three-way table described above include all those in which the expected frequencies match their observed counterparts in the one-dimensional marginals. One can also construct models that impose a uniform distribution on one or more of these marginals by dropping reference to a factor altogether. For example, eliminating $\lambda_{B(j)}$ from the model $[AC][B]$ leaves the log-linear form

$$\log \mu_{ijk} = \lambda + \lambda_{A(i)} + \lambda_{C(k)} + \lambda_{AC(ik)} \qquad (3.23)$$

This model implies that $\mu_{ij_1k} = \mu_{ij_2k}$ for any j_1 and j_2, so that a proportion $1/b$ of the frequency falls at each level of factor B, in the manner of the two-way models described in Section 2.12.

Expected frequencies for these constant-frequency models are found by analyzing the subscript-sensitive part of the model, then allocating these frequencies equally over the levels of the missing subscripts. For Model 3.23, where i and k are involved but j is not, the frequencies for the subscripted component are taken from the AC marginal and are divided by b, giving

$$\hat{\mu}_{ijk} = \frac{x_{i+k}}{b}$$

Had the AC association term been lacking from Model 3.23, the model would conjoin the unrelatedness of A and C with the division of frequency equally over the levels of B, giving the expected frequencies

$$\hat{\mu}_{ijk} = \frac{x_{i++}x_{++k}}{x_{+++}b} \qquad (3.24)$$

Models with two or more constant factors also exist. The simplest of these models has no subscripted terms at all, expressing uniform probability over all cells:

$$\log \mu_{ijk} = \lambda \quad \text{and} \quad \hat{\mu}_{ijk} = \frac{x_{+++}}{abc} \qquad (3.25)$$

The constant-frequency models are not commonly used. There are two reasons for their rarity. First, hypotheses of constant frequency are uncommon. Most research concerns the association of factors rather than their absolute level. One only tests for the uniformity of a categorization (as a null hypothesis) when one is interested in determining whether one category is more or less likely than others. More often, one wants to know whether the category frequency varies with another factor. Second, the constant-frequency models combine several unrelated effects. For example, the model leading to Equation 3.24 mixes assertions of the constancy of B, the unrelatedness of A and C, and unrelatedness of B to A and C. Unless this combination has a specific interpretation, its parts are easier to study separately. For example, if one was specifically interested in the uniformity of the B distribution, that question is better studied in the marginal B distribution obtained by collapsing over A and C. Because of its apparent simplicity, Model 3.25 places even stronger restrictions on the data: three types of marginal uniformity combined with all the varities of unrelatedness implied by $A \perp\!\!\!\perp B \perp\!\!\!\perp C$.

For these reasons, and to simplify the later exposition, the constant-frequency models do not appear further in this book. The principal reason to be familiar with them is that some computer programs generate and test them. One needs to know how to recognize them. Typically, they are indicated by dropping the reference to the constant factors; for example, Model 3.23 is denoted by [AC].

3.8. THE HIERARCHICAL LATTICE OF MODELS— DIFFERENCE TESTS

The models developed in Sections 3.2 to 3.6 form a hierarchy, from complete independence, [A][B][C], through the models that allow some association, [AB][C], [AB][BC], and [AB][AC][BC], to the saturated model, [ABC]. Each model in this series contains those preceding it as special cases, so that the simpler models can be obtained from the more complex ones by eliminating some of their parameters. For example, the model [AB][BC] has the log-linear form of Equation 3.18:

$$\log \mu_{ijk} = \lambda + \lambda_{A(i)} + \lambda_{B(j)} + \lambda_{C(k)} + \lambda_{AB(ij)} + \lambda_{BC(jk)} \qquad (3.26)$$

When $\lambda_{BC(jk)} = 0$ for all j and k, it becomes the model [AB][C] (Equation 3.14):

$$\log \mu_{ijk} = \lambda + \lambda_{A(i)} + \lambda_{B(j)} + \lambda_{C(k)} + \lambda_{AB(ij)} \qquad (3.27)$$

The hierarchical relationship connecting these and similar models creates a lattice, shown in Figure 3.4. Simple models appear toward the top of this diagram and more complicated ones toward the bottom. Each line in the diagram connects two models that have a direct hierarchical relationship to each other: the

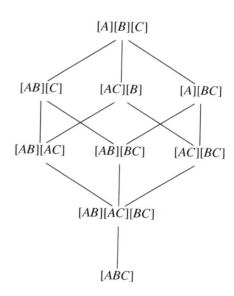

FIGURE 3.4. The hierarchical lattice of three-way models

simpler of the pair can be made from the more complex by eliminating a set of parameters. Models not so connected—for example, $[AB][C]$ and $[AC][BC]$—do not have a hierarchical relationship, even though one of them may be more complex than the other and may have more parameters. The constant-frequency models are not included in this diagram, although they are part of a larger lattice (see Problem 3.6).

The hierarchical structure lets one test whether a particular set of parameters plays a critical role in explaining the data. Consider again the models $[AB][C]$ and $[AB][BC]$, whose log-linear representations (Equations 3.26 and 3.27) differ by the parameters λ_{BC}. If both models fit equally well, then λ_{BC} makes no overall contribution to the model. Of course, since the model $[AB][BC]$ has every parameter in the model $[AB][C]$ as well as some extra ones, it almost certainly fits a set of data better, even when $[AB][C]$ is correct in the population. But this gain comes the expense of some degrees of freedom. The improvement in fit must be substantial before λ_{BC} is deemed essential. A comparison of these models tests the pair of hypotheses

$$H_0: \lambda_{BC(jk)} = 0 \qquad \text{for all } j \in \mathcal{B}, k \in \mathcal{C}$$
$$H_1: \lambda_{BC(jk)} \neq 0 \qquad \text{for some } j \in \mathcal{B}, k \in \mathcal{C}$$

The context of this test includes any possible AB association and excludes any AC association.

The test statistic comparing two models is the difference between their goodness-of-fit statistics, either G^2 or X^2. If the more complete model fits the data adequately, this difference has approximately a chi-square distribution with degrees of freedom equal to the difference in the degrees of freedom of the two tests. For reasons discussed in Section 4.5, the mathematical basis for this statistic is clearer for the likelihood ratio statistic G^2 than for the Pearson X^2. In practice, either can be used. In this book, these differences are denoted by ΔX^2 or ΔG^2 using the letter Δ to explicitly indicate that they are differences. In research reports they are commonly written simply as X^2 or G^2.

With the data of Table 3.1, the test of λ_{BC} in the context of λ_{AB} is

$$
\begin{array}{lll}
[AB][C]: & G^2(6) = 67.49 & \\
[AB][BC]: & G^2(4) = 7.92 & \qquad (3.28) \\
\hline
& \Delta G^2(2) = 59.57 &
\end{array}
$$

The change in G^2 is clearly significant so the hypothesis of no BC association is rejected and one conlcudes that some $\lambda_{BC(jk)} \neq 0$.

The difference tests are a useful adjunct to the tests for conditional independence. Suppose that one wishes to look for the association of two factors, A and B, in a context that includes a third factor, C. The hypothesis $A \perp\!\!\!\perp B|C$ tests for any relationship between the factors. This test will detect both direct relationships between A and B and interactions with C. Frequently, the largest and most important part of the relationship is the direct association, expressed by λ_{AB}. This term is tested by the difference between the null model $[AC][BC]$ and a model that adds the two-factor association, $[AB][AC][BC]$. This comparison concentrates the important portion of the association in fewer degrees of freedom than does the test of conditional independence. It is frequently a more powerful way to detect association than a test of conditional independence.

The same type of differences can test more than one type of parameter at once. Any two models for which the parameters of one are a subset of the parameters of the other can be used. In the lattice picture, the more general model lies below the simpler one along a sequence of descending lines. For such a pair of models, one takes the difference in statistic value and in degrees of freedom. For example, a test for the necessity of any two-factor term in a model for Table 3.1 is given by the comparison

$$
\begin{array}{ll}
[A][B]: & G^2(7) = 169.28 \\
[AB][AC][BC]: & G^2(2) = 2.85 \\
\hline
& \Delta G^2(5) = 166.43
\end{array}
$$

Obviously, two-factor associations are present in these data.

The conclusions that one draws from difference tests are limited in two respects, both concerning effects other than the one being tested. The first involves terms that are omitted from the alternative model. Differences in G^2 or X^2 test what they are supposed to test only when the more complete model provides a valid description of the data. When that model fails to fit, tests of its components are of doubtful value. Of course, when the alternative model is roughly correct, even if not exactly, the resulting tests are still informative. In the example at hand, the more complex model has $G^2(4) = 7.92$, which is satisfactory.

The other limitation to the conclusion concerns the context in which the test is made, as given by the simpler model. The results can change when additional associations are introduced into this model. In the example in Display 3.28, λ_{AC} never appears. It is conceivable (although unlikely, given the size of the effect) that the introduction of λ_{AC} into both models could reduce ΔG^2 sufficiently to eliminate the need for the λ_{BC}. An adequate fit of $[AB][AC]$ would imply that λ_{BC} is needed only when λ_{AC} is lacking. In that case, whether one prefers to treat λ_{BC} as a necessary addition to $[AB][C]$ or as unnecessary in $[AB][AC]$ depends on the investigation from which the data were obtained, specifically of which of $[AB][BC]$ and $[AB][AC]$ is easiest model to interpret. In fact, $[AB][AC]$ is unsatisfactory here ($G^2(4) = 24.67$) and the conclusions about λ_{BC} are unaltered.

3.9. THE HIERARCHY PRINCIPLE

A reader familiar with analysis-of-variance designs may notice the absence of several models from Figure 3.4. For example, there is no model with the log-linear form

$$\log \mu_{ijk} = \lambda + \lambda_{AB(ij)} + \lambda_{C(k)} \tag{3.29}$$

The nearest thing to it is the model $[AB][C]$, which has two additional terms:

$$\log \mu_{ijk} = \lambda + \lambda_{A(i)} + \lambda_{B(j)} + \lambda_{C(k)} + \lambda_{AB(ij)} \tag{3.30}$$

Neither the independence notation nor the bracket notation can specify the former model. Without moving to a larger class of descriptions, models like Equation 3.29 are excluded.

The difference between Models 3.29 and 3.30 is that the latter obeys a rule known as the *hierarchy principle*. This rule states that whenever a model contains a λ term with a particular set of subscripts, it must also contain all lower-order λ terms involving those subscripts. If λ_{AB} is part of a model, then the hierarchy principle requires that λ, λ_A and λ_B also appear. Models such as Equation 3.30 that obey this principle are known as *hierarchical models*; models such as Equation 3.29 that do not are *nonhierarchical models*. The bracket notation can express any hierarchical model, but no nonhierarchical model.

Almost all the models in this book are hierarchical. Among the basic log-linear models, only models such as Equation 3.30 that can be written in the bracket notation are used. At first, this limitation may seem restrictive, since it precludes the study of certain combinations of effects. In fact, the restriction has little practical effect. Most research questions translate either into assertions of unrelatedness and conditional-independence or into questions about the association of specific sets of factors. Hierarchical models suffice to investigate both types of relationship.

When fitting a model as a description of data, one might find that a non-hierarchical model like Equation 3.29 fits nearly as well as the hierarchical Model 3.30. Although use of the simpler model (as measured by the number of parameters) is tempting, its adoption usually increases the complexity of the explanation in terms of psychological constructs. The hierarchical log-linear models can always be interpreted as implying agreement between the observed frequencies and the expected frequencies in certain marginal tables (as in Figure 3.1 or Equations 3.11). These matched marginals naturally express the design of an experiment (the number of observations in the conditions) and introduce associations among various factors into the model. In contrast, the fit of a nonhierarchical model is hard to understand. The parameters in these models still obey the constraints that make them sum to 0—if they were free, the model would be hierarchical. To give the model a plausible interpretation, one must explain why these hold. Inevitably, such explanations are strained.

Occasionally one finds situations where nonhierarchical hypotheses seem plausible. Even here, one can usually reinterpret the problem to avoid using non-hierarchical models, as the following example shows. Suppose that all members of a sample of children are asked which of two other children, a boy and a girl, they would pick to play with. The responses classified by sex form a 2×2 table:

Playmate
chosen (P)
boy   girl

		boy	girl
Sex of	male	x_{mb}	x_{mg}
child (C)	female	x_{fb}	x_{fg}

The degree of association in this table measures the extent to which males tend to select a boy and females a girl (or vice-versa). The logical null hypothesis to test in this table is one that asserts that the choice of a boy or girl playmate does not depend on the sex of the choosing child. This hypothesis is expressed by the model $C \perp\!\!\!\perp P$, which treats the number of children and the number of choices of each target child as fixed marginal frequencies.

There is another way to examine these data. One can ask whether either sex has a disproportionate tendency to chose a same-sex playmate. This hypothesis leads to a different set of constraints. Obviously, the number of children examined (factor C) is fixed by the design. For the new hypothesis, one also wishes to make the total number of same-sex and different-sex choices agree with their observed values and to test whether their allocation over C is balanced. Unfortunately, the same-sex and different-sex frequencies are not marginals: they are the diagonal sums $x_{mb} + x_{fg}$ and $x_{mg} + x_{fb}$. To hold them fixed, a nonhierarchical model seems to be needed, one based on C and the CP association. However, in this nonhierarchical form, the problem feels unnatural and ungainly. The situation is simplified if the table is recast as

Sex of choice
(D)
same   diff

		same	diff
Sex of	male	x_{mb}	x_{mg}
child (C)	female	x_{fg}	x_{fb}

Here the hypothesis of homogeneous similarity of sex preference is expressed by a model of independence, $C \perp\!\!\!\perp D$. This model obeys the hierarchy principle and is easier to comprehend.

3.10. PARALLELS TO THE ANALYSIS OF VARIANCE

The log-linear models look like analysis of variance models. There is an obvious similarity between the saturated two-factor model for the mean frequency,

$$\log \mu_{ij} = \lambda + \lambda_{A(i)} + \lambda_{B(j)} + \lambda_{AB(ij)} \tag{3.31}$$

and the analysis-of-variance model for a cell mean in a two-factor design,

$$\mu_{ij} = \mu + \alpha_i + \beta_j + \gamma_{ij} \qquad (3.32)$$

Furthermore, the sum-to-zero constraints on the parameters are the same. Pursuing this similarity, one is tempted to call λ_A and λ_B "main effects" and to call λ_{AB} an "interaction."

Unfortunately, this parallel is deceptive and not precisely in the spirit of the two terms. The confusion arises because the two-factor analysis of variance really involves three variables: the two classification (independent) variables and the measured (dependent) variable. The last of these has no dimension in the table of data. However, had the measured variable been categorical it would have had explicit representation. Specifically, think of the third example experiment from Section 3.1, which had two design factors (instructions and practice) and one outcome measure (retention). If retention is measured as a numerical score, then the analysis of variance is proper and one interprets the experiment as a two-way instruction-by-practice layout, appropriately described by Model 3.32. If the retention scores are categorical, a three-way table results, making Model 3.31 inadequate.

The two-factor categorical Model 3.31 refers to a simpler design. Suppose that factor A has the role of an independent variable or predictor and that B is the dependent variable or outcome. The proper analogy to this situation — one independent and one dependent variable—is a one-way analysis of variance, with the model

$$\mu_i = \mu + \alpha_i$$

Matching Equation 3.31 to this model, λ best corresponds to the average sample size, $\lambda_{A(i)}$ to the relative difference in the sizes of the samples, $\lambda_{B(j)}$ to the common effect across the groups (the grand mean μ), and $\lambda_{AB(ij)}$ to the differences among the groups (the effects α_i).

As the term is conventionally used in discussing the analysis of variance, an *interaction* refers to the modulation of the magnitude of the relationship between two variables (the dependent and an independent variable) by a third variable. This is exactly the situation described by the model [ABC] for the three-way case: the form of the AC association differs at levels of B (recall Sections 3.5 and 3.6). Thus, the three-variable log-linear models best embody the relationships implied in a two-factor analysis of variance. The parameters λ_C, λ_{AC}, λ_{BC}, and λ_{ABC} are the frequency counterparts of the parameters on the right hand side of the analysis of variance model (Equation 3.32).

In describing research, it seems smart to avoid using the expression *main effect* for single-variable terms like λ_A and *interaction* for terms like λ_{AB}. The latter are more clearly described as two-factor associations. Although some authors use the word "interaction" in the frequency-model context to refer to two-factor associations, this word is better reserved for terms of the complexity of λ_{ABC}, at least in discussing experimental results. Consistency of terminology here makes it less confusing to go from one type of design to another. The correspondence is actually quite simple: because the dependent factor is given explicitly in a frequency table, effects in that analysis involve one more subscript than do the corresponding effects in the analysis of variance.

3.11. COUNTING PARAMETERS AND DEGREES OF FREEDOM

The formulae for the number of degrees of freedom that are given in Sections 3.2 to 3.6 were not fully explained. They derive from a few simple principles. In essence each degree of freedom in a test is a dimension of variation by which the observed data can deviate from a model. Calculation of the degrees of freedom amounts to counting these dimensions.

Each cell in a table of data constitutes one place where the observed and expected frequencies can differ. An $a \times b \times c$ table contains abc cells, so if the expected frequencies are given without regard to the data, there are abc places where they can disagree. A statistic testing a set of a priori frequencies has abc degrees of freedom. In fact, the expected frequencies are never given a priori, but are selected to agree with the observed data in certain ways. Certainly they are chosen so that their total agrees with the observed total; usually they are made to agree with some of the marginal tables as well. Each constraint on the expected frequencies brings them closer to the observed frequencies and reduces the number of degrees of freedom by 1. Using the symbol $\#(X)$ to indicate the number of Xs, the rule is

$$df = \#(\text{cells in table}) - \#(\text{constraints on expected frequencies}) \quad (3.33)$$

A good way to find the number of constraints on the expected frequencies is to count the parameters in the model that is being fit. Each freely chosen parameter represents one way in which the expected frequencies are made to agree with the data and in effect provides one constraint on their values. In these terms, Equation 3.33 becomes

$$df = \#(\text{cells in table}) - \#(\text{free parameters estimated}) \quad (3.34)$$

For the log-linear models, the number of parameters is obtained by counting the number of unconstraineed λ's in the model.†

---

†A more rigorous treatment of the degrees of freedom is geometric. The n frequencies in an n-cell table fall at a point in an n-dimensional space. The predictions of a model with p free parameters fall into a p-dimensional subspace of this space. The deviations from the model lie outside the prediction space, so are in a subspace that is orthogonal to the model, which is an $(n - p)$-dimensional subspace of the original space. The number of degrees of freedom available for a test equals the dimensionality of this subspace.

A little care is needed to count the parameters. As noted above, most of the models have too many parameters to let them to be estimated unambiguously. Unique values are obtained by imposing constraints on the parameter values, usually by forcing them to sum to zero over any subscript (e.g., Equations 3.8 and 3.15). Each such constraint reduces the number of free parameters by 1. For example, there are a different parameters $\lambda_{A(i)}$, but only $a - 1$ of them are free, since after the first $a - 1$ are specified, the fact that $\Sigma\lambda_{A(i)} = 0$ determines the last value. This idea generalizes to a rule for counting free parameters:

$$\#(\text{free parameters}) = \#(\lambda \text{ parameters}) - \#(\text{constraints}) \qquad (3.35)$$

This formula applies both to parameters of a single type, such as λ_A described above, and to all parameters in a model. Consider how it works for the two-factor term $\lambda_{AB(ij)}$. There are ab raw values, which are subject to the estimation constraints

$$\sum_i \lambda_{AB(ij)} = \sum_j \lambda_{AB(ij)} = 0$$

There are b constraints in the first set and a in the second. However, these constraints are not completely free: one of them follows from the others. For example, if one knows that the sums across the rows and down all but one of the columns are zero, one can deduce that the last column also sums to zero:

$$
\begin{array}{ccccc|c}
\lambda_{11} & \lambda_{12} & \cdots & \lambda_{1,b-1} & \lambda_{1b} & 0 \\
\lambda_{21} & \lambda_{22} & \cdots & \lambda_{2,b-1} & \lambda_{2b} & 0 \\
\vdots & \vdots & & \vdots & \vdots & \vdots \\
\lambda_{a1} & \lambda_{a2} & \cdots & \lambda_{a,b-1} & \lambda_{ab} & 0 \\
\hline
0 & 0 & \cdots & 0 & ? & \leftarrow \text{This must be 0}
\end{array}
$$

Thus, there are $a + b - 1$ independent constraints in Equation 3.35, not $a + b$. The number of free parameters is

$$\#(\text{free } \lambda_{AB} \text{ parameters}) = ab - (a + b - 1) = (a - 1)(b - 1)$$

Under most circumstances the counting need not be done in such detail. In a complete table of parameters subject to summation constraints in every direction, the number of free elements is the product of the dimensions of the table, each reduced by 1. Thus, the $a \times b$ array of λ_{AB} has $(a - 1)(b - 1)$ free parameters. To get the number of free parameters in a model, one sums these quantities over the λ terms, remembering that the unsubscripted λ counts as one parameter. For example, the log-linear form of the model $[A][BC]$ is

$$\log \mu_{ijk} = \lambda + \lambda_{A(i)} + \lambda_{B(j)} + \lambda_{C(k)} + \lambda_{BC(jk)}$$

Taking each λ in turn, the count of free parameters is

$$\#(\text{free parameters}) = 1 + (a - 1) + (b - 1) + (c - 1)$$
$$+ (b - 1)(c - 1)$$
$$= a + bc - 1$$

The table contains abc cells, so completing Equation 3.34 gives

$$df_{[A][BC]} = abc - (a + bc - 1) = (a - 1)(bc - 1)$$

A similar analysis gives the degrees of freedom shown in Figure 3.1 for tests of the other three-way models.

For most analyses, the procedure just described works correctly. However, it breaks down when portions of the table are missing. Missing data sufficient to cause a problem with the degrees of freedom occur under two circumstances. First, by happenstance the observed table may contain so many zeros that some of the fitted marginals are empty and certain parameters cannot be estimated. Second, some cells in a complete table may be intrinsic voids, either because that combination of factors is impossible or because these cells have been excluded as part of a specialized analysis. These possibilities are discussed in Section 5.5 and Chapter 10, respectively. In both cases, one must count the data cells, parameters, and constraints separately and apply Equations 3.34 and 3.35 to find the number of degrees of freedom. The general treatment of degrees of freedom is also necessary for the association models in Chapters 11 and 13.

3.12. ASSOCIATION IN TWO AND THREE DIMENSIONS

The various forms of independence and dependence in a three-dimensional table can be confusing. To one accustomed to thinking of relationships in two-way arrays, the three-factor effects are difficult at first. To help clarify them, this section looks at some situations in which the three-dimensional view is necessary.

Central to an understanding of the higher-order associations is the distinction between ordinary independence and conditional independence. The former is two-dimensional, the latter is fundamentally three-dimensional. They are not the same. It is quite possible for two-factor independence to hold when conditional independence does not, or vice versa. One normally has no assurance that the association that one measures in the marginal table has any particular relationship to the conditional association in the complete table. Each type of association makes a different statement about the data, and it is important to keep them clear.

Consider the difference between the two hypotheses. Suppose that two measures of performance in some skilled task (factors A and B) are collected in a population of subjects of varying abilities. Say that the hypothesis $A \perp\!\!\!\perp B$ is rejected, indicating that over the entire population the scores on A and B go together. Now classify the subjects by the amount of practice they have had on the task. Well-practiced subjects tend to score well on both tasks, while poorly-practiced subjects receive low scores on both. If the amount of practice varies substantially over the population, then it may account for much of the observed association between A and B. By examining the conditional-independence model $A \perp\!\!\!\perp B|P$, one restricts attention to the association at given levels of practice. This restricted association is much attenuated from the unconditional form, perhaps even eliminated. In this example, simple association says something about the relationship in the full population, and the conditional association helps to understand how that association came about.

As this example shows, the (conditional) independence or dependence of two factors is not a property of those factors per se, but of the factors in a particular context. When a factor is added to an analysis, what had seemed to be a fundamental association can disappear, or two factors that had been independent can become related. The selection of which factors to include in an analysis is a decision that cannot be performed automatically. One must understand what conditional independence means in the various contexts and choose the factors in a table carefully. This point is neither new nor exotic: a chapter on partial association making most of the points raised here is found in Yule (1911).

The distinction between direct and conditional dependence has a parallel in the difference between direct and partial association measured by correlation coefficients with continuous variables. The simple correlation coefficient measures a bivariate relationship in isolation, while the partial correlation excludes the variation that depends on a third variable. Correlation coefficients are less general than categorical measures in that they treat only the linear components of the association, rather than any form of relationship.

The conditioning effect of a third variable can be dramatic enough to reverse the direction of the conditional probabilities, in a phenomenon known as *Simpson's paradox* (Simpson, 1951; although awareness of the effect predates this paper). For example, suppose that one is interested in the probability that a disorder improves following one of two different forms of treatment, t_1 and t_2. Treatment t_1 is more effective than treatment t_2, in that for any patient

$$P(\text{improve}|t_1) > P(\text{improve}|t_2)$$

Now suppose that the population of patients is composed of two subpopulations, p_1 and p_2. In both subpopulations treatment t_1 is more effective than treatment t_2, but the patients in the first subpopulation have a poorer prognosis than those in the second subpopulation. Specifically, let

$$P(\text{improve}|t_1, p_1) = 0.5 \quad \text{and} \quad P(\text{improve}|t_2, p_1) = 0.4$$

$$P(\text{improve}|t_1, p_2) = 0.8 \quad \text{and} \quad P(\text{improve}|t_2, p_2) = 0.7$$

An investigator sets out to compare the treatments. In a good design the proportion of each treatment group drawn from each subpopulation is approximately the same. However, sometimes it is impossible to randomly assign subjects to the treatments. Suppose that treatment and subpopulation are confounded so that 70% of the patients given t_1 are from subpopulation p_1 and 70% of those given t_2 are from p_2. Then

$$P(\text{improve}|t_1) = P(\text{improve}|t_1, p_1)P(p_1|t_1) + P(\text{improve}|t_1, p_2)P(p_2|t_1)$$
$$= (0.7)(0.5) + (0.3)(0.8) = 0.59$$

while

$$P(\text{improve}|t_2) = (0.3)(0.4) + (0.7)(0.7) = 0.61$$

The relative worth of the treatments is reversed. Of course, the problem is that t_1 has mainly been given to the subpopulation with generally poor outcomes and t_2 to the more successful subpopulation. An analysis that considers only treatment and improvement gives an incorrect conclusion. A better analysis conditions on the subpopulation.

A well-known and effective illustration of these effects concerns sex discrimination in admission to graduate school (Bickel, Hammel, & O'Connell, 1975). Suppose that two academic departments in a university (factor D) accept students into graduate school. From each pool of applicants, some are accepted and others rejected (factor A). Some hypothetical results when acceptance is classified by sex (factor S) for each department are shown at the top of Table 3.2. Although there is a slight excess of frequency in the minor diagonals (i.e., $\hat{\alpha} < 1$), there is no significant AS association for either department. However, when the two departments are combined (Table 3.2, second panel), an association appears. The association is appreciable, statistically significant, and in the direction of excess frequency on the major diagonal ($\hat{\alpha} > 1$). From approximately equal acceptance rates, there is now a bias toward accepting males.

The phenomenon here is the same as in the treatment example. The departments differ both in the sex distribution of their applicants and in the proportion of students that are accepted, as shown by the other two marginal distributions at the bottom of Table 3.2. The department to which the preponderance of female students apply is the one that is hardest to get into. Because more females apply to this difficult department, a smaller proportion of them are accepted. The locus of the association in the marginal AS table lies in this relationship, rather than in any AS association at levels of D. To express it in another way, A and S are not independent, but are conditionally independent given D, as shown by the good fit of the model $A \perp\!\!\!\perp S|D$, which has $X^2(2) = 0.16$.

The interpretation of a situation like this involves more than simply listing the significant associations. Which associations are important depends on the way in which the factors are deemed to influence one another. If acceptance takes place

TABLE 3.2
Hypothetical Data for Admission to Graduate School

Three-way Classification

	Dept. 1		Dept. 2	
	Accept	Reject	Accept	Reject
Male	23	16	3	25
Female	7	4	7	47

Dept. 1: $\hat{\alpha} = 0.82$, $X^2 = 0.08$

Dept. 2: $\hat{\alpha} = 0.81$, $X^2 = 0.09$

Data Collapsed over Department

	Accept	Reject
Male	26	41
Female	14	51

$\hat{\alpha} = 2.31$
$X^2 = 4.65$

Data Collapsed over Acceptance Outcome

	Male	Female
Dept. 1	39	11
Dept. 2	28	54

$\hat{\alpha} = 6.84$

Data Collapsed over Sex of Applicant

	Accept	Reject
Dept. 1	30	20
Dept. 2	10	72

$\hat{\alpha} = 10.80$

at the department level, after the number of slots available to the department has been determined and a pool of applicants to the department collected, then both the acceptance ratio and the sex ratio are antecedent to the acceptance process. If so, the department actions are better expressed by separate tables for each department than by the pooled table. The relationship between the characteristics of the applicants and their acceptance should be examined in the three-dimensional table, conditioned on the department. By this logic, the reason for the association between sex and acceptance in the marginal table lies not in the action of accepting an applicant, but in such matters as the department size and the distribution of the applicants' interests.

This argument against two-way treatment does not apply to the other pairs of factors in this example. Acceptance follows the formation of the departmental applicant pool, so there is no reason to condition on acceptance when the department-by-sex association is examined. Separate DS tables for accepted and rejected applicants are not helpful in understanding what is going on, nor does the hypothesis $D \perp\!\!\!\perp S|A$ test a meaningful question. Conditioning the acceptance by department relationship on sex is also problematic.

3.13. ELIMINATING A FACTOR FROM A TABLE

The discussion in the last section indicates that there can be a substantial difference between analyses of the association of two factors via two-way and three-way tables, both in the results and in the interpretation. Neither the large nor the small analysis is uniformly preferable. An analysis in a small table is simpler to understand and, because the frequencies are larger, statistically more robust. An analysis in the full table allows effects of greater complexity to be discovered. The researcher must decide which analysis to run.

The easiest decision occurs when one factor is irrelevant to the other association. In this case, one collapses the data immediately to the smaller table. In many sets of data, some factors are logically subsequent to others. The later factors should never condition earlier relationships. Consider a sample of patients who arrive at a clinic and are classified by sex (factor S) and the duration of their symptoms (factor D). They receive some treatment, the success of which is evaluated 6 months later (factor T). If one wishes to see whether there is a sex-duration relationship, the factor T should not enter into the analysis. The treatment had not been applied when S and D were measured, so conditioning on T makes no sense and the model $S \perp\!\!\!\perp D|T$ is meaningless. For this test one looks at the hypothesis $S \perp\!\!\!\perp D$ in the SD marginal. In contrast, when one looks at whether the effectiveness of the treatment is related to the patient's sex, effects due to differences in the duration of symptoms should be excluded using the hypothesis is $S \perp\!\!\!\perp T|D$. Likewise, the last paragraph of the discussion of the graduate admission example justified the appropriateness of two-way tables in examining the association of department to the applicant's sex or the department's acceptance proportion. In cases like these, the conditional hypothesis is meaningless and should not be tested.

The situation is more difficult when the factors have no clear temporal or causal order. Here both the conditional and the unconditional analyses can be done. The two analyses express different questions, however, and should not be confused. The graduate-admission example illustrates the difference. The two-way table of sex by acceptance is where one goes to see whether different proportions of males and females are accepted into the university. It correctly estimates the overall differences, but says nothing about the actual process of admission, which takes place at the department level. The three-factor view is necessary to understand the effects at this level and to understand why the overall association occurs.

Pooling the levels of a factor is appropriate only when the pooled groups reflect a real population about which an inference can be made. In many designed experiments, the levels of certain factors are artificially constructed or sampled. Combining these subsamples creates an meaningless ensemble. For example, suppose that one has collected two measures of cognitive functioning from 25 left-handed students and 25 right-handed students. When studying the relationship of the two measures to each other, there is no justification for collapsing over handedness. The analysis in the full table is preferable. The pooled result would refer to a nonexistent population in which left- and right-handed students were equally prevalent. If one wished to make an inference about the association of the questions in the population of students at large, one would weight the subpopulations in proportion to their natural frequency.

The reasons for working in a larger or smaller table given above do not depend on the data. They apply regardless of whether the unconditional analysis and the conditional analysis give the same results or different results. However, when the two procedures give the same outcome, it is frequently better to work in the collapsed table, since the simpler table is easier to report and has larger cell frequencies. In a three-way table, one can safely collapse over a factor whenever that factor is unrelated to at least one of the other factors. Specifically, estimates of the parameters λ_{AB} are affected by the presence of a third factor C only when C is directly associated to both A and B. When both λ_{AC} and λ_{BC} are nonzero or when they interact in a nonzero λ_{ABC}, then removing factor C alters the AB relationship. This result makes intuitive sense: The AB association is affected by removing C only when C is part of a mediating path between A and B. When either branch of this path is absent, elimination of C has no effect.

Tests exist for these conditions. If one can reject both the hypotheses $A \perp\!\!\!\perp C|B$ (thereby showing an AC link) and $B \perp\!\!\!\perp C|A$ (showing an AB link), one cannot eliminate C on empirical grounds. Put in model-fitting terms, one can collapse C unless a model containing both λ_{AC} and λ_{BC} (or λ_{ABC}) is required, that is, unless one of the models $[AC][BC]$, $[AB][AC][BC]$, or $[ABC]$ is required. The empirical justification for collapsing is always more delicate then when the choice is driven by the a priori reasoning, since one is put in the position of accepting the validity of a model. The decision to collapse requires a feeling for the power of the tests: one would not want to conclude that $\lambda_{AC} = 0$, say, only because one's data were so bad that one could not detect any but enormous exceptions. A further discussion of the rules for collapsing a factor appears in Section 5.11.

Much additional work has been done on the problem of pooling several 2×2 tables, particularly when tables showing the association between a risk factor and the appearance of a disease are to be combined over several populations in which both the risk factor and the disease prevalence varies. The problem in the 2×2 case is simpler than in general, since the association in each table is expressed by a single odds ratio. Several procedures for pooling odds ratios over independent groups have been devised (Cornfield, 1956; Gart, 1962, 1970; Mantel, 1977; Mantel & Haenszel, 1959), besides those based on the log-linear models described in this book. These techniques are nicely reviewed by Fleiss (1981, Chapter 10) and are not covered here.

PROBLEMS

3.1. Consider the three-way table:

	$-b_1-$		$-b_2-$		$-b_3-$	
	a_1	a_2	a_1	a_2	a_1	a_2
c_1	12	13	18	26	25	29
c_2	14	17	13	48	56	61

a. Test the hypotheses $AB \perp\!\!\!\perp C$ and $A \perp\!\!\!\perp B|C$.
b. What is the simplest hierarchical log-linear model that fits these data? Hint: Put your findings into a hierarchical lattice similar to Figure 3.4. To save work, the model $[AB][AC][BC]$ has $X^2 = G^2 = 3.47$.

3.2. Find a formula for G^2 for the model $[AB][AC]$ comparable to Equations 3.6 or 3.13.

3.3. Test to see whether the effects in the data of Problem 2.1b and 2.6 are the same.

3.4. Consider a three-way table with frequencies

	a_1		a_2	
	c_1	c_2	c_1	c_2
b_1	10	20	20	10
b_2	20	10	10	20

Show that although $A \perp\!\!\!\perp B \perp\!\!\!\perp C$ does not hold (calculate the expected frequencies), the relationships $A \perp\!\!\!\perp B$, $A \perp\!\!\!\perp C$, and $B \perp\!\!\!\perp C$ are true in the two-way marginals.

3.5. Suppose that the study described in Problem 2.1a (a test for the recall of a person in the same or a different room) is expanded. Two groups of subjects are run, one tested at a delay of 1 hour, the other at a delay of 1 week. What tests answer the following questions:
a. Is there any effect of delay?
b. Is there a relationship between the room of test and the amount of retention?
c. Does this relationship change with the delay?

3.6. The constant-frequency models of Section 3.7 fit into the lattice of models shown in Figure 3.4. Draw a complete lattice for a three-way table that includes these models.

3.7. Does the constant-frequency model $[B][C]$ fit the data in Problem 3.1?

3.8. A researcher uses a packaged computer program to analyze data from the first example in Section 3.1 (call the questions A, B, and C). On part of the computer output a model identified as $[AB]$ is fitted to the three-way table. Both X^2 and G^2 for this model are impressively significant. Pleased, the researcher reports the presence of an AB association, citing these statistic values. Identify at least two serious errors. What is the proper test for an AB association?

3.9. Make up a $2 \times 3 \times 2$ tables of 150 "observations" that fit the following models (but no simpler model):
a. $[AB][AC]$
b. $[AB][AC][BC]$

3.10. Use the rules in Section 3.10 to derive a formula for the number of degrees of freedom for tests of the models
a. $[A][B][C]$
b. $[AB][AC]$
c. $[AB][AC][BC]$

3.11. Which of the following models obey the hierarchy principle? For the model(s) that violate this principle, what is the proper hierarchical model that contains all the listed effects?
a. $\lambda + \lambda_{A(i)} + \lambda_{B(j)} + \lambda_{C(k)} + \lambda_{AC(ik)}$
b. $\lambda + \lambda_{B(j)} + \lambda_{C(k)} + \lambda_{AC(ik)}$
c. $\lambda + \lambda_{B(j)} + \lambda_{C(k)}$
d. $\lambda + \lambda_{A(i)} + \lambda_{AB(ij)} + \lambda_{AC(ik)}$

3.12. Consider the following divided-attention experiment. A subject performs one of three tracking tasks of different difficulties, t_1, t_2, or t_3. During each trial, a small light in the lower right corner of the apparatus may or may not flash (factor F, levels y and n). At the end of the trial the subject states whether the light flashed or not (factor R, levels y and n). Thus, each trial falls into one cell of a $3 \times 2 \times 2$ table. Suppose that data from many trials are collected for a subject and that the experimenter believes that they can be treated as independent and identically-distributed observations. The data are:

| | $-t_1-$ | | $-t_2-$ | | $-t_3-$ | |
	r_y	r_n	r_y	r_n	r_y	r_n
f_y	79	21	57	43	86	14
f_n	22	78	42	58	50	50

a. Which of the nine three-factor models ($[F][T][R]$ through $[FTR]$) should not be fitted to these data? Draw the lattice of permissible models.
b. How would you answer the following questions? Identify the model(s) you would fit and describe what their rejection and retention would mean.
  i. Is there any detection of the light at all?
  ii. Is there any difference in the detectibility of the light as a function of the tracking task t_i?
  iii. If a difference is found in ii, is there any detection for each task alone?
c. Run the tests in b.

3.13. A developmental psychologist observes the onset of the ability to perform three different tasks. A group of children is given the three tasks and each child is classified as to whether he or she is capable of doing each task. Thus, each child falls in one cell of a $2 \times 2 \times 2$ table.

a. Which three-factor models are consistent with the constraints of this experiment?

b. The experimenter observes an association between the ability to do tasks A and B in the marginal AB table, with an excess of frequency in the *yes-yes* and *no-no* cells. However, theory suggests that this association is secondary to the development of the skill measured by the third task, C, so that children who can solve task C can also solve A and B, but those who cannot solve C are likely to fail A and B. How should the experimenter test to see whether the association between A and B can be explained by C.

c. Can the experimenter show that the skill measured by C causes the A and B scores rather than, say, A causing B and C? If so, how?

3.14. Devise a table of frequencies that shows Simpson's paradox, using a situation like the example of the effectiveness of a treatment in Section 3.12. Test for the unrelatedness of treatment and improvement in the two-way and three-way tables. If you have access to a computer program, fit models that add the parameter λ_{TI} to the unrelatedness models in the two-way and three-way tables. How do the estimates of these parameters differ in the two contexts?

3.15. To assess the effects of socioeconomic status (SES) on cognitive development, an investigator gives a battery of Piagetian conservation tasks to three groups of children chosen from a local preschool (low SES, middle SES, and high SES—factor E) at each of two age groups ($2\frac{1}{2}$–$3\frac{1}{2}$ and $3\frac{1}{2}$–$4\frac{1}{2}$ years of age—factor A). Each child is classified into one of two categories, as conserving or as failing to conserve. Frequencies are as follows:

Age: SES:	—	young	—	—	old	—
	lo	md	hi	lo	md	hi
Conserve: yes	9	13	10	33	12	17
no	18	23	33	12	8	12

An analysis of the SES-Conservation association in the marginal table shows a significant effect:

SES:	lo	md	hi
Conserve: yes	42	25	27
no	30	31	45

$G^2(2) = 6.48$
$p < 0.05$

Apparently, an association between SES and Conservation has been shown. What is the difficulty with this conclusion? Explain the difficulty and run the proper analysis.

4 The Statistical Basis of Sampling and Testing

This chapter presents some statistical theory. As the review of inferential procedures in Sections 1.3 and 1.4 mentions, estimates and tests are based on probabilistic models of the population and of the sampling scheme by which the data are generated. The models used in the analysis of frequency data are different from the normal-distribution models commonly used with continuous data. These sampling models are examined in Sections 4.1 and 4.2. The remainder of the chapter describes how the standard statistical operations of estimation and testing apply to these models.† Throughout the chapter three-way tables are used, but the discussion applies to tables of any size.

For some readers, this chapter may appear to be a digression. After all, one can become reasonably adept in applying statistical procedures without understanding their mathematical underpinnings. However, both curiosity and more sophisticated use demand deeper treatment. The sampling models are particularly important because they affect the interpretation of the results. Nevertheless, readers who are uncomfortable with the more formal aspects of statistics should not let the details bog them down. The important thing to get from this chapter is a general understanding of the sampling models and of how the tests work. The details—and most of the larger equations—can be passed over until a later reading.

---

†Most of the material in this chapter can be found in any standard text on mathematical statistics. For details on the basic distributions, see Feller (1968) or Johnson & Kotz (1969). Kendall & Stewart (1979) have an extensive discussion of the likelihood material in Sections 4.3 and 4.5. A less technical treatment of much of this material is given by Hays (1988).

4.1. SAMPLING DISTRIBUTIONS FOR FREQUENCIES

Most of the multifactor models for frequency data are based on one or both of two important probability distributions, the multinomial distribution and the Poisson distribution. These are the place to start an investigation of the statistical models. Because designs with completely constrained marginal distributions are rare in multiway tables, the hypergeometric distribution (which was used in the exact tests of Section 2.11) is not needed.

The Multinomial Distribution

The binomial distribution and its generalization, the multinomial distribution, describe the frequencies that arise when a fixed number of probabilistically identical objects are distributed randomly into a set of categories. For example, one might take a random sample of people and classify them by place of birth into one of several regional categories. The sampling and classification of a person are described as a random event (i.e., one whose outcome is uncertain until it is observed) that takes values indexed by the index set $\mathcal{A}$ (the regions). Denote the probability that this event takes the ith value by π_i. Because each observation of an event has one and only one value, the sum of the π_i over $i \in \mathcal{A}$ is 1. Now suppose that N observations are made, each one independent of all the others, and let X_i be the number of times that event i occurs. Since the N observations are random events, the X_i are random variables. Under these conditions, the X_i have a *multinomial distribution*, in which the probability that they take the particular values $x_1, x_2, \ldots, x_a$ is

$$P(x_1, x_2, \ldots, x_a) = B \prod_{i \in \mathcal{A}} \pi_i^{x_i} \qquad (4.1)$$

The symbol $\prod$ here indicates that the product of the terms is to be taken, just as Σ represents summation. The notational conventions described for Σ in Section 2.2 apply also to $\prod$. The constant B is known as a *multinomial coefficient* and has the value

$$B = \frac{N!}{x_1! \, x_2! \, \ldots \, x_{a-1}! \, x_a!} \qquad (4.2)$$

The multinomial distribution is most familiar in the case where $a = 2$. Random events with two outcomes are known as *Bernoulli events*. Frequently one of the outcomes is somewhat arbitrarily called a *success* and the other a *failure*. Let π be the probability of a success and suppose that X successes are observed in N observations. The random variable X is now said to have a *binomial distribution*. The number of failures is completely determined by X and N and need not be separately listed. So Equation 4.1 becomes

85

$$P(x) = \frac{N!}{x! \, (N - x)!} \, \pi^x \, (1 - \pi)^{N-x} \tag{4.3}$$

The constant here is frequently written using the conventional symbol for the *binomial coefficient*:

$$\binom{N}{x} = \frac{N!}{x! \, (N - x)!} \tag{4.4}$$

The mean (or expected value) and variance of the binomial distribution are readily found. For a binomial random variable X with the distribution of Equation 4.3,

$$E(X) = N\pi \quad \text{and} \quad \text{var}(X) = N\pi(1 - \pi) \tag{4.5}$$

More generally, the mean and variance of X_i in a multinomial distribution are given by Equations 4.5 with the appropriate π_i, and the covariance of two counts is

$$\text{cov}(X_i, X_j) = -N\pi_i\pi_j \tag{4.6}$$

It is frequently useful to think of a multinomial distribution as composed of binomials. In particular, if one subdivides one category of a multinomial or binomial distribution in a binomial manner, the result is still multinomial. For example, one may decide to divide the large category "East" in the birthplace example into the two smaller categories "Northeast" and "Southeast". Formally, this result is easy to demonstrate. Let A be an event that has a binomial distribution with probability α over a sample of size N. The probability that x_A such events are observed is

$$P(x_A) = \frac{N!}{x_A!(N-x_A)!} \, \alpha^{x_A}(1 - \alpha)^{N-x_A}$$

Now take the $N - x_A$ events that are not A and further classify them as B or C. Let the probability that this reclassification produces a B be $\beta = p(B|not\ A)$. Thus, the conditional distribution of the number of B events given the number of opportunities is binomial:

$$P(x_B|N - x_A) = \frac{(N - x_A)!}{x_B!(N-x_A-x_B)!} \, \beta^{x_B}(1 - \beta)^{N-x_A-x_B}$$

Since $N - x_A$ not-A events means that x_A occurrences of event A, this probability can also be denoted $P(x_B|x_A)$. Combining the two distributions to get the joint distribution of x_A and x_B gives

$$P(x_A,x_B) = P(x_A)P(x_B|x_A)$$

$$= \left(\frac{N!}{x_A!(N-x_A)!} \alpha^{x_A}(1-\alpha)^{N-x_A} \right)$$

$$\times \left(\frac{(N-x_A)!}{x_B!(N-x_A-x_B)!} \beta^{x_B}(1-\beta)^{N-x_A-x_B} \right)$$

$$= \frac{N!}{x_A!x_B!(N-x_A-x_B)!} \alpha^{x_A}[(1-\alpha)\beta]^{x_B}[(1-\alpha)(1-\beta)]^{N-x_A-x_B}$$

This is a multinomial distribution over the set $\{A, B, C\}$, as a comparison to Equations 4.1 and 4.2 shows. The probabilities $(1 - \alpha)\beta$ and $(1 - \alpha)(1 - \beta)$ are the unconditional probabilities of B and C, respectively. This type of combination is used in Chapters 7 and 11 to justify treating a complex multinomial effect as a series of more comprehensible binomials.

The Poisson Distribution

The other important model for discrete events is the *Poisson distribution*. It arises most naturally from a count of random events during a fixed period of time. Suppose that one makes observations for an interval of time and occasionally detects an event of some sort. These events occur haphazardly in time. A prototypical example of such events is the arrival of customers at some sort of service facility. To satisfy the requirement for a Poisson model, the events must be independent of each other, in the sense that the occurrence or nonoccurrence of an event at one time has no influence on the occurrence or nonoccurrence of an event at any later time. Whether or not a customer appears at 10:30 does not influence whether a different customer arrives at 10:36. During the interval that one observes, a total of X events take place. One would like to know the distribution of this count.

The *Poisson process* is the simplest model for a sequence of independent random events of this type. Formally, this process is governed by three rules that describe the events during very short time intervals of length Δt (strictly, that describe the events in the limit as $\Delta t \rightarrow 0$). First, for small Δt the chance of an event during the interval is proportional to the length of the interval. Denote the constant of proportionality by ρ, so that the probability of an event in the interval is $\rho\Delta t$. Second, the probability of two or more events in this very short interval is essentially zero, certainly vanishingly smaller than the probability of a single event. Third, what happens in one interval is independent of what happens in any other interval. From these assumptions, one can derive the properties of events in a longer interval of length T. In particular, the distribution of the number of events is

$$P(x \text{ events}) = \frac{e^{-\rho T}(\rho T)^x}{x!}$$

where x is zero or any positive integer. For convenience, one can replace ρT by the symbol μ, to give

$$P(x \text{ events}) = \frac{e^{-\mu}\mu^x}{x!} \qquad (4.7)$$

A distribution following this probability function is known as a *Poisson distribution*.†

The probability that no events are observed in a Poisson process is $e^{-\mu}$. In some situations, one can only detect classes with positive counts. To describe these situations, the distribution is conditioned on at least one event taking place, giving the *truncated Poisson distribution*. Now x takes only positive integer values (not zero), and

$$P(x \text{ events}|x>0) = \frac{P(x \text{ events}, x>0)}{P(x>0)} = \frac{e^{-\mu}\mu^x}{(1-e^{-\mu})x!} \qquad (4.8)$$

The term in the denominator is $1 - P(X=0)$.

The Poisson distribution has a simple mean and variance:

$$E(X) = \text{var}(X) = \mu \qquad (4.9)$$

(which is why the symbol μ was used). For the truncated form of the distribution,

$$E(X) = \frac{\mu}{1-e^{-\mu}} \quad \text{and} \quad \text{var}(X) = \frac{\mu[1-(1+\mu)e^{-\mu}]}{(1-e^{-\mu})^2} \qquad (4.10)$$

For a Poisson process during an interval of length $T = 1$, an average of $\mu = \rho$ events occur; thus ρ is said to be the *rate* at which events take place.

The underlying logic of a multinomial process is different from that of a Poisson process. A multinomial count is limited by the total number of events, so that x is always less than some bound N. In contrast, the number of Poisson events has no upper bound. Thus, binomial or multinomial distributions are valuable as descriptions of a fixed set of events divided among alternatives— tallies of some property over a sample of size N—while the Poisson distribution models the open ended count of events during a fixed observation period. The difference in the distributions underlies their use in larger-scale sampling models.

Notwithstanding their differences, the binomial and the Poisson distributions are sometimes similar. When N is very large and π is very small, so that only a moderate number of successes occur, then binomial probabilities are almost identical to Poisson probabilities. The parameters of the two distributions are related by $\mu = N\pi$. Thus, if one is counting the occurrence of a rare property over the members of a large city, it makes little difference which model one uses.

---

†See Wickens (1982) or, more elaborately, Feller (1968) for a deeper treatment of the Poisson process.

Although strictly binomial, with N equal to the city's population, the Poisson probabilities are essentially the same and are much easier to calculate—think of what $N!$ must be.

4.2. SAMPLING MODELS FOR FREQUENCY TABLES

To make statistical inferences about a frequency table, one needs sampling models that give the probability of a particular table. These models must reflect the uncertain elements of the data in a plausible manner and must accommodate the constraints of the experimental design. Single multinomial or Poisson sampling distributions are not enough here. More elaborate models are needed.

The probability models for most frequency tables are formed from three basic building blocks:

- Where a given number of observations are classified into categories, a multinomial (or binomial) distribution results.
- Where observations are tallied for a fixed period of time, a Poisson distribution results.
- Where a quantity is fixed by design, it has no distribution.

Assembled in various combinations, these three units provide sampling models for most situations. The remainder of this section describes several particular cases for tables in three-dimensions. An extension to more than three factors follows straightforwardly.

Pure Multinomial Sampling

Suppose that N individuals are sampled and are classified and tallied according to a three-dimensional taxonomy. A ready example is an opinion survey, in which each member of a sample of predetermined size is asked three questions. The probability model for this situation is straightforward. Each of the abc cells in the table represents a combination of answers to the questions and each cell has a probability in the population. Each individual falls into exactly one cell; thus, the distribution of events is multinomial. Let cell i,j,k have probability π_{ijk} and observed frequency x_{ijk}. Denote the complete table of data by the boldface letter $\mathbf{x}$. By adapting Equations 4.1 and 4.2, to the three-dimensional notation, the probability of a set of data is obtained:

$$P(\mathbf{x}) = \left(\frac{N!}{\prod\limits_{\text{cells}} x_{ijk}!} \right) \prod\limits_{\text{cells}} \pi_{ijk}^{x_{ijk}} \qquad (4.11)$$

Pure Poisson Sampling

Now consider a similar situation, except that the total sample size is not fixed. Instead, one watches a series of events for a fixed duration, giving each event a three-dimensional classification. For example, one looks at the records of a clinic and counts the number of patients who present with a given combination of three symptoms during the course of a year. Since the observations are unrelated, the number of counts in each cell of the table can plausibly be described by an independent Poisson process. If the rate parameter for a cell is ρ_{ijk} so the expected number of events during the interval is $\mu_{ijk} = \rho_{ijk}T$, then the distribution of the number of events in that cell during an interval of length T is given by the Poisson distribution (Equation 4.7),

$$P(x_{ijk}) = \frac{e^{-\mu_{ijk}}\pi_{ijk}^{x_{ijk}}}{x_{ijk}!} \tag{4.12}$$

This equation takes care of one cell, but there are abc cells in the table. For a full model, the individual distributions are combined. The independence of the individual events means that the counts in the different cells are independent of each other. Since the joint probability of several cells is the product of the individual probabilities, the complete probability distribution is

$$P(\mathbf{x}) = \prod_{\text{cells}} P(x_{ijk}) = \prod_{\text{cells}} \frac{e^{-\mu_{ijk}}\pi_{ijk}^{x_{ijk}}}{x_{ijk}!}$$

If one lets $\mu = \Sigma\mu_{ijk}$ stand for the total expected frequency, this equation becomes

$$P(\mathbf{x}) = \left(\frac{e^{-\mu}}{\prod\limits_{\text{cells}} x_{ijk}!}\right)\prod_{\text{cells}} \pi_{ijk}^{x_{ijk}} \tag{4.13}$$

Product Multinomial Sampling

Neither the pure multinomial nor the pure Poisson sampling rule describes investigations in which certain sets of marginal frequencies are constrained by design. As the examples in Sections 2.3 and 3.1 suggest, there are many such studies. For example, one might select 90 subjects from each of two age groups, then randomly assign each subject to one of three training conditions, forming six groups of 30 subjects in all. In such cases, the frequencies associated with the two-way classification of groups do not have a sampling distribution. It is improper to treat them as if they were random.

Suppose, in particular, that a two-dimensional array of conditions corresponding to the i and j subscripts is constrained by the investigator to contain n_{ij}

subjects in the manner of the age-by-training example. The values of the n_{ij} need not be equal, although it is usually good experimental design to make them so. Then the members of each of these ab subpopulations are classified into one of the c categories of the index set $\mathscr{C}$, say by a measure of performance in the example. This classification is the random aspect of the process. Consider the i,jth subpopulation. There are n_{ij} observations distributed over c cells, a probabilistic event represented by the multinomial distribution. Let $\pi_{k|ij}$ be the probability that an observation from the i,jth subpopulation falls in category k; then the distribution for that subpopulation is

$$P(x_{ij1}, \ldots, x_{ijc}) = \frac{n_{ij}!}{x_{ij1}! \, x_{ij2}! \, \ldots \, x_{ijc}!} \, \pi_{1|ij}^{x_{ij1}} \, \pi_{2|ij}^{x_{ij2}} \, \ldots \, \pi_{c|ij}^{x_{ijc}} \quad (4.14)$$

To get a sampling model for the full set of data, this distribution is combined with those of the other subpopulations. Events in different subpopulations are independent, so the joint probability is the product of the separate probabilities from Equation 4.14:

$$P(\mathbf{x}) = \prod_{i,j} P(x_{ij1}, \ldots, x_{ijc})$$

$$= \left(\frac{\prod_{i,j} n_{ij}!}{\prod_{\text{cells}} x_{ijk}!} \right) \prod_{\text{cells}} \pi_{k|ij}^{x_{ijk}} \quad (4.15)$$

When one of the three factors is fixed and the other two are sampled, a similar product multinomial model is produced (see Problem 4.1).

Poisson-multinomial Sampling

In product-multinomial sampling, the number of occurrences of each subpopulation is fixed by design. By observing for a fixed duration, designs are created which the observations in the subpopulations occur as Poisson events. Again suppose that the subscripts i and j determine subpopulations and that the index k denotes a multinomial classification. The number of observations of the i,jth population, x_{ij+}, obeys a Poisson law with rate ρ_{ij} and mean frequency $\mu_{ij} = \rho_{ij}T$:

$$P(x_{ij+}) = \frac{e^{-\mu_{ij}} \mu_{ij}^{x_{ij+}}}{x_{ij+}!}$$

Within each subpopulation, the sampling is multinomial, following Equation 4.14. For the full set of data, these rules combine to give

$$P(\mathbf{x}) = \prod_{i,j} P(x_{ij1}, \ldots, x_{ijc} | x_{ij+}) P(x_{ij+})$$

$$= \prod_{i,j} \left(\frac{x_{ij}!}{x_{ij1}! \, x_{ij2}! \, \ldots \, x_{ijc}!} \, \pi_{1|ij}^{x_{ij1}} \pi_{2|ij}^{x_{ij2}} \cdots \pi_{c|ij}^{x_{ijc}} \right) \left(\frac{e^{-\mu_{ij}} \mu_{ij}^{x_{ij+}}}{x_{ij+}!} \right)$$

$$= \left(\frac{e^{-\mu}}{\prod_{\text{cells}} x_{ijk}!} \right) \prod_{\text{cells}} (\pi_{k|ij} \mu_{ij})^{x_{ijk}}$$

(4.16)

Again, μ is the total expected frequency. Note that this formula is identical to that of the pure Poisson model (Equation 4.13) if μ_{ijk} in that formula is replaced by $\pi_{k|ij} \mu_{ij}$.

Other Models

Other sampling models are constructed along the same lines. They all start with subpopulation frequencies that are either fixed by design or generated by Poisson processes. They combine these frequencies with multinomial distributions of responses within subpopulations. Each model leads to a formula for $P(\mathbf{x})$ that is similar to Equations 4.11, 4.13, 4.15, and 4.16. As far as statistical tests are concerned, it turns out that the differences among the models are not important. For reasons to be developed in Section 4.4, samples generated according to any of the models are tested in the same way. In spite of this similarity, discrimination among the models is useful, for the interpretation of a set of data depends on the model that underlies it. The way in which the data are organized determine what questions about them are meaningful. The models help to make this organization clear.

4.3. LIKELIHOOD FUNCTIONS AND MAXIMUM-LIKELIHOOD ESTIMATORS

Like any probability model, the models in the last section depend on various parameters, denoted there by π or ρ. In any real situation, the value of these parameters are unknown; indeed, the whole purpose of the investigation is to find out about them. The first step in any inference procedure is to estimate their values. There are several ways to make these estimates. The procedure that is used most often in this book is known as *maximum-likelihood estimation.*

Maximum-likelihood estimation starts with a set of data and a probability model for those data that expresses their probability in terms of various unknown parameters. One's goal is to find values for the parameters that are concordant with the data. Under the probability model, the chance of obtaining a particular set of data is greater with some sets of parameters than with others. For example, the probability of observing 3 successes in 10 independent Bernoulli events is

0.2601 when the probability of a success is $\pi = 1/3$, but only 0.0031 when $\pi = 3/4$. Accordingly, 1/3 is a more reasonable choice for the value of π than is 3/4. By plotting the probability of 3 successes in 10 trials as a function of π, as in Figure 4.1, one can see that the greatest chance of 3 successes occurs when $\pi \approx 0.3$. This is the *maximum-likelihood estimate*: the set of parameter values that makes the observed data most likely to have happened.

More formally, consider a probability model such as one of those discussed in the last section. As constructed, this model gives probabilities as functions of the data, holding the parameters fixed. However, in the estimation situation, one has a specific set of data and the parameters are unknown. To reflect this difference, the formulae are treated as functions of the parameters, with the data fixed. As such, they are called *likelihoods* and denoted by L(parameters), rather than P(data). The maximum-likelihood estimates are those parameters that maximize the likelihood, in other words, the set of parameters for which the given data have the greatest probability of occurring.

As an illustration of the maximum-likelihood procedure, consider the pure Poisson sampling model. The parameters are the rates ρ_{ijk} and the likelihood (adapted from Equation 4.13) is

$$L(\rho_{111}, \rho_{112}, \ldots, \rho_{abc}) = \prod_{\text{cells}} \frac{e^{-\rho_{ijk}T}}{x_{ijk}!} (\rho_{ijk}T)^{x_{ijk}} \qquad (4.17)$$

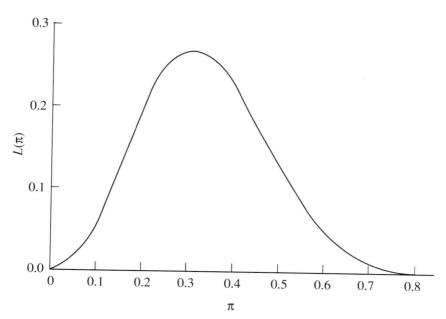

FIGURE 4.1. Likelihood function for three successes in 10 Bernoulli trials with unknown success probability π

The maximum-likelihood estimate of the ρ_{ijk} are the values that maximize this function, which, as the next paragraph shows, are

$$\hat{\rho}_{ijk} = \frac{x_{ijk}}{T} \tag{4.18}$$

This is a very natural result: the rate is estimated by the average frequency with which events take place.

Deriving Equation 4.18 is a relatively straightforward exercise in differential calculus. Rather than work with L directly, it is easier to take the logarithm of L, which has a maximum at exactly the same place (remember that the logarithm is a monotonic function). It also turns products into sums and eliminates the need for double subscripts and superscripts. Equation 4.17 becomes

$$\log L(\rho_{111}, \ldots, \rho_{abc}) = \sum_{\text{cells}} [-\rho_{ijk}T - \log(x_{ijk}!) + x_{ijk} \log(\rho_{ijk}T)]$$

To maximize this function with respect to any parameter, say ρ_{111}, one differentiates it, sets the result to zero, and solves. The derivative of a sum is the sum of derivatives, so

$$\frac{\partial \log L}{\partial \rho_{111}} = \sum_{\text{cells}} \frac{\partial}{\partial \rho_{111}} [-\rho_{ijk}T - \log(x_{ijk}!) + x_{ijk} \log(\rho_{ijk}T)]$$

Only the first term of the sum depends on ρ_{111}; the rest vanish when the derivative is taken and

$$\frac{\partial \log L}{\partial \rho_{111}} = \frac{\partial}{\partial \rho_{111}} [-\rho_{111}T - \log(x_{111}!) + x_{111}\log(\rho_{111}T)]$$

$$= -T + \frac{x_{111}}{\rho_{111}}$$

Setting this equation to zero and solving for ρ_{111} give the estimate x_{111}/T. Because very small or very large values of ρ_{111} fit less well than intermediate values, $\log L$ is concave downward and this extremum is a maximum. A similar argument applies for any other set of subscripts, giving Equation 4.18.

The estimates in Equation 4.18 are simple, in part because a saturated model is being fit and there is one unknown ρ_{ijk} for every x_{ijk}. However, the same maximum-likelihood principle can estimate parameters for unsaturated models, such as the various independence models described in Chapters 2 and 3. To fit these models, one replaces $\log \mu_{ijk}$ by a linear model with parameters λ, $\lambda_{A(i)}$, $\lambda_{B(j)}$, etc. The likelihood is then maximized with respect to these parameters. Although estimates can be obtained in this way, a more intuitive estimation strategy, based on the marginal frequencies, is possible. This procedure is discussed in the next section.

Beyond their conceptual simplicity, maximum-likelihood estimates have many desirable properties. One can show that they tend to be close to the true population value, converging to it as the samples get large (i.e., they have the statistical properties known as *consistency* and asymptotic lack of *bias*). The situation is even nicer for the frequency table models. These models are all members of a general class known as *exponential distributions*. For this class of models, the maximum-likelihood estimates extract all the information that is possible from the data (i.e., they are *sufficient*; see Hogg & Craig, 1978, Chapter 10). Furthermore, when the maximum-likelihood procedure is applied to frequency tables, it leads to a straightforward computational procedure, which is discussed in Sections 4.4 and 5.2.

Maximizing the likelihood is not the only way to estimate parameters; there are also *least-squares estimates* and *minimum chi-square estimates*. Both procedures minimize a measure of discrepancy between the model and the data. The conventional Pearson X^2 statistic measures the deviation of the theoretical μ_{ijk} from the observed x_{ijk}. Good estimates of the μ_{ijk} make X^2 small, and the minimum chi-square estimates are those parameters that make X^2 the smallest. Similarly, least-squares estimates minimize the squared deviation between observed and expected quantities, such as

$$\sum_{\text{cells}} (x_{ijk} - \mu_{ijk})^2 \quad \text{or} \quad \sum_{\text{cells}} (p_{ijk} - \pi_{ijk})^2$$

The techniques in Chapter 12 are based on a variant of these least-squares estimates.

Both the least-squares and the minimum-chi-square procedures lead to satisfactory estimates; indeed, for large samples their values do not differ appreciably from maximum-likelihood estimates. As the sample size goes to infinity, all the estimates converge to the same values. Hence, almost all the discussion of how to apply or interpret the models does not depend on the estimation procedure. Any method can be used without altering either the logic of the testing situations or the final conclusions.

4.4.   ESTIMATES OF CELL FREQUENCIES AND THE EQUIVALENCE OF THE SAMPLING MODELS

The expected cell frequencies $\hat{\mu}_{ijk}$, which are estimates of the mean frequencies under the various models for independence or partial independence, are central to the fitting or testing of any model. This section connects these estimates to the sampling models in Section 4.2. It also introduces two important facts about the maximum-likelihood estimators for these models: first, they can be obtained from the marginal distributions, and second, the same estimates of the cell frequencies are obtained for any of the sampling models.

Consider the probability models in Section 4.2 (Equations 4.11, 4.13, 4.15, and 4.16). Although the structure of these models differs in detail, they all have the same general form. All of them can be written as

$$P(\text{data}) = \left(\begin{array}{c} \text{term depending} \\ \text{on data and} \\ \text{total frequency} \end{array} \right) \prod_{\text{cells}} (\text{parameter}_{ijk})^{x_{ijk}}$$

For either of the Poisson models (Equation 4.13 or 4.16) the parameter in this equation is μ_{ijk} and the first term involves the total expected frequency, μ. For the multinomial models, where the total sample size is fixed by design, μ is not needed and the parameter is a multiple of μ_{ijk}, either $\pi_{ijk} = \mu_{ijk}/N$ in Equation 4.11 or $\pi_{k|ij} = \mu_{ijk}/n_{ij}$ in Equation 4.15. Thus, in all cases the probability of the data is

$$P(\mathbf{x}) = K(\mathbf{x})A(\mu) \prod_{\text{cells}} \mu_{ijk}{}^{x_{ijk}}$$

where $K(\mathbf{x})$ depends only on the data $\mathbf{x}$, and $A(\mu)$ depends only on μ. When treated as a function of the parameters, this expression is a likelihood function and may be denoted $L(\boldsymbol{\mu})$ where the boldface $\boldsymbol{\mu}$ indicates collectively all the μ_{ijk}. Taking the logarithm puts $L(\boldsymbol{\mu})$ into additive form:

$$\log L(\boldsymbol{\mu}) = \log K(\mathbf{x}) + \log A(\mu) + \sum_{\text{cells}} x_{ijk} \log \mu_{ijk} \qquad (4.19)$$

What Equation 4.19 says is important. The same form is obtained for all the sampling models in Section 4.2 (as well as for the models that could have been constructed for other sampling schemes). Thus, any property that can be shown to follow from Equation 4.19 holds for all the sampling models. In particular, the only portion of $\log L(\boldsymbol{\mu})$ that is affected by the relative size of the individual cell frequencies is the final sum. This sum is the same for all the sampling models.

Now consider the problem of fitting an unsaturated hierarchical linear log-frequency model to data. The direct approach to estimation is to substitute the linear model for $\log \mu_{ijk}$ into Equation 4.19, and then to maximize the likelihood with respect to the new parameters λ, $\lambda_{A(i)}$, etc. As it happens, this is not the easiest solution. One can continue to work with the μ_{ijk}, finding estimates $\hat{\mu}_{ijk}$ that maximize $L(\boldsymbol{\mu})$ subject to the constraints imposed by the log-linear model. Instead of estimates of the λ's, one gets a set of conditions that the $\hat{\mu}_{ijk}$ must satisfy. These conditions are pleasingly simple: when the estimated expected frequencies are summed into a marginal table corresponding to a parameter of the log-frequency model, the sum agrees with the observed data. Thus, if the model contains $\lambda_{AB(ij)}$, then when maximum-likelihood estimates are found,

$$x_{ij+} = \sum_{k} \hat{\mu}_{ijk}$$

Intuitively, this result is easy to justify. A hierarchical model that involves a particular term has one free parameter available to fit every cell of the corresponding marginal distribution. For example, the presence of $\lambda_{AB(ij)}$ in a model gives ab parameters, one for every i,j combination (remember that in a hierarchical model the presence of λ_{AB} means that λ, λ_A, and λ_B are also present). These parameters are used to fit the expected frequencies to the marginal distributions, then the rest of the table is extrapolated from these frequencies.

The importance of this result is twofold. First, it says that as far as maximum-likelihood estimates are concerned, the sampling models of Section 4.2 are all the same. Second, it gives criteria that suffice to determine the μ_{ijk}. These estimates must be such that (1) the observed and expected frequencies are the same for any marginal table corresponding to a term in the model, and (2) no other associations are present. Estimates of the other parameters—the λ's, $\hat{\pi}$'s, or $\hat{\rho}$'s—follow from the $\hat{\mu}_{ijk}$. This part of the computation is described in Sections 5.2 and 5.3.

Specifically, take the model $[AB][C]$. It has the log-linear representation

$$\log \mu_{ijk} = \lambda + \lambda_{A(i)} + \lambda_{B(j)} + \lambda_{C(k)} + \lambda_{AB(ij)} \qquad (4.20)$$

When maximum-likelihood estimates are found, the observed and expected frequencies match in the relevant marginal tables:

$$\sum_{j,k} \hat{\mu}_{ijk} = x_{i++}, \quad \sum_{i,k} \hat{\mu}_{ijk} = x_{+j+},$$

$$\sum_{i,j} \hat{\mu}_{ijk} = x_{++k}, \quad \text{and} \quad \sum_{k} \hat{\mu}_{ijk} = x_{ij+} \qquad (4.21)$$

The first two of these sums are are redundant—they are obtained if the last sum is further summed over j or i, respectively. In Section 3.3, estimates for this model were given:

$$\hat{\mu}_{ijk} = \frac{x_{ij+} \, x_{++k}}{x_{+++}}$$

It is easy to show that these values fulfill the two criteria for maximum-likelihood estimates. First, as a little calculation demonstrates, they satisfy Equations 4.21. Second, no extraneous associations are involved, since $\hat{\mu}_{ijk}$ fits Model 4.20. Thus, they are the proper estimates.

The matching of marginal distributions is sufficiently important that some readers may wish to see a more formal demonstration (others can skip to the next section). The following partial proof is adapted from Birch (1963).

Consider the Poisson sampling model (Equation 4.13). For this model the constant $A(\mu)$ in the likelihood function (Equation 4.19) is $e^{-\mu}$, so $\log A(\mu) = -\Sigma \mu_{ijk}$. With a little rearranging, the log-likelihood is

$$\log L(\boldsymbol{\mu}) = \log K(\mathbf{x}) + \sum_{\text{cells}} [x_{ijk} \log \mu_{ijk} - \mu_{ijk}]$$

Now suppose that $\log \mu_{ijk}$ is given by a hierarchical linear model; specifically take Model 4.20, above, which expresses the model $[AB][C]$. Denote the likelihood function by $L(\boldsymbol{\lambda})$ to indicate that its fundamental parameters are now the λ's. To maximize the $L(\boldsymbol{\lambda})$ it is differentiated with respect to its parameters and the result set to 0. Consider first the unsubscripted parameter λ. The derivative is

$$\frac{\partial \log L(\boldsymbol{\lambda})}{\partial \lambda} = \frac{\partial}{\partial \lambda} \log K(\mathbf{x}) - \sum_{\text{cells}} \left(x_{ijk} \frac{\partial \log \mu_{ijk}}{\partial \lambda} - \frac{\partial \mu_{ijk}}{\partial \lambda} \right)$$

Because $K(\mathbf{x})$ does not depend on λ, the first term on the right of this equation vanishes. The model that is to be fitted is linear in $\log \mu_{ijk}$, so the expression is easier to work with if second term of the sum is replaced by one that uses the logarithm. This is accomplished with the identity

$$\frac{d\mu}{d\lambda} = \mu\left(\frac{1}{\mu}\frac{d\mu}{d\lambda}\right) = \mu \frac{d \log \mu}{d\lambda}$$

The result is

$$\frac{\partial \log L(\boldsymbol{\lambda})}{\partial \lambda} = - \sum_{\text{cells}} (x_{ijk} - \mu_{ijk}) \frac{\partial \log \mu_{ijk}}{\partial \lambda} \qquad (4.22)$$

The derivative on the right is obtained from the original model,

$$\frac{\partial \log \mu_{ijk}}{\partial \lambda} = \frac{\partial}{\partial \lambda} (\lambda + \lambda_{A(i)} + \lambda_{B(j)} + \lambda_{C(k)} + \lambda_{AB(ij)}) = 1$$

With this substitution, Equation 4.22 is

$$\frac{\partial \log L(\boldsymbol{\lambda})}{\partial \lambda} = - \sum_{\text{cells}} (x_{ijk} - \mu_{ijk})$$

$$= \sum_{\text{cells}} \mu_{ijk} - x_{+++} \qquad (4.23)$$

This derivative is zero at the maximum-likelihood estimate of λ, a situation satisfied only when the overall sums of the observed and expected frequencies agree.

The other parameters are treated similarly. Consider $\lambda_{A(i)}$. These parameters are subject to the constraint $\Sigma \lambda_{A(i)} = 0$, which means that one need only estimate $\lambda_{A(i)}$ for $i = 1, 2, \ldots, a - 1$, after which the final term is

$$\lambda_{A(a)} = - \sum_{i=1}^{a-1} \lambda_{A(i)} \qquad (4.24)$$

As in the case of λ, the first step is to differentiate $\log L(\lambda)$ with respect to $\lambda_{A(i)}$ for any $i \neq a$. The process proceeds as far as Equation 4.22, where the derivative of $\log \mu_{ijk}$ is substituted. Because of the constraint in Equation 4.24, this derivative is more complicated than it was for λ:

$$\frac{\partial \log \mu_{ljk}}{\partial \lambda_{A(i)}} = \begin{cases} 1, & l=i \\ -1, & l=a \\ 0, & \text{otherwise} \end{cases}$$

Substituting this result into an equation similar to Equation 4.22, the derivatives of all terms except those subscripted by i or a vanish, leaving

$$\frac{\partial \log L(\lambda)}{\partial \lambda_{A(i)}} = \sum_{j,k} [x_{ijk} - \mu_{ijk} - (x_{ajk} - \mu_{ajk})]$$

$$= x_{i++} - \sum_{j,k} \mu_{ijk} - x_{a++} + \sum_{j,k} \mu_{ajk}$$

Setting this equation to zero, rearranging the terms, and replacing μ_{ijk} by $\hat{\mu}_{ijk}$ to indicate the maximum-likelihood estimate, gives

$$x_{i++} - x_{a++} = \sum_{j,k} \hat{\mu}_{ijk} - \sum_{j,k} \hat{\mu}_{ajk} \tag{4.25}$$

Although this equation has been derived for $i \neq a$, it also holds (trivially) when $i = a$. Summing it over i from 1 to a gives

$$x_{+++} - ax_{a++} = \sum_{\text{cells}} \hat{\mu}_{ijk} - a \sum_{j,k} \hat{\mu}_{ajk}$$

The sums of x_{ijk} and $\hat{\mu}_{ijk}$ over all cells are equal, as was shown at Equation 4.23, so the first terms on either side drop out leaving

$$x_{a++} = \sum_{j,k} \hat{\mu}_{ajk}$$

Substituting this in Equation 4.25 shows that for any i,

$$x_{i++} = \sum_{j,k} \hat{\mu}_{ijk}$$

The sums of x_{ijk} and $\hat{\mu}_{ijk}$ in the A marginals agree.

The same analysis applies to the other terms in the log-linear model. The argument depends on the hierarchical nature of the model, since the proof for each higher-order term (e.g., λ_{AB}) depends on having shown the result for lower-order terms (i.e., λ, λ_A, and λ_B). The final conclusion is simple: for any parameter in a hierarchical log-linear model for μ_{ijk}, the corresponding sums of the data and the maximum-likelihood estimates are the same.

4.5. LIKELIHOOD-RATIO TESTS

The likelihood function provides both a means to estimate parameters and a way to test their values. It is the basis of *likelihood-ratio tests*, which compare the fits of hierarchically related models. For example, to test whether a particular parameter takes a given value, one can compare a model in which the parameter is fixed at this value to one where it is free.

Specifically, one starts with a probabilistic model for a set of data based on a set of p nonredundant parameters $\omega_1, \omega_2, \ldots, \omega_p$. In the present context, these are probably λ's, but could be π's, ρ's, or any other parameterization. Denote this model by $\mathcal{M}$ and the likelihood function for a particular set of data by $L(\omega)$. Suppose that one is interested in testing whether the parameters $\omega_{q+1}, \omega_{q+2}, \ldots, \omega_p$ take particular values—perhaps are equal to 0. The other q parameters, $\omega_1, \omega_2, \ldots, \omega_q$ remain free. To see the effect of this restriction, one constructs a second model that is identical to $\mathcal{M}$ except that the values of $\omega_{q+1}, \ldots, \omega_p$ are fixed.† Denote the restricted model by $\mathcal{M}^*$ and its restricted parameter set by ω^*. Since $\mathcal{M}^*$ is a special case of $\mathcal{M}$, the models are hierarchically related in the manner of the lattice of Figure 3.4. The likelihood function for $\mathcal{M}^*$, denoted by $L^*(\omega^*)$, is the same as that of $\mathcal{M}$ except for the restrictions imposed on the $p - q$ fixed elements. What is needed now is a way to compare the adequacy of $\mathcal{M}$ and $\mathcal{M}^*$.

Maximum-likelihood estimates for the parameters of $\mathcal{M}$ and $\mathcal{M}^*$ are obtained by maximizing $L(\omega)$ and $L^*(\omega^*)$, respectively. Denote these estimates by hats as usual. One can do a better job maximizing $L(\omega)$ than $L^*(\omega^*)$, because one has more parameters to work with. In $\mathcal{M}^*$ one is stuck with the $p - q$ values that were fixed when it was created from $\mathcal{M}$, but in $\mathcal{M}$ these are free. Thus, at their respective maxima, $L^*(\hat{\omega}^*) \leq L(\hat{\omega})$. Equality is nearly impossible; almost surely $\mathcal{M}^*$ has the smaller maximum likelihood. The size of this difference indicates the importance of the restrictions. If the maximum for $\mathcal{M}$ is only slightly larger than that for $\mathcal{M}^*$, then the restrictions do little damage, and the assignments that fix the parameters are not far from wrong. If $L(\hat{\omega})$ is much larger than $L^*(\hat{\omega}^*)$, the assignment had best be rejected. One sensible choice of a statistic to compare the two likelihoods is their ratio, known appropriately as the *likelihood ratio*,

$$r = \frac{L(\hat{\omega})}{L^*(\hat{\omega}^*)}$$

Because the numerator is at least as large as the denominator, $r \geq 1$. The more that r exceeds 1, the more one can be sure that $\mathcal{M}^*$ should be rejected in favor of $\mathcal{M}$. A test based on this statistic is known as a *likelihood-ratio test*.

---

†More correctly, $p - q$ restrictions are imposed on the parameter space of $\mathcal{M}$ to form that of $\mathcal{M}^*$, so that the dimensionality of the space spanned by the parameters of $\mathcal{M}$ is $p - q$ greater than the dimensionality of the parameter space of $\mathcal{M}^*$. For the present discussion it suffices to think of parameters as set to fixed values.

To use the likelihood ratio to test the restrictions, one must know its sampling distribution. Suppose that the restricted model $\mathcal{M}^*$ is correct and that the sample size is large. Then under a wide range of conditions (which are satisfied for all the models in this book) an approximately χ^2 distributed statistic is

$$R = 2 \log r = 2 \log \frac{\text{maximum unrestricted likelihood}}{\text{maximum restricted likelihood}}$$

$$= 2 \log L(\hat{\omega}) - 2 \log L^*(\hat{\omega}^*) \qquad (4.26)$$

The number of degrees of freedom associated with R equals the differences in the number of independent parameters in the models, which here is $p - q$. If R exceeds the upper-tail critical value of $\chi^2(p - q)$ at the selected significance level, the parameter restrictions are rejected. If R is less than this value, the restrictions are retained.

When calculating the degrees of freedom, one must be sure to count only parameters that are free and are independent of one another. However, it is often convenient to use a parameterization which involves more quantities than are really necessary. The parameters of the log-linear model are a case in point: if all a values of $\lambda_{A(i)}$ are free, one does not need to include λ in the model. However, the model is conceptually simpler with a full complement of parameters. To avoid problems in estimation, one restricts λ_A to sum to zero. When this is done, the number of restrictions must be subtracted from the number of apparent parameters to get the number of free parameters. Thus, the a parameters $\lambda_{A(i)}$ are subject to one restriction $\Sigma\lambda_{A(i)} = 0$, leaving $a - 1$ degrees of freedom and the ab parameters $\lambda_{AB(ij)}$ are subject to $a+b - 1$ restrictions, leaving $(a - 1)(b - 1)$ degrees of freedom (recall the discussion of Section 3.11). Only the change in the free parameter count determines the degrees of freedom.†

Two important caveats attach to the likelihood-ratio test. First, the sample size must be adequate for the chi-square approximation to be accurate. When only a few observations go into calculating the likelihoods, the discrete distribution that results is poorly approximated by χ^2, and the use of this distribution in a test is improper. Rules of thumb governing sample size here are similar to those discussed for two-way tests in Section 2.5. The second problem concerns the adequacy of model $\mathcal{M}$. When $\mathcal{M}$ is true, R has either a central or noncentral χ^2 distribution, depending on the truth of $\mathcal{M}^*$, which makes a test possible. But when $\mathcal{M}$ is inappropriate, then a test of the values of its parameters makes no sense at all. Such a *specification error* in $\mathcal{M}$ renders the results of a likelihood-ratio test meaningless (or any other test, for that matter). One must give thought to the model $\mathcal{M}$, as well as the difference between $\mathcal{M}$ and $\mathcal{M}^*$, a point that is easily overlooked.

---

†More strictly, the number of degrees of freedom equals the difference in dimensionality between the space spanned by the parameters of $\mathcal{M}$ and that spanned by the parameters of $\mathcal{M}^*$. When a set of p parameters is subject to r (linear) restrictions, they now span a $p - r$ dimensional space. This geometric description is the ultimate reference in counting degrees of freedom.

The form of the sampling models for frequency tables further simplifies the likelihood-ratio tests. The likelihood under any of the sampling models has the form given above in Equation 4.19:

$$\log L(\mu) = \log K(\mathbf{x}) + \log A(\mu) + \sum_{\text{cells}} x_{ijk} \log \mu_{ijk} \qquad (4.27)$$

The data are the same for both $\mathcal{M}$ and $\mathcal{M}^*$, so that $K(\mathbf{x})$ and $A(\mu)$ are also the same. With this likelihood, the likelihood-ratio statistic (Equation 4.26) is

$$R = 2 \log L(\hat{\omega}) - 2 \log L^*(\hat{\omega}^*)$$

$$= 2 \left[\left(\log K(\mathbf{x}) + \log A(\mu) + \sum_{\text{cells}} x_{ijk} \log \hat{\mu}_{ijk} \right) \right.$$

$$\left. - \left(\log K(\mathbf{x}) + \log A(\mu) + \sum_{\text{cells}} x_{ijk} \log \hat{\mu}^*_{ijk} \right) \right]$$

$$= 2 \sum_{\text{cells}} x_{ijk} \log \frac{\hat{\mu}_{ijk}}{\hat{\mu}^*_{ijk}} \qquad (4.28)$$

Now consider a test in which the saturated model $\mathcal{M}_s$ plays the role of the unrestricted model $\mathcal{M}$. A comparison of some $\mathcal{M}^*$ to $\mathcal{M}_s$ is, in effect, a test of the goodness of fit of $\mathcal{M}^*$. In a saturated model, the likelihood is maximized when the expected frequencies are the same as the data, that is, when $\hat{\mu}_{ijk} = x_{ijk}$. Then Equation 4.28 is

$$R = 2 \sum_{\text{cells}} x_{ijk} \log \frac{x_{ijk}}{\hat{\mu}^*_{ijk}} \qquad (4.29)$$

This is exactly the G^2 statistic introduced in Section 2.8, known there as the *likelihood-ratio statistic*. The basis for the name is now apparent.

The difference tests using G^2 introduced in Section 3.8 are also likelihood-ratio tests. To show this, let $L(\mathbf{x})$ stand for the likelihood of the saturated model, obtained by substituting x_{ijk} for μ_{ijk} in Equation 4.27, and let $\mathcal{M}$ and $\mathcal{M}^*$ be two hierarchically related unsaturated models. The G^2 statistics for these models are likelihood-ratio tests against the saturated model, specifically

$$G^2 = 2 \log L(\mathbf{x}) - 2 \log L(\hat{\lambda})$$

$$G^{2*} = 2 \log L(\mathbf{x}) - 2 \log L(\hat{\lambda}^*)$$

The difference between these test statistics is

$$\Delta G^2 = G^{2*} - G^2 = 2 \log L(\hat{\lambda}) - 2 \log L(\hat{\lambda}^*)$$

This difference is the likelihood-ratio test statistic for the restriction of $\mathcal{M}$ to $\mathcal{M}^*$, as a comparison to Equation 4.26 shows. This argument gives the difference tests on G^2 a more exact statistical basis than exists for other statistics, such as X^2. Changes in the values of those statistics also yield reasonable tests, although they lack this foundation.

PROBLEMS

4.1. Consider a design in which fixed samples of size n_i subjects are chosen from each of a subpopulations. Then, each individual is classified into one cell of a $b \times c$ table. Write the sampling model for $P(\mathbf{x})$ in this situation.

4.2. How does the model in Problem 4.1 change when the subpopulations consist of the collection of all individuals of a different types who are observed during a fixed time interval?

4.3. What is the relationship between parameter estimates obtained by maximizing the likelihood and those obtained by minimizing G^2? Hint: the answer is simple: complicated calculations are not needed.

4.4. Show that $p = x/N$ is the maximum-likelihood estimate of π in the binomial distribution of Equation 4.3. Note: this problem is straightforward if you know how to use the derivative to maximize a function — here log $L(\pi)$. If this use of calculus is novel, do not attempt the problem.

4.5. Construct an exact formula for a likelihood-ratio test of the hypothesis that $\lambda_{AC} = 0$ in the context of the model $\mathcal{M} = [AB][AC]$.

5 Fitting and Testing Models

Chapters 2 and 3 described the way in which models in two and three dimensions are constructed and tested. Chapter 4 covered the mathematical basis of these operations in more detail. This chapter combines these ideas and generalizes them to tables of any size. When results from Chapter 4 are used, they are briefly restated.

5.1. THE HIERARCHY OF MEANINGFUL MODELS

An enormous number of models for a frequency table can be written. Fortunately, only a very small proportion of these are relevant to any particular study. Generally, one's problems arise less from the lack of an applicable model than from having too many of them. Thus, one's first task in all but the simplest investigations is to winnow out the irrelevant models and select the most useful ones. For this task, an overview of the range of potential models is valuable.

To begin, one can organize the totality of models into sets of diminishing size, starting with the most general collection and then specializing. Each of the following sets includes the subsequent sets as special cases.

1. *All models for the expected frequencies.* Obviously, this is a very large and diverse collection. The most useful members are the linear models, including linear models for the cell frequencies, for the logarithms of the frequencies, and occasionally for other functions of the cell probabilities. Nonlinear models are less useful, except in certain special cases. Models can also be constructed by imposing particular constraints on the frequencies—most notable here are the

models created by equating certain marginal probabilities. Generally, the set of all models is too broad to be useful, and one wants to restrict attention to more limited classes. In what follows, most attention is paid to the models for the logarithm of the cell frequencies, although some other types of models are discussed in Chapters 12 and 13.

2.   *Linear models for the logarithm of the expected frequencies.* These are known as log-linear models. They include all the models discussed in Chapters 2 and 3 and most of those in the rest of this book (some multiplicative models are discussed in Chapter 11). For most purposes, this set is larger than necessary, for it contains many models that have no simple meaning in terms of common research designs.

3.   *Hierarchical linear log-frequency models.* One way to tighten up the set of log-linear models is to restrict attention to models that obey the *hierarchy principle*. This rule, which was introduced in Section 3.9, states that whenever a linear model contains a λ parameter that depends on a set of subscripts, it must also contain every λ parameter whose subscripts are subsets of this set. So a model that contains the parameter λ_{AB} also contains λ, λ_A, and λ_B. The hierarchy principle eliminates models that include high-order associations and hold low-order ones constant. Fortunately, these nonhierarchical models almost never describe useful hypotheses about a study. The problem is not that lower-order terms are never zero, but that it is hard to generate design constraints or to construct hypotheses that preclude their appearance. A second benefit of restricting one's attention to hierarchical models is more mechanical: as the discussion in Section 4.4 shows, a simple rule links the terms in a hierarchical log-frequency model to the marginal distributions. This connection is the basis of the fitting algorithm presented in the next section.

4.   *Models of independence and conditional independence.* The set of models is further restricted by considering only those hierarchical linear log-frequency models that correspond to hypotheses of independence or conditional independence. So far, the only example of a model that is excluded by this restriction is [AB][AC][BC], but there are many more examples in higher-way tables. Since a great many specific hypotheses can be couched in conditional independence terms, these models are more valuable than their relative prevalence would suggest. Beyond the simple independence and quasi-independence models, such as $A \perp\!\!\!\perp B$ or $A \perp\!\!\!\perp C|B$, this set includes models that combine the independence or conditional independence of several sets of factors into a single compound model. With this inclusion, the collection of conditional-independence models is nearly identical to the set of models that are described by graphs, a connection to be explored further in Sections 6.3 and 6.5.

For many analyses, the third set—the hierarchical linear log-frequency models—is the most useful. Most of its members have comprehensible interpretations and are not hard to fit. However, two additional restrictions usually apply, even to this set. The first is consistency with the sampling design. Quantities that are fixed by the investigator must be included in the model. In particular, where a marginal distribution is determined by the design, the model must contain parameters to represent it. They form the irreducible base against which other effects are tested. Without them, a model may be retained or rejected for reasons completely unrelated to the performance of the subjects.

The second restriction is the exclusion of the constant-frequency models. These are models in which one or more of the factors of the table make no appearance, for example the model $[A][B]$ in a three-way table. As noted in Section 3.7, omitting a factor from a model altogether implies both that the factor is unrelated to any other factor in the table and that the frequencies at all levels of the factor are the same. In most research situations, one is not interested in the second part of this compound hypothesis. Particularly in larger tables, the elimination of the constant-frequency models costs the researcher little. Accordingly, one demands that every factor occur in the model at least as a simple λ parameter, factor A as λ_A, factor B as λ_B, and so forth.

A set of models, such as the ones just described, naturally organizes itself into a hierarchical lattice similar to the one shown above in Figure 3.4. It underlies most subsequent analysis. This lattice is formed by connecting any pair of models together that differ only by a single variety of λ parameter. Thus, $[AB][BC]$ is connected in one direction to $[AB][C]$ and $[A][BC]$, which lack λ_{BC} and λ_{AB}, respectively, and in the other to $[AB][AC][BC]$, which adds λ_{AC}. Usually, it is convenient to put the simpler models toward the top of the lattice. Although with practice one learns to use the lattice implicitly, it is often useful to write out part of it explicitly.

Consider, for example, an investigation involving 8 groups of undergraduate students, classified by sex (factor S, 2 levels) and year in school (factor Y, 4 levels). Each student is asked two questions (factors A and B). These two questions serve to locate each student in one cell of a two-way AB table. For a given type of student, following the logic in Section 4.1, the distribution of frequencies into these cells is multinomial. A similar AB table is formed from each of the 8 subsamples of students. Suppose that the investigator has fixed the size of the subsamples, by including 60 subjects of each type. This feature of the design gives the sampling model for the four-way table a product multinomial form (Section 4.2, see Equation 4.15). The mathematical form of this model is less important than the restrictions that it imposes. In constructing models for the data, one is free to change the parameters relating to the associations with A and B, but must consider only models that keep the SY marginal frequencies fixed at 60 per cell. To do this, one includes λ_{SY} (and so also λ_S and λ_Y) in every model. Strictly speaking, these quantities are not parameters in the sense of statistical inference, since they do not correspond to any population characteristics. However, in a minor violation of notational convention, they will still be indicated by the Greek letter λ. To avoid the constant frequency models, the parameters λ_A and λ_B are also included. Thus, the nucleus of any reasonable model is

$$\log \lambda_{ijkl} = \lambda + \lambda_{S(i)} + \lambda_{Y(j)} + \lambda_{SY(ij)} + \lambda_{A(k)} + \lambda_{B(l)} \qquad (5.1)$$

In bracket notation, this model is denoted by $[SY][A][B]$; in independence terms, it is $SY \perp\!\!\!\perp A \perp\!\!\!\perp B$.

The minimal model, having the smallest possible number of parameters, is maximally restricted and usually fails to fit the data. To accommodate more elaborate effects, other terms are added to Equation 5.1, while keeping consistent with the hierarchy principle. Part of the resulting lattice of models is shown in Figure 5.1. If this figure were complete, it would contain 73 four-factor models, each including λ_{SY}, λ_A, and λ_B. The remaining 41 four-factor models that do not involve λ_{SY} are excluded, along with 11 models that omit A, B, or both. The restriction to hierarchical models excludes 1946 candidate models, all of which are otherwise consistent with the design. Among the 73 acceptable models, 30 express hypotheses of independence or conditional independence. These form a sublattice of Figure 5.1 and are marked by asterisks.

It is important to realize that the construction of the model lattice is based on the logic of the design and not on considerations of goodness of fit. When the samples are of equal size and there are few higher-order associations, the value of G^2 or X^2 may be but little altered by removing mandatory terms such as λ_{SY}. However, the models thus created are logically uninterpretable. The degrees of freedom for tests of these models are incorrect, since they mix references to true parameters and to experimental constraints. Chapter 6 tells how to construct this lattice in more detail.

5.2. ESTIMATION OF THE EXPECTED FREQUENCIES: THE ITERATIVE PROPORTIONAL FITTING ALGORITHM

A model can be fit to a frequency table in several ways. In this section a scheme is described that is based on the marginal frequency distributions, as emphasized in the work of Goodman (e.g., 1970) and the book by Bishop, Fienberg, and Holland (1975). Other algorithms can be used, such as Newton-Raphson iteration (Haberman, 1974a, 1978, 1979), weighted least squares (Grizzle, Starmer, & Koch, 1969; also chapter 11, below), iterated least squares (McCullagh & Nelder, 1983), and minimum discrimination information (Gokhale & Kullback, 1978; Ireland & Kullback, 1968; Ku, Varner, & Kullback, 1971). In fact, when applied to the same hypothesis, these methods are nearly equivalent. In this respect, although each method has its advantages and disadvantages, the choice among them is not critical. Estimates based on the marginal frequency distributions are described here because of their comparative simplicity and connection to hypotheses of independence. Readers who plan to use another estimation

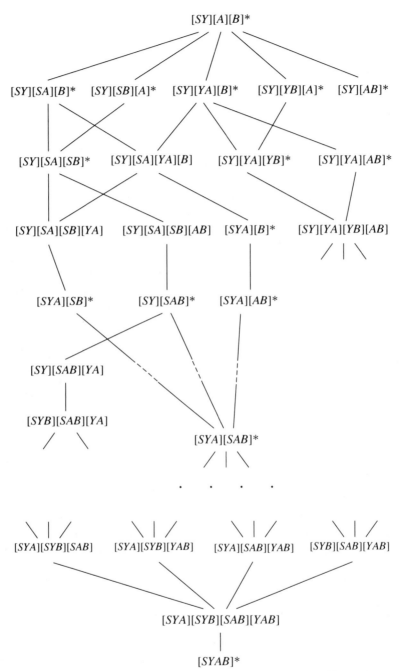

FIGURE 5.1. A portion of the hierarchical lattice of models for a four-way design with two factors fixed. Many models and their associated links are omitted. Asterisks indicate models that can be interpreted in terms of conditional independence.

108

procedure need not abandon this book, however, since all but this section and next apply unchanged.

For all the models in Chapters 2 and 3 except $[AB][AC][BC]$, explicit formulae for the expected frequencies can be written (e.g., Equations 3.2, 3.12, and 3.16). Such models are called *direct models*. Unfortunately, closed formulae do not always exist; models without them are known as *indirect models*. For example, the model $[AB][AC][BC]$ is indirect. With more factors, the proportion of indirect models is much greater.

The distinction between direct and indirect models is important only if one needs closed estimation formulae. In practice, the computation in all but the simplest cases is likely to be done on a computer, so a single algorithm that works for both types of models is more useful. For the hierarchical log-linear models, a simple scheme follows from the rules for maximum-likelihood estimation. As shown in Section 4.4, the use of maximum-likelihood estimates imposes restraints on the marginal frequency tables. For any parameters in the model, the marginal subtables of the data and the expected frequencies agree. Thus, to estimate the expected frequencies, one need only construct a table which (1) agrees with the observed marginal frequencies for terms that are in the model and (2) contains no other associations. These two criteria suffice to determine the maximum-likelihood estimates; if a table can be found for which both hold, it contains the desired result.

For example, the four-factor model $[AB][BCD]$ has log-frequency form

$$\log \mu_{ijkl} = \lambda + \lambda_{A(i)} + \lambda_{B(j)} + \lambda_{C(k)} + \lambda_{D(l)} + \lambda_{AB(ij)} + \lambda_{BC(jk)} \\ + \lambda_{BD(jl)} + \lambda_{CD(kl)} + \lambda_{BCD(jkl)} \quad (5.2)$$

All the terms in this equation are generated by applying the hierarchy principle to the highest-order terms λ_{AB} and λ_{BCD}. For the maximum-likelihood estimates, the inclusion of these parameters in the model means that

$$\sum_{k,l} \hat{\mu}_{ijkl} = x_{ij++} \quad \text{and} \quad \sum_{i} \hat{\mu}_{ijkl} = x_{+jkl} \quad (5.3)$$

The other parameters in Model 5.2 lead to similar equations involving x_{i+++}, x_{+jk+}, etc., but these are subsumed by Equations 5.3 and are true whenever these equations hold.

A set of $\hat{\mu}_{ijkl}$ is needed that fits Equations 5.3 and that does not contain any other associations. These frequencies are generated by an algorithm known as *iterative proportional fitting*.† The way in which this procedure operates is

---

†The iterative proportional fitting algorithm was developed by Deming and Stephan (1940) to adjust one table of data to another set of marginal distributions, a slightly different use from that made here (see Haberman, 1979, Chapter 9 for examples). For a discussion of the statistical properties of the algorithm, with proofs or references thereto, see Bishop, Fienberg, & Holland (1975, Chapter 3).

straightforward. It starts with a table of equal frequencies that shows no association at all. Then, one by one, the constrained marginal distributions are examined. For a particular marginal configuration, the observed and expected frequencies are summed and compared. If they do not agree, the expected frequencies are inflated or deflated proportionally so that the table fits. Because exactly the same changes are made to every element that contributes to a particular marginal cell, this operation does not introduce any higher-order associations. When the adjustment of one marginal distribution is completed, attention is turned to the next marginal table. This procedure continues until all the observed and expected marginal tables agree. The adjusted table now contains the $\hat{\mu}$.

This procedure is general and applies to both direct models and indirect models. The maximum-likelihood estimates of the expected frequencies are unique, which means that the iterative algorithm gives the same result as the closed-form equations, where the latter exist. This is a nice result: one need not worry about whether the model is direct. At the occasional cost of a little extra computing, one can always use the iterative scheme.

The iterative proportional fitting algorithm is most simply illustrated in a two-way table, although, because the independence model is direct, it is not strictly necessary. The sequence of steps is shown in Table 5.1. Under the model of independence, $A \perp\!\!\!\perp B$ or $[A][B]$, the observed and expected marginal frequencies must agree in both the rows and the columns:

$$\sum_j \hat{\mu}_{ij} = x_{i+} \quad \text{and} \quad \sum_i \hat{\mu}_{ij} = x_{+j}$$

The goal is to find a set of frequencies that satisfies these equations, but is without any other association. The algorithm starts with a table of identical frequencies, which satisfies the no-association criterion but not the marginal-sums criteria (Table 5.1, step 0). The marginal frequencies in this table disagree badly with the observed data, but they can be fixed. Consider row a_1. Here $x_{1+} = 35$, but $\hat{\mu}_{ij}$ sums to 3. This discrepancy is corrected if every entry in that row of the $\hat{\mu}$ table is multiplied by $35/3 = 11.667$ (step 1a). A similar adjustment to row a_2 corrects its frequencies (step 1b). Because all the entries in each row have been changed in the same way at the same time, no row-column dependencies are introduced and the independence in the table is not compromised. The columns sums are still incorrect, requiring another round of adjustment. The first column sum is too small—it is 24.667 and should be 39—so every score in it is multiplied by $39/24.667 = 1.581$ (step 2a). Correcting the next two columns (the multipliers are 0.365 and 1.054), completes the column adjustment (steps 2b and 2c). The row sums in the table are still correct, so the estimated expected frequencies under the model $[A][B]$ have been obtained. It is easy to verify that they are the same as those given by the conventional formula for independence (e.g., Equation 2.3).

TABLE 5.1
Fitting a Model by Iterative Proportional Adjustment
of the Marginal Distributions

Observed Frequencies

	b_1	b_2	b_3	
a_1	13	5	17	35
a_2	26	4	9	39
	39	9	26	74

Step 0: A Table with No Association

	b_1	b_2	b_3	
a_1	1	1	1	3
a_2	1	1	1	3
	2	2	2	

Step 1a: Adjust Row a_1

	b_1	b_2	b_3	
a_1	11.667	11.667	11.667	35.000
a_2	1.000	1.000	1.000	3.000

Step 1b: Adjust Row a_2

	b_1	b_2	b_3	
a_1	11.667	11.667	11.667	35.000
a_2	13.000	13.000	13.000	39.000
	24.667	24.667	24.667	

Step 2a: Adjust Column b_1

	b_1	b_2	b_3
a_1	18.446	11.667	11.667
a_2	20.554	13.000	13.000
	39.000	24.667	24.667

Steps 2b and 2c: Adjust Columns b_2 and b_3

	b_1	b_2	b_3	
a_1	18.446	4.257	12.297	35.000
a_2	20.554	4.743	13.703	39.000
	39.000	9.000	26.000	

When it is applied to indirect models, without closed estimates, the iterative scheme works in the same way. However, with these models the correction applied to one marginal distribution alters the other marginal distributions. In the example of Table 5.1, fitting the columns in step 2 did not alter the row sums that had been adjusted in step 1. In general, the agreement of one set of marginal frequencies is lost when others are adjusted. When this happens, the solution is simple: use proportional adjustment again to readjust the expected frequencies and bring the defective marginal distribution back to agreement. Of course, the new adjustment may disrupt another distribution, which must in turn be fixed, but the magnitude of these corrections get smaller and smaller as one proceeds. Eventually, the inaccuracies become less than any desired value as the estimates converge. The expected frequencies are obtained to whatever accuracy one wishes.†

Application of the iterative proportional fitting algorithm, especially to a large table, takes a lot of calculation. This work is best left to a computer. In a computer program, the iterative algorithm is usually visible to the user only in some terminology and a few specialized results. Programs often report the number of iterations that are required to obtain the expected frequencies. The user may be able to set the limit for the number of iterations or the criterion for deciding that an approximation to the expected frequencies is sufficiently accurate. Sometimes, with a complicated model and a table with many blank cells, a failure to reach the desired accuracy within the specified number of iterations may be reported. Increasing the allowable number of iterations or relaxing the criterion for convergence may solve this problem (but see the discussion in Section 5.6).

5.3. ESTIMATION OF THE LOG-LINEAR PARAMETERS

The frequency models are expressed with parameters that are more fundamental than the cell expectations. The parameters λ of the log-linear model are one example; the probability and rate parameters (π and ρ) of the sampling models in Section 4.2 are others. Estimates of these parameters follow easily once the $\hat{\mu}$ have been found. Usually π and ρ are simple functions of μ within the context of the appropriate sampling model (those given in Chapter 4), and the same functions apply to the estimates. For example, in a two-way table, the conditional

---

†The accuracy that is required before a set of expected frequencies is deemed to fit depends on the standards of the user. Because different computer programs use different standards of accuracy, results computed by different programs may differ in the last few places, although not substantially. Calculations for the examples in this book have used a conservative criterion for convergence.

probability of column j given row i, denoted $\pi_{j|i}$, is estimated by dividing $\hat{\mu}_{ij}$ by the fixed marginal frequency x_{i+}. Using the estimates from Table 5.1 yields

$$\hat{\pi}_{2|1} = \frac{\hat{\mu}_{12}}{x_{1+}} = \frac{4.257}{35} = 0.122$$

Estimates of the λ's are more complicated, since they do not derive from any single $\hat{\mu}$. The fitting algorithm ensures the existence of a set of $\hat{\lambda}$'s that is consistent with the calculated $\hat{\mu}$'s. In essence, they are found by solving the log-linear model for the parameters. The form of the hierarchical models makes this easy to do. The procedure is easiest to see in an example. Consider the model $[AB][BC]$ in three dimensions, which has log-linear form

$$\log \mu_{ijk} = \lambda + \lambda_{A(i)} + \lambda_{B(j)} + \lambda_{C(k)} + \lambda_{AB(ij)} + \lambda_{BC(jk)} \qquad (5.4)$$

The maximum-likelihood estimates $\hat{\mu}_{ijk}$ are chosen to be consistent with this model and so obey an analogous equation,

$$\log \hat{\mu}_{ijk} = \hat{\lambda} + \hat{\lambda}_{A(i)} + \hat{\lambda}_{B(j)} + \hat{\lambda}_{C(k)} + \hat{\lambda}_{AB(ij)} + \hat{\lambda}_{BC(jk)} \qquad (5.5)$$

There are abc such equations, one for each cell. This system of equations is solved for the $\hat{\lambda}$'s. However, these equations alone are not enough to separate one λ from another. For example, one can increase every $\hat{\lambda}_{A(i)}$ by a constant and decrease every $\hat{\lambda}_{B(j)}$ by the same constant without changing their sum. To complete the solution, further equations, known as *identifying restrictions*, are needed. The usual choice are the sum-to-zero constraints, which for this model are

$$\sum_i \hat{\lambda}_{A(i)} = \sum_j \hat{\lambda}_{B(j)} = \sum_k \hat{\lambda}_{C(k)} = \sum_i \hat{\lambda}_{AB(ij)} = \sum_j \hat{\lambda}_{AB(ij)}$$

$$= \sum_j \hat{\lambda}_{BC(jk)} = \sum_k \hat{\lambda}_{BC(jk)} = 0 \qquad (5.6)$$

(cf. Equations 2.22, 3.8, or 3.15). With these restrictions, $\hat{\lambda}$ reflects the overall frequency in the table, $\hat{\lambda}_A$ reflects the marginal effects of the A classification, and so forth.

The combination of Equations 5.5 and 5.6 is best solved by starting with the low-order terms and working up. Summing Equation 5.5 over the entire table gives

$$\sum_{\text{cells}} \log \hat{\mu}_{ijk} = \sum_{\text{cells}} \hat{\lambda} + \sum_{\text{cells}} \hat{\lambda}_{A(i)} + \sum_{\text{cells}} \hat{\lambda}_{B(j)} + \sum_{\text{cells}} \hat{\lambda}_{C(k)}$$

$$+ \sum_{\text{cells}} \hat{\lambda}_{AB(ij)} + \sum_{\text{cells}} \hat{\lambda}_{BC(jk)}$$

$$= abc\hat{\lambda} + bc \sum_i \hat{\lambda}_{A(i)} + ac \sum_j \hat{\lambda}_{B(j)} + ab \sum_k \hat{\lambda}_{C(k)}$$

$$+ c \sum_{i,j} \hat{\lambda}_{AB(ij)} + a \sum_{j,k} \hat{\lambda}_{BC(jk)}$$

The constraints of Equation 5.6 make all the remaining sums in this expression vanish, so

$$\sum_{\text{cells}} \log \hat{\mu}_{ijk} = abc\hat{\lambda}$$

Solving for $\hat{\lambda}$ gives the estimate

$$\hat{\lambda} = \frac{\sum\limits_{\text{cells}} \log \hat{\mu}_{ijk}}{abc} \tag{5.7}$$

Now consider $\hat{\lambda}_{A(i)}$. When Equation 5.5 is summed over the unused subscripts j and k, the remaining sums again are zero:

$$\sum_{j,k} \log \hat{\mu}_{ijk} = \sum_{j,k} \hat{\lambda} + \sum_{j,k} \hat{\lambda}_{A(i)} + \sum_{j,k} \hat{\lambda}_{B(j)} + \sum_{j,k} \hat{\lambda}_{C(k)}$$

$$+ \sum_{j,k} \hat{\lambda}_{AB(ij)} + \sum_{j,k} \hat{\lambda}_{BC(jk)}$$

$$= bc\hat{\lambda} + bc\hat{\lambda}_{A(i)} + c \sum_j \hat{\lambda}_{B(j)} + b \sum_k \hat{\lambda}_{C(k)}$$

$$+ c \sum_j \hat{\lambda}_{AB(ij)} + \sum_{j,k} \hat{\lambda}_{BC(jk)}$$

$$= bc\hat{\lambda} + bc\hat{\lambda}_{A(i)}$$

The unknown $\hat{\lambda}_{A(i)}$ is

$$\hat{\lambda}_{A(i)} = \frac{\sum\limits_{j,k} \log \hat{\mu}_{ijk}}{bc} - \hat{\lambda} \tag{5.8}$$

The other parameters are found in the same way: sum over the unused subscripts, apply the identifying restrictions, and subtract the hierarchically lower-order terms.

As a specific example, consider the data from the example at the start of Chapter 3 (Table 3.1). The model [AB][BC] fits these data satisfactorily, with the expected frequencies shown at the top of Table 5.2. First logarithms are taken,

TABLE 5.2
Calculating the Parameters of the Log-linear Model from the
Expected Frequencies

Expected Frequencies $\hat{\mu}_{ijk}$

| | a_1 | | | a_2 | | |
	c_1	c_2	c_3	c_1	c_2	c_3
b_1	6.346	7.212	1.442	15.654	17.789	3.558
b_2	24.601	49.201	137.197	1.399	2.798	7.803

Logarithms of Expected Frequencies log $\hat{\mu}_{ijk}$

| | a_1 | | | a_2 | | |
	c_1	c_2	c_3	c_1	c_2	c_3
b_1	1.848	1.976	0.366	2.751	2.879	1.269
b_2	3.203	3.896	4.921	0.336	1.029	2.054

Calculation of the Parameters

$$\hat{\lambda} = \frac{26.528}{12} = 2.21$$

$$\hat{\lambda}_{A(1)} = \frac{16.210}{6} - 2.211 = 0.49$$

$$\hat{\lambda}_{A(2)} = \frac{10.318}{6} - 2.211 = -0.49$$

Other Parameters

$\hat{\lambda}_B$:   −0.36 0.36

$\hat{\lambda}_C$:   −0.18 0.23 −0.06

	a_1	a_2
$\hat{\lambda}_{AB}$: b_1	−0.94	0.94
b_2	0.94	−0.94

	c_1	c_2	c_3
$\hat{\lambda}_{BC}$: b_1	0.63	0.34	−0.97
b_2	−0.63	−0.34	0.97

then Equations 5.7, 5.8, and so forth, are used to obtain the parameter estimates. Note that the sets of parameters sum to zero, as they should. If one needs to do so, one can reconstruct the $\hat{\mu}_{ijk}$ from the $\hat{\lambda}$'s, in the manner of Table 2.4.

This three-dimensional analysis generalizes without difficulty to other models and to more extensive tables. One starts by estimating the parameters with the fewest subscripts and works from them to parameters with many subscripts.

The interpretation of the parameters of a log-linear model is often a subtle matter, one that depends on the details of the particular investigation (examples will be given in Chapters 6 and 7). There are two approaches to the problem. One approach is to look at the patterns that are present in tables of parameters such as those in Table 5.2. For this examination, the $\hat{\lambda}$'s are the most useful. Cells with positive terms have an excess of frequency relative to a model in which that term is missing; negative values indicate a comparable deficiency. Thus, the parameter estimates $\hat{\lambda}_A$ in Table 5.2 show that there is a relative excess of frequency in a_1, and the pattern in $\hat{\lambda}_{AB}$ shows that the AB association takes the form of a surplus of observations on the a_1b_2-a_2b_1 diagonal.

The symmetry of the logarithmic parameters about zero makes the $\hat{\lambda}$'s useful when one looks for overall patterns, but it is harder to given an intuitive meaning to their logarithmic scale. When one wishes to discuss the effect on specific conditions or combinations of factors, it is often useful to convert the parameterization to a form that is closer to the raw frequencies. By exponentiating a model for log μ, one creates a model for μ and changes it from log-linear to multiplicative form. Denote the exponential e^λ, with whatever subscripts, by β. With this transformation, the model for $[AB][BC]$ in Equation 5.5 becomes

$$\hat{\mu}_{ijk} = e^{\hat{\lambda}} e^{\hat{\lambda}_{A(i)}} e^{\hat{\lambda}_{B(j)}} e^{\hat{\lambda}_{C(k)}} e^{\hat{\lambda}_{AB(ij)}} e^{\hat{\lambda}_{BC(jk)}}$$

$$= \hat{\beta} \hat{\beta}_{A(i)} \hat{\beta}_{B(j)} \hat{\beta}_{C(k)} \hat{\beta}_{AB(ij)} \hat{\beta}_{BC(jk)}$$

The parameters of the new model express the excesses or deficiencies in multiplicative form. For example, $\hat{\lambda}_{AB(12)} = \hat{\lambda}_{AB(21)} = 0.94$ in Table 5.2, so that $\hat{\beta}_{AB(12)} = \hat{\beta}_{AB(21)} = 2.56$. This value implies that the presence of the AB association in the model makes the 1,2 and 2,1 cells about $2\frac{1}{2}$ times larger than they would be were there no such association. The comparable effect for the cells on the other diagonal is $\hat{\beta}_{AB(11)} = \hat{\beta}_{AB(22)} = 0.39$. To compare the particular effect in one cell with that in another, the ratio of the corresponding $\hat{\beta}$'s is used. So the difference between the minor and major diagonals of the AB effect is $\hat{\beta}_{AB(12)}/\hat{\beta}_{AB(11)} \approx 6.5$. This is a substantial ratio, which is clearly evident in the expected frequencies of Table 5.2. Many packaged programs can print out the parameters of both log-linear and multiplicative versions of the models.

5.4. STANDARD ERRORS AND STANDARDIZED PARAMETER ESTIMATES

Like the estimates of any parameter, the $\hat{\lambda}$'s are random variables. In a replication of the study, they would almost certainly have different values. This fluctuation is described by the sampling distribution of the estimates. When the sample size is large, the sampling distributions of the $\hat{\lambda}$'s are roughly normal, centered about the true value, and so are fully characterized by their standard errors.

When the standard errors are large, the parameters are only weakly determined; when small, they are more exact. Knowledge of this variability helps to determine how much one can rely on the estimates.

For the rest of this section, let $\hat{\lambda}$ without subscript stand for any parameter of a log-linear model that is not fixed by the design (e.g., $\hat{\lambda}$, $\hat{\lambda}_{A(i)}$, $\hat{\lambda}_{AB(ij)}$, etc.), let $\hat{\lambda}$ be its estimate, and let $\sigma_{\hat{\lambda}}$ be the standard error of $\hat{\lambda}$. If $\sigma_{\hat{\lambda}}$ is known, then the *standardized parameter estimate* is

$$\zeta_{\hat{\lambda}} = \frac{\hat{\lambda}}{\sigma_{\hat{\lambda}}} \tag{5.9}$$

For a rough interpretation of their magnitudes, these ratios can be referred to tables of the standard normal distribution (as in Appendix A.4). When $\lambda = 0$, values of $\zeta_{\hat{\lambda}}$ greater than about 2 (strictly, 1.96) appear only about 5% of the time.† Likewise, confidence intervals for λ can be constructed. Denote the two-sided critical value from the standard normal distribution by z_α. Then with probability $1 - \alpha$,

$$\hat{\lambda} - z_\alpha \sigma_{\hat{\lambda}} \le \hat{\lambda} \le \hat{\lambda} + z_\alpha \sigma_{\hat{\lambda}} \tag{5.10}$$

Like the $\hat{\lambda}$'s, the standard errors $\sigma_{\hat{\lambda}}$ are population characteristic and must be estimated. When working with direct models and maximum-likelihood estimates, the procedure is conceptually straightforward. One inserts the formula used to estimate the $\hat{\mu}$'s into the formula for estimating the parameters (e.g., Equations 5.7 and 5.8 in the last section) and obtains a single equation that expresses the $\hat{\lambda}$'s as functions of the original data. These turn out to be linear functions of the log x_{ijk}. The sampling models provide estimates of the variances of log x_{ijk}. Since the variance of a linear combination of observations is easy to work out, estimates of $\sigma_{\hat{\lambda}}$ are obtained (Lee, 1977). Variance estimates for indirect models are more difficult to find and require other procedures. In either case, the equations for $\sigma_{\hat{\lambda}}$ are sufficiently complicated that a detailed presentation is inappropriate here.

Many computer programs compute standard errors of the parameter estimates along with the estimates themselves, allowing rough tests and confidence intervals to be constructed using Equations 5.9 and 5.10. However, these results should be interpreted cautiously, particularly in small samples, for several reasons. First, programs are usually based on pure Poisson or multinomial sampling models and do not incorporate any constraints of the design other than the total sample size. Second, the tests and variance estimates are correct only asymptoti-

---

†However, note that a difference of 2 between the values of ζ for two different parameters does not mean that the corresponding λ's differ. Both estimates are random variables and they are not necessarily independent. If the full covariance matrix of the estimates is found, the methods described in Chapter 12 can be used to test for differences in parameter value.

cally, when the sample size is large. Third, the estimates of $\sigma_{\hat{\lambda}}$ are subject to sampling fluctuation, and this inaccuracy should properly be accommodated in the tests. Consequently, the standard normal distribution understates the descriptive levels in Equation 5.9 and creates somewhat too narrow intervals in Equation 5.10. Fourth, the model contains many parameters, all of which are tested, creating multiple-inference problems. Even when the chance of an error in any one test is properly regulated, the chance of an error somewhere among the tests is much greater. Finally, the value 0 is only an arbitrary center imposed by the identification constraints and frequently has no particular meaning in terms of the design. The pattern of the parameter estimates over the full set of subscripts is likely to be more informative.

To continue the example in the last section, suppose that factor A is not fixed by the design, so that the $\hat{\lambda}_{A(i)}$ are random variables. The estimated large-sample standard error of $\hat{\lambda}_{A(I)}$ is 0.106. Hence, the standardized parameter value is

$$z_{A(1)} = \frac{0.491}{0.106} = 4.61$$

This value is large enough to imply that the true value of $\lambda_{A(1)}$ is nonzero. By Equation 5.10, an approximate 95% confidence interval for $\lambda_{A(1)}$ is

$$0.491 - (2)(0.106) \leq \lambda_{A(1)} \leq 0.491 + (2)(0.106)$$

$$0.28 \leq \lambda_{A(1)} \leq 0.70$$

Similar calculations can be made for the other parameters.

5.5. TESTS OF OVERALL FIT AND DEGREES OF FREEDOM

Once the expected frequencies have been found, a test of the model's fit is given by either the Pearson or the likelihood-ratio statistic,

$$X^2 = \sum_{\text{cells}} \frac{(x - \hat{\mu})^2}{\hat{\mu}} \quad \text{and} \quad G^2 = 2\sum_{\text{cells}} x \log \frac{x}{\hat{\mu}}$$

(with appropriate subscripts on x and $\hat{\mu}$). Application of these formulae is straightforward.

The greatest danger for a neophyte in using these tests is confusion about the interpretation of the resultant fit or failure of the model. It is possible to get turned around and think one has shown exactly what one has not. Some of the difficulty stems from the standard, but nonintuitive nature of hypothesis-testing procedures; another problem is that one may approach a problem by fitting models rather than testing effects. A model does not fail because of its content but because of what it is missing. When the model fits, it means that nothing important has been excluded, but this does not show that the model is right, for a simpler model could also fit. Likewise, the failure of a model does not indicate that its terms are unnecessary, but only shows that more are needed.

Return, for example, to the two questions asked of the college students in Section 5.1, and suppose that one wishes to know whether the answer to question A is associated with the answer to question B. Recall that the variables of sex (S) and year (Y) are present, so that AB associations may be mediated by these two variables. Suppose that one is interested in testing for the presence of an AB association and wishes to exclude any direct association of A and B with S and Y from influencing the test. The wrong way to do the analysis is to see whether a model that contains λ_{AB}, along with the other associations, fits the data. Say that the model [SYA][SYB][AB] is satisfactory. The improper argument says that the presence of λ_{AB} implies the existence of an AB association. This conclusion is a mistake. Showing that λ_{AB} can be included does not show that it is needed. The proper procedure is to fit a model that excludes λ_{AB} and to examine it as a null hypothesis. The appropriate hypothesis is of the conditional independence of A and B given S and Y, i.e., $A \perp\!\!\!\perp B|SY$. This hypothesis is tested by the fit of the model [SYA][SYB]. A failure of this model demands at least an AB association. A successful fit indicates that no interquestion association is present, at least to the extent that a null hypothesis can be established as correct.

The degrees of freedom for these tests are obtained by the procedure introduced in Section 3.11. Two equations are used:

$$\text{degrees of freedom} = \#(\text{data cells}) - \#(\text{free parameters}) \quad (5.11)$$

$$\#(\text{free parameters}) = \#(\text{parameters}) - \#(\text{constraints}) \quad (5.12)$$

For example, the three-way model [AB][BC] used in the last two sections is

$$\log \mu_{ijk} = \lambda + \lambda_{A(i)} + \lambda_{B(j)} + \lambda_{C(k)} + \lambda_{AB(ij)} + \lambda_{BC(jk)} \quad (5.13)$$

There are abc cells in the data table, giving the first term of Equation 5.11. Equation 5.12 can be evaluated, by counting the λs and the number of identifiability constraints. However, if there are no marginal zeros, it is easier to examine the parameters and their constraints at the same time. Originally, one degree of freedom is associated with each λ. However, the constraints act to reduce the number of free values for each dimension of the table to one fewer than its number of levels. Thus, there are $a - 1$ degrees of freedom associated with λ_A, $(a - 1)(b - 1)$ associated with λ_{AB}, and so on. In place of Equation 5.12 compute

$$\begin{aligned}
\#(\text{free parameters}) &= 1 + (a - 1) + (b - 1) + (c - 1) + (a - 1)(b - 1) \\
&\quad + (b - 1)(c - 1) \\
&= b(a + c - 1) \quad (5.14)
\end{aligned}$$

The order of these terms matches that of Equation 5.13. Then by Equation 5.11,

$$df = abc - b(a + c - 1) = (a - 1)b(c - 1)$$

5.6.   EMPTY CELLS

Under most circumstances a few empty cells in a table of data present no difficulties to the analysis. Usually an observed frequency of zero only means that the cell is rare, which may or may not be consistent with the model and is incorporated into the test statistics. However, where many cells are empty, adjustments in the degrees of freedom are sometimes necessary. The most obvious case occurs when a line of zeros in the data table causes a marginal cell used by the fitting algorithm to be zero. If so, the effects represented by these cells cannot be studied. If, by chance, no left-handed female machinists are sampled in a survey, then nothing can be said about the opinion of left-handed female machinists as a separate category. Their opinions may or may not be consistent with a model that is to be fitted, but without observations, one cannot tell. The analysis must be adapted to exclude the unobserved cells.

The effect of these empty cells is to reduce the degrees of freedom for a test. The empty marginal cell prevents estimation of one of the model's parameters and blocks the empty data cells from contributing to the test. Both the number of data cells and the number of free parameters in Equation 5.11 are smaller than they would otherwise be. Where the number of zeros is sufficient to empty a two-dimensional array in a marginal table, both the number of parameters eliminated and the number of restrictions rendered moot must be considered in evaluating Equation 5.12. A packaged computer program may or may not make these corrections automatically—one should check to be sure.

Two examples illustrate this point. First consider fitting the model $[AB][BC]$ to the data in Table 5.3. The cell b_2c_1 in the BC margin of this table is empty. This void means that when any model that includes λ_{BC} is fitted, the cells $a_1b_2c_1$ and $a_2b_2c_1$ have expected frequencies of zero. These zeros reduce the number of usable data cells from 24 to 22. With these cells gone, the parameter $\lambda_{BC(21)}$ is irrelevant, which produces a concomitant decrease in the number of parameters to be estimated. The model $[AB][BC]$ now has only 15 free parameters instead of 16. Thus, the number of degrees of freedom for a test of this model decreases from 8 to 7. Note that the other zeros in the data, which do not create marginal voids, do not affect the degrees of freedom.

The second example, in Table 5.4, shows the effects of a more extensive pattern of zeros. Suppose that the model $[AB][AC]$ is fitted to a $3 \times 5 \times 2$ table with the arrangement of filled and empty cells denoted by X and 0 at the top of the table. Without zeros, this model is tested with 12 degrees of freedom. However, there are so many zeros that voids appear in both the AB and the AC

TABLE 5.3
Fitting the Model [AB][BC] to a Table with Empty Cells

Pattern of Zeros in the Original Data

	c_1				c_2				c_3			
	b_1	b_2	b_3	b_4	b_1	b_2	b_3	b_4	b_1	b_2	b_3	b_4
a_1	5	0	7	8	9	8	3	12	6	3	5	11
a_2	10	0	6	7	8	1	0	9	0	2	8	11

Model

$$\log \mu_{ijk} = \lambda + \lambda_{A(i)} + \lambda_{B(j)} + \lambda_{C(k)} + \lambda_{AB(ij)} + \lambda_{BC(jk)}$$

Marginal Distributions

AB:

20	11	15	31
18	3	14	27

BC:

15	0	13	15
17	9	3	21
6	5	13	22

Degrees-of-Freedom Calculation Ignoring Zeros

   #(data cells) = abc = 24

   #(free parameters) = $b(a + c - 1)$ = 16

   Degrees of freedom = 24 − 16 = 8

Corrected Degrees-of-Freedom Calculation

   #(data cells) = 24 − 2 = 22

   #(free parameters) = 16 − 1 = 15

   Degrees of freedom = 22 − 15 = 7

---

marginal tables. One can neither estimate the parameters corresponding to these marginal zeros nor draw information from the empty cells that cause them. So 4 parameters are lost from the λ_{AB} and 1 is lost from the λ_{AC}. To see how many data cells are left, one determines the pattern of zeros that is forced on the expected frequencies by the empty marginal cells. Any cell that is connected by the model to a marginal void must have $\hat{\mu}_{ijk} = 0$. These cells are identified by marking them in a table the size of the original table of data, as shown toward the bottom of Table 5.4. There are 10 zeros and 20 nonzero cells here. Only the latter contribute to the test. With this correction, the test has 7 degrees of freedom.

The treatment of zeros depends on the model that is fit. For example, the model [A][B][C] fit to the pattern of zeros in Table 5.4 has no marginal zeros and

TABLE 5.4
Calculation of Degrees of Freedom for the Model [AB][AC]
When Many Cells are Empty

Pattern of Zeros in the Original Data

	c_1					c_2				
	b_1	b_2	b_3	b_4	b_5	b_1	b_2	b_3	b_4	b_5
a_1	X	X	X	0	X	X	0	0	X	X
a_2	0	0	0	0	0	X	0	0	0	X
a_3	0	X	X	X	X	0	0	0	X	X

Degrees-of-Freedom Calculation Ignoring Zeros

#(data cells) = 30

#(free parameters) = 1 + 2 + 4 + 1 + 8 + 2 = 18

Degrees of freedom = 30 − 18 = 12

Pattern of Zeros in the Fitted Marginal Tables

AB:

X	X	X	X	X
X	0	0	0	X
0	X	X	X	X

AC:

X	X
0	X
X	X

Pattern of Zeros Induced in $\hat{\mu}_{ijk}$ *Under Model [AB][AC]*

X	X	X	X	X	X	X	X	X	X
0	0	0	0	0	X	0	0	0	X
0	X	X	X	X	0	X	X	X	X

Corrected Degrees-of-Freedom Calculation

#(data cells) = 20

#(free parameters) = 1 + 2 + 4 + 1 + 4 + 1 = 13

Degrees of freedom = 20 − 13 = 7

requires no correction to the degree-of-freedom calculation, while the model [AC][BC] removes a pattern of cells different from those in Table 5.4. Thus, when there are many zeros, tests of different models may be based on different sets of observations. This variation creates interpretation problems, some solutions for which are discussed in later chapters. The problem is most serious for higher-order models.

Sometimes the problem of accidental zeros takes a more insidious form. In a multiway table, certain patterns of zeros can affect the tests without any vacant marginal cells. These problems usually involved the highest-order interactions. The simplest such case occurs when the model $[AB][AC][BC]$ is fitted to a 2 × 2 × 2 table with zeros at opposite corners:

$$
\begin{array}{cc|cc}
0 & X & X & X \\
X & X & X & 0
\end{array}
\qquad (5.15)
$$

Although there is nothing obviously untoward about this pattern, the two zeros render the parameters λ_{ABC} incapable of test. As an indication of the problem, the three-dimensional cross-product ratio evaluates to $\hat{\alpha} = 0/0$, which is undefined. In effect, the model $[AB][AC][BC]$ is saturated and when it is tested, a perfect fit is obtained ($X^2 = G^2 = 0$). This result is the tip-off that something is wrong. Fortunately, estimation problems of this sort affect only the most complicated models for a particular table. In the example, the parameters and expected frequencies of less saturated models can be estimated and tests of them against $[AB][AC][BC]$ are valid. The degrees of freedom for tests of the goodness of fit of these models—which in effect are against the model $[ABC]$—are too large by 1.

In tables with many categories, some of the high-order association parameters may not be estimable even though the test statistics for those associations are nonzero. The almost-saturated models still differ from the saturated model by several parameters that can be estimated, even if others cannot. For example, in a 3 × 3 × 4 table, the most complex unsaturated model, $[AB][AC][BC]$ differs from the saturated model by 36 parameters on 12 degrees of freedom. One may be able to pick out a pair of rows and a pair of columns for which the pattern of zeros looks like Display 5.15. That component of the test is undefined.

The fact that a few empty cells are underdetermined is not obvious from summary statistics. Fortunately, there are warning signs. When association terms are compromised, the iterative fitting algorithm tends to converge very slowly and to create near zero estimates of $\hat{\mu}$ for some cells in which $x = 0$. Usually a program passes its iteration limit without reaching convergence, leaving $\hat{\mu}$ nearly zero but not exactly so. The combination of slow convergence and near zero estimates suggests that there is a problem. However, even when one is warned, it is difficult to locate the trouble and properly correct the degrees of freedom. One can treat the offending cells as structural zeros, adjusting the degrees of freedom downward (as explained in Chapter 10), or one can break the test into single degree of freedom components to identify those that are undefined (see Sections 11.1 and 12.9). Both these analyses require a painful degree of meticulousness that is usually unnecessary. The degrees of freedom are off only for global tests of goodness of fit and for tests of the highest-order interactions. In the first case, the errors that are induced are conservative, in the sense that one overestimates the number of degrees of freedom that is used to pick the critical value of the χ^2

comparison distribution. Because the χ^2 distribution shifts to the right with increasing degrees of freedom, it becomes harder to reject the models. This built-in conservatism forces weaker inferences, which are appropriate in a thinly filled table. As for the high-order terms, the quantity of data is probably insufficient to test them anyway. Sparse tables do not support inferences to elaborate models. Fortunately, difference tests of lower-order parameters are unaffected by the zeros.

It is sometimes suggested that empty cells be avoided by artificially replacing them with a small positive number, often $\frac{1}{2}$. This increment helps estimation of the logit and the odds ratio (see Sections 7.2 and 9.1) and it makes the technical problem go away, but its effects on inference are less clear. When cells about which no information is available are replaced by constants, spurious effects and nonexistent degrees of freedom are fabricated. Where there are few zeros, the problem is negligible, but where there are many, it seems best to attempt a more careful analysis of the degrees of freedom and, most important, to recognize the limits of the data.

5.7.   DIFFERENCES BETWEEN MODELS

With more than three factors, simple tests of fit or failure, which compare a model to the saturated model, are insufficiently discriminating. A model is rejected in an overall goodness-of-fit test when it lacks any parameters that are necessary to a good explanation of the data. The failure of a simple model does not identify the important associations.

Better tests are provided by comparisons between specific models within the hierarchical lattice of models. These tests allow specific sets of parameters to be examined. Tests of this type were introduced in Section 3.8, and their statistical basis—the likelihood ratio test—was discussed in Section 4.5. The general procedure, as it applies to hierarchical log-linear models, is reviewed here. Let the symbol $\mathcal{M}$ represent any model for the data and let $\mathcal{M}^*$ represent another model that differs from it only by the deletion of some of its parameters. Most generally, any set of parameters can be removed; for the moment, consider removal of all the λ's of a particular type. Model $\mathcal{M}$ is connected to model $\mathcal{M}^*$ by an ascending line or series of lines in lattice diagrams such as Figures 3.4 or 5.1. For example, if $\mathcal{M}$ is the model $[ABC][CD]$, then $\mathcal{M}^*$ could either be the model $[ABC][D]$, which differs by λ_{CD}, or $[AB][AC][BC][CD]$, which differs by λ_{ABC}, or could be one of many other models that differ by several sets of parameters. Not every set of parameters can be removed at any time. If λ_{ABC} remains in the model, the hierarchy principle prevents the removal of λ_A, λ_{AB}, etc.

Let λ_d stand for the deleted parameters. Clearly, model $\mathcal{M}$, which contains both λ_d and all the parameters of $\mathcal{M}^*$, fits any set of data at least as well as $\mathcal{M}^*$ does, since by setting λ_d to 0 the models become the same. Thus, G^2 or X^2 for

$\mathcal{M}^*$ is larger than the corresponding statistic for $\mathcal{M}$. The difference between them gives an indication of how valuable λ_d is to the model: if X^2 or G^2 for $\mathcal{M}^*$ is only slightly larger than the corresponding statistic for $\mathcal{M}$, then there is little point to putting λ_d in the model for that set of data. If the difference is large, λ_d provides significant help.

As Section 4.5 described, the statistical necessity of λ_d is tested by the difference between the overall test statistics for Models $\mathcal{M}$ and $\mathcal{M}^*$. If G^2 is used, the difference ΔG^2 is a likelihood-ratio test; if X^2 is used, ΔX^2 is an approximation to this test. For large samples, both ΔG^2 and ΔX^2 have roughly a χ^2 distribution. The number of degrees of freedom for either test equals the number of free parameters associated with the set λ_d. Normally, this is the difference in the degrees of freedom for tests of $\mathcal{M}$ and $\mathcal{M}^*$. If there are enough zeros in the data to empty one or more cells of the marginal tables on which the λ_d depend, a problem arises. Because of the zeros, the cells contributing to G^2 for $\mathcal{M}$, which contains λ_d, are not the same as those contributing to G^2 for $\mathcal{M}^*$, which does not. If so, the hypothesis being tested is more complicated than $\lambda_d = 0$, since it entails the introduction of these cells. An adjustment that corrects the tests is described in Section 10.1.

Difference tests are most useful when a particular substantive question is tied to a set of parameters within a model. For example, suppose that data have been collected on the opinion of a group of voters on a forthcoming referendum. Ancillary information has also been obtained, including age, political party, and geographical location. Call these factors R, A, P, and G, respectively, with, say, 3, 4, 3, and 5 levels. One might ask whether there are geographical differences in preference. Clearly, the basic GR association is embodied in the parameters λ_{GR}. One place to test for these parameters is in the marginal GR table. However, effects in this table may be secondary to geographical differences in the other factors, such as in age or party registration. One may wish to look for geographical effects over and above these associations. Thus, these associations should be part of the context in which λ_{GR} is tested. The most general test is made with $\mathcal{M} = [APG][APR][GR]$ and $\mathcal{M}^* = [APG][APR]$. If one had evidence for the lack of an age by party interaction with R, the pair $\mathcal{M} = [APG][AR][PR][GR]$ and $\mathcal{M}^* = [APG][AR][PR]$ could be used instead. For either pair, the difference is distributed on 8 degrees of freedom (assuming no problems with zeros), since there are this many free parameters in the 5×3 table of λ_{GR}.

One advantage of the difference test is apparent when one compares it with another test of GR association. Rejection of the conditional-independence hypothesis $G \perp\!\!\!\perp R|AP$ (i.e., the model $[APG][APR]$) indicates a GR association. However, this is a test of the parameters λ_{GR}, λ_{AGR}, λ_{PGR}, and λ_{APGR} and is conducted on 96 degrees of freedom. It is likely that the greater part of the association of G to R (if any) appears in the first order GR association and much less in the complicated terms such as λ_{AGPR}. Combining these higher-order terms in the same test with λ_{GR} mixes the effects, thereby diluting the test of GR

association and weakening its power. The difference test is more precise and is the better choice. As noted below, it also makes less severe demands on sample size.

Although these difference tests examine the hypothesis $\lambda_d = 0$, their outcome does not depend solely on the association that λ_d represents. The balance of the models—the base $\mathcal{M}^*$ to which λ_d is added to give $\mathcal{M}$—also has an effect. Accordingly, one cannot speak of a test of a set of parameters in isolation from how that test is made. The graduate admission example from Section 3.12 illustrates this point. When the parameters λ_{SA} are tested by comparing the models $\mathcal{M}^* = [DS][DA]$ and $\mathcal{M} = [DS][DA][SA]$, the result is $\Delta G^2(1) = 0.1670 - 0.0003 = 0.17$, implying that the parameters are unnecessary. Tests based on $\mathcal{M}^* = [D][S][A]$, $\mathcal{M}^* = [DS][A]$, or $\mathcal{M}^* = [S][DA]$, however, all give $\Delta G^2(1) \approx 4.7$, which is significant. Clearly, the context is important. Of course, one would not normally run all these tests, but would use extrastatistical information to select one of them, as discussed in Section 3.12.

The inconsistent results in the last example can be attributed to the failure of the simpler version of the model $\mathcal{M}$ to fit accurately. This failure casts doubt on tests of λ_{SA} in the corresponding contexts. However, poor fit is not the entire problem. Particularly in many-way tables, one finds cases where a particular association is necessary with one choice of $\mathcal{M}^*$ and not with another, while $\mathcal{M}$ cannot be rejected in either case. For example, one may find that both $[AB][AC]$ and $[AB][BC]$ fit a three-way table satisfactorily, that no term significantly improves the fit of either model, and that no term can be removed without appreciable loss. Without outside information, the status of λ_{AC} and λ_{BC} is unclear. The appropriate way to deal with such a situation is to try to understand what the full model means and not to evaluate its parts in isolation. The essential point was made as far back as Section 1.2: the design must dictate the analysis. The problems arise when one tries to avoid having to think about the multidimensional relationships present in the data or attempts a purely data-driven analysis.

Difficulties in the attribution of effects are not unique to frequency models, but occur in statistics whenever explanatory variables are associated (i.e., are *nonorthogonal*). For example, the effectiveness of a variable in a multiple regression equation can either increase or decrease as other variables are introduced into the equation or are removed. Dummy variables used in the analysis of variance or covariance show the same effects, leading to interpretation ambiguities when the sample sizes are unequal (e.g., Appelbaum & Cramer, 1974; Cramer & Appelbaum, 1980; Overall & Spiegel, 1969; etc.). The solution is the same as it is for frequency tables: to move from the interpretation of individual effects to an appreciation of the full pattern of relationships, from hypothesis testing toward the fitting of models and an appreciation of the context in which the tests are made. The equal-sample analysis of variance is the principal exception to the need to interpret effects in context. These balanced designs displace the labor of interpretation onto the subject-assignment process. The equal sample sizes create artificial populations in which the tests of individual associations—the analysis of variance effects—are unrelated to their context. The result is a particularly tidy analysis. With other designs, effects cannot be made orthogonal, and the overlapping explanatory power of the variables must be considered.

A final point concerns sample size. The χ^2 reference distribution is a large-sample approximation to the true sampling distribution of ΔX^2 and ΔG^2, just as it is for the goodness-of-fit statistics X^2 and G^2. When the sample size is adequate to support the overall tests, it also supports difference tests. However, a second set of asymptotic theorems applies to the difference tests (Haberman, 1977; Fienberg, 1979). These show that the distribution of the difference statistics approaches a χ^2 distribution as the sample size gets large, even when the table simultaneously expands so that the expected cell sizes remain finite. The critical requirement is that the sample size per degree of freedom in the difference test becomes large. Although specific rules for the application of this principle are lacking, it is clear that tests based on ΔX^2 or ΔG^2 may be referred to a χ^2 distribution in situations where the sample is inadequate to support goodness-of-fit tests of the component models $\mathcal{M}$ and $\mathcal{M}^*$, as long as the sample is an appreciable multiple of the difference in degrees of freedom. To return to the opinion poll example, there are 180 cells in the $4 \times 3 \times 5 \times 3$ table of age, party, geographical region, and preference (factors A, P, G, and R). A substantial sample is required to test the goodness of fit for hypotheses such as $G \perp\!\!\!\perp R|AP$—following the principle of requiring an average of 4 observations per cell mentioned in Section 2.5, the study needs 720 observations. The difference test of the hypothesis that $\lambda_{GR} = 0$ is based on 8 degrees of freedom and certainly requires a smaller sample—a couple of hundred should easily suffice. If one is not interested in the higher-order associations, these tests are a much more efficient way to investigate the lower-order relationships, even when one wishes to condition the tests on other factors in the design.

5.8. RELATIVE CHANGES IN FIT

Although the descriptive level of the test statistics, hence their significance or lack of it, is a valuable thing to examine, one must not depend too much on statistical significance alone. For one thing, fitting a model is useful even when violations of the assumptions associated with the χ^2 approximation—small sample size, empty cells, the presence of potential dependencies between observations—make it risky to trust the probability values. For another, the presence of a significant effect does not tell whether that effect is large enough to be interesting. To get this information, one needs to know something about the relative sizes of the effects.

The measures of relative effect size that are easiest to calculate are based on the X^2 and G^2 statistics. Instead of interpreting their values directly, one relates their size to their total change through the hierarchical lattice of models. This lattice begins with the simplest model that is consistent with the design and ends with the saturated model (e.g., Figure 5.1). The goodness-of-fit statistics for any other model fall between those of these extreme models. So, to get an idea of where each model lies between these endpoints, one writes their test statistics as a percentage of the total change. The increments between models are particularly helpful. Large relative changes indicate big increments in fit and that the difference between the models may be of practical significance. Small changes usually mean trivial differences. These interpretations are true regardless of whether the effects in question are statistically significant. The additive nature of the G^2 statistic over a series of models makes it particularly satisfactory for this purpose.

Consider the example of Section 5.1 involving the two questions (A and B) asked of college students, who were also classified by sex and year (S and Y), and assume the hypothetical data in Table 5.5. The simplest acceptable model for these data is [SY][A][B], the most complicated is [$SYAB$], and the range of intermediate models in Figure 5.1 lies between them. From this hierarchy can be selected a series of models, each adding terms to the previous model. One such series of 6 models, along with brief interpretations and statistics measuring their fit is given in Table 5.6. This series starts with the independence model [SY][A][B] and ends with [$SYAB$]. The leftmost columns of numbers in the table gives G^2 and its degrees of freedom. The difference in G^2 between the extreme models is 271.70. The next column assigns to each model the percentage of this change that is still unmade (i.e., based on the proportion $1 - G^2/271.70$). The final three columns give ΔG^2, degrees of freedom, and percentage change for the difference between successive models. These proportions clearly show that the bulk of the dependence effects in Table 5.5 is embodied in the association of the two responses. Over half the change comes with the introduction of λ_{AB}. The association between the responses and the respondent's sex is also quite

TABLE 5.5
Hypothetical Data for Eight Groups of Students Asked Two Questions

		a_1		a_2	
		b_1	b_2	b_1	b_2
s_1	y_1	40	11	3	6
	y_2	41	4	5	10
	y_3	30	9	8	13
	y_4	23	7	11	19
s_2	y_1	20	4	9	27
	y_2	17	2	9	32
	y_3	10	5	10	35
	y_4	10	2	9	39

TABLE 5.6
Various Models Fitted to the Data in Table 5.5

Model	Interpretation	Overall fit			Differences		
		G^2	df	%	ΔG^2	df	%
[SY][A][B]	Independence	271.70	22	0.0			
[SY][AB]	Associated responses	116.21	21	57.2	155.49	1	57.2
[SY][YA][YB][AB]	Association to year	94.13	15	65.4	22.08	6	8.1
[SY][SA][SB][YA][YB][AB]	Association to year and sex	9.73	13	96.4	84.40	2	31.1
[SY][SAB][YAB]	Simple interactions	3.17	9	98.8	6.56	4	2.4
[SYAB]	Higher-order interactions	0.00	0	100.0	3.17	9	1.2

important, accounting for 31% of the change, even in the context of year and interquestion association. The higher-order interactions are unimportant.

This relative change measure has been proposed by several authors (e.g., Bentler & Bonnet, 1983; Goodman, 1972b; Haberman, 1978). The temptation to draw a parallel to regression statistics is strong—for example, Goodman and Haberman refer to the ratio as R^2. However, one cannot trust intuitions developed from multiple-regression theory here. Test statistics are not variances, so their relative size lacks the explained-variance interpretation that gives R^2 its meaning in regression statistics (although, as will be seen in Section 9.4, G^2 behaves like the dispersion measure H defined below). If one wishes to have a statistic that expresses an idea comparable to explained variance, one must find more appropriate measures.

The difficulty in applying the conventional definition of variance to categorical data is that the categories lack a center or mean about which to measure variation. However, there are several variance-like measures of dispersion that indicate the extent to which observations are distributed over a range of categories rather than being concentrated in any one of them (Efron, 1978; Haberman, 1982; Magidson, 1981). Consider a one-dimensional probability distribution π_1, $\pi_2, \ldots, \pi_b$. One dispersion measure, known as the *concentration*†, is defined as

$$C(\boldsymbol{\pi}) = 1 - \sum_j \pi_j^2 \tag{5.16}$$

The concentration is zero when all the probability falls in one category and is maximal when the categories are equally likely. A second measure is known variously as the *entropy*, the *information*, or the *uncertainty*, is

$$H(\boldsymbol{\pi}) = - \sum_j \pi_j \log_2 \pi_j \tag{5.17}$$

Note that the base of the logarithm here is 2.‡ The properties of the entropy and concentration measures are similar, so to avoid duplication the discussion in this

---

†The concentration measure has been independently invented several times in a diverse collection of fields. It is sometimes identified by the names of Gini and of Simpson, but it seems better to avoid eponyms here and use a (somewhat) descriptive name. For a generalized diversity index that subsumes both the concentration and the entropy, see Patil & Taillie (1982).

‡Recall that to change a logarithm from base a to base b, one divides by the logarithm of the new base, $\log_b x = (\log_a x)/(\log_a b)$, so that

$$H(\boldsymbol{\pi}) = - 1.4427 \sum_j \pi_j \log_e \pi_j = - 3.3219 \sum_j \pi_j \log_{10} \pi_j$$

When calculating the ratio $\hat{\eta}_H$ below, any base can be used, since the same factor appears in both numerator and denominator.

section uses $C(\boldsymbol{\pi})$ only. The interpretation of Equation 5.17 is discussed in Section 9.4.

These definitions extend to measures of dispersion for a multiway table. Under multinomial or product-multinomial sampling models or under Poisson models conditioned on total frequency, the theoretical probabilities take the form of one probability distribution for each population sampled. Thus, for the student example, there are 8 populations, indexed by combinations of S and Y (corresponding to the rows of Table 5.5), each with 4 probabilities, indexed by combinations of A and B (the columns). To simplify the notation, let the single index i indicate the population and let j index the probabilities within the populations, as if a two-way table were in use. Suppose that a model has been fitted to these data. Denote the conditional probability of category j for population i under that model by $\hat{\pi}_{j|i}$ and this distribution collectively by $\hat{\boldsymbol{\pi}}_i$. These probability estimates are obtained from the expected frequencies as $\hat{\mu}_{ij}/x_{i+}$, dividing by the observed marginal frequency x_{i+} because the fitting algorithm ensures that this sum is the same as the corresponding sum of the expected frequencies. Then the concentration index for population i associated with the model is given by Equation 5.16 as

$$C(\hat{\boldsymbol{\pi}}_i) = 1 - \sum_j \pi_{j|i}^2$$

To obtain a measure of concentration for the entire collection of data, the $C(\hat{\boldsymbol{\pi}}_i)$ are averaged over the populations. Since the number of observations of each population may be different, the $C(\hat{\boldsymbol{\pi}}_i)$ are weighted in this average by proportion of the sample that comes from that population, or x_{i+}/x_{++}. So, the composite measure of dispersion for the model is

$$C(\hat{\boldsymbol{\pi}}) = \sum_i \frac{x_{i+}}{x_{++}} C(\hat{\boldsymbol{\pi}}_i) \tag{5.18}$$

A comparable measure, $H(\hat{\boldsymbol{\pi}})$ uses the entropy. When the model does not fit well and poorly articulates the differences among the populations, these quantities are large. They are smaller when the model fits well, although they do not equal zero unless the model perfectly categorizes each population into one and only one cell. In this sense, $C(\hat{\boldsymbol{\pi}})$ and $H(\hat{\boldsymbol{\pi}})$ are analogous to measures of unexplained variance in a regression or analysis-of-variance design.

A brief example illustrates these calculations. The top panel of Table 5.7 shows the expected frequencies for the model $[AB][BC]$ fit to the three-way data from Table 3.1, as calculated in Display 3.17 of Section 3.4. Suppose that factors A and B define fixed populations (the rows). The conditional probabilities under this model are shown in the second panel. The lack of an AC term in the model means that these probabilities do not vary with factor A. For each row the concentration, calculated by Equation 5.18, appears in the first column to the right of the table. The last column gives the sample-size weights. Averaging the

TABLE 5.7

Calculation of the Concentration for the Model $[AB][BC]$

Fitted to the Data from Table 3.1

Expected Frequencies $\hat{\mu}_{ij}$ under $[AB][BC]$

		c_1	c_2	c_3	x_{i+}
a_1	b_1	6.35	7.21	1.44	15
	b_2	24.60	49.20	137.20	211
a_2	b_1	15.65	17.79	3.56	37
	b_2	1.40	2.80	7.80	12
					275

Conditional Probabilities $\hat{\pi}_{j|i}$ and the Concentration

		c_1	c_2	c_3	$C(\hat{\pi}_i)$	$\dfrac{x_{i+}}{x_{++}}$
a_1	b_1	0.423	0.481	0.096	0.581	0.054
	b_2	0.117	0.233	0.650	0.509	0.767
a_2	b_1	0.423	0.481	0.096	0.581	0.134
	b_2	0.177	0.233	0.650	0.509	0.044

$$C(\hat{\pi}) = \sum_i \frac{x_{i+}}{x_{++}} C(\hat{\pi}_i) = 0.523$$

four concentrations according these weights gives the overall concentration for this model: $C(\hat{\pi}) = 0.523$.

For the four-way student data, Table 5.8 shows the concentration and entropy measures calculated for the same models that were analyzed in Table 5.6. The minimal model is $[SY][A][B]$, which has the most diverse predictions and the largest dispersion scores. As one moves through the sequence of models in Table 5.6, the dispersion gets smaller as the models articulate the patterns in the data better. The minimum value is realized with the saturated model. A similar decrease in $H(\hat{\pi})$ with increasing complexity of the model holds for any other hierarchical sequence, and $C(\hat{\pi})$ normally follows this pattern. Models that make similar predictions have almost the same dispersion, and those that make substantially different predictions have larger differences.†

These residual-dispersion statistics are not yet measures of the proportional

---

†Because the concentration and entropy measures behave like sums of squares or variances for continuous variables, they can be partitioned and used to construct analogs to the analysis of variance (Light & Margolin, 1971; Margolin & Light, 1974).

TABLE 5.8
Analysis of Concentration and of Entropy for the Data in Table 5.5

Model	Concentration			Entropy		
	$C(\hat{\pi})$	$\eta_C,\%$	$\Delta\nu_C,\%$	$H(\hat{\pi})$	$\eta_C,\%$	$\Delta\nu_C,\%$
$[SY][A][B]$	0.749	0.0	10.1	1.997	0.0	11.7
$[SY][AB]$	0.673	10.1	2.0	1.763	11.7	1.7
$[SY][YA][YB][AB]$	0.658	12.1	7.9	1.730	13.4	6.3
$[SY][YA][YB][SA][SB][AB]$	0.599	20.0	0.2	1.603	19.7	0.5
$[SY][YAB][SAB]$	0.597	20.2	0.2	1.593	20.2	0.2
$[SYAB]$	0.596	20.4		1.589	20.4	

reduction in the variability that is accounted for by a model. To get such a ratio, one first selects the minimum model that is consistent with the design. For the example, this is the model $[SY][A][B]$. Let $\hat{\pi}_0$ be the predictions of this model. The associated concentration $C(\hat{\pi}_0)$ is the amount of dispersion that potentially could be interpreted by a more elaborate model. For any other model $\mathcal{M}$ with expected probabilities $\hat{\pi}_{\mathcal{M}}$, define the relative reduction in dispersion for $\mathcal{M}$ as

$$\hat{\eta}_C(\mathcal{M}) = \frac{C(\hat{\pi}_0) - C(\hat{\pi}_{\mathcal{M}})}{C(\hat{\pi}_0)} \tag{5.19}$$

The relative-reduction character of this statistic makes it analogous to such measures as the correlation ratio η^2 and proportion of variance ω^2 statistics in the analysis of variance or to R^2 in multiple regression. A comparable definition based on $H(\hat{\pi})$ gives a statistic $\hat{\eta}_H$. These statistics are shown in Table 5.8, both the relative reduction of dispersion accounted for by each model and the difference between models. They lead to essentially the same conclusions as did the relative G^2 statistics in Table 5.6: most of the effect is in the AB association and in the link to sex.

Unlike the G^2 statistic, $C(\hat{\pi})$ and $H(\hat{\pi})$ for the saturated model are nonzero. This fact indicates that a considerable amount of residual variation is present in the data that is not explained by the population classification. Indeed, the models serve to reduce the dispersion by only about 20%. While the smallness of this figure may seem disconcerting at first, it is appropriate for data like these. One hardly expects to account for most of the diversity of opinion by such general factors as sex or year in school. Presumably, the introduction of additional predictive information might increase this figure. Inclusion of the residual dispersion in $\hat{\eta}_C$ or $\hat{\eta}_H$ makes these statistics more realistic measures of the relative effects than are their test-statistic-based counterparts. For simply sorting out large and small effects, however, any of the measures can be used.

5.9. STANDARDIZED CELL DEVIATES

When constructing a model for a set of data, one is pulled by two contradictory goals: to make the model simple and to make it complete. A sufficiently complex model will fit adequately; one can then look at estimates of its parameters to try to understand what is happening. However, when a model is too complicated, its very inclusiveness defies interpretation. Then it may be more useful to fit a simple model, even though it is statistically rejected, and to look at the way that the data deviate from it. This approach is particularly valuable when only a few cells violate the simple model. For example, when one cell in a multiway table is out of line, the highest order interaction may be needed to fit the data, although the structure is otherwise simple.

There are several ways to examine how a simple model fails to fit the data. The most direct way, described in this section, is to look at the deviation between the fitted model and the data. More elaborate approaches—removing certain cells from the table or constructing models that describe the deviation—are covered in Chapters 10 and 11. The use of deviations is particularly valuable when one is exploring the data without any strong preconceptions of what one will find or what hypotheses to test.

The simplest way to characterize a model's failure to fit a set of data is by the difference between the observed frequencies, x, and expected frequencies, $\hat{\mu}$ (omitting the subscripts for simplicity and generality). However, $x - \hat{\mu}$ is not itself a useful measure, for its size depends on the overall frequency. A discrepancy of a particular size is a more serious violation of a model when the expected frequency is small than when it is large. For example, the difference of 15 between $\hat{\mu} = 5$ and $x = 20$ is serious, while the same difference between $\hat{\mu} = 205$ and $x = 220$ is less substantial.

A good way to avoid this difficulty is to express the difference relative to its statistical fluctuation by forming a *standardized deviate*. The standardization gives this measure a distribution that is roughly unrelated to the size of $\hat{\mu}$. The most obvious standarized deviates are the *components of the Pearson chi-square*,

$$z_p = \frac{x - \hat{\mu}}{\sqrt{\hat{\mu}}} \qquad (5.20)$$

These deviates are so named because the sum of z_p^2 over the cells of a table is X^2.

A two-way example is shown in Table 5.9. First, a model of independence is fitted. This model is rejected with $G^2(6) = 18.20$. The standardized residual in the first cell is

$$z_{11} = \frac{12 - 16.93}{\sqrt{16.93}} = -1.20$$

Similar calculations give standardized deviates for the other cells. In the table of standardized deviates, cell 1,2 has a large positive residual, while other residuals

TABLE 5.9
Calculation of Standardized Deviates in a 3 × 4 Table

Observed Frequencies

12	18	3	10
18	3	7	10
20	6	9	11

Expected Frequencies

16.93	9.14	6.43	10.50
14.96	8.08	5.69	9.28
18.11	9.78	6.88	11.23

Standardized Deviates $z_P = \dfrac{x - \hat{\mu}}{\sqrt{\hat{\mu}}}$

-1.20	2.93	-1.35	-0.15
0.79	-1.79	0.55	0.24
0.44	-1.21	0.81	-0.06

in that row and column are negative. This pattern suggests the presence of excess frequency in that cell. If so, then the negative entries in the other cells may be an artifact of the excess, since the equality of observed and expected marginal sums in the rows and columns displaces $\hat{\mu}$ for these cells downward—remember that the row and column sums are constrained to equal the observed totals. The question of whether this excess suffices to explain the dependence is answered more exactly in Section 10.2.

A motivation for Equation 5.20 comes from the Poisson sampling model (Equation 4.13). Under this model, each cell is an independently generated Poisson variate with both mean and variance equal to the parameter μ. Subtracting this mean from x and dividing by the standard deviation creates the standardized variable

$$\zeta = \frac{x - E(X)}{\sigma_X} = \frac{x - \mu}{\sqrt{\mu}} \tag{5.21}$$

Replacing μ by its estimate gives Equation 5.20.

There are other ways to standardize the deviations besides Equations 5.20 and 5.21. Freeman and Tukey (1950) pointed out that for observations from a Poisson distribution, the quantity $\sqrt{x} + \sqrt{x + 1}$ has a mean nearly equal to

$\sqrt{4\mu + 1}$ and has unit variance. From this result, a second type of standardized deviate, known as the *Freeman-Tukey deviate†*, is formed:

$$z_{FT} = \sqrt{x} + \sqrt{x + 1} - \sqrt{4\hat{\mu} + 1} \qquad (5.22)$$

The properties of z_{FT} are similar to those of the components of the Pearson statistic. The components of the likelhood-ratio statistic G^2 can also be used as a deviation measure,

$$z_{LR} = 2x \log \frac{x}{\hat{\mu}} \qquad (5.23)$$

This measure lacks the approximate unit variance of z_P and z_{FT}. Neither z_{FT} nor z_{LR} provide much practical benefit over the components of X^2.

When μ is large, the Poisson distribution is approximately normal, and the population standardized residuals (such as ζ in Equation 5.21) have roughly a standard normal distribution. This suggests that criteria appropriate to this distribution can be used to identify cells that are significantly discrepant—at the 5% level one would reject the fit if the absolute value of z_P exceeded 1.96. Such tests are not exact. First, the variance of z_P is less than 1 when the cells are not independent observations, as they are, say, if a model of homogeneous rows or columns holds (Haberman, 1973). Second, when μ is replaced by $\hat{\mu}$, as in Equation 5.20, the distribution of z_P is altered, analogously to the change to a t distribution for normal scores when the standard deviation is estimated. Third, since the table contains many cells, one is running many tests, with consequent changes in the family-wise error rate. Corrections are available for these problems: one can adjust the variances to accommodate the first two problems and apply Bonferroni-type corrections to deal with the multiple tests. Usually, these corrections are unnecessary. When exploring data, there is no need to be pedantic about significance levels. Classification of residuals as discrepant or not is most useful when the model fails, but does so in a relatively small number of cells. To spot these, a criterion that is larger than about $2\frac{1}{2}$ and that marks about 10% of the cells as exceptional usually suffices.

The detection of deviates can complement the estimation of parameters in more elaborate models, as the example in Table 5.10 shows. If the model [AB][C] is fitted to those data, it fails badly with $G^2(10) = 234.26$. The pattern of standardized deviations in the two BC tables formed by fixing the level of A are similar—for example, the signs of the deviations agree for 7 of the 9 pairs. This rough regularity suggests a consistency of behavior that might be captured

---

†The sum of the squared Freeman-Tukey deviates has an asymptotic χ^2 distribution with the same number of degrees of freedom as X^2 or G^2. Thus, it may be used as a test statistic. However, there is no reason to prefer it to other statistics; indeed, its small-sample properties may be slightly worse than those of X^2 (Larntz, 1978).

TABLE 5.10
Standardized Residuals and Parameter Estimates

Observed Frequencies

	a_1			a_2		
	c_1	c_2	c_3	c_1	c_2	c_3
b_1	54	90	27	37	148	36
b_2	221	601	92	18	67	10
b_3	110	20	33	22	4	7

Standardized Deviates z_p for Model [AB][C]

	a_1			a_2		
	c_1	c_2	c_3	c_1	c_2	c_3
b_1	0.6	−1.0	1.1	−3.4	1.7	1.4
b_2	−2.7	3.0	−2.3	−1.8	1.6	−0.6
b_3	9.1	−7.7	2.6	4.1	−3.5	1.4

Estimates of λ_{BC} in Model [AB][BC]

	c_1	c_2	c_3
b_1	−0.43	0.43	0.00
b_2	−0.30	0.64	−0.34
b_3	0.73	−1.07	0.34

by adding λ_{BC} to the model. In fact, the model [AB][BC] is almost satisfactory, with $G^2(6) = 13.75$, and certainly fits a great deal better than [AB][C]. To a considerable extent, estimates of λ_{BC} from this model mirror the pattern of the deviates.

5.10. POWER CALCULATIONS

If an estimate of power or a sample-size calculation is needed, the principles of Section 2.9 generalize to multiway tables directly. First, one identifies two models: a general model, $\mathcal{M}$, that fits perfectly in the population and a restriction of that model, $\mathcal{M}^*$, to which the power calculations apply. Where overall fit is concerned (as in Section 2.9), the saturated model plays the role of $\mathcal{M}$. Next, one establishes cell probabilities for the general model. For notational simplicity, ignore the subscript designating the cell, and denote the probabilities by π. For a given sample size, N, the expected frequencies under $\mathcal{M}$ are $\mu = N\pi$. Next the probabilities π^* under the restricted model are derived and the noncentrality parameter of the χ^2 distribution is determined, using the same equations that applied above (Equation 2.29 and 2.30). For the Pearson statistic X^2,

$$\omega = N \sum_{\text{cells}} \frac{(\pi - \pi^*)^2}{\pi^*} = \sum_{\text{cells}} \frac{(\mu - \mu^*)^2}{\mu^*} \qquad (5.24)$$

and for the likelihood-ratio statistic G^2,

$$\omega = 2N \sum_{\text{cells}} \pi \log \frac{\pi}{\pi^*} = 2 \sum_{\text{cells}} \mu \log \frac{\mu}{\mu^*} \qquad (5.25)$$

These values can be referred to Figure A3, which relates $\sqrt{\omega}$ to the power $1 - \beta$.

The main difficulty is the specification of π and π^*. Probabilities under $\mathcal{M}$ may be drawn from the theory being tested or from results of a previous experiment. They should represent an alternative to $\mathcal{M}^*$ of interesting magnitude. The probabilities under $\mathcal{M}^*$ are derived from those under $\mathcal{M}$ by forcing them to fit $\mathcal{M}^*$. The same model-fitting algorithms used to fit ordinary data are used here, starting with either π or μ. In this way standard programs can do most of the numerical work, including calculation of Equations 5.24 and 5.25.

In particular, suppose that one were interested in replicating the college student questionnaire of Section 5.8 and wanted to have a 90% power of detecting a conditional SA association when no associations higher than second order are present. This test compares the models $\mathcal{M} = [SY][YA][YB][SA][SB][AB]$ and $\mathcal{M}^* = [SY][YA][YB][SB][AB]$. The best estimate of the cell probabilities for $\mathcal{M}$ are obtained from the previous study by fitting $\mathcal{M}$ to those data (given in Table 5.5). The fitted frequencies are shown in Table 5.11, as is the rest of the calculation. The conditional probabilities $P(a_k b_l | y_i s_j)$ are estimated by the response proportions $\hat{\mu}_{ijkl}/x_{ij++}$. If the new experiment is to have equal samples in the eight groups,

$$\pi_{ijkl} = \hat{P}(a_k b_l y_i s_j) = \frac{\hat{\mu}_{ijkl}}{8 x_{ij++}}$$

With minor rounding adjustments to make each subpopulation sum to 0.125, this equation gives the values of π_{ijkl} shown in the table. To get π^*, fit Model $\mathcal{M}^*$ to these probabilities, using whatever program one prefers. If the fitting program does not accept nonintegral values as data, each proportion can be multiplied by a constant, say 1000, and then the fitted expected values scaled back down to proportions. The program that fits $\mathcal{M}^*$ reports a comparison of π to π^* with "G^2" $= 0.095$, a value that cannot be referred to a χ^2 distribution but that gives the summation term in the noncentrality parameter (Equation 5.25). Hence $\omega = 0.095N$. The difference between $\mathcal{M}$ and $\mathcal{M}^*$ is tested on 2 degrees of freedom. With these degrees of freedom, Figure A3 indicates that $\omega = 3.55^2 = 12.6$ is

TABLE 5.11
Sample-size Calculations for a Difference Test in a Four-way Table

Expected Frequencies for the Model [SY][YA][YB][SA][SB][AB]

| | s_1 | | | | s_2 | | | |
| | a_1 | | a_2 | | a_1 | | a_2 | |
	b_1	b_2	b_1	b_2	b_1	b_2	b_1	b_2
y_1	84.9	17.2	7.3	15.6	41.1	12.7	16.7	54.5
y_2	80.1	12.2	12.5	20.2	33.0	7.7	24.4	59.9
y_3	66.0	15.8	12.3	31.0	22.2	8.1	19.6	75.2
y_4	54.6	12.2	17.4	40.9	15.1	5.1	22.9	81.8

Estimated Probabilities π_{ijkl} for the Full Model

| | s_1 | | | | s_2 | | | |
| | a_1 | | a_2 | | a_1 | | a_2 | |
	b_1	b_2	b_1	b_2	b_1	b_2	b_1	b_2
y_1	0.085	0.017	0.007	0.016	0.041	0.013	0.017	0.054
y_2	0.080	0.012	0.013	0.020	0.033	0.008	0.024	0.060
y_3	0.066	0.016	0.012	0.031	0.022	0.008	0.020	0.075
y_4	0.055	0.012	0.017	0.041	0.015	0.005	0.023	0.082

Estimated Probabilities π^*_{ijkl} for the Restricted Model [SY][YA][YB][SB][AB]

| | s_1 | | | | s_2 | | | |
| | a_1 | | a_2 | | a_1 | | a_2 | |
	b_1	b_2	b_1	b_2	b_1	b_2	b_1	b_2
y_1	0.078	0.010	0.015	0.023	0.049	0.020	0.009	0.047
y_2	0.070	0.006	0.023	0.026	0.044	0.013	0.014	0.054
y_3	0.057	0.009	0.021	0.038	0.031	0.015	0.011	0.068
y_4	0.046	0.006	0.027	0.046	0.024	0.011	0.014	0.077

needed to give a power of 0.9. Thus, $12.6 = 0.095N$, or $N \approx 133$. Since there are 8 subpopulations, a sample of about 17 subjects from each year and sex combination suffices. Of course, this sample size is appropriate only for the test between the specific $\mathcal{M}$ and $\mathcal{M}^*$ postulated above. Other tests with the same design may require more or fewer subjects. One should also recognize that these calculations make no allowance for the effects of small samples on the quality of the χ^2 approximation. Where the power calculations ask for only a few observations per cell, one should augment the sample. Thus, in the last example, one may feel that 17 subjects for each 4-level AB classification is a bit light and prefer a sample of, say, 25 subjects per year-sex combination.

5.11. COLLAPSING TO A SMALLER TABLE

The reduction of a large table to a smaller one by omitting some dimensions of classification is an important operation. One often begins with more variables than accuracy or simplicity demands and eliminates the unwanted ones during the analysis. The actual operation of reduction is simple: one sums over the unneeded subscript(s) to form a smaller table. Collapsing should not be done without thought, however, to ensure that violence is not done to the associations under study. The discussion of two- and three-dimensional tables in Sections 3.12 and 3.13 showed that collapsing can introduce bias (recall Simpson's paradox). One needs to know when one is safe.

There are many reasons to reduce a table. Foremost, a simple table is easier to understand than a large one and is easier to explain. If one is interested in the associations among a few factors, one wants to study them in a table that includes the smallest number of additional factors. Moreover, because its cells contain larger frequencies, a small table usually yields more stable tests than a large one. Finally, it may aid the interpretation of a table to know that the associations among a set of factors is invariant with respect to another set. This invariance may be explicit or implicit in the original study, for whenever one does not measure a variable, one is put in the same place as if that variable had been measured and then ignored.

As Section 3.13 pointed out, the simplest justification for collapsing a table is based on the meaning of the factors. Some associations are more fundamental than others, and these associations may be studied in smaller tables. For example, if the factors are causally ordered, later factors are best eliminated from a study of the earlier ones. In particular, suppose that one is studying the relationship between a performance measure P and a type of training T in a group of subjects for which sex (S), age (A), and prior experience (E) have been measured. To study the relationships among S, A, and E, it is more appropriate to collapse over T and P than to use the five-way table, since conditioning one's conclusions about the characteristics of the subject populations on the treatment or its outcome makes no sense whatsoever. In contrast, the treatment-performance relationship may well be conditioned by S, A, and E, and so is better studied in the full table. These sorts of theoretical justification override the empirical rules for collapsing a table that are discussed in the rest of this section and should be employed wherever possible.

Without a theoretical basis, the justification for collapsing must depend on the observed configuration of the data, that is, on the model that fits the table. With some patterns of association, a variable can be eliminated without harm, while with other patterns the effects change. A three-way table described by the model $[AB][BC]$ cannot be collapsed over variable B without altering the AC association (recall Section 3.12). However, collapsing over C in this table leaves the AB association unaltered.

Concerns about the effects of collapsing a table arise in two situations. First, one may be interested in a particular association and wish to know that this association or set of λ parameters is not altered when some irrelevant variables are eliminated. What happens to other relationships is not important. Second, one may be interested in the model that fits a complete subtable, including all associations among those factors. One needs to know when the relationships in the subtable accurately reflect those that would be measured in the entire set of data, that is, when the subtable model is a simple restriction of the complete model. Clearly, these two sorts of questions are related, but they reflect sufficiently different practical problems to make them worthy of separate discussion.

Examining Parameters

Suppose that the full set of factors is divided into three disjoint sets, $\mathcal{S}$, $\mathcal{T}$, and $\mathcal{U}$. One is interested in the relationship among the factors $\mathcal{S}$ and wishes to eliminate the factors in the set $\mathcal{U}$ from the table, leaving a table with the factors $\mathcal{S} \cup \mathcal{T}$. To make collapsing valid, the parameters of the log-frequency model involving $\mathcal{S}$ should be unchanged in the reduced model. However, associations among the members of $\mathcal{T}$ or between those of $\mathcal{S}$ and $\mathcal{T}$ may be altered by the collapsing, since these are not of concern. One says, then, that the $\mathcal{S}\mathcal{T}\mathcal{U}$ table is *collapsible over $\mathcal{U}$ with respect to $\mathcal{S}$*. The simplest case occurs when one wishes eliminate a factor C when studying λ_{AB} in a three-way table. In this case, $\mathcal{S} = \{A,B\}$, $\mathcal{T}$ is empty, and $\mathcal{U} = \{C\}$.

When $\mathcal{S}$ consists of two factors (or two sets of factors), say $\mathcal{S} = \{A,B\}$, and $\mathcal{U}$ contains only a single dichotomous variable U, a simple rule determines if collapsing is possible (Bishop, Fienberg, & Holland, 1975; Simpson, 1951). For $\lambda_{\mathcal{S}}$ to be unaffected by the elimination of U, at least one member of $\mathcal{S}$ must be conditionally independent of U. Extending the conditional independence notation to allow sets, one must have either $A \perp\!\!\!\perp U|B\mathcal{T}$ or $B \perp\!\!\!\perp U|A\mathcal{T}$, or both. When $\mathcal{U}$ contains two or more factors or a factor with more than two levels, this conditional-independence condition is sufficient to ensure collapsibility, but is not necessary (Shapiro, 1982; Whittemore, 1978). However, the exceptions to the rule are a result of a balancing of effects among the levels and are specialized enough that one need only worry about the conditional-independence rule.

In the five-way example with a treatment and performance (T and P), measured in a subject population classified by sex, age, and experience (S, A, and E), suppose that one wished to see whether sex effects can be ignored in studying the TP association. Thus, $\mathcal{S} = \{T,P\}$, $\mathcal{T} = \{A,E\}$, and $\mathcal{U} = \{S\}$. Since sex is a dichotomous variable and $\mathcal{S}$ contains two factors, the first version of the rule applies. To collapse over S, either $P \perp\!\!\!\perp S|AET$ or $T \perp\!\!\!\perp S|AEP$ must hold. These hypotheses are tested by the models [AETP][AEST] and [AETP][AESP], respectively. If the five-way table is sparsely populated, a more powerful test for the most common type of dependence is obtained by looking at the low-order parameters, comparing these models to $[AETP][AEST][SP]$ and $[AETP][AESP][ST]$, respectively.

In practice, one is often interested in something more than collapsibility in this sense. One's real concern is that the collapsed coefficients give an accurate picture of what is going in all the subpopulations that one has combined by collapsing over $\mathcal{U}$. It is not enough for $\lambda_{\mathcal{S}}$ to be the same in both the $\mathcal{STU}$ table and the $\mathcal{ST}$ table. In addition, the relationships involving the factors in $\mathcal{S}$ should not interact with the factors in $\mathcal{U}$. This situation, known as *strict collapsibility*, makes more stringent demands on the data. The conditions for strict collapsiblity are simple: the variables in which one is interested must be conditionally independent of the eliminated variables given the remaining variables. This relationship is expressed by the conditional-independence hypothesis $\mathcal{S} \perp\!\!\!\perp \mathcal{U}|\mathcal{T}$, which is tested by the fit of $[\mathcal{ST}][\mathcal{TU}]$ in the full table. This model must be retained (with adequate power) to let collapsing to proceed. Since the associations are likely to manifest themselves in lower-order effects, a comparison of the model $[\mathcal{ST}][\mathcal{TU}]$ to the model $[\mathcal{ST}][\mathcal{SU}][\mathcal{TU}]$ often has more power to detect problems than does the goodness-of-fit test, especially when the frequencies in the $\mathcal{STU}$ table are small. For the example above, preservation of the TP table after collapsing over S and A would require that $PT \perp\!\!\!\perp SA|E$.

Collapsing of Models

The second type of collapsing rule concerns the conditions under which a set of factors can be eliminated without altering any residual relationship. In effect, this case is like strict collapsibility when $\mathcal{T}$ is empty. A table with a certain pattern of associations is said to be *collapsible* over some of its factors (the set $\mathcal{U}$) when doing so does not affect the associations among the retained factors (the set $\mathcal{S}$).

First note the form that the collapsed model must have. If a parameter relates factors of $\mathcal{S}$ in the $\mathcal{SU}$ model, the same parameter must be present in the model over $\mathcal{S}$ only. For this to be true, the model that applies to the subtable must be a simple restriction of the model for the full table, obtained by deleting the unused factors from it. For example, consider eliminating D and E from a five-way table described by the model $[ABD][BCD][CED]$. Striking D and E from the full model leaves $[AB][BC][C]$, which becomes $[AB][BC]$ after the redundant $[C]$ is removed. If the original table is collapsible, then it is collapsible to this model. Of course, one cannot always collapse to this model; it was shown in Chapter 3 that when a table fitted by the model $[AB][BC]$ is collapsed over B, the result is not necessarily fitted by $[A][C]$. Further conditions are needed.

These conditions can be written in at least two ways (Asmussen & Edwards, 1983). In terms of expected frequencies, a table is collapsible if the expected frequencies obtained from the model in the marginal table are the same as those obtained by summing frequencies from the full model in the larger table. Specifically, let $\mu_{\mathcal{SU}}$ denote the expected frequencies for a model that accurately describes the full $\mathscr{S}\mathscr{U}$ table and let $\mu_{\mathscr{S}}$ denote the frequencies for the collapsed model involving only the factors in $\mathscr{S}$. The table is collapsible if and only if

$$\mu_{\mathscr{S}} = \sum_{\mathscr{U}} \mu_{\mathscr{S}\mathscr{U}}$$

An alternative definition of collapsibility uses the λ parameters. A table is collapsible when all λ parameters in common to saturated models in the collapsed and uncollapsed tables have the same values. Thus, in reducing an $ABCD$ table to an AB table, the parameters λ, λ_A, λ_B, and λ_{AB} must not change. If the proper model for either table is unsaturated, some of the parameters are zero. In particular, if an unsaturated model fits the reduced table, the corresponding parameters must be zero in the larger table in order for the table to be collapsible.

The conditions for this type of collapsibility to hold are somewhat confusing when they are stated as a general theorem (for an accurate statement, see Asmussen & Edwards, 1983). As an algorithm that verifies whether collapsing is possible, they are fairly direct. Six steps are required:

1. Select a model $\mathcal{M}$ that is acceptable for the full table (i.e., over $\mathscr{S} \cup \mathscr{U}$).
2. Collapse $\mathcal{M}$ by deleting factors in $\mathscr{U}$ from it and removing redundant terms, as illustrated above. This is the candidate for a reduced model on $\mathscr{S}$.
3. If the model just found does not describe the reduced table, then collapsing is not possible. Otherwise, the algorithm continues.
4. Again starting with $\mathcal{M}$, delete the factors of $\mathscr{S}$ from every bracketed term. The result is a collection of subsets of factors from $\mathscr{U}$, one from each bracketed term. Remove any redundant subsets.
5. For each of these subsets, create a subset of $\mathscr{S}$ by listing every member of $\mathscr{S}$ that is directly connected to one of the $\mathscr{U}$-subset members by a λ parameter of $\mathcal{M}$.
6. Compare the results of steps 3 and 5. If every subset from step 5 is a λ parameter in the reduced model (i.e., is part of a bracketed term), then collapsing can be done. If any subset is not part of the reduced model, then collapsing is not permissible.

As an example, consider the elimination of $\mathscr{U} = \{D,E\}$ from a table with factors A, B, C, D, and E to leave $\mathscr{S} = \{A,B,C\}$. The analysis proceeds as follows:

1. Suppose that the model $\mathcal{M} = [ABD][BE][CE]$ fits in the $\mathscr{S}\mathscr{U}$ table.
2. By deleting D and E from $\mathcal{M}$, the potential reduced model $[AB][C]$ is obtained.
3. Suppose that this model adequately fits the $\mathscr{S}$ table.

4. Deleting the factors of $\mathcal{S}$ from the first bracketed term of $\mathcal{M}$ turns $[ABD]$ into D. The other two terms both give E, so the subsets of $\mathcal{U}$ are $\{D\}$ and $\{E\}$.
5. In $\mathcal{M}$, factor D is connected to variables A and B from $\mathcal{S}$, while the factor E is connected to B and C (from the second and third terms of $\mathcal{M}$). These produce two subsets $\{A,B\}$ and $\{B,C\}$.
6. The corresponding λ terms are λ_{AB} and λ_{BC}. Although λ_{AB} appears in the putative reduced model from step 2, λ_{BC} does not. Thus, this collapsing is not possible.

Although one cannot collapse both D and E in this example, note that it is possible to collapse the five-way table over D without damaging the results. The factors of $\mathcal{S}$ linked to D are A and B, which are combined in the parameter λ_{AB} of the original model.

All the above rules are described in population terms. Of course, except when working at the theoretical level, one does not have access to the populations. For samples, if the empirically derived models fit exactly, the same rules would apply. However, in real data the presence of sampling fluctuation means that even when a parameter is absent from the true population model, the sample estimate of it is usually nonzero (albeit not significantly so). Accordingly, collapsing a variable that is statistically unrelated to any others in the table typically causes some minor, nonsystematic changes in the other estimates.

In deciding empirically to collapse a model, one should recognize that the rules depend on the model that fits the full table. Selecting this model means, in effect, accepting a null hypothesis. Statistically, this action is on a much less solid footing than is rejecting a hypothesis, the more so since the test that confirms the model may be conducted in a table with small cell frequencies. One must proceed cautiously here, after satisfying one's concerns about power and goodness of fit.

PROBLEMS

5.1. Which of the following models is consistent with the design in Section 5.1 (two questions asked to 8 groups of college students)?

a. $[S][Y][A][B]$
b. $[SY][AB]$
c. $[ABS][AY]$
d. $[ASY][BY]$

5.2. Use the iterative proportional fitting procedure to fit the model $[AB][AC]$ to the table

	b_1		b_2	
	c_1	c_2	c_1	c_2
a_1	8	12	7	8
a_2	6	3	21	2

Check your results using estimates from the closed formula for $\hat{\mu}_{ijk}$.

5.3. Draw the hierarchical lattice of models for a four-factor design in which the frequencies of three factors are constrained by the design. *Hint*: there are 19 models in the lattice.

5.4. Complete the estimation of the parameters in the example in Section 5.3.

5.5. Estimate the parameters of the log-linear model [AB][AC] for the data given in Problem 5.2. *Note*: the expected frequencies are

	b_1		b_2	
	c_1	c_2	c_1	c_2
a_1	8.57	11.43	6.43	8.57
a_2	7.59	1.41	19.41	3.59

5.6. How many degrees of freedom are associated with tests of the following models in a four-way table. Assume that no marginal cells are empty.

a. [ABC][D]

b. [AB][AD][BC][CD]

c. [ABC][ABD][BCD]

5.7. For a three-way table with the pattern of zeros given in Table 5.4, determine the degrees of freedom for tests of the models [AB][AC], [AC][BC], and [AB][AC][BC]. Remember that the number of expected zeros is not the same for all models.

5.8. Suppose that the pattern of filled and empty cells in a four-way table is

		c_1					c_2					c_3				
		d_1	d_2	d_3	d_4	d_5	d_1	d_2	d_3	d_4	d_5	d_1	d_2	d_3	d_4	d_5
a_1	b_1	X	X	X	X	X	X	X	X	X	X	X	X	X	X	X
	b_2	X	0	0	X	X	X	X	0	X	X	0	X	0	X	X
	b_3	X	X	X	0	X	0	0	0	0	0	0	X	X	0	X
	b_4	X	X	X	0	X	0	0	0	0	0	0	0	X	0	X
a_2	b_1	X	X	X	X	X	X	X	X	X	X	X	X	X	X	X
	b_2	X	0	0	X	X	X	X	0	X	X	X	X	0	X	X
	b_3	X	0	X	0	0	0	0	0	0	0	X	0	X	0	X
	b_4	X	X	X	0	X	X	0	X	0	X	0	X	X	0	0

a. How many degrees of freedom are associated with tests of the models $[ABC][D]$, $[ABC][BD]$, and $[ABC][BCD]$?

b. For this pattern of zeros, calculate the degrees of freedom for tests of the BD and BCD association in the most restrictive context (e.g., the first of these compares the model $B \perp\!\!\!\perp D|AC$ with the same model to which λ_{BD} has been added).

5.9. Find η_C for the model $[AB][AC]$ that was fitted in Problems 5.2 and 5.5. Assume that factors A and B define populations. Hint: Notice that $C(\hat{\pi})$ for the marginal distribution of factor C is the concentration for the model $[AB][C]$.

5.10. The concentration $C(\hat{\pi})$ for the model $[AB][AC]$ in the three-way table of Problems 5.2 and 5.5 is the same as $C(\hat{\pi})$ for one of the two-way marginal tables. Which one? Explain why.

5.11. ℰ† The probability distribution associated with a $2 \times 2 \times 2$ table with $\lambda_{A(1)} = 0.2$, $\lambda_{B(1)} = 0.0$, $\lambda_{C(1)} = -0.3$, $\lambda_{AB(11)} = -0.8$, and $\lambda_{AC(11)} = 0.4$ is

	b_1		b_2	
	c_1	c_2	c_1	c_2
a_1	0.0503	0.0412	0.2490	0.2039
a_2	0.0750	0.3041	0.0151	0.0614

What is the power of a test with 200 subjects in this context to detect an effect with $\lambda_{BC(11)} = 0.5$?

5.12. ℰ What sample size is required to have a power of 90% to reject the hypothesis $\lambda_{CD} = 0$ in the context $C \perp\!\!\!\perp D|AB$? A guess at the data is

		c_1			c_2		
		d_1	d_2	d_3	d_1	d_2	d_3
a_1	b_1	9	2	12	9	2	17
	b_2	9	13	1	14	7	7
	b_3	7	5	8	5	3	20
a_2	b_1	14	14	9	6	9	17
	b_2	12	4	3	2	1	12
	b_3	12	3	19	2	2	9

5.13. Which four-way models are consistent with dropping factor D from an $ABCD$ table? What if one is interested only in the AB relationship within the three-way collapsed table?

5.14. Can D and E be eliminated from a table for which the following models fit without altering the relationships among the other variables?

---

†Problems marked by ℰ require a computer, usually with some form of packaged log-frequency analysis program.

a. [ABD][ACD][BE][CE]

b. [ABD][BCD][BE][CE]

5.15. ℰ One of the best ways to learn how an algorithm works is to go through its operation in detail. This is an important function of numerical examples. For some of the present algorithms, too much arithmetic is required to make problems of this type practical. Then writing a computer program is very revealing. If you know how to program, try writing the following programs, using whatever language you know well. *Note*: to do a thorough job writing a statistical program, one must worry about catching errors (e.g., negative frequencies on input) and handling special cases (e.g., marginal zeros), and must be concerned with the accuracy of the numerical routines (e.g., Equation 2.25 is a more accurate way to calculate G^2 than is Equation 2.26). For this problem, ignore these complications.

a. Write a program to estimate the expected frequencies in a two-way table for the model of unrelatedness, using the iterative proportional fitting algorithm. Calculate X^2 and G^2.

b. Write a program to fit and test the model [AB][AC][BC] in a three-way table.

c. Modify these programs to calculate estimates of the parameters of the log-linear model.

6 Testing Specific Hypotheses

Chapter 5 shows how to estimate and test the parameters of any complete hierarchical log-linear frequency model. As far as the mechanics of calculation are concerned, that chapter contains most of what one needs to know. But deciding how to apply the procedures is often more confusing than the procedures themselves. When there are many factors, the number of possible models is large: excluding constant-frequency models, there are 2 models for two factors ([A][B] and [AB]), 9 for three factors (recall Figure 3.4), 114 for four factors, and the number increases rapidly in larger tables. By the time 10 factors are involved, the number of models is enormous—there are 115,974 hypotheses of complete independence and 3,475,978 of complete or conditional independence, including those that postulate equal frequencies over some of the factors (Good, 1975). These only touch the full set of possible models. An idea of the vastness of the number of 10-factor models is gained when one realizes that there are 45 pairwise combinations of factors, hence $2^{45} = 35,184,372,088,832$ models involving only pairwise associations. Obviously, a strategy is needed to cope with this plethora.

One must fall back on one's knowledge of the source of the data to conduct the search. Roughly, one can distinguish three levels of knowledge, which gives rise to three strategies by which a problem can be approached:

- In a well-specified situation, there are definite hypotheses that one wants to test and models that one wants to fit. These give the most exact and most powerful results, but make the strongest demands on one's prior understanding of the investigation.
- Sometimes one factor in the investigation can be viewed as an outcome, whose

148

value is conceptually "caused" by the other factors. This predictor-outcome logic eliminates many candidate models and greatly simplifies the generation of hypotheses and the search for a satisfactory model.

- The most difficult situation arises when one has little a priori knowledge to bring to the investigation and is simply searching for a good model. One's conclusions from this exploratory analysis are inevitably much weaker than when more structure can be imposed.

The next three chapters discuss problems in the selection and interpretation of models, roughly treating these three situations in order. As they are read, keep in mind that the choice of how best to approach a problem is to some degree a matter of one's interests, tastes, and standards, so can be treated differently by different investigators. Frequently, there are several satisfactory analyses, and one cannot be dogmatic about which is best (which is not to say that there are not plenty of incorrect approaches). Ultimately, facility comes only through familiarity with both the statistical procedures and the substantive areas to which they apply.

6.1.   SOME DETECTION DATA

Much of this chapter is an extended example that uses the data from an experiment on the detection of weak stimuli.† Suppose that a subject is attempting to detect a weak signal—it could be a light, a tone, a pattern, or whatever—that is, the subject says whether the signal is there or not. On a particular trial, the subject is presented with a stimulus that either includes this weak signal (the signal-present condition) or does not (the signal-absent condition). Because the signal is weak, the two types of stimulus are readily confused. The subject rates each stimulus on a six-point scale, from 1 when sure that no signal is present through 6 when sure that the signal is there. A single trial provides little information about the detection process, so the subject is given many similar trials—here 2000 of them—for one-half of which the signal is present and one-half absent. Thus, each trial is classified into one cell of a 2×6 table (Table 6.1). Had the signal been strong, all the responses would have fallen into the $a1$ and $p6$ cells. Because the signal was weak, there was a good deal of confusion and at least one response appears in every cell. Nevertheless, cells $a1$ and $p6$ are the most heavily populated, indicating that the signal was detectable to some extent.

The first step in using frequency models to analyze these data is to decide which sampling model describes the design. The basic structure of the experi-

---

† These data are drawn from Olzak (1986); see Olzak & Wickens (1983). The usual approach to such data uses signal detection theory (e.g., Green & Swets, 1966; McNicol, 1971). The treatment presented here does not replace a signal-detection analysis, but is a complementary approach.

TABLE 6.1
Data from a Signal-Detection Task

		Response					
		1	2	3	4	5	6
Signal	Absent (a)	524	296	125	44	10	1
	Present (p)	92	65	78	180	238	347

ment is clear: the designation of a trial as signal or as noise is controlled by the experimenter and thus is not a random component of any model. For each stimulus type, the subject's behavior generates a distribution of responses. This pattern indicates a product-multinomial sampling model in which the stimulus type is given and the response is random.

The data in Table 6.1 are simple, and only a few hypotheses apply to them. The most important hypothesis concerns whether the signal could be detected at all. If the presence of the signal had no effect on the subject, then the same multinomial distribution would fit both rows of the table. If detection were possible, then different distributions would apply. Different distributions are expressed as an association between the stimulus presented (the row factor, S) and the subject's response (the column factor, R). Testing for detection amounts to assessing the homogeneity of the distributions by testing the model $S \perp\!\!\!\perp R$. This hypothesis is tested by the conventional test for heterogeneity in a two-way table (Chapter 2) or, more formally, by a comparison of the model $[S][R]$ to the saturated model $[SR]$.

Before one applies the statistical tests to these (or any) data, the applicability of the sampling models should be examined. The problems posed by this example are not routine. The unit of observation in this experiment is the single trial. Since all the observations are collected from the same subject, the potential for violation of trial-to-trial independence is substantial. The product-multinomial sampling rule, on which analysis is based, requires each response to be independent of all other responses. Clearly, the best realization of this condition occurs when every observation comes from a different subject. For this investigation, such an experiment would be absurdly inefficient; on this count (and others) the within-subject procedure is necessary. Yet the assumption of independence is crucial to the relationship between the test statistic and the theoretical χ^2 distribution. Breakdowns in independence cast doubt on the accuracy of this approximation.

There is no unambiguously satisfactory solution here. On the one hand, for psychophysical experiments with trained observers, the assumption of independent trials is both conventional and reasonable. On the other, some dependence is probable. Fortunately, doubts about the independence assumptions do not invalidate the use of the frequency models as descriptive devices. Even without independence, they can still be fitted and their parameters examined. From this exploratory point of view, one ignores significance tests altogether. More realistically, one can go ahead with the tests, but interpret any probability statements with caution. If one avoids placing much faith on results of precarious significance and emphasizes the relative sizes of the changes in fit when interpreting the models, one is reasonably safe.

With this design, another of the basic sampling assumptions is also at risk: that of the homogeneity of the observations. If the observations are not probabilistically identical, there is no assurance that the model that fits the aggregate data also fits the individual parts. In the present example, there is reason for concern. Two thousand trials take a lot of time, and one may reasonably doubt whether the behavior of the subject remained constant throughout. The data were collected during several sessions, and this fact, along with the possibility that the subject became fatigued during a single session, calls homogeneity into question. In fact, for experiments such as this, homogeneity is frequently a more serious problem than is the independence of the observations. One should examine experimental procedure with some suspicion on these grounds. For this example, assume that this examination allows the analysis to proceed. In a real problem, one should be more cautious, attempting to demonstrate homogeneity through subsidiary tests and demanding that any conclusion can be replicated in the results from different sessions or different subjects.

With these considerations completed, turn to the test. Of course, the effect in Table 6.1 is so substantial that a test is unnecessary, but in any case the hypothesis $S \perp\!\!\!\perp R$ is rejected with $G^2(5) = 1322.9$. Obviously, some form of stimulus-sensitive behavior is taking place.

As just described, the experiment has little room for complicated analysis. Actually, the data in Table 6.1 are collapsed from a larger design that includes two other factors as well. The full experiment consisted of two detection tasks, such as the one just described, that were performed simultaneously. The stimulus was a compound, combining signals of two different types, each of which might or might not be present. For example, these might be lights of two different colors, tones of two frequencies, or two different patterns (in fact, they were two gratings of different spatial frequencies). One signal had a high frequency, and the other had a low frequency. In all, there were four types of stimuli, formed from the combinations of two factors H and L, each taking values of present (p) or absent (a). One fourth of the trials (i.e., 500 of them) were of each of the four types.

To this compound stimulus the subject made a compound response, composed of two ratings, each on the six-point scale. One of these, call it X, indicated how sure the subject was that the H component of the stimulus was present. The second response, Y, rated the L component. The full set of data form a four-way table (Table 6.2). Table 6.1 is the HX marginal distribution of this table.

The sampling picture for Table 6.2 is essentially the same as for the simplified

TABLE 6.2
Data from a Concurrent-task Detection Experiment

| | | H = a | | | | | | H = p | | | | | |
		X = 1	2	3	4	5	6	1	2	3	4	5	6
	Y = 1	69	6	1	1	0	0	10	5	2	11	16	28
	2	34	20	10	3	1	0	8	5	11	43	27	38
L = a	3	43	24	13	9	1	0	9	6	7	28	32	45
	4	78	40	20	6	0	1	8	6	14	19	23	22
	5	32	38	17	5	4	0	4	5	7	6	18	18
	6	5	14	3	2	0	0	0	1	2	3	5	8
	Y = 1	4	1	0	0	0	0	5	0	1	4	4	9
	2	5	3	2	1	0	0	0	1	3	6	9	27
L = p	3	8	6	3	1	0	0	2	3	2	11	27	20
	4	36	25	18	3	1	0	9	12	11	10	23	31
	5	83	69	26	6	1	0	16	7	5	19	33	40
	6	127	50	12	7	2	0	21	14	13	20	21	61

data in Table 6.1. A product-multinomial sampling model is still appropriate. The four combinations of H and L give four stimulus types, and the combinations of X and Y create a 36-level multinomial distribution of responses. The frequencies of the HL combinations are controlled by the experimental design, so any meaningful model that includes both factors must accommodate the frequency of these events by including λ_{HL} terms. Thus, the lattice of acceptable models is similar to the one described in Section 5.1 for the experiment in which college students responded to two questions (Figure 5.1).

With the introduction of the two new factors, it is no longer obvious how to analyze the data. It is easy enough to collapse Table 6.2 to various two-way tables similar to Table 6.1. However, the point of the experiment was to search for more complicated associations among the stimuli and responses. To do so, Table 6.2 must be analyzed in its complete four-way form. There are 73 different four-factor hierarchical log-linear models that contain the parameter λ_{HL} and 38 possible models on collapsed versions of the table. This is a sufficiently large number that some strategy for their use is necessary. Fitting each one to the data separately is not satisfactory. Even if one could find a way to adjust the type I error probability to compensate for the multiplicity of tests, the tangle of results would be almost impenetrable. Among 111 outcomes, there inevitably would be contradictions and ambiguities.

To oversimplify slightly, two approaches to the analysis of these data are possible. First, one may try to formulate and test specific hypotheses about the factors or about specific parameter values. Second, one can examine meaningful models for all the data. In a carefully designed experiment such as this one, these strategies can be worked out almost completely in advance. Of course, an approach by hypothesis testing and one by model fitting work with the same data and are closely related. Their relationship is developed in the final sections of this chapter.

One would not routinely apply all the procedures described in this chapter to a single set of data. Along with other techniques to be described in Chapters 7 and 8, they constitute part of the variety of approaches one should have at the back of one's mind when looking at a set of data. In seeking to understand the data, one will probably explore several approaches, but will follow up only those that are most productive. Certainly a finished research report presents only the analyses that give the clearest picture of the data.

6.2. HYPOTHESES OF INDEPENDENCE AND CONDITIONAL INDEPENDENCE

The models of conditional independence provide the tools to construct specific hypotheses. Suppose that one asks whether two factors are related. By the logic of hypothesis testing, this question is investigated by positing a model in which they are unrelated and testing whether that model fits. If this model can be rejected, then a link between the factors has been shown.

If only two factors are involved, unrelatedness is expressed as independence, homogeneity, or the like, which for factors A and B is represented by $A \perp\!\!\!\perp B$. However, in many situations one wants to test for unrelatedness in the context of one or more factors that may mediate an observed association. To exclude these context factors, say C, D, and E, one investigates the conditional independence hypothesis, $A \perp\!\!\!\perp B|CDE$ rather than simple independence. The only way that this hypothesis can be rejected is for A and B to be associated over and above whatever common association with C, D, and E is present.

As far as testing goes, the procedure is straightforward. Conditional independence translates to a linear log-frequency model that is readily fitted and tested. For example, the hypothesis $A \perp\!\!\!\perp B|CDE$ is equivalent to the model $[ACDE]$ $[BCDE]$. The test is easy to run, since the resulting model is direct and has expected frequencies that are given by a closed formula,

$$\hat{\mu}_{ijklm} = \frac{x_{i+klm}x_{+jklm}}{x_{++klm}}$$

Each numerator term is indexed by one of the test factors and the context factors, while the denominator is from the marginal distribution of the context factors. When an iterative program is used to fit the model, the directness of the estimates means that convergence occurs after the first cycle, and little computer time is necessary.

The hardest part is deciding the appropriate context for the test. Here, one needs an idea about the ordering of the factors or about the priority of the possible explanations for a relationship. Generally speaking, the proper context for a test includes all the factors that are directly related to the factors in question and that are more important sources of explanation than the relationship being tested.

The psychophysics example may help to understand this. Consider first the test of the relationship of the presence or absence of the high-frequency component of the stimulus, H, to its proper response, X. This linkage expresses a principal portion of the subject's task. Accordingly, any HX association that is observed should be attributed first to a direct linkage between H and X. The factors L and Y are irrelevant to this test. No specific context is required, and the proper test for the HX relationship is the hypothesis $H \perp\!\!\!\perp X$, as examined in Table 6.1.

Testing the relationship between the responses is different. Plausibly response X somehow influences response Y (or vice versa). A test for XY connection is not as simple as it is for HX, however. One cannot use a two-way table here. Both X and Y unquestionably depend on the presence or absence of the signals, and explanations based on these signals have priority over the less clear XY associations. Thus, the signal conditions H and L are the appropriate context in which to run the test. The conditional-independence hypothesis $X \perp\!\!\!\perp Y|HL$ is investigated instead of simple independence, $X \perp\!\!\!\perp Y$. For the data in Table 6.2, the proper model is $[HLX][HLY]$, which is rejected with $X^2(95) = 207.13$. A zero in the HLX marginal distribution reduces the degrees of freedom for this test from 100 to 95, as described in Section 5.6.

This test can be refined by looking at the first-order association parameters λ_{XY}, to see whether they make a significant contribution. Interesting effects often reside in the lower-order portions of the association rather than in the higher-order parts. Further, when the number of factors is large and the total frequency in the table is insufficient for adequate tests of overall fit, difference tests may be more accurate. For these data, the λ_{XY} are tested by comparing the conditional-independence model to one that introduces these parameters. Using G^2 as a test statistic gives

$$
\begin{array}{lll}
[HLX][HLY]: & G^2(95) = 221.43 \\
[HLX][HLY][XY]: & G^2(70) = 94.05 \\
\hline
& \Delta G^2(25) = 127.38
\end{array}
$$

These results attribute the bulk of the effect to λ_{XY} and leave the residual model only at the borderline of significance (the critical value of $\chi^2(70)$ at the 5% level is 90.53).

The other interesting set of relationships for these data relate the responses to the inappropriate signals, that is, Y to H and X to L. These effects include cases where the presence of one signal acts to potentiate or to inhibit the response to the other signal. Clearly, these effects can be tested with the same type of conditional-independence hypothesis that was appropriate for XY relationships. These tests are shown in the upper parts of the two panels of Table 6.3. The two null hypotheses are $H \perp\!\!\!\perp Y|LX$ and $L \perp\!\!\!\perp X|HY$, which have statistic values sufficient to be rejected, although not by a substantial amount. The test of first-order λ parameters tends to implicate λ_{HY} but not λ_{LX}. The degrees of freedom in both goodness-of-fit tests are influenced by marginal zeros, but the difference tests are unaffected.

Another approach to these tests is often preferable. In one's theoretical considerations, one may wish to give explanatory priority to signal-response associations before those relating responses to responses. If that is the case, then the HY and LX relationships are preceded by the HX and LY associations, but not by the XY links. Consider H and Y. In this view, the test just run is unnecessarily

TABLE 6.3
Tests of λ_{HY} and λ_{LX} for the Data in Table 6.2

Tests of HY Association

Model	df	G^2	X^2
Tested in full four-way table			
$H \perp\!\!\!\perp Y|LX$ or [HLX][LXY]	55	84.70	87.75
[HLX][LXY][HY]	50	47.95	44.63
Difference	5	36.75	43.12
Tested in reduced HLY table			
$H \perp\!\!\!\perp Y|L$ or [HL][LY]	10	134.81	129.86
[HL][LY][HY]	5	15.38	15.01
Difference	5	119.43	114.85

Tests of LX Association

Model	df	G^2	X^2
Tested in full four-way table			
$L \perp\!\!\!\perp X|HL$ or [HLY][HXY]	54	82.98	77.07
[HLY][HXY][LX]	49	72.89	66.99
Difference	5	10.10	10.08
Tested in reduced HLX table			
$L \perp\!\!\!\perp X|H$ or [HL][HX]	10	19.49	19.00
[HL][HX][LX]	5	3.55	3.16
Difference	5	15.94	15.84

complicated, since it introduces the *XY* relationship into the context for the test (recall that $H \perp\!\!\!\perp Y|LX$ is tested by the model $[HLX][LXY]$, which includes λ_{XY}). Factor *X* has no direct influence on the *HY* relationship, and so it does not belong. The proper signal for *Y* (i.e., *L*) is relevant, however, and should appear. Accordingly, the appropriate place to construct the test is in the three-way *HLY* table, using the hypothesis $H \perp\!\!\!\perp Y|L$. Tests of this type appear in the bottom portions of the two panels of Table 6.3. The results are more decisive, particularly for λ_{HY}. Another reason to prefer tests in a three-way table to those in the four-way table will appear in the discussion of the decomposition of a model in Section 6.5.

6.3. GRAPHICAL MODELS

When one has specific questions to be answered, the most direct approach is to construct specific hypotheses that test them, in the manner of the last section. At other times, one is more concerned with an overall description of the data and wishes to formulate a complete model that embodies a more extensive set of effects. These models are generally more complicated than the independence or conditional-independence hypotheses and amalgamate several effects in a single statement. Their parameters can be used to describe the data in ways that transcend pure hypothesis tests. Of course, not all models that can be fit to a table make sensible statements about the data. Many models are inconsistent with what one knows about the source of the data. One's best strategy is to base the models that one fits on the logic of the investigation. This section describes one way to construct these models.†

When first developing a model it is useful to restrict one's attention to models that can be represented graphically. As one thinks about how the factors in an investigation are related, it is natural to denote them by points and to use a line between two of them to indicate some form of fundamental association. Specifically, returning to the graduate admission example of Section 3.12, one denotes the three factors (department, sex, and acceptance to school) by three points:

If one postulates that sex-department and department-acceptance associations are present, one draws lines that connect those points:

---

†This section, and much of the use of graphical models elsewhere in this chapter, draws heavily on Darroch, Lauritzen, & Speed (1980) and Edwards & Kreiner (1983).

The lack of a direct sex-admission relationship is indicated by the absence of a line between S and A. This picture, with two connections present, is equivalent to the model $[DS][DA]$.

With only three factors, a picture is not really necessary. Diagrams are more useful when more factors are involved. Suppose, for example, that one is studying the effectiveness of an advertising campaign at effecting a change of opinion regarding a particular product. Subjects are sampled and are classified on three different demographic factors: age, sex, and education (A, S, and E, respectively). Two questions are asked of each subject, concerning the importance of the product and the product that the subject currently uses (I and P). Then the subjects are exposed to one of several advertisements (T, for "treatment"), and finally a product choice rating (C) is taken. Among the first five factors, the investigator decides that (1) the relationships among age, sex, and education are not of concern and can be allowed to take any form; (2) the importance rating is likely to depend on all three of these factors; and (3) the previous product use depends on the importance rating and education, but not directly on either age or sex. To express these relationships as a diagram, one connects A, S, and E to each other, connects I to each of these, and connects P to I and E. The result is the picture

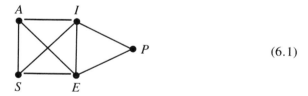

(6.1)

Before looking at the last two factors (T and C), consider how this graphical representation is turned into a model. The process is simple and consists of two steps. First, one locates every set of factors within which each node is connected to every other node. In graph theory, these sets are known as *cliques*. In Diagram 6.1, the sets $\{A,S,E,I\}$ and $\{E,I,P\}$ are cliques. The set $\{I,S,E,P\}$ is not a clique because there is no link between S and P. Where one clique is contained within another, as the clique $\{A,S,E\}$ is contained within the clique $\{A,S,E,I\}$, only the larger set need be listed. The second step turns this list of maximal cliques into a model. One simply lists each clique as a bracketed term. Thus, Diagram 6.1 translates to the model $[ASEI][EIP]$.

Although this procedure converts any diagram to a model, the reverse is not always possible. Not every model can be represented as a diagram. Accordingly, one speaks of the set of *graphical models*, which is smaller than set of hierarchical linear log-frequency models. The difference arises because the graphs do not distinguish higher-order associations from dense nets of lower-order associations. The smallest example of a nongraphical model is [AB][AC][BC] in a three-way table, which has links between all three pairs of factors. To avoid ambiguity, cliques are taken to describe saturated parameterizations, so that [ABC] is a graphical model but [AB][AC][BC] is not. This choice allows most graphical models to be interpreted in conditional independence terms, as Section 6.5 discusses further. Since independence hypotheses are intuitively appealing, the graphical models are particularly useful.

The link between graphical models and conditional independence points up one of their limitations. More subtle hypotheses concerning particular association parameters cannot be expressed in their terms. It is common enough for two factors to be associated—that is, conditionally dependent—yet for this association to be simple and free of interaction with other factors. Such relationships usually cannot be described graphically. Hence, in looking at a large table, one may need to switch between the classes of models. An illustration of the interplay of the classes appears in the next section, with graphical models guiding the overall formation of models and the hierarchical log-frequency models refining it.

To return to the advertising example, suppose that the investigator further postulates that (4) the choice (C) is related to the treatment, to importance, and to previous preference (T, I, and P); and (5) the magnitude of the TC association is modulated by education (E). The first assumption introduces links from C to T, I, and P; the second implies the presence of ETC terms and so is represented by a triangular clique involving these three factors. The resulting graph is

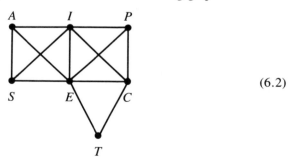

$$(6.2)$$

The corresponding model, obtained by extracting cliques from Diagram 6.2, is [ASEI][EIPC][ECT].

Readers who are familiar with *path analysis* from multiple regression may note a similarity between these diagrams and those used in that field (e.g., Pedhazur, 1982; Duncan, 1975). The parallel is not complete, however. In path analysis, one can give direction to the linkages and assign weights that indicate their importance. This attribution is problematic with frequency tables, although attempts at depicting path structure have been made (e.g., Goodman, 1972b, 1973a,b). The unordered nature of categorizations in frequency analysis makes the analysis less satisfactory than in multiple regression and creates ambiguity in the determination of path coefficients (see Fienberg, 1980, Chapter 7). Accordingly, this book does not treat numerical coefficients, although the notion of a causal ordering of factors is often used to select plausible hypotheses or models and is essential to most of Chapter 7.

6.4. CONSTRUCTING A SENSIBLE HIERARCHY OF MODELS

Return now to the psychophysics example, and consider the models that can be fitted to the full table. These models go beyond those that form the hypothesis tests in Section 6.2, in that they posit a pattern of relationships that encompasses the entire table, rather than examining a single link. If one decides to work with this type of model, it pays to construct a series of them, starting with simple models and progressing to the more complex, each based on a particular explanation of the data. The next few paragraphs consider some of these possibilities, making heavy use of the graphical principles from the last section.

1. *Random responding.* The simplest possibility is that the subject's responses are totally random, unrelated to the stimulus or to each other. In graphical terms, this state of affairs is depicted as

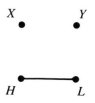

Only the *HL* connection, which expresses the experimenter's manipulation of the frequency of the signal combinations, is present. The model corresponding to this graph is *[HL][X][Y]*.

2. *Undetectable signals.* If the signals are completely subliminal, a slightly different model applies. The signal classifications (*H* and *L*) are unrelated to the responses (*X* and *Y*), but a relationship between the responses is possible—the subject, after all, makes both of them. Graphically the picture is

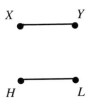

The model here is [*HL*][*XY*].

3. *Detectable signals.* If the signals are detectable, links between *H* and *X* and between *L* and *Y* appear in the diagrams. A useful version of this model is without an *XY* link:

In bracket form, this model is [*HL*][*HX*][*LY*]. In essence, this model describes the response pattern of a subject who is doing exactly what the experimenter requested: making responses that are uninfluenced by any systematic effect other than the appropriate signal. As such, it is the base model to which more complicated forms of association are added. If there is reason to think that one signal is detectable and the other is undetectable, one can construct models in which only one of the two response links is present, specifically, the models [*HL*][*HX*][*Y*] and [*HL*][*LY*][*X*] or their graphical equivalents.

4. *Association to the unrelated signal.* Other linkages can be added to the model of detectable signals. A model in which the responses are influenced by both the appropriate and the inappropriate signals is denoted graphically as

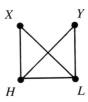

This model is [*HLX*][*HLY*] and describes the conditional-independence hypothesis $X \perp\!\!\!\perp Y | HL$. A more restricted, nongraphical version of this model, which retains only the pairwise parameters, is [*HL*][*HX*][*HY*][*LX*][*LY*]. The latter model excludes interaction among the factors.

Because of the priority that one gives to explanations based on the proper

signal (H for X and L for Y), there is no reason to examine a model that includes only links to the inappropriate signals,

This model gives no help in interpreting the experiment, and one should not complicate one's task by fitting it.

5. *Response-response association.* In the same manner as in the last model, a link between the responses added to the detectable-signals model gives

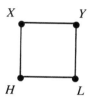

The bracket representation of this model includes 4 two-factor terms, [HL][HX] [LY][XY].

6. *All pairwise associations.* The two-factor sources of association can be combined into a nongraphical model that associates every pair of factors without interaction, [HL][HX][HY][LX][LY][XY]. If this model fits, it indicates that the four-factor table can be described accurately by a series of two-way tables of association parameters. The connections between factors are pure and free of interaction. Failure of the pairwise-association model indicates that the relationship between at least one pair of factors is modulated by a third factor.

7. *Interaction models.* Beyond the pairwise-association model are various models that introduce one or more set of three-factor parameters. The meaning of these models is best described by interactions of effects. For example, the model [HLX][HY][LY][XY] introduces λ_{HLX} to the pairwise-association model and, compared to that model, implies that the detectibility of the high-frequency signal (measured by the parameters λ_{HX}) is modulated by the low-frequency signal. Because of one's preference for the proper signal as an explanatory concept, this description of λ_{HLX} is more useful than the formally equivalent assertion that LX associations are modulated by H. Other interaction models involving different three-factor λ terms are interpreted in similar ways.

8. *Complete association.* To cap the series of models, the saturated model allows the possibility of associations of all types. This model, once again, is graphical:

Since it places no restrictions on the data, the saturated model inevitably fits perfectly and is the recourse if all other models fail to fit. If it is needed, at least one interaction involving all four factors is present.

When a four-factor interaction is detected, one should be aware that it does not necessarily indicate a substantive relationship among the factors. If a single cell in the table is exceptional, in the sense of having an excess or a deficiency of frequency relative to the value that would fit a simpler model, then the highest-order interaction often appears. In such a case, it may be more profitable to treat that cell as an explicit anomaly, using models of the type discussed in Section 10.2.

To visualize the relationships among the models, one can array them in a lattice diagram (Figure 6.1). This diagram contains only a subset of the 73 potential models for these data. As just described, they are selected for their interpretability. The relative sparseness of this lattice makes it easier to understand and prevents the testing of the models from becoming unduly burdensome. The models are evaluated using the conventional fitting and testing procedures. Goodness-of-fit statistics are shown in Figure 6.1, as are their differences. These statistics are expressed both as G^2 (or ΔG^2) and as percentages of the total difference between the random responding model and the saturated model. The latter values help to separate large and small effects, regardless of their statistical significance. The variability-reduction statistics of Section 5.8 could equally well be used.

One can use Figure 6.1 to help select a model for further work. Two contrasting needs govern this choice. On the one hand, a model that fails to include a necessary term is unsatisfactory. As the discussion of collapsing in Sections 3.13 and 5.11 suggests, when parameters that should be part of the model are missing, the estimates of the remaining parameters can be biased. On the other hand, estimating unnecessary parameters increases the variability of all the estimates, making them inaccurate, even if not biased. Models that are too complex are hard to understand as well. Thus, one must try to pick a model that includes all the important effects, while not arbitrarily including effects of little relevance. For the data here, an examination of the tests in Figure 6.1 indicates that all the two-factor associations are necessary and that higher-order terms are only slightly useful. A more detailed analysis of the three-way associations implicates only λ_{LXY}, and this not heavily. Hence, one may chose to work with the model

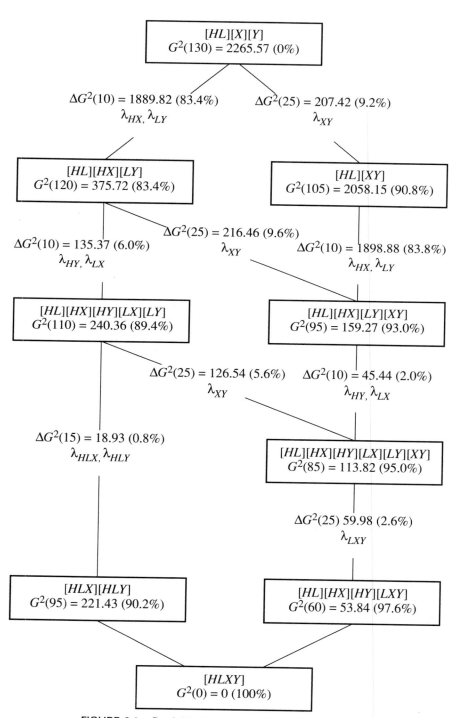

FIGURE 6.1. Partial lattice of models fitted to Table 6.2

163

[HL][HX][HY][LX][LY][XY] or the model [HL][HX][HY][LXY], depending on whether one is more concerned about simplicity or completeness. The latter model, which provides a satisfactory fit to the data, is the better choice if parameters are to be estimated, even if little use is to be made of the $\hat{\lambda}_{LXY}$.

Of course, one is not limited to the models in Figure 6.1. After examining the fits of the models in this lattice, one may decide to expand one area of the lattice and to ignore others, in an attempt to rationally select the best possible model. In practice one often abandons a rational consideration of the meaning of the models here and uses something like the stepwise search procedures described in Chapter 8.

However it is selected, the choice of a specific model is an assertion that one knows something about the process and about how the factors are related. This knowledge is embodied in the model's parameters, and one logically turns next to an examination of their values. The parameters in the model [HL][HX][HY][LXY] that are not fixed by design include the three-way association, all the pairwise associations except λ_{HL}, and the single-factor parameters λ_X and λ_Y. These are shown in Table 6.4. Because there are only two levels to the stimulus factors, there is no need to list parameters for both signal-absent and signal-present conditions. The constraints of the estimation procedure make the parameter values in one of these conditions the negative of the corresponding values in the other. It is easier to think of responding to a signal than of not responding to its absence, so the estimates for the signal-present condition are the more natural choice here.

The first pair of parameter estimates in Table 6.4, $\hat{\lambda}_X$ and $\hat{\lambda}_Y$, is not very useful. They give information about the subject's use of the categories, but their values are difficult to interpret since they combine information over the signal-present and signal-absent conditions. The next pair of estimates, $\hat{\lambda}_{HX}$ and $\hat{\lambda}_{LY}$, show the direct association to the signals. There is an appreciable association here, which has an ascending pattern and indicates a greater frequency of high-numbered responses in the signal-present condition. The HY and LX associations, given by the next pair of estimates, are much smaller; there appears to be a small inhibitory effect of H on Y (its presence gives more low-valued responses) and no consistent LX association.

The interresponse association is embodied in the values of $\hat{\lambda}_{XY}$. The general pattern in this array puts positive entries in the block that match a low response to one signal (1, 2, or 3) with a high response to the other (4, 5, or 6). Similarly numbered responses are less likely to occur together. The exception to this pattern is the cell where both responses are 1, where $\hat{\lambda}_{XY(11)}$ is positive and substantial. Apparently, this response combination is more likely than can be predicted from the other effects. This anomaly raises the question of whether it alone accounts for the observed XY association. To test whether this is so, one needs to repeat the analysis, ignoring the data in this cell. Procedures for testing the contribution of a specific cells are discussed in Chapter 10.

TABLE 6.4
Parameter Estimates for the Signal-present Condition of the Model
[HL][HX][HY][LXY] Fitted to Table 6.2

	X or Y					
	1	2	3	4	5	6
	Overall relative frequencies					
$\hat{\lambda}_X$	0.89	0.48	0.13	0.17	−0.39	−1.29
$\hat{\lambda}_Y$	−1.01	−0.23	0.10	0.55	0.62	−0.03
	Association to proper signal					
$\hat{\lambda}_{HX}$	−1.46	−1.28	−0.77	0.12	1.04	2.35
$\hat{\lambda}_{LY}$	−0.65	−0.61	−0.39	0.03	0.49	1.13
	Association to opposite signal					
$\hat{\lambda}_{HY}$	0.29	0.26	0.07	−0.06	−0.37	−0.19
$\hat{\lambda}_{LX}$	0.07	−0.06	0.00	−0.10	−0.02	0.10
	Response-response association ($\hat{\lambda}_{XY}$)					
Y 1	1.04	−0.56	−0.81	0.09	−0.03	0.27
Y 2	−0.36	−0.24	0.20	0.28	−0.10	0.22
Y 3	−0.34	−0.16	−0.15	0.25	0.39	0.01
Y 4	0.12	0.24	0.52	−0.28	−0.18	−0.42
Y 5	−0.23	0.28	0.21	−0.27	0.19	−0.17
Y 6	−0.23	0.44	0.03	−0.07	−0.27	0.09
	Interaction with XL ($\hat{\lambda}_{LXY}$)					
Y 1	−0.27	−0.27	0.25	0.27	0.01	0.01
Y 2	−0.30	−0.03	0.04	−0.17	0.09	0.36
Y 3	−0.25	0.09	−0.12	0.01	0.35	−0.08
Y 4	−0.17	0.17	0.08	−0.17	0.05	0.04
Y 5	0.22	0.13	−0.13	0.14	−0.20	−0.16
Y 6	0.76	−0.08	−0.11	−0.08	−0.30	−0.18

Although they are presented in Table 6.4, the estimates of λ_{LXY} are more complicated and do not warrant the space for interpretation here. Generally speaking, one approaches them by looking at how the XY relationship interacts with L. Much of this analysis depends on how one explains λ_{XY}. To extract the interaction pattern, one may wish to combine $\hat{\lambda}_{XY}$ and $\hat{\lambda}_{LXY}$, making two XY tables, one for $L = a$ and one for $L = p$.

The results to this point leave the analysis truncated. In a real treatment of these data, one would relate the model and its parameter estimates to the properties of the visual system. That analysis, in turn, would feed back and suggest new models to test and parameters to examine. This book is not the place to follow that track, however.

The observant reader may have noticed that except in the qualitative interpretation of the $\hat{\lambda}$'s, no use has been made of the ordering of the responses—for example, of the fact that the response $X = 2$ lies between $X = 1$ and $X = 3$. Of course, using this information can add power to one's analysis, but an explicit model for ordered association is required. Such models are discussed in Chapters 11 and 13. However, for some purposes, these detailed models do not improve the analysis. They require specific assumptions about the form that the association takes. These assumptions can be at odds with the data and so interfere with the tests. For the type of general questions addressed here, simple association models are at least as useful. In any case, the use of the ordered models with the current data involves the particulars of a signal-detection analysis to a degree that is inappropriate for the present discussion. An application using both types of model is given by Wickens & Olzak (in press).

6.5.   DECOMPOSITION OF MODELS

As Section 6.3 described, the absent links in a graphical model correspond to assertions that those factors are fundamentally unrelated. For most graphs, these assertions are equivalent to hypotheses of conditional independence. In the detection example, consider the graph of the model that allowed response association to both signals:

The lack of a connection between X and Y in this figure implies that $X \perp\!\!\!\perp Y|HL$. When more links are missing, the graphical model is equivalent to several conditional-independence hypotheses, one for each absent link. For example, a test of the detectable-signals model, which has the diagram

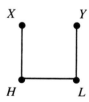

jointly assesses conditional independence involving H and Y, L and X, and X and Y. Deciding that a graphical model fits a set of data amounts to the joint retention of all the conditional-independence hypotheses implied by its missing links. Conversely, the failure of a graphical model to fit can be attributed to conditional dependence in one or more of the links.

An attractive consequence of this analysis is the division of the test statistic for the composite model into portions associated with each of the links. This procedure applies primarily to graphical models, for which the links can be unambiguously defined, and is one of the reasons why these models are useful. At first thought, one might suspect that this decomposition combines the tests of conditional independence for each of the missing links, with the remaining factors serving as the context of the tests. For example, with the detectable-signals model in the graph just above, these tests are $H \perp\!\!\!\perp Y|LX$, $L \perp\!\!\!\perp X|HY$, and $X \perp\!\!\!\perp Y|HL$. However, the additive partition is not quite so simple, since the graphical models sometimes make stronger assertions and some of the tests of conditional independence have more general contexts. Before returning to the analysis of the detectable-signals model, a simpler example is helpful.

The simplest case where decomposition is possible is in a three-way table. Consider the graduate admission example from Section 3.12 (Table 3.2). The three factors are department, D, sex of applicant, S, and acceptance to school, A. The model of complete independence, $[D][S][A]$, is easily rejected, with $G^2(4) = 58.98$. This model is the starting point for the decomposition and is graphically represented by

The failure of complete independence may involve any of the three absent links in this graph. As will be shown, a minimum condition for complete three-way independence is that two pairs of factors be completely independent of each other and that the third pair be conditionally independent given the other factors. Thus, the model $[S][D][A]$ jointly implies that $S \perp\!\!\!\perp D$, $A \perp\!\!\!\perp D$, and $A \perp\!\!\!\perp S|D$. The first two of these hypotheses are tested in two-way tables, the last in the full table. Failure of any of these hypotheses leads to failure of the composite model. To put it another way, a test of the composite model combines these three tests. Both the values of G^2 and their degrees of freedom add to that of the full model, as shown by the test statistics in Table 6.5. If the tests are run with X^2 the summation is not exact, although one's conclusions are generally the same.

Symbolically, one can write this combination of tests as

$$[S][D][A] \equiv (S \perp\!\!\!\perp D) \cap (A \perp\!\!\!\perp D) \cap (A \perp\!\!\!\perp S|D) \tag{6.3}$$

The symbol $\equiv$, which relates the composite model on the left to the conditional-independence hypotheses on the right, may be read "is equivalent to," and since all three of the independence model on the right-hand side must hold, their combination is indicated by the intersection symbol $\cap$, which may be read "and." Strictly, the set of all possible tables that exactly satisfy complete independence is the intersection of the set of tables for which $S \perp\!\!\!\perp D$, the set for which

TABLE 6.5
Additive Decomposition of Independence for the
Graduate Admission Example

| Hypothesis | Tested by | | G^2 | X^2 | df |
	Model	Table			
$S \perp\!\!\!\perp D$	$[S][D]$	SD	24.98	23.90	1
$A \perp\!\!\!\perp D$	$[A][D]$	AD	33.83	33.61	1
$S \perp\!\!\!\perp A|D$	$[SD][AD]$	SDA	0.17	0.16	2
	$[S][D][A]$	SDA	58.98	63.51	4

$A \perp\!\!\!\perp D$, and the set for which $A \perp\!\!\!\perp S|D$. However, this set description is not particularly important in the interpretation of Equation 6.3.†

The decomposition in Equation 6.3 is not unique. There are actually three ways to partition G^2 for three-way independence. These differ in which two pairs of factors are tested for full independence:

$$[S][D][A] \equiv (S \perp\!\!\!\perp D) \cap (A \perp\!\!\!\perp D) \cap (A \perp\!\!\!\perp S|D)$$

$$\equiv (S \perp\!\!\!\perp D) \cap (A \perp\!\!\!\perp S) \cap (A \perp\!\!\!\perp D|S)$$

$$\equiv (A \perp\!\!\!\perp S) \cap (A \perp\!\!\!\perp D) \cap (S \perp\!\!\!\perp D|A)$$

Not all these decompositions are meaningful in a particular situation. For the graduate admission data, the first row is most consistent with the acceptance process. Neither the conditional-independence hypothesis $S \perp\!\!\!\perp D|A$ nor $A \perp\!\!\!\perp D|S$ makes much sense here. Acceptance to graduate school follows application rather than precedes it, so the SD relationship cannot be conditioned on A, which rules out $S \perp\!\!\!\perp D|A$. The model $A \perp\!\!\!\perp D|S$ also lacks a simple interpretation, unless perhaps acceptance quotas are assigned to departments separately by sex. Accordingly, one is directed to the first of the three decompositions.

In formulating rules for partitioning a model, the use of graphs is very helpful. The basic principle is to add one link at a time, dividing the original model into a test of conditional independence and a further model. Consider the model $[S][D][A]$ and suppose that one concentrates first on the SD link. The complete independence model is the intersection of a test of this link and the balance of the

---

†More algebraic treatments of model decomposition are given by Goodman (1970, 1971), Bishop, Fienberg, & Holland (1975, Section 4.6), Reynolds (1977, Section 6.6). The graphical emphasis here derives largely from Edwards & Kreiner (1983). The decomposition of all graphical models with 5 or fewer factors is given by Darroch, Lauritzen, & Speed (1980).

graph with that link included. Temporarily indicate the link to be tested by a dotted line. Graphically the model decomposes into one graph with a marked link and another graph with that link filled in. The first term represents a test for *SD* association, the second term is a test of the other parts of the original model.

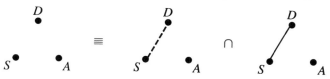

The hypothesis marked by the dotted line can be simplified. If factor *A* is unrelated to *S* and *D*, as that part of the picture shows, then it has no influence on a test of the *SD* link. So it is dropped from the picture, leaving

Finally, a test of a link is the same as fitting a model without that link, so dropping the dotted link returns to the normal graphical notation:

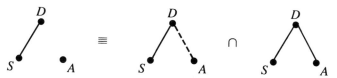

In symbolic form, this decomposition is

$$[S][D][A] \equiv (S \perp\!\!\!\perp D) \cap [SD][A] \qquad (6.4)$$

The right-hand model here is still composite (it lacks two links), so the decomposition process is repeated. By concentrating on a test of the *DA* linkage, the model [SD][A] is divided into

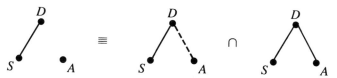

Again, the first term on the right can be simplified. The link that attaches *S* to *D* is not germane to the *AD* test, since it connects to only one of the tested members and is not a mediating path for the association (remember the rules for collapsing in Section 5.11). It is dropped from the picture, leaving

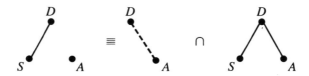

The second model on the right is a conditional-independence hypothesis, so this breakdown is

$$[SD][A] \equiv (A \perp\!\!\!\perp D) \cap (S \perp\!\!\!\perp A|D) \tag{6.5}$$

The graphs on the right lack only single links, so no further decomposition is possible. By combining Equations 6.4 and 6.5, the full breakdown in Equation 6.3 is produced.

This procedure is readily formalized. Start with the graph of a model, and repeat the following three steps either as far as desired or until no more divisions are possible:

1. Select a pair of factors that are unconnected in the graph (subject to the restriction noted below).
2. Decompose the model into the intersection of a test of the missing link and the model that results when the link is filled in.
3. Convert the test of the link to a conditional-independence hypothesis by deleting any factors that are not on direct paths connecting the tested factors.

If the residual model formed in step 2 has more than one missing link, then the steps can be repeated. Otherwise the residual model is already a conditional-independence hypothesis, and decomposition is complete.

One restriction must be added to these rules, because certain graphical models cannot be decomposed. A model that contains a closed path of more than three steps without cross-connection does not reduce to conditional-independence hypotheses. The simplest such graph is a four-step loop:

This model cannot be decomposed further. Thus, when choosing a link in step 1, one should either be sure that such graphs are not produced or be prepared to stop with that step. Squares or larger loops that are cross-linked to make triangles are not a problem; for example, the graph is an appropriate depiction of the conditional independence of two corner factors.

As an illustration of these rules, consider the detectable signals model again. This model is described by the graph

In the first step of the procedure, either of the absent links *HY* or *LX* can be chosen. Choice of the *XY* link stops the decomposition process, since adding it produces a square. If *HY* is chosen, step 2 gives

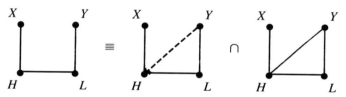

Factor *X* is irrelevant to the *HY* test as diagramed, but *L* is not (it is connected to both *H* and *Y*). The resulting test is conducted in a three-way table, and

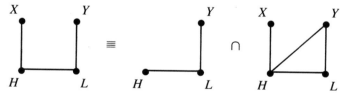

The next cycle can be based on either of the remaining links, *LX* or *XY*. Since *HY* was chosen in the first cycle, selection of *LX* next is more symmetric. The decomposition based on this link is

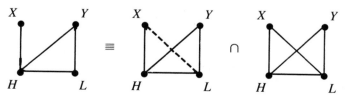

Again, one factor is not needed for the conditional-independence test, and Y is dropped from the test of the XL link:

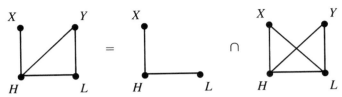

The final graph lacks only one edge, so it is a conditional-independence hypothesis and the process is complete. Combining these two steps in symbolic form gives the full decomposition,

$$[HL][HX][LY] \equiv (H \perp\!\!\!\perp Y|L) \cap (L \perp\!\!\!\perp X|H) \cap (X \perp\!\!\!\perp Y|HL)$$

Tests of these hypotheses are shown in Table 6.6. Exact additivity is compromised here because a marginal zero alters the degrees of freedom for the model $[HLX][HLY]$ (it would be 100 in a complete table). Nevertheless, the three hypotheses closely partition the fit of the detectable-signals model.

In closing this discussion, a pair of warnings should be noted. Although the analysis-of-variance-like additive partitions shown in Tables 6.5 and 6.6 are attractive, they are only as valuable as their tests are meaningful. For example, no considerations of additivity can improve the two breakdowns of the graduate-admission data that are inconsistent with the admission process. Nor is the existence of the additive decomposition a reason to confine oneself to graphical models if a more profitable analysis can be made using nongraphical models, nor does it say that models that are not part of an additive decomposition are in any way bad. Second, one need not test every link in the graph. Some links are not interesting. In the advertisement evaluation example in Section 6.3 (Diagram 6.2), the link between the treatment condition and, say, sex (factors T and S) represents only accidents of random sampling and is not a hypothesis one is compelled to test. Indeed, for an experiment such as that one, where one factor

TABLE 6.6
Additive Decomposition of the Detectable-signals Model

Hypothesis	Tested by		G^2	df
	Model	Table		
$H \perp\!\!\!\perp Y\|L$	$[HL][LY]$	HLY	134.81	10
$L \perp\!\!\!\perp X\|H$	$[HL][HX]$	HLX	19.49	10
$X \perp\!\!\!\perp Y\|HL$	$[HLX][HLY]$	$HLXY$	221.43	95
	$[HL][HX][LY]$	$HLXY$	375.72	120

(choice, C) is of primary interest, the predictor-outcome analysis described in the next chapter is usually more productive than a graphical decomposition.

PROBLEMS

Note: Chapters 6, 7, and 8 concern ways of approaching a complex set of data. The best exercise here is to take a set of data and work with it. Some problems of this sort are given below, but by far the best set of data is a familiar one. Think of an investigation that involves at least 4 cross-classified factors in a field you know. Propose at least three or four hypotheses to be tested. Describe the subtables and models that these tests need. If you have data and a computer, run the tests and analyze them. It is a good idea to work on this problem with one or more other people, so you can discuss the hypotheses and argue about the tests. Remember, there is more than one way to test some hypotheses. Continue working with these examples in Chapters 7 and 8.

6.1. Suppose that one wished to test for the presence of any three-way associations in the signal-detection data.
a. What test simultaneously examines all three-way terms?
b. If the result of this test is deemed significant, one might decide to test the individual three-way terms. How is this done? Be sure to control for post-hoc errors.
c. 𝒞. Run the tests on the data in Table 6.2.

6.2. 𝒞. The data in Table 6.7 were collected from a different subject in the same

TABLE 6.7
Data from a Different Subject in the Same Experiment as Table 6.2

		$H = n$						$H = s$					
		$X = 1$	2	3	4	5	6	1	2	3	4	5	6
$L = n$	$Y = 1$	271	8	25	16	4	0	101	6	23	41	43	102
	2	28	2	6	5	0	0	7	2	1	6	6	16
	3	41	5	6	3	1	0	11	0	5	6	13	19
	4	26	5	4	5	0	1	10	1	1	10	8	17
	5	14	1	6	2	3	0	9	3	2	6	6	6
	6	4	1	4	2	1	0	2	2	1	3	3	2
$L = s$	$Y = 1$	62	3	7	2	2	0	20	2	12	15	19	43
	2	10	3	2	3	1	0	0	2	3	3	1	12
	3	28	1	3	5	3	0	7	1	4	4	6	34
	4	23	11	7	5	2	0	13	1	3	4	12	36
	5	50	11	14	4	6	0	18	3	10	10	14	25
	6	123	33	36	24	13	3	48	8	21	23	19	44

psychophysical experiment discussed in this chapter. Analyze these data, using the same logic that was employed in this chapter.

a. Are HX and LY links present?

b. Are there HY and LX links? Test both in the presence of an XY association and its absence.

c. Is there an XY association?

d. Are there higher-order associations?

6.3. Homogeneity of the observations in data such as in the signal-detection example is always a concern. For example, the subject's performance may improve over the course of an experiment. How would you reclassify the data and analyze them to detect such effects?

6.4. A researcher is studying the effects of family interaction patterns on child pathology. The subject population consists of a group of families having a child with a behavior disorder. These families serve as units ("subjects") in the analysis. When referred to the clinic, each family is classified according to the diagnosis of the child into one of two categories (factor D, levels d_1 and d_2). The investigator has no control over the referral, hence over the size of these samples. The families are also classified as to whether they contain both natural parents, one parent and one step-parent, or a single parent only (factor P, levels "both", "step", and "single"). At the time that the child enters treatment (but after the diagnosis is made), the interaction pattern in the family is accessed. A 5 minute conversation among the family members is recorded and rated by trained raters. Two classification are obtained. One indicates the amount of aggressive exchange in the conversation (factor A, levels "low," "medium," and "high"). The other indicates the frequency of unconventional interaction patterns or bizarre speech elements in the conversation (factor U, same levels as A).

a. What frequency models can appropriately be fitted to the four-way $DPAU$ table of data? Explain, but do not list them all.

b. How would you test the following questions?

    i. Is there a relationship between the diagnosis category and the aggressiveness rating?

    ii. Is there a relationship between the diagnosis category and the unconventionality rating?

    iii. Does the diagnosis-aggressiveness relationship in (i) interact with family composition?

    iv. Is there a simple association between the aggressiveness and the unconventionality ratings?

c. Suppose that a non-null effect is found in parts b(i) and b(ii), above. This association makes the researcher wonder whether any effects found by the test in b(iv) are a consequence of differences in diagnosis category. Is this a plausible reason for concern (statistically speaking)? Explain how to test for AU association that exceeds that explicable by diagnosis differences. Is there any association that cannot be explained by the diagnosis and family composition differences, taken together?

d. The family composition factor is a bother, and the researcher wishes that it would go away. Of course, it could be removed from the analysis by collapsing over it.

   i. What are the advantages and disadvantages of collapsing the table in this way?

   ii. What properties must the data have to let this factor be eliminated without altering any other findings?

6.5 ℰ. Consider the data in Tables 6.1 and 6.7. One important set of questions concerns the consistency of the two subjects. Run appropriate tests for the following questions:

a. Does the model developed in Section 6.3 apply to both sets of data, using the same parameters?

b. Does the model developed in Section 6.3 apply to both sets of data, using different parameters?

c. Do the two subjects use the categories of X and Y with different frequencies?

d. Are there other differences between the subjects than those tested by (c)?

6.6. Which of the following models are graphical?

a. $[AB][C][D]$

b. $[AB][AC][BD][CD]$

c. $[AB][AC][BC][CD]$

d. $[AB][BCD]$

e. $[ABC][BCD]$

f. $[ABC][BCD][AB]$

g. $[ABCD]$

6.7. Two groups of college students are obtained, one containing 20 female students and the other containing 30 males (factor S). Each subject is given a test that classifies her or him as left-brain dominant or right-brain dominant (factor D). The subjects are then given a spatial-skill task to solve and are classified as succeeding or failing (factor T). Which of the following are valid decompositions of the model $[S][D][T]$? Which is most consistent with the design?

a. $(S \perp\!\!\!\perp D) \cap (D \perp\!\!\!\perp T) \cap (S \perp\!\!\!\perp T)$

b. $(S \perp\!\!\!\perp D) \cap (D \perp\!\!\!\perp T|S) \cap (S \perp\!\!\!\perp T|D)$

c. $(S \perp\!\!\!\perp T) \cap (D \perp\!\!\!\perp T) \cap (S \perp\!\!\!\perp D|T)$

d. $(S \perp\!\!\!\perp D) \cap (D \perp\!\!\!\perp T) \cap (S \perp\!\!\!\perp T|D)$

6.8. Show that for the psychophysical data

$$[HL][X][Y] \equiv (H \perp\!\!\!\perp X) \cap (L \perp\!\!\!\perp Y) \cap [HL][HX][LY]$$

How would the summary in Table 6.6 be modified to include these results?

6.9. Devise a sensible decomposition of the model $[D][P][A][U]$ in Problem 6.4.

6.10. Which of the models in Problem 6.6 can be interpreted in conditional-independence terms?

6.11. Draw graphs for the following models and reduce them to conditional-independence hypotheses:

a. [ABC][AD]

b. [AB][AC][AD]

c. [AB][AC][BD]

7

Predictor–Outcome Models

In many investigations, one's principal interest is in the way that one factor is influenced by several other factors. For example, one can ask how a set of precursor conditions leads a subject to remember one word and to forget another, how a collection of demographic and opinion characteristics relates to a person's choice of a particular product or vote for a particular candidate, and so on. The notable thing about these situations is that only the influences on a single factor—called here the *outcome factor*—are important. Relationships among the other factors—the *predictors*—are of less interest.

7.1. PREDICTOR-OUTCOME LOGIC

Prediction situations result from many different designs. The simplest occurs when only one factor is sampled, with the values of the others being determined by the investigator. For example, an experimenter may randomly assign subjects to a factorial combination of instruction conditions, and then look at how these predictors influence the subject's solution to a problem. In such a design, all associations except those to the final factor are part of the experimental design. In other studies, the predictor-outcome logic is not intrinsic. Even when all factors are sampled, the investigator may decide to treat one factor as the outcome and the others as predictors. A political poll is a nice example. Although the designer of the sampling procedure has no control over, say, the number of Democrats or supporters of gun control legislation in the sample, these factors can still be viewed as predictors of voting preference. This type of organization is particularly obvious when the predictors are measured before the outcome classification is determined.

Of course, many investigations cannot be put into predictor-outcome terms. For example, the psychophysical study in Chapter 6 involves two response factors (X and Y) that are potentially associated. However, many investigations do have a single outcome factor, and even in cases where the predictor-outcome structure is not part of the original design it can be useful as a way to organize one's approach to a problem. The big advantage of working with a single outcome factor is that one does not need to worry about the relationships among the predictors. By doing so, the set of potential models for the data is greatly reduced, with a concomitant simplification of interpretation.

One might be tempted to speak of the predictors as *independent variables* and to call the outcome factor a *dependent variable*. However, although these terms imply a predictor-outcome structure, they refer to characteristics of the experimental design. It is preferable to keep them for that use. As the poll example shows, predictor-outcome logic applies to situations where none of the factors are independent by design. In some sources, the terms *explanatory variable* (or *factor*) and *response variable* (*factor*) are used instead of *predictor* and *outcome*.

Speaking abstractly, suppose that categorizations A, B, C, and D are used to predict the categorization Y. If one is concerned only with the way that these predictors influence Y, the relationships among the predictors are irrelevant. These relationships are not random characteristics from the predictor-outcome viewpoint, and they should be chosen to match the observed relationships. In effect, the analysis is conditioned on the observed pattern of the predictors. Accordingly, every model that is investigated includes the multiway association among all the predictors, embodied in the parameters λ_A, λ_B, . . ., λ_{ABCD} and symbolized by the term [ABCD] in the bracketed specification of the model. This reasoning is analogous to that which demands that all the associations of a set of manipulated factors be included in a model, except that here the justification is the logic of the analysis rather than the probabilistic basis of the model.

It is worth reemphasizing why the parameters that express relationships among the predictors should appear, even when a simpler model fits equally well. Even if the models [ABY][CY][DY] and [ABCD][ABY][CY][DY] fit a set of data equally well, the latter model should be used. When the full [ABCD] term is not included, the degrees of freedom and the variation associated with the differences among A, B, C, and D are mixed with those describing the relationship of these factors to Y. This muddling of effects alters the tests of relationships to Y and can give these tests either a positive or a negative bias. Including all *ABCD* associations in every tested model removes these associations from tests involving Y. In fact, as is shown more explicitly in Section 7.3, the parameters associated with any *ABCD* relationship effectively vanish from many of these inferences. A related reason for using the larger model involves communication of the research. Composite results are always more difficult to comprehend and to explain to someone else. The predictor-outcome logic makes the analysis clearer. By failing to include all the predictors, one defeats this logical structure.

In summary, in a predictor-outcome analysis the simplest valid model has the form [all predictors][outcome], for example, [ABCD][Y]. This model represents independence of the outcome factor from the predictors, $Y \perp\!\!\!\perp ABCD$. Were this model to fit, there would be little more to say. If it fails, then additional parameters are necessary to describe the way in which the predictors influence the outcome.

The predictor-outcome procedure developed here is analogous to the use of multiple regression with continuous (or at least ordinal) variables. In multiple regression, one has a single outcome variable Y and a set of predictors X_1, X_2, . . ., X_p, and one wants to examine the parameters of an underlying linear model

$$Y = \beta_0 + \beta_1 X_1 + \beta_2 X_2 + \ . \ . \ . \ + \beta_p x_p + \text{error}$$

The error component in this model is (usually) a normally distributed random quantity that spreads the individual scores away from the expected value of Y implied by the values of $X_1, X_2, \ . \ . \ ., X_p$. The frequency models differ from this formulation in two respects. First, a linear model describes the logarithm of the expected frequencies instead of the frequencies themselves. Second, the random character is expressed by a sampling model such as those discussed in Section 4.2 instead of an added error. However, most of the testing logic with which one may be familiar from multiple regression theory carries over to the predictor-outcome analysis of frequency models. One further difference should be noted. In multiple regression, the ordered nature of the variables makes any combination of them have a particular functional form; for example, the product $X_i X_j$ defines a multiplicative interaction. Because most such functions are unrealistic, one usually does not look systematically at all combinations of variables. With the unordered categorization of frequency tables (as with the analysis of variance), it is more common to examine all the potential higher-order associations. These associations are represented in the frequency analysis by parameters such as λ_{ABY} or λ_{ABCY} that relate the outcome factor to more than one predictor.

The predictor-outcome logic makes one think of the outcome factor as if it had a separate probability distribution for each combination of the predictors. One speaks of the conditional probability of outcome y_k given the prediction values a_i and b_j—the probability $\pi_{k|ij}$ in the notation of Chapter 4—rather than the unconditional probability of a cell, π_{ijk}. One does this even when, as with the political poll, the data are not properly described by a product-multinomial rule. It is natural to think of the conditional probability of candidate preference in the subpopulation of, say, Democrats under 40, even if these attributes were sampled in the poll. These conditional distributions are easier to comprehend. The simplicity of this representation is characteristic of the gains that one gets from adopting the predictor-outcome point of view.

7.2. DICHOTOMOUS OUTCOME FACTORS—
THE LOGIT

An important simplification of the form of a predictor-outcome model is possible when the outcome is dichotomous. Consider such a factor, Y. Because Y is dichotomous, the probabilities of its two levels are redundant:

$$P(y_2|\text{predictors}) = 1 - P(y_1|\text{predictors})$$

One need not analyze both of these probabilities—either one of them is sufficient. Alternatively, they can be combined in a single measure. The latter course is more useful: one recasts the model from one that describes log μ to one that describes another quantity known as the logit. As the next section shows, models for the logit are simpler than the log-frequency models.

The condensation of the two levels of Y starts by expressing the probabilities as the relative odds, defined in Section 2.6. The *odds* of the event y_1 are given by the ratio

$$\text{odds}_Y = \frac{P(y_1)}{1 - P(y_1)} = \frac{P(y_1)}{P(y_2)}$$

This ratio is near zero when y_1 is unlikely, equals 1 when $P(y_1) = \frac{1}{2}$, and is large when y_1 is more likely than not. Just as log μ is often a better choice for a model than μ, the logarithm of the odds, known as the *logit*, is at least as easy to interpret as the odds. Denote the logit by η:

$$\eta = \log(\text{odds}_Y) = \log \frac{P(y_1)}{1 - P(y_1)} \qquad (7.1)$$

Then $\eta = 0$ when $P(y_1) = \frac{1}{2}$ (i.e., when $\text{odds}_Y = 1$), $\eta > 0$ when $P(y_1) > \frac{1}{2}$, and $\eta < 0$ when $P(y_1) < \frac{1}{2}$. The logit is symmetric about zero, in the sense that a given sized deviation of $P(y_1)$ from $\frac{1}{2}$ yields the same absolute value of η. For example, if $P(y_1) = 0.3$, then the odds are 0.429 and $\eta = -0.847$, while if $P(y_1) = 0.7$, then the odds are 2.333 and $\eta = 0.847$. The symmetry of the logit makes it a better candidate for modeling than the unmodified odds.

A natural estimator of the logit from data is obtained by substituting estimates of $P(y_1)$ into Equation 7.1. If there are x_1 observations of y_1 in n trials, this estimate is

$$\hat{\eta} = \log \frac{x_1/n}{(n - x_1)/n} = \log \frac{x_1}{n - x_1} \qquad (7.2)$$

Unfortunately, when $\eta \neq 0$, this estimate is biased, that is, $E(\hat{\eta}) \neq \eta$. Moreover, it is undefined when $x_1 = 0$ or $x_1 = n$. An estimator that solves both problems adds $\frac{1}{2}$ to each frequency:

$$\hat{\eta}_c = \log \frac{x_1 + \frac{1}{2}}{n - x_1 + \frac{1}{2}} \qquad (7.3)$$

(Anscombe, 1956; Haldane, 1955; see Gart & Zweifel, 1967). Using Equation 7.3 instead of Equation 7.2 reduces the extreme values of $\hat{\eta}$ slightly and avoids the nasty surprises that occur when all the observed events happen to be of one type. For large samples, there is little difference between the two estimators, unless $P(y_1)$ is very near 0 or 1. However, the problem of bias is more complicated when one is interested in the parameters of a model for logits rather than in the logits themselves. The appropriate "correction" apparently depends on the model that is fitted and the amount of data used (Gart, Pettigrew, & Thomas, 1985). To avoid these complications, Equation 7.2 is used to estimate the logit in any model calculation.

In a multiway table, the probabilities that go into the logit are conditioned on a set of predictors. So, for predictors A and B of Y, the logit for the combination $a_i b_j$ is

$$\eta_{ij} = \log \frac{P(y_1 | a_i b_j)}{1 - P(y_1 | a_i b_j)} \qquad (7.4)$$

The logit is closely related to the idea of association. Consider a 2×2 table, and let η_1 and η_2 be the logits in the two rows. The magnitude of association in the table is measured by the odds ratio,

$$\alpha = \frac{\mu_{11} \mu_{22}}{\mu_{12} \mu_{21}}$$

Taking the logarithm gives

$$\log \alpha = \log \frac{\mu_{11}}{\mu_{12}} - \log \frac{\mu_{21}}{\mu_{22}} = \eta_1 - \eta_2$$

Thus, the difference between the logits is a direct measure of association.

7.3. LOGIT MODELS

The link between association and the difference in logits suggests describing the relationship among several populations by some form of logit model. Where the model says that the logits in two conditions are the same, those conditions are homogeneous; where they differ, there is an association between the conditions and the outcome categorization. In particular, suppose that one has two predictors, A and B, and a binary outcome classification Y, with logits defined as in Equation 7.4. The variation in the logit with two predictors is readily described by a saturated linear model,

$$\eta_{ij} = \nu + \nu_{A(i)} + \nu_{B(j)} + \nu_{AB(ij)} \qquad (7.5)$$

Identification constraints are necessary to complete this model. These are the same as for the log-frequency models: commonly, each parameter sums to zero over any of its subscripts.

Model 7.5 is a saturated model, with enough parameters to give any value to each of the ab logits. Unsaturated models are formed by dropping parameters from the saturated version. Thus, a model that allows both factors A and B to influence Y but does not let them interact is

$$\eta_{ij} = \nu + \nu_{A(i)} + \nu_{B(j)} \tag{7.6}$$

The simplest logit model, which corresponds to homogeneity of all the conditions, is

$$\eta_{ij} = \nu \tag{7.7}$$

Linear models for the logit are closely related to linear model for log μ. In fact, their predictions are identical and the parameters of the logit model are multiples of the log-frequency model's parameters. To see the connection, first note that for a dichotomous classification the difference in log frequency equals the logit. Consider the case of two predictors. Multiplication of the numerator and denominator of the definition of the logit (Equation 7.4) by x_{ij+} converts the probabilities into expected frequencies:

$$\eta_{ij} = \log \frac{x_{ij+}P(y_1|a_ib_j)}{x_{ij+}[1 - P(y_1|a_ib_j)]}$$

$$= \log \frac{\mu_{ij1}}{\mu_{ij2}} = \log \mu_{ij1} - \log \mu_{ij2}$$

The three-way table is represented by a saturated log-frequency model

$$\log \mu_{ijk} = \lambda + \lambda_{A(i)} + \lambda_{B(j)} + \lambda_{Y(k)} + \lambda_{AB(ij)} + \lambda_{AY(ik)}$$
$$+ \lambda_{BY(jk)} + \lambda_{ABY(ijk)} \tag{7.8}$$

Substituting this model into the equation for η_{ij} gives

$$\eta_{ij} = \log \mu_{ij1} - \log \mu_{ij2}$$
$$= \lambda + \lambda_{A(i)} + \lambda_{B(j)} + \lambda_{Y(1)} + \lambda_{AB(ij)} + \lambda_{AY(i1)} + \lambda_{BY(j1)} + \lambda_{ABY(ij1)}$$
$$- (\lambda + \lambda_{A(i)} + \lambda_{B(j)} + \lambda_{Y(2)} + \lambda_{AB(ij)} + \lambda_{AY(i2)}$$
$$+ \lambda_{BY(j2)} + \lambda_{ABY(ij2)})$$
$$= (\lambda_{Y(1)} - \lambda_{Y(2)}) + (\lambda_{AY(i1)} - \lambda_{AY(i2)}) + (\lambda_{BY(j1)} - \lambda_{BY(j2)})$$
$$+ (\lambda_{ABY(ij1)} - \lambda_{ABY(ij2)})$$

Any parameter that does not involve Y appears in both log μ_{ij1} and log μ_{ij2}, but with opposite sign. So it vanishes from η_{ij}. Because Y is dichotomous, the identification constraints on the λ's mean that each y_2 term is the negative of the corresponding y_1 term, $\lambda_{Y(2)} = -\lambda_{Y(1)}$, $\lambda_{AY(i2)} = -\lambda_{AY(i1)}$, etc. These substitutions give

$$\eta_{ij} = 2\lambda_{Y(1)} + 2\lambda_{AY(i1)} + 2\lambda_{BY(j1)} + 2\lambda_{ABY(ij1)}$$

Matching this equation to the linear model for η_{ij} (Equation 7.5) shows that

$$\nu = 2\lambda_{Y(1)}, \quad \nu_{A(i)} = 2\lambda_{AY(i1)}, \quad \nu_{B(j)} = 2\lambda_{BY(j1)},$$
$$\text{and} \quad \nu_{AB(ij)} = 2\lambda_{ABY(ij1)} \tag{7.9}$$

The same argument applies to estimates of the parameters, $\hat{\nu}$ and λ.

The parallel between logit and log-frequency models means that a linear logit model can be fitted using programs designed to work with log-linear models for μ. One constructs the corresponding log-frequency model, fits it, and then converts its parameters using Equations 7.9. Those parameters that do not involve the outcome factor Y do not enter the logit model at all.†

For unsaturated logit models, the same rules apply, except that certain of the ν's and λ's are zero. For example, the logit model without ν_{AB} (Equation 7.6) derives from a log-frequency model with $\lambda_{ABY} = 0$—the model $[AB][AY][BY]$ —and the constant logit model (Equation 7.7) is developed from the model $[AB][Y]$,

$$\log \mu_{ijk} = \lambda + \lambda_{A(i)} + \lambda_{B(j)} + \lambda_{Y(k)} + \lambda_{AB(ij)}$$

In each case, Equations 7.9 relate the parameters of the two models. In every case the log-frequency model contains the complete parameterization of the predictors, here those implied by the term $[AB]$.

The logit models contain no information that is not present in the original log-frequency model, for the ν's derive completely from the λ's. The logit models' value lies in their greater simplicity, which makes them easier to interpret. Not only does each term in the logit model have one fewer subscript than the corresponding λ, but also there are fewer terms. For example, the saturated logit model in Equation 7.5 contains half as many terms as the frequency model in Equation 7.8, although both describe the same data. For unsaturated models, the gain is even greater. Basically, this simplification is a consequence of the predictor-outcome organization: Using the logit frees the model from the relationships among the predictors.

As an example of the construction of a logit model, consider a sample of the data collected in interviews with 647 heroin addicts undergoing treatment in methadone maintenance programs (Anglin, McGlothlin, & Speckart, 1981).‡ Among the questions that were asked were the following:

- County of residence (factor C: urban, suburban, or rural)
- Socioeconomic status (SES; factor S: low or not low)

---

†The parameters of Equation 7.5 can also be estimated directly; see Cox (1970) and the least-squares methods in Sections 12.4 and 13.3. The direct methods allow logit models to be fitted when some of the predictors are numerical variables rather than categorizations.

‡I thank M. Douglas Anglin for the use of these data.

- Were both parents present in the home up to the time that the subject was 16 years old (factor P: yes or no)
- Age at time of first heroin use (factor F: age < 18, age ≥ 18)

The raw frequency table relating these factors is shown at the top of Table 7.1.

Suppose that one wishes to predict the age of first use (factor F) based on C, S, and P. Logits for F can be defined with either $P(<18)$ or $P(\geq 18)$ in the numerator. This choice determines what a positive logit means. For this example, define

$$\eta_{ijk} = \log \frac{P(<18|c_i s_j p_k)}{P(\geq 18|c_i s_j p_k)} \tag{7.10}$$

With this definition, positive values are associated with younger first use. Applying this transformation to the frequency data produces the table of logits in the bottom part of Table 7.1. The prevailing negative values in this table reflect the lower incidence of young first use.

Consider the model in which SES is a simple predictor and in which the county and the parents' presence interact:

$$\eta_{ijk} = \nu + \nu_{S(i)} + \nu_{C(j)} + \nu_{P(k)} + \nu_{CP(jk)} \tag{7.11}$$

TABLE 7.1
Results from a Survey of Heroin Users, with Derived Logits

Original Frequencies

			County					
			Urban		Suburban		Rural	
Parents	SES	First Use:	<18	≥18	<18	≥18	<18	≥18
Yes	Low		32	65	21	20	10	40
	Not low		34	97	14	28	8	23
No	Low		41	42	18	22	6	13
	Not low		41	45	3	13	1	10

Logits

		County		
Parents	SES	Urban	Suburban	Rural
Yes	Low	−0.709	0.049	−1.386
	Not low	−1.048	−0.693	−1.056
No	Low	−0.024	−0.201	−0.773
	Not low	−0.093	−1.466	−2.303

This model may have been suggested by previous theory or as the result of a systemic search—its origin is not important to the present discussion. To fit it, it is first converted to a log-frequency model. In this version, it includes parameters matching those in Equation 7.11 with F added to each one (i.e., λ_F, λ_{SF}, λ_{CF}, λ_{PF}, and λ_{CPF}) as well as a constant λ and seven terms relating the predictors S, C and P to one another (λ_S, λ_C, . . ., λ_{SCP}). In bracket notation, this model is $[CSP][SF][CPF]$. It adequately fits Table 7.1, with $G^2(5) = 6.21$ and $X^2(5) = 6.02$.

The parameters of the logit model are obtained by doubling those of the log-frequency model. Only parameters that involve the factor F are used. The estimates of λ_F are $\hat{\lambda}_{F(<18)} = -0.365$ and $\hat{\lambda}_{F(\geq 18)} = 0.365$. The first of these (first use age < 18) is used to get the logit parameter, since it was this category that appeared in the numerator of the logit (Equation 7.10). The estimate of ν is twice that of $\lambda_{F(<18)}$, so $\hat{\nu} = -0.730$. The association to SES is embodied in λ_{SF}, which is estimated to be

		<18	≥ 18
		\multicolumn{2}{c}{F}
S	low	0.086	-0.086
	not low	-0.086	0.086

Again the estimates for the <18 subjects are doubled, giving $\hat{\nu}_{S(low)} = 0.172$ and $\hat{\nu}_{S(not\ low)} = -0.172$. The positive value of $\hat{\nu}_{S(low)}$ indicates a tendency for a younger age of first use in the low-SES group. The complete set of parameter estimates is shown in Table 7.2. The last of these parameters, $\hat{\nu}_{CP}$, describes the interaction of C and P. Unlike the double-subscripted λ parameters, this parameter measures a true interaction in the analysis-of-variance sense, representing the modulation of the effect of one factor on F by the level of another factor. Frequently these interaction effects are easier to understand if they are combined with the simple associations. The net CP effect is described by the sum $\hat{\nu}_C + \hat{\nu}_P + \hat{\nu}_{CP}$,

		urban	suburban	rural
		\multicolumn{3}{c}{C}
P	yes	-0.15	0.42	-0.57
	no	0.67	0.14	-0.51

This table clearly shows the relatively older first use for the rural group and the interaction with the parents' presence in the urban and suburban cells.

As described in Section 5.4, standardization of the parameters by dividing them by their standard errors can be helpful. Since each $\hat{\nu}_X$ is twice the corresponding λ_{XY}, the size of the standard error also is double. Thus, the standard-

TABLE 7.2
Parameters of a Logit Model Fitted to Table 7.1

$\hat{\nu} = -0.73$

$\hat{\nu}_{S(low)} = 0.17$ $\hat{\nu}_{S(not\ low)} = -0.17$

$\hat{\nu}_{P(yes)} = -0.10$ $\hat{\nu}_{P(no)} = 0.10$

$\hat{\nu}_{C(urban)} = 0.26$ $\hat{\nu}_{C(suburban)} = 0.28$ $\hat{\nu}_{C(rural)} = -0.54$

$\hat{\nu}_{CP}$:

		C		
		Urban	Suburban	Rural
P	Yes	−0.31	0.24	0.07
	No	0.31	−0.24	−0.07

ized values of $\hat{\nu}_X$ and $\hat{\lambda}_{XY}$ are the same. The interpretation of these standardized values is unchanged.

7.4.   LOGITS FOR MULTILEVEL CATEGORIES

A single odds or a single logit cannot completely describe an outcome factor with more than two levels. When multilevel classification is present, more logits are needed. Each additional category requires another logit, so to completely describe a c-level categorization, $c - 1$ logits are needed. These should be selected to reflect the design. For example, suppose that one has data on a three-level categorization from an opinion poll, with categories *yes*, *no*, and *don't know*. Two logits are needed to represent the three categories. A natural choice is to treat the know/don't-know aspect of these data as one logit and the yes/no aspect as another:

$$\eta^{(know)} = \frac{P(\text{yes or no})}{P(\text{don't know})} \quad \text{and} \quad \eta^{(opinion)} = \frac{P(\text{yes})}{P(\text{no})} \tag{7.12}$$

The superscripts here differentiate the logits. In the full analysis, each logit also carries indices to designate the levels of the predictors.

The analysis of these multiple logits presents no new difficulties. One repeats the procedures that are used for a single logit several times. The separate analyses makes particularly good sense when, as in the poll example, the two logits describe different substantive points and may be fitted by different models. So, the analysis of $\eta^{(know)}$ tells how the presence or absence of an opinion varies over the predictors, and the analysis of $\eta^{(opinion)}$ tells how the opinion varies among those who express it. Where the outcome factor consists of an undifferentiated set of categories, the choice of logit definition is less obvious, and the logit approach may be less useful.†

Many different logits can be formed from a set of categories by picking one set as the positive event, whose probability appears in the numerator, and another set as the negative events that appear in the denominator. With four categories there are 25 ways to pick two nonempty sets, with five there are 90, and the number increases rapidly thereafter. Obviously, it is pointless to look at all the implied logits. Two considerations influence the appropriate choice. The first and more important is that the logits express meaningful questions about the study. One picks the logits to contrast interesting and meaningful sets of categories, not according to some arbitrary schema. Second, logits should be selected so that they are, to the extent possible, unrelated to one another.

To ensure that the logits capture nonredundant information from the outcome factor, they must satisfy several restrictions. These strictures are analogous to the rules for the decomposition of an analysis-of-variance effect into orthogonal contrasts. The first rule limits the number of logits that can be formed without redundancy. Just as a dichotomous category is represented by a single logit, a c-level categorization can support no more than $c - 1$ logits before all the information in the data is used up. Whenever a set of c or more logits is formed from c categories, at least one of them is a linear combination of others. Not every set of $c - 1$ logits is linearly independent, but any set of more than $c - 1$ surely overlaps.

The second rule forces each logit in the set to capture different information from the data. The set is selected so that any pair of categories is contrasted across the numerator and denominator of a logit exactly once. Before general rules for constructing such a set of logits are presented, consider two examples. The logits for the poll example just described (Equation 7.12) are an example of a breakdown that combines the data in two nonredundant tests. In contrast, a redundant pair of logits is

$$\eta^{(1)} = \frac{P(\text{yes})}{P(\text{no})} \quad \text{and} \quad \eta^{(2)} = \frac{P(\text{yes})}{P(\text{no}) + P(\text{undecided})}$$

Here $P(\text{yes})$ is contrasted with $P(\text{no})$ in both logits. Thus, any difference between these probabilities is reflected in both $\eta^{(1)}$ and $\eta^{(2)}$. Normally the set of logits in Equations 7.12 is easier to interpret and so is preferable to this one.

For a second example, consider some psychophysical data, similar to those in Chapter 6, in which a yes/no decision is recorded along with a high/low confi-

---

†Another approach to multilevel categorization treats the set of logits as a multivariate outcome and constructs a multivariate log-linear model for it. For a four-level category, one writes $\eta = [\eta^{(1)}, \eta^{(2)}, \eta^{(3)}]$, and then works with η. This procedure makes most sense when the univariate logits have little individual meaning. The multivariate approach is not developed here. Where the categories are ordered, models described in Chapter 13 can be used.

dence rating. The result is the four-level set of categories in the outcome factor: yes-high (*yh*), yes-low (*yl*), no-low (*nl*), and no-high (*nh*). These 4 categories determine 3 logits. Three sets of logits are shown in Table 7.3. The first scheme revolves around the yes/no distinction. One logit combines the two yes categories and compares them to the two no categories; the second and third ratios examine confidence ratings within these categories, as shown in the first part of the table. Other schemes are based on the ordering of the categories, which runs from a clear assertion of a signal by a *yh* response to definite denial by *nh*. The second set in Table 7.3 is of this type. The choice of which scheme to use (or whether another one is better) depends on the particular questions that one would like to answer. The first scheme is more appropriate if one's emphasis is on the yes/no decision, the second if the ordering is to be emphasized.

The third set of logits in Table 7.3 shows an unsatisfactory combination. Here each logit compares a category to all the others. In some ways, this scheme is natural and obvious. The 4 logits have a parallel structure, and their parameters are easy to estimate (each is double the corresponding λ parameter from an ordinary log-frequency model). Separately, each logit is completely acceptable—indeed, the first of these is the same as the first member of the second set—but in combination they are unsatisfactory. For one thing, there are too many of them. Selecting 3 logits from the 4 helps, but there are other problems. The logits still violate the rule that separates any pair of categories across a logit only once. For example, the *yh* and *yl* cells stand on opposite sides of both comparison 1 and comparison 2, so that both logits are influenced by this difference. Models for both sets of logits are likely to be retained or rejected together: their tests are not independent. Any set of 3 of these logits contains at least one such pair.

TABLE 7.3
Three Sets of Logits Applying to a Four-level Categorization

Logit Measures		Numerator	Denominator
First set			
1.	Yes responses	*yh, yl*	*nl, nh*
2.	High confidence given yes	*yh*	*yl*
3.	High confidence given no	*nh*	*nl*
Second set			
1.	*yh* responses	*yh*	*yl, nl, nh*
2.	*yl* given not *yh*	*yl*	*nl, nh*
3.	*nl* given *no*	*nl*	*nh*
Third set			
1.	Yes-high vs. others	*yh*	*yl, nl, nh*
2.	Yes-low vs. others	*yl*	*yh, nl, nh*
3.	No-low vs. others	*nl*	*yh, yl, nh*
4.	No-high vs. others	*nh*	*yh, yl, nl*

This type of contamination does not occur with the first two sets of logits in Tables 7.3. In these cases, any pair of groups is divided exactly once between the positive and the negative event. Consider the first set. Comparisons 2 and 3 each involve a contrast between categories that are pooled in comparison 1. Diagrammatically, the hierarchical nature of this division can be pictured as a tree

$$
— (1)\underset{(3)}{\overset{(2)}{<}}\begin{array}{l} -yh \\ -yl \\ -nh \\ -nl \end{array}
\qquad (7.13)
$$

The numbered nodes indicate logits, and the two branches going into the node are the categories in the numerator and the denominator of the logit. These categories are pooled when they participate in another logit nearer to the tree's root (the left-hand side). Similarly, the tree representing the second set of logits is

$$
— (1)\overset{(2)}{<}\ \overset{(3)}{<}\begin{array}{l} -nl \\ -nh \\ -yl \\ -yh \end{array}
\qquad (7.14)
$$

The relationship among the logits imposed by putting them into this type of tree is necessary for them to form a nonredundant set. If a tree cannot be drawn—as it cannot for the third set of logits in Table 7.3—the questions are not separate.

A complete decomposition of the categories in this way creates an exact partitioning of G^2 into parts associated with each of the logits. Each logit implies a table of frequencies in which the outcome factor is reduced to two levels by dropping or pooling categories. If the same predictor-outcome log-frequency model is fitted to each of these tables, the value of G^2 for a complete division sums to G^2 for that model in the original table. In this way, one may be able to localize an overall effect into one or two simple contrasts. A related partitioning is discussed in Section 11.1.

The use of independent tests is a good idea and helps to organize one's questions about an experiment, but it is not mandatory. The content of the investigation must drive the statistics, rather than the other way round. For one thing, there is never an obligation to examine all the independent logit models that can be formed. If fewer questions are interesting, then fewer logits are needed. For example, in the opinion poll, one might be interested only in developing an elaborate model for $\eta^{(\text{opinion})}$, and skip over a complex analysis of $\eta^{(\text{know})}$, particularly if most respondents express opinions. Second, in some cases the important a priori questions are not independent. Lack of independence should not prevent one from asking these questions. The failure of independence should be considered when the results are interpreted and one should ask oneself whether there are better ways to get at one's questions, but independence alone should not override the construction of meaningful logits.

7.5. SERIAL PREDICTOR-OUTCOME STAGES

In laying out the plan for an analysis, it is sometimes useful to employ a staged structure. One first postulates a causal ordering to the factors, and then uses this ordering to collapse the table or to adopt a predictor-outcome analysis. The analysis of relationships among a subset of the factors is carried out separately from the analysis that uses this subset to predict later factors.

The first step is to order the factors. Frequently, some factors logically precede others. Opinion in June precedes that in September; the demographics of a child's situation precede that child's actions as an adult; the manipulation of experimental conditions precedes the subjects' responses. For example, one might decide that the four classifications of the addicts (Table 7.1) could be ordered in influence, placing the county and SES first, the parental situation next, and the addiction age last. By using arrows to indicate the directions of influence, one gets the diagram

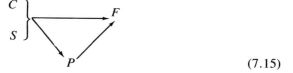

$$(7.15)$$

The organization of factors into ordered sequences in this way has received considerable scrutiny in the branch of multiple regression theory known as *path analysis* (e.g., Duncan, 1975). One can distinguish between *recurrent models*, for which all connections between factors consist of arrows that point in one direction only, and *nonrecurrent models*, in which the causal link between some of the factors is bidirectional. Except for the relationship between S and C, Diagram 7.15 shows a recurrent structure.

The advantage of constructing something like Diagram 7.15 is that it simplifies the range of tenable hypotheses and allows some collapsing of the table. One need not work with all four factors simultaneously, attempting to find a composite model, since the structure of the diagram justifies an analysis in three stages:

1. Study the relationship of county and SES in the CS table.
2. Study the relationship of these factors to P in the CSP table. Because the CS relationships have been treated in the first stage, a predictor-outcome analysis can be used, so that the CS term appears in every model.
3. Study the relationship of C, S, and P to F. Again, the predictor-outcome analysis is used, with C, S and P as predictors. This is the analysis in Section 7.2.

This staged procedure partitions the totality of effects into three comprehensible packages.

It is neither necessary to introduce the factors into a staged analysis one at a time, nor to make every factor dependent on those that have already been chosen. Consider six factors to which the following pattern can be assigned:

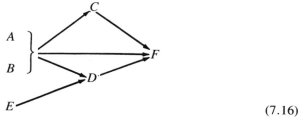

$$(7.16)$$

This figure suggests using A and B as predictors of C in the ABC table and the set $\{A,B,E\}$ as predictors of D in the $ABDE$ table. Factor F is examined in the $ABCDF$ table with predictors A, B, C, and D. At no time need the entire $ABCDEF$ table be examined, which is valuable if the total frequency is not great.

In this way, the magnitude of the interpretive task falling on the researcher is greatly reduced, since many useless models can be ignored. However, these analyses do not verify structures such as Diagrams 7.15 and 7.16. Although the failure of a model to fit indicates that a path has been omitted from one of these diagrams, a good fit does not show that a diagram is correct. Furthermore, neither result says anything about the causal relationships imputed to the factors. Instead, the assumption of a causal structure provides a way to let extrastatistical information influence the course of the analysis. A different researcher, starting with a different view of the process, could draw the arrows differently and come up with different interpretations of the same table of data. Such an occurrence is not a matter for statistical concern, reflecting, as it does, the multiplicity of potential explanations available in the world. Naturally, these differences of interpretation are often the occasion for nonstatistical arguments.

7.6.   GLOBAL MODELS FROM SERIAL STAGES

The procedures in the last section produce a nested series of models, each predicting one factor from several others. Factor A may predict B in one model, and these two factors predict C in another. Each model is proper in itself, although neither describes the entire set of data. The individual models must be combined to get a description of the complete table. The resultant model can be tested to give a composite measure of fit for the whole series of stages.

A composite model is constructed in three steps. First, the factors are divided into a set of predictors and a single outcome factor. Next, two models are fit, one to the set of predictors, the other in predictor-outcome form to the whole table. Call the first of these the *marginal model* and the second the *predictive model*. Finally, the two models are combined into the *composite model* by weighting the rows of the predictive model by the expected frequences in the marginal model.

Consider the addict data of Table 7.1. As discussed above (see Diagram 7.15), factors C, S, and P are viewed as predictors of F, completing the first step. In the second step, one model is fit to the three predictors and another model is used to predict F from them. Say that these models are $[CS][CP][SP]$ and $[CSP][CPF][SF]$, respectively. Both fits are satisfactory, with $G^2(2) = 3.19$ and $G^2(5) = 6.21$. Their expected frequencies are shown in the top panels of Table 7.4. To illustrate the third step, consider the low-SES, urban, no-parents group. The predictive model puts 32.07 of the 97 members of this group into the <18 category and 64.93 in the ≥ 18 category. These are proportions of 0.3306

TABLE 7.4
Formation of a Composite Model

Expected Frequencies $\hat{\mu}^{(M)}$ for the Marginal Model $[CS][CP][SP]$

		Low			Not Low		
P	S C	Urban	Suburb	Rural	Urban	Suburb	Rural
Yes		94.25	45.31	48.45	133.75	37.69	32.55
No		85.75	35.69	20.55	83.25	20.31	9.45

Expected Frequencies $\hat{\mu}^{(P)}$ for the Predictive Model $[CSP][CPF][SF]$

P	S	C F	Urban		Suburban		Rural	
			<18	≥ 18	<18	≥ 18	<18	≥ 18
Yes	Low		32.07	64.93	19.03	21.97	12.22	37.78
	Not low		33.93	97.07	15.97	26.03	5.78	25.22
No	Low		43.91	39.09	15.91	24.09	4.85	14.15
	Not low		38.09	47.91	5.09	10.91	2.15	8.85

Combination of Frequencies in Composite Model

$$\hat{\mu}^{(C)}_{ijkl} = \frac{\hat{\mu}^{(P)}_{ijkl}\hat{\mu}^{(M)}_{ijk}}{x_{ijk+}}$$

P	S	C F	Urban		Suburban		Rural	
			<18	≥ 18	<18	≥ 18	<18	≥ 18
Yes	Low		31.16	63.08	21.04	24.27	11.84	36.60
	Not low		34.64	99.11	14.33	23.36	6.07	26.49
No	Low		45.37	40.39	14.19	21.50	5.25	15.30
	Not low		36.87	46.38	6.47	13.84	1.84	7.60

and 0.6694. The composite model applies these proportions to the 94.25 observations that are allocated to the no-low-urban category by the marginal model. Thus, the composite expected frequencies are $(0.3306)(94.25) = 31.16$ and $(0.6694)(94.25) = 63.09$, as shown in the bottom panel of Table 7.4.

More generally, denote the expected frequencies for the composite model, the predictive model, and the marginal model by $\hat{\mu}^{(C)}$, $\hat{\mu}^{(P)}$, and $\hat{\mu}^{(M)}$, respectively. Suppose that there are three predictors indexed by i, j, and k, and one outcome factor indexed by l. For a particular combination of i, j, and k, the proportion of observations in category l under the predictive model is $\hat{\mu}_{ijkl}^{(P)}/x_{ijk}$. Applying this proportion to the expected frequency $\hat{\mu}_{ijk}^{(M)}$ under the marginal model gives the composite expected frequencies,

$$\hat{\mu}_{ijkl}^{(C)} = \frac{\hat{\mu}_{ijkl}^{(P)}\,\hat{\mu}_{ijk}^{(M)}}{x_{ijk+}} \qquad (7.17)$$

This formula generalizes readily to other numbers of predictors. Because the parameters on the right hand side are maximum-likelihood estimates, the $\hat{\mu}^{(C)}$ maximize the likelihood for the composite model (Goodman, 1973b).

When the expected frequencies for the composite model in Table 7.4 are fitted to the observed data, a test statistic value of $G^2 = 9.40$ is obtained. This statistic is the sum of the G^2 statistics for the two component models (which are 3.19 and 6.21). In fact, one always has

$$G_C^2 = G_P^2 + G_M^2 \quad \text{and} \quad df_C = df_P + df_M$$

In the example, the overall statistic has $5 + 2 = 7$ degrees of freedom.

In Equation 7.17 the marginal expected frequencies are obtained by fitting a single model, but the argument leading to that equation is not altered if they derive from a composite model at an earlier serial stage. For example, the $\hat{\mu}_{ijk}^{(M)}$ could have been obtained by combining the predictions of a two-factor marginal model, $\hat{\mu}_{ij}^{(M)}$, with those of a three-factor predictive model, $\hat{\mu}_{ijk}^{(P)}$. If so, the three-stage expected frequencies in the full table are

$$\hat{\mu}_{ijkl}^{(C)} = \frac{\hat{\mu}_{ijkl}^{(P)}\hat{\mu}_{ijk}^{(P)}\hat{\mu}_{ij}^{(M)}}{x_{ijk+}x_{ij++}} \qquad (7.18)$$

This generalization extends to as many serial stages as necessary.

Equations 7.17 and 7.18 have an unfamiliar form, involving the product of the expected frequencies from other models. For some combinations of models, the $\hat{\mu}^{(C)}$ simplify to a hierarchical log-linear model, but for many other combinations they do not. This failure occurs whenever the predictive part of the model implies a structure for the predictors that is inconsistent (in log-linear terms) with that demanded by the marginal model (see Asmussen & Edwards, 1983, for specific rules). For example, the frequencies at the bottom of Table 7.4 cannot be produced by a hierarchical log-linear model. In this sense, the composite models go beyond the forms that have appeared so far in this book. This extension does

not cause interpretational problems, however, since appeal to the comprehensible form of the component models is immediate.

The composite model is valuable when one wishes to assemble an overall
description of one's data. However, in many other circumstances it is unnecessary. Before bothering to construct it, and before presenting it to others, one
should consider whether it provides any new information. When one's interest is
in the individual sub-models that make up the composite model, then their
combination may reveal nothing new, particularly if one must return to the pieces
to interpret it. Moreover, since the test of the composite model confounds the
tests of its several parts, its value is limited in a hypothesis-testing framework.

PROBLEMS

7.1. Estimate the logits for the data in Problem 2.1a.

7.2. In a four-way table with factors V, W, X, and Y, with Y treated as an outcome,
what is the log-frequency model that corresponds to the following logit models?

a. $\eta_{ijk} = \nu + \nu_{V(i)} + \nu_{W(j)} + \nu_{X(k)} + \nu_{VW(ij)}$

b. $\eta_{ijk} = \nu + \nu_{V(i)} + \nu_{W(j)} + \nu_{X(k)} + \nu_{VW(ij)} + \nu_{VX(ik)} + \nu_{WX(jk)}$

7.3. Subjects are classified as left-handed, right-handed, or of mixed handedness. It is
desired to represent this handedness factor by logits. Devise at least two such sets of
logits. Describe circumstances under which each would be useful (for example, the types
of questions that each would help answer).

7.4. ℰ Consider a three-way classification with the data

	$-b_1-$		$-b_2-$		$-b_3-$	
	y_1	y_2	y_1	y_2	y_1	y_2
a_1	39	16	23	2	18	2
a_2	33	24	19	7	7	10

Show that these data fit the logit model

$$\eta_{ij} = \nu + \nu_{A(i)} + \nu_{B(j)}$$

Estimate its parameters.

7.5. Which of the following sets of logits is the better representation of a 5-level
classification?

a. $\eta^{(1)} = \dfrac{P(y_1, y_2, y_3)}{P(y_4, y_5)}$, $\eta^{(2)} = \dfrac{P(y_4)}{P(y_5)}$, $\eta^{(3)} = \dfrac{P(y_1)}{P(y_2, y_3)}$, $\eta^{(4)} = \dfrac{P(y_2)}{P(y_3)}$

b. $\eta^{(1)} = \dfrac{P(y_1, y_2)}{P(y_3, y_4, y_5)}$, $\eta^{(2)} = \dfrac{P(y_4)}{P(y_5)}$, $\eta^{(3)} = \dfrac{P(y_1)}{P(y_2, y_3)}$, $\eta^{(4)} = \dfrac{P(y_3)}{P(y_4)}$

7.6. Fit a logit model to the data from Problem 3.12.

7.7. Two further variables were measured in the addict survey described in Section 7.3: whether the subject had an alcohol-related arrest (factor L) and whether the subject had been arrested before the time of first use (factor A). Draw a plausible path-type structure, and devise a plan to analyze the relationships among the compete set of variables.

7.8. ℰ Consider the three-factor data from Problem 7.4.
a. Show that $A \perp\!\!\!\perp B$ in the AB table.
b. Combine the fit of this model with that of the logit model in Problem 7.4 to give a single set of predicted frequencies for the three-way table. What would the statistic G^2 equal for a goodness of fit test of these frequencies?

7.9. Consider a four-factor model $[ABC][Y]$. Using the procedure in Section 6.4, show that this model can be written as a series of conditional-independence hypotheses,

$$[ABC][Y] \equiv (A \perp\!\!\!\perp Y) \cap (B \perp\!\!\!\perp Y | A) \cap (C \perp\!\!\!\perp Y | AB)$$

How is this decomposition related to the stage models of Sections 7.5 and 7.6?

8

Analyzing Unstructured Tables

The last two chapters have described some techniques for investigating tables of data when the context of the investigation allows structure to be imposed and specific hypotheses to be tested. Unfortunately, there are some sets of data where this cannot be done. One may lack the information to formulate specific hypotheses and be unwilling to posit a predictor-outcome structure, yet still want to analyze the results. Obviously, starting with weaker assumptions about the data, one must draw weaker conclusions in the end. Nevertheless, there is much one can do; this chapter considers some options.

8.1. WORKING WITH A LARGE TABLE

Sometimes one is confronted with a set of data in which many categorizations are collected simultaneously. The results of a survey are a good example: dozens or even hundreds of individual responses can be collected from each respondent. If v classifications are obtained, each observation falls conceptually into one cell of a v-dimensional table. However, when v is larger than about 8, the table has so many cells that the data cannot actually be put into this form. With a dozen two-level categorizations, a table with $2^{12} = 4096$ cells is produced; if half of these have three levels, there are 46656 cells. Obviously, one doesn't get much from writing out this table, although it is sometimes conceptually useful to picture the data that way.

The analysis of this table must balance two opposing tendencies. To keep the analysis simple, one wants to work in small marginal subtables, ignoring as many of the factors as possible. The low-order associations that appear in these

196

tables are easier to interpret and explain. Working against the simplicity is the fear of missing something. Only by including a factor in a table can one be sure that it does not interact with other effects and that collapsing over it does not alter other relationships. To guard against these omissions, one wants to include as many factors as possible. The trick is to find a satisfactory balance between too many factors and too few.

One can almost always rule out fitting a single model to the entire table. The most obvious problem is the sample size. Without an enormous pool of observations, most of the cells contain zeros or small frequencies. The expected frequencies are tiny numbers, violating the minimum sample-size rules of Section 2.5. The accuracy of the χ^2 approximation to the sampling distribution of X^2 or G^2 is bad, forcing one to make decisions using poor quality tests. Inconsistencies appear, both between the X^2 and G^2 statistics and across tests of different models. Moreover, the empty cells probably make a modification of the degrees of freedom necessary, complicating both computation and interpretation.

A less apparent problem is the plethora of potential models that can be fit to a multiway table. The number of models increases much more rapidly than the number of factors. Most of these models are neither interesting nor plausible. The computational labor alone prevents one from fitting more than a tiny fraction of them. Even if they could be fit, the process of sorting through them is tedious, confusing, and fraught with ambiguity. One must recognize that small quantities of data do not tell much about higher-order associations, no matter how much one is interested in them. The number of parameters in a high-order model is great, and when it approaches the number of observations, one is helpless.

In the end, the appropriate analysis is likely to be an interplay among at least three approaches to the data: an approach based on a priori grounds, one based on the analysis of small subtables, and one based on larger tables. Each contributes its own information; each has its own limits. One draws what information one can from each source and hopes to work toward an explanation that clearly and accurately expresses the data. In doing so, one must take a hand in the analysis. It cannot be turned over to automatic procedures such as computer algorithms.

One's first recourse should be to an a priori analysis. How this is done depends on the particular problem one is studying and is hard to discuss in the abstract. Generally, one decides that the relationships among some factors are important and that those among others (even if they exist) are uninteresting. The latter ones may be of no theoretical importance, they may be excluded by the source of the data, or they may be too well known to bother with. One concentrates on tables that include interesting combinations of factors. Selecting subsets of factors in this way is an extension of the procedures in Chapter 6 and 7, although with a looser set of questions. The graphical representation discussed in Chapter 6 is often helpful here.

Sometimes a good way to simplify the situation is to coalesce several factors into a single multilevel variable. For example, a survey may have recorded 10 binary questions that are thought to measure the respondent's current happiness. Rather than treating them as 10 separate factors, they can be subsumed in a single happiness variable that ranges from 0 to 10. The combination reduces the number of factors to be analyzed, and provides a more stable estimate of the common characteristics than do its separate parts. Any differences among the components that are lost in the combination can be studied in separate tables if one wishes. The combined variable is analyzed using the ordinal techniques of Chapter 13 or, if it is sufficiently graded, by multiple regression or the analysis of variance.

The second approach to a large table is to look at the associations in the subtables formed by taking all combinations of a few factors at a time. A common strategy here is to look at the two-way associations obtained from all pairs of factors. With somewhat more work, one can also look at factor triplets. In this endeavor, one is often abetted by the computer package one is using; many packages contain routines that print all pairwise subtables of a set of factors. This analysis allows one to spot some unexpected associations and to group factors that hang together. It is sometimes a reasonable way to scan a large and unfamiliar set of data.

The exhaustive pairwise (or triplet) approach has several limitations. Perhaps most seriously, these tests tell nothing about any higher-order associations. Interactions, which are often more interesting than pairwise associations, are only detected in a multifactor table.† The table must contain at least as many factors as are in the association: a four-way association is studied in at least a four-way table. Another difficulty stems from the mass of tests. The number of pairwise tests increases as the square of the number of factors, and is soon too large to make interpretation easy. It is difficult to avoid capitalizing on sampling accidents in one's selection of results, and inevitably contradictions and ambiguities appear. Some form of multiple-comparison correction, such as the Bonferroni adjustment of significance levels, is necessary. Because there are so many tests, one tends to focus on statistically significant results. Yet statistical significance is not an indicator of practical importance. For one thing, not all close associations revealed by pairwise tests are worth following up. Many questionnaires contain redundant items whose similarity is not particularly interesting—the 10 happiness items mentioned above would lead to 45 such tests. For another, the lack of an association where it is expected can be more important than the presence of a significant result. These absences get lost when there are too many positive findings.

Drawing on the results from a priori analysis and from the fitting of small

---

†The situation contrasts with that in much of continuous multivariate statistics. Those procedures are based on the correlation matrix, which derives from pairwise relationships. Nevertheless, the analysis is acceptable since inferences are based on the multivariate normal distribution, which does not involve higher-order associations. The stronger model lets one get more from the data. Such assumptions are inappropriate for categorical models.

subsets, one tries to form subsets of the factors to which models can be fitted and with which hypotheses can be tested. Usually these sets contain from 3 to 6 factors. One wants to make tables that involve interesting relationships and that are small enough to meet the minimum sample size rules of Section 2.5.

8.2. STEPWISE SEARCH FOR A MODEL

Where one can do so, the best way to find useful results is through tests of meaningful hypotheses, as was done in Chapter 6. However, these types of tests are not always possible, for in many situations—surveys are often an example—sufficiently detailed prior hypotheses are not available. In these cases, one can make a guided search through the lattice of potential association models, looking for a simple model that adequately describes the data.

This change of tactic is made at some cost. By searching among a large collection of potential alternatives, one abandons a crucial portion of the hypothesis-testing logic. Instead of examining a single model (or set of models) that can be retained or rejected, one looks at a series of models and accepts one because it cannot be rejected. Since any member of a large family of models may be selected, problems arise concerning the control of error rate and capitalization on chance effects. The conclusions that follow from this process are weaker than those that come from a strict hypothesis-testing framework. Thus, these search methods are appropriate only for less structured situations and should be avoided if clear hypotheses can be formulated.

What one would like to do is to fit all the models that are consistent with the design and to pick the one that best combines good fit with relative simplicity. However, when more than three factors are involved, the enormous number of potential models precludes an exhaustive search. As noted above, with as few as four factors, there are 114 candidate models to be examined.

Another possibility that comes to mind is to test each type of parameter by itself—test λ_A, λ_B, λ_{AB}, and so on—then put together a model from those that are found necessary. This is more or less what one does in the orthogonal analysis of variance, where each main effect and each interaction is tested separately to create a composite picture of the data. However, that strategy is too simple for frequency data. Here the situation is more like that of multiple regression or the unequal-sample analysis of variance: the tests are not independent and one must worry about the context in which the test is run. Although something like the testing of individual terms is described in Section 8.4, it is not a complete answer. A freer method of search is necessary.

One common search procedure is known as *stepwise search*. In it, one proceeds from one model to the next, a single step at a time. One starts with a reasonable candidate model, which may derive from previous research, from a logical analysis of the design, from the preliminary tests in Section 8.4, or from any other source. Then, one looks at models that differ from it by only a single set of parameters. Parameters in the model are candidates for removal, and parameters out of the model are candidates for inclusion. If a new model is more satisfactory, it is adopted and the process is repeated. Thus one moves one step at a time through the lattice of permissible models toward better fitting alternatives. Of course, at every step the constraints imposed by the hierarchy principle and by the design of the investigation are respected. Eventually, a model is reached from which no further step is acceptable, and the process stops. This stepping operation is essentially the same as the stepwise procedures used in other areas of statistics, particularly in multiple regression.

Two variants of the stepwise search procedure are commonly found. In a *stepwise step-up search* one starts with a simple model and adds terms to it, moving toward more and more complicated models. A *stepwise step-down search* works exactly the opposite way: One starts with a complicated model, often the saturated model, and removes terms from it, making it simpler and simpler. In either case the goal is a model of intermediate complexity.

In absolute measure, a model with more parameters always fits better than one that omits some parameters. Extra parameters cannot hurt the fit. Accordingly, one needs a criterion for a "best fitting" model. No single rule is totally satisfactory, for often several models can be deemed "best" on purely statistical grounds. At least five criteria for a satisfactory model present themselves:

- A satisfactory model is readily interpretable.
- A satisfactory model accounts for a large portion of the variability in the data.
- A satisfactory model cannot be rejected by an overall goodness-of-fit test.
- A satisfactory model contains no term that can be removed without causing a substantial deterioration of fit.
- A satisfactory model omits no term that substantially improves the fit if it is added to the model.

Unfortunately, for many sets of data these criteria cannot be satisfied simultaneously.

Often the first three criteria must be balanced against one another. For example, one may be faced with a choice between a simple, interpretable model that explains most of the variation but that can be rejected by a significance test and a complicated model that is statistically sound but hard to understand. When the sample is large, statistical tests often indicate the necessity of parameters whose actual contribution to understanding the data is very small (recall the relative-change statistics in Section 5.8). For example, for the detection data in Chapter 6, the model $[HL][HX][HY][LY][XY]$ is nearly acceptable, with a descriptive level slightly over 1%, while the simplest model that formally fits is $[HL][HX]$ $[HY][LXY]$, which has 30 additional parameters. It is not at all obvious which model is more useful. The model that one prefers depends on what one intends to do with the results, so the choice is partly a matter of taste and of the goals of the research. If one is trying to frame a general description of the phenomenon, the simpler model is better; but if one is selecting a model to examine its parameter estimates, a more complicated model that is sure to fit well is better. At an early stage in one's work, one concentrates on large effects; later probes small effects.

When to stop stepping depends on one's criteria for a satisfactory model. One pair of rules is the following:

- Stop stepping up (adding terms) when the upper-tail χ^2 area for G^2 (or X^2) falls below a preset criterion.
- Stop stepping down (deleting terms) when the upper-tail χ^2 area for G^2 (or X^2) exceeds a preset criterion.

Using the upper-tail areas of a χ^2 distribution here instead of the raw test statistics allows differences in degrees of freedom between models to be accommodated. A second pair of rules is formulated in terms of the changes in fit:

- Stop stepping up when the upper-tail χ^2 area for ΔG^2 (or ΔX^2) for all unentered sets of parameters falls below a preset criterion.
- Stop stepping down when the upper-tail χ^2 area for ΔG^2 (or ΔX^2) for all sets of parameters in the model exceeds a preset criterion.

In formulating the criteria, it is tempting to use the conventional significance levels to indicate fit or failure of a model. However, although the upper-tail χ^2 areas are useful to compare statistics with differing degrees of freedom, these values have no probabilistic interpretation in a stepwise search. The problem is that the stepwise selection procedure biases all the test statistics with respect to the χ^2 distribution. This bias arises because the choice in the stepwise procedures is not taken into account by the statistical tests. Consider the addition of parameters. The term chosen to add to the model at a particular step has the largest ΔG^2 among several alternatives. Even if there are no real effects, so that each term's ΔG^2 has a standard χ^2 sampling distribution, the process of selection gives the largest of them a distribution that is biased upward relative to a χ^2 distribution. A similar influence affects the overall statistic value: when a term is added, G^2 drops more than expected, so that a χ^2 distribution overestimates how well it fits. An analogous bias affects the deletion of terms: the distribution of the smallest of several ΔG^2 or ΔX^2 statistics is less than expected from a χ^2 distribution (possibly noncentral), and thus the deletion of this term also inflates the overall statisic.

There is no satisfactory way to accommodate the biases induced by selection into a proper statistical test, except by testing the resultant models with a new sample. Accordingly, one should never speak of the statistics obtained in stepwise procedures as "significant" or "not significant". The choice of model should be based on other criteria, such as its interpretability or the relative sizes of the changes.

As the example in the next section shows, it is wise to carry the stepping process beyond the point where these rules first tell one to stop. Sometimes a term that fails to meet the criterion for inclusion or elimination at one step becomes important at a later step. More frequently, the hierarchy principle excludes important high-order terms from consideration until some less important-looking lower-order terms are in the model. In this respect, stepping with hierarchical models is unlike ordinary stepwise multiple regression where all terms are potentially candidates at any stage and the late appearance of important effects is rarer.

Of course, it would be most convenient if both step-up and step-down procedures selected the same model and if this model were the best model in the entire hierarchy of permissible models. However, neither event is guaranteed. Whatever criterion is used, the stepwise procedures respond only to local properties of the lattice and thus can overlook good models not on the locally optimal path. This property makes it possible to devise patterns of association for which the step-up and step-down procedures lead to different results or for which the best model according to some other criterion is missed. There is some evidence that step-up searches are less powerful than step-down searches and so are more likely to omit effects from the final model (Oler, 1985). In any case, stepwise analyses are not the definitive means for finding the "right" model. At best, they provide useful information that contributes to a sensible search.

8.3.   EXAMPLES OF STEPWISE SEARCH

One goal of the addiction survey described in Section 7.2 was to look at predictors of treatment outcome. Each subject was classified into three classes depending on the success of the methadone treatment: daily drug use (a poor outcome), occasional use, and little or no use. Call this factor O and abbreviate the categories by dy, oc, and no. Now consider an attempt to predict the outcome based on the factors SES, county, and age at first use (S, C, and F, respectively), along with two additional factors:

- Has the subject ever had an alcohol-related arrest (factor L: yes or no)?
- Was the subject ever arrested prior to first heroin use (factor A: yes or no)?

There are five predictors, S, C, F, L, and A, and one outcome, O. The data are shown in Table 8.1. Without a theory that provides specific questions to test, one can start by using a stepwise search to fit a model. Several search strategies are possible, three of which are considered here.

TABLE 8.1
Data on Drug Addiction Treatment Outcome

			L Yes						L No					
			A Yes			A No			A Yes			A No		
S	C	F	dy	oc	no	dy	oc	no	dy	oc	no	dy	oc	no
Low	Urban	<18	13	7	12	4	4	4	7	3	7	4	4	4
		≥18	18	20	27	0	3	4	5	10	10	0	8	2
	Suburban	<18	3	9	7	3	3	1	3	1	3	1	2	3
		≥18	8	11	10	1	0	0	3	3	1	1	3	1
	Rural	<18	3	2	2	1	0	4	0	0	2	1	0	1
		≥18	7	9	14	0	3	1	1	5	4	3	2	4
Not Low	Urban	<18	16	4	9	5	2	6	8	5	5	3	8	4
		≥18	23	22	22	6	4	5	8	19	17	6	5	5
	Suburban	<18	4	3	0	1	1	1	2	2	1	2	0	0
		≥18	3	8	17	1	0	1	2	3	2	1	0	3
	Rural	<18	0	0	2	3	1	0	0	0	1	1	0	1
		≥18	1	7	5	0	1	1	2	1	3	0	0	12

Stepwise Step-up Search

The simplest model consistent with the prediction goal is $[SCLFA][O]$, which serves as a starting point. This model does not fit ($G^2(94) = 146.03$), indicating that terms must be added to it. Into this context, any of the parameters λ_{SO}, λ_{CO}, λ_{PO}, λ_{FO}, or λ_{AO} can be introduced to produce a new hierarchical model. Each model is fitted, G^2 is calculated, and ΔG^2 for the introduction of the new parameters is found. Since the degrees of freedom associated with the different terms are not the same, these statistics are standardized by calculating upper-tail χ^2 areas. These areas are denoted $UT\chi^2$ in the tables below, rather than as descriptive levels or "p-values", since they do not have a probabilistic interpretation. These tests are shown as Step 1 in Table 8.2. Of the terms tested, the first-use factor, λ_{FO} (marked by the asterisk), makes the largest change in G^2 with the smallest number of degrees of freedom, so is the best candidate for inclusion.

The process now repeats, starting the second step with the model just selected, $[SCFLA][FO]$. This step introduces λ_{CO} and leads to the model $[SCFLA][CO][FO]$. With the third step it is possible to add the three-factor term λ_{CFO}, while remaining true to the hierarchy principle, since the three two-factor terms λ_{CF}, λ_{CO}, and λ_{FO} are now present. In fact, this term gives the largest change. The change at this step is small and is not significant by standard criteria, so at this point one might decide to stop, particularly since the fourth step yields only a small improvement. However, the fifth step introduces λ_{CLO}, which makes a more substantial contribution. The appearance of this larger change points out the necessity of continuing the stepping process beyond the point where the changes first diminish before one decides to stop.

One might stop with the model $[SCFLA][CFO][CLO]$ particularly if one were interested only in the simpler effects. However, although the next steps introduce only terms that make insubstantial contributions, a larger change occurs in step 9 when λ_{SCFO} is introduced. This term could not have been entered earlier, since the necessary three-factor parameters were lacking. From this point on, no larger changes occur, making the model $[SCFLA][SCFO][CLO]$ the last sensible place to stop. In fact, the difference between the models at steps 5 and 9 is only $\Delta G^2(12) = 18.73$, which, in view of the bias that is part of the selection process, may not be a big enough change to support the additional complexity of the later model.

Stepwise Step-down Search

Just as one can step up from a simple model, one can start with a complex model and step down. The saturated model is a potential starting point for the process, although starting with a simpler model saves computation, particularly when the table is large. In the present case, there are not enough data to say much about the highest order associations, so a plausible beginning is the model that contains all four-way associations along with the complete set of predictor terms:

[SCFLA][SCFO][SCLO][SCAO][SFLO][SFAO][SLAO][CFLO][CFAO]
[CLAO][FLAO]

This model is almost satisfactory ($G^2(19) = 33.30$), although the many small cells make the statistic untrustworthy and the degrees of freedom too large. One cell in the marginal $CFLO$ table is zero, reducing the count of degrees of freedom by 3 from what it would be for a complete table. Now one lists the λ terms that can be removed from this model without violating the hierarchy principle. These terms are the ones whose letters appear in the brackets in the specification of the model. The parameters λ_{SCFLA} are not removed, since their presence is mandated by the design. Each term is tested to check the effect of its removal. One deletes the term whose ΔG^2 has the largest upper-tail χ^2 area and that leaves behind the best-fitting model, as shown in step 1 of Table 8.3.

The model with λ_{CFLO} deleted creates a minor problem here, since a zero in that marginal table eliminates four cells. These appear when the term is deleted. To avoid contaminating the test of λ_{CFLO} with the introduction of these cells, they are excluded from the data used to fit the unrestricted model, using methods explained in Chapter 10. For all other models, the $CFLO$ marginal distribution is included, which automatically eliminates these cells from both the restricted and the unrestricted models. The rate of convergence of many of these models is exceptionally slow, which implies that some high-order zeros of the type described in Section 5.6 are present. No correction for these zeros has been made here, so that the number of degrees of freedom for some of the full models is suspect. In any case, these difficulties vanish after the fifth step.

On the first step, λ_{FLAO} is chosen for removal (marked by an asterisk in Table 8.3). This table also shows the second and third steps of the search in detail. Notice that the terms λ_{SCAO} and λ_{SCLO} are removed before λ_{SLAO}, even though the latter has the smaller ΔG^2, because they have more degrees of freedom and a larger upper-tail χ^2 area. To save space in Table 8.3, only the terms eliminated in steps 4-13 are shown. At the end of step 13 the model [SCFLA][SCFO][SFLO] [CLO] is reached. As step 14 shows, elimination of any of these terms makes a larger change than any others that have come before ($CLAO$ on step 9 is the possible exception). This is a reasonable place to stop. As it happens, step 13 is also the point where any further deletion results in a model that can be rejected by 5% criteria, although this is less important than the fact that the further deletions start to remove terms that have consistently had large values of ΔG^2 and small upper-tail area.

If a packaged computer program with an automatic stepwise step-down feature is used, one must be careful not to let the program tamper with terms implied by the design. In a predictor-outcome analysis, the associations among the pre-

TABLE 8.2
Stepwise Step-up Search for a Model for the Data in Table 8.1. The Most Valuable Term at Each Stage is Marked by an Asterisk

Step	Term	New Model	G^2	df	$UT\chi^2$	ΔG^2	df	$UT\chi^2$
0	—	[SCFLA][O]	146.03	94	0.000	—	—	—
1	SO	[SCFLA][SO]	144.62	92	0.000	1.41	2	0.494
	CO	[SCFLA][CO]	135.97	90	0.001	10.06	4	0.039
	FO*	[SCFLA][FO]	130.89	92	0.005	15.15	2	0.000
	LO	[SCFLA][LO]	144.28	92	0.000	1.75	2	0.417
	AO	[SCFLA][AO]	145.88	92	0.000	0.15	2	0.928
2	SO	[SCFLA][SO][FO]	128.71	90	0.005	2.18	2	0.337
	CO*	[SCFLA][CO][FO]	122.01	88	0.010	8.88	4	0.064
	LO	[SCFLA][FO][LO]	128.91	90	0.004	1.98	2	0.372
	AO	[SCFLA][FO][AO]	129.96	90	0.004	0.93	2	0.629
3	SO	[SCFLA][SO][CO][FO]	120.10	86	0.009	1.91	2	0.386
	LO	[SCFLA][CO][FO][LO]	119.79	86	0.009	2.21	2	0.331
	AO	[SCFLA][CO][FO][AO]	121.38	86	0.007	0.62	2	0.733
	CFO*	[SCFLA][CFO]	116.52	84	0.011	5.49	4	0.241
4	SO	[SCFLA][SO][CFO]	114.86	82	0.010	1.45	2	0.483
	LO*	[SCFLA][CFO][LO]	114.57	82	0.010	1.91	2	0.385
	AO	[SCFLA][CFO][AO]	115.88	82	0.008	0.06	2	0.971

5	SO	[SCFLA][SO][CFO][LO]	112.63	80	0.010	1.94	2	0.378
	AO	[SCFLA][CFO][LO][AO]	114.28	80	0.007	0.29	2	0.865
	CLO*	[SCFLA][CFO][CLO]	101.89	78	0.036	12.69	4	0.013
	FLO	[SCFLA][CFO][FLO]	114.46	80	0.007	0.12	2	0.944
6	SO*	[SCFLA][SO][CFO][CLO]	99.98	76	0.034	1.90	2	0.386
	AO	[SCFLA][CFO][CLO][AO]	101.31	76	0.028	0.57	2	0.751
	FLO	[SCFLA][CFO][CLO][FLO]	101.37	76	0.028	0.52	2	0.772
7	AO	[SCFLA][SO][CFO][CLO][AO]	99.31	74	0.026	0.68	2	0.713
	SCO	[SCFLA][SCO][SFO][CLO]	96.25	72	0.030	3.74	4	0.443
	SFO*	[SCFLA][SFO][CFO][CLO]	96.73	74	0.039	3.25	2	0.196
	SLO	[SCFLA][SLO][CFO][CLO]	99.34	74	0.028	0.64	2	0.726
	FLO	[SCFLA][SO][CFO][CLO][FLO]	99.45	74	0.026	0.53	2	0.767
8	AO	[SCFLA][SFO][CFO][CLO][AO]	96.05	72	0.031	0.68	2	0.713
	SCO*	[SCFLA][SCO][SFO][CFO][CLO]	93.38	70	0.032	3.35	4	0.502
	SLO	[SCFLA][SFO][SLO][CFO][CLO]	95.98	72	0.031	0.75	2	0.688
	FLO	[SCFLA][SFO][CFO][CLO][FLO]	96.09	72	0.031	0.64	2	0.725
9	AO	[SCFLA][SCO][SFO][CFO][CLO][AO]	92.76	68	0.025	0.63	2	0.731
	SLO	[SCFLA][SCO][SFO][SLO][CFO][CLO]	92.59	68	0.025	0.80	2	0.672
	FLO	[SCFLA][SCO][SFO][CFO][CLO][FLO]	92.78	68	0.025	0.61	2	0.739
	SCFO*	[SCFLA][SCFO][CLO]	83.16	66	0.075	10.22	4	0.037
10	AO	[SCFLA][SCFO][CLO][AO]	82.53	64	0.059	0.63	2	0.729
	SLO*	[SCFLA][SCFO][SLO][CLO]	82.45	64	0.060	0.71	2	0.701
	FLO	[SCFLA][SCFO][CLO][FLO]	82.56	64	0.059	0.60	2	0.741

TABLE 8.3
Stepwise Step-down Search for a Model for the Data in Table 8.1.
Only the First Three and the Last Steps are Shown in Detail.
The Term to be Eliminated in These Stages is Marked by Asterisks

Step	Term Removed	G^2	df	$UT\chi^2$	ΔG^2	df	$UT\chi^2$
0	—	33.30	19	0.022			
1	SCFO	45.31	23	0.004	12.01	4	0.017
	SCLO	37.08	23	0.032	3.78	4	0.437
	SCAO	35.67	23	0.045	2.37	4	0.668
	SFLO	37.07	21	0.017	3.77	2	0.152
	SFAO	38.11	21	0.013	4.81	2	0.090
	SLAO	34.67	21	0.031	1.37	2	0.505
	CFLO[†]	38.02	23	0.025	4.72	4	0.317
	CFAO	40.54	23	0.013	7.24	4	0.124
	CLAO	46.01	23	0.003	12.71	4	0.013
	FLAO*	33.34	21	0.043	0.04	2	0.980
2	SCFO	45.42	25	0.007	12.07	4	0.017
	SCLO	37.12	25	0.056	3.77	4	0.438
	SCAO*	35.74	25	0.076	2.40	4	0.663
	SFLO	37.11	23	0.032	3.77	2	0.152
	SFAO	38.14	23	0.025	4.79	2	0.091
	SLAO	34.67	23	0.056	1.33	2	0.515
	CFLO[†]	38.09	25	0.045	4.74	4	0.315
	CFAO	40.78	25	0.024	7.44	4	0.114
	CLAO	46.80	25	0.005	13.46	4	0.009
3	SCFO	46.36	29	0.022	10.62	4	0.031
	SCLO*	39.45	29	0.093	3.70	4	0.447
	SFLO	39.75	27	0.054	4.01	2	0.135
	SFAO	39.44	27	0.058	3.70	2	0.157
	SLAO	37.42	27	0.087	1.68	2	0.432
	CFLO[†]	40.63	29	0.074	4.89	4	0.299
	CFAO	42.80	29	0.047	7.06	4	0.133
	CLAO	49.97	29	0.009	14.23	4	0.007
4	SLAO	40.99	31	0.108	1.55	2	0.462
5	CFLO[†]	46.16	35	0.098	5.17	4	0.270
6	CFAO	50.38	42	0.176	3.39	4	0.495
7	SFAO	55.11	44	0.122	4.74	2	0.094
8	FAO	55.53	46	0.159	0.41	2	0.814
9	CLAO	64.29	50	0.092	8.77	4	0.067
10	LAO	64.43	52	0.116	0.14	2	0.934
11	CAO	69.66	56	0.104	5.23	4	0.265
12	SAO	73.41	58	0.084	3.75	2	0.154
13	AO	73.98	60	0.106	0.57	2	0.752
14	SCFO	84.92	64	0.041	10.94	4	0.027
	SFLO	81.71	62	0.047	7.74	2	0.021
	CLO	87.91	64	0.025	13.98	4	0.008

[†]Cells where the CFLO marginal-frequency sum is zero have been excluded from the test of this model.

dictors are often small, and the program happily removes them. In the present example, if λ_{SCFAL} had not been preserved, it would have been removed at an early step and the program eventually would have come to rest with a model that was inconsistent with the design. This result would not be useful. The flow of a step-down stepwise analysis should be controlled or corrected by the researcher, unless the automatic features of the program allow a mandatory term to be specified.

Instead of pure step-up or step-down searches, one can employ a mixed strategy, either adding or deleting a term at each stage. This type of stepping is most appropriate when one starts from a plausible model in the middle of the lattice of models. Although this starting model may be close to correct, it might contain a few extra terms or omit a few important ones. One can use a bidirectional stepwise search to make the final adjustments. The procedures described in the remainder of this section and in the next section can be used (among others) to generate a potential starting model.

Stepping with Conditional Independence Models

One difficulty with the step-down procedure is that many complicated models must be fitted. Most are indirect (i.e., without closed estimates) and their convergence is slow, excruciatingly so if there are many empty cells. Much of this work is avoided if one advances through the lattice by larger steps. One way to take big steps is to stick to graphical models, removing one link at a time instead of a single λ parameter (Edwards & Kreiner, 1983; Wermuth, 1976). This procedure is particularly effective when a predictor-outcome structure is not imposed or when several outcome factors are used, so that the number of testable links is large.

As an illustration, consider the joint prediction of L, and O from S, C, F, and A. One starts with the saturated model—that is, a single clique of all factors—then removes a link at a time, retaining the clique $\{S,C,F,A\}$ in all models. As Figure 8.1 shows, there are 9 potentially removable links among the factors. From the saturated model, deletion of a single link eliminates λ_{SCFLAO} and four of the six sets of fifth-order parameters. For example, deleting the link between S and L leaves the model $S \perp\!\!\!\perp L|CFAO$ or [SCFAO][CFLAO]. This model is direct and can be fitted with little difficulty. Among all models created by deleting a single link, the one that fits best is retained as the basis of the second step. The degrees of freedom for these models are complicated by the presence of many marginal zeros in the five-way tables, which make different adjustments in the degrees of freedom necessary for each model. Properly, one should modify each test to put the selection of zeros on the same footing, but these adjustments usually do not affect the search and one can normally ignore them.

The search shown in Table 8.4 descends rapidly, eliminating the links SL, LO, CL, and FL, to arrive at the model [SCFAO][LA], from which no link can be

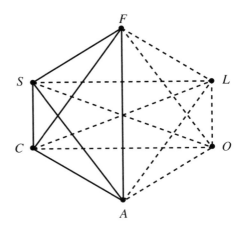

FIGURE 8.1.   Required links (solid) and removable links (dashed) for the prediction of factors *L* and *O* from *S, C, F,* and *A*

eliminated without creating a substantially worse fit. At this point, one could stop, or could use this model as the starting point for a search base on individual λ terms, as described above. In either case, much work has been saved.†

8.4.   TESTS OF INDIVIDUAL PARAMETERS

Most of the work of selecting a model could be saved if there was a way to test the individual λ terms in isolation. As a first try, one can look at the parameters of the saturated model to see which have large values relative to their standard errors. Then a model can be made up that uses these terms. Unfortunately, the saturated model is usually not the best place to conduct a test of individual terms. The model probably has many surplus parameters, the uncertainty of whose estimation raises the standard error of all the other estimates. This excess variability makes the real parameters look less important than they should be, so that one tends to overlook important terms. Better tests are run in a context that is closer to the final model.

However, as has been emphasized several times already, there is no unequivocal way to test whether a set of parameters is necessary to all models. It is always possible that the introduction or removal of one set of parameters may change the significance of another set. Nevertheless, some parameters are necessary in almost every model, while others are almost always useless. If *C* is nearly

---

†The number of models that need to be examined can be further reduced by testing at later stages only those edges or sets of edges that were found to be unnecessary earlier (Edwards & Kreiner, 1983; Edwards & Havránek, 1985; Havránek, 1984). Investigators with many sets of data to examine may find these methods useful.

independent of A and B and is worthless as a predictor of Y, then λ_{CY} should never be necessary, regardless of the status of A and B. Brown (1976) has suggested two tests that help to rule out unlikely terms and to pick likely ones. These tests examine what he refers to as *marginal association* and *partial association*.

The *marginal association* of a set of factors is their association in the marginal table that is formed by collapsing over all the other factors in the design. A four-way table with factors A, B, C, and D, shows an AD marginal association if λ_{AD} is necessary in a model for the two-way AD table formed by collapsing over B and C. To show this association, the model [A][D] must be rejected in this table. Similarly, to show an ABD marginal association, the model [AB][AD][BD] must be rejected in the ABD marginal table. Because the test of marginal association involves only the factors specifically being tested, there is no opportunity for the presence of other factors to influence it. The test is conducted in the simplest possible context.

In contrast, *partial association* is tested in the complete table, in a context that involves all other associations involving the same number of factors.† An AD partial association is present in the four-way table if λ_{AD} cannot be removed from a model that contains all 6 sets of two-way associations, [AB][AC][AD][BC][BD] [CD]. In this way, the test gives other factors a substantial chance to influence the effect.

Where the logic of the model implies that certain parameters must be present, Brown's partial association can be modified to accommodate them. In the predictor-outcome case, the complete association among all predictors should be included in every model, even when this term is of higher order than the term being tested. If A, B, and C are predictors of Y, then the test of AY partial association is better conducted in the context of [ABC][BY][CY] than of [AB][AC][BC][BY] [CY]. If a packaged computer program is used for these tests, one should be sure that this term in included. However, the two contexts are unlikely to produce substantially different results, and, since these tests are mainly advisory, either definition can generally be used.

There is no assurance that the tests of marginal association and partial association agree with each other, and for most sets of data there are some conflicts. However, because they differ so much in context, it is likely that whenever the two tests agree, they also agree with the results in other contexts. A set of parameters that is deemed necessary by both tests is likely to be needed in other models. Similarly, a set of parameters that is worthless in both contexts is likely to remain worthless in another context. Thus, the tests are likely to sort most of

---

†This is Brown's use of the term *partial association*. Other authors use it differently, defining a lack of partial association to be equivalent to conditional independence (e.g., Birch, 1964, 1965). The limited context here makes it unnecessary to fit models with high-order terms in what may be a sparse table. For a comparison and additional examples, see Benedetti & Brown, 1978).

TABLE 8.4
Stepwise Step-down Search for a Graphical Model for the Data in Table 8.1.
Asterisks Mark the Links Dropped at Each Stage

Step	Link	New Model	G^2	df	UT_{χ}^2	ΔG^2	df	UT_{χ}^2
0	—	[SCFLAO]	0.00	0	1.000			
1	SL*	[SCFAO][CFLAO]	27.65	30	0.589	27.65	30	0.589
	SO	[SCFLA][CFLAO]	74.01	43	0.002	74.01	43	0.002
	CL	[SCFLA][SFLAO]	55.29	42	0.082	55.29	42	0.082
	CO	[SCFLA][SFLAO]	102.72	64	0.002	102.72	64	0.002
	FL	[SCFAO][SCLAO]	29.90	29	0.419	29.90	29	0.419
	FO	[SCFLA][SCLAO]	79.07	46	0.000	79.07	46	0.000
	AL	[SCFLO][SCFAO]	65.93	30	0.000	65.93	30	0.000
	AO	[SCFLA][SCFLO]	66.49	46	0.026	66.49	46	0.026
	LO	[SCFLA][SCFAO]	51.90	36	0.141	51.90	36	0.141
2	SO	[SCFA][CFLAO]	80.42	55	0.014	52.77	25	0.001
	CL	[SCFAO][FLAO]	67.35	54	0.105	39.70	24	0.023
	CO	[SCFA][SFAO][CFLA][FLAO]	116.56	84	0.011	88.91	54	0.002
	FL	[SCFLO][CLAO]	53.96	48	0.257	26.31	18	0.093
	FO	[SCFA][SCAO][CFLA][CLAO]	105.51	72	0.006	77.86	42	0.001
	AL	[SCFAO][CFLO]	83.94	47	0.001	56.29	17	0.000
	AO	[SCFA][SCFO][CFLA][CFLO]	85.10	69	0.091	57.45	39	0.029
	LO*	[SCFAO][CFLA]	58.31	54	0.320	30.66	24	0.164

3	SO	[SCFA][CFAO][CFLA]	111.08	84	0.026	52.77	30	0.006
	CL*	[SCFAO][FLA]	71.96	62	0.181	13.65	8	0.091
	CO	[SCFA][SFAO][CFLA]	121.24	92	0.022	62.93	38	0.007
	FL	[SCFAO][CLA]	71.48	60	0.147	13.17	6	0.040
	FO	[SCFA][SCAO][CFLA]	121.24	84	0.004	64.54	30	0.000
	AL	[SCFAO][CFL]	102.84	60	0.000	44.53	6	0.000
	AO	[SCFA][SCFO][CFLA]	103.72	84	0.071	45.41	30	0.035
4	SO	[SCFA][CFAO][FLA]	124.73	92	0.013	52.77	30	0.006
	CO	[SCFA][SFAO][FLA]	134.89	100	0.012	62.93	38	0.007
	FL*	[SCFAO][LA]	78.07	64	0.111	6.11	2	0.047
	FO	[SCFA][SCAO][FLA]	136.51	92	0.002	64.54	30	0.000
	AL	[SCFAO][FL]	109.60	64	0.000	37.63	2	0.000
	AO	[SCFA][SCFO][FLA]	117.37	92	0.038	45.41	30	0.035
5	SO	[SCFA][CFAO][LA]	162.49	94	0.000	84.29	30	0.000
	CO	[SCFA][SFAO][FL]	172.53	102	0.000	94.45	38	0.000
	FO	[SCFA][SCAO][FL]	174.14	94	0.000	96.07	30	0.000
	AL	[SCFAO][L]	109.80	65	0.000	31.73	1	0.000
	AO	[SCFA][SCFO][LA]	123.48	94	0.022	45.41	30	0.035

the relevant parameters, even if a few sets are retained by one test and rejected by the other. The status of these last parameters is ambiguous and must be investigated further.

For example, consider the data on the addicts from the last section (Table 8.1). To examine the parameters λ_{SO} two tests are run:

- *Marginal association*: Collapse the data into the *SO* marginal table

		Outcome		
		dy	*oc*	*no*
SES	low	90	122	128
	high	98	96	123

In this table, the model [S][O], which lacks λ_{SO}, is tested. This test gives $G^2(2) = 1.41$. The models is not rejected, so no marginal association is present.

- *Partial association*: In the full table look at the necessity of λ_{SO} in the context of the model containing the requisite *SCFLA* term as well as the other 4 two-factor associations:

[SCFLA][CO][FO][LO][AO]	$G^2(84) = 119.53$
[SCFLA][SO][CO][FO][LO][AO]	$G^2(82) = 117.24$
Difference (λ_{SO})	$\Delta G^2(2) = 2.29$

Again, no association is indicated.

Together, these results imply that λ_{SO} is unlikely to be necessary in any model. Of course, it could still be forced into a model through application of the hierarchy principle if a higher-order term such as λ_{SAO} has to be included.

The full set of tests for two- and three-factor parameters, using G^2, appear in Table 8.5. The two-factor partial-association tests work in the manner just described. An asterisk indicates a result in the upper 5% of the χ^2 distribution, a dagger one in the upper 10%. From these tests, λ_{CO} and λ_{FO} are candidates for inclusion in a model. The three-factor tests operate in a similar way, with the tests of marginal association being conducted in three-way tables and the tests of partial association deleting one term from a model that contains *SCFLA* and the 10 terms linking pairs of predictors to *O*. From this portion of the analysis, λ_{CLO} is a candidate for inclusion, and λ_{SAO} has ambiguous status. One can test for four-way terms with a similar procedure, but in view of the difficulty in supporting four-way associations with the amount of data present, stopping here is sensible. So, the model [SCFLA][SAO][CLO][FO] is a potential candidate for further analysis. It is an ideal place to start a bidirectional stepwise analysis.

One must be careful not to read Table 8.5 (or similar ones produced by

TABLE 8.5
Tests of Partial Association and Marginal Association
for the Drug Treatment Example

Term	df	Marginal Association	Partial Association
SO	2	1.41	119.53 − 117.24 = 2.29
CO	4	10.06*	125.73 − 117.24 = 8.49†
FO	2	15.15*	132.66 − 117.24 = 15.42*
LO	2	1.75	119.35 − 117.24 = 2.21
AO	2	0.15	117.57 − 117.24 = 0.33
SCO	4	4.77	84.86 − 80.90 = 3.96
SFO	2	2.61	84.83 − 80.90 = 3.39
SLO	2	0.61	81.39 − 80.90 = 0.49
SAO	2	3.81	86.94 − 80.90 = 6.04*
CFO	4	5.49	86.90 − 80.90 = 6.00
CLO	4	11.49†	88.94 − 80.90 = 8.04†
CAO	4	7.06	86.45 − 80.90 = 5.55
FLO	2	0.13	81.94 − 80.90 = 1.04
FAO	2	0.79	81.37 − 80.90 = 0.47
LAO	2	0.70	81.03 − 80.90 = 0.13

*Result in the upper 5 percent of a χ^2 distribution
†Result in the upper 10 percent of a χ^2 distribution

packaged programs) as if it were the summary table from an analysis of variance. The tests do not measure the significance of orthogonal effects and cannot be treated as such. One would not normally present these tables or the tests that they contain as part of a research report, as one might do with the results of an analysis of variance. Rather, they are an intermediate step in an ongoing analysis.

8.5. CROSS VALIDATION

Any of these data-directed search procedures select some parameters for inclusion in a model from a much larger set of candidates. This selection operation is not accounted for by conventional statistical tests. It biases these tests, making them fit too well. Thus, the descriptive levels of X^2 or G^2 cannot be used to evaluate the adequacy of the model. If possible, after selecting a model in one of these ways, one should attempt to confirm the model through independent means. The best way to do this is through cross-validation in a new sample.

When the original sample is large, a reasonable scheme is to sequester a portion of the sample—one-third, one-quarter, or the like—and to use the remainder of the sample to develop a model. After this model has been found, through whatever combination of search strategies, it is tested in the reserved sample. Ideally, the derived model should fit the validation sample, everything that the model contains being necessary and nothing essential being missing. Unfortunately, the samples may disagree. The principal problem is the positive bias induced by the search. If much selection of terms has been done, the original model may contain terms that are not required by the reserved sample. As long as the size of the cross-validation sample is sufficient to give reasonable power, one may use it to eliminate these excess terms. The simpler model here is the better choice.

The original fitting process generates both a model and a set of parameter estimates. As the model is cross-validated in the new sample, the original estimates may or may not be used. One can either transport the estimates with the model to the reserved data for testing or can estimate the parameters of the selected model anew. The former procedure tests both the chosen model and the estimated parameters, the latter only the model. The appropriate degrees of freedom are different in the two cases. If the original parameter estimates are used, the test statistic is distributed on the number of cells minus the number of restrictions imposed by the design. If new estimates are obtained, a degree of freedom must be subtracted for each estimate, as in the usual test. Since only the selection of terms for inclusion is subject to bias, there is not so much reason to cross validate the estimates. Most canned programs accept a model to be fit more easily than they take a model with its parameters given, so reestimation of the parameters is the usual choice here. Of course, one would be concerned if the pattern of the estimates was substantially different in the two samples, even if the same model held.

Once a model has been chosen and validated, the separation of the samples need not be maintained. The original sample was split to help distinguish between true and fortuitous effects. After a model has been selected, all the data can be used to obtain the greatest possible precision in the estimates of the parameters of the log-frequency or logit models.

Cross-validation procedures themselves are subject to a degree of bias. The original sample in which the search is done, as a sample, is subject to statistical fluctuation. Thus, one may find an incorrect model or, if one hits on the correct population model, may inaccurately estimate its parameters. However, the cross-validation procedure treats the tested model as if it were an error-free population statement. This discrepancy biases the cross-validation test toward rejection. This bias can be estimated and is least when the original sample is as large as possible (Chase, 1972; Fienberg, 1979). Thus, it is best to split the original pool of data unequally and to sequester the smallest proportion consistent with adequate power in the cross-validation test. Placing most of one's resources into the initial selection of a model is the best strategy.

The principal difficulty with cross validation is the cost in subjects. Where large samples are cheap, one may be able to divide the data into portions of sufficient size to perform the necessary tests. Where the subjects are difficult to obtain, the increased imprecision that arises because of the split sample negates the value of the cross validation. In such cases, only a single estimation and testing sequence is possible. Any validation would need to be conducted as part of subsequent investigations. Obviously, unvalidated results must be viewed with greater caution than validated ones. This trade-off is no different from numerous others encountered elsewhere in statistics. With less data, one is forced to make more extrastatistical assumptions, and to draw weaker conclusions. With more data, conclusions more completely supported by empirical evidence are possible.

There are other ways besides cross-validation to examine the accuracy with which a model has been chosen. In particular, a procedure known as the *bootstrap* should be considered. Bootstrap assessments of a statistical analysis are performed by simulating the analysis many times, using synthetic samples drawn from the data. In brief, one thinks of the observed data as a population, selects samples from it with replacement, fits models to each of the samples, and observes the stability of the model selection process. Details and examples (not specifically concerned with frequency data) are given in Diaconis & Efron (1983), Efron (1982), and Efron & Gong (1983). Bootstrap investigations require a very large amount of computation and at this point are probably better suited to a general discussion of a statistical technique than to the routine evaluation of results.

PROBLEMS

8.1. ℰ Starting with the tentative model for the addict data developed at the end of Section 8.4, run bidirectional stepwise tests to see whether a better model can be found.

8.2. ℰ Find the best model for the detection data from Chapter 6, using both step-up and step-down procedures. Be sure to respect the design constraints. Fit the data from
a. Table 6.2
b. Table 6.7

8.3. In a bidirectional search with 5 factors, you have reached the model [ABC][ADE][BD][CD]. What terms are candidates for inclusion in this model and for deletion from it? What new models result?

8.4. ℰ Find a simple model for Table 7.1.
a. Allow any model.
b. Keep within the predictor-outcome structure.

8.5. ℰ Run tests for marginal association and partial association on the data in Table 7.1. Include potential terms of all orders. What plausible model do you obtain?

9

Measures of Effect Size

One often wishes to follow tests of significance by calculation of a measure of the size of the effect. It is not enough to decide that an association is real; one wants to know how big it is. However, neither the value of a test statistic nor its descriptive level is satisfactory as an effect-size measure. Both indicate how likely the result is if the null hypothesis distribution is true, and so they are influenced by the size of the sample. For any alternative to the null hypothesis, X^2 and G^2 get larger and the descriptive level smaller as N increases. An adequate measure of the effect cannot vary in this way.

Many measures of association have been proposed, often specialized for particular purposes, and it is neither reasonable nor very helpful to make an exhaustive survey here. Many are considered in a series of papers by Goodman and Kruskal (1954, 1959, 1963, 1972); these and others are discussed in such sources as Bishop, Fienberg, & Holland (1975, Chapter 11), Liebetrau (1983), and Reynolds (1977). This chapter treats a selection of the more useful ones that apply to unordered categories. The association models in Sections 11.3 and 11.4 generate others. Some measures that apply when the categories form an ordered sequence are deferred until Sections 13.8 to 13.10.

9.1. THE ODDS RATIO AND RELATED ASSOCIATION MEASURES

The simplest measure of association, and the one that is most directly attuned to the type of log-frequency analysis discussed in this book, is the *odds ratio* or *cross-product ratio*, α. This ratio was introduced in Section 2.6 for 2×2 tables.

To review that discussion, α is the ratio of the odds in the first row (or column) to that in the second row (or column). In terms of population probabilities, π_{ij}, the ratio is

$$\alpha = \frac{\pi_{11}\pi_{22}}{\pi_{12}\pi_{21}} \tag{9.1}$$

When no association is present, the two rows (or two columns) are proportional to each other and $\alpha = 1$. When the association between rows and columns is in the direction of excess frequency on the major diagonal (π_{11} and π_{22}), then $\alpha > 1$; otherwise, $\alpha < 1$. The relationship between positive and negative associations is reciprocal: associations of $\alpha = a$ and $\alpha = 1/a$ are of equivalent magnitude and opposite direction.

For sample data, the obvious estimate of this ratio substitutes the sample proportions for the probabilities:†

$$\hat{\alpha} = \frac{p_{11}p_{22}}{p_{12}p_{21}} = \frac{x_{11}x_{22}}{x_{12}x_{21}} \tag{9.2}$$

This is a maximum-likelihood estimate of α for a product binomial sampling model in which one factor is fixed by design. However, the estimate is biased, tending to overestimate the true value of α. Much of this bias is removed by adding 1 to each of the denominator cells, giving the estimate

$$\hat{\alpha}_c = \frac{x_{11}x_{22}}{(x_{12}+1)(x_{21}+1)} \tag{9.3}$$

(see Jewel, 1986). Unlike Equation 9.2, this adjusted estimate remains defined when either x_{12} or x_{21} is zero, although what any particular estimate of α means when cells are zero is obscure. If the sample sizes are large, this correction has a negligible effect.

To use the cross-product ratio in a table with more than two levels of categorization, the table must be decomposed into 2×2 tables. An $a \times b$ table of frequencies is turned into an $(a - 1) \times (b - 1)$ table of ratios by applying Equation 9.2 or 9.3 to adjacent 2×2 subtables. Thus, Table 9.1 shows a 3×4 array of frequencies and the corresponding 2×3 table of odds ratios (calculated using the uncorrected estimate, Equation 9.2). These ratios are useful in identifying where the associations are strong or weak, but they do not summarize the association in a single number.

The cross-product ratio generalizes to describe the association in tables with more than two dimensions. As Sections 3.5 and 3.6 discuss, a three-way associa-

---

†In this book "hats" distinguish sample estimates from population parameters. This distinction is not always maintained by other authors; for example, one often finds α used to indicate sample values. This remark also applies to the other measures discussed below.

TABLE 9.1
Representing Association by a Table of Odds Ratios

Original Frequencies

	b_1	b_2	b_3	b_4
a_1	23	26	44	31
a_2	39	16	12	7
a_3	41	28	48	58

Odds Ratios

	b_1-b_2	b_2-b_3	b_3-b_4
a_1-a_2	0.363	0.443	0.828
a_2-a_3	1.665	2.286	2.071

tion is one in which the two-way associations at different levels differ, as, for example, in the pair of tables

$$
\begin{array}{cc}
\begin{array}{cc} 23 & 26 \\ 39 & 16 \end{array} & \begin{array}{cc} 16 & 5 \\ 7 & 29 \end{array} \\
\hat{\alpha}_1 = 0.363 & \hat{\alpha}_2 = 13.257
\end{array}
$$

Just as the ratio of the odds measures the difference between the effects in the rows of a two-way table, so the ratio of odds ratios measures the difference between the two-way effects. For the three-dimensional example above, $\hat{\alpha} = 0.363/13.257 = 0.027$. The interpretation of this cross-product ratio is similar to that of the two-dimensional odds ratio.

This scheme is readily extended to more than three binary classifications. Thus, the d-dimensional cross-product ratio is the ratio of two cross-product ratios in $d - 1$ dimensions. It equals 1 when there is no d-factor association. These ratios keep their cross-product character. For example, in three dimensions, the ratio is

$$
\hat{\alpha} = \frac{x_{111}x_{122}x_{212}x_{221}}{x_{112}x_{121}x_{211}x_{222}}
$$

In this ratio, the frequencies with subscripts summing to odd numbers appear in the numerator and those with subscripts summing to even numbers appear in the denominator. A similar rule holds for any cross-product ratio, although whether the odd or even subscripts appear on the top may change, depending on the number of factors and the most natural assignment of what a "positive" association means. Presumably, corrections for bias could be made to these estimates in the manner of Equation 9.3, but the nature of these corrections seems not to have been studied.

If all the observed frequencies are nonzero, an estimate of the sampling variance of α is

$$\hat{\mathrm{var}}(\hat{\alpha}) = \hat{\alpha}^2 \sum_{\text{cells}} \frac{1}{x_{ij}} \tag{9.4}$$

The sum in this equation includes the four cells that are used to calculate $\hat{\alpha}$. For the bias-corrected estimate $\hat{\alpha}_c$, a similar formula applies, but with x_{12} and x_{21} augmented by 1. Knowledge of the variance of $\hat{\alpha}$ and $\hat{\alpha}_c$ is less useful than one might suspect, however, because the sampling distribution is highly asymmetric. The range of potential values stretches from the no-association point of $\alpha = 1$ all the way to infinity on the positive side but only down to zero on the negative side. So the variance is always larger on the right of a point than on the left. This asymmetry makes statistical inference problematic. Confidence intervals are particularly bad, since a symmetric interval about $\hat{\alpha}$, such as one might ordinarily construct, is inappropriate. The construction of an asymmetric confidence interval for α has received considerable study, and several procedures have been proposed (for reviews and evaluations, see Gart, 1971; Gart & Thomas, 1972, 1982). The procedure described in the next paragraphs gives a good interval for most work, although the procedure of Cornfield (1956; see the references just cited) is somewhat more accurate.

A solution to the problems caused by the asymmetric distribution of $\hat{\alpha}$ is to transform α to a measure centered about zero and for which coefficients of equal absolute value represent equal association. An effective transformation is the logarithm: one works with the quantity $\beta = \log \alpha$ instead of α. Under independence, $\beta = 0$. Its values range symmetrically over the real numbers, taking unbounded positive or negative values when one cell of the table is empty. Most inferential problems for frequencies are much easier to solve on a logarithmic scale, a fact that is evident in the importance of log-linear and logit models in the earlier chapters of this book. The symmetry of β also makes it a better measure to use when comparing effects across several 2×2 tables.

The natural estimate of β is $\hat{\beta} = \log \hat{\alpha}$. This estimate, like that of α, is biased, but since the transformation from α to β is nonlinear, the bias is not the same. An estimate with only slight bias is given by adding $\frac{1}{2}$ to each cell,

$$\hat{\beta}_c = \log \frac{(x_{11}+1/2)(x_{22}+1/2)}{(x_{12}+1/2)(x_{21}+1/2)} \tag{9.5}$$

This correction is the same as the bias correction for the logit discussed in Section 7.2 (Equation 7.3). Again, the addition of the constant eliminates the problems caused by empty cells.

The sampling variability of $\hat{\beta}$ is quite straightforward, estimated by

$$\hat{\text{var}}(\hat{\beta}) = \sum_{\text{cells}} \frac{1}{x_{ij}} \tag{9.6}$$

For $\hat{\beta}_c$, the frequencies in this formula are replaced by $x_{ij}+\frac{1}{2}$.

The variance of $\hat{\alpha}$ and $\hat{\beta}$ (Equations 9.4 and 9.6) illustrates an important theorem that is often used to obtain standard errors. If the random variable Y is some function $f(X)$ of a random variable X, then

$$\text{var}(Y) \approx \left(\frac{df(x)}{dx}\right)^2 \text{var}(X) \tag{9.7}$$

This formula is developed by approximating $f(X)$ near any point by a linear function $f(X) = kX$ with a slope $k = df/dx$ that matches that of $f(X)$ at the point, and then applying the elementary rule $\text{var}(kX) = k^2\text{var}(X)$. Thus, Equation 9.7 is exact for linear functions and accurate for small variances unless $f(X)$ is violently nonlinear. In particular, letting $\beta = f(\alpha) = \log \alpha$ in this formula transforms Equation 9.4 to Equation 9.6. The multivariate equivalent of Equation 9.7—finding the variance by linearizing a transformation—is sometimes known at the *delta method*. It is extremely useful for deriving the variability of association coefficients and is the source of the variance results reported below.

Finding a confidence interval for β follows a conventional course. The large-sample distribution of $\hat{\beta}$ is nearly normal, with an estimated standard error $s_{\hat{\beta}}$, that is the square root of Equation 9.6. So, if z is the appropriate confidence limit for a normal distribution,

$$\hat{\beta} - zs_{\hat{\beta}} \le \beta \le \hat{\beta} + zs_{\hat{\beta}} \tag{9.8}$$

Since α and β are related, this interval also implies an interval for the odds ratio. The endpoints of this interval are the values of α that are transformed to the left- and right-hand sides of Equation 9.8. Since $\alpha = e^\beta$, exponentiating both terms gives the interval for α,

$$\hat{\alpha}/\exp(zs_{\hat{\beta}}) \le \alpha \le \hat{\alpha} \exp(zs_{\hat{\beta}}) \tag{9.9}$$

As an example, consider the 2×2 table at the upper left of Table 9.1. For this table, using the bias-reduced estimate (Equation 9.5) gives

$$\hat{\beta}_c = \log \frac{(23+\frac{1}{2})(16+\frac{1}{2})}{(26+\frac{1}{2})(39+\frac{1}{2})} = \log 0.370 = -0.993$$

The standard error is

$$s_{\hat{\beta}_c} = \sqrt{\frac{1}{23.5} + \frac{1}{26.5} + \frac{1}{39.5} + \frac{1}{16.5}} = 0.408$$

For a 95% confidence interval, $z \approx 2$, and

$$\hat{\beta}_c - zs_{\hat{\beta}_c} = -1.81 \le \beta \le \hat{\beta}_c + zs_{\hat{\beta}_c} = -0.18$$

Exponentiation gives the interval for α:

$$e^{-1.81} = 0.16 \le \alpha \le e^{-0.18} = 0.84$$

This interval is not symmetric about $\hat{\alpha} \approx 0.370$, but is wider toward the upper side.

A table larger than 2×2 gives rise to several odds ratios, as in Table 9.1. Testing these raises the problem of simultaneous inference. Goodman (1964a,b) has generalized Scheffé's simultaneous inference procedure (Scheffé, 1953, 1959; see also Miller, 1981) to the family of all odds ratios formed by selecting two rows and two columns from a larger table. To obtain a set of confidence intervals that jointly hold at a certain confidence level, one must widen each interval relative to its uncorrected size. The appropriate correction replaces z in Equations 9.8 and 9.9 by the square root of the χ^2 statistic that is used to test for significance in the full table, that is, by $\sqrt{\chi^2(a-1)(b-1)}$. There are 6 degrees of freedom in Table 9.1, so for a 95% interval the $z \approx 2$ used with no correction is replaced by $z = \sqrt{12.59} = 3.54$, making an interval almost twice as wide. Since Goodman's procedure corrects for a larger set of odds ratios than is in use here, this interval is conservative. With the limited number of tests, Bonferroni corrections are less conservative—for example, in Table 9.1, instead of using a value of z that cuts off 2.5% of a normal distribution in each tail, one bases the value on a tail area of $2.5\%/6 = 0.42\%$. The normal statistic now is $z = 2.64$, substantially less than that demanded by Goodman's rule.

The confidence-interval procedure extends readily to higher dimensions. For a v-dimensional cross-product ratio, the sum in Equation 9.6 include all the 2^v cells that go into calculating α. With this understanding, the formulae for the confidence intervals are identical to those given above.

The unbounded character of both α and $\log \alpha$ can be inconvenient. Other transformations of α restrict the range to a finite interval. Two measures, bounded between -1 and 1, are Yule's *coefficient of association*,[†]

$$Q = \frac{\alpha - 1}{\alpha + 1} \qquad (9.10)$$

and his *coefficient of colligation*,

$$Y = \frac{\sqrt{\alpha} - 1}{\sqrt{\alpha} + 1} \qquad (9.11)$$

(see Yule, 1900 and 1912, respectively). Although in most respects these coefficients are simply rescalings of α to an appropriate range, they can be interpreted more directly. The association measure Q is the same as the 2×2 Goodman-

[†]Here, as in several other places in this chapter, the convention of representing population parameters by Greek letters is violated to maintain a conventional symbol.

Kruskal γ coefficient, described in Section 13.8, and can be interpreted with reference to the concordance or discordance of two randomly chosen observations, as discussed there. The colligation coefficient is somewhat more complicated: if the original table is adjusted without changing the association, so that all the marginal frequencies are $1/2$, then Y is the Pearson correlation coefficient calculated by assigning scores of (say) 0 and 1 to the two categories of each factor. In either case, one must be careful not to carry over one's intuitions about correlation coefficients for continuous data to Q or Y. In particular, neither coefficient measures the proportion of variance that the two classifications have in common, as does the squared correlation coefficient. Parallels to variance measures are better drawn by the measures in Sections 9.3 and 9.4.

Sample estimates of Y and Q are obtained by substituting $\hat{\alpha}$ for α in Equations 9.10 and 9.11, or, with a little algebra, can be written in terms of the original frequencies. Sampling variances, transformed from $\text{var}(\hat{\alpha})$ with Equation 9.7, are

$$\hat{\text{var}}(\hat{Q}) = \frac{(1 - \hat{Q}^2)^2}{4} \sum_{\text{cells}} \frac{1}{x_{ij}} \quad \text{and} \quad \hat{\text{var}}(\hat{Y}) = \frac{(1 - \hat{Y}^2)^2}{16} \sum_{\text{cells}} \frac{1}{x_{ij}} \quad (9.12)$$

These variances allow tests to be made and confidence intervals to be constructed.

For most purposes there is little reason to choose one of these two statistics over the other. Except in special circumstances, they are mainly useful as rescalings of $\hat{\alpha}$. The association measure Q may be slightly more common.

9.2. MEASURES OF ASSOCIATION BASED ON PEARSON'S X^2

Although the test statistics X^2 and G^2 are not satisfactory measures of association, certain transformations of them are valid association measures. Because the test statistics are not limited to 2×2 tables, they are a more convenient way to summarize the overall effect than is the odds ratio.

Consider the Pearson test statistic,

$$X^2 = \sum_{\text{cells}} \frac{(x_{ij} - \hat{\mu}_{ij})^2}{\hat{\mu}_{ij}}$$

When the overall sample size—call it N—is doubled without any change in the underlying probabilistic association, then both x_{ij} and $\hat{\mu}_{ij}$ double, so the numerator quadruples and X^2 doubles. Thus, for a given effect, the size of X^2 is directly proportional to N. One way to turn X^2 into a sensible measure of effect is to adjust the statistic's value as if it came from a sample of some standard size. Dividing X^2 by N sets this size to 1. The resulting coefficient is conventionally denoted Φ^2. Taking the square root gives the sample estimate of the *phi coefficient*:

$$\hat{\Phi} = \sqrt{X^2/N} \tag{9.13}$$

For the data in Table 9.1, $N = 373$ and $X^2 = 40.64$, so $\hat{\Phi}^2 = 40.64/373 = 0.109$ and $\hat{\Phi} = 0.330$.

Combining the definitions of $\hat{\Phi}^2$ and X^2, one obtains

$$\hat{\Phi}^2 = \sum_{\text{cells}} \frac{(p_{ij} - \hat{\pi}_{ij})^2}{\hat{\pi}_{ij}} \tag{9.14}$$

where $p_{ij} = x_{ij}/x_{++}$ are the sample proportions and $\hat{\pi}_{ij} = p_{i+}p_{+j}$ are the expected frequencies under the hypothesis of no association. This formula points up an illuminating characteristic of the effect-size measures: because their values do not depend on the size of the sample, they can always be calculated from the proportions without reference to the frequencies.

The statistic $\hat{\Phi}^2$ is directly related to the noncentrality parameter used in the power calculations of Sections 2.9 and 5.10. If the $\pi_{ij}^{(1)}$ are the alternative probabilities and the $\pi_{ij}^{(0)}$ are the probabilities under the null hypothesis, then the noncentrality parameter is

$$\omega = \sum_{\text{cells}} \frac{(\pi_{ij}^{(1)} - \pi_{ij}^{(0)})^2}{\pi_{ij}^{(0)}}$$

When the alternative effect is estimated from another study by $\hat{\pi}_{ij}^{(1)} = p_{ij}$, then Equation 9.14 is obtained and $\omega = \Phi^2$.

Both X^2 and $\hat{\Phi}^2$ are never negative and both are zero when no association is present. The maximum value of $\hat{\Phi}^2$ in a two-way table occurs when there is a perfect association, for example, in a table such as

10	0	0	0
0	18	0	0
0	0	12	0

In this table $\hat{\Phi}^2 = 2$, a result that does not depend on the particular frequencies used. More generally, the maximum value of $\hat{\Phi}^2$ is 1 less than the minimum of the number of rows and the number of columns. Scaling $\hat{\Phi}^2$ down by this proportion gives an association measure for an $a \times b$ table known as *Cramèr's coefficient* (Cramèr, 1946),

$$\hat{\phi}' = \sqrt{\frac{\Phi^2}{\min(a,b) - 1}} \tag{9.15}$$

With this scaling $\hat{\phi}'$ lies between 0 (no association) and 1 (complete association). For the data in Table 9.1, $\hat{\Phi}^2$ is divided by 2, and so $\hat{\phi}' = 0.233$.

Cramèr's statistic is most valuable when it is used to compare tables that have both different sizes and different total frequencies. The composite measure reduces them to a common ground. Several other ways to scale X^2 have been proposed (for example, those associated with Pearson and with Tschuprow), but they have no particular advantage over ϕ'. However, these statistics lack an intuitive interpretation other than as a scaling of X^2, which limits their usefulness.†

9.3. MEASURES OF PREDICTIVE ASSOCIATION

Many association measures have been proposed that have a more solid intuitive base than the rescalings of X^2 and α. Several are founded on the prediction of one classification from the other. When there is an association between two discrete factors A and B, then knowing A allows one to say more about B than if one does not know A. If one has a way to quantify certainty, then a measure of the value of A based on the gain of certainty in B is

change of certainty in B = (certainty of B when A is known)
$\qquad$ − (certainty of B when A is unknown)

Expressed as uncertainty rather than certainty, this difference is

change of certainty in B = (uncertainty of B) − (uncertainty of B given A)

The change of certainty is not yet a reasonable effect measure, for its size depends on the initial uncertainty of B. To make a proper measure, the change in uncertainty is expressed relative to its initial value as

$$\text{measure} = \frac{\text{(uncertainty of } B) - \text{(uncertainty of } B \text{ given } A)}{\text{(uncertainty of } B)} \qquad (9.16)$$

When A is unassociated with B, there is no reduction in uncertainty, the two numerator terms are equal, and the measure is zero. When knowing A eliminates all uncertainty in B, the relative reduction is 1.

Equation 9.16 lacks a definition of "uncertainty." When the comparable analysis is made with continuous variables, the natural way to measure uncertainty is by the variance; then Equation 9.16 yields the correlation ratio η^2, the variance-reduction statistic ω^2, or the squared multiple-correlation coefficient. As Section 5.8 mentioned, with discrete categorization there is no best way to quantify uncertainty. Depending on the circumstances, several different measures can be used. One definition is treated in this section, two others in the next.

One way to define the uncertainty of a categorization is by the frequency of

---

†Although interpretations of $\hat{\Phi}^2$ and $(\hat{\phi}')^2$ as relative reductions in errors can be made (see the next section), these are sufficiently forced that they do not contradict this assertion (Blalock, 1958).

errors that one makes when one guesses an outcome. Suppose that one is asked to predict which of several categories is going to occur. The way to make the fewest errors is to pick the most probable category. For example, if one must make a choice among 3 categories with probabilities 0.5, 0.3, and 0.2, one should predict the first category. This strategy makes one right one-half the time, while any other pattern of guesses produces more errors. Now consider a two-way table with rows denoted by factor A and columns by factor B. Suppose that the column category is to be predicted. If the row categorization is unknown, the choice of B must be based on its marginal distribution. If the categorization of A is known, a separate choice can be made in each row of the table. If the optimum choice is not the same for all a_i, fewer errors result. Using the probability of a guessed error as a measure of uncertainty in Equation 9.16 creates the *coefficient of predictive association*, conventionally denoted by λ_B, in which the subscript B indicates the factor to be predicted. Note that this λ_B should not be confused with the parameter λ_B of a log-frequency model.

Calculation of the predictive association is easiest to see in an example. Consider the data of Table 9.1, shown again in Table 9.2. In each row of this table, the largest value is italicized. If A is unknown, then the best choice of B is b_3, which occurs 104 times out of 373. If b_1, b_2 or b_4 occur, an error results; thus, the probability of an error on an unconditional guess of B is estimated to be 0.721, as shown in the bottom panel of the table. Knowing A improves the prediction. If a_1 takes place, then b_3 is the best choice; if a_2, then b_1; and if a_3,

TABLE 9.2
Calculation of the Predictive-association Statistic
for the Data from Table 9.1

Original Data with Row Maxima Italicized

	b_1	b_2	b_3	b_4	
a_1	23	26	*44*	31	
a_2	*39*	16	12	7	
a_3	41	28	48	*58*	
	103	70	*104*	96	373

Calculation of Predictive Association

$$\hat{P}(\text{error in } B) = \frac{103 + 70 + 96}{373} = 0.721$$

$$\hat{P}(\text{error in } B|A) = \frac{23 + 26 + 31 + 16 + 12 + 7 + 41 + 28 + 48}{373} = 0.622$$

$$\hat{\lambda}_B = \frac{\hat{P}(\text{error in } B) - \hat{P}(\text{error in } B|A)}{\hat{P}(\text{error in } B)} = \frac{0.721 - 0.622}{0.721} = 0.138$$

then b_4. These are the italicized values in Table 9.2. The probability that an error is made with this guessing scheme is estimated from the counts in the unchosen cells of the table to be 0.622, which is less than the unconditional 0.721. These two estimates are combined in a relative-reduction coefficient,

$$\hat{\lambda}_B = \frac{\hat{P}(\text{error in } B) - \hat{P}(\text{error in } B|A)}{\hat{P}(\text{error in } B)} \tag{9.17}$$

From Table 9.2, $\hat{\lambda}_B = 0.138$.

The value of λ_B (or of $\hat{\lambda}_B$) ranges from 0 to 1, but its meaning differs from that of the measures discussed earlier. A value of $\hat{\lambda}_B = 0$ does not indicate the absence of an association, in the sense that G^2, X^2, or $\hat{\alpha}$ is zero. Instead, it implies that there is no advantage to knowing A when B is to be guessed. Although $X^2 = 0$ means that $\hat{\lambda}_B = 0$, it is fairly common for $X^2 \neq 0$, yet for the same column to be most frequent in every row, so that $\hat{\lambda}_B = 0$. Thus, prediction in this sense—which should not be confused with the weaker sense of prediction in the predictor-outcome schemes of Chapter 7—is not the same as association. When one wants to predict specific outcomes, $\hat{\lambda}_B$ is the quantity by which the relationship should be measured; if association without prediction is of interest, another measure should be used.

The steps involved in calculating $\hat{\lambda}_B$ are readily combined in a single formula. Let m be the value of j that maximizes the marginal distribution p_{+j}, and let $m(i)$ be the value of j that selects the maximum in the ith row (i.e., that picks out the underlined elements of Table 9.2). Then p_{+m} is the proportion of correct responses under optimal guessing without information about A, and $p_{i,m(i)}$ is the proportion if a_i is known to have occurred. The proportions of errors are 1 minus these quantities. So, filling in the terms of Equation 9.17 yields

$$\hat{\lambda}_B = \frac{\left(1 - p_{+m}\right) - \left(1 - \sum_i p_{i,m(i)}\right)}{1 - p_{+m}}$$

$$= \frac{\sum_i p_{i,m(i)} - p_{+m}}{1 - p_{+m}} \tag{9.18}$$

Using the frequencies instead of the proportions gives

$$\hat{\lambda}_B = \frac{\sum_i x_{i,m(i)} - x_{+m}}{x_{++} - x_{+m}} \tag{9.19}$$

Applying this formula to the data in Table 9.2 gives

$$\hat{\lambda}_B = \frac{(44 + 39 + 58) - 104}{373 - 104} = 0.138$$

When both factors are sampled and when the value of $\hat{\lambda}_B$ is neither 0 nor 1, the large-sample variance of $\hat{\lambda}_B$ is

$$\hat{\text{var}}(\hat{\lambda}_B) = \frac{\left(x_{++} - \sum_i x_{i,m(i)}\right)\left(x_{+m} + \sum_i x_{i,m(i)} - 2 \sum_{m(i)=m} x_{im}\right)}{(x_{++} - x_{+m})^3} \quad (9.20)$$

The final sum in this equation includes only the entries from those rows where the largest column frequency is in the same column that has the largest marginal frequency. The asymptotic sampling distribution of $\hat{\lambda}_B$ is roughly normal, so this variance can be used to construct hypothesis tests and confidence intervals for $0 < \lambda_B < 1$. The hypotheses $\lambda_B = 0$ and $\lambda_B = 1$ have a special status in this test: they are retained only when the corresponding sample statistic is 0 or 1. For the example data,

$$\hat{\text{var}}(\hat{\lambda}_B) = \frac{(373 - 141)(104 + 141 - 2 \times 44)}{(373 - 104)^3} = 0.00187$$

Hence $s_{\hat{\lambda}} = 0.043$ and a 95% confidence interval ($z \approx 2$) goes from 0.05 to 0.22.

Prediction of A is a different operation from prediction of B, so it is not surprising that the predictive association λ_A is different from λ_B. The difference in formulae is trivial: the roles of A and B (and their subscripts) are interchanged in Equations 9.17 to 9.20. Let n and $n(j)$ maximize the frequency down the columns in the manner of m and $m(i)$. Then, in parallel to Equation 9.19,

$$\hat{\lambda}_A = \frac{\sum_j x_{n(j),j} - x_{n+}}{x_{++} - x_{n+}} \quad (9.21)$$

In Table 9.2, row a_3 is largest in every column, so $\sum x_{n(j),j} = x_{n+}$ and $\hat{\lambda}_A = 0$. For $\hat{\lambda}_A$ other than 0 or 1, a variance formula analogous to Equation 9.20 applies. For the current example, $\hat{\lambda}_A = 0$ and no sampling variance can be estimated.

In this example, knowing A helps to predict B ($\hat{\lambda}_B = 0.14$), but knowing B does not help with A ($\hat{\lambda}_A = 0$). This difference does not create practical difficulties in interpretation, for prediction normally precedes only in one direction. In a given situation, one coefficient is more meaningful than the other, so a composite measure of prediction in both directions is rarely needed. Nevertheless, a symmetric measure has been devised. In effect, this measure describes what happens if one is asked to predict A from B one-half the time and B from A the other half of the time. Both types of errors go into the measure of uncertainty. The numerators and the denominators of $\hat{\lambda}_A$ and $\hat{\lambda}_B$ are pooled, and their ratio is found, giving

$$\lambda_{AB} = \frac{\sum_i x_{i,m(i)} + \sum_j x_{n(j),j} - x_{+m} - x_{n+}}{2x_{++} - x_{+m} - x_{n+}} \quad (9.22)$$

There are several ways to extend the measures of predictive association to more than two dimensions. These follow logically from an analysis of what is known, uncertain, and to be predicted in the problem, and they are based on principles analogous to those of the two-dimensional measures. With a little practice, one can devise a statistic that is appropriate to one's particular application (e.g., Problem 9.8).

9.4. MEASURES OF INFORMATION TRANSMISSION

The predictive-association measures take into account only the largest probability in a row (or column). A more variance-like measure should use the entire distribution. Two such dispersion measures are described in Section 5.8. For any distribution $\pi_1, \pi_2, \ldots \pi_b$, the *concentration* and the *entropy*, respectively, are defined as

$$C(\boldsymbol{\pi}) = 1 - \sum_j \pi_j^2 \tag{9.23}$$

and

$$H(\boldsymbol{\pi}) = - \sum_j \pi_j \log_2 \pi_j \tag{9.24}$$

(Equations 5.16 and 5.17). When they are used to compare the saturated model to a model of unrelatedness, the coefficients η_C and η_H (Equation 5.19) are effect-size measures of the type described here. For example, η_H is the relative difference in entropy between a model in which the rows and columns are unrelated and one in which the predictions match the data,

$$\eta_H = \frac{H(\text{no association}) - H(\text{saturated association})}{H(\text{no association})}$$

Calculation is done as described in Section 5.8 or as amplified below.

The interpretation of the entropy measure is worth a digression. The basis of this measure lies in the mathematical theory of communication (Shannon, 1948; Shannon & Weaver, 1949; see Coombs, Dawes, & Tversky, 1970; Garner, 1962; Krippendorff, 1986; Luce, 1960).[†] Suppose that one is about to receive a "message" consisting of a single event taken from a b-level probabilistic categorization. Equation 9.24 defines the *entropy*, the *information*, or the *uncertainty* (all three terms have been used) of this message. It measures the extent to which

---

[†] Entropy can be used as a central concept in the analysis of frequency tables, beyond the association measures described here (e.g., Krippendorff, 1986). For another development of the information concept for frequency tables, see Gokhale and Kullback (1978).

the distribution of messages is scattered evenly over the *b* alternatives. When one category dominates, $H(\pi)$ is small, and when the categories are equiprobable it is large. Using Equation 9.24, the four-level distribution with probabilities 0.62, 0.21, 0.14, and 0.03, has entropy

$$H(\pi) = - [0.62 \log_2 0.62 + 0.21 \log_2 0.21 + 0.14 \log_2 0.14 + 0.03 \log_2 0.03]$$

$$= -[(0.62)(-0.690) + (0.21)(-2.252) + (0.14)(-2.837) + (0.03)(-5.059)]$$

$$= 1.45$$

Referring to $H(\pi)$ as both the "information" and the "uncertainty" of a message may seem curious; one ordinarily thinks of information as what one knows, but the larger $H(\pi)$, the more variable the distribution. However, from the point of view of communication, the definition makes sense. Information about an unknown event is more useful as one knows less about the event. If all the observations fall into a single category, there is no uncertainty in the outcome, and learning about the event conveys no information. One learns nothing that one did not already know, so $H = 0$. At the other extreme, if all the categories are equally probable, then one's uncertainty about the situation is maximal and the largest amount of information is gained by finding out which event takes place. With equal probabilities, H takes its largest value, which is $\log_2 b$.

The use of base 2 for the logarithms gives a nice interpretation to H: it is the average number of dichotomous decisions, or *bits of information*, necessary to make the classification. For example, consider classifying an event into a four-cell distribution. Certainly, two questions suffice; the following two will do:

1. Is the event in the set $\{a_1, a_2\}$?
2. Is the event in the set $\{a_1, a_3\}$?

$$(9.25)$$

The pattern of yes and no answers to these questions pins down the event to a single possibility. If the frequencies in the four cells are the same, this pair of questions is the best that one can do. However, with an uneven distribution, one can devise a more efficient questioning scheme. Suppose that the probabilities of the four categories are those in the example above (0.62, 0.21, 0.14, and 0.03) and that one asks the following questions, stopping when one knows the event:

1. Is the event a_1?
2. Is the event a_2?
3. Is the event a_3?

$$(9.26)$$

When event a_1 occurs only the first question is necessary, which happens 62% of the time. On 21% of the events a_2 occurs and two questions are needed. Only for the remaining 17% of events need all three questions be asked. The many times that one gets away with a single question more than compensate for the occasions when three questions are necessary. The long-term average number of questions required is $(1)(0.62) + (2)(0.21) + (3)(0.17) = 1.55$. This is less than the two questions that are always needed under Scheme 9.25. Different questioning schemes yield different averages, some higher, others lower. No scheme can reduce the average below $H(\boldsymbol{\pi})$ questions. One can get arbitrarily close to this limit with a sufficiently clever scheme (which may need to code several events at once). In the example, $H(\boldsymbol{\pi}) = 1.45$ bits, slightly better than Scheme 9.26.

Returning to the association coefficient, Section 5.8 showed how to calculate statistics such as η_H for any model. In a two-way table, the calculations are simpler. Say that the rows of the table (factor A) are used to predict the columns (factor B). The entropy of the distribution of B is calculated from the marginal distribution. Denote this entropy by $H(B)$, then

$$H(B) = -\sum_j P(b_j) \log_2 P(b_j) = -\sum_j \pi_{+j} \log_2 \pi_{+j} \tag{9.27}$$

For the ith row of the table, the entropy is

$$H(B|a_i) = -\sum_j P(b_j|a_i) \log_2 P(b_j|a_i) = -\sum_j \left(\frac{\pi_{ij}}{\pi_{i+}}\right) \log_2 \left(\frac{\pi_{ij}}{\pi_{i+}}\right) \tag{9.28}$$

Combining these values over A gives the average entropy of B when A is known:

$$H(B|A) = \sum_i P(a_i)H(B|a_i) = \sum_i \pi_{i+}H(B|a_i) \tag{9.29}$$

Knowing A increases one's certainty about B, so $H(B) \geq H(B|A)$. In information-theoretic terms, the difference between these two entropies is the amount of information that A gives about B, or the *information transmitted between A and B*,

$$T(A,B) = H(B) - H(B|A) \tag{9.30}$$

Intuitively, $T(A,B)$ is a measure of how much A tells one about B. Small values imply that A and B are unrelated, and large values mean that much of the variation in A reappears in B's classification. The statistic η_H is the proportion of the entropy of B that derives from A,

$$\eta_H(B) = \frac{T(A,B)}{H(B)} = \frac{H(B) - H(B|A)}{H(B)} \tag{9.31}$$

Sample estimates of the quantities in Equations 9.27 to 9.31 are calculated in the obvious way: one substitutes p_{ij} for π_{ij} throughout.

A measure like η_H is most appropriate when one classification determines the other. Consider some confusion data (adapted and modified from Miller & Nicely, 1955). Consonant-vowel stimuli are presented in noise and the subject

TABLE 9.3
Calculation of the Relative Entropy Statistics
for Some Confusion Data

Confusion Data

		Subject's Response (R)						
		ba	da	ga	va	tha	za	zha
	ba	235	4	0	34	27	1	0
	da	0	189	48	0	4	8	11
Stimulus	ga	0	74	161	0	4	8	25
Presented (S)	va	19	0	2	177	29	4	1
	tha	7	0	10	64	105	18	0
	za	0	17	23	4	22	132	26
	zha	0	2	3	1	1	9	191

Conversion to Conditional Probabilities and Calculation of the Entropy Statistics

	ba	da	ga	va	tha	za	zha	$\hat{H}(R\|s_i)$	$\hat{P}(s_i)$
ba	.781	.013	.000	.113	.090	.003	.000	1.056	0.177
da	.000	.727	.185	.000	.015	.031	.042	1.225	0.153
ga	.000	.272	.592	.000	.015	.029	.092	1.514	0.160
va	.082	.000	.009	.763	.125	.017	.004	1.162	0.136
tha	.034	.000	.049	.314	.515	.088	.000	1.707	0.120
za	.000	.076	.103	.018	.098	.589	.116	1.862	0.132
zha	.000	.010	.014	.005	.005	.044	.923	0.531	0.122
$\hat{P}(r_j)$	.154	.168	.145	.165	.113	.106	.149	2.789	

$$\hat{H}(R|S) = \sum_i \hat{P}(s_i)\hat{H}(R|s_i) = 1.290$$

$$\hat{\eta}_H(R) = \frac{\hat{H}(R) - \hat{H}(R|S)}{\hat{H}(R)} = \frac{2.789 - 1.290}{2.789} = 0.537$$

attempts to identify them. The data form the confusion matrix at the top of Table 9.3. One does not need a statistical test to see that there is considerable association in this table. Nevertheless, information transmission is imperfect, since the off-diagonal entries are nonzero. Take the conditional probabilities of the responses (factor R) within each row (determined by the stimulus factor S) and calculate the information using the sample equivalent of Equations 9.27 and 9.28. The results are at the bottom of the table. Note that the uncertainty when s_i is known is much less than the unconditional $\hat{H}(R) = 2.789$. The final column gives the row proportions. Using them to average the 7 values of $\hat{H}(R|s_i)$, the conditional information is $\hat{H}(R|S) = 1.290$ (Equation 9.29). Then the relative reduction statistic $\eta_H(B) = 0.537$ is calculated by Equation 9.31.

Combining Equations 9.27 to 9.31 into a single formula gives

$$\eta_H(B) = \frac{\sum_{\text{cells}} \pi_{ij} \log \frac{\pi_{i+}\pi_{+j}}{\pi_{ij}}}{\sum_{j} \pi_{+j} \log \pi_{+j}} \tag{9.32}$$

The subscript 2 has been dropped from the logarithm here, since any type of logarithm gives the same answer in Equation 9.32, as long as numerator and denominator use the same base. Sample estimates are obtained by replacing π_{ij} by p_{ij}.

Expressed using the frequencies, the estimate of the transmitted information is

$$\hat{T}(A,B) = \frac{1}{x_{++}} \sum_{i,j} x_{ij} \log_2 \frac{x_{ij}x_{++}}{x_{i+}x_{+j}}$$

Except for the base of the logarithm and the absence of the factor 2, the summation term is the statistic G^2 in a test of unrelatedness, so that

$$\hat{T}(A,B) = \frac{G^2}{2(\log 2)x_{++}} = 0.7213\frac{G^2}{x_{++}} \tag{9.33}$$

Thus, the relative entropy is

$$\hat{\eta}_H(B) = \frac{G^2}{2\left(x_{++} \log x_{++} - \sum_j \pi_{+j} \log \pi_{+j}\right)} \tag{9.34}$$

The principal part of Equation 9.33 is G^2 divided by the sample size. This form is reminiscent of the phi coefficient of Section 9.2. However, because of their relationship to information theory, the coefficients $\hat{T}$ and η_H have a stronger process interpretation than do $\hat{\Phi}$ and $\hat{\phi}'$.

The relative transmission from B to A, denoted by $\eta_H(A)$ or $\hat{\eta}_H(A)$, is readily calculated by changing the roles of A and B and of i and j in Equations 9.27 to 9.34. A composite measure is constructed by pooling the numerators and denominators of the original ratios to give

$$\eta_H(AB) = \frac{2T(A,B)}{H(A) + H(B)} \tag{9.35}$$

However, this ratio is harder to interpret than the directional measures, inasmuch as the tie to the process of information transmission is weakened.

The relationship between G^2 and $\hat{\eta}_H$ (Equation 9.34) lets one easily test the hypothesis that $\eta_H = 0$. This hypothesis is rejected whenever the hypothesis of nonassociation is rejected with a G^2 test. The variance of $\hat{\eta}_H$ is

$$\text{var}[\hat{\eta}_H(B)] = \frac{\displaystyle\sum_{\text{cells}} \pi_{ij}\left[H(B) \log_2\left(\frac{\pi_{i+}\pi_{+j}}{\pi_{++}}\right) - T(A,B)\log_2\pi_{+j}\right]^2}{x_{++}[H(B)]^4} \tag{9.36}$$

where $H(B)$ and $T(A,B,)$ are defined by Equations 9.27 and 9.30 (see Agresti, 1986). Confidence intervals are constructed using this quantity. For Table 9.3, $s_{\hat{\eta}_H(R)} = 0.012$ and a 95% confidence interval stretches from 0.51 to 0.56.

Turn now to the extension of these ideas to multi-way tables. One such application appeared in Section 5.8, where the entropy was calculated for the expected frequencies under a series of models. Another approach, which is more consistent with the interpretation of entropy as information, uses the relationship between information transmission and independence. It is treated in the remainder of this section.

The information-transmission statistics are extended to three-way classifications in two ways. The simplest way is to treat a pair of factors as determining a single categorization. When a two-level factor A and a three-level factor B are combined in a single six-level categorization, their joint transmission to a third factor is denoted $T(AB,C)$. Calculation of this quantity follows the formulae for the two-way case (Equations 9.27, 9.29, and 9.30), with

$$T(AB,C) = H(C) - H(C|AB) = H(AB) - H(AB|C) \tag{9.37}$$

In the second extension to three dimensions, the transmission between two of the factors is conditioned on levels of the third. Specifically, consider the transmission between factors A and B given factor C. When C is restricted to level c_k, the transmission between A and B is

$$T(A,B|c_k) = H(B|c_k) - H(B|A \cap c_k)$$

(cf. Equation 9.30). The *conditional information transmission* is the average of these two-way transmission statistics over C:

$$T(A,B|C) = \sum_k P(c_k)T(A,B|c_k)$$

Using the definition of $T(A,B|C_k)$ and of conditional information (Equation 9.29), this equation becomes

$$T(A,B|C) = H(B|C) - H(B|AC) \tag{9.38}$$

Information transmission in higher-dimensional tables derives from the same principles. For example, among the transmission statistics in a four-way table are the types $T(A,BCD)$, $T(AB,CD)$, $T(AB,C|D)$, and $T(A,B|CD)$. All of these quantities can be calculated using extensions of the three-way formulae (Equations 9.37 and 9.38).

Some algebraic manipulation of the estimate of $T(A,B|C)$ from Equation 9.38 shows that it is proportional to the G^2 statistic that tests the hypothesis $A \perp\!\!\!\perp B|C$. The constant of proportionality is $1/(2x_{+++}\log 2)$, as in the two-way case of Equation 9.33. This relationship lets one exploit the decomposition of the independence models that was described in Section 6.5. The same additive partitioning applies to information transmission.† For example, suppose that A and B predict Y. The unrelatedness of Y to the predictors breaks into two hypotheses:

$$AB \perp\!\!\!\perp Y \equiv (A \perp\!\!\!\perp Y) \cap (B \perp\!\!\!\perp Y|A)$$

(cf. Equation 6.5). Each of these hypotheses has an associated G^2 statistic, and when these are expressed as information transmission the result is

$$T(AB,Y) = T(A,Y) + T(B,Y|A) \qquad (9.39)$$

Thus, the total information transmitted from the predictors to the outcome is the sum of the transmission from A to Y and that from B to Y when A is held constant.

To create association coefficients, the components of Equation 9.39 are expressed relative to the entropy of Y. Three relative-reduction coefficients are produced. Two of these are standard information-transmission statistics,

$$\eta_H(A,Y) = \frac{T(A,Y)}{H(Y)} \quad \text{and} \quad \eta_H(AB,Y) = \frac{T(AB,Y)}{H(Y)} \qquad (9.40)$$

The third is a conditional statistic that can be constructed in two ways, depending on the choice of denominator. Using the denominator $H(Y)$ gives the statistic

$$\eta'_H(B,Y|A) = \frac{T(B,Y|A)}{H(Y)} \qquad (9.41)$$

Combined with the unconditional coefficients in Equations 9.40, this definition preserves the additive relationship of Equation 9.39:

$$\eta_H(AB,Y) = \eta_H(A,Y) + \eta'_H(B,Y|A)$$

The value of $\eta'_H(B,Y|A)$ is bounded by $1 - \eta_H(A,Y)$, so is not a fully conditional coefficient. In this sense, a better choice of denominator is $H(Y|A)$, which gives

$$\eta_H(B,Y|A) = \frac{H(Y|A) - H(Y|AB)}{H(Y|A)} = \frac{T(B,Y|A)}{H(Y|A)} \qquad (9.42)$$

The difference between $\eta'_H(B,Y|A)$ and $\eta_H(B,Y|A)$ is analogous to the difference between the part (or semi-partial) correlation coefficient and the partial correlation coefficient in continuous-variable statistics. The first expresses the influence of B on Y given A relative to the total variation of Y, the second expresses it relative to the variation in Y after the effects of A have been removed.

---

†For a different development of the partioning of information transmission, see McGill (1954).

An example, using some of the drug-addiction data from Table 7.1, is shown in Table 9.4. Consider SES and county as predictors of the age of first use. Suppose that county is given first status as a predictor, so that its effects are to be extracted first. Accordingly, one looks first at the CF relationship, then at the conditional relationship of S to F:

$$CS\perp\!\!\!\perp F \equiv (C\perp\!\!\!\perp F) \cap (S\perp\!\!\!\perp F|C)$$

The top section in Table 9.4 also shows the calculation of the entropy statistics $H(F)$, $H(F|C)$, and $H(F|SC)$. The bottom portion of the table shows the calculation of the transmission coefficients, both as entropy differences and in their relationship to tests of independence hypotheses. The final column in this panel shows the additive association coefficients produced by dividing the transmission statistics by $\hat{H}(F) = 0.9375$. These ratios are additive, like G^2 and T. The partial association coefficient $\eta_H(S,F|C)$ is calculated at the bottom of the table. The association coefficients are small in all cases, indicating that only a small part of the uncertainty of F is removed when C and S are known.

TABLE 9.4
Calculation of Relative Entropy Statistics Using Data from Table 7.1

Original Frequencies

County	SES	First Use <18	First Use ≥18	$\hat{H}$	$\hat{p}$	
urban	Low	73	107	0.974	0.278	
	Not low	75	142	0.930	0.335	
suburban	Low	39	42	0.999	0.125	
	Not low	17	41	0.872	0.090	
rural	Low	16	53	0.781	0.107	
	Not low	9	33	0.750	0.065	$\hat{H}(F|CS) = 0.9182$
urban		148	249	0.953	0.614	
suburban		56	83	0.972	0.215	
rural		25	86	0.760	0.172	$\hat{H}(F|C) = 0.9256$
		229	418	0.938		$\hat{H}(F) = 0.9375$

Calculation of Entropy Statistics

Relationship	Hypothesis	G^2	$\hat{T}$	$\hat{\eta}_H$
C to F	$C \perp\!\!\!\perp F$	17.31	0.0119	0.0127
S to F given C	$S \perp\!\!\!\perp F|C$	6.63	0.0074	0.0079
SC to F	$SC \perp\!\!\!\perp F$	10.69	0.0193	0.0206

$$\hat{\eta}_H(B,Y|A) = \frac{0.9256 - 0.9182}{0.9256} = \frac{0.0074}{0.9256} = 0.0080$$

The concentration measure (Equation 9.23) is the basis of another association coefficient η_C (see Problem 9.9). This measure, which has many of the properties of η_H but lacks its interpretation and its relationship to independence, was proposed by Goodman & Kruskal (1954), where it is denoted τ_b.†

9.5. A MEASURE OF AGREEMENT

The coefficients described in the last four sections are measures of overall association in one form or another. The more the factors covary in a consistent manner, the greater the coefficient. For some problems, these general measures of association are not helpful. There are many specific types of association, and one needs specialized coefficients to study them. For example, where the categories are ordered, one may wish to measure the extent to which high-ranked categories go together. Measures of this type are discussed in Chapter 13. Another specific form of association is agreement in classification. If the factors of a two-way table have the same categories, one can measure the tendency for the classification of an item to be the same on both factors. For example, when studying the reliability of two raters or judges who are classifying a series of instances, it is not enough for the two ratings to be associated. If the behavior is consistent, the ratings should be the same.

Suppose, for example, that patients are assigned to one of 4 diagnoses, d_1 to d_4, on the basis of the transcript of an interview. Two raters separately classify the same 100 patients, giving the 4×4 array shown in Table 9.5. If the raters' judgments are consistent, most observations fall into the diagonal cells of this table. Any other consistent association, appearing in the off-diagonal cells, means that the raters diagnose the patients differently. An index is needed that summarizes the diagonal tendency.

In passing, note that one must resist any temptation to cast these observations into a 2×4 table of raters by ratings, with 100 observations in each row. To do so violates a basic assumption of the χ^2 test, since then a pair of observations provides two counts, which are dependent. Even if one ignores this problem or corrects for it, the hypothesis that is tested in such a table is not of identical classification by the judges. Recasting the data into two rows loses the relationship between the two diagnoses of each patient. If anything, the equal use of the categories is tested. The proper way to investigate that hypothesis is discussed in Sections 10.7 and 12.3.

Consider the problem in terms of the population probabilities, π_{ij}. The total proportion of agreement is the sum of the probabilities on the main diagonal, $\Sigma\pi_{ii}$. By itself, this sum is not a good measure of association. If the judges

---

†This association measure should not be confused with the Kendall concordance coefficient, also known as τ_b, which is described in Section 13.10.

TABLE 9.5
Classification of 100 Interview Transcripts
into Four Diagnostic Categories by Two Raters

		Rater B				
		d_1	d_2	d_3	d_4	
	d_1	6	2	4	2	14
Rater	d_2	4	17	14	5	40
A	d_3	1	3	20	0	24
	d_4	1	3	6	12	22
		12	25	44	19	100

behaved independently, the proportion of observations in cell i,i would be $\pi_{i+}\pi_{+i}$ and the total proportion on the diagonal would be $\Sigma\pi_{i+}\pi_{+i}$. This sum depends on the marginal distributions; it is large if both judges put most of the observations in one category. To make a good measure, the apparent agreement, $\Sigma\pi_{ii}$, must be corrected for these chance events. Subtracting $\Sigma\pi_{i+}\pi_{+i}$ and expressing the result relative to the probability of agreement give the *coefficient of agreement*:

$$\kappa = \frac{P(\text{observed agreement}) - P(\text{chance agreement})}{\text{maximum possible agreement} - P(\text{chance agreement})}$$

$$= \frac{\sum_i \pi_{ii} - \sum_i \pi_{i+}\pi_{+i}}{1 - \sum_i \pi_{i+}\pi_{+i}} \tag{9.43}$$

(Cohen, 1960)†. An equivalent definition stated in terms of disagreement, which more closely parallels the measure of uncertainty (Equation 9.16), is

$$\kappa = \frac{P(\text{chance disagreement}) - P(\text{actual disagreement})}{P(\text{chance disagreement})}$$

When probabilities are substituted, this form is the same as Equation 9.43.

Replacing the probabilities in Equation 9.43 by their sample proportions gives an estimate of κ. Converted to frequencies, this estimate is

---

†The adjustment $\Sigma\pi_{i+}\pi_{+i}$ is not strictly correct as a measure of accidental agreement, since π_{i+} and π_{+i} reflect both chance effects and true agreement. Separation of these sources requires a model for the agreement, such as Equation 9.45 below, and the concept of quasi-independence discussed in Chapter 10 (see Section 10.3). For most uses, the κ coefficient as defined by Equation 9.43 is satisfactory.

$$\hat{\kappa} = \frac{x_{++} \sum_i x_{ii} - \sum_i x_{i+}x_{+i}}{x_{++}^2 - \sum_i x_{i+}x_{+i}} \tag{9.44}$$

For example, applied to the data in Table 9.5, the agreement is

$$\hat{\kappa} = \frac{100(6 + 17 + 20 + 12) - (14 \times 12 + 40 \times 25 + 24 \times 44 + 22 \times 19)}{100^2 - (14 \times 12 + 40 \times 25 + 24 \times 44 + 22 \times 19)} = 0.388$$

Since $\hat{\kappa}$ does not measure simple association, its magnitude is not tested by X^2 or G^2. Its large-sample distribution is approximately normal, so that a test can be performed with an ordinary z ratio if the standard error of $\hat{\kappa}$ is known. This standard error can be estimated under two different assumptions (Fleiss, Cohen, & Everitt, 1969): in general and when the true value of κ is zero. Formulae for these estimates are given in more general versions below (Equations 9.50 and 9.51). The unrestricted standard error could, in principle, be used to construct a confidence interval for κ; the restricted estimate is appropriate for tests of the hypothesis that $\kappa = 0$. Unfortunately, unless the sample is quite large, the unrestricted approximation is inaccurate (unless $\kappa = 0$), which limits its use in confidence intervals (Cicchetti & Fleiss, 1977; Fleiss & Cicchetti, 1978). In an $a \times a$ table, a minimum sample size of $16a^2$ is suggested. The estimate of the variance when $\kappa = 0$ is more robust and allows the useful hypothesis of chance agreement of the classifications to be tested.

To continue the example, if $\kappa = 0$ then $\hat{var}_0(\hat{\kappa}) = 0.00324$ (the subscript $_0$ indicates the restricted estimate). Thus, the standard error of $\hat{\kappa}$ is 0.057 and a test of the null hypothesis that $\kappa = 0$ yields the test statistic $z = 0.388/0.057 = 6.82$. This statistic exceeds the 1.96 criterion for a 5% test in a normal distribution, so the hypothesis of only chance agreement can be rejected. The total sample size of 100 is too small to use the unrestricted variance estimate (which is 0.00424) for confidence-interval calculation.

The model for the data that underlies the κ statistic combines two effects: overall independence, which determines the accidental agreement, and an increment in frequency in the diagonal cells. In the log-linear spirit of this book, such a model is written as

$$\log \mu_{ij} = \lambda + \lambda_{A(i)} + \lambda_{B(j)} + \delta_{ij} \tag{9.45}$$

Here the λ's provide the usual expression of independence and δ_{ij} is nonzero only on the diagonal,

$$\delta_{ij} = \begin{cases} \delta_i, & \text{if } i = j, \\ 0, & \text{otherwise} \end{cases} \tag{9.46}$$

Model 9.45 captures the idea behind the κ statistic, although it does not imply the specific form of κ described here (Equation 9.43). It can be used to develop the model for agreement further, as is discussed briefly in Sections 10.3 and 11.2 below.

The kappa statistic admits many modifications. Many of these weight the disagreements unequally, so that some are treated as less serious than others (Cohen, 1968). The *weighted kappa* statistic assigns to each combination of classifications a weight w_{ij} between 0 and 1. Weights near 0 indicate disagreement and those near 1 indicate agreement. Usually, the perfect-agreement cells on the diagonal receive the weight $w_{ii} = 1.0$. For example, with an ordered set of categories, one can use a monotonic function of the magnitude of the difference between i and j, such as

$$w_{ij} = 1 - \frac{|i-j|}{a-1} \tag{9.47}$$

With the weights incorporated, the observed agreement is $\Sigma w_{ij}\pi_{ij}$ and the agreement by chance is $\Sigma w_{ij}\pi_{i+}\pi_{+j}$, both sums running over all the cells in the table. With these values, the weighted coefficient of agreement is

$$\kappa_w = \frac{\displaystyle\sum_{\text{cells}} w_{ij}\pi_{ij} - \sum_{\text{cells}} w_{ij}\pi_{i+}\pi_{+j}}{1 - \displaystyle\sum_{\text{cells}} w_{ij}\pi_{i+}\pi_{+j}} \tag{9.48}$$

An estimate of κ_w is obtained by replacing the probabilities π_{ij} with p_{ij}, or by using the frequencies:

$$\hat{\kappa}_w = \frac{\displaystyle x_{++}\sum_{\text{cells}} w_{ij}x_{ij} - \sum_{\text{cells}} w_{ij}x_{i+}x_{+j}}{x_{++}^2 - \displaystyle\sum_{\text{cells}} w_{ij}x_{ij}x_{+j}} \tag{9.49}$$

The large-sample variance of this estimate is

$$\hat{v}\text{ar}(\hat{\kappa}_w) = \frac{1}{x_{++}(1-P_c)^2}\left(\sum_{\text{cells}} [w_j - (1-\kappa_w)(\overline{w}_{i+} + \overline{w}_{+j})]^2 p_{ij}\right.$$
$$\left. - [\kappa_w - (1-\kappa_w)P_c]^2\right) \tag{9.50}$$

where

$$P_c = \sum_{\text{cells}} w_{ij}p_{i+}p_{+j}$$

is the probability of chance agreement and

$$\overline{w}_{i+} = \sum_j w_{ij}p_{+j} \quad \text{and} \quad \overline{w}_{+j} = \sum_i w_{ij}p_{i+}$$

Once again, the restriction to large-samples applies: Equation 9.50 should not be used for confidence intervals unless x_{++} is quite large. Under the assumption that $\kappa = 0$, the estimated variance is

$$\hat{var}_0(\hat{\kappa}_w) = \frac{1}{x_{++}(1 - P_c)^2}\left(\sum_{\text{cells}} [w_{ij} - \overline{w}_{i+} - \overline{w}_{+j}]^2 p_{i+}p_{+j} - P_c^2\right) \qquad (9.51)$$

This variance may be used to test whether $\kappa_w = 0$. It is more robust than Equation 9.50, and can be used in moderately-sized samples.

The unweighted κ statistic (Equations 9.43 and 9.44) is a special case of the weighted statistic, obtained by setting the weights for the diagonal cells to 1 (perfect agreement) and the weights of all other cells to 0 (perfect disagreement). Thus, a computer program need implement only Equations 9.49, 9.50, and 9.51 to calculate both weighted and unweighted coefficients.

As an example of the weighted statistic, suppose that the linear pattern of weights defined by Equation 9.45 is used with the data of Table 9.5. The weights are

	d_1	d_2	d_3	d_4
d_1	1.0000	0.6667	0.3333	0.0000
d_2	0.6667	1.0000	0.6667	0.3333
d_3	0.3333	0.6667	1.0000	0.6667
d_4	0.0000	0.3333	0.6667	1.0000

Then the weighted agreement is $\Sigma w_{ij}p_{ij} = 0.787$ and the chance figure is $P_c = 0.646$. Hence, $\hat{\kappa}_w = 0.398$. The null variance is 0.00442 and a test of the hypothesis that $\kappa_w = 0$ gives the test statistic $z = 5.99$.

The statistics κ and κ_w are simple and transparent, which is one of their great virtues. However, one should keep a few warnings in mind while using them (see, e.g., Light, 1971). The first warning derives from the use of the independence model to determine chance agreement. For most real categorizations, various types of association among the categories are likely to be present. Often two categories are more readily confusable with each other than they are with a third category, as the category *agree very much* is closer to the category *agree somewhat* than it is to *disagree somewhat*. The κ statistic makes no use of the quality of fit of the independence model, in effect treating any association involving the diagonal as an indication of agreement. To a degree, the weighted κ statistic allows the off-diagonal cells to enter the calculation, but the core model is still independence. A better measure of agreement may come from a more realistic base model that includes some form of partial association.

A second point to note is that in summarizing the amount of agreement, the κ statistics make no assertion about the nature of this agreement. Many different patterns of diagonal excess yield the same value of κ. Thus, it is possible for two pairs of observers to have the same degree of agreement, as measured by $\hat{\kappa}$, yet for the character of this agreement to be very different. If two raters have the same $\hat{\kappa}$ when compared to a standard rater, one cannot say that they are doing the same thing. Thus, one must be careful when drawing conclusions about multiple raters using the κ statistic.

There have been several attempts to define agreement statistics that avoid some of these difficulties (e.g., Agresti, 1988; Darroch & McCloud, 1986; Tanner & Young, 1985ab). Some versions of these models are described briefly later in this book, although the models that combine agreement with other models of association are not sufficiently developed at this point to be included. There have also been attempts to develop agreement indices for more than two observers (Conger, 1980; Fleiss, 1971, 1981; Light, 1971; Tanner & Young, 1985b). A generalization of κ_w to tables that are not square appears in Hubert (1978).

PROBLEMS

9.1. For the frequency table

	b_1	b_2
a_1	26	12
a_2	11	18

estimate the cross-product ratio α and its logarithm β, find the phi-coefficient $\hat{\Phi}$, estimate the predictive association λ_B and the information transmission $\eta_H(B)$.

9.2. Test the hypothesis that each of the coefficients in problem 9.1 equals the value that it would take if no association were present.

9.3. Calculate confidence intervals for the coefficients α, β, λ_B, and $\eta_H(B)$, using the data in Problem 9.1.

9.4. Derive the variance of $\hat{Y}$ and $\hat{Q}$ (Equations 9.12) by applying Equation 9.7 to the variance of $\hat{\alpha}$.

9.5. Consider the three-way table data formed by combining the results in Problems 2.1b and 2.6.
a. Estimate the three-factor cross-product ratio α. How would you interpret this coefficient?
b. Test the hypothesis that $\alpha = 1$ and construct a confidence interval for α. Remember that the three-dimensional coefficient has the same problems with asymmetry that affected the two-dimensional odds ratio, so inference should be approached through log α as in Equation 9.9.

9.6. An experiment and its replication give the following two 3 $\times$ 4 tables of frequencies and associated tests of independence:

Experiment:

14	17	26	30
3	17	11	27
18	24	9	4

$N = 200$
$X^2 = 37.510$
$G^2 = 41.399$

Replication:

11	6	13	21
2	4	3	18
13	6	2	1

$N = 100$
$X^2 = 30.586$
$G^2 = 32.983$

a. Which version of the experiment shows the largest effect? Why?
b. How would you test to see whether the effects in the two tables are the same (do not run the test)?

9.7. By what proportion does a knowledge of the species of a bird in Problem 2.1c reduce the errors that one makes in predicting its nesting location?

9.8. The predictive-association coefficient generalizes to three dimensions. Consider a three-factor table of data in which A and B are predictors of an outcome factor Y:

		y_1	y_2	y_3
	b_1	15	4	5
a_1	b_2	7	3	8
	b_3	13	19	5
	b_1	10	6	9
a_2	b_2	6	14	16
	b_3	4	18	16

a. How many errors are made in predicting Y when
   i. No information is available about either A or B
   ii. A is known and B is not
   iii. Both A and B are known
b. Use these counts to define three relative error-reduction effect-size statistics:
   i. A coefficient $\lambda_{Y(A)}$ that measures the relative reduction in errors when A is known. Note that this statistic is the same as λ_Y in the marginal AY table.
   ii. A coefficient $\lambda_{Y(AB)}$ that measures the reduction when both predictors are known.
   iii. A coefficient $\lambda_{Y(B|A)}$ that measures the reduction in errors provided by B when the classification of A is known,

$$\lambda_{Y(B|A)} = \frac{\#(\text{errors}|A) - \#(\text{errors}|A \text{ and } B)}{\#(\text{errors}|A)}$$

9.9. In defining the predictive-association coefficient λ_B, the most probable category is always predicted. Another approach is to match the distribution of the predictions to that of the factor being predicted. So, if category b_j has probability π_j, then it is chosen for a proportion π_j of the predictions. Develop an uncertainty-reduction coefficient for a two-way table using this definition. Throughout, apply the results to the table in Problem 2.1,

a. If A is unknown, the distribution of predictions of B matches that factor's marginal distribution. What is the probability of an error for these predictions? Show that this probability is the same as the measure of concentration $C(\pi)$ in Equation 9.23.

b. What is the probability of a correct prediction of a category if the row category A is known?

c. Use these results to construct a relative-reduction coefficient. Show that the result is the coefficient η_C originally discussed in Section 5.8 (Equation 5.19).

9.10. A 5-level distribution of probabilities is 0.10, 0.60, 0.05, 0.20, and 0.05.
a. What is the entropy $H(\pi)$?
b. Devise a questioning scheme to identify an outcome. On the average, how many questions does it require? How does this compare to the entropy?

9.11. Calculate the information transmission statistic η_H for the data in Tables 2.2 and 2.3.

9.12. Using the data from Problem 9.8, find the relative information transmission from A to Y and from B to Y given A. The following sums may be helpful: $\Sigma p_{i++}\log p_{i++} = -0.6868$, $\Sigma p_{ij+}\log p_{ij+} = -1.7570$, $\Sigma p_{++k}\log p_{++k} = -1.0967$, $\Sigma p_{i+k}\log p_{i+k} = -1.7460$, and $\Sigma p_{ijk}\log p_{ijk} = -2.7512$.

9.13. The detection data discussed in Chapter 6 are subject to the decomposition

$$[HL][X][Y] \equiv (H \perp\!\!\!\perp X) \cap (L \perp\!\!\!\perp Y) \cap (H \perp\!\!\!\perp Y|L) \cap (L \perp\!\!\!\perp X|H) \cap (X \perp\!\!\!\perp Y|HL)$$

(see Table 6.6 and Problem 6.8). Use G^2 statistics to define a series of association coefficients $\eta_H(H,X)$, $\eta_H(L,Y)$, $\eta_H(H,Y|L)$, $\eta_H(L,X|H)$, and $\eta_H(X,Y|HL)$. Use the statistics from Chapter 6 to calculate their values.

9.14. Find the coefficient of agreement κ for the data in Problem 9.1. Test whether it is nonzero.

9.15. Two problems are given to a group of 6-year old subjects. For each problem, the subjects are classified as able to solve the problem, requiring instruction to solve the problem, or unable to solve it (s, i, and u, respectively). The results are

		Problem 2		
		s	i	u
	s	17	5	1
Problem 1	i	3	12	4
	u	4	6	8

Show that there is a significant amount of consistency in ability across the problems.

10

Structurally Incomplete Tables

The discussion so far has applied to complete cross-classification tables in which observations can fall into every cell. Any empty cells are accidents of sampling. This type of empty cell is known as a *random zero*. Random zeros have an effect on the analysis only when they are sufficiently prevalent to block out an entire section of a table or to compromise the test of a high-order interaction. The treatment of random zeros problems, which largely consists of adjustments to the degrees of freedom, was discussed in Section 5.6.

The present chapter considers the treatment of data in which certain cells are excluded from consideration. These vacancies may be intrinsic to the phenomenon being studied or may be part of a hypothesis under test. They are never accidents of sampling. They are known as *structural voids* or as *structural zeros*, the former term being more general since the cells in question may have non-zero observed frequencies. Data tables with structural voids lack a complete factorial structure. Their analysis requires a modification of the concept of independence, although in other respects the procedures are fundamentally the same. Models involving structural voids allow some very precise hypotheses to be tested and are a powerful adjunct to the models of unrelatedness in complete tables.

10.1. STRUCTURAL VOIDS AND QUASI-INDEPENDENCE

The most direct type of structural void occurs when something in the world that one is observing prevents counts from falling into certain cells of what would otherwise be a factorial table. An obvious example of such an impossibility occurs in a cross-classification of hospital admissions by sex: although pregnant males may have a cell in the table, none are observed. Another example occurs when subjects are asked to select two preferred objects from a set of alternatives. A set of data for choices among 6 alternatives is shown in Table 10.1. Since the subjects are not permitted to make the same choice twice, the cells on the diagonal are necessarily empty. To distinguish these structural zeros from random zeros, they are marked by dashes rather than zeros.

If one treats the impossible cells in Table 10.1 as frequencies of zero, they assert themselves as dependencies in a test of independence ($G^2(25) = 198.03$). The vacant diagonal makes rejection of independence a foregone and uninteresting conclusion. Neither the absence of pregnant men nor the fact that subjects followed instructions and did not record the same choice twice is worth a statistical test. Instead, one would like to test more subtle hypotheses of independence, concerning the relationship of the rows and columns when the structural zeros are ignored.

What one really wants to do with Table 10.1 is to ignore the missing diagonal and inspect the off-diagonal cells for association, to see whether the second choices show a tendency to be related to the first choices. As discussed in Chapter 2, the hypothesis of independence in a full table implies that an additive log-frequency model fits the data,

$$\log \mu_{ij} = \lambda + \lambda_{A(i)} + \lambda_{B(j)} \tag{10.1}$$

In the deficient table, this model can still apply to the valid cells. If Model 10.1 fits, it indicates that, other than the constraint not to pick the same category twice, the first and second choices are unrelated. An incomplete table for which Equation 10.1 holds is said to show *quasi-independence*. The quasi-independence and the independence models are the same for any cell to which they both apply; the difference between them arises only because certain cells are excluded from the quasi-independence model.

The missing cells make it impossible to calculate $\hat{\mu}_{ij}$ for the quasi-indepen-

TABLE 10.1
Hypothetical First- and Second-choice Preference Data

		Second Choice					
		a_1	a_2	a_3	a_4	a_5	a_6
	a_1	—	15	13	8	3	8
	a_2	16	—	5	8	7	6
First Choice	a_3	18	14	—	10	4	6
	a_4	6	3	2	—	13	34
	a_5	1	1	1	3	—	7
	a_6	2	3	2	23	8	—

dence model by a direct formula such as $x_{i+}x_{+j}/x_{++}$. However, the iterative proportional fitting algorithm still applies if the structural voids are ignored in determining the adjustments. Maximum-likelihood parameter estimates are obtained by adjusting expected frequencies so that the observed and expected marginal distributions are equal, exactly as in Section 5.2. Where the usual distributional and sampling assumptions hold, X^2 or G^2 test statistics can be calculated, again using only the filled cells. The tally of degrees of freedom follows from the usual rules for counting cells, parameters, and constants discussed in Section 5.5 and parameter estimates from the procedures of Sections 5.3 and 5.4.

Take Table 10.1 as an example. The fitting algorithm starts with a table of ones. Summing the legitimate cells across the first row gives 5 (the structurally empty cell 1,1 is ignored), while the actual data sum to 47. Thus, the entries in the first row of the $\hat{\mu}$ table are multiplied by $47/5 = 9.40$. Similar corrections are made to the other rows, and then to the columns. In a complete two-way table, these two adjustments give maximum-likelihood estimates of μ_{ij} (as they did in Table 5.1). Where there are structural voids, repeated iteration cycles are necessary before convergence occurs, just as with the indirect multifactor models. For the data in Table 10.1, this operation gives the expected frequencies in Table 10.2. The frequencies for the vacant cells on the diagonals (shown in parentheses) are obtained by applying the corrections to the initial value of 1 in these cells, even though they do not figure in determining the size of the correction. The interpretation of these numbers is discussed in Section 10.3.

The observed x_{ij} and expected $\hat{\mu}_{ij}$ from Tables 10.1 and 10.2 are compared using either of the test statistics. Only the structurally valid cells (not the structural zeros) are used. The fit is $X^2 = 106.06$ or $G^2 = 103.80$. There are 30 valid data cells in the table, and there are 13 estimated parameters (one λ and 6 each of λ_A and λ_B), less the 2 constraints that make both the λ_A and the λ_B sum to zero. Thus, there are $30 - (13 - 2) = 19$ degrees of freedom. This figure is 6 less than the 25 degrees of freedom that would apply to a test of complete indepen-

TABLE 10.2
Expected Frequencies for Table 10.1 Under Quasi-independence

		Second Choice					
		a_1	a_2	a_3	a_4	a_5	a_6
	a_1	(9.9)	8.1	5.3	13.0	6.9	13.7
	a_2	8.5	(6.9)	4.6	11.2	5.9	11.8
First Choice	a_3	0.0	8.1	(5.4)	13.1	7.0	13.8
	a_4	13.1	10.6	7.0	(17.1)	9.1	18.1
	a_5	2.6	2.1	1.4	3.4	(1.8)	3.6
	a_6	8.7	7.1	4.7	11.4	6.1	(12.1)

dence, a difference that corresponds to the 6 missing cells. In this example, the test-statistic values are sufficient to reject quasi-independence, even though they are considerably reduced from those of the pure independence model. Apparently, there is some form of association between the first and second choices.

The cells that are ignored need not actually be empty to make the quasi-independence model appropriate. For example, consider the confusion data presented in Table 9.3, shown again in the top panel of Table 10.3. The diagonals in this table, which match the same category in rows and columns, represent correct responses and have a special status. Pure independence is certainly rejected here, but that result predominantly indicates the prevalence of correct responses. It is more interesting to ask whether association is present in the off-diagonal cells. Quasi-independence here implies that when a correct response is not made, the error is unrelated to the original stimulus. By treating the diagonal of this table as void, a quasi-independence model is fitted, giving the expected frequencies in the lower panel of the figure. Quasi-independence is rejected ($G^2(29) = 647.44$); one concludes that incorrect responses are related to the original stimulus.

TABLE 10.3
A Quasi-independence Model Fitted to the
Confusion Data from Table 9.3

Observed Frequencies

		Subject's Response (R)						
		ba	da	ga	va	tha	za	zha
	ba	235	4	0	34	27	1	0
	da	0	189	48	0	4	8	11
Stimulus	ga	0	74	161	0	4	8	25
Presented (S)	va	19	0	2	177	29	4	1
	tha	7	0	10	64	105	18	0
	za	0	17	23	4	22	132	26
	zha	0	2	3	1	1	9	191

Expected Frequencies under Quasi-independence with the Diagonal Void

		Subject's Response (R)						
		ba	da	ga	va	tha	za	zha
	ba	(3.4)	13.1	12.8	13.4	12.6	6.7	7.5
	da	4.3	(16.5)	16.2	16.9	15.8	8.4	9.4
Stimulus	ga	6.6	25.7	(25.1)	26.3	24.6	13.1	14.7
Presented (S)	va	3.3	12.9	12.6	(13.2)	12.3	6.5	7.4
	tha	5.9	22.8	22.3	23.3	(21.9)	11.6	13.0
	za	5.0	19.2	18.8	19.6	18.4	(9.8)	11.0
	zha	0.9	3.4	3.3	3.5	3.2	1.7	(1.9)

In some situations, the structural zeros may block the table into several pieces that can be studied separately. For example, the pattern of empty cells

$$
\begin{array}{cccccc}
X & X & X & - & - & - \\
X & X & X & - & - & - \\
- & - & - & X & X & X \\
- & - & - & X & X & X \\
\end{array}
$$

(where X is a filled cell) is really two 2 × 3 tables. The parameters needed to express one of these subtables do not apply to the other subtable. When this situation occurs, the table fragments can be fitted and tested in isolation, although the test statistics (with their degrees of freedom) can be summed into a single composite value, if desired. The separate pieces of the table are usually sufficiently obvious that their analysis does not need discussion here (see Bishop, Fienberg, & Holland 1975, Section 5.2.2, for details).

In this way, almost any hypothesis that can be written for a complete table can be written and tested in an incomplete table, the only limitation occurring if the voids are so extensive as to take all degrees of freedom away from the test or to remove a section of the table completely. Higher-dimensional incomplete tables are fitted and tested in the same way, as are models involving various forms of partial association. Their interpretation is similar to that of a complete table, save that the conclusion applies only to the cells that are actually present.

The incomplete-table procedures let one avoid the problems that are created when random zeros cause certain cells to drop out of difference tests. For example, in the detection data of Chapter 6, the cells with $H = s$, $L = n$, and $X = 6$ are all zero, so that when models involving λ_{HLX} are fitted, no parameter involving this combination can be estimated. However, these cells are available for simpler models that do not involve the HLX marginal frequencies. The ephemeral character of these zeros confounds comparisons involving λ_{HLX}. Specifically, consider a test of whether the HLX association adds anything to the model $[HL][HX][HY]$ $[LXY]$. The natural way to run this test is to add the parameters λ_{HLX} to the base model. If both models are fit normally, the difference test is

$[HL][HX][HY][LXY]$	$G^2(60) = 54.84$
$[HLX][HY][LXY]$	$G^2(50) = 47.95$
Difference	$\Delta G^2(10) = 5.89$

The model $[HLX][HY][LXY]$ here both introduces the new parameters and drops the 6 cells. Neither the test statistic nor the degrees of freedom are the same as they would be if the table were complete. It is hard to tell what biases the missing cells create. A proper test excludes the 6 cells that are not testable in the second model from both models, treating them as structural voids. This modification changes the fit of the first model, giving

[HL][HX][HY][LXY]	$G^2(54) = 52.51$
[HLX][HY][LXY]	$G^2(50) = 47.95$
Difference, λ_{HLX}	$\Delta G^2(4) = 4.56$

The test statistic and the degrees of freedom have both changed appreciably, although for these data the conclusion remains the same. Since no estimate of the parameter $\lambda_{HLX(sn6)}$ can be made, there are 4 degrees of freedom associated with the difference test, even though the HLX configuration forms a $2 \times 2 \times 6$ table and would ordinarily involve 5 degrees of freedom.

10.2. ANOMALOUS CELLS

Sometimes the failure of a model of independence (or quasi-independence) to fit a table can be entirely attributed to a few cells. The exceptional nature of these cells may be predicted from theory or may be discovered by a post hoc examination of residuals. In either case, one would like to know whether the independence or quasi-independence model holds for the balance of the table. To test this hypothesis, the questionable cell is designated a structural void, and the simpler model is applied to the revised table.

For example, consider the 3×4 array in Table 10.4. Independence is rejected here ($G^2(6) = 18.20$). To try to understand the nature of the dependence, the expected frequencies are calculated and standardized residuals obtained (using Equation 5.20 from Section 5.9). Among the residuals, that of cell 1,2 is large and positive, while the other residuals in that row and column are negative. This pattern suggests an anomaly involving the frequency x_{12}. To check if this cell is the only anomaly, a model of quasi-independence is fitted to the table with the questionable cell structurally omitted. The resulting model fits well ($G^2(5) = 2.46$), indicating quasi-independence in the balance of the table and that the source of the original discrepancy has been identified.

Pure independence is a special case of quasi-independence. The latter model can be thought of as containing extra parameters that are used to adjust the values of the deleted cells to make the fit in those cells perfect. For example, one way to write the model for Table 10.4 with x_{12} ignored is

$$\log \mu_{ij} = \lambda + \lambda_{A(i)} + \lambda_{B(j)} + \delta_{12(ij)} \tag{10.2}$$

where δ_{12} takes any value in cell 1,2 and is zero in all other cells. One does not ordinarily fit the quasi-independence model in this form, but it shows that independence and quasi-independence are hierarchically related so that a difference test based on the two models is appropriate (Table 10.4, bottom). The statistical significance of ΔG^2 indicates that $\delta_{AB(12)} \neq 0$ and that cell 1,2 carries a reliable portion of the failure of independence. Following Model 10.2, one can view Table 10.4 as combining independence with excess frequency in cell 1,2.

TABLE 10.4
Analysis of a Table with a Single Anomalous Cell

Observed Data

12	18	3	10
18	3	7	10
20	6	9	11

Expected Frequencies under Independence

16.9	9.1	6.4	10.5
15.0	8.1	5.7	9.3
18.1	9.8	8.9	11.2

Standardized Deviates z_P

−1.20	2.93	−1.35	−0.15
0.79	−1.79	0.55	0.24
0.44	−1.21	0.81	−0.06

Test for Significance of the Anomalous Cell 1,2

[A][B] in full table	$G^2(6) = 18.20$
[A][B] in table with cell 1,2 excluded	$G^2(5) = 2.46$
$\delta_{12} = 0$ in Model 10.2	$\Delta G^2(1) = 15.74$

Using a χ^2 distribution directly to interpret ΔG^2 makes sense if there is good reason, other than the data, to select the particular cell for examination. If this test is done as part of the post hoc location of anomalous cells, error control is important. Potentially, one could run the same test for every cell of the table, creating a family of tests over which the type I error rate is inflated. For tables of moderate size, a correction based on the Bonferroni inequality is easy to apply. To fix the error rate to a nominal value of α_F over an $a \times b$ table, divide α_F by the number of cells, running each test at the α_F/ab level. Critical values for these tests are provided in Appendix A.2. Using $\alpha_F = 0.05$ for the 12 tests from Table 10.4 gives a criterion value of 8.21 (from row 12 and column 1 of Table A.2). Thus, cell (1,2) is a significant anomaly, even when identified post hoc. Of course, because of this correction, post hoc analysis is less powerful than a planned analysis. An analysis strategy driven by the logic of the problem, if possible, is more desirable.

Following the reasoning mentioned in Section 9.1, a type I error can also be limited by comparing ΔG^2 to the critical value of χ^2 with $(a - 1)(b - 1)$ degrees of freedom at the desired α_F level. This value is handy when one has only standard χ^2 tables available, but it is conservative relative to the Bonferroni correction and so is less powerful. Applied to Table 10.4, the critical value of $\chi^2(6)$ at $\alpha = 0.05$ is 12.59, appreciably greater than the Bonferroni corrected value of 8.18.

The signal detection data in Chapter 6 provide some further examples of the examination of specific cells. Tests there indicated that the parameters λ_{XY} were necessary, and examination of estimates of these parameters suggested that much of this need could be attributed to the $X = 1$, $Y = 1$ response. Before attempting to interpret the remainder of the λ_{XY} table, one should check to see whether λ_{XY} is needed only because of the special nature of the $X = 1$, $Y = 1$ cells. In the original analysis (Section 6.2), λ_{XY} was deemed necessary when the model $[HLX][HLY][XY]$ was compared to $[HLX][HLY]$ and found to fit significantly better. Fits of these models, with and without the $X = 1$, $Y = 1$ cells, and the difference tests between them, are

	Including (1,1)	Excluding (1,1)
$[HLX][HLY]$	$G^2(95) = 221.43$	$G^2(91) = 152.30$
$[HLX][HLY][XY]$	$G^2(70) = 94.05$	$G^2(67) = 80.03$
λ_{XY}	$\Delta G^2(25) = 127.38$	$\Delta G^2(24) = 72.27$

The tests on the right allow the hypothesis of no response interaction in the remainder of the table to be tested. The difference of G^2 is still significant, so $\lambda_{XY} = 0$ can be rejected, although not by so large an amount.

These results also allow the reliability of the $X = 1$, $Y = 1$ anomaly to be assessed. The deletion of four $X = 1$, $Y = 1$ cells corresponds to the introduction of 4 additional parameters that fit their exact values. Thus, the models with and without the cells are related hierarchically and can be compared to identify whether the four cells are out of line. The difference between the fits of the model $[HLX][HLY]$ is $\Delta G^2(4) = 221.43 - 152.30 = 69.13$, which clearly indicates an effect in the selected cells. Although smaller, the result of deleting the cells from the model $[HLX][HLY][XY]$ is also significant ($\Delta G^2(3) = 14.02$), implying that the effects in these cells cannot be completely accounted for by the single two-way parameter $\lambda_{XY(11)}$. Tests of this type are helpful in explaining the nature of the LXY association.

Where some of the observations in a set of data have been damaged, the quasi-independence model can be used to smooth over the defect. Perhaps a cell of one's table has been incorrectly recorded and it is now impossible to go back and recover the original entry; perhaps a mistake in the experimental procedure has invalidated the results in one condition. Instead of abandoning the investigation, one can use the incomplete-table procedure to analyze the remainder of the data, fitting models of whatever complexity is needed.

10.3. ESTIMATES OF MISSING CELLS

An unsaturated log-frequency model that is fitted to an incomplete table gives estimated expected values for the missing cells as well as for the complete ones. These estimates are obtained by applying the model for log $\hat{\mu}$ to the structural voids, even though they had no role in originally fitting the model. When the cell's classification is meaningless (as with pregnant men) the resulting numbers are of no interest. However, when the cells contain meaningful but unobserved frequencies, the estimates may be useful. Essentially, they tell what the value in the missing cell would be if the model for the rest of the table held there as well.

In the last section a missing-cell procedure was used to identify an anomalous cell (Table 10.4). When a significant anomaly is found, the size of the deviation is determined by subtracting the observed frequency from its estimate under the missing-cell model. For Table 10.4, the quasi-independence model fits the data if cell 1,2 is excluded. The parameter estimates for this model are

$$\hat{\lambda} = 2.07$$

$$\hat{\lambda}_{A(1)} = -0.27, \ \hat{\lambda}_{A(2)} = 0.03, \ \hat{\lambda}_{A(3)} = 0.23,$$

$$\hat{\lambda}_{B(1)} = 0.72, \ \hat{\lambda}_{B(2)} = -0.71, \ \hat{\lambda}_{B(3)} = -0.25, \ \hat{\lambda}_{B(4)} = 0.24,$$

Based on these values, the predicted entry in cell 1,2 is

$$\log \hat{\mu}_{12} = \hat{\lambda} + \hat{\lambda}_{A(1)} + \hat{\lambda}_{B(2)} = 1.09$$

$$\hat{\mu}_{12} = e^{1.09} = 3.0$$

The observed $x_{12} = 18$. Thus, the anomaly in this cell consists of an excess of about 15 individuals.

Estimates of missing cells can be produced directly by the iterative proportional fitting algorithm. To do so, any adjustments used to fit the included cells are applied to the missing portion of the table, even though the excluded cells do not influence the size of these adjustments. As the included cells converge to their maximum-likelihood estimates, the excluded cells converge to values that are consistent with the relevant log-frequency model. Calculated in this way, the missing-cell estimates are a by-product of the estimation procedure and have almost no computational cost.

One application of the missing-cell estimates is to correct data for guessing according to a model. Consider, for example, the confusion data in Table 10.3. The frequency with which the subject correctly identified the stimulus is not simply the sum of the diagonal frequencies, since some of these correct responses were lucky guesses. To find the true number of correct responses, one must estimate the amount of lucky guessing and subtract it from the correct-response frequency. There are many models for the incorrect responses. The simplest treats the subject as either knowing the response or guessing. Under this all-or-none model of knowledge, guesses are independent of the true answer. If so, then Table 10.3 is the sum of a table showing independence (the guesses) and a diagonal table (the true identifications). These tables can be reconstructed by using the quasi-independence model. The diagonals of the original table are treated as structural zeros, and the remainder of the table is used to estimate their value. For the confusion data, the expected frequencies under the quasi-independence model are shown at the bottom of Table 10.3. The parenthesized entries on the diagonal are derived from the off-diagonal data. The diagonal contains 1190 entries in the original data and 91.8 in the new estimates. Presumably, the latter are guesses that happened to be correct. Thus, one estimates that on $1190 - 92 = 1098$ trials the subject properly identified the response.

The quasi-independence model also provides a test of the adequacy of the all-or-none description of the behavior on which the correction is based. If one assumes independence of the observations (an assumption that should not be made without some careful consideration), there are plenty of degrees of freedom available to test how well the quasi-independence model fits. When this model can be rejected, as it can for the example above, then the subject must have been basing answers on some form of partial information. In that case, the estimates of the diagonal frequencies are inadequate; indeed, the whole notion that responses are either known or guessed is called into question. More subtle models of partial association are needed, including some discussed in the next chapter. If these models can be put in log-linear form, then estimates of the diagonal cells can be obtained from them, in the same manner as in the quasi-independence model. With some such more sophisticated models, better corrections can be made.

In the discussion of Cohen's κ statistic in Section 9.5 a model was presented that combined independence with agreement on the diagonal (Equations 9.45 and 9.46). In the language of the current chapter, the portion of this model describing chance agreement amounts to quasi-independence of the off-diagonal cells. This description is identical to the model for correction for guessing described in the present section and can be fit in the same way. The incomplete-table procedures are easily used to estimate chance values of the diagonal cells and a coefficient of excess agreement analogous to κ derived (Problem 9.2).

10.4. CHOICE MODELS

The quasi-independence model has applicability beyond the treatment of structurally empty cells. An important part of its power comes from its use in the construction of models that test various specialized hypotheses. The remaining four sections of this chapter describe models of this sort, as does Section 11.2.

A somewhat surprising place where the quasi-independence model appears is in the theory of choice developed by Bradley & Terry (1952), then extended and given an axiomatic basis by Luce (1959). Suppose that subjects are asked to choose among pairs of alternatives. Sometimes one alternative is chosen, sometimes the other. For example, in an experiment by Estes (in 1960) 117 undergraduate subjects were asked to select which of a pair of famous people they would like to meet and talk to (cited by Atkinson, Bower, & Crothers, 1965, who discuss Luce's axiomitization and its application to these data in more detail). All possible combinations from a set of four names were given, resulting in the data shown at the top of Table 10.5. For example, of the 117 subjects given a choice between Eisenhower and Churchill, 67 chose Eisenhower and 50 chose Churchill. Throughout the table, entries on opposite sides of the main diagonal come from the same pair and sum to 117. The diagonal entries do not correspond to possible comparisons, and so are structurally void.

Reasonably enough, the probability that a person is chosen depends on the alternative with which he is paired. The Bradley-Terry-Luce choice model describes data such as these by assigning to each alternative a_i a scale value $v(a_i)$. To convert this scale value to the probability that a_i is chosen from a set of possibilities, the size of $v(a_i)$ is compared to the sum of the scale values for the alternatives involved in that particular choice. The probability of choosing Eisenhower over Churchill, for example, is the ratio of $v(E)$ to $v(E) + v(C)$. More generally, for choices from the set $\{a_i, a_j\}$,

$$P(\text{select } a_i \text{ from } \{a_i, a_j\}) = \frac{v(a_i)}{v(a_i) + v(a_j)} \tag{10.3}$$

TABLE 10.5
Results from a Pairwise Choice Experiment
(from Atkinson, Bower, & Crothers, 1965)

Pairwise Choice Data

			Paired with			
			E	C	H	F
	Dwight Eisenhower	(E)	—	67	94	96
Person Chosen	Winston Churchill	(C)	50	—	89	94
	Dag Hammarskjold	(H)	23	28	—	70
	William Faulkner	(F)	21	23	47	—

Data Reorganized as Choices by Pair

				Tested Pair		
		{E,C}	{E,H}	{E,F}	{C,H}	{C,F}	{H,F}
	E	67	94	96	—	—	—
Chosen person	C	50	—	—	89	94	—
	H	—	23	—	28	—	70
	F	—	—	21	—	23	47

Although Equation 10.3 may not appear familiar, it is actually a log-linear model of quasi-independence (Fienberg & Larntz, 1976). To see why, suppose that n_{ij} observations of the pair $\{a_i, a_j\}$ are made. Let μ_{ij} be the expected number of choices of a_i. This expectation equals n_{ij} times the probability of choice from Equation 10.3, so taking the logarithm gives

$$\log \mu_{ij} = \log[n_{ij} P(\text{select } a_i \text{ from } \{a_i, a_j\})]$$

$$= \log \frac{n_{ij} v(a_i)}{v(a_i) + v(a_j)}$$

$$= \log v(a_i) + \log \frac{n_{ij}}{v(a_i) + v(a_j)} \qquad (10.4)$$

The first term on the right-hand side depends on the stimulus chosen, the second on the particular pair but not the choice. By recasting the data so that rows in the table correspond to choices and columns to pairs, Model 10.4 becomes a quasi-independence model, to which the standard fitting and testing algorithms apply.

The Estes data are reorganized in this form at the bottom of Table 10.5. The quasi-independence model fits this table well ($X^2(3) = 0.74$), indicating that the data are consistent with the choice model. As Equation 10.4 suggests, the row parameters are the logarithms of the scale values. Estimates of these λ's are 0.815, 0.565, -0.533, and -0.847, and exponentiation gives scale values of 2.26, 1.76, 0.59, and 0.43. These estimates result from the usual standardization that makes the λ_A sum to zero. With the scaling model, it is more conventional to use a different standardization, one that fixes one parameters at zero and expresses the others relative to it. With Eisenhower as the standard, the λ_A are 0, -0.250, -1.348, and -1.662, and the scale values are 1.00, 0.78, 0.26, and 0.19. The change of standard has no effect on the choice probabilities predicted by Equation 10.3.

One advantage of this formulation of the Bradley-Terry-Luce choice model is that it can be extended to choices among more than two alternatives. For three alternatives, the denominator of Equation 10.3 is adjusted to include 3 weights,

$$P(\text{select } a_i \text{ from } \{a_i, a_j, a_k\}) = \frac{v(a_i)}{v(a_i) + v(a_j) + v(a_k)}$$

To fit this model, one simply fills in additional cells in the second formulation of Table 10.5 and proceeds as before (see Problem 10.3).

10.5. ESTIMATION OF POPULATION SIZE

Another example where a missing cell must be estimated occurs when the size of a population is to be approximated from several partial samples of the population. Consider a population of v entities that one wishes to count—fish in a lake, for example, crimes committed in a city, baseball players whose name one knows, or something of the sort. A count is performed, by capturing and marking fish, by collecting crime statistics, by giving a free-recall test, or by other appropriate means. This approach tallies some of the members of the population but misses others, so the total count is less than A. To get at the missing entities, a second sample is taken, if possible in a different way from the first. Some of the individuals that are detected in the second sample are also part of the first sample, although probably some new individuals are observed and not all the old ones reappear. The observations are classified by whether they occurred in each of the samples and are tabulated in an incomplete table:

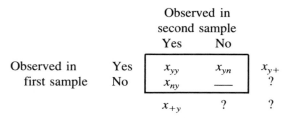

		Observed in second sample Yes	Observed in second sample No	
Observed in first sample	Yes	x_{yy}	x_{yn}	x_{y+}
	No	x_{ny}	—	?
		x_{+y}	?	?

If the value of x_{nn} in the missing cell were known, the four entries in the table would sum to A. The incomplete table methodology suggests a way to estimate the missing frequency (Fienberg, 1972). First, a model of quasi-independence is fitted to the table. From this an estimate of x_{nn} is obtained, and adding this estimate to the observed counts gives an estimate of the total frequency $\hat{v}$.

With two samples, $\hat{v}$ can be found algebraically. Under independence, the cross-product ratio is 1. This applies approximately to the sample values, so one expects that

$$\hat{\alpha} = \frac{x_{yy}\,x_{nn}}{x_{yn}\,x_{ny}} = 1$$

Solving for x_{nn} gives the estimates

$$\hat{x}_{nn} = \frac{x_{yn}\,x_{ny}}{x_{yy}}$$

and

$$\hat{v} = x_{yy} + x_{yn} + x_{ny} + \hat{x}_{nn} = \frac{x_{y+}x_{+y}}{x_{yy}} \qquad (10.5)$$

This estimate is sometimes known as the *Petersen estimate* (Petersen, 1894; see LeCren, 1965).

The estimate in Equation 10.5 is somewhat naive, for it is based on an assumption of independence, which is rarely realistic. Some fish are more readily captured than others, some crimes more visible, some players more easily recalled. Such tendencies put larger frequencies in x_{yy} and the missing x_{nn} than the model predicts. A better analysis requires a model that permits dependencies among the observations. Fitting such a model requires further samples to be taken. Suppose that three samples are available, making an incomplete $2 \times 2 \times 2$ table with 7 cells. These allow the 7 parameters of a model with the 3 two-way associations to be fitted. These associations better accommodate the shy and the readily caught individuals and so give a more accurate estimate of the missing cell. If more probes of the population are available, estimation can be preceded by a test of the model. Four samples give a 23 table with 15 cells. A model with every two-way association, $[AB][AC][AD][BC][BD][CD]$, contains 11 parameters. After this model has been fitted and used to estimate the expected frequencies, there remain 4 degrees of freedom to test whether it is satisfactory. If it can be retained, one is more sure of the estimate $\hat{v}$.

Whatever model is fitted, the highest-order association cannot be estimated because of the missing cell and must always be assumed to be zero. In effect, this association represents an excess or a deficiency in the unobserved cell. Unfortunately, this association has a relatively high chance of occurring. There is always the possibility that some sequestered subpopulation has remained undetected in all the samples. Only better and more varied schemes for probing the population can help here. Statistical elaboration can never wholly substitute for good and clever experimentation.

In many practical circumstances, the situation is more complicated than these simple models indicate. To estimate the missing cell in this way, one must work with a *closed population*, in which no individuals enter or leave between the first and last counts. This would not happen if some fish were stocked or lost from the population, if new crimes were committed, or if more players' names were learned. These *open populations* demand more complex procedures. There are many other models for multiple-capture data in both open and closed populations that are not based on the log-frequency models (see Seber, 1982, 1986 for reviews). Recently linear log-frequency models have been applied to open populations (Cormack, 1981, 1985). These models go considerably beyond the model described in this section. A researcher who anticipates much use of the multiple-recapture methodology should look at this work.

10.6.   SYMMETRY AND QUASI-SYMMETRY

Tables in which the rows and the columns use the same classification scheme are common. The two judges' ratings discussed in Section 9.5 (Table 9.4) are an example, as are the confusions in Tables 9.3 and 10.3 or the paired choices in Table 10.5. The square structure of these tables allows many specialized hypotheses to be formulated. The quasi-independence models for tables with deleted diagonals, discussed in Section 10.2, are one example. Others are described in this section and the next, and many others are discussed by Goodman (1972a; see also Smith, 1973).

One important form of association is symmetry. A square table is said to be symmetric when the elements on opposite sides of the main diagonal are equal, that is, when $\mu_{ij} = \mu_{ji}$. It is often of interest to know when a set of data shows symmetry and when symmetry can be rejected. A test of symmetry is easily devised: the expected entry in cell i,j is the average of the entries on either side of the diagonal,

$$\hat{\mu}_{ij} = \hat{\mu}_{ji} = \frac{x_{ij} + x_{ji}}{2} \qquad (10.6)$$

The diagonal cells are not specified by a symmetry hypothesis and can be ignored, both in computing $\hat{\mu}$ and in calculating a test statistic. For example, the data table at the top of Table 10.6 generates, by Equation 10.6, the expected frequencies in the middle panel. Based on the six off-diagonal cells, test statistics are $X^2 = 4.56$ and $G^2 = 4.62$. Six cells contribute to these statistics, but 3 parameters are needed to calculate the $\hat{\mu}$ (one for each diagonal pair). Thus, the statistics are distributed on $6 - 3 = 3$ degrees of freedom, and the model of symmetry cannot be rejected. In effect, one can think of this analysis as combining three separate tests, each one testing for equal distribution on a diagonal pair. More generally, in an $a \times a$ table, there are $a(a - 1)$ off-diagonal cells and half

TABLE 10.6
Testing for Symmetry about the Diagonal

Original Data

36	26	19
32	27	21
25	11	18

Expected Frequencies under Symmetry

—	29	22
29	—	16
22	16	—

Symmetry as Quasi-independence

k = 1			k = 2		
—	26	19	—	32	25
32	—	21	26	—	11
25	11	—	19	21	—

that many parameters, leaving $a(a - 1)/2$ degrees of freedom for the symmetry model.

Although the symmetry of a table of data may not be important in itself, it is an important precursor to other analyses. For example, many multidimensional-scaling models presuppose a matrix of distances between objects (see, e.g., Kruskal & Wish, 1978). Since the distance from object a_i to object a_j is the same as that from a_j to a_i, this matrix should be symmetric. The test of symmetry allows the appropriateness of these models to be evaluated. If symmetry cannot be rejected in the data, one concludes that the data may be thought of as distances, and a multidimensional-scaling algorithm can be applied to the symmetric expected frequencies. If symmetry is rejected, then the scaling solution cannot fully describe the data.

In the form expressed by Equation 10.6, the symmetric $\hat{\mu}_{ij}$ are not formed by fitting marginal distributions, hence they are not readily calculated by an ordinary log-frequency computer program. An ingenious trick turns the symmetry model into one of quasi-independence and lets it be fitted. First, a three-dimensional table is created, in which the first layer is the original table and the second is the transpose of that table, as shown at the bottom of Table 10.6. The diagonals are ignored. Call the frequencies in this table y_{ijk}; formally, they are defined by

$$y_{ijk} = \begin{cases} —, & \text{if } i = j \\ x_{ij}, & \text{if } i \neq j \text{ and } k = 1 \\ x_{ji}, & \text{if } i \neq j \text{ and } k = 2 \end{cases} \qquad (10.7)$$

The marginal frequencies in this table derive from those in the original table:

$$y_{ij+} = x_{ij} + x_{ji}, \quad y_{++k} = x_{++}, \quad \text{and} \quad y_{+++} = 2x_{++}$$

Thus, when the model $[AB][C]$ is fitted to the y_{ijk}, the expected frequencies are

$$\hat{\mu}_{ijk} = \frac{y_{ij+} y_{++k}}{y_{+++}} = \frac{x_{ij} + x_{ji}}{2}$$

In this way, the symmetric expected frequencies of Equation 10.6 are created.

Although the expected frequencies estimated from the expanded table are correct, the test statistics calculated by a standard program are incorrect. There are two problems, both of which arise from redundancies in the y-table. First, each cell of the x-table appears twice in the y-table, so that the statistics X^2 or G^2 as calculated are twice as large as they should be. Second, the duplicate cells and parameters are counted in the degrees of freedom calculations. Thus, fitting the model $[AB][C]$ to the bottom panel of Table 10.6 apparently gives $X^2(8) = 9.13$. For the correct test, G^2 or X^2 is divided by 2 and evaluated against a χ^2 distribution with the proper $a(a - 1)/2$ degrees of freedom. The program does the tedious work of fitting and calculating, however.

For many sets of data in which symmetric tendencies are suspected, the pure symmetry model is inappropriate. Consider the first and second choices of Table 10.1. Pure symmetry is unlikely in this table—if a_i is preferred to a_j, one would expect $x_{ij} > x_{ji}$. Nevertheless, once this preference is taken into account, the residual association may be symmetric. Such a model is appropriate if the association represents an underlying phenomenon, such as confusion among the alternatives, that is more or less symmetric. In essence, the resulting *quasi-symmetry model* moves the symmetric aspect from the observed frequencies to the association parameters. To the quasi-independence model of unrelated first- and second-choice preferences is added a symmetric association term, so that the complete model is

$$\log \mu_{ij} = \lambda + \lambda_{A(i)} + \lambda_{B(j)} + \lambda_{AB(ij)} \tag{10.8}$$

with $\lambda_{AB(ij)} = \lambda_{AB(ji)}$ (Caussinus, 1966).

The quasi-symmetry model can be fitted to data with the same three-dimensional table used for the symmetry test. In the table of y_{ijk}, quasi-symmetry is expressed by the model [AB][AC][BC]. The AC and BC terms allow different marginal frequencies to be accommodated, while, because of the two transposed layers of the C dimension, the parameters $\lambda_{AB(ij)}$ are forced to be symmetric. Once again, a standard computer program attributes double the proper test statistic to this model and gives an incorrect number of degrees of freedom. Corrections analogous to those for the pure symmetry model must be employed. The numbers of free parameters associated with the four terms on the right of Equation 10.8 are 1, $a - 1$, $a - 1$, and $a(a - 3)/2$, respectively, the last of these reflecting the a constraints that make each row sum to zero. Subtracting the parameters from the number of observations, gives the degrees of freedom for the test:

$$df_{QS} = (a^2 - a) - \left[1 + (a - 1) + (a - 1) + \frac{a(a - 3)}{2} \right]$$

$$= \frac{(a - 2)(a - 1)}{2}$$

For the choice data of Table 10.1, the quasi-independence model was rejected, with $G^2(19) = 103.80$. The quasi-symmetry model is not rejected; indeed, it fits very well, with $G^2(10) = 5.05$. The parameters of the model (Table 10.7) show the popular and unpopular choices and the symmetric nature of their association.

The quasi-symmetry model turns up in an unexpected place involving the Bradley-Terry-Luce choice model discussed in Section 10.4. For pairwise choices, the two models are identical (Fienberg & Larntz, 1976). Thus, fitting a quasi-symmetry model directly to the original table of data in the top panel of Table 10.5 gives the correct expected frequencies. Naturally, the scale values of the choice model are related to the parameters of the quasi-symmetry model.

TABLE 10.7
Parameter Estimates for the Quasi-symmetry Model
Fitted to the Choice Data in Table 10.1

λ_A:	0.34	0.28	0.40	0.27	−1.11	−0.18
λ_B:	−0.12	−0.14	−0.63	0.44	0.01	0.44
λ_{AB}:	—	1.10	1.24	−0.03	−0.62	−0.24
	1.10	—	0.79	−0.22	0.13	−0.29
	1.24	0.79	—	−0.08	−0.38	−0.40
	−0.03	−0.22	−0.08	—	0.70	1.37
	−0.62	0.13	−0.38	0.70	—	0.94
	−0.24	−0.29	−0.40	1.37	0.94	—

Under the latter model, each cell receives a contribution from both the row and the column factor; because of this, log $v(x)$ is the difference between the row and column parameters:

$$\log v(a_i) = \hat{\lambda}_{A(i)} - \hat{\lambda}_{B(i)}$$

With the appropriate normalization, the same scale values found from the pair-by-choice table are obtained. However, the quasi-symmetry interpretation of the choice model is less general than that described in Section 10.4, since it cannot accommodate choices among more than two alternatives.

10.7.   MARGINAL HOMOGENEITY

Another natural question about a square table concerns whether the marginal distribution in the rows and columns is the same. Such a state is interesting when the classifications refer to the same categorization, as, for example, with preferences, choices among judges, classification of the same thing at two different times, or the like. The corresponding condition on the frequencies is straightforward:

$$\mu_{i+} = \mu_{+i}, \quad \text{for all } i \in \mathcal{A} \tag{10.9}$$

Data for which this relationship holds are said to show *marginal homogeneity*.

Although it is simple, the hypothesis of marginal homogeneity cannot be tested directly with the type of hierarchical log-linear models discussed so far in this book. The difficulty is that Hypothesis 10.9 is not log-linear. It is linear, but not logarithmic, and it cannot be translated to a set of conditions for a log-linear model without imposing additional restrictions. One has two alternatives: either to abandon the log-linear models (and their associated fitting algorithms) or to test a specialized form of the marginal-homogeneity hypothesis that can be written in log-frequency form. Section 12.3 describes a test of the former sort; the present section, one of the latter.

One context in which marginal homogeneity can be tested is symmetry of association. The important observation is that the symmetry model implies marginal homogeneity, while quasi-symmetry does not. If a set of symmetric frequencies, with $\mu_{ij} = \mu_{ji}$, is summed over one subscript, say j, the marginal homogeneity condition of Equation 10.9 is obtained. In contrast, the different row and column parameters of the quasi-symmetry model (Equation 10.8) allow different marginal distributions. This hierarchical relationship, with one model implying marginal homogeneity and the other not, allows a test. When quasi-symmetry holds, the difference between this model and the pure symmetry model tests for marginal homogeneity. The difference test has $a - 1$ degrees of freedom, which is the difference between the degrees of freedom of the two models. It is also the number of additional parameters needed to make the marginals unequal.

As a numerical example, consider the two judges' data given in Section 9.5, shown again in Table 10.8. Do the judges make the four diagnoses with equal frequency? Before launching into a test based on quasi-symmetry, one should consider the plausibility of that context. A critical arbitrator is the test of fit of the quasi-symmetry model: if it does not fit, one should not go ahead with the test. One should also ask whether quasi-symmetry is plausible as a description of the processes that one believes underlie the data. In this example, there is no reason to think of the intrinsic confusions between categories as other than symmetric. An interpretation of the frequencies in Table 10.8 is the combination of symmetric confusions of the underlying disorders and a tendency for the judges to use the categories in somewhat different ways. If this is an adequate description of the choices, quasi-symmetry applies and the test of marginal homogeneity is appropriate. The test of fit below further justifies the use of the test.

When one is satisfied with the assumptions, the models are fitted. If a program for fitting incomplete factorial tables is available, one duplicates the table in transpose and fits the three-dimensional models corresponding to symmetry

TABLE 10.8
Classification of 100 Interview Transcripts into Four Diagnostic Categories
by Two Raters (from Table 9.5)

| | | Rater B | | | |
		d_1	d_2	d_3	d_4
	d_1	6	2	4	2
Rater	d_2	4	17	14	5
A	d_3	1	3	20	0
	d_4	1	3	6	12

and quasi-symmetry. Marginal homogeneity is tested by the difference of these statistics. For the data in Table 10.8 the results are

Symmetry	$G^2(6) =$	19.49
Quasi-symmetry	$G^2(3) =$	3.16
Marginal homogeneity	$\Delta G^2(3) =$	16.34

The quasi-symmetry model is satisfactory, so an interpretation of the difference test is reasonable. The test of marginal homogeneity is significant, indicating that equal use of the categories can be rejected in favor of a conclusion that the judges use the diagnostic categories to different extents.

For the example here, the quasi-symmetry context seems plausible. In other cases there may be intrinsic asymmetry. For example, if one were looking at the way that a survey of opinion changed from February to June (measured on the same subjects), there would be no reason to assert the symmetric association required by the quasi-symmetry context. Then one is wiser to avoid this context, even if the quasi-symmetry model appears to fit, and to use a more general test of the hypothesis. An unrestricted test of marginal homogeneity must be formulated using linear models for μ_{ij} instead of log-linear models. Section 12.3 describes how these tests can be run. For a theoretical interpretation of the quasi-symmetry model in rating data, see Darroch & McCloud (1986).

There are many ways to extend the models of symmetry, quasi-symmetry, and marginal homogeneity to tables in more than two dimensions. Most apply to tables in which three or more factors have identical classifications. These models are straightforward enough, but are sufficiently specialized that they are not covered here (for examples, see Bhapkar, 1979; Bishop, Fienberg, & Holland, 1975, Section 8.3). In any case, most of the complicated models involving marginal homogeneity are easier to formulate using the linear-models approach of Chapter 12.

PROBLEMS

10.1. ℰ The following table is fitted by a simple model, except for a violation in one cell. Identify the anomaly and show that the model otherwise fits.

15	7	4	10
9	6	18	6
20	11	3	14

What is the magnitude of the violation?

10.2. At the end of Section 10.3 it was noted that quasi-independence model underlies Cohen's κ statistic. Expected frequencies for off-diagonal quasi-independence for the data in Table 9.5 are

	Rater B			
	d_1	d_2	d_3	d_4

		d_1	d_2	d_3	d_4
	d_1	(1.1)	2.6	4.1	1.3
Rater A	d_2	3.8	(9.2)	14.6	4.6
	d_3	0.9	2.1	(3.3)	1.1
	d_4	1.4	3.3	5.3	(1.7)

Use these estimates to construct a κ-like measure of agreement. A test of the fit of these frequencies gives $X^2(5) = 2.27$. What does this statistic indicate?

10.3. In the experiment by Estes on choices in Section 10.4, choices from the three-member sets $\{E, C, H\}$ and $\{C, H, F\}$ were also collected. The numbers of subjects choosing each alternative were, respectively, 60, 42, and 15, and 76, 23, and 18.
a. Describe how to combine these data with those in Table 10.5 and to obtain a single estimate of the parameters $v(x)$.
b. $\mathscr{C}$ Calculate the new scale values.

10.4. In a multiple-recapture experiment, three samples are taken. Assume that only the three-way association is necessarily zero.
a. Devise a formula analogous to Equation 10.5 to estimate v.
b. Apply this estimate to the three-sample data,

Sample 1		Yes		No	
Sample 2		Yes	No	Yes	No
Sample	Yes	324	79	117	62
3	No	36	54	147	——

c. $\mathscr{C}$ Is there evidence that estimates from these data based on pairs of samples (e.g., Equation 10.5) would be invalid here?

10.5 Consider the table of data.

	b_1	b_2	b_3	b_4	b_5
a_1	15	19	9	10	5
a_2	10	7	9	10	4
a_3	6	6	4	3	14
a_4	58	28	5	15	1
a_5	5	4	11	2	8

These are rewritten as a three-way table, introducing factor C,

15	19	9	10	5	15	10	6	58	5
10	7	9	10	4	19	7	6	28	4
6	6	4	3	14	9	9	4	5	11
58	28	5	15	1	10	10	3	15	2
5	4	11	2	8	5	4	14	1	8

They are submitted to a standard frequency-analysis program and all three-factor models are fitted. The reported statistic values and degrees of freedom are

Model	G^2	df
[A][B][C]	263.28	40
[AB][C]	103.40	24
[AC][B]	216.59	36
[A][BC]	216.59	36
[AB][AC]	56.71	20
[AB][BC]	56.71	20
[AC][BC]	169.91	32
[AB][AC][BC]	21.62	16

Interpret these results.

10.6. ℰ Use the methods in this chapter to test the data in Problem 9.15 to see whether the distribution of solutions for problem 1 is the same as that for problem 2.

10.7. Subjects are asked to choose which of four statements they agree with most. They then see videotapes of a series of lectures designed to influence their opinions. Two weeks later, a new rating of the four statements is taken. The data are

		Delayed choice			
		s_1	s_2	s_3	s_4
Initial	s_1	28	7	18	11
choice	s_2	5	12	6	6
	s_3	5	5	15	1
	s_4	0	3	9	15

The investigator would like to know whether the opinions have changed. Can this question reasonably be tested by the marginal-homogeneity test presented in Section 10.7?

10.8. Consider the matrix of confusions that was given in Table 10.3. Explain what each of the following models means (if anything). Answer in terms of the experiment, not the statistical model.

a. Independence
b. Quasi-independence (off diagonal)
c. Symmetry
d. Quasi-symmetry

10.9. ℰ Problem 5.15a asked for a program to be written that estimated the expected frequencies for the two-factor model of independence by using the iterative proportional fitting algorithm. Modify this program to accommodate structural voids. Be sure to calculate test statistics and degrees of freedom correctly. Test the program on examples from this chapter.

11
Descriptions of Association

The discussion to this point has made heavy use of the concepts of independence and unrelatedness. Most models have been put in these terms. Of course, any model for a multifactor table other than complete independence is also a description of dependence, in the sense that it allows dependencies among the combinations of factors that are not specifically asserted to be unrelated. Nevertheless, the models are built around the supposition that certain parameters of the saturated model are zero. When these models are rejected, one does not have very sophisticated ways to describe the association. One can list the values of the relevant λ parameters or can examine the residuals from a simpler model, but these are only general tabulations. One needs a better way to characterize dependence.

For binary factors, association models are not necessary. There is only one degree of freedom to the association in a 2×2 table, so one can use any of the effect-size measures from the Chapter 9 to express it. However, the association in a larger two-way table has multiple components, just as the test of unrelatedness is on several degrees of freedom. There is room for further analysis of the association. One approach is to partition the overall association effect into single degree-of-freedom parts that represent separate components of the association. This approach is described in Section 11.1. A second approach, which occupies the remainder of the chapter, describes the association using a model with fewer free parameters than there are degrees of freedom for the original association.

Most of the discussion in this chapter applies to two-way tables, where the association models are by far the most common. In tables of higher dimensionality, the number of forms of specific dependence is very large and the association models proliferate rapidly. The hierarchical log-linear models discussed in

268

the earlier chapters are often more tractable here. Nevertheless, all the procedures in this chapter can extend to multiway tables in one way or another. The extensions of the models in Sections 11.1 and 11.2 are fairly natural and the reader can probably generalize them without much aid. Multifactor versions of the multiplicative-association model in Section 11.3 and the maximum-correlation models in Sections 11.4 and 11.5 are briefly covered in Section 11.6.

11.1.   THE EXTRACTION OF SUBTABLES

The most direct way to study the pattern of association within a large table is to chop it up into subtables and examine these tables separately. The principle is simple: a big table is reduced to a smaller one by dropping some categories from the classification, by combining categories, or by a mixture of omission and combination. For example, dropping the first column and combining the second two rows change the table from

$$
\begin{array}{ccc}
56 & 21 & 17 \\
81 & 18 & 54 \\
93 & 21 & 60
\end{array}
\qquad \text{to} \qquad
\begin{array}{cc}
21 & 17 \\
39 & 114
\end{array}
$$

Of course, one does this only if the second table isolates an interesting aspect of the larger table.

Many 2×2 subtables can be extracted from a larger table. For a factor with a categories, there are $(3^a - 2^{a+1} + 1)/2$ ways to select two nonempty sets of factors.† This count applies to every dimension of the table. So, from a 4×5 table, one can form $25 \cdot 90 = 2250$ different 2×2 subtables. Obviously, the information in these subtables is highly redundant. This overlap induces two problems. The first is the control of type I error over so many tests. The second is how to select a set of subtables that captures all the information in the original table without repeating the same tests.

The multiple comparison problem has a reasonably direct solution. In Section 9.1, it was pointed out that simultaneous confidence intervals for odds ratios can be constructed by using the χ^2 statistic appropriate to the entire table instead of $\chi^2(1)$ (Goodman, 1964a; see also Gabriel, 1966). The odds ratios are examples of extracted 2×2 tables, formed by selecting a pair of rows and a pair of

---

†Each of the a categories may be in either of the two pooled sets or may be excluded, creating 3^a possibilities. No testable table is produced when either of the pooled sets is empty, so the 2^a partitions in which the first set is empty and the 2^a partitions in which the second set is empty (one of which, where both are empty, has already been counted) must be subtracted. Finally, the order of the two sets is unimportant, necessitating division by 2.

columns and throwing out the rest. The set of extractable tables here is more extensive than the odds ratios, since the pooling of rows or columns is allowed. Nevertheless, the same correction seems appropriate. As is shown later in this section, the test statistic G^2 in any subtable is always less than G^2 for the entire table. So, if a subtable is tested against a $\chi^2[(a-1)(b-1)]$ distribution, then when it is deemed significantly associated, so also is the entire $a \times b$ table. For the 3×3 table above, one tests the extracted subtables using a $\chi^2(4)$ distribution: at 5%, the critical value is 9.49, rather than the uncorrected criterion of 3.84.

The second problem, that of finding a nonoverlapping collection of subtables, is solved by choosing them so that their test statistics partition the test statistic for the original table into a set of additive components. The test for association in an $a \times b$ table is based on $(a-1)(b-1)$ degrees of freedom. So the table can be divided into this many 2×2 subtables, each of which is tested on one degree of freedom. If the decomposition is properly done, the $G^2(1)$ statistics for the subtables sum to the overall statistic $G^2[(a-1)(b-1)]$ for the full table. This additivity ensures that different aspects of the original table are captured by each of the subtables and that the ensemble of subtables exhausts the association. This partitioning is analogous to the partitioning of the sum of squares by an orthogonal decomposition in the analysis of variance.

The easiest way to exhaustively partition a table is to apply to each factor the pictorial scheme used in Section 7.3 to decompose a polytomous variable into logits. The categories of each factor are divided into a series of pairwise comparisons such that (1) any combination of categories appears at most once and (2) categories once cast into separate partitions are not recombined as part of another partition. If the partitioning is carried to the point that each category appears by itself exactly once, then a complete breakdown into individual degrees of freedom results. Otherwise some tables with dimensions larger than 2 remain. Of course, these larger tables are subject to further decomposition.

To take a specific example, suppose that one is studying the strategies by which subjects find and correct a defect in a faulty electronic circuit. Three groups of subjects are used, and the solutions are classified into four categories according to their sophistication (Table 11.1, top). The test for independence in a 3×4 table has 6 degrees of freedom, so a decomposition into six 2×2 subtables is possible. There are many potential subdivisions, and one should attempt to select a meaningful one. For example, one might partition the table according to the division shown in tree form in Figure 11.1. The rows are divided to decompose that factor into (1) a comparison of the two student groups (dropping the instructors) and (2) a comparison of the instructors to the students (combining the two years). The four columns are partitioned by (1) comparing the two least organized methods (dropping the last two columns), (2) comparing the most organized methods (dropping the first two columns), and (3) pooling each of these two pairs and comparing them. The combination of these two divisions breaks the original table into six 2×2 subtables, shown at the bottom

TABLE 11.1
Classification of Solutions for Three Groups of Subjects and the
Decomposition of this Table into Single-degree-of-freedom Subtables

Original Two-way Classification

	Trial and Error	*Undirected Search*	*Directed Search*	*Insightful Solution*
1st Year Students	23	9	2	6
3d Year Students	11	12	5	3
Instructors	0	3	18	7

$$G^2(6) = 54.23$$
$$X^2(6) = 47.32$$

Subtables Expressing this Association

	T&E	US
1st Year	23	9
3d Year	11	12

$$G^2(1) = 3.28$$
$$X^2(1) = 3.28$$

	DS	IS
	2	6
	5	3

$$G^2(1) = 2.35$$
$$X^2(1) = 2.29$$

	Poor	Good
	32	8
	23	8

$$G^2(1) = 0.34$$
$$X^2(1) = 0.34$$

	T&E	US
Student	34	21
Instructor	0	3

$$G^2(1) = 5.53$$
$$X^2(1) = 4.48$$

	DS	IS
	7	9
	18	7

$$G^2(1) = 3.27$$
$$X^2(1) = 3.27$$

	Poor	Good
	55	16
	3	25

$$G^2(1) = 39.47$$
$$X^2(1) = 36.88$$

<u>Division of the rows</u>

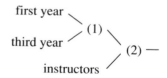

<u>Division of the columns</u>

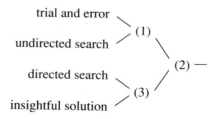

FIGURE 11.1. Graphical representation of the decomposition in Table 11.1

of Table 11.1. The subtable at the upper left of this array is a 2 × 2 segment from the upper left of the original table, while the lower-right subtable is formed by poolings of both rows and columns:

21	9	2	6
11	12	5	3
0	3	18	7

The significance tests of these tables identify the major source of the association in the last subtable.

These 6 subtables exhaustively partition the original association. The six individual G^2 statistics in Table 11.1 sum to G^2 for the full table. This additivity is a consequence of the form of the likelihood-ratio test and so is only approximately true for X^2. As is usually the case in such situations, the choice of statistic does not substantially alter the conclusions, and either statistic is satisfactory in practice. The important point is that the subtables obey the breakdown rules just described.†

Of course, one is not limited to dichotomies when subdividing a table, nor must examine all the subtables that are part of a complete breakdown. The 2 × 2 subtables give the finest division and the maximum number of unrelated subtables, but the analysis should go this far only when the separate subtables are meaningful. If one needs to examine only some of the 2 × 2 tables, or finds it appropriate to leave subtables larger than 2 × 2, this is fine. One should not run useless tests just because they fall out of the decomposition or ignore meaningful ones because they do not.

The decomposition into additive components permits a different approach to the simultaneous comparison problem. If one can specify in advance how to break the table into subtables, the family of tests over which type I error should be controlled contains at most $(a - 1)(b - 1)$ members. This is many fewer than when all possible tables are considered. For a family of this size, the Bonferroni inequality discussed in Section 1.4 gives smaller critical values than do tests based on the $\chi^2[(a - 1)(b - 1)]$ distribution. For the 3 × 4 table above, there are 6 subtables, so Bonferroni-corrected tests are run at the $\alpha_F/6$ level. If one selects α_F of 10%, the table in Appendix A.2 shows a critical value of 5.73. Correction for all possible subtables at this level uses a critical value drawn from a $\chi^2(6)$ distribution, which is 10.64. Of course, the former correction depends on the fact that one's family size is really 6 and is inappropriate if the decomposition into single degree-of-freedom tests has been made after examining the data.

---

†Other partitioning formulae provide an exact partition of X^2 (Irwin, 1949; Kimball, 1954; Lancaster, 1949, 1950; see also Bresnahan & Shapiro, 1966; Castellian, 1965; Gilula & Krieger, 1983). These are conceptually less clear than the partitioning scheme just described (Shaffer, 1973) and do not add explanatory power.

11.2. MODELS WITH HOMOGENEOUS ASSOCIATION PARAMETERS

In many forms of dependency, association is present throughout a table in simple form. In these cases, isolating parts of the table, in the manner of the last section, is not a very useful strategy. Most of the subtables show significant association. A better approach is to construct a model that explicitly represents the association. The remainder of this chapter presents various models of this type. These models are useful both as simple descriptions of a table of data and because they isolate important effects in a few parameters. Confining the association effects to a small set of parameters improves both the precision and the power of the analysis. Detailed hypotheses can be tested when the appropriate assumptions (independence, homogeneity, and large sample size) are satisfied. When statistical testing cannot be supported, a model can still be fitted and its parameters used as a compact summary of the data.

One type of partial-association model is constructed by dividing the cells of the table into sets that have the same association parameter in a log-linear model. These models look similar to the saturated model of complete dependence,

$$\log \mu_{ij} = \lambda + \lambda_{A(i)} + \lambda_{B(j)} + \lambda_{AB(ij)} \tag{11.1}$$

However, unlike the saturated model, in which $\lambda_{AB(ij)}$ is free, these models constrain this parameter to a few distinct values. The result is a model that implies dependence of the rows and columns, but in a less general way than when the association is arbitrary.

As an example, consider a two-way table that classifies a group of patients according to the severity of a disorder before and after treatment (factors B and A in Table 11.2). Independence fails in this table. The interpretation of the factors as states at two points in time makes certain patterns of dependence particularly interesting. If the treatment is effective, the column classification (after treatment) tends to be higher than the row classification (before), which puts an excess of frequency in the upper right-hand portion of the table. This pattern suggests a specific model. Instead of letting λ_{AB} be free, use a single parameter to increment all the frequencies in the upper triangular portion of the table and to decrement all of them in the lower portion. This restriction replaces the general model of Equation 11.1 by a model that explicitly specifies this triangular asymmetry,

$$\log \mu_{ij} = \lambda + \lambda_{B(i)} + \lambda_{A(j)} + \lambda_{T(ij)} \tag{11.2}$$

The parameter $\lambda_{T(ij)}$ takes only two values, δ when $i < j$ and $-\delta$ when $i > j$. Since the cells on the diagonal of the table, where $i = j$, do not contribute information about whether a change in a patient's state is for the better or the worse, they are structurally ignored, in the manner of the quasi-independence models of Chapter 10 (but see Problem 11.3). This parameter pattern is shown at

TABLE 11.2
A Classification of Patients Before and After Treatment
and an Analysis of Their Improvement
by the Triangles Parameter Model

Observed Data

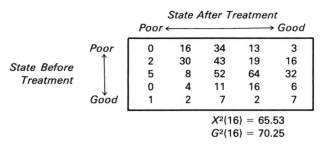

	State After Treatment			
	Poor ⟵————————⟶ Good			

Poor	0	16	34	13	3
	2	30	43	19	16
	5	8	52	64	32
	0	4	11	16	6
Good	1	2	7	2	7

State Before Treatment

$X^2(16) = 65.53$
$G^2(16) = 70.25$

Pattern of Parameters

—	δ	δ	δ	δ
−δ	—	δ	δ	δ
−δ	−δ	—	δ	δ
−δ	−δ	−δ	—	δ
−δ	−δ	−δ	−δ	—

Test of the Association Parameter, $\hat{\delta} = 0.80$

Quasi-independence	$G^2(11)$	= 35.54
Triangles parameter model	$G^2(10)$	= 13.45
Triangle parameter ($\delta = 0$)	$\Delta G^2(1)$	= 22.09

the bottom of Table 11.2. The resulting model is known as the *triangles parameter model* (Goodman, 1972a).

If $\delta = 0$, the triangles parameter model implies quasi-independence in the off-diagonal cells. Its association parameter gives a compact way to indicate the extent to which the treatment, if it changes the patient's classification, leads to improvement or deterioration. This single number is a more convenient description than is a collection of association parameters from a saturated model. For Table 11.2, a fit of the triangles parameter model (using the procedure described below) gives $\hat{\delta} = 0.80$. This value indicates a considerable drift of observations toward the upper triangle. As Equation 11.2 shows, after differences in row and column frequencies are accounted for, values of log μ_{ij} in the upper and lower triangular portions differ by 2δ—the coefficient 2 here combines $+\delta$ in the upper triangle with $-\delta$ in the lower. Thus, for comparable row and column frequencies, there are $e^{2\delta} \approx 5$ times as many observations in the upper triangle.

To test the fit of the triangles parameter model, its degrees of freedom are needed. The parameter δ adds one parameter to those of the quasi-independence model, so the triangles parameter model is tested on one fewer degree of freedom than the quasi-independence model. Since the quasi-independence model in an $a \times a$ table has $a(a - 3) + 1$ degrees of freedom, the triangles parameter model has $a(a - 3)$ degrees of freedom. Unless $a > 3$, no degrees of freedom are available for a test and the triangles parameter model is the same as the saturated model. Since the quasi-independence model and the triangles parameter model are hierarchically related, the difference in their goodness-of-fit statistics tests the hypothesis that $\delta = 0$. This test, shown in Table 11.2, clearly substantiates the presence of a triangles effect. It is a good way to look for an improvement effect, since all the difference between triangles is concentrated in a single degree of freedom. For the present example, the satisfactory fit of the triangles parameter model indicates that this effect captures all the nonrandom variation in the data.

The categories in Table 11.2 are ordered (from poor to good). This ordering makes the triangular structure of the parameters plausible. A substantial proportion of the models of this type that have been proposed use an ordering of the categories to define the sets. However, association models can also be constructed for categories that are organized in other ways. Recall the preference data from Table 10.1, shown again at the top of Table 11.3. A model of quasi-independence does not fit these data. Now suppose that this dependence results from two clusters of preference, with second choices being made most often from the same set as the first choice. In particular, suppose that subjects who make their first choice from the set $\{a_1, a_2, a_3\}$ tend to make their second choice from the same set, and suppose that the same consistency applies to the set $\{a_4, a_5, a_6\}$. This pattern could occur if the sets are collections of nearly equivalent alternatives. A model that expresses the blocked alternatives is formed by setting the association parameters to β when the cell represents the choice of two alternatives from the same set and to $-\beta$ when the choices are from different sets (Table 11.3, second panel). Except for the different arrangement of the association parameters, this *block-association model* is the same as Model 11.2 and is fitted and tested in the same way. As the test at the bottom of Table 11.3 shows, the single parameter β picks up almost all the departure from independence.

The cells can be divided into more than two sets. For example, the *diagonals parameter model* posits homogeneous strips with equal association parameters running along the major diagonals:

$$
\begin{array}{cccc}
\lambda_4 & \lambda_5 & \lambda_6 & \lambda_7 \\
\lambda_3 & \lambda_4 & \lambda_5 & \lambda_6 \\
\lambda_2 & \lambda_3 & \lambda_4 & \lambda_5 \\
\lambda_1 & \lambda_2 & \lambda_3 & \lambda_4
\end{array}
$$

TABLE 11.3
Block-dependence Model Fitted to First- and
Second-choice Data from Table 10.1

Observed Data

		Second Choice					
		a_1	a_2	a_3	a_4	a_5	a_6
	a_1	—	15	13	8	3	8
	a_2	16	—	5	8	7	6
First Choice	a_3	18	14	—	10	4	6
	a_4	6	3	2	—	13	34
	a_5	1	1	1	3	—	7
	a_6	2	3	2	23	8	—

Pattern of Association Parameters

—	β	β	$-\beta$	$-\beta$	$-\beta$
β	—	β	$-\beta$	$-\beta$	$-\beta$
β	β	—	$-\beta$	$-\beta$	$-\beta$
$-\beta$	$-\beta$	$-\beta$	—	β	β
$-\beta$	$-\beta$	$-\beta$	β	—	β
$-\beta$	$-\beta$	$-\beta$	β	β	—

Tests of Association Parameter, $\hat{\beta} = 0.66$

Quasi-independence	$G^2(19)$	$= 103.80$
Block dependence	$G^2(18)$	$= 11.57$
Presence of blocks ($\beta = 0$)	$\Delta G^2(1)$	$= 92.23$

(Goodman, 1972a). Similarly, the block-association model can readily use more than one division of each factor.

The constant-parameter association models can be expressed in a more general form (following Caussinus, 1966). In each model the cells, except for structural voids, are partitioned into mutually exclusive and exhaustive sets. Let $\mathcal{S}_1$, $\mathcal{S}_2, \ldots, \mathcal{S}_s$ be such a partition. The upper and lower triangles of Model 11.2 are such sets, as are the blocks in Table 11.3 and the bands of the diagonals parameter model. A *set-association model* assigns the same association parameter to all members of a set. Denote the parameter pertaining to $\mathcal{S}_k$ by $\lambda_{S(k)}$, then the loglinear expression of the set-association model is

$$\log \mu_{ij} = \lambda + \lambda_{A(i)} + \lambda_{B(j)} + \lambda_{S(k)} \tag{11.3}$$

To uniquely identify the λ_S, one conventionally sets their sum to zero,

$$\sum_k \lambda_{S(k)} = 0$$

Alternatively, the value of one of the $\lambda_{S(k)}$ can be fixed, say by setting $\lambda_S = 0$ for the least-chosen set. Either way, there are $s - 1$ free parameters associated with a s-element partition. These are subtracted from the $(a - 1)(b - 1)$ degrees of freedom of the independence model to get the degrees of freedom for a test of Model 11.3.

Several of the models presented in earlier chapters can be recast in set-association form. For example, the paired cells across the diagonals of the symmetry models in Section 10.6 are sets. Defined in this way, Model 11.3 expresses quasi-symmetry. The density of sets in this model is sufficiently great that it interferes with the degrees-of-freedom formulae; they do not follow from the usual set-association formulation, but are found as described in Chapter 10 or by a more detailed analysis of the parametric dependencies. The symmetry model is a simpler form of Model 11.3, in which λ_A and λ_B have been dropped to leave only λ and λ_S.

Models that have several partitions of the cells are formed in the same way. For each different partition, a term is added to the log-linear set model. For example, if $\mathscr{S}_1, \mathscr{S}_2, \ldots, \mathscr{S}_s$ and $\mathscr{T}_1, \mathscr{T}_2, \ldots, \mathscr{T}_t$ are two distinct partitions of the cells, the two-factor set-association model is

$$\log \mu_{ij} = \lambda + \lambda_{A(i)} + \lambda_{B(j)} + \lambda_{S(k)} + \lambda_{T(l)} \tag{11.4}$$

By crossing sets appropriately, more complex patterns of association can be developed with Model 11.4 than are possible with a single term.

Model 11.4 lets several sources of association be combined. For example, Goodman (1979a; see also Agresti, 1983b) has proposed combining the diagonals parameter model with the symmetry model to produce the *diagonals parameter symmetry model*. This model, which is tested on $(a - 1)(a - 2)/2$ degrees of freedom, gives expected frequencies similar to those from a quantized bivariate normal distribution.

Models 11.3 and 11.4 look exactly like the model of complete quasi-independence in three-way and four-way tables, complete because they contain only single-factor terms and quasi because the combinations of subscripts do not have a full factorial layout. Since the model is, in effect, a quasi-independence model, it can be fitted by the same algorithms. For maximum-likelihood estimates of μ_{ij} under these models, the appropriate marginal sums of observed and expected frequencies are the same. For the rows and columns the equations are the usual ones:

$$x_{i+} = \sum_j \hat{\mu}_{ij} \quad \text{and} \quad x_{+j} = \sum_i \hat{\mu}_{ij}$$

For the sets they equate within-set sums; for Model 11.3,

$$\sum_{(i,j) \in \mathscr{S}_k} x_{ij} = \sum_{(i,j) \in \mathscr{S}_k} \hat{\mu}_{ij}$$

One makes iterative adjustments to $\hat{\mu}_{ij}$ until these equations are satisfied, then the parameters are extracted by solving the log-linear model as in Section 5.3. In this view, the rows and columns are partitions of the observations, like the sets, and have exactly the same formal standing in the analysis.

The parallel between set association and quasi-independence lets one fit set models with programs designed to fit quasi-independence models to factorial tables. No special-purpose programs are needed. The data are recast as an incomplete table by making the set factor S an explicit dimension. For the examples of Tables 11.2 and 11.3, these expanded representations are shown in Table 11.4. Each level of k contains the data associated with one of the sets. The models are tested by fitting the quasi-independence model $[A][B][S]$ to these tables, giving the results reported above. The number of degrees of freedom for the factorial quasi-independence model is the same as that of the set association model. It is calculated normally, unless the partition of sets involves some anomaly that produces a linear dependency among the parameters (e.g., a set that is the same as a row or a column). Multiple-partition models are fitted by introducing additional dimensions; for example the two-partition model (Equation 11.4) is fitted as $[A][B][S][T]$ in four dimensions.

As a third example of the set-association model, return to the problem of estimating the agreement between two raters that was discussed in connection with Cohen's coefficient κ in Section 9.5. The implicit model underlying this

TABLE 11.4
Incomplete Tables Used to Fit Tables 11.2 and 11.3
as Factorial Quasi-independence Models

For Table 11.2 and Model 11.2:

	k = 1					k = 2				
—	16	34	13	3	—	—	—	—	—
—	—	43	19	16	2	—	—	—	—
—	—	—	64	32	5	8	—	—	—
—	—	—	—	6	0	4	11	—	—
—	—	—	—	—	1	2	7	2	—

For Table 11.3:

		k = 1						k = 2			
—	15	13	—	—	—	—	—	—	8	3	8
16	—	5	—	—	—	—	—	—	8	7	6
18	14	—	—	—	—	—	—	—	10	4	6
—	—	—	—	13	34	6	3	2	—	—	—
—	—	—	3	—	7	1	1	1	—	—	—
—	—	—	23	8	—	2	3	2	—	—	—

statistic combines independence with excess diagonal frequency (Equations 9.45 and 9.46):

$$\log \mu_{ij} = \lambda + \lambda_{A(i)} + \lambda_{B(j)} + \delta_{ij}$$

where the δ_{ij} are the increments due to agreement,

$$\delta_{ij} = \begin{cases} \delta_i, & \text{if } i = j \\ 0, & \text{otherwise} \end{cases}$$

In an $a \times a$ table, this model contains a parameters representing agreement, one for each diagonal cell. The set-association model provides a simpler representation (Tanner & Young, 1985a). The increments δ_i are set to the same value δ in all diagonal cells, making δ an indicator of the amount of added frequency and a measure of overall agreement. This definition of δ_{ij} does not obey the usual identification constraint, in that its two values sum to δ instead of zero. With the parameterization used in this section (Equation 11.3), δ_{ij} equals $\lambda_{S(1)}$ in the cells on the diagonal and $\lambda_{S(2)}$ in the remainder of the table, with $\lambda_{S(1)} = -\lambda_{S(2)}$. The translation between this representation and the more intuitive parameter δ is simple: δ is just twice $\lambda_{S(1)}$.

When applied to the table of rater frequencies in Table 9.5, the constant-δ or *diagonal-set model* fits with $X^2(8) = 4.43$. The estimate of $\lambda_{S(1)}$ is 0.72, so $\delta = 1.44$. An index of the excess frequency in the diagonal cells is found by comparing the observed diagonals with the expected frequencies from the quasi-independence portion of the model, in the manner of Problem 10.2.

Since the diagonal-set model is a restriction of the independence model, the hypothesis that $\delta = 0$ is tested by comparing test statistics for the two models. For Table 9.1, under independence $G^2(9) = 47.69$, and for the set-association model $G^2(8) = 5.96$, so the absence of agreement is rejected with $\Delta G^2(1) = 41.73$. Clearly, the raters agree with each other, at least some of the time.

Many set-association models can be constructed on these principles (see Goodman, 1972a; 1979a; 1985, Section 3). They are readily tailored to particular experimental situations and hypotheses. All that one needs to build a model is a rationale for grouping the cells into sets. This need is also one of their limitations: in many circumstances it is difficult to select these sets on any rational basis.

11.3. MULTIPLICATIVE-ASSOCIATION MODELS

When a justification for the sets of constant association parameters of the set-association model is lacking, an approach based on a graded pattern of association may be more elegant. The remainder of this chapter describes two such approaches (another appears in Chapter 13). In each, a numerical parameter is assigned to every row and to every column, then the association is written as a function of these row and column scores. The models are chosen so that a pair of rows (or columns) with similar patterns of association have nearly the same parameter values. Thus, the parameters of these models scale the rows and columns with respect to the association present in the table.

Two-factor association is described by the parameter λ_{AB} of a log-linear model. Consider how one might write this parameter as a combination of row and column scores. Two seemingly natural choices do not work. A linear model for λ_{AB} turns out to be no different from the additive log-linear model for μ_{ij} that expresses independence (Problem 11.7). A log-linear model for λ_{AB} comes closer, but is unsatisfactory because $\log \lambda_{AB}$ is undefined when λ_{AB} is negative. A successful solution skips the logarithmic part and writes λ_{AB} as a product of row and column terms. Specifically, let $\xi_{A(i)}$ and $\xi_{B(j)}$ be sets of row and column parameters, respectively, and let ϕ be a single scalar. Then the *multiplicative-association model* is

$$\log \mu_{ij} = \lambda + \lambda_{A(i)} + \lambda_{B(j)} + \phi \xi_{A(i)} \xi_{B(j)} \qquad (11.5)$$

The parameters $\lambda, \lambda_{A(i)},$ and $\lambda_{B(j)}$ accommodate the marginal frequencies, and the association is

$$\lambda_{AB(j)} = \phi \xi_{A(i)} \xi_{B(j)} \qquad (11.6)$$

Because of this product term, Equation 11.5 is not a log-linear model. The term produced by the product of the two scales is said to be *bilinear*, so Equation 11.5 is a *log-bilinear model*.

As written in Equation 11.5, the multiplicative-association model is over-parameterized. As always, the parameters λ_A and λ_B need to be subjected to the familiar summation constraints. The constraints on the association parameters are a little more complicated. To get unique estimates, both ξ_A and ξ_B require not one but two restrictions. Usually, one of these restrictions locates the center of the parameter sequence, and the other fixes its spread. There are two natural ways to impose these restrictions. One constrains the sums and sums of squares of the parameters; in sample terms,

$$\sum_i \hat{\xi}_{A(i)} = 0 \quad \text{and} \quad \sum_i \hat{\xi}^2_{A(i)} = 1$$

$$\sum_j \hat{\xi}_{B(j)} = 0 \quad \text{and} \quad \sum_j \hat{\xi}^2_{B(j)} = 1 \qquad (11.7)$$

The other fixes the means and variances with respect of the marginal probability distributions,

$$\sum_i p_{i+}\hat{\xi}_{A(i)} = 0 \quad \text{and} \quad \sum_i p_{i+}\hat{\xi}^2_{A\,(i)} = 1$$

$$\sum_j p_{+j}\hat{\xi}_{B(j)} = 0 \quad \text{and} \quad \sum_j p_{+j}\hat{\xi}^2_{B(j)} = 1$$

$$(11.8)$$

With either choice, $\hat{\phi}$ is a measure of the overall magnitude of the association, and $\hat{\xi}_A$ and $\hat{\xi}_B$ create a scaling of the categories based on their association.

If one is only interested in obtaining unique estimates for the parameters, either set of constraints can be used. However, their interpretations are not equivalent. When the categories of a factor represent separate populations, whose frequency of observation is determined by the experimenter, there is no intrinsic marginal distribution for that factor—another investigator might assign subjects differently. Then the distribution-based constraints (Equation 11.8) are not estimates of any consistent population characteristics. The non-distributional constraints (Equations 11.7) give the same weight to each population and are more appropriate. In contrast, where the frequencies of both categories are sampled, the mean and variance are sensible constructs and Equations 11.8 apply. The distinction between these standardizations is most important when one want to interpret the magnitude of the association. If one is only interested in the positions of the categories relative to each other, either standardization does the job.

Because of the additional parameters, Model 11.5 is harder to fit than the independence model. However, maximum-likelihood estimates can be found by an iterative procedure similar to that used for the simpler models. Details of this algorithm are given by Goodman (1979c, where this model is known as the "Row and Column Effect Model II"). Other estimation techniques can also be applied.

As an example, suppose that one has survey data in which subjects make a 7-alternative choice (factor C). This tabulation is crossed with a 5-level demographic classification of the subject (factor D). Such a table appears at the top of Table 11.5. The middle portion of Table 11.5 gives estimates of the parameters of this model. If the data are drawn from a single sample, so that both marginal distributions are sampled, then both standardizations of ξ_C and ξ_D are meaningful. Both are shown, although the parameters expressing the marginal frequencies are only given for the equally-weighted standardization of Equations 11.7.

The values of $\hat{\xi}_C$ and $\hat{\xi}_D$ order the categories by the similarities of their association. For example, the alternatives c_2 and c_4 have similar values of $\hat{\xi}_C$, indicating similar association patterns, while c_1 and c_5 are different. If they are consistent with other aspects of the design, similarities of ξ can be used to justify combining two categories that show a similar relationship to the other factor. At the bottom of Table 11.5, the original data are rearranged to put the categories in the order of the parameter values. If the marginal frequencies are similar, this reorganization places the larger cells near the principal diagonal of the table. The

TABLE 11.5
Fitting the Multiplicative-association Model

Original Data

		c_1	c_2	c_3	c_4	c_5	c_6	c_7
					Choices			
	d_1	5	15	8	9	24	29	15
	d_2	44	66	7	40	5	7	8
Demographic Category	d_3	12	14	3	11	1	15	1
	d_4	24	29	5	23	9	16	3
	d_5	7	16	4	5	4	15	1

Parameter Estimates

Association parameters scaled to zero sum and unit sum of squares:

$\hat{\lambda}$:   2.32
$\hat{\lambda}_D$:   0.22   0.39   −0.41   0.21   −0.42
$\hat{\lambda}_C$:   0.30   0.82   −0.69   0.34   −0.42   0.36   −0.73

$\hat{\phi}$:   2.70
$\hat{\xi}_D$:   0.74   −0.62   −0.22   −0.17   0.15
$\hat{\xi}_C$:   −0.50   −0.36   0.10   −0.39   0.50   0.30   0.34

Association parameters scaled to zero mean and unit variance:

$\hat{\phi}$:   0.49
$\hat{\xi}_D$:   1.68   −1.04   −0.03   −0.15   0.49
$\hat{\xi}_C$:   −0.98   −0.60   0.68   −0.69   1.78   1.24   1.32

Data Reorganized to be Concordant with the Associative Scaling

	c_1	c_4	c_2	c_3	c_6	c_7	c_5
d_2	44	40	66	7	7	8	5
d_4	24	23	29	5	16	3	9
d_3	12	11	14	3	15	1	1
d_5	7	5	16	4	15	1	4
d_1	5	9	15	8	29	15	24

associative structure is emphasized, which may be a useful way to report the data if the categories are not intrinsically ordered.

The fitting of the multiplicative-association model can be viewed in a purely descriptive sense, using the parameters ξ_A and ξ_B to summarize the relationship in a table of frequencies. This scaling can be profitable, even when the data do not obey the sampling assumptions that are necessary for statistical testing. When these assumptions can be made—independence, complete categorization, and reasonable sample size—these estimates can be supplemented with statistical tests.

Two sorts of tests are available for the multiplicative-association model. One tests whether the multiplicative term explains any non-chance variation, the other whether the model fits the data. The second type of test is straightforward. The usual X^2 and G^2 statistics are used to compare the observed and expected frequencies under the model, then these statistics are referred to a χ^2 distribution. In addition to the λ's, the multiplicative-association model has $a - 2$ free values of ξ_A, $b - 2$ free values of ξ_B, and the parameter ϕ. Counting these parameters and subtracting from the number of cells gives $(a - 2)(b - 2)$ degrees of freedom for the test. Rejection indicates that the data contain association components that are not represented by the simple multiplicative-association model.

Tests of the second type are more complicated. The model of independence is a special case of the multiplicative-association model, created when $\phi = 0$. Because of this hierarchy, one might expect that tests of the importance of the multiplicative-association parameters would be given by the difference in X^2 or G^2 between fits of the independence model and of the multiplicative-association model. However, there is a degree of selection involved in fitting the multiplicative-association model that the χ^2 likelihood-ratio testing procedure does not take into account. As Section 11.5 explains, a saturated association model contains several unrelated terms of the form $\hat{\phi}\hat{\xi}_A\hat{\xi}_B$. The estimation of ξ_A and ξ_B is done in a way that maximizes $\hat{\phi}$ and gives the model the maximum improvement in fit over independence. Under the null hypothesis of unrelatedness, the largest of these terms is selected. Just as the maximum of several random variables tends to take larger values than does any particular single variable, the selection process lets the model explain more of the association than would be expected from reference to a χ^2 distribution.†

Although not χ^2, the sampling distribution of the difference statistics is known. When independence holds in the population, both ΔX^2 and ΔG^2 have the same large-sample distribution as does the largest eigenvalue (or characteristic root) of a Wishart matrix (Haberman, 1981). Some critical values of this distribution are shown in the table in Appendix A.5. This table is indexed by the number of rows and columns in the original data, and it is symmetric in these arguments. A comparison of this table to the χ^2 distribution shows that the correct critical values are much larger, except when a or b is 2. For example, in a table the size of Table 11.5, where $a = 5$ and $b = 7$, the 5% critical value for the largest root statistic is 21.62, while the apparent χ^2 distribution (with 9 degrees of freedom) gives 16.92. Clearly, incorrectly using a χ^2 distribution substantially biases the tests toward significance.

The parameter ϕ in the multiplicative-association model gives a measure of the magnitude of the associative relationship. As such, it is an association measure, like those described in Chapter 9. It measures the amount of association

---

†The selection effects give a negative bias to tests of the overall fit of the multiplicative-association model relative to a $\chi^2[(a-2)(b-2)]$ distribution. This bias vanishes when the null hypothesis is substantially false or when N is large.

that is captured by the pair of scales ξ_A and ξ_B. Its usefulness in this role is increased by transforming it to the range from -1 to $+1$. When the parameters can appropriately be estimated under the distributional identification constraints (Equations 11.8), a conversion to this range is

$$\hat{\rho}_\phi = \frac{\sqrt{1+4\hat{\phi}^2} - 1}{2\hat{\phi}} \tag{11.9}$$

Why one chooses this improbable-looking transformation is not obvious. Its form comes from the relationship between multiplicative association and a latent normal distribution, which is explained in Section 13.6. For the example, $\hat{\phi} = 0.493$, and so $\hat{\rho}_\phi = 0.410$. Where the distributional constraints are not used, $\hat{\phi}$ can be treated as if it were an odds ratio and converted to a range from -1 to 1 using one of the transformations described in Section 9.1.

When the scale parameters ξ_A and ξ_B are treated as free parameters, as they are in the models described here, the maximum-likelihood estimate $\hat{\phi}$ of ϕ is not unbiased. The estimates of ξ_A and ξ_B are chosen to maximize the apparent association, which allows $\hat{\phi}$ to capitalize on any chance effects that are present as a result of sampling accidents. Bias of this type may be familiar from multiple-regression theory, where the optimal character of the estimates of the regression coefficients means that the sample multiple-regression coefficient overestimates the corresponding population quantity. In practice, this bias often has little effect on an analysis, if one only intends to use $\hat{\phi}$ as an indicator of the effect. This bias should be borne in mind, however, when the association in two samples of differing size is to be compared, particularly in small samples where the bias can be substantial. The proper way to compare two samples uses a version of the three-dimensional models mentioned in Section 11.6.

The multiplicative-association model accommodates structural voids in the same manner as the independence models. The choice data with excluded diagonal in Table 11.3 are a good example. The fit of the multiplicative-association model to these data appears adequate, with $X^2(10) = 6.95$. With the standardizations of Equations 11.7, the association parameter is estimated as $\hat{\phi} = 3.88$, the scores for the first choices in the rows ($\hat{\xi}_F$) as

$$-0.49 \quad -0.31 \quad -0.40 \quad 0.40 \quad 0.30 \quad 0.50$$

and those for the second choices in the columns ($\hat{\xi}_S$) as

$$-0.43 \quad -0.37 \quad -0.40 \quad 0.37 \quad 0.31 \quad 0.53$$

The block structure of the original table is clearly visible in the grouping of these parameters (see Problem 11.8).

For some purposes, it is convenient to view the multiplicative-association model as a description of the odds ratios from 2×2 subtables. A large two-way table yields many of these coefficients, each formed by selecting two rows and two columns. Using rows i and k and columns j and l gives the ratio

$$\alpha_{(ik)(jl)} = \frac{\mu_{ij}\mu_{kl}}{\mu_{il}\mu_{jk}} \tag{11.10}$$

Taking the logarithm and substituting the expected frequencies under the multiplicative-association model (from Equation 11.5) give

$$\log \alpha_{(ik)(jl)} = \phi(\xi_{A(i)} - \xi_{A(k)})(\xi_{B(j)} - \xi_{B(l)}) \tag{11.11}$$

Writing the model in this form shows that the magnitude of the association in the subtable depends on the difference between the parameters of the selected rows and the difference between the parameters of the selected columns. In this form, the assertion made earlier concerning the scaling of association becomes clearer: rows and columns with similar values of $\chi_{A(i)}$ or $\chi_{B(j)}$ are nearly independent of each other, while those for which both coefficients are different are highly associated.

A potential instability of the multiplicative-association model should be noted. The association term in this model, like that of the maximum-correlation model in the next section, is the largest of several similar terms. If one multiplicative association term clearly dominates all other terms in the population, it almost certainly determines the model. However, if the underlying association is composed of two or more similarly sized multiplicative components, replications of the study may sometimes produce a model based on one of them, sometimes one based on the other, as sampling accidents favor one component or another. The danger of this instability is greatest when the model fits poorly and leaves much variability unexplained. If a substantial part of the association is not captured by the multiplicative-association model as it is described here, one should move to the multicomponent forms of the models in Section 11.5.

11.4. MAXIMUM-CORRELATION MODELS

In the multiplicative-association model, a product term, $\phi\xi_A\xi_B$, is added to the logarithm of the expected frequencies under independence (Equation 11.5). Another important model for association effects, here referred to as the *maximum-correlation model*, adds such a product term directly to μ_{ij} instead of to $\log \mu_{ij}$. The resulting model is not log-linear, but has numerous other interpretations.†

When the rows and columns of a two-way table are independent, the probability of an observation in cell i,j is the product of the row probability distribution, $\pi_{A(i)}$, and the column probability distribution, $\pi_{B(j)}$, or

---

†Most of the material in this section and the next appears in Greenacre (1984), Lebart, Morineau, & Warwick (1984), or Nishisato (1980). These references should be consulted for the subtleties of the methods and for citations of the extensive primary literature.

$$\pi_{ij} = \pi_{A(i)}\pi_{B(j)}$$

In the maximum-correlation model, a product term is added to this description, to give

$$\pi_{ij} = \pi_{A(i)}\pi_{B(j)}(1 + \rho\psi_{A(i)}\psi_{B(j)}) \qquad (11.12)$$

As with the homologous parameters in the multiplicative-association model, the scores $\psi_{A(i)}$ and $\psi_{B(i)}$ can be interpreted as scalings of the rows and columns categories with respect to the association. The magnitude of this association is measured by ρ.

Two constraints on ψ_A and ψ_B are required to identify them. The natural choice is to fix their mean and variance with respect to the corresponding marginal distribution. For factor A, the restrictions are

$$\sum_i \pi_{A(i)}\psi_{A(i)} = 0 \quad \text{and} \quad \sum_i \pi_{A(i)}\psi_{A(i)}^2 = 1 \qquad (11.13)$$

Similar restrictions apply to ψ_B. A standardization based on the simple sums and sums of squares (analogous to Equations 11.7 for the multiplicative-association model) can also be used, but is less natural for this model.

The structure of the maximum-correlation model is simple, and the model can be developed in several different ways. Consequently, it has been independently invented and named several times. Each of these developments emphasizes some characteristic of the association in a two-way table. The following paragraphs describe several approaches, which together give a richer feeling for the model than any one does alone.

Each approach starts with a set of numerical scores a_i associated with the rows of a two-way table and another set b_j associated with the columns. In keeping with the constraints on the theoretical parameters (Equation 11.13), the mean and variance of these scores with respect to the marginal distribution of the data is fixed; for factor A,

$$\sum_i p_{i+}a_i = 0 \quad \text{and} \quad \sum_i p_{i+}a_i^2 = 1 \qquad (11.14)$$

The scores are chosen both to obey these constraints and to optimize some property of the data. When so chosen, they are estimates of the parameters ψ_A and ψ_B of the model (Equation 11.12). The three approaches differ in what is optimized, but not in the resulting estimates.

The first approach emphasizes the model as an expression of linear association. Using the scores a_i and b_j, one calculates a Pearson correlation coefficient from the contingency table, treating it as if it were a grouped frequency distribution. With the constraints of Equation 11.14, this correlation is

$$r = \sum_{\text{cells}} p_{ij}a_ib_j \qquad (11.15)$$

Obviously, the size of r depends on a_i and b_j, some choices giving large values and others small values. The notion behind this model is that an optimal representation of the association is obtained by selecting a_i and b_j so that r is a maximum. In this way the maximal linear component of the association is extracted. This interpretation of the model is the source of the name *maximum-correlation model* used here.

The second approach to the model emphasizes the mutual dependence between the rows and the columns. It is known as *reciprocal averaging* and arises from an attempt to write the row and column scores as linear combinations of each other. Starting with the row scores a_i, one assigns to each column their average value, as determined by the distribution in that column:

$$b'_j = \sum_i \left(\frac{x_{ij}}{x_{+j}}\right) a_i \qquad (11.16)$$

The quantity in parenthesis here is the conditional proportion of the observations in column j that come from row i. Likewise, new scores for the rows are obtained by averaging the column values,

$$a'_i = \sum_j \left(\frac{x_{ij}}{x_{i+}}\right) b_j \qquad (11.17)$$

In general, there is no reason for the averages a'_i and b'_j to bear any relationship to the original scores a_i and b_j. However, there are certain ways to select a_i and b_j so that the averaging changes only their spread, not the relative placement of the categories:

$$a'_i = ra_i \quad \text{and} \quad b'_j = rb_j \qquad (11.18)$$

For all such choices, $r < 1$. Among these alternatives, the pair of scales associated with the largest value of r is the optimal choice.

The third development of the model, known as *dual scaling* or *optimal scaling*, emphasizes the assignment of scores as a way to maximize discrimination among the categories. Consider the columns of the tables as groups of x_{+j} observations. To each observation in row i of any column assign the score a_i. So, a count of $x_{23} = 5$ indicates five instances of the score a_2 in the third group. For some assignments of these scores there is little difference among the column means; for others the differences are larger. To measure the separation of the groups, run an analysis of variance. A large effect is indicated by a large value of the F statistic or, equivalently, by a large value of the *correlation ratio*,

$$r^2 = \frac{SS_{\text{between groups}}}{SS_{\text{total}}} \qquad (11.19)$$

By this criterion, the optimal choice of scores makes F and r^2 as large as possible. Optimum scores are attached to the columns in the same way, by treating the rows as groups. These optimal row scores give the same r^2 as the optimal column scores.

Each of these maximization problems can be given a rigorous mathematical formulation. The three interpretations lead to the same result, which turns out to be an eigenvalue problem. Thus, they have the same solution. The optimum scores a_i and b_j are estimates of the parameters $\psi_{A(i)}$ and $\psi_{B(j)}$ of Equation 11.12. The maximal association, measured by r in Equations 11.15, 11.18, and 11.19, has the same role in the model as ρ. As in the case of ϕ and $\hat{\phi}$ for the multiplicative-association model, the maximized correlation is not an unbiased estimate of ρ, however, since the optimization procedure can capitalize on sampling accidents that are unique to the sample. For example, even if complete independence holds in a population, there is usually some haphazard association in a sample, so that $r > 0$ even though $\rho = 0$. In small samples, this bias is appreciable (O'Neill, 1978b).

The reciprocal averaging procedure gives an iterative method to estimate the model's parameters. One starts with a set of arbitrarily chosen scores, $a_i^{(0)}$, and applies Equation 11.16 to calculate b_j. Next, Equation 11.17 is applied to change these score to new values, a_i'. These are rescaled to the proper mean and variance (Equation 11.14) and denoted $a_i^{(1)}$. Again using Equations 11.16, 11.17, and 11.14, $a_i^{(1)}$ is transformed into $a_i^{(2)}$. As this process is repeated, the parameters converge to their optimum values, $\hat{\psi}_{A(i)}$ and $\hat{\psi}_{B(j)}$. The adjustment of the spread that is required to give both $a_i^{(n)}$ and $a_i^{(n+1)}$ a unit variance equals r^2, as implied by Equations 11.18.

Another way to view the maximum-correlation model is as a description of the residuals from independence. The marginal distributions π_A and π_B in the maximum-correlation model are estimated by the observed marginal proportions. Inserting these estimates into the formula for μ_{ij} (following Equation 11.12) gives the sample version of the model,

$$\hat{\mu}_{ij} = \frac{x_{i+}x_{+j}}{x_{++}}\left(1 + \hat{\rho}\hat{\psi}_{A(i)}\hat{\psi}_{B(j)}\right) \tag{11.20}$$

The term outside the parenthesis on the left-hand side of this equation is the expected frequency under independence, $x_{i+}x_{+j}/x_{++}$. Let e_{ij} denote these frequencies and suppose that the model approximately describes a set of data with frequencies x_{ij}. Rearranging Equation 11.20 gives

$$\frac{x_{ij} - e_{ij}}{e_{ij}} \approx \hat{\rho}\hat{\psi}_{A(i)}\hat{\psi}_{B(j)} \tag{11.21}$$

This reorganization shows that the association term is a model for the relative deviations of the data from independence. This description is analogous to the interpretation of the multiplicative-association model as a model for $\lambda_{AB(ij)}$ in Equation 11.6.

As an example of the parameters of this model, consider the data that were analyzed by the multiplicative-association model in Table 11.5. Estimates of the maximum-correlation models parameters, ρ, ψ_D (demographic category), and ψ_C (choices), are shown in the bottom three lines of Table 11.6. The estimates of the association parameters are similar to those of the multiplicative-association model and are interpreted in a similar way.

Tests of the fit of the maximum-correlation model are almost the same as those described for the multiplicative-association model. A test of the overall fit is obtained by comparing the expected frequencies from Equation 11.20 to the observed data using X^2 or G^2 and referring the result to a χ^2 distribution with $(a - 2)(b - 2)$ degrees of freedom. To test for differences from the independence model, one uses ΔX^2, ΔG^2, or the equivalent statistic $x_{++}\rho^2$, which is somewhat easier to calculate. Under independence, when $\rho = 0$, all three of these statistics have the Wishart root distribution tabulated in the table in Appendix A.5 (O'Neill, 1978a). Probably the easiest way to run a test is to divide the critical value from this table by x_{++} to get a critical value for $\hat{\rho}^2$. For the 500 observations in the 5×7 array in Table 11.5, the 5% level of the Wishart largest root statistic is 21.62, so the critical correlation is

$$\sqrt{\frac{21.62}{500}} = 0.208$$

The observed $\hat{\rho} = 0.46$ in Table 11.6 exceeds this value, so a significant association component is present.

In the numerical example of Tables 11.5 and 11.6, the association parameters from the maximum-correlation model are similar to those of the multiplicative-association model. This is not a coincidence. Although the outward form of the two models is different, both represent the deviations from independence by the product of a row scale, a column scale, and an association coefficient (compare

TABLE 11.6
Parameters of the Maximum-correlation Model
Fitted to the Data in Table 11.5

Sample Size							
N: 500							
Marginal Proportions							
$\hat{\pi}_{i+}$:	0.21	0.35	0.11	0.22	0.10		
$\hat{\pi}_{+j}$:	0.18	0.28	0.05	0.18	0.09	0.16	0.06
Association Parameters							
$\hat{\rho}$:	0.46						
$\hat{\psi}_{D(i)}$:	1.77	−0.94	−0.18	−0.26	0.37		
$\hat{\psi}_{P(j)}$:	−0.91	−0.62	0.58	−0.69	1.87	1.16	1.44

Equations 11.6 and 11.21).† The similarity in the bilinear representation gives them a similarity in their information content that in some circumstances overrides the difference in form. When the amount of association in the table is not large and when both models fit well, they give similar results. Under these circumstances, the choice between the two models is not of great consequence as far as the representation of the data is concerned. When the association is substantial the predictions of the two models differ substantially, which can have an appreciable effect on the quality of their fits.

There are reasons other than goodness of fit to prefer one formulation to the other. As always, interpretational matters are most important. The circumstances that favor one model over the other are far from clear, but some differences can be identified. In the multiplicative-association model, the bilinear association term expresses a relationship among the log μ_{ij}, whereas in the maximum-correlation model the relationship is to μ_{ij} (or π_{ij}). Thus, the first model is more attuned to log-linear association effects, the other to linear effects. This difference gives the multiplicative-association model an advantage when one is studying association, for which the representation is essentially on a logarithmic scale. The maximum-correlation model is more natural for linear effects (which are not much emphasized in this book). The process by which the data came about also influences the choice of model. If one believes that the data derive from a categorized bivariate normal distribution (as described in Section 13.6, below), then the multiplicative-association model applies (Goodman, 1981a, 1985). When the association derives from the influence of an unmeasured latent categorical variable, then the maximum-correlation model results (Gilula, 1984; Goodman, 1987). For further discussion of the differences between the models, see Gilula, Krieger, & Ritov (1988), and Goodman (1985, 1986, 1987).

11.5. MULTIPLE ASSOCIATION TERMS

The models in the last two sections are not saturated (unless a or b is 2) and may leave considerable association unexplained. They can be generalized by intro-

---

†Readers familiar with power series will recall that $e^x = 1 + x + x^2/2! + \cdots$. By using this identity, the frequencies of the multiplicative-association model (Equation 11.5) are

$$\mu_{ij} = A_i B_j \exp(\phi\xi_{A(i)}\xi_{B(j)})$$
$$= A_i B_j (1 + \phi\xi_{A(i)}\xi_{B(j)} + \phi^2\xi_{A(i)}^2\xi_{B(j)}^2/2 + \ldots)$$

This series differs from the maximum-correlation model (Equation 11.12) only in the third and higher terms. When ϕ is small, these terms are small and the models make similar predictions. When the association is substantial, the models differ. For another treatment of the parallel between models, see Goodman (1981a).

ducing additional association terms. Consider the maximum-correlation model (Equation 11.12),

$$\pi_{ij} = \pi_{A(i)}\pi_{B(j)}(1 + \rho\psi_{A(i)}\psi_{B(j)}) \qquad (11.22)$$

To better fit the data, one can add a second association component, with a new pair of scales and a new correlation. Denoting the two sets of parameters by a subscript on ρ and a parenthesized superscript on the ψ's, the expanded model is

$$\pi_{ij} = \pi_{A(i)}\pi_{B(j)}(1 + \rho_1\psi_{A(i)}^{(1)}\psi_{B(j)}^{(1)} + \rho_2\psi_{A(i)}^{(2)}\psi_{B(j)}^{(1)}) \qquad (11.23)$$

Without further constraints, the parameters of Equation 11.23 cannot be estimated. First, the mean and variance of the new terms are constrained to zero and one (as in Equation 11.13). Moreover, the two association terms have the same form, so the distinction between them is ambiguous. To separate them, one extends the maximum-correlation principle: the first set, consisting of ρ_1, $\psi_A^{(1)}$, and $\psi_B^{(1)}$, is chosen to capture as much of the association as possible—i.e., so that ρ_1 is maximal. Next, ρ_2, $\psi_A^{(2)}$, and $\psi_B^{(2)}$ are used to express the largest portion of the association that remains uninterpreted. In Equation 11.21 the first association term was interpreted as a description of the residuals from independence. Now the second association term is the best bilinear fit to the residuals after removal of both marginal-frequency effects and the first association term. The first set captures the largest correlational component of the association, the second the next largest.

As long as there is uninterpreted association, one can introduce more terms. The general multiterm maximum-correlation model is

$$\pi_{ij} = \pi_{A(i)}\pi_{B(j)}\left(1 + \sum_{k=1}^{K} \rho_k\psi_{A(i)}^{(k)}\psi_{B(j)}^{(k)}\right) \qquad (11.24)$$

Each set of scores is selected to have a mean of zero and a variance of one (as in Equations 11.13) and is chosen so that ρ_k is maximal, subject to the constraint that no term duplicates association already expressed in a lower-numbered term. The latter restriction forces the scores to satisfy an *orthogonality restriction*. This restriction states that for any two series of terms, i.e., with $k \neq l$,

$$\sum_i \pi_{A(i)}\psi_{A(i)}^{(k)}\psi_{A(i)}^{(l)} = 0 \quad \text{and} \quad \sum_j \pi_{B(j)}\psi_{B(j)}^{(k)}\psi_{B(j)}^{(l)} = 0$$

Comparable equations using $\hat{\pi}$ and $\hat{\psi}$ apply to the estimates. Constraints similar to these may be familiar from the definition of orthogonality in other branches of statistics, for example, in the extraction of orthogonal components in the analysis of variance or in the definition of principal components in multivariate analysis.

The number of association terms that appear in Equation 11.24 depends on the size of the original data table. For a complete table, the model is always saturated when K is 1 less than the smaller of the number of rows or columns. Except in a few unlikely circumstances, a series of exactly this many uniquely defined such terms exist (Lancaster, 1958). Unless the table contains structural voids or dependencies among the rows or columns, models with smaller values of K are unsaturated. Of course, many sets of data do not require a full complement of terms to achieve an adequate fit.

The ordering of terms, so that $\rho_k \geq \rho_l$ for any $k > l$, has important consequences. Because each correlation is the largest possible, the low-numbered terms are the same, regardless of how many other terms are in the model. The parameters ψ_A, ψ_B and ρ of the single-term model (Equation 11.22) are identical to $\psi_A^{(1)}$, $\psi_B^{(1)}$, and ρ_1 in the multiterm models (Equations 11.23 and 11.24). Similarly, the $k = 2$ parameters are the same in Equations 11.23 and 11.24. Any model with a few association terms is a special case of all models that have more terms. Accordingly, one need not fit the unsaturated models separately. First, the saturated model is fitted, then the high-numbered terms are peeled away to get the restricted versions.†

The value of the multiterm correlation models lies in the way that the parameters $\psi_A^{(k)}$ and $\psi_B^{(k)}$ reduce the important aspects of the association to a few pairs of scales. Only those sets of parameters that make a substantial contribution to the association need be retained; the others can be dropped. The Pearson statistic measuring departure from independence is proportional to the sum of squared correlations,

$$X^2_{A \perp\!\!\!\perp B} = x_{++} \sum_k \hat{\rho}_k^2 \qquad (11.25)$$

Accordingly, $\hat{\rho}_k^2$ is a good indicator of an association term's importance to the model. One can decide qualitatively how many sets of association scores to keep in one's model by looking either at the squared correlations or at their size relative to their sum over all terms. A plot of these proportions is helpful: one sees quickly when the size of the squared correlations has fallen to a negligible proportion of the total.

For an example, return to the choice data in Table 11.5. Table 11.7 shows the results of fitting the full multiterm model (Equation 11.24) to these data. Because the smaller dimension of the table has 5 levels, there are 4 sets of association terms. The top part of the table presents the correlations, their squares, and the size of the squares as a percentage of their sum (0.257). The last quantity is

---

†In linear-algebraic terms, the multiterm maximum-correlation model is obtained from a *singular value decomposition* of the data. That is, the contingency table **X**, treated as a matrix, is rewritten as a product $\mathbf{A'\Lambda B}$ in which the rows of **A** and **B** are category scores and Λ is a diagonal matrix that contains the correlations. This formulation reduces the estimation problem to one for which computational algorithms are readily available (e.g., Press, Flannery, Teukolsky, & Vetterling, 1986).

TABLE 11.7
Multivariate Maximum-correlation Model (Correspondence
Analysis) Fitted to Data from Table 11.5

Analysis of the Correlations

k	$\hat{\rho}_k$	$\hat{\rho}_k^2$	%	Rough Graph (■ = 4%)
1	0.456	0.208	80.9	████████████████████
2	0.198	0.039	15.3	████
3	0.084	0.007	2.7	■
4	0.053	0.003	1.1	I
		0.257	100.0	

Scale Values, $\hat{\psi}^{(k)}$

	Row Scales		Column Scales	
i or j	$k = 1$	$k = 2$	$k = 1$	$k = 2$
1	1.768	0.729	−0.912	−0.038
2	−0.936	0.752	−0.619	0.112
3	−0.184	−1.796	0.585	−0.378
4	−0.265	−0.154	−0.692	0.267
5	0.374	−1.741	1.869	1.302
6			1.158	−1.790
7			1.442	2.332

Coordinate Values, $f^{(k)}$

	Row Scales		Column Scales	
i or j	$k = 1$	$k = 2$	$k = 1$	$k = 2$
1	0.806	0.145	−0.416	−0.007
2	−0.427	0.149	−0.282	0.022
3	−0.084	−0.356	0.267	−0.075
4	−0.121	−0.031	−0.316	0.053
5	0.171	−0.345	0.853	0.258
6			0.528	−0.355
7			0.658	0.463

graphed. The first two components capture $80.9 + 15.3 = 96.2\%$ of the association. Apparently, the two-term model (Equation 11.23) is an adequate representation of these data. The middle portion of the table gives the scores associated with these terms. The estimates for $k = 1$ are those of the single-term maximum-correlation model in the last section (Table 11.6).

The statistical tests available for the multiterm maximum-correlation model are similar to those that apply to its single-term version. A satisfactory test of whether there is any unexplained association is conducted with the usual X^2 and

G^2 statistics. If the K-term model (Equation 11.23) is necessary, in that ρ_1 to ρ_K are all nonzero, then the hypothesis that $\rho_k = 0$ for $k > K$ is tested against the hypothesis that at least one additional ρ_k is nonzero by referring these statistics to a χ^2 distribution with $(a - K - 1)(b - K - 1)$ degrees of freedom.

Tests for the individual correlations are less satisfactory. Since the largest correlation is the same regardless of how many terms are included in the model, the hypothesis that $\rho_1 = 0$ is still tested by comparing $x_{++}\hat{\rho}_1^2$ to the Wishart root distribution in Appendix A.5, as described in the last section. One would like similar tests that look at the other ρ_k. Since $x_{++}\hat{\rho}_1^2$ is a test statistic for the first term, one might hope that other components of Equation 11.25 could be examined in the same way. Unfortunately, when $k > 1$ the distribution of $x_{++}\hat{\rho}_k^2$ (or of ΔX^2 and ΔG^2) depends on the particular effects that are associated with lower-numbered terms (O'Neill, 1978b, 1981). This dependence makes it impossible to tabulate critical values, except in the very special case of independence when all the ρ_k are zero. However, these tests are not useful, since one does not care about ρ_2 unless one has already rejected $\rho_1 = 0$. Because the critical values of the higher coefficients are less than those in Table A.5, one can use that table for a conservative test, but this comparison is not helpful beyond the second or third term. One turns to the type of qualitative analysis discussed above, which is usually adequate for the descriptive treatment appropriate to this model. Comparable selection problems—deciding how many dimensions to retain in a final model—appear in other branches of multivariate statistics, for example in discriminant analysis, principal components analysis, factor analysis, or multidimensional scaling (see, e.g., Harris, 1985, Sections 4.4 and 4.5).

Just as the maximum-correlation model has several independent origins, the multi-term model derives from several sets of principles (well taxonomized by Tenenhaus & Young, 1985). Each of the interpretations of the maximum-correlation model in the last section has its multicomponent form. The model is heavily used in the French school of statistics, where it is the basis for *l'analyse des correspondances*, known in English as *correspondence analysis*† (Benzécri et al., 1973; Greenacre, 1984, Lebart, Morineau, & Warwick, 1984).

When only a few scales suffice to represent the data, the association can be described geometrically, by plotting the scores. In particular, when the association is two-dimensional, as in the example in Table 11.7 the relationships among the categories can be plotted in the plane. Plotting $\hat{\psi}_A^{(k)}$ and $\hat{\psi}_B^{(k)}$ directly is a

---

†The words *correspondance* (French) and *correspondence* (English) are not exact cognates. The French word includes the idea of connection or association, making it more appropriate for the topic at hand than the English word. One might translate the procedure as the analysis of relationship or the analysis of association. *L'analyse des correspondances* is more than the use of Model 11.24: it embodies a particular style of interpretation and a philosophy of data analysis (see Benzécri et al., 1973, Section IIA no 1). For example, the French work heavily emphasizes the descriptive nature of the techniques and avoids almost entirely any treatment of hypothesis tests.

bit deceptive, however. As defined as unidimensional scales, both sets of scores are standardized to unit variance, even though they carry unequal proportions of the effect. A multi-dimensional plot better represents the data if one multiplies the coordinates by the correlation before graphing. Instead of the original scores, one plots

$$f^{(k)}_{A(i)} = \hat{\rho}_k \hat{\psi}^{(k)}_{A(i)} \quad \text{and} \quad f^{(k)}_{B(j)} = \hat{\rho}_k \hat{\psi}^{(k)}_{B(j)} \tag{11.26}$$

With this adjustment, the variance of each dimension is proportional to the size of its contribution to X^2 in Equation 11.25. These coordinates are shown in the bottom panel of Table 11.7 and are plotted in Figure 11.2.

Row points (demographic category)

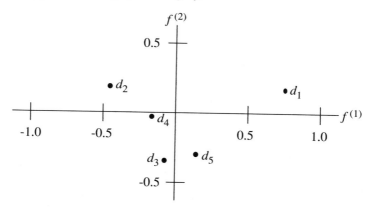

Column points (products)

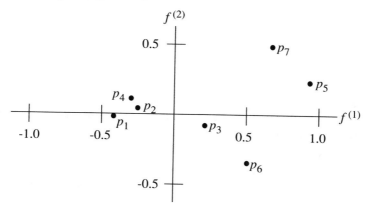

FIGURE 11.2. Plots of the coordinates from Table 11.8

Plots such as Figure 11.2 put points representing categories that have similar association patterns close to each other, and those that are different at widely separated points. As with other derived multidimensional representations, such as factor analysis or multidimensional scaling, external characteristics of the categories may help to assign meaning to the dimensions of the space. The original axes are not critical now, and one may find it useful to redistribute the variability among the dimensions by rotating the axes before interpreting them.

Because the scales of the row and column plots are similar, the two sets of scores can be plotted on a single graph. This dual plot is useful, since it puts related row and column points near to each other. As the dual scaling formulae indicate (Equations 11.16 and 11.17), a row that largely contains observations from one column is represented by a point that is very close to the column point.† For further discussion of graphical interpretation in correspondence analysis, see Greenacre (1984) and Greenacre & Hastie (1987).

The multiplicative-association model also has a multiterm form. The extension is made by adding bilinear terms to that model (Equation 11.5) in a process completely comparable to that of the maximum-correlation model (Goodman, 1985, 1986). Thus, the multiterm association model is

$$\log \mu_{ij} = \lambda + \lambda_{A(i)} + \lambda_{B(j)} + \sum_{k=1}^{K} \phi_k \xi_{A(i)}^{(k)} \xi_{B(j)}^{(k)} \tag{11.27}$$

Summation and orthogonality constraints, similar to those of the maximum-correlation model apply to the $\xi_{A(i)}^{(k)}$ and $\xi_{B(i)}^{(k)}$. As in that model, saturation is attained when K is one less than the smaller of the number of rows or the number of columns. Similar forms of graphical interpretation can be made. Most statements about the correlation model in this section have a counterpart for the association model. However, parameter estimation is typically different, in that the estimates for models with small K are not the same as the comparable parameters in models with larger K.

Because of its earlier development and its use in correspondence analysis, the multiterm correlation model has been much more widely used than the multiterm association model. The discussion concerning the differences between these models at the end of the last section applies to the multiterm forms as well. The situations under which one model is preferable to another are not fully clear, although because of its logarithmic character the association model is probably the better way to introduce association into a context of probabilistic independence.

---

†One must not overinterpret the distances between row and column points. In particular, one should avoid attributing to them the properties of the *unfolding model* from multidimensional scaling (Coombs, 1964), which uses the intercategorization distances as the fundamental indication of the distance between row and column entities.

11.6. MULTIDIMENSIONAL ASSOCIATION MODELS

Both the multiplicative-association model and the maximum-correlation model express the association between one multilevel classification scheme in the rows of a two-way table and another in the columns. The relationship that these models capture is essentially bivariate: the association measures are analogous to correlation coefficients and correlation is a bivariate concept. If one wishes to express the association in a multiway table, one must extend these procedures. Broadly speaking, there are two approaches that one may take: either one expands the models to involve three (or more) factors or one reduces the data to a two-dimensional configuration.

Consider the first approach first. There are many ways to extend the two-dimensional association models to higher dimensionality (see, e.g., Agresti, 1984, Chapter 8; Agresti & Kezouh, 1983; Clogg, 1982). The *partial-association models* connect pairs of factors by means of association terms similar to those of the two-way model. For example, the multiplicative-association version of this model for three-dimensional data uses three bilinear product terms,

$$\log \mu_{ijk} = \lambda + \lambda_{A(i)} + \lambda_{B(j)} + \lambda_{C(k)} + \phi_{AB}\xi_{A(i)}\xi_{B(j)} + \phi_{AC}\xi_{A(i)}\xi_{C(k)}$$
$$+ \phi_{BC}\xi_{B(j)}\xi_{C(k)} \qquad (11.28)$$

Each pairwise association term describes the association between two factors when the third is held constant, which is why they are called partial associations. For example, if k is fixed in Equation 11.28, the last two terms depend only on i and j, respectively, and can be absorbed into $\lambda_{A(i)}$ and $\lambda_{B(j)}$ for that slice.

As Equation 11.28 is written, the ξ's in different terms are not differentiated. For example, $\xi_{A(i)}$ is part of both the AB and the AC association terms. One can expand the model by allowing them to differ. Thus, $\xi_{A(i)}$ could legitimately represent different scales when paired with B and with C. Depending on which scales are the same and which are different, eight variant models are produced.

Another way to extend the association models to multiple factors uses the concept of *conditional association*. Here one singles out two factors, constructs an association model for them, and investigates the way that parameters of that model vary over the additional factor(s). Using the multiplicative representation of association, this model in three dimensions is

$$\log \mu_{ijk} = \lambda + \lambda_{A(i)} + \lambda_{B(j)} + \lambda_{C(k)} + \lambda_{AC(ik)} + \lambda_{BC(jk)}$$
$$+ \phi_{AB}^{(k)}\xi_{A(i)}^{(k)}\xi_{B(i)}^{(k)} \qquad (11.29)$$

where the superscript $^{(k)}$ indicates the level of the third factor. The association in the AB dimensions is constrained by the form of the multiplicative-association model, while the parameters $\lambda_{AC(ik)}$ and $\lambda_{BC(jk)}$ allow arbitrary patterns of association to appear in the AC and BC marginals. If the bilinear association term is deleted from Model 11.29, the resulting model represents the conditonal-independence hypothesis $A \perp\!\!\!\perp B|C$. Thus, Model 11.29 adds association to this assertion: its emphasis is on the AB tables at levels of C. One uses it to look at how the association terms depend on k. This type of model is developed in more detail in Section 13.4, using as a base the additive-association model of Section 13.3.

As a brief example of how the conditional approach is used, suppose that the survey leading to the demographic-category-by-choice data in Table 11.5 is replicated at three different times. The surveys combine in a three-dimensional table with factors of demographic category, choice, and the time of the survey (D, C, and T, respectively). A complete analysis of this table has several stages, the logic of which follows from the discussion of Chapter 6. To begin, one can investigate changes in demographic category over time in the TD marginal table and look for changes in preference over time by testing the hypothesis $C \perp\!\!\!\perp T|D$. If no three-factor association is present, as indicated by an acceptable fit of the model $[TD][TC][CD]$, then one can investigate the DC association by fitting the version Model 11.29 in which the multiplicative assocation of D and C is present but is not allowed to vary with time (the index k in Equation 11.29). If three-factor association is present, one studies how the DC association changes with time, by examining how the parameters of the multiplicative term vary with k. If the time-varying model fits, then any changes that have taken place in the amount of association are measured by $\phi^{(k)}$ and any changes in the relative placement of the choice alternatives with respect to each other are measured by $\xi_C^{(k)}$. Hypotheses of both sorts are tested by difference statistics. The conditional models are particularly useful when the conditioning factor has only two levels.

There are numerous versions of the multiway multiplicative-association model other than those in Equations 11.28 and 11.29. One can include parameters to fit various combinations of the marginals, can allow the association terms to vary with the levels of any of the factors, and can introduce multiterm representations of any particular association. A selection of such models is presented in Section 8 of Goodman (1986). In general, the problems associated with using these models come more from difficulties in finding an interpretable representation and de-limiting the set of plausible models, than from finding a model that fits the data.

The models of Equations 11.28 and 11.29 contain many parameters and allow many variants. They are better adapted to the examination of specific hypotheses or the representation of specific effects than they are to general description. As description, they lose the simplicity of the two-dimensional plots such as Figure 11.2. The other general approach attempts to salvage the simple plots by reduc-ing the multiway table to a two-way layout so that the bivariate association models can still be applied. This approach is a common part of the correspon-dence-analysis approach, known as *multiple correspondence analysis*. How the reduction to two dimensions is made depends on the data one wishes to analyze. The remainder of this section describes several possibilities.

One common form of multidimensional data occurs when the link between a single categorization and a series of other factors is being studied. Surveys often yield this type of data, the single factor being some classification of the respondents and the other factors being their responses to a series of questions. For example, suppose that the data in Table 3.1, shown again at the top of Table 11.8, relate a three-level subject classification (factor C) to two yes-no questions (factors A and B). Rather than work with the separate CA and CB tables, one assembles them into a single 3×4 table, shown in the middle panel of Table 11.8. Obviously, this table violates the sampling assumptions needed for statistical inference (in particular, each respondent appears twice). Nevertheless, the association models are still satisfactorily for descriptive purposes. They yield a representation with a point for each of the respondent categories and a point for each answer to each question. The organization of this table emphasizes the relationship between the classification of the subjects and the answers to the

TABLE 11.8
Three Two-dimensional Representations
of the Three-way Data from Table 3.1

Original Data (from Table 3.1)

| | a_1 | | a_2 | |
	b_1	b_2	b_1	b_2
c_1	7	22	15	4
c_2	5	49	20	3
c_3	3	140	2	5

Assemblage of the CA and the CB Tables

	a_1	a_2	b_1	b_2
c_1	29	19	22	26
c_2	54	23	25	52
c_3	143	7	5	145

Burt Table

	a_1	a_2	b_1	b_2	c_1	c_2	c_3
a_1	226	0	15	211	29	54	143
a_2	0	49	37	12	19	23	7
b_1	15	37	52	0	22	25	5
b_2	211	12	0	223	26	52	145
c_1	29	19	22	26	48	0	0
c_2	54	23	25	52	0	77	0
c_3	143	7	5	145	0	0	150

questions. It is unaffected by any association among the questions (factors A and B) or by any three-way effects.

The omission of the interquestion association in the last example is reasonable when one is concentrating on how a given classification (the subjects) is linked to the others (the questions). It is less appropriate when all combinations of the factors are of interest, as would be the case with the responses to a set of three questions. All two-way relationships appear in a configuration known as a *Burt table*, in which every category appears both in the rows and in the columns (Table 11.8, bottom panel). This table contains within it all the two-factor subtables relating pairs of factors. There is considerable redundancy in the Burt table. It is symmetric, each subtable appears twice, and the blocks along the diagonal consist primarily of zeros. However, this redundancy is not a problem for the analysis. Either the row points or the column points give a representation of all categories, based on all two-way associations.

The Burt table still involves only the two-way effects. If one wishes to capture higher association effects, a more elaborate configuration is required. One can create this representation by letting the rows or columns be factorial combinations of two or more factors. For example, if one wishes to allow for ABC association in Table 11.8, one can analyze the original table in top panel as a 3 × 4 configuration. This analysis introduces the three-factor association in the relationship between C and the combinations of A and B. As a second example of this approach, recall the four-way configuration from Chapter 5 in which groups of students were asked two questions (Table 5.5). To emphasize the association between the subject groups and the responses, one can cross the eight combinations of year and sex with the the four combinations of the responses A and B. The result is the 8 by 4 $SY \times AB$ table that appears in Table 5.5. The association here includes both direct and higher-order portions. A graph of the solution contains a point for each combination of student classification and a point for each combination of responses. Similarities and differences involving the sexes, the years, or the questions are investigated by relating the points informally. In this form, the analysis essentially scales the failure of the model $SY \perp\!\!\!\perp AB$ (or $[SY][AB]$) to fit the data (cf. Equation 11.21). This treatment is quite different from the search for association terms that followed from the fitting of the log-frequency models in Section 5.8.

A limitation of the analysis just described is that both simple and complex effects are lumped together and must be separated informally. It is also possible to scale only the complex portion of the association. The maximum-correlation model can be interpreted as a description of the deviations from independence. The association models can also be used to examine deviations from more complicated models (Escofier, 1983; van der Heijden & de Leeuw, 1985). Suppose, in the college-student example, that one wishes to look at the way in which the joint association between A and B is related to sex and year. The $SY \times AB$ table described in the last paragraph is unsatisfactory, since a solution based on it is influenced by the association between SY and A and between SY and B as well as that related to the association of A and B. One can exclude all but direct AB association by fitting a model of direct association, $A \perp\!\!\!\perp B|SY$ (or $[SYA]$ $[SYB]$), and then analyzing the deviations of the data from this model, $x_{ijk} - \hat{\mu}_{ijk}$, configuring these as an $SY \times AB$ table. A graphical display of the higher-order association is obtained.

The multidimensional methods are complicated and none of them is uniformly satisfactory. The problem really is the inherent complexity of multifactor association. There is no automatic algorithm that makes such association clear, nor can one choose the best representation without quite a bit of thought. As this book has emphasized, it is particularly difficult to force multiway relationships into a two-way form.

PROBLEMS

11.1. Consider the following 3×4 table of data:

	b_1	b_2	b_3	b_4
a_1	51	31	18	32
a_2	17	23	36	38
a_3	41	39	30	80

For a test of independence in this table, $X^2 = 35.37$ and $G^2 = 33.89$. Decompose the table into a complete set of single-degree-of-freedom tables according to a decomposition that aggregates category a_1 with a_2 to compare to a_3, and that first combines b_1 with b_2 to compare to b_3, then combines these to compare to b_4. Show that the G^2 statistics are additive. Which subtables are significant by an uncorrected test, by Goodman's simultaneous single degree-of-freedom test, and by a test corrected with the Bonferroni inequality.

11.2. Will the following breakdowns of a 4×3 table result in additivity of the component tests of independence?

a. (a_1, a_2) vs. (a_3, a_4), a_1 vs. a_2, a_3 vs. a_4, (b_1, b_2) vs. b_3, and b_1 vs. b_2.
b. (a_1, a_2, a_3) vs. a_4, (a_1, a_2) vs. a_3, a_1 vs. a_3, b_1 vs. b_3, and b_2 vs. b_3.

11.3. The triangles-parameter model can be generalized to allow the major diagonal to be treated differently from the two triangular sections, with

$$\lambda_{T(ij)} = \begin{cases} \delta_1 & \text{if } i < j \\ \delta_2 & \text{if } i = j \\ \delta_3 & \text{if } i > j \end{cases}$$

a. Formulate this model as an incomplete model in a three-way table.
b. ℰ Fit your model to Table 11.2.

11.4. Arange the following models for an ordered square table into a hierarchical lattice:

- independence
- quasi-independence excluding the diagonals
- complete dependence
- symmetry
- quasi-symmetry
- the symmetric and asymmetric forms of the triangles parameter model
- both forms of the diagonals parameter model
- the model in Problem 11.3

11.5. € Test the hypothesis that stimuli in the sets {ba,va,tha} and {da,ga,za,zha} from Table 10.3 are more readily confused with members of the same set than with members of the other set.

11.6. Suppose that the choices in Table 11.3 are such that the chances of making a second choice from the set $\{a_1,a_2,a_3\}$ is different from that of $\{a_4,a_5,a_6\}$.

a. Modify the block-association model of Table 11.3 to describe this situation.
b. How could this model be tested using a program designed to work with incomplete factorial data?
c. € Run the tests.

11.7. One might try to construct an association model by describing the association parameter $\lambda_{AB(ij)}$ as a sum of two parameters, $\gamma_{A(i)} + \gamma_{B(j)}$. In fact, this is not an association model. Show that when a model for log μ_{ij} is written using this description of λ_{AB}, the parameters γ_A and γ_B combine with λ_A and λ_B to give the model for independence.

11.8. Suppose that a set of data is well fit by the block-association model. What happens when the multiplicative-association model is fit to these data?

11.9. Consider an 2 × b table to which the multiplicative-association model has been fit. It is desired to express the binary factor as logits.

a. Put in logit form, what does the multiplicative-association model look like?
b. More generally, in an a × b table, define a logit that compares rows i and k for the jth column by

$$\text{logit}_{j(i,k)} = \log \frac{\pi_{ij}}{\pi_{kj}}$$

Show that under the multiplicative-association model, this logit is a linear function of the column scores and that the parameters of this function depend on the pair of columns selected to form the logit,

$$\text{logit}_{j(i,k)} = \alpha_{ik} + \beta_{ik}\xi_j$$

Thus, the model reflects a simple pattern of change over the rows.

11.10. The multiplicative-association model is fit to the data of Problem 11.1. Under the constraints of Equation 11.8, estimates of the parameters of this model are

$$\hat{\lambda} = 3.504,$$
$$\hat{\lambda}_A = -0.090, -0.238, 0.328,$$
$$\hat{\lambda}_B = -0.010, -0.101, -0.260, 0.371,$$
$$\hat{\xi}_A = -1.332, 1.319, 0.134,$$
$$\hat{\xi}_B = -1.487, -0.256, 1.356, 0.480,$$
$$\hat{\phi} = 0.256$$

Interpret these results. Is the assumption of a single bilinear pattern of association tenable?

11.11. Why is it unreasonable to fit the multiterm association models of Section 11.5 to a $2 \times b$ table?

11.12. Consider a 3×4 table containing 24 observations:

4	2	2	0
1	3	4	1
1	1	1	5

When the maximum-correlation model is fitted to this table, the row scores are -1.000, -0.366, and 1.366; the column scores are -0.796, -0.460, -0.460, and 1.716; and the correlation is 0.628. Use these values to demonstrate the three interpretations of the model.

a. As a grouped bivariate frequency distribution, a correlation of 0.628 is obtained (Equation 11.15).

b. When either the row or the column scores are averaged, the other set of scores is obtained, with spread reduced by a factor of 0.628 (Equations 11.16–11.18).

c. If the data are interpreted as four groups of 6 scores (or 3 groups of 8 scores), their values being given by the parameter estimates above, then the correlation ratio from an analysis of variance is $(0.628)^2 = 0.394$ (Equation 11.19).

11.13. When the multiterm maximum-correlation model is fit to the data in Problem 11.1, the following scale values $\hat{\psi}^{(k)}$ are obtained:

i or j	Row scores		Column scores	
1	1.377	-0.638	1.511	-0.371
2	-1.248	-1.126	0.257	-0.153
3	-0.208	1.119	-1.277	-1.527
4			-0.542	1.219

The correlations $\hat{\rho}^{(k)}$ are 0.246 and 0.144. Convert these results to appropriate coordinates and plot them.

12 Least-squares Models

The approach to frequency tables presented so far in this book has emphasized independence and association as explanatory concepts. Moreover, the maximum-likelihood principle has been used for model-fitting and parameter estimation, specifically accomplished by the iterative fitting of the constrained marginal distributions. Neither of these emphases is essential. This chapter presents an alternative approach. In particular, it describes

- an interpretation of frequency tables based on linear models for functions of the data that need not be either logarithmic or hierarchical
- parameter estimation using a weighted least-squares criterion of fit, with associated statistical tests

The linking of these two concepts is not essential, for one can employ weighted least-squares estimates with association models and can use maximum-likelihood estimates to fit nonhierarchical and non-log-linear models. However, as Section 12.10 discusses, the interpretation and the estimation methods fit naturally together. The change of approach alters the flavor of the analysis, introducing a broader class of models and placing a heavier reliance on the parameters of the linear models. Otherwise, the differences are not great, for tests of similar hypotheses give essentially identical results. For example, the tests are still expressed as χ^2-distributed statistics with the familiar degrees of freedom, taking almost the same values as do their maximum-likelihood counterparts.

Some knowledge of elementary matrix algebra is needed for what follows. Many texts on multiple regression in multivariate statistics contain an adequate review (e.g., Green, 1976; Harris, 1985; Tatsuoka, 1971, among many other

304

possibilities). Only simple matrix operations are used in this chapter: transposition, addition, subtraction, multiplication, and inversion. Readers who wish to skip this chapter can do so without jeopardizing any of Chapter 13, except Section 13.6.

The discussion in this chapter follows the treatment of Grizzle, Starmer, & Koch (1969; see also Grizzle & Williams, 1972; Koch, Landis, Freeman, Freeman, & Lehnen, 1977; Williams & Grizzle, 1972—the 1977 article contains a useful summary of the method). The mechanism is a bit ponderous in places, but the ideas are straightforward. The reader should not lose sight of the motivation behind the formal matrix expressions.

12.1. LINEAR AND LOG-LINEAR HYPOTHESES FOR A SINGLE POPULATION

The simplest application of least squares estimates to a linear model is for a single population of observations, where each observation can fall into any class. Such a situation may be modeled by the pure multinomial or pure Poisson models of Section 4.2, but not, say, by a product multinomial model where the observations come from separately sampled subpopulations (a case that is treated in Section 12.8). As with any of the methods, the goal is to describe the relationships in the distribution with a linear or log-linear model.

To introduce the formalism, consider a simple example: the test of independence applied to the 2×2 table of data that first appeared in Section 2.3 (Table 2.2, shown with corresponding probabilities in Table 12.1). These data de-

TABLE 12.1
Observed Frequencies of Correct Solution as Classified by
the Approach to a Problem (from Table 2.2) and These Frequencies
Converted to Probabilities

Frequencies, x_{ij}

		Solution Accuracy Correct	Error
Approach Chosen	a	26	115
	b	54	136

Probabilities, p_{ij}

		Solution Accuracy Correct	Error
Approach Chosen	a	0.078	0.347
	b	0.163	0.411

scribed the cross-classification of two approaches to a problem (factor A, for "approach") with the successfulness of the solution (factor S, for "solution"). As usual, let x_{ij} be the frequencies, π_{ij} the population probabilities, and $p_{ij} = x_{ij}/x_{++}$ the corresponding sample proportions. The analysis can be conducted with either the frequencies or the proportions, with the same outcome. Since it is a little easier to interpret the magnitude of sizes of probabilities than of frequencies, p_{ij} and π_{ij} are used here.

To configure the data for matrix operations, the probabilities are written as a single column vector

$$\boldsymbol{\pi} = \begin{bmatrix} \pi_{11} \\ \pi_{12} \\ \pi_{21} \\ \pi_{22} \end{bmatrix}$$

These column vectors are denoted here by lowercase boldface letters (matrices use uppercase boldface letters). To save space in printing, a column vector is often written as the transpose of a row vector, with a prime denoting the transposition,

$$\boldsymbol{\pi} = [\pi_{11}, \pi_{12}, \pi_{21}, \pi_{22}]'$$

The sample estimate of $\boldsymbol{\pi}$ is the vector

$$\mathbf{p} = [p_{11}, p_{12}, p_{21}, p_{22}]' = [0.078, 0.347, 0.163, 0.411]'$$

Finally, let $\log \boldsymbol{\pi}$ and $\log \mathbf{p}$ denote vectors of element-by-element logarithms, so that

$$\log \mathbf{p} = [-2.544, -1.057, -1.813, -0.889]'$$

Many useful hypotheses are expressed as linear functions of $\boldsymbol{\pi}$ or $\log \boldsymbol{\pi}$. For example, testing for independence corresponds to testing whether the odds ratio α is zero (recall Section 2.6). In turn, this condition implies that a linear function of the logarithm of the π_{ij} is zero:

$$\log \alpha = \log \frac{\pi_{11} \pi_{22}}{\pi_{12} \pi_{21}}$$

$$= \log \pi_{11} - \log \pi_{12} - \log \pi_{21} + \log \pi_{22} = 0 \qquad (12.1)$$

In matrix terms, this independence condition is written as

$$\log \alpha = \begin{bmatrix} 1 & -1 & -1 & 1 \end{bmatrix} \begin{bmatrix} \log \pi_{11} \\ \log \pi_{12} \\ \log \pi_{21} \\ \log \pi_{22} \end{bmatrix} = 0 \qquad (12.2)$$

or

$$\mathbf{A} \log \boldsymbol{\pi} = 0 \qquad (12.3)$$

where $\mathbf{A}$ is the 1×4 matrix in Equation 12.2. If this equality is rejected, association is present.

A test of Hypothesis 12.3 is constructed from linear statistical theory. Let y denote the sample estimate of log α:

$$y = \log \hat{\alpha} = \mathbf{A} \log \mathbf{p}$$

$$= [1 \ -1 \ -1 \ \ 1] \log \begin{bmatrix} 0.078 \\ 0.347 \\ 0.163 \\ 0.411 \end{bmatrix} = -0.563$$

The statistical question now is whether y differs from zero by more than its sampling variability makes likely. If an estimate of the sampling variability of y is available, then one tests Hypothesis 12.3 by dividing y by its standard error or, equivalently, by the statistic

$$W^2 = \frac{y^2}{\text{var}(y)}$$

If y is approximately normal, then $y/SE(y)$ has roughly a standard normal distribution under the hypothesis of independence, and W^2 is distributed as $\chi^2(1)$. By a calculation described in the next section, var(y) is found to be 0.0730, and so $W^2 = 4.34$. Since this statistic exceeds the criterion of 3.84 for a 5% test, the hypothesis of independence is rejected.

With this example as a guide, the notation can be generalized. The probabilities in the n-element vector $\boldsymbol{\pi}$ must sum to 1, so they constitute at most $n - 1$ independent quantities. Let $f_i(\boldsymbol{\pi})$, $i = 1, 2, \ldots, m$, be a set of functions of $\boldsymbol{\pi}$ that are jointly linearly independent of one another (i.e., no function can be written as a linear combination of the others). Since the number of independent functions cannot exceed the number of independent observations, $m \leq n - 1$. In the example, only one function was defined, with $f_1(\boldsymbol{\pi}) = \log \alpha$ (Equation 12.3). Write these functions as a column vector,

$$\mathbf{f}(\boldsymbol{\pi}) = [f_1(\boldsymbol{\pi}), f_2(\boldsymbol{\pi}), \ldots, f_m(\boldsymbol{\pi})]'$$

Hypotheses to be tested are expressed by using $\mathbf{f}(\boldsymbol{\pi})$, either by equating it to $\mathbf{0}$ (as in this section) or by writing it as a linear model (Section 12.4). The sample vector corresponding to $\mathbf{f}(\boldsymbol{\pi})$ is

$$y = \mathbf{f}(\mathbf{p}) = [f_1(\mathbf{p}), f_2(\mathbf{p}), \ldots, f_m(\mathbf{p})]'$$

This vector summarizes the relevant portions of the data; the statistical tests ask whether it is far from $\mathbf{0}$ or whether it violates a particular linear model.

For most practical purposes, only a few forms of function are important. These are described in general in the next section; for this section, two suffice. The first is linear: each $f_i(\boldsymbol{\pi})$ is a linear combination of the π_j. In vector notation, for a matrix $\mathbf{A}$,

$$\mathbf{f}(\boldsymbol{\pi}) = \mathbf{A}\boldsymbol{\pi} \tag{12.4}$$

The other form is a linear combination of logarithms of linear combinations:

$$\mathbf{f}(\boldsymbol{\pi}) = \mathbf{A}_2\log(\mathbf{A}_1\boldsymbol{\pi}) \tag{12.5}$$

where $\mathbf{A}_1$ and $\mathbf{A}_2$ are matrices of constants. Frequently, $\mathbf{A}_1$ is an identity matrix, so that Equation 12.5 becomes

$$\mathbf{f}(\boldsymbol{\pi}) = \mathbf{A} \log \boldsymbol{\pi}$$

This is the form used in the example above.

The simplest useful hypothesis about the data sets the functions to zero:

$$\mathbf{f}(\boldsymbol{\pi}) = \mathbf{0} \tag{12.6}$$

This is the multivariate form of the independence hypothesis tested above. A test of this hypothesis is direct. Let $\mathbf{y} = \mathbf{f}(\mathbf{p})$ be the sample estimate of $\mathbf{f}(\boldsymbol{\pi})$, let $\mathbf{S_y}$ be the covariance matrix of $\mathbf{y}$, and compute the statistic

$$W^2 = \mathbf{y}'\mathbf{S_y}^{-1}\mathbf{y} \tag{12.7}$$

If Hypothesis 12.6 is true, than W^2 has asymptotically a $\chi^2(m)$ distribution.[†] The number of degrees of freedom equals the number of functions in $\mathbf{f}(\boldsymbol{\pi})$.

The test statistics W^2 are sometimes known as *Wald statistics*, after their original use (in a more general context) by Wald (1943; see Bhapkar & Koch, 1968). This statistic was shown by Neyman (1949) to have an asymptotic χ^2 distribution. For frequency data, the Wald statistic has another interpretation. The *modified chi-square statistic* is created by replacing the expected frequency in the denominator of the Pearson X^2 statistic formula by the observed value,

$$X_1^2 = \sum_{\text{cells}} \frac{(x - \hat{\mu})^2}{x}$$

(Bhapkar, 1966). The Wald statistic is equal to the minimum value that X_1^2 attains over all choices of $\hat{\mu}$ that are consistent with the hypotheses that is being tested. It is, thus, a *minimum modified chi-square statistic*.

The requirement that the functions be mutually independent should be noted. Specifically, it means that no function is a linear combination of the other functions. In matrix terms, the matrix $\mathbf{A}$ in Equation 12.4 must be of full rank and contain no more than $n - 1$ rows. When redundant functions are present, the hypothesis $\mathbf{f}(\boldsymbol{\pi}) = \mathbf{0}$ appears to impose more constraints than it actually does. The practical consequence is to make $\mathbf{S_y}$ singular, so that Equation 12.7 cannot be evaluated. In several of the examples below, the most obvious set of functions is redundant in this way and one or more functions must be eliminated.

[†]The symbol W^2 in Equation 12.7 is not standard notation (which varies from author to author). I have used this letter to distinguish this statistic from X^2 and G^2.

As a more extensive example of model construction, consider the $2 \times 2 \times 3$ contingency table used as an example in Section 3.1 (Table 3.1), reproduced here as Table 12.2. The theoretical probabilities in this table are assembled into the vector

$$\boldsymbol{\pi} = [\pi_{111}, \pi_{112}, \pi_{113}, \pi_{121}, \pi_{122}, \pi_{123}, \pi_{211}, \pi_{212}, \pi_{213}, \pi_{221}, \pi_{222}, \pi_{223}]'$$

Suppose that one wishes to test for the lack of a three-way association, a hypothesis that in earlier chapters is examined by fitting the model $[AB][AC][BC]$. Now the first step is to express the lack of association as a condition on functions of $\boldsymbol{\pi}$. The three-way relationship is measured by the value of the three-factor cross-product ratios. There are three of these ratios, comparing columns by pairs (first to second, first to third, and second to third, respectively):

$$\alpha_{12} = \frac{\pi_{111}\pi_{122}\pi_{212}\pi_{221}}{\pi_{112}\pi_{121}\pi_{211}\pi_{222}}, \quad \alpha_{13} = \frac{\pi_{111}\pi_{123}\pi_{213}\pi_{221}}{\pi_{113}\pi_{121}\pi_{211}\pi_{223}},$$

$$\text{and} \quad \alpha_{23} = \frac{\pi_{112}\pi_{123}\pi_{213}\pi_{222}}{\pi_{113}\pi_{122}\pi_{212}\pi_{223}}$$

These three ratios are not independent, for $\alpha_{13} = \alpha_{12}\alpha_{23}$, so that the values of two of them determine the third. If three-way association is lacking, all three must equal 1, but it suffices to work with any pair of them. Let $f_1(\boldsymbol{\pi}) = \log \alpha_{13}$ and $f_2(\boldsymbol{\pi}) = \log \alpha_{23}$. For the ordering of the parameters shown above, the functions in matrix form are

$$\mathbf{f}(\boldsymbol{\pi}) = \mathbf{A} \log \boldsymbol{\pi}$$
$$= \begin{bmatrix} 1 & 0 & -1 & -1 & 0 & 1 & -1 & 0 & 1 & 1 & 0 & -1 \\ 0 & 1 & -1 & 0 & -1 & 1 & 0 & -1 & 1 & 0 & 1 & -1 \end{bmatrix} (\log \boldsymbol{\pi})$$

The null hypothesis to be tested is $\mathbf{f}(\boldsymbol{\pi}) = \mathbf{0}$.

Once the hypothesis is formulated, the test proceeds directly. With the data in Table 12.2, the sample estimate of $\mathbf{f}(\boldsymbol{\pi})$ is

$$\mathbf{y} = \mathbf{f}(\mathbf{p}) = \begin{bmatrix} 0.460 \\ -1.253 \end{bmatrix}$$

TABLE 12.2
Three-way Table of Frequencies from Table 3.1

| | a_1 | | | a_2 | | |
	c_1	c_2	c_3	c_1	c_2	c_3
b_1	7	5	3	15	20	2
b_2	22	49	140	4	3	5

Its covariance matrix, determined by the methods in the next section, is

$$\mathbf{S_y} = \begin{bmatrix} 1.545 & 1.040 \\ 1.040 & 1.644 \end{bmatrix}$$

The null hypothesis of no three-way association is tested by the statistic

$$W^2(2) = \mathbf{y'S_y^{-1}y} = 2.72$$

This hypothesis cannot be rejected: no evidence for three-factor association is present. This result is essentially the same as that obtained for the comparable hypothesis in Section 2.5 where the statistics $X^2(2) = G^2(2) = 2.83$ were found.

12.2. COVARIANCES MATRICES

The covariance matrix of the vector $\mathbf{y} = \mathbf{f(p)}$, denoted $\mathbf{S_y}$, is part of the test statistic W^2 (Equation 12.7) and is needed in many other places below. Its construction is covered in this section. However, a detailed knowledge of how $\mathbf{S_y}$ is obtained is not necessary in order to construct models in matrix form, to appreciate how the weighted least-squares analysis works, or to use a packaged computer program. A reader who is willing to take the covariance matrices on faith can skim this section.

The matrix $\mathbf{S_y}$ is found in two steps: first the covariance matrix of $\mathbf{p}$ is obtained, then it is transformed to $\mathbf{S_y}$. The first step follows from the sampling models discussed in Chapter 4. For a single sample, the distribution of $\boldsymbol{\pi}$ is either multinomial or pure Poisson. The latter case reduces to the multinomial if the analysis is made conditional on total sample size. Then, following Equations 4.5 and 4.6, the covariance matrix of $\mathbf{p}$, based on N observations, is

$$\boldsymbol{\Sigma_p} = \frac{1}{N} \begin{bmatrix} \pi_1(1-\pi_1) & -\pi_1\pi_2 & \cdots & -\pi_1\pi_n \\ -\pi_1\pi_2 & \pi_2(1-\pi_2) & \cdots & -\pi_2\pi_n \\ \vdots & \vdots & & \vdots \\ -\pi_1\pi_n & -\pi_2\pi_n & \cdots & \pi_n(1-\pi_n) \end{bmatrix}$$

The factor $1/N$ appears here rather than the N in Equations 4.5 and 4.6 because proportions, not frequencies, are involved. The values of the π_i are unknown, so they are estimated by sample proportions p_i to give an estimate of the covariance matrix,

$$\mathbf{S_p} = \frac{1}{N} \begin{bmatrix} p_1(1-p_1) & -p_1p_2 & \cdots & -p_1p_n \\ -p_1p_2 & p_2(1-p_2) & \cdots & -p_2p_n \\ \vdots & \vdots & & \vdots \\ -p_1p_n & -p_2p_n & \cdots & p_n(1-p_n) \end{bmatrix} \tag{12.8}$$

The second part of the calculation, which turns S_p into S_y, calls on a general theorem that gives the variance of a function of a multivariate random variable. This theorem states that if x is a random vector with covariance matrix S_x and if $y = f(x)$ is a reasonably smooth function of x, then

$$S_y \approx HS_xH'$$ (12.9)

where H is a matrix whose elements are the partial derivatives of these functions with respect to the probabilities,

$$h_{ij} = \frac{\partial f_i(x)}{\partial x_j}$$ (12.10)

Equation 12.9 is exact if the functions are linear and approximate otherwise. The approximation is poor when the variability of x is large in comparison to the nonlinearity of $f(x)$. Equations 12.9 and 12.10 are the multivariate generalization of the variance transform described in Chapter 9 (Equation 9.7). They are quite general and are widely used in statistics.

At first glance, these partial derivatives are forbidding. Fortunately, only a few types of functions are needed for the treatment of frequency data. Four rules cover most important cases:

1. *Linear functions.* If $y = f(x)$ is linear, it is described by the matrix product

$$y = Ax$$

The variance transformation matrix H is equal to A, so $S_y = AS_xA'$. This transformation is central to linear multivariate statistics.

2. *Logarithmic functions.* If

$$y = \log x$$

then h_{ij} is zero except when $i = j$, in which case $h_{ii} = 1/x_i$. In matrix terms, $H = D_x^{-1}$ where D_x is everywhere 0 except for the entries of x lying on the diagonal.

3. *Exponential functions.* If

$$y = e^x$$

(i.e., each element of x is exponentiated), then a rule similar to the logarithmic case applies, except that the diagonal elements in H are those of y and no reciprocal is needed; in the notation of rule 2, $H = D_y$.

4. *Composition of functions.* If $f(x)$ is found by applying two transformations one after the other,

$$y = f_2[f_1(x)]$$

then $H = H_2H_1$, where H_1 and H_2 are the derivative matrices of f_1 and f_2, respectively.

Applying these rules yields the variances of the last sections. For example, consider a logarithmic transformation

$$\mathbf{f}(\boldsymbol{\pi}) = \mathbf{A}_2 \log(\mathbf{A}_1 \boldsymbol{\pi})$$

(Equation 12.5). This function is composed of three parts, a linear transformation, followed by a logarithmic transformation, followed by another linear one. Applying rule 4 twice breaks the overall $\mathbf{H}$ into the product of three separate matrices. Then using rules 1 and 2 to express the individual parts gives

$$\mathbf{H} = \mathbf{A}_2 \mathbf{D}^{-1} \mathbf{A}_1$$

where $\mathbf{D}$ contains the elements of the vector $\mathbf{A}_1 \mathbf{p}$ on its diagonal.

Now consider how all this applies to the first example in the last section, the test of independence in the 2×2 Table 12.1. The estimated covariance matrix $\mathbf{S_p}$ is obtained by substituting the sample proportions into Equation 12.8 to give

$$\mathbf{S_p} = \begin{bmatrix} 0.000219 & -0.000082 & -0.000039 & -0.000098 \\ -0.000082 & 0.000685 & -0.000171 & -0.000431 \\ -0.000039 & -0.000171 & 0.000412 & -0.000202 \\ -0.000098 & -0.000431 & -0.000202 & 0.000731 \end{bmatrix}$$

The transformation $f(\boldsymbol{\pi}) = \log \alpha$ (Equations 12.2 and 12.3) consists of taking the logarithm followed by a linear transformation. Thus, applying rules 1, 2, and 4 gives

$$\mathbf{H} = \mathbf{A}\mathbf{D_p}^{-1} = [1 \ -1 \ -1 \ \ 1] \begin{bmatrix} 0.0785 & 0.0 & 0.0 & 0.0 \\ 0.0 & 0.3474 & 0.0 & 0.0 \\ 0.0 & 0.0 & 0.1631 & 0.0 \\ 0.0 & 0.0 & 0.0 & 0.4108 \end{bmatrix}^{-1}$$

$$= [12.731 \ -2.878 \ -6.130 \ \ 2.434]$$

This matrix is applied to $\mathbf{S_p}$ to obtain $\mathbf{S_y}$, which is only a single number here:

$$\mathbf{S_y} = \mathbf{H}\mathbf{S_p}\mathbf{H}' = [0.0730]$$

This variance was used above to test whether the observed value of $\mathbf{y}$ equaled zero.

When no observations happen to fall into a cell, the estimated probability in that cell is zero. This zero propagates through the corresponding row and column of $\mathbf{S_p}$ (as calculated by Equation 12.8), creating two problems. First, if observations might have been obtained in that cell, the true variance should not be zero. Second, the vacant row and column make the covariance matrix singular. The seriousness of these problems depends on the particular functions in use. The variability of a function that depends heavily on empty cells is underestimated unless a correction is made. If the zeros are sufficiently prevalent to create a singularity in the covariance matrix of $\mathbf{y}$, this is even more serious, since computation cannot proceed unless $\mathbf{S_y}$ can be inverted.

To avoid these zeros, one can insert a small number into the empty cell. Presumably, the empty cell is rare, but not impossible, so replacing the zero by a small positive frequency does not greatly violate the data. The substituted value need not be an integer: sometimes $1/2$ is used, sometimes the reciprocal of the number of categories (Berkson, 1955; Grizzle, Starmer, & Koch, 1969). In either case, the result is a complete covariance matrix, and one can proceed with the analysis as if there had been no zeros.

The problem of empty cells is considered again in Section 12.9.

12.3. HOMOGENEOUS MARGINAL DISTRIBUTIONS

One reason to adopt a direct linear models approach is that it permits hypotheses to be tested that cannot be expressed by a hierarchical log-linear model. One of the most useful of the non-log-linear hypotheses is the hypothesis of marginal homogeneity. Since this hypothesis equates sums of probabilities, it is linear not log-linear. To test it with log-linear models, additional constraints have to be imposed. This was done in Section 10.7 with the quasi-symmetry model, but if one has no reason to assert this model, a more general test is better. The least-square methods allow marginal homogeneity to be tested without the ancillary assumption (Bhapkar, 1966, 1979).

For an explicit example, return to data that represented the classification of a set of interviews by two raters (Table 9.5, analyzed for marginal homogeneity in Section 10.7, shown again as Table 12.3). These observations are drawn from a single population and plausibly have a multinomial sampling distribution.

The test of marginal homogeneity in Table 12.3 is a test of the hypothesis

$$H_0: \pi_{i+} = \pi_{+i}, \quad i = 1, 2, 3, 4 \tag{12.11}$$

against an alternative of inequality. Substituting for i here, expanding the sums implied by the "+" subscripts, and rearranging terms give a set of four equations

TABLE 12.3
Classification of 100 Interview Transcripts into Four Diagnostic Categories
by Two Raters (from Table 9.5)

		Rater B				
		d_1	d_2	d_3	d_4	
	d_1	6	2	4	2	14
Rater A	d_2	4	17	14	5	40
	d_3	1	3	20	0	24
	d_4	1	3	6	12	22
		12	25	44	19	100

$$\pi_{12} + \pi_{13} + \pi_{14} - \pi_{21} - \pi_{31} - \pi_{41} = 0$$
$$\pi_{12} - \pi_{21} - \pi_{23} - \pi_{24} + \pi_{32} + \pi_{42} = 0$$
$$\pi_{13} + \pi_{23} - \pi_{31} - \pi_{32} - \pi_{34} + \pi_{43} = 0 \qquad (12.12)$$
$$\pi_{14} + \pi_{24} + \pi_{34} - \pi_{41} - \pi_{42} - \pi_{43} = 0$$

These equations are the functions whose values are to be tested, but they are not independent of one another. For example, the first equation is the sum of the last three. This dependence is not surprising, for it reflects the same redundancy in the original hypothesis: if three of the categories have equal marginal probabilities, then the marginal probabilities of the remaining category are perforce equal. Dropping any one equation leaves a satisfactory set. Using the first three members of Equations 12.12 gives a linear transformation $\mathbf{f}(\boldsymbol{\pi}) = \mathbf{A}\boldsymbol{\pi}$, with

$$\boldsymbol{\pi} = [\pi_{11}, \pi_{12}, \pi_{13}, \ldots, \pi_{43}, \pi_{44}]'$$

and

$$\mathbf{A} = \begin{bmatrix} 0 & 1 & 1 & 1 & -1 & 0 & 0 & 0 & -1 & 0 & 0 & 0 & -1 & 0 & 0 & 0 \\ 0 & 1 & 0 & 0 & -1 & 0 & -1 & -1 & 0 & 1 & 0 & 0 & 0 & 1 & 0 & 0 \\ 0 & 0 & 1 & 0 & 0 & 0 & 1 & 0 & -1 & -1 & 0 & -1 & 0 & 0 & 1 & 0 \end{bmatrix}$$

$$(12.13)$$

Before the calculations proceed, the observed zero in the data must be dealt with. Although it creates no problem in calculating the function values $\mathbf{y} = \mathbf{Ap}$, it would, incorrectly, be assigned a variance of zero by the formulae in the last section. To give a more realistic value, the zero is replaced by a small number. Since there are a total of 16 cells in the table, $1/16$ is a reasonable choice. After this substitution, the frequencies are converted to a vector of probabilities, $\mathbf{p}$, then this is transformed by Equation 12.13 to

$$\mathbf{y} = \mathbf{Ap} = [0.0200, \quad -0.1499, \quad 0.1992]'$$

The function $\mathbf{f}(\boldsymbol{\pi})$ is a pure linear transformation, so following the first rule in the last section, the covariance matrix of $\mathbf{y}$ is

$$\mathbf{S_y} = \mathbf{AS_pA'} = \begin{bmatrix} 0.00139 & 0.00063 & 0.00046 \\ 0.00063 & 0.00287 & -0.00140 \\ 0.00046 & -0.00140 & 0.00240 \end{bmatrix}$$

The resulting text statistic is

$$W^2(3) = \mathbf{y}'\mathbf{S_y}^{-1}\mathbf{y} = 17.07$$

There are 3 degrees of freedom because 3 functions are tested. The critical value of a $\chi^2(3)$ distribution at the 5% level is 7.81, so the hypothesis of equal use of the categories can be rejected. This result compares with $G^2(3) = 16.34$ obtained from the log-linear analysis in Section 10.7. Unlike with that test, no assumption of quasi-symmetry is necessary.

12.4. FITTING LINEAR MODELS TO f(π)

The procedures discussed so far test the hypothesis that certain functions of the probabilities are zero, that is, $\mathbf{f}(\boldsymbol{\pi}) = \mathbf{0}$. For simple situations, this test is sufficient, but for more complicated hypotheses, such as the difference tests in the earlier chapters, a more elaborate scheme is necessary. This is provided by fitting a linear model to the functions $\mathbf{f}(\boldsymbol{\pi})$,

$$f_i(\boldsymbol{\pi}) = \beta_1 x_{i1} + \beta_2 x_{i2} + \ldots + \beta_r x_{ir}, \quad i = 1, 2, \ldots, m \quad (12.14)$$

As with the comparable models in multiple regression or the analysis of variance, the x_{ij} are derived from the design of the study or the hypotheses being tested, while the parameters β_j are unknown. In matrix terms, the x_{ij} form a *design matrix* $\mathbf{X}$, and the β_j form a *parameter vector*, $\boldsymbol{\beta}$, so that Equations 12.14 consolidate to

$$\mathbf{f}(\boldsymbol{\pi}) = \begin{bmatrix} f_1(\boldsymbol{\pi}) \\ f_2(\boldsymbol{\pi}) \\ \vdots \\ f_m(\boldsymbol{\pi}) \end{bmatrix} = \mathbf{X}\boldsymbol{\beta} = \begin{bmatrix} x_{11} & x_{12} & \cdots & x_{1r} \\ x_{21} & x_{22} & \cdots & x_{2r} \\ \vdots & \vdots & & \vdots \\ x_{m1} & x_{m2} & \cdots & x_{mr} \end{bmatrix} \begin{bmatrix} \beta_1 \\ \beta_2 \\ \vdots \\ \beta_r \end{bmatrix} \quad (12.15)$$

Of course, even when Model 12.15 is true, the observed data are subject to sampling fluctuation and do not fit perfectly. Fitting the data to this model is where the weighted least squares come in.

The same general ideas underlie most methods of parameter estimation. Conceptually, a comparison between the data and the predictions of the model is made for every possible assignment of values to the unknown parameters. The parameter set that produces the maximum agreement is selected as the parameter estimate. In practice, one never examines all the potential parameter values directly. The optimum set is found through some algebraic or numerical procedure. Different estimation methods match the model and the data in different ways. For the maximum-likelihood procedure (recall Sections 4.3 and 4.4), the measure of agreement is the probability of the observed data given the parameter set. The least-squares procedure uses a different criterion, that of squared error. This criterion is the basis of linear multiple-regression theory, and least-squares estimates are likely to be most familiar in that context (see almost any book on multiple regression, such as Draper & Smith, 1981).

Suppose that Model 12.15 is to be fitted to data $y_1, y_2, \ldots, y_m$. For a given vector of parameter values $\mathbf{b}$, the predicted values of y_i are

$$\hat{y}_i = b_1 x_{i1} + b_2 x_{i2} + \ldots + b_r x_{ir}, \quad i = 1, 2, \ldots, m$$

(cf. Equation 12.14). In matrix terms,

$$\hat{\mathbf{y}} = \mathbf{X}\mathbf{b}$$

These predictions may or may not lie close to the observed data. The total squared error of prediction is

$$E = \sum_{i=1}^{m} (\text{observed} - \text{predicted})^2 = \sum_{i=1}^{m} (y_i - \hat{y}_i)^2$$

$$= (\mathbf{y} - \mathbf{Xb})'(\mathbf{y} - \mathbf{Xb}) \tag{12.16}$$

Then the *least-squares estimates* are the values $\hat{\beta}_1, \hat{\beta}_2, \ldots, \hat{\beta}_r$ of $b_1, b_2, \ldots, b_r$ that minimize E; in vector form $\hat{\boldsymbol{\beta}}$.

The error criterion just described is not quite satisfactory for frequency data. Equation 12.16 weights each observation y_i equally in determining the squared error. However, the y_i do not necessarily have equal variance, and so their errors are not of equal importance. Deviations that have small variance should be given more weight than deviations with larger variance. To make this correction, the squared error is redefined as the *weighted squared error*: if y_i has variance σ_i^2 then

$$E = \sum_{i=1}^{m} \left[\frac{y_i - \hat{y}_i}{\sigma_i} \right]^2 \tag{12.17}$$

A second problem concerns correlation among the y_i. One wishes to compensate for this correlation by reducing the weight of related observations so as to count any portion of the discrepancy only once. This problem, along with that of unequal variance, is solved by modifying E to take the full covariance matrix of $\mathbf{y}$ into consideration. If $\boldsymbol{\Sigma}_\mathbf{y}$ is the covariance matrix of $\mathbf{y}$, then in matrix terms the error is

$$E = (\mathbf{y} - \mathbf{Xb})'\boldsymbol{\Sigma}_\mathbf{y}^{-1}(\mathbf{y} - \mathbf{Xb}) \tag{12.18}$$

Note that Equation 12.18 reduces to Equation 12.17 when the y_i are uncorrelated and to Equation 12.16 when they have equal variance.

Of course, without the true probabilities $\boldsymbol{\pi}$, the value of $\boldsymbol{\Sigma}_\mathbf{y}$ is unknown. As discussed in Section 12.2, an estimate $\mathbf{S}_\mathbf{y}$ of this value is obtained by replacing each probability by its observed value. With this estimate, the error criterion becomes

$$E = (\mathbf{y} - \mathbf{Xb})'\mathbf{S}_\mathbf{y}^{-1}(\mathbf{y} - \mathbf{Xb}) \tag{12.19}$$

Developing a formula for the *weighted least squares estimates* $\hat{\boldsymbol{\beta}}$ that minimizes Equation 12.19, is best done with the matrix calculus. It is not necessary to follow the details of this derivation here—they can be found in many multivariate statistics texts, including those cited above. The result is important:

$$\hat{\boldsymbol{\beta}} = (\mathbf{X}'\mathbf{S}_\mathbf{y}^{-1}\mathbf{X})^{-1}\mathbf{X}'\mathbf{S}_\mathbf{y}^{-1}\mathbf{y} \tag{12.20}$$

These parameter estimates are linear functions of the data vector **y** (if $\mathbf{S_y}$ is taken as given), so their variance is calculated by the first of the variance-transformation rules that were described in Section 12.2. This calculation gives

$$\mathbf{S_{\hat{\beta}}} = (\mathbf{X'S_y^{-1}X})^{-1} \tag{12.21}$$

The minimum value of E, calculated by replacing **b** by $\hat{\boldsymbol{\beta}}$ in Equation 12.19, provides a test statistic for the hypothesis that the model fits a set of data. The measure is another form of the Wald statistic,

$$W^2(m - r) = (\mathbf{y} - \mathbf{X\hat{\beta}})'\mathbf{S_y^{-1}}(\mathbf{y} - \mathbf{X\hat{\beta}}) \tag{12.22}$$

For large samples, this statistic is distributed as $\chi^2(m - r)$ when the model fits. The number of degrees of freedom is the difference between the number of independent observations, m, and the number of parameters that are fitted, r.

Further restrictions on a model that has been fitted in this way are tested by looking at the effects of constraining the parameter values. Let **C** be a $c \times r$ matrix whose rows form a linearly independent set. Then the restriction $\mathbf{C\beta} = \mathbf{0}$ fixes the value of c linear combinations of the parameters. If the overall model fits, the hypothesis that this restriction holds is tested by the statistic

$$W^2(c) = (\mathbf{C\hat{\beta}})'[\mathbf{C(X'S_y^{-1}X)^{-1}C'}]^{-1}(\mathbf{C\hat{\beta}}) \tag{12.23}$$

This Wald statistic is distributed as $\chi^2(c)$ under the null hypothesis. In the logic of hypothesis testing, Equations 12.22 and 12.23 play the same role as G^2 and ΔG^2 (or X^2 and ΔX^2) did in the likelihood-based procedures.

12.5. THREE TESTS OF TWO-FACTOR INDEPENDENCE

There is enough freedom in the model-fitting and parameter-testing procedures to allow most hypotheses to be tested in several equivalent ways. This section illustrates these options for tests of independence in a two-way table. In Section 12.1 this hypothesis was tested by examining the logarithms of the odds ratios to see whether they were nonzero. This section describes two other ways to make this test. Although these tests do not introduce any new hypotheses, they illustrate how the fitting and testing mechanisms described abstractly in the last section operate.

Consider how the table of data that was used to test independence in Section 12.1 (Table 12.1) is represented in a model. This 2×2 table contains 4 probabilities and is subject to one constraint (they sum to 1), so 3 functions are needed to represent it in full. Many sets of 3 functions can be used. The set that is most consistent with the analysis strategies used elsewhere in this book is a set of log-linear functions that reflects the two-factor structure of the data. The first function in this set, $f_A(\boldsymbol{\pi})$, measures the difference between cells in one row and those in the other (the approach to the problem, factor A):

$$f_A(\boldsymbol{\pi}) = \log \pi_{11} + \log \pi_{12} - \log \pi_{21} - \log \pi_{22}$$

A similar function picks up the variation between the columns (the accuracy of the subjects' solutions, factor S):

$$f_S(\boldsymbol{\pi}) = \log \pi_{11} - \log \pi_{12} + \log \pi_{21} - \log \pi_{22}$$

The association between A and S is captured by a function that expresses $\log \alpha$:

$$f_{AS}(\boldsymbol{\pi}) = \log \pi_{11} - \log \pi_{12} - \log \pi_{21} + \log \pi_{22}$$

These three functions describe the three dimensions of variation that are possible within the four probabilities of a 2×2 table.

To clarify the meaning of these functions, it may be helpful to look at them in two other ways. The first is in relation to the parameters of a log-linear model for $\boldsymbol{\pi}$. The saturated model, written in terms of probabilities, is

$$\log \pi_{ij} = \log \frac{\mu_{ij}}{x_{++}} = \lambda + \lambda_{A(i)} + \lambda_{S(j)} + \lambda_{AS(ij)} - \log x_{++}$$

The division by x_{++} (or subtraction of $\log x_{++}$) converts the means to proportions. The usual strictures that make the parameters sum to zero over any of their subscripts still apply. Now use this model to expand $f_A(\boldsymbol{\pi})$, giving

$$\begin{aligned}
f_A(\boldsymbol{\pi}) &= \log \pi_{11} + \log \pi_{12} - \log \pi_{21} - \log \pi_{22} \\
&= \lambda + \lambda_{A(1)} + \lambda_{S(1)} + \lambda_{AS(11)} - \log x_{++} \\
&\quad + \lambda + \lambda_{A(1)} + \lambda_{S(2)} + \lambda_{AS(12)} - \log x_{++} \\
&\quad - \lambda - \lambda_{A(2)} - \lambda_{S(1)} - \lambda_{AS(21)} + \log x_{++} \\
&\quad - \lambda - \lambda_{A(2)} - \lambda_{S(2)} - \lambda_{AS(22)} + \log x_{++} \\
&= 2(\lambda_{A(1)} - \lambda_{A(2)}) + \lambda_{AS(11)} + \lambda_{AS(12)} - \lambda_{AS(21)} - \lambda_{AS(22)}
\end{aligned}$$

Substituting the constraint $\lambda_{A(2)} = -\lambda_{A(1)}$ and the similar relationships for λ_{AS}, reduces the result to

$$f_A(\boldsymbol{\pi}) = 4\lambda_{A(1)}$$

The size of $f_A(\boldsymbol{\pi})$ is a measure of the magnitude of the λ_A parameter and an indication of the extent to which one approach is favored over the other. Similarly, the other two functions capture the other two parameters:

$$f_S(\boldsymbol{\pi}) = 4\lambda_{S(1)} \quad \text{and} \quad f_{AS}(\boldsymbol{\pi}) = 4\lambda_{AS(11)}$$

Thus, assigning a nonzero value to a function is equivalent to including the corresponding λ in a log-linear model for μ.

The second interpretation of the functions may appeal to readers who are familiar with the construction of dummy contrasts in the analysis of variance. Except for the logarithms, the three functions are those that are ordinarily used to express the main effect of A, the main effect of S, and the AS interaction in a two-way design, although the meaning of these "main effects" and "interactions" is not the same as in the analysis of variance (recall Section 3.10). Contrasts of this sort are explained in most books on multiple regression and in many analysis-of-variance texts. The association function $f_{AS}(\boldsymbol{\pi})$ is constructed in the manner of interaction contrasts, by taking the product of the coefficients from the same terms in $f_A(\boldsymbol{\pi})$ and $f_S(\boldsymbol{\pi})$. This operation is pictured in Table 12.4. Each coefficient in the bottom line is the product of the two coefficients above it. This mechanical procedure is a straightforward way to generate functions, particularly for designs in higher dimensions.

In matrix notation, the functions are

$$\mathbf{f}(\boldsymbol{\pi}) = \begin{bmatrix} f_A(\boldsymbol{\pi}) \\ f_S(\boldsymbol{\pi}) \\ f_{AS}(\boldsymbol{\pi}) \end{bmatrix} = \mathbf{A} \log \boldsymbol{\pi} = \begin{bmatrix} 1 & 1 & -1 & -1 \\ 1 & -1 & 1 & -1 \\ 1 & -1 & -1 & 1 \end{bmatrix} \begin{bmatrix} \log \pi_{11} \\ \log \pi_{12} \\ \log \pi_{21} \\ \log \pi_{22} \end{bmatrix} \qquad (12.24)$$

Using the proportions from Table 12.1 gives the observed function values

$$\mathbf{y} = \mathbf{f}(\mathbf{p}) = \begin{bmatrix} -0.899 \\ -2.410 \\ -0.563 \end{bmatrix}$$

By the methods of Section 12.2, these variables have the covariance matrix

$$\mathbf{S_y} = \begin{bmatrix} 0.0730 & 0.0186 & 0.0409 \\ 0.0186 & 0.0730 & 0.0213 \\ 0.0409 & 0.0213 & 0.0730 \end{bmatrix}$$

Under independence, the functions $f_A(\boldsymbol{\pi})$ and $f_S(\boldsymbol{\pi})$ can take any values, but $f_{AS}(\boldsymbol{\pi})$ is zero. One way to describe this situation is to fit a model that includes parameters for the functions $f_A(\boldsymbol{\pi})$ and $f_S(\boldsymbol{\pi})$ and sets $f_{AS}(\boldsymbol{\pi})$ to zero. Let

$$\boldsymbol{\beta} = \begin{bmatrix} \beta_A \\ \beta_S \end{bmatrix} \quad \text{and} \quad \mathbf{X} = \begin{bmatrix} 1 & 0 \\ 0 & 1 \\ 0 & 0 \end{bmatrix}$$

so that

$$\mathbf{f}(\boldsymbol{\pi}) = \begin{bmatrix} f_A(\boldsymbol{\pi}) \\ f_S(\boldsymbol{\pi}) \\ f_{AS}(\boldsymbol{\pi}) \end{bmatrix} = \mathbf{x}\boldsymbol{\beta} = \begin{bmatrix} 1 & 0 \\ 0 & 1 \\ 0 & 0 \end{bmatrix} \begin{bmatrix} \beta_A \\ \beta_S \end{bmatrix} = \begin{bmatrix} \beta_A \\ \beta_S \\ 0 \end{bmatrix}$$

When this model is applied to the data, the parameter estimates are

$$\hat{\boldsymbol{\beta}} = (\mathbf{X}'\mathbf{S_y}^{-1}\mathbf{X})^{-1}\mathbf{X}'\mathbf{S_y}^{-1}\mathbf{y} = \begin{bmatrix} -0.583 \\ -2.246 \end{bmatrix}$$

TABLE 12.4
Construction of an Association Function as a
Dummy Interaction Contrast

Function	Representing	Coefficients of			
		$\log \pi_{11}$	$\log \pi_{12}$	$\log \pi_{21}$	$\log \pi_{22}$
f_A	Approach frequencies	1	1	−1	−1
f_S	Response frequencies	1	−1	1	−1
f_{AS}	AS association	1	−1	−1	1

(Equation 12.20). The Wald statistic testing the fit of this model is

$$W^2(1) = (y - X\hat{\beta})'S_y^{-1}(y - X\hat{\beta}) = 4.34$$

(Equation 12.22). The same result was obtained by the direct test of $\log \alpha$ in Section 12.1.

Equation 12.21 gives the covariance matrix of the parameter estimates:

$$S_{\hat{\beta}} = (X'S_y^{-1}X)^{-1} = \begin{bmatrix} 0.0500 & 0.0067 \\ 0.0067 & 0.0668 \end{bmatrix}$$

The diagonal elements of this matrix are estimates of the variance of β_A and β_S under the model. If the model fits, these can be used to obtain confidence intervals for the parameters, using a normal reference distribution. For example, a 95% interval for β_A is

$$-0.583 - 1.96\sqrt{0.0500} \leq \beta_A \leq -0.583 + 1.96\sqrt{0.0500}$$

$$-1.021 \leq \beta_A \leq -0.145$$

The third way to express independence in the 2×2 table uses the constraint matrices. By adding a third parameter to β, a saturated model is formed, with

$$\beta = \begin{bmatrix} \beta_A \\ \beta_S \\ \beta_{AS} \end{bmatrix} \quad \text{and} \quad X = \begin{bmatrix} 1 & 0 & 0 \\ 0 & 1 & 0 \\ 0 & 0 & 1 \end{bmatrix}$$

The design matrix here is an identity, so fitting the model is trivial: the parameter estimates are the same as the original function values. In the context of this model, independence means that the parameter expressing AS association is zero, that is, $\beta_{AS} = 0$. This is a hypothesis of the type $C\beta = 0$, where C the 1×3 matrix

$$C = [0 \quad 0 \quad 1]$$

A test, now using Equation 12.23, gives $W^2(1) = 4.34$ yet again.

To summarize this series of tests, three ways to examine independence in a two-factor table are

- to show that the association parameters are zero (as in Section 12.1)
- to fit and test a model that excludes association
- to fit a model that includes association, and then test whether the association parameters can be eliminated

These three types of test are readily available from the weighted least-squares approach to model fitting. Of course, only one method would be used in any particular problem.

12.6. TESTING MODELS IN A FACTORIAL TABLE

One of the most common forms of single-population data is a complete factorial cross-classification. The types of functions described in the last section are particularly useful when these tables are analyzed, as the following example shows. As data, take the three-factor example from Chapter 3 that was used in Section 12.1 (with data reproduced as Table 12.2). Log-linear models that are fitted to this table are interpreted in the same way as were the comparable models in other chapters of this book. Specifically, consider the problem of testing whether the parameters associating B and C are required in a model that is without AC or ABC linkage. Such a test corresponds to using ΔG^2 or ΔX^2 to compare the models $[AB][BC]$ and $[AB][C]$. A systematic approach to this test involves three steps: first, functions are defined that express the dimensions of the table; second, the more general model is fitted; and third, this model is restricted to the limited form. The three steps are summarized in Table 12.5 and are explained below. The essential parts of the three operations are embodied in the matrices A, X, and C, respectively.

Most of the work is in the definition of the functions. Just as with the two-way case, these have the form of linear dummy contrasts representing differences between conditions in factorial designs in other areas of statistics. As in Section 12.1, order the 12 probabilities in π as

$$\pi = [\pi_{111}, \pi_{112}, \pi_{113}, \pi_{121}, \pi_{122}, \pi_{123}, \pi_{211}, \pi_{212}, \pi_{213}, \pi_{221}, \pi_{222}, \pi_{223}]'$$

The function that captures the direct effect of A contrasts the first six values of $\log \pi_{ijk}$ (for which $i = 1$) with the second six (for which $i = 2$):

$$f_A(\pi) = [1 \quad 1 \quad 1 \quad 1 \quad 1 \quad 1 \quad -1 \quad -1 \quad -1 \quad -1 \quad -1 \quad -1] \log \pi$$

Similarly, $f_B(\pi)$ contrasts with the six cells with $j = 1$ to those with $j = 2$:

$$f_B(\pi) = [1 \quad 1 \quad 1 \quad -1 \quad -1 \quad -1 \quad 1 \quad 1 \quad 1 \quad -1 \quad -1 \quad -1] \log \pi$$

TABLE 12.5
Testing the Necessity of BC Terms in the Model $[AB][BC]$

1. Function Definition

$$\mathbf{f}(\boldsymbol{\pi}) = \begin{bmatrix} f_A(\boldsymbol{\pi}) \\ f_B(\boldsymbol{\pi}) \\ f_{C_1}(\boldsymbol{\pi}) \\ f_{C_2}(\boldsymbol{\pi}) \\ f_{AB}(\boldsymbol{\pi}) \\ f_{AC_1}(\boldsymbol{\pi}) \\ f_{AC_2}(\boldsymbol{\pi}) \\ f_{BC_1}(\boldsymbol{\pi}) \\ f_{BC_2}(\boldsymbol{\pi}) \\ f_{ABC_1}(\boldsymbol{\pi}) \\ f_{ABC_2}(\boldsymbol{\pi}) \end{bmatrix} = \mathbf{A}\log\boldsymbol{\pi} = \mathbf{A}\begin{bmatrix} \log \pi_{111} \\ \log \pi_{112} \\ \log \pi_{113} \\ \log \pi_{121} \\ \log \pi_{122} \\ \log \pi_{123} \\ \log \pi_{211} \\ \log \pi_{212} \\ \log \pi_{213} \\ \log \pi_{221} \\ \log \pi_{222} \\ \log \pi_{223} \end{bmatrix}$$

$$\mathbf{y} = \mathbf{A}\log\mathbf{p}$$
$$= [0.270,\ -4.968,\ 0.788,\ 1.253,\ -9.573,\ -2.795,\ -2.331,\ 4.936,\ 4.374,\ 0.460,\ -1.253]'$$

2. Definition and Fit of Model $[AB][BC]$

$$\mathbf{f}(\boldsymbol{\pi}) = \mathbf{X}\boldsymbol{\beta} = \begin{bmatrix} 1 & 0 & 0 & 0 & 0 & 0 & 0 \\ 0 & 1 & 0 & 0 & 0 & 0 & 0 \\ 0 & 0 & 1 & 0 & 0 & 0 & 0 \\ 0 & 0 & 0 & 1 & 0 & 0 & 0 \\ 0 & 0 & 0 & 0 & 1 & 0 & 0 \\ 0 & 0 & 0 & 0 & 0 & 0 & 0 \\ 0 & 0 & 0 & 0 & 0 & 0 & 0 \\ 0 & 0 & 0 & 0 & 0 & 1 & 0 \\ 0 & 0 & 0 & 0 & 0 & 0 & 1 \\ 0 & 0 & 0 & 0 & 0 & 0 & 0 \\ 0 & 0 & 0 & 0 & 0 & 0 & 0 \end{bmatrix}\begin{bmatrix} \beta_A \\ \beta_B \\ \beta_{C_1} \\ \beta_{C_2} \\ \beta_{AB} \\ \beta_{BC_1} \\ \beta_{BC_2} \end{bmatrix}$$

$$\hat{\boldsymbol{\beta}} = (\mathbf{X}'\mathbf{S_y}^{-1}\mathbf{X})^{-1}\mathbf{X}'\mathbf{S_y}^{-1}\mathbf{y}$$

$$= [-0.278, \ -4.438, \ -0.786, \ 0.799, \ -10.702, \ 5.919, \ 4.934]'$$

$$W^2(4) = (\mathbf{y} - \mathbf{X}\hat{\boldsymbol{\beta}})'\mathbf{S_y}^{-1}(\mathbf{y} - \mathbf{X}\hat{\boldsymbol{\beta}}) = 8.38$$

3. Test of the Restriction $\boldsymbol{\beta}_{BC} = \mathbf{0}$

$$\mathbf{C}\boldsymbol{\beta} = \begin{bmatrix} 0 & 0 & 0 & 0 & 0 & 1 & 0 \\ 0 & 0 & 0 & 0 & 0 & 0 & 1 \end{bmatrix} \begin{bmatrix} \beta_A \\ \beta_B \\ \beta_{C_1} \\ \beta_{C_2} \\ \beta_{AB} \\ \beta_{BC_1} \\ \beta_{BC_2} \end{bmatrix} = \begin{bmatrix} 0 \\ 0 \end{bmatrix}$$

$$W^2(2) = (\mathbf{C}\hat{\boldsymbol{\beta}})'[\mathbf{C}(\mathbf{X}'\mathbf{S_y}^{-1}\mathbf{X})^{-1}\mathbf{C}']^{-1}(\mathbf{C}\hat{\boldsymbol{\beta}}) = 29.98$$

There are 3 levels of C, so two functions are necessary to pick up all the differences among them. As in the comparable problem of defining contrasts in the analysis of variance, there is some choice here. The way that these two functions are defined does not affect the significance tests, although it alters the individual functions' values and their interpretation. Contrasts reflecting the differences between $k = 1$ and $k = 3$ and between $k = 2$ and $k = 3$ are adequate. These are

$$f_{C_1}(\pi) = [1 \quad 0 \ -1 \quad 1 \quad 0 \ -1 \quad 1 \quad 0 \ -1 \quad 1 \quad 0 \ -1] \log \pi$$

$$f_{C_2}(\pi) = [0 \quad 1 \ -1 \quad 0 \quad 1 \ -1 \quad 0 \quad 1 \ -1 \quad 0 \quad 1 \ -1] \log \pi$$

To represent the joint association of two factors, products of the coefficients of the individual functions are taken, in the manner of Table 12.4. For example, multiplying the coefficients of $f_A(\pi)$ and $f_B(\pi)$ gives

$$f_{AB}(\pi) = [1 \quad 1 \quad 1 \ -1 \ -1 \ -1 \ -1 \ -1 \ -1 \quad 1 \quad 1 \quad 1] \log \pi$$

Two functions each for AC, BC, and ABC are defined similarly, one from $f_{C_1}(\pi)$, the other from $f_{C_2}(\pi)$. These complete the transformation from probabilities into contrast functions shown at the top of Table 12.5.

The unrestricted model $[AB][BC]$ must fit A, B, C, AB, and AC terms, so has the parameter vector

$$\beta = [\beta_A, \ \beta_B, \ \beta_{C_1}, \ \beta_{C_2}, \ \beta_{AB}, \ \beta_{BC_1}, \ \beta_{BC_2}]'$$

Most of the work in constructing this model has already been done with the function definitions. The design matrix $\mathbf{X}$ need only select the appropriate elements of $\mathbf{f}(\pi)$, as shown in the middle of Table 12.5. Fitted and tested by Equations 12.20 and 12.22, this model cannot be rejected at conventional levels of significance.

The difference between this model and one without any BC link is tested by fixing $\beta_{BC_1} = 0$ and $\beta_{BC_2} = 0$ using the restriction matrix in the third part of Table 12.5. When it is tested by using Equation 12.23, this restriction is rejected. Thus, the lack of BC association is not tenable in this analysis. This conclusion is not substantially different from that obtained by likelihood methods with G^2 or X^2 (cf. Section 3.8 and Display 3.28).

Table 12.6 shows a summary of the analysis of this model. The first line gives the overall fit of the model, testing whether significant variation has been excluded from it. This is the test in the middle portion of Table 12.5. The remaining lines describe a more detailed examination of the effects and parameters of the model. Each line shows either a parameter estimate and a test of whether it is zero, or a composite test that all the parameters of a particular effect are null. Each of these tests is generated by a restriction of the model and is tested with W^2 using Equation 12.23. This portion of the table has a seductive similarity to an analysis-of-variance table, as if each effect or parameter is being tested in isola-

TABLE 12.6
Summary of Tests of a Model with *AB* and *BC* Association
(Table 12.5) Applied to the Data in Table 12.2

Parameter or Test	$\hat{\beta}$	W^2	df
Test of model		8.38	4
Analysis of parameters			
A effect	−0.28	0.05	1
B effect	−4.44	9.71	1
C effect		4.33	2
C_1	−0.78	0.51	1
C_2	0.80	0.57	1
AB association	−10.70	66.67	1
BC association		29.98	2
BC_1	5.92	29.19	1
BC_2	4.93	21.56	1

tion. However, a null value of a lower-order parameter (β_A, β_B, β_{C_1}, or β_{C_2} in this model) implies a nonhierarchical representation of the data that may have little or no practical interpretation. Furthermore, these estimates and tests are specific to the model from which they are produced. In another context (say the saturated model) they may be different. So, one might not mention all these tests in a final report of the analysis and would stick with those that pertain to readily interpretable hypotheses.

12.7.   LOGIT MODELS

The examples in the last section do not use the full power of the linear models. The direct fitting of logit models more completely uses this machinery. As defined in Chapter 7, these models are linear functions of the log-odds or logit, η. The saturated logit model for a three-way table with a dichotomous third factor is

$$\eta_{ij} = \log \frac{\pi_{ij1}}{\pi_{ij2}} = \beta + \beta_{A(i)} + \beta_{B(j)} + \beta_{AB(ij)} \qquad (12.25)$$

The parameters of the linear model are denoted by β here rather than v as in Chapter 7. The natural way to fit Model 12.25 is to use the functions $\mathbf{f}(\boldsymbol{\pi})$ to construct the logits, then to fit and test a model for these.

Consider, for example, the data from the drug-use survey to which a logit model was fitted in Chapter 7 (Table 7.1, shown again as Table 12.7). With *P*, *C*, and *S* as predictors of the fourth factor *F*, the tendency for early first drug use is expressed by the logit

TABLE 12.7
Heroin User's Survey Data (from Table 7.1)

Parents	SES	County First use	Urban <18	Urban ≥18	Suburban <18	Suburban ≥18	Rural <18	Rural ≥18
Yes	Low		32	65	21	20	10	40
	Not low		34	97	14	28	8	23
No	Low		41	42	18	22	6	13
	Not low		41	45	3	13	1	10

$$\eta_{ijk} = \log \frac{\pi_{ijk1}}{\pi_{ijk2}}$$

These logits are constructed by the transformation $\mathbf{f}(\boldsymbol{\pi}) = \mathbf{A}\log \boldsymbol{\pi}$, as shown at the top of Table 12.8. In Chapter 7, these data were fitted by the model

$$\eta_{ijk} = \beta + \beta_{S(i)} + \beta_{C(j)} + \beta_{P(k)} + \beta_{CP(jk)} \qquad (12.26)$$

(Equation 7.11). Fitting the same model here requires the vector of parameters

$$\boldsymbol{\beta} = [\beta, \beta_S, \beta_{C_1}, \beta_{C_2}, \beta_P, \beta_{CP_1}, \beta_{CP_2}]'$$

If the order of the logits in $\mathbf{y}$ is such that the index of factor P changes most rapidly and that of S most slowly, Model 12.26 is expressed by the design matrix in the middle of the table. As the summary at the bottom shows, the model fits well, as measured by an overall statistic of $W^2(5) = 5.82$, calculated by Equation 12.22. The parameter estimates are similar to the estimates of the comparable parameters obtained by maximum-likelihood calculation (Section 7.3) and are interpreted as described in that section. Although tests for all factors are reported in the summary table, the presence of the CP interaction makes it difficult to interpret the tests of C and P alone. One does better to study the interaction by looking at the parent effect (which appears negligible in the average) for the different counties, as described in Section 7.3.

The same type of construction can be used to model the way in which another summary statistic varies across a series of indexed variables. For example, suppose that one wonders whether the association within a 2 × 2 table changes over levels of one or more additional factor. To look at this variation, use the functions $f_i(\boldsymbol{\pi})$ to express the desired quantity, here the logarithms of the cross product ratios in the individual tables. Then a linear model is fitted to these values, allowing one to examine how these functions are related to the other factors (see Problem 12.10).

Logits can form part of a more intricate model, taking their basic data from a combination of the original probabilities. An important example of such a situation occurs when repeated observations have been made on the same subjects and one wishes to compare the marginal distributions of the table. These hypotheses involve descriptions that are not log-linear and their test makes full use of the power of the weighted-least-squares formulation. As a specific example, imagine an experiment in which undergraduate subjects are given descriptions of four people and are asked to decide whether they would go out on a date with each person. The four descriptions are identical except in two places where adjectives are inserted. At each place, the inserted adjective may give either a positive or a negative characterization—for example, at one place either "cheerful" or "moody" might be inserted. The experimenter is interested in the way that these changes influence the acceptability of the person.

One's first impulse with this design is to cross-classify the subjects' ratings with the 2×2 array of conditions, as in the top panel of Table 12.9. There are two predictors and one dichotomous outcome factor, suggesting that a logit model may be useful. However, with these data, each subject provides a response for each of the four descriptions, so that the observations in the four rows of this table are not independent. This dependence violates the usual sampling models, which allow each subject only one entry in the table. The correct organization of the data is as a $2 \times 2 \times 2 \times 2$ table in which each factor is the classification of one of the four descriptions (Table, 12.9, second panel). The table presented first gives the marginal distributions of this array.

The function definitions in the weighted least-squares approach let one go from the second table to the first, while accounting for the associations among the multiple responses. This analysis is shown in the middle portion of Table 12.9. The functions $f(\pi)$ are given by the general logarithmic transformation of Equation 12.5. Two steps are required: first, a linear transformation $\mathbf{A}_1$ reduces π to the four sets of marginals; second, these marginal pairs are expressed as logits by taking the logarithm and applying a second linear transformation, $\mathbf{A}_2$. With the data reduced to logits, a linear logit model is readily fitted. The parameters of this model express the overall positiveness of the rating (β), the effects of each of the adjective pairs (β_1 and β_2), and their interaction (β_{12}). The influence of the adjective manipulation is determined from these parameters. For example, the hypothesis that the effects of the adjectives do not interact (in a logit sense) is the hypothesis that $\beta_{12} = 0$. To show that one of the adjective pairs has a greater effect on the preference than the other, one tests whether the hypothesis $\beta_1 = \beta_2$ can be rejected (presumably after one has decided to retain a model without an interaction). For Table 12.9, the additive model (without β_{12}) fits with $G^2(1) = 0.46$, and the test of effect homogeneity is rejected with $G^2(1) = 10.35$.

Many experiments in which attention is directed to the relationship of a few marginal distributions can be approached in this way. The major limitation to this approach is the number of subjects that are required. The factorial combination of the responses rapidly produces tables with many cells. Thus, if a third adjective pair is added to the descriptions, there are 8 descriptions, so that the data are represented in a $2^8 = 256$ cell table. Since some of the descriptions are likely to be much more desirable or undesirable than others, a very large sample is

TABLE 12.8
Fitting a Logit Model to Table 12.7

Construction of the Logits

$\mathbf{f}(\boldsymbol{\pi}) = \mathbf{A} \log \boldsymbol{\pi}$

$$=$$

log π

Fitting Model 12.26

$\mathbf{f}(\boldsymbol{\pi}) = \mathbf{X}\boldsymbol{\beta} =$

$\begin{bmatrix} \beta \\ \beta_S \\ \beta_{C_1} \\ \beta_{C_2} \\ \beta_P \\ \beta_{CP_1} \\ \beta_{CP_2} \end{bmatrix}$

Summary of the Model

Parameter or Test	$\hat{\beta}$	W^2	df
Test of model		5.82	5
Analysis of parameters			
Intercept	−0.70	38.56	1
SES	0.16	3.50	1
County		7.41	2
C_1	0.24		
C_2	0.27		
Parents	−0.11	1.08	1
CP association		6.87	2
CP_1	−0.29		
CP_2	0.24		

TABLE 12.9

Analysis of a Logit Model Fitted to the Marginal Distributions
of a Factorial Table

Adjective Effects and Logits

First	Second	yes	no	logit
	Adjective			
positive	positive	137	36	1.336
positive	negative	50	123	-0.900
negative	positive	80	93	-0.150
negative	negative	18	155	-2.153

Proper Data Configuration

| | | pos-pos | yes | | no | |
| | | pos-neg | | | | |
neg-pos	neg-neg		yes	no	yes	no
yes	yes		3	8	1	2
	no		18	34	0	14
no	yes		1	3	0	0
	no		26	44	1	18

Construction of the logits

$$\mathbf{f}(\boldsymbol{\pi}) = \mathbf{A}_2 \log \mathbf{A}_1 \boldsymbol{\pi}$$

$$= \begin{bmatrix} 1 & -1 & 0 & 1 & -1 & 0 & 0 & 0 & 0 \\ 0 & 0 & 0 & 0 & 0 & 0 & 1 & -1 & 0 \\ 0 & 0 & 0 & 0 & 0 & 0 & 0 & 1 & -1 \end{bmatrix} \log \begin{bmatrix} 1 & 1 & 1 & 1 & 1 & 1 & 1 & 0 & 0 & 0 & 0 & 0 & 0 & 1 & 0 & 1 & 0 & 1 \\ 0 & 0 & 0 & 0 & 0 & 0 & 0 & 1 & 1 & 1 & 1 & 1 & 1 & 0 & 1 & 0 & 1 & 0 \\ \cdots \end{bmatrix} \boldsymbol{\pi}$$

Fitting an Additive Model

$$\mathbf{f}(\boldsymbol{\pi}) = \mathbf{X}\boldsymbol{\beta} = \begin{bmatrix} 1 & 1 & 1 & 1 \\ 1 & 1 & -1 & -1 \\ 1 & -1 & 1 & -1 \\ 1 & -1 & -1 & 1 \end{bmatrix} \begin{bmatrix} \beta \\ \beta_1 \\ \beta_2 \\ \beta_{12} \end{bmatrix}$$

Summary of the Models

Parameter	$\hat{\beta}$	W^2	df
Full Model			
Intercept	-0.47	19.25	1
Adjective 1 (β_1)	0.68	41.41	1
Adjective 2 (β_2)	1.06	158.23	1
Interaction (β_{12})	0.68	0.46	1
Additive Model			
Intercept	-0.49	24.12	1
Adjective 1 (β_1)	0.70	45.47	1
Adjective 2 (β_2)	1.07	167.70	1

necessary if most of the cells are to have an adequate size. When the frequency is inadequate, one can collapse the table so that only pairwise relationships are examined in any part of the analysis.

12.8.   THE ANALYSIS OF MULTIPLE POPULATIONS

The least-squares methods extend readily to investigations where the data are drawn from several populations. In one sense, the procedure is exactly the same as in the single-population case: the data are summarized in a set of functions, a linear model is fitted to these functions, and parametric restrictions are tested. However, the structure imposed by a multiple-population design suggests certain natural organizations of the analysis. Typically, the frequencies observed in different populations are independent of one another and all populations use the same set of functions. The within-population aspects of the design can be concentrated in these functions, while the between-population aspects are picked up in the design matrix.†

Suppose that there are p populations and that the members of each population are classified into n categories. Within the kth population, there is a theoretical probability vector $\boldsymbol{\pi}_k$ and sample estimates $\mathbf{p}_k$ over the n categories. These vectors are constructed as in the single-population case and are complete probability distributions summing to 1. The n probabilities from each population are transformed by a set of m functions into the vector $\mathbf{f}_k(\boldsymbol{\pi}_k)$. These functions express the relevant within-populations structure of the data. For example, a set of cross-classifications might be resolved into contrast functions such as those described in Section 12.6 (Table 12.5). In the sample, these functions produce the vector $\mathbf{y}_k$. The covariance matrix of $\mathbf{y}_k$, denoted $\mathbf{S}_{\mathbf{y}_k}$, is calculated as in the single-population case.

Now the between-population part of the design comes into play. The vectors $\mathbf{f}_k(\boldsymbol{\pi}_k)$ and $\mathbf{y}_k$ are strung together into the single vectors $\mathbf{f}(\boldsymbol{\pi})$ and $\mathbf{y}$ of length pm. Since the within-population structure is usually the same for all populations, the same functions are often applied to each, although this is not strictly necessary. Then a linear model $\mathbf{f}(\boldsymbol{\pi}) = \mathbf{X}\boldsymbol{\beta}$ is constructed that ties together the within-population effects. Its parameters can consolidate or contrast information over the separate populations. Finally, hypotheses about the relationship of the popu-

---

†The difference between single- and multiple-population models is mainly one of interpretation. Just as the results of the maximum-likelihood analysis methods are the same for all the sampling models in Section 4.2, so the same values of W^2 are obtained for a given hypothesis regardless of which factors are deemed to constitute populations, as long as the same log-linear models are fitted (Woolson & Brier, 1981). This equivalence may not apply to models that are not log-linear.

lations are tested by applying linear contrasts to $\boldsymbol{\beta}$. Because the same sort of linear models are fit here as in the single-population case, the same formulae for fitting and testing are used (Equations 12.20 to 12.23).

The covariance matrix of $\mathbf{y}$ is a combination of the individual covariance matrices $\mathbf{S}_{\mathbf{y}_k}$. Observations from different populations are independent of one another and, if no function combines probabilities from more than one population, this independence is maintained through the transformation. Thus, the covariance between observations from different populations is zero, and $\mathbf{S}_\mathbf{y}$ has a block-diagonal form:

$$\mathbf{S}_\mathbf{y} = \begin{bmatrix} \mathbf{S}_{\mathbf{y}_1} & \mathbf{0} & \cdots & \mathbf{0} \\ \mathbf{0} & \mathbf{S}_{\mathbf{y}_2} & \cdots & \mathbf{0} \\ \vdots & \vdots & & \vdots \\ & & & \\ \mathbf{0} & \mathbf{0} & \cdots & \mathbf{S}_{\mathbf{y}_p} \end{bmatrix} \tag{12.27}$$

where the $\mathbf{0}$'s indicate matrices of the appropriate zeros. The same form applies to $\mathbf{S}_\mathbf{y}^{-1}$: it is constructed of diagonal blocks that contain $\mathbf{S}_{\mathbf{y}_k}^{-1}$.

Now turn to a specific example. Consider a portion of the data presented in Section 5.8 (Table 5.5). The situation involved two questions (A and B) that were put to college students who were classified into populations based on sex and year in school (S and Y). To reduce the size of the matrices in this example, only the first and last years (y_1 and y_3) are analyzed, although there is no problem in using the full design. Thus, there are $p = 4$ populations, each indexed by an SY combination. For each population, a 2×2 table of observations is collected (factors A and B). Using rows for the populations and columns for the observations within populations, the data are shown at the top of Table 12.10. There is no intrinsic meaning to the total frequency in each population (otherwise they would not constitute separate populations), so each row is converted to proportions by dividing each entry by the sum for that row (Table 12.10, middle).

The data from each population have an organization as a 2×2 table, and so are described by the same set of three functions that were used to analyze a single such table in Section 12.5 (Equation 12.24):

$$\mathbf{f}_k(\boldsymbol{\pi}) = \begin{bmatrix} f_A(\boldsymbol{\pi}) \\ f_B(\boldsymbol{\pi}) \\ f_{AB}(\boldsymbol{\pi}) \end{bmatrix} = \mathbf{A} \log \boldsymbol{\pi} = \begin{bmatrix} 1 & 1 & -1 & -1 \\ 1 & -1 & 1 & -1 \\ 1 & -1 & -1 & 1 \end{bmatrix} \begin{bmatrix} \log \pi_{11} \\ \log \pi_{12} \\ \log \pi_{21} \\ \log \pi_{22} \end{bmatrix} \tag{12.28}$$

The first of these functions measures the difference in frequency between a_1 and a_2 responses, the second the difference between b_1 and b_2, and the third the association of the classifications. Together, they are applied to each of the four populations, creating four 3-element vectors (Table 12.10, bottom).

TABLE 12.10
Data from Two Questions Asked to Four Groups of Students (Extracted from Table 5.5)

Frequency Data

	a_1 b_1	a_1 b_2	a_2 b_1	a_2 b_2
s_1y_1	40	11	3	6
s_1y_4	23	7	11	19
s_2y_1	20	4	9	27
s_2y_4	10	2	9	39

(Subpopulations; Responses)

Subpopulations Converted to Proportions

	a_1 b_1	a_1 b_2	a_2 b_1	a_2 b_2
s_1y_1	0.667	0.183	0.050	0.100
s_1y_4	0.383	0.117	0.183	0.317
s_2y_1	0.333	0.067	0.150	0.450
s_2y_4	0.167	0.033	0.150	0.650

(Subpopulations; Responses)

Transformation to Function Values (Equation 12.28)

	f_A	f_B	f_{AB}
s_1y_1	3.196	0.598	1.984
s_1y_4	−0.261	0.643	1.736
s_2y_1	−1.111	0.511	2.708
s_2y_4	−2.865	0.143	3.076

(Subpopulations; Functions)

To construct the interpopulation model, the 4 three-element sample vectors (the y_i) are combined into the single vector y shown in Table 12.11. The population structure shows clearly in the block-diagonal form of the covariance matrix S_y, which is calculated from Equation 12.27 and is also shown in Table 12.11. This matrix contains nonzero entries only within a population.

Now the models are fitted. First consider a model that suggests that the pattern of the four responses does not vary with year or sex. This model implies that corresponding function values are the same in the four populations. It is represented by the design

Table 12.11
Sample probability vector and covariance matrix for the data in Table 12.10.

$\mathbf{Y} =$ [3.196 0.598 1.984 −0.261 0.643 1.736 −1.111 0.511 2.708 −2.865 0.143 3.076]'

$\mathbf{S}_y =$

3.196	0.598	1.984	−0.261	0.643	1.736	−1.111	0.511	2.708	−2.865	0.143	3.076
0.616	−0.232	0.101	0.0	0.0	0.0	0.0	0.0	0.0	0.0	0.0	0.0
−0.232	0.616	−0.384	0.0	0.0	0.0	0.0	0.0	0.0	0.0	0.0	0.0
0.101	−0.384	0.616	0.0	0.0	0.0	0.0	0.0	0.0	0.0	0.0	0.0
0.0	0.0	0.0	0.330	−0.138	−0.061	0.0	0.0	0.0	0.0	0.0	0.0
0.0	0.0	0.0	−0.138	0.330	0.043	0.0	0.0	0.0	0.0	0.0	0.0
0.0	0.0	0.0	−0.061	0.043	0.330	0.0	0.0	0.0	0.0	0.0	0.0
0.0	0.0	0.0	0.0	0.0	0.0	0.448	−0.274	−0.126	0.0	0.0	0.0
0.0	0.0	0.0	0.0	0.0	0.0	−0.274	0.448	0.152	0.0	0.0	0.0
0.0	0.0	0.0	0.0	0.0	0.0	−0.126	0.152	0.448	0.0	0.0	0.0
0.0	0.0	0.0	0.0	0.0	0.0	0.0	0.0	0.0	0.737	−0.485	−0.314
0.0	0.0	0.0	0.0	0.0	0.0	0.0	0.0	0.0	−0.485	0.737	0.463
0.0	0.0	0.0	0.0	0.0	0.0	0.0	0.0	0.0	−0.314	0.463	0.737

$$
f(\boldsymbol{\pi}) = \mathbf{X}\boldsymbol{\beta} =
\begin{bmatrix}
1 & 0 & 0 \\
0 & 1 & 0 \\
0 & 0 & 1 \\
1 & 0 & 0 \\
0 & 1 & 0 \\
0 & 0 & 1 \\
1 & 0 & 0 \\
0 & 1 & 0 \\
0 & 0 & 1 \\
1 & 0 & 0 \\
0 & 1 & 0 \\
0 & 0 & 1
\end{bmatrix}
\begin{bmatrix}
\beta_A \\
\beta_B \\
\beta_{AB}
\end{bmatrix}
\tag{12.29}
$$

In effect, this model asserts that entries in the columns of the table of function values (Table 12.10, bottom) are homogeneous. It is not satisfactory and is rejected with $W^2(9) = 46.51$.

Model 12.29 does not describe complete independence of the four factors. It expresses the relationship $SY \perp\!\!\!\perp AB$. The SY term arises because the population frequencies are presupposed by the model; the AB term because the third function, which measures AB association, is fitted by β_{AB}. Had this function been set to zero by dropping the third column of $\mathbf{X}$, a model equivalent to $[SY][A][B]$ would have been formed.

Parameters may be added to Model 12.29 to measure variation in the function values among the populations. For example, a parameter entered with one sign for females and the other for males measures the extent of sex variation in the corresponding function. If these parameters are introduced for both population classifications by both responses, the result is the model

$$
f(\boldsymbol{\pi}) = \mathbf{X}\boldsymbol{\beta} =
\begin{bmatrix}
1 & 1 & 1 & 0 & 0 & 0 & 0 \\
0 & 0 & 0 & 1 & 1 & 1 & 0 \\
0 & 0 & 0 & 0 & 0 & 0 & 1 \\
1 & 1 & -1 & 0 & 0 & 0 & 0 \\
0 & 0 & 0 & 1 & 1 & -1 & 0 \\
0 & 0 & 0 & 0 & 0 & 0 & 1 \\
1 & -1 & 1 & 0 & 0 & 0 & 0 \\
0 & 0 & 0 & 1 & -1 & 1 & 0 \\
0 & 0 & 0 & 0 & 0 & 0 & 1 \\
1 & -1 & -1 & 0 & 0 & 0 & 0 \\
0 & 0 & 0 & 1 & -1 & -1 & 0 \\
0 & 0 & 0 & 0 & 0 & 0 & 1
\end{bmatrix}
\begin{bmatrix}
\beta_A \\
\beta_{SA} \\
\beta_{YA} \\
\beta_B \\
\beta_{SB} \\
\beta_{YB} \\
\beta_{AB}
\end{bmatrix}
\tag{12.30}
$$

With the added associations, this model fits nicely: $W^2(5) = 4.53$.

The satisfactory fit of this model can be followed by testing hypotheses about the individual parameters. These are summarized for the association parameters in Table 12.12. Compound hypotheses can also be tested, two of which are shown. If by jointly testing both sex association parameters with a constraint matrix $\mathbf{C}$ one finds that the hypothesis $\beta_{SA} = \beta_{SB} = 0$ can be retained, then any connection between the sex factor and the responses can be dropped from the model. Table 12.12 shows that such a hypothesis is rejected for both sex and year. Both population factors are necessary to understand the variation in the responses. This variation appears stronger for question A than for question B. Empirically, one might choose a simpler model for these data, using β_A, β_{SA}, β_{YA}, β_B, and β_{AB}. The fit of this model is satisfactory, with $G^2(7) = 5.29$. Thus, variation in question B with sex and year may be entirely mediated by the association with A.

The association between the two responses is measured by the parameter β_{AB}. This parameter expresses the common value of the third function derived from each of the four populations. It equals the logarithm of the cross-product ratio,

$$f_{AB}(\boldsymbol{\pi}) = \log \pi_{11} - \log \pi_{12} - \log \pi_{21} + \log \pi_{22}$$
$$= \log \frac{\pi_{11}\pi_{22}}{\pi_{12}\pi_{21}} = \log \alpha$$

The good fit of the present model indicates that a single value for this association is satisfactory, while the test in Table 12.12 indicates that its value is nonzero. The estimate of β_{AB} from this model is a more satisfactory way to determine the common association over all the populations than is the odds ratio in the marginal AB table. Were both A and B related to S and Y, averaging over the populations would potentially bias the estimate (recall the discussion of Simpson's paradox in Section 3.12). Where one needs estimates of the magnitude of association pooled across several populations, this mode of estimation is more appropriate than pooling.

TABLE 12.12
Summary of Tests of Model 12.30 with the Data in Table 12.10

Parameter or Test	$\hat{\beta}$	W^2	df
Test of model		4.53	5
Analysis of parameters			
A effect	−0.27		1
B effect	0.31		1
AB association	2.24	41.97	1
Association to sex		32.57	2
SA effect	1.57	19.87	1
SB effect	0.29	0.75	1
Association to year		19.48	2
YA effect	1.31	14.18	1
YB effect	0.06	0.03	1

12.9. MISSING CELLS AND STRUCTURAL ZEROS

The weighted least-squares procedures can be used with data where cells are missing, either by accident or for structural reasons, although not so transparently as can the maximum-likelihood treatment of hierarchical log-linear models. In essence, the analysis is unchanged. The missing cells remove data points, which alters the parametric constraints. The model is revised to take these deletions into consideration, and then is tested as before. The only real difficulties arise in tailoring the model to the pattern of missing cells.

A few random zeros are not generally a problem. Their effect is mainly on the covariance matrix. As noted above, when an observed frequency is zero, the estimate of that probability is zero, as are the corresponding row and column of the covariance matrix. These zeros underestimate the true variability and reduce the rank of S_p. In itself, the reduction of rank is not necessarily a problem. However, if the singularities carry through the functions to create singularities in S_y, the weighted least-squares algorithm collapses. Usually, it suffices to replace the empty cell by a small number, which gives both a nonzero variance and a nonsingular covariance matrix.

If there are many missing cells, further problems may emerge. When these fall in particular patterns, some of the functions may be completely undefined. Substituting small numbers for the missing cells is not much help here; a better solution is to eliminate the ill-defined function. In effect, the conclusions become conditional on the absence of these cells. Computationally, the model is adapted to accidentally missing cells in the same way as it is adapted to structural vacancies, discussed next. This loss of information affects the iterative likelihood procedures as well, manifesting itself there either as empty marginal cells or as slow convergence of an association term (recall Section 5.6).

Structural voids are different. Clearly there is no justification for assigning any frequency, small or not, to these cells or for attributing a nonzero variance to them. They simply are not part of π or p. Eliminating these cells shortens the vectors by one or more elements. With these reduced vectors, the analysis proceeds as usual. The difficulty is that both the functions and the design matrix may need modification. For example, with missing cells the type of factorial decomposition used in the last section must be changed. Sometimes the functions that measure a particular association are uncomputable, at other times their contrasts are no longer properly balanced.

Consider the case of a 3×3 table with one structural void:

25	17	10
—	35	18
16	22	29

Ordinarily, the association within a complete 3×3 table involves 4 degrees of freedom and a set of 4 contrasts. With the missing cell, one of these contrasts is lost, so that the test of quasi-independence depends on 3 functions.

Selecting these functions requires attention, since they are not necessarily the same as the natural choices for the complete table. For example, suppose that one represented the association in the full table by the logarithms of the odds ratios from the 2×2 tables formed from adjacent rows and columns, so that $\mathbf{f}_{ij}(\boldsymbol{\pi})$ is the log odds ratio for the table with upper left-hand corner at cell i,j:

$$f_{11}(\boldsymbol{\pi}) = \log \pi_{11} - \log \pi_{12} - \log \pi_{21} + \log \pi_{22}$$

$$f_{12}(\boldsymbol{\pi}) = \log \pi_{12} - \log \pi_{13} - \log \pi_{22} + \log \pi_{23}$$

$$f_{21}(\boldsymbol{\pi}) = \log \pi_{21} - \log \pi_{22} - \log \pi_{31} + \log \pi_{32} \qquad (12.31)$$

$$f_{22}(\boldsymbol{\pi}) = \log \pi_{22} - \log \pi_{23} - \log \pi_{32} + \log \pi_{33}$$

Both $f_{11}(\boldsymbol{\pi})$ and $f_{21}(\boldsymbol{\pi})$ involve the missing cell in position $(2,1)$. However, the omission of one cell should reduce the number of functions by one, so both cannot be eliminated. The two defective functions must be replaced by a single function that captures the portion of their variability that does not depend on π_{21}. A satisfactory choice is a function that expresses the log odds ratio involving rows 1 and 3 and columns 1 and 2:

$$f_5(\boldsymbol{\pi}) = \log \pi_{11} - \log \pi_{12} - \log \pi_{31} + \log \pi_{32}$$

The 3 functions $f_{12}(\boldsymbol{\pi})$, $f_5(\boldsymbol{\pi})$ and $f_{22}(\boldsymbol{\pi})$ describe the 3 components of association that do not involve $\pi_{21}(\boldsymbol{\pi})$. A test of quasi-independence in the incomplete table is a test of whether these functions are simultaneously zero. The procedure of Section 12.1 can be used, giving $W^2(3) = 13.66$.

Another type of problem arises if one is constructing contrasts to express the row or column effects in this table (as in Section 12.5, see Equation 12.24) or is constructing a between-population model (as in Section 12.8). In a complete 3×3 table, the differences on a logarithmic scale in the A marginal are described by a pair of functions such as

$$f_{A_1}(\boldsymbol{\pi}) = \log \pi_{11} + \log \pi_{12} + \log \pi_{13} - \log \pi_{21} - \log \pi_{22} - \log \pi_{23}$$

$$f_{A_2}(\boldsymbol{\pi}) = \log \pi_{21} + \log \pi_{22} + \log \pi_{23} - \log \pi_{31} - \log \pi_{32} - \log \pi_{33}$$

$$(12.32)$$

Again suppose that π_{21} is structurally absent. If one deletes this term, Equations 12.32 become

$$f'_{A_1}(\boldsymbol{\pi}) = \log \pi_{11} + \log \pi_{12} + \log \pi_{13} - \log \pi_{22} - \log \pi_{23}$$

$$f'_{A_2}(\boldsymbol{\pi}) = \log \pi_{22} + \log \pi_{23} - \log \pi_{31} - \log \pi_{32} - \log \pi_{33} \qquad (12.33)$$

These functions are zero when the proportions in each margin are equal but, because of the unbalanced number of cells in the rows, are nonzero when the cell probabilities are equal. If one wishes equal cell probabilities to imply no effect, then one must give more weight to the row that has fewer cells. Since there are 3 probabilities in one row and 2 in the other, these weights stand in a 2:3 relationship. It is easiest to use integer weights, revising the functions to

$$f''_{A_1}(\boldsymbol{\pi}) = 2 \log \pi_{11} + 2 \log \pi_{12} + 2 \log \pi_{13} - 3 \log \pi_{22} - 3 \log \pi_{23}$$
$$f''_{A_2}(\boldsymbol{\pi}) = 3 \log \pi_{22} + 3 \log \pi_{23} - 2 \log \pi_{31} - 2 \log \pi_{32} - 2 \log \pi_{33}$$
(12.34)

Obviously, the use of Equations 12.33 gives different answers from Equations 12.34 (although a test of independence gives the same $W^2(3) = 13.66$). One formulation is not more correct than the other. They differ in what is implied by the lack of an A effect. This interpretation should determine one's choice.

Where more cells are missing, the appropriate functions are harder to pick out. For example, in a 3×3 table with structurally absent diagonals, only a single contrast is needed to express association—that is, violation of quasi-independence. Specifically, consider the table

—	18	35
39	—	62
12	9	—

None of the functions that would normally represent association (such as Equations 12.31) can be used. Five functions are required to express the relationships among the 6 filled cells. Each of the marginal effects involves 3 levels, so requires 2 functions. A good choice for these functions is

$$f_{A_1}(\boldsymbol{\pi}) = \log \pi_{12} + \log \pi_{13} - \log \pi_{21} - \log \pi_{23}$$
$$f_{A_2}(\boldsymbol{\pi}) = \log \pi_{21} + \log \pi_{23} - \log \pi_{31} - \log \pi_{32}$$
$$f_{B_1}(\boldsymbol{\pi}) = -\log \pi_{12} + \log \pi_{21} + \log \pi_{31} - \log \pi_{32}$$
$$f_{B_2}(\boldsymbol{\pi}) = \log \pi_{12} - \log \pi_{13} - \log \pi_{23} + \log \pi_{32}$$

To complete the set of functions, a fifth function is needed to represent the association. This function should be chosen to be orthogonal to the other four, so that it extracts only the variability that does not depend on the marginal distributions. The required function is

$$f_{AB}(\boldsymbol{\pi}) = \log \pi_{12} - \log \pi_{13} - \log \pi_{21} + \log \pi_{23} + \log \pi_{31} - \log \pi_{32}$$

Quasi-independence holds when $f_{AB}(\boldsymbol{\pi}) = 0$, a hypothesis that is tested in any of the usual ways, giving $W^2(1) = 0.023$.

In these ways, models for designs with missing cells are written. Often, as in the first example, the conditional model is a relatively straightforward restriction of the model for the similar hypothesis in a complete table. However, with many zeros, as in the last example, selection of the appropriate model is more difficult. Some time studying the relationships in the data is necessary before the model can be written. For these models, an iterative fit to the marginal frequencies is simpler.

In the discussion of multiple populations in Section 12.7, the same set of functions was applied to every population. If certain cells are missing from one population or another, due to structural impossibilities or certain patterns of random zeros, the populations must be treated separately, using different functions. For example, one might find that, by accident or design, one question in a survey was not asked to subjects from one population. Information about this question and its associations is lacking, but the rest of the data from that population can still be used. Although the defect damages the parallel between populations, with appropriate modification the type of interpopulation models discussed in Section 12.8 can still be applied. Further detail is given by Grizzle & Williams (1972).

12.10. WEIGHTED LEAST-SQUARES AND MAXIMUM-LIKELIHOOD METHODS

A look back at the examples in this chapter shows that all the analyses except those involving marginal homogeneity were based on hierarchical log-linear models. Thus, they could have been performed using the maximum-likelihood estimates obtained by iterating on the appropriate marginal distributions. The values of the test statistics X^2 or G^2 would not differ substantially from W^2 and the same conclusions would be reached. So, in most situations, either approach can be used.

Because of this similarity, the decision to use one method rather than another is often more a matter of personal preference than anything else. One is most efficient working with techniques that one knows well. Using design and restriction matrices to construct a test feels natural to somebody who has done a lot of work with similar models in continuous multivariate statistics. To this worker, the parallels to the general linear model in multiple regression and the analysis of variance are easy to exploit. In contrast, a researcher who is not facile with linear models may find the expression of hypotheses as sets of linear contrasts to be unnatural and the resulting large matrices to be confusing. This user will likely find the concepts of probabilistic independence and conditional independence, with their graphical representation, to be a more palatable way to describe hypotheses.

Of course, a sophisticated user exploits both approaches, moving from independence concepts to log-linear models as the need arises. In this regard, it is worth remembering that maximum-likelihood estimates do not apply exclusively to hierarchical models, nor does the use of matrix representation imply that weighted least-squares estimates are used. In particular, an extension of the matrix formulation in this chapter can provide maximum-likelihood estimates for any log-linear model. As a brief example, consider the model $[AB][BC]$ in a $2 \times 2 \times 2$ table. In matrix notation, the log-linear form of this model is

$$
\log \boldsymbol{\mu} =
\begin{bmatrix}
\mu_{111} \\
\mu_{112} \\
\mu_{121} \\
\mu_{122} \\
\mu_{211} \\
\mu_{212} \\
\mu_{221} \\
\mu_{222}
\end{bmatrix}
= \mathbf{X}\boldsymbol{\lambda} =
\begin{bmatrix}
1 & 1 & 1 & 1 & 1 & 1 \\
1 & 1 & 1 & -1 & 1 & -1 \\
1 & 1 & -1 & 1 & -1 & -1 \\
1 & 1 & -1 & -1 & -1 & 1 \\
1 & -1 & 1 & 1 & -1 & 1 \\
1 & -1 & 1 & -1 & -1 & -1 \\
1 & -1 & -1 & 1 & 1 & -1 \\
1 & -1 & -1 & -1 & 1 & 1
\end{bmatrix}
\begin{bmatrix}
\lambda \\
\lambda_{A(1)} \\
\lambda_{B(1)} \\
\lambda_{C(1)} \\
\lambda_{AB(11)} \\
\lambda_{BC(11)}
\end{bmatrix}
\qquad (12.35)
$$

Clearly non-hierarchical log-linear models can be written in this way. With the model in this form, several iterative maximum-likelihood estimation algorithms apply. One approach directly maximizes the likelihood under Equation 12.35 using what is known as Newton-Raphson iteration (Haberman, 1974a, 1978, 1979; see Agresti, 1984, Appendix B). Another approach uses a series of weighted least squares estimates (as in this chapter) in which the covariance matrix $\mathbf{S_p}$ is based on estimates of $\hat{\boldsymbol{\pi}}$ that are calculated from the log-linear model and the current parameter approximations (e.g., McCullagh & Nelder, 1983; Nelder & Wedderburn, 1972). Either procedure gives estimates that are the same as those obtained by the iterative proportional fitting algorithm.

Beyond matters of preference, there are some more fundamental reasons to choose one method over another. The real advantage of the weighted least-squares analysis is the large number of models that it can fit. Clearly, the generality of the function transformations in Section 12.2 is very great. Models that violate the hierarchy principle and that are not log-linear can be constructed. The marginal-homogeneity models discussed in Sections 12.3 and 12.7 are examples of what is gained. The first of these models is linear in the probabilities and the second combines both linear and log-linear aspects. However, one should not overestimate the value of this generality. In most situations, one is not hampered by a restriction to hierarchical log-frequency models. Most commonly, the wider classes of models lack interpretation and only serve to complicate the discussion and confuse the user.

Another important difference between the methods concerns the treatment of zeros. Unless random zeros are common enough to create holes in the model by rendering some parameters irrelevant, they are nearly transparent to either method. Structural zeros are another matter, as are multiple random zeros. They are easily accommodated when frequencies are adjusted to fit the marginal distributions, but where an explicit design matrix must be constructed, new functions or new parameterizations must be devised. As Section 12.9 illustrated, the proper modification is not always obvious. In these situations, the least-squares procedure is considerably harder to use.

In summary, when both methods apply, the results are roughly similar. The least-squares analysis is favored by (1) its closer links to the multivariate models from conventional parametric statistics and (2) the greater number of hypotheses that can be tested. The analysis based on the marginal distributions is favored by (1) its conformity with hypotheses of (conditional) independence and quasi-independence and (2) the smooth way in which it accommodates random and structural zeros. The salience of these points depends on the problem to which they are applied.

PROBLEMS

Note: All calculation in these problems requires a computer, hence should be indicated by $\mathscr{C}$. However, much of the value of an exercise is obtained by setting up the problem and defining $\mathbf{X}$, $\boldsymbol{\beta}$, $\mathbf{C}$ as needed. If you do not have access to an appropriate computer program†, state the proper models and tests.

12.1. Reanalyze the data in Problem 2.1 using the weighted least-squares procedures.

12.2. Test the hypotheses of Problem 3.1a.

12.3. Test whether the two problems in Problem 9.13 are solved with equal proficiency.

12.4. Analyze the data in Problem 10.7.

12.5. Fit the set-association model and the related model of Problem 11.6 to the data in Table 11.3.

12.6. Set up a test of marginal homogeneity by constructing functions to give the marginal probabilities, then equating them using contrast matrices. Apply the method to the data from Problem 10.7.

12.7. Reanalyze the data in Problem 7.4 using the weighted least-square procedures.

12.8. How would the differences among the three experiments that were described at the start of Section 3.1 be reflected in a weighted least-squares analysis? Set up the transformations and an appropriate model in each case.

12.9. Consider a questionnaire study in which one question classifies the respondents into three categories, those who answered "Yes," those who answered "No," and those who refused to answer. The respondents are also classified by the 2-level factor A and the 3-level factor B. Set up transformation matrices to define two logits, the first expressing a Yes/No contrast, the second contrasting the respondents who answered with those who did not. How does one test whether the association between the relative frequency of positive responses (versus No's) and classification factor A varies with B?

12.10. A survey asks subjects to indicate agreement or disagreement with two statements, A and B. The survey is given to three populations of subjects, p_1, p_2, and p_3, giving the data

---

† Note that PROC CATMOD in SAS can be used (SAS Institute, 1985).

A:	p_1 Agree	p_1 Disagree	p_2 Agree	p_2 Disagree	p_3 Agree	p_3 Disagree
B Agree	13	42	18	29	17	44
B Disagree	17	28	33	20	47	22

Define a weighted least-squares model based on functions that express log α for each population. Use this model to estimate the common value of log α that occurs across the populations and to test whether this value adequately represents the association or whether log α must be indexed by population.

12.11. Is statement A in Problem 12.10 answered "Yes" more often than is statement B? Does this difference vary over the three populations?

12.12. Reanalyze the data in Problem 3.12 using the weighted least-square procedures.

12.13. An experiment is designed to manipulate the proportion of subjects who adopt a cooperative strategy in a Prisoner's dilemma conflict. This is done by two statements that can be inserted in the instructions for the task (factors A and B). Four groups are run, based on factorial combinations of these statements. The data are

		Cooperate yes	Cooperate no
A	B	yes	no
Absent	Absent	13	17
Absent	Present	7	23
Present	Absent	19	11
Present	Present	16	14

Use a logit model to investigate the following assertions:

a. Each statement has an effect on the subjects' strategy.
b. These effects are not of comparable magnitude, statement A having a larger influence.
c. The effects of the statements do not interact.

12.14. Test for quasi-independence in the table

25	11	13
51	—	8
17	12	5

12.15. [Harder] As defined in Sections 5.8 and 9.4, the entropy, $H(\pi) = \Sigma\ \pi \log \pi$, measures the diversity of responses in a distribution. Suppose that you wish to see whether the variability of a classification differs among three subpopulations of subjects. A natural approach is to let $f(\pi) = H(\pi)$ and use a linear model to test for differences among the subpopulations. Apply the rules in Section 12.2 to find the variance transform for this function and set up the analysis.

13

Ordered Categories

The analysis procedures presented up to now treat the categorizations as nominal. The order in which the categories are listed in the table is arbitrary, insofar as the analysis is concerned. However, many factors are intrinsically ordered. Several examples have already appeared in this book: the classification of college students by year is ordered, as are the detection responses X and Y in Chapter 6 and the three levels of drug use in Chapter 8. There is information in these orderings that can aid the analysis and strengthen the conclusions that one draws. This chapter looks at ways to accommodate the ordering of categories.

13.1. VARIETIES OF ORDERED-CATEGORY ANALYSIS

A table based on an ordered categorization can be analyzed in several ways, depending on how much one is willing to assume about the ordering. If one distrusts the ordering, the ordered factor can be treated as if it were unordered, and the table analyzed by using the models discussed in earlier chapters. At the other extreme, one can take the categorization very seriously, assign numbers to the categories (e.g., the integers 1, 2, 3, . . .), and then analyze the data as if these were numerical scores, using parametric statistical procedures such as the t test, the analysis of variance, or multiple regression and correlation. Often, neither of these approaches is completely satisfactory.

Treating an ordered factor as if it were unordered wastes much of its information. If one rejects independence in an unordered two-way table, one often turns to a model of complete dependence (unless an association model like those in Chapter 11 is appropriate). In an $a \times b$ table, complete dependence introduces ab

345

parameters, λ_{AB}, on $(a - 1)(b - 1)$ degrees of freedom. To accommodate ordering, one can look for patterns in these parameters or examine the residuals from the expected frequencies under independence. In contrast to the unordered models, partial-association models based on the ordering require far fewer parameters—sometimes only one for the association part. Generally, estimation in a model with many parameters is less accurate than in a model with fewer parameters, and hypothesis tests are less powerful. Thus, one pays for the generality of association in the unordered case with diminished precision. If one wants to make statements that involve the ordering, then tests making specific use of the ordering are preferable.

When the number of categories is large and well graded, one may apply conventional parametric procedures to the data. A many-leveled ordered categorization is close to a continuous scale and if the sample size is adequate, there is little difference between the results. For example, one may choose to summarize the association in a large two-way ordered table by a Pearson correlation instead of using one of the association models described below. Again, a test for the homogeneity of several populations on an ordered variable may sometimes be conducted with an analysis of variance. These techniques are familiar and give specific, well-understood results.

When the number of categories is not large, there are reasons to prefer other procedures. Probably the most serious problem with the conventional analysis is the difference between the sampling models for the categorical data and the normal distribution postulated by most parametric statistical techniques. The statistical model for the dependent variables in the parametric approach specifies that they have univariate or multivariate normal distributions, while the sampling distributions for the frequency methods are binomial or Poisson with marginal parameters that are generally left free. For some tests, the central limit properties of the mean saves the situation for the parametric tests—the sampling distribution of the mean of a reasonably large sample is nearly normal even when the parent distribution is not. For other statistics, particularly those involving variability and interfactor association, large samples do not help. What starts nonnormal stays non-normal. A second problem with the parametric method concerns the assignment of scale values to the categories. Most of these methods require the data to be converted from an ordinal to a numeric scale. Unless there is an a priori reason for a particular assignment of numbers to the categories, one must choose the values arbitrarily, often by selecting consecutive integers. The importance of the scale-value issue is somewhat equivocal, however. On the one hand, versions of the parametric methods are available in which category scores are assigned on the basis of the data (for example, the monotone analysis of variance; see Kruskal, 1965) or that choose assignments that minimize the possible disagreement (e.g., Abelson & Tukey, 1963). On the other hand, several of the frequency methods also require the assignment of scales (for example, the uniform-association model described in Section 13.2). Perhaps the most telling reason to use categorical methods is simply that it is more satisfactory to use a procedure that is specifically constructed for the type of data one is analyzing than an approximation based on another model. The relationship between the normal distribution and the ordered categorical models is important and motivates several of the categorical models discussed below.

When both the unordered models and a parametric analysis are inappropriate, one must turn to a class of models specifically designed for ordered categorical data. Several analysis schemes that use the ordering but that do not assume specific scores or spacing lie between the treatment of an ordered factor as unordered and as continuous. These are the principal topic of this chapter.†

One way to picture the difference between the ordered and the unordered models for a set of data is in terms of the transformations that can be applied to the table without changing the outcome of the analysis (McCullagh, 1978). Consider a four-level categorization. There are $4! = 20$ orders in which the four categories can be listed. Of these orders, only two are consistent with an intrinsic ordering of the classification: one that lists the categories in ascending order, the other in descending order. An analysis procedure based on properties of the table that are independent of order should yield the same result regardless of which of the 20 orders is used. Such a procedure is said to be *permutationally invariant*, since it gives the same result for every permutation of the categories. Except for some models in Chapter 11, the models and tests discussed up to this point are permutationally invariant. In contrast, an analysis procedure that uses ordering should not give the same answer when the categories are arbitrarily shuffled. The only time that the same results should be obtained is when the sequence of categories is reversed. Because the same result is obtained when the categories are read forward or backward, these procedures are said to be *palindromically invariant*. Most of the models that apply to ordered tables, including all those in this chapter, are palindromically invariant.

An example may help to make these invariance properties concrete. Consider a hypothetical two-way table obtained by counting the number of errors made by subjects who have received various degrees of training on a task (Table 13.1, upper panel). Both factors in this table are ordered. A model of independence fails to fit these data ($G^2(6) = 43.64$). Now rewrite this table with the order of the rows and columns permuted (Table 13.1, lower panel). The test of independence is unchanged by this shuffling: exactly the same expected frequencies are obtained and the same values of X^2 and G^2. Similarly, the multiplicative-associa-

---

†There are many more of these models than can be reasonably described in this chapter. Specifically, the approaches based on the stereotype ordered regression model of Anderson (1984) or deriving from the generalized linear model (McCullagh, 1980; McCullagh & Nelder, 1983) are not treated here. Most of the work on ordered categorical data is recent, and it likely that new approaches will be developed and the older ones refined further. A more extensive treatment of many of the models in this chapter is given by Agresti (1983a).

TABLE 13.1
Hypothetical Data from a Simple Training Experiment
Organized in Ways that are Consistent and
Inconsistent with the Category Ordering

Data with the Categorizations Ordered

		Number of Errors Made			
		0	1	2	≥3
Training	Low	15	14	10	45
	Moderate	46	26	14	30
	High	42	15	7	8

Data with the Categorizations Permuted

		Number of Errors Made			
		0	2	1	≥3
Training	High	42	7	15	8
	Low	15	10	14	45
	Moderate	46	14	26	30

tion model of Section 11.3, which is also permutationally invariant, gives the same statistics and the same estimated parameters in both tables. Unlike these models, an analysis that uses the order gives different results in the two tables. The fit should be the same only if one completely reverses the order, writing *high*, *moderate*, and *low*, or ≥3, 2, 1, and 0.

The appropriateness of some of the ordered models depends on the sampling assumptions underlying the data. If the data derive from a set of populations (as in Table 13.1), they are best described by a product-multinomial sampling model. If they are sampled from a single population, they follow a pure multinomial or Poisson model. The distinction is important when an analysis makes use of the marginal distributions or when it postulates a single underlying multivariate distribution. For a dimension such as the amount of training, these concepts have no population counterparts and no intrinsic meaning. They could be different in another study without altering the phenomenon being investigated. As an example of the single-population situation, suppose that subjects are asked to rate their agreement with two statements. Hypothetical data using four-point ordered scales appear in Table 13.2. These data have a bivariate form, for which both marginal distributions estimate meaningful population characteristics. Obviously, both types of data—the single-population and the multiple-population—occur in practice. In analyzing them, one must be sure not to apply interpretations to the latter type that are based on the assumptions of the former.

Whatever sampling model applies, the goal of all the ordered-category models is to use the ordering to interpret association. When the factors are associated,

TABLE 13.2
Hypothetical Data Comparing Rating of Two Questions

		Question B			
		Strongly Disagree	Weakly Disagree	Weakly Agree	Strongly Agree
Question A	Strongly Disagree	2	10	15	13
	Weakly Disagree	7	17	20	20
	Weakly Agree	40	40	42	12
	Strongly Agree	35	31	47	6

one wishes to describe their relationship, using as few parameters as possible. In this respect this chapter concerns partial-association models, like those in Chapter 11.

One variety of ordered-category model has already been discussed in Chapter 11. As noted in Section 11.2, the set-association models are often designed around a square table with ordered factors. Recall that these models imposed patterns on the association parameters λ_{AB}. Any such model for which the parameter pattern depends on the sequence in which the categories are written is automatically an ordered-category model. Changing this order changes the pattern, so the model is palindromically invariant, but not permutationally invariant. For example, in the triangles parameter model (Equation 11.2) the triangular pattern of association parameters is preserved only for a specific ordering or its reverse. Similarly, the diagonals parameter model and the diagonals parameter symmetry model are based on the ordered listing of categories.

Another type of ordered-association model works with the odds ratios discussed in Section 11.3. Although the multiplicative-association model is permutationally invariant, other models for the odds ratios are intolerant of permutation and use the ordering. These impose a structure on the odds ratios formed from adjacent categories,

$$\hat{\alpha}_{ij} = \frac{x_{ij}x_{i+1,j+1}}{x_{i+1,j}x_{i,j+1}} \tag{13.1}$$

(here the + indicates addition, not summation over a subscript). Again, the adjacency makes the model responsive to the ordering. Models of this type are discussed in Sections 13.2 to 13.4.

A somewhat stronger assumption about the categories that is still consistent with palindromic invariance is that they are represented by a numerical scale. Each category is assigned a number. In models of this type, the association is expressed with these scale values. These values can be constructed from the observed data rather than by a priori assignment, so that they are consistent with an ordinal relationship. They can be defined and estimated in several ways; their use is discussed in Sections 13.5 and 13.6. As will be seen, the association and the scale approaches are not exclusive: the scale models imply values for the α_{ij}, and the association models attach numerical values to the categories.

By their nature, the ordered-category procedures are tied to the sequence of their categorizations. Usually they are most sensitive to effects that vary monotonically with the ordering. Other effects are likely to be ignored. For example, association standing in a U-shaped relationship to the ordering of a factor may remain uninterpreted. If one expects such effects, one should use other types of models. The discussion of the multicomponent association models in Section 11.5 showed that a full accounting of association requires a series of terms. Most of the ordered-association models pick up only the term that matches the ordering. This restriction is both their strength and their limitation. They gain much because they use the external information carried by the ordering to focus their attention, but they risk an incomplete treatment of more complex patterns of association. If the fit of an ordered model is inadequate, one should turn to models that can express a wider range of possibilities.

13.2. THE UNIFORM-ASSOCIATION MODEL

An important class of association models is based on the odds ratio (see Duncan, 1979; Goodman 1979c, 1985, Section 2). One such model, the multiplicative-association model, was described in Section 11.3. This model expressed the odds ratio as a multiplicative function of a set of row coefficients and a set of column coefficients (Equation 11.5). As presented there, this model is invariant under permutation of the classification and so is not specifically an ordered category model. Other forms for the association parameters are more closely linked to the ordering.

Consider the table of odds ratios relating pairs of adjacent categories (Equation 13.1). Denote these by α_{ij} in the population and $\hat{\alpha}_{ij}$ in the sample. For the training-and-error data in Table 13.1, there are $(a - 1)(b - 1) = 6$ two-by-two subtables relating adjacent pairs of rows and columns—the same number as the degrees of freedom for a test of independence. Each subtable produces an odds ratio, as shown in Table 13.3; for example, the subtable formed by the first two rows and the first two columns gives the ratio $(15 \times 26)/(14 \times 46) = 0.606$. All these ratios are less than 1, which indicates a relative paucity of observations on the major diagonal of the 2×2 subtables. An association of this nature implies that fewer errors are made by the more highly trained groups. Note also that all the ratios are of similar size.

The ordering is important to this analysis, since it determines which categories are adjacent to which. This characteristic of the ratios is palindromically invariant, but is changed by other permutations. That other orderings produce

TABLE 13.3
Odds Ratios from Adjacent 2 × 2 Tables Formed from Table 13.1
and Fit of the Uniform-association Model

Original Data

| | | Number of Errors Made | | | |
		0	1	2	≥3
Training	Low	15	14	10	45
	Moderate	46	26	14	30
	High	42	15	7	8

Odds Ratios of Adjacent Subtables

	0-1	1-2	2-3
Low-moderate	0.606	0.754	0.476
Moderate-high	0.632	0.867	0.533

Expected Frequencies under Uniform Association

| | | Number of Errors Made | | | |
		0	1	2	≥3
Training	Low	15.4	13.8	11.8	43.0
	Moderate	44.6	25.5	13.8	32.1
	High	43.0	15.6	5.4	8.0

less tidy results is easily seen when one looks at the odds ratios for the permuted array at the bottom of Table 13.1:

| 4.000 | 0.653 | 6.027 |
| 0.457 | 1.327 | 0.359 |

This table is not as simple as Table 13.3 and is less easily described. There is no hope of summarizing it by a single value.

The strategy now is to build a model for the odds ratios in Table 13.3. The simplest picture is of a uniform degree of association:

$$\alpha_{ij} = \theta \qquad (13.2)$$

If $\theta = 1$, then independence is implied. For $\theta \neq 1$, a model of specific dependence results, known as the *uniform-association model*. If this model fits, it implies that the association measured in the 2 × 2 subtables formed from adjacent pairs of rows and columns is homogeneous. In this sense, the association is uniform throughout the table.

There are several ways to fit the uniform-association model to data. The details of the estimation algorithms are not treated here (for discussions see Agresti, 1984; Fienberg, 1980, Section 4.4; Goodman, 1979c, 1985; and Haberman, 1974b). In the main, these procedures generalize the estimation techniques that apply to unordered tables. To briefly illustrate, recall that for maximum-likelihood estimates under independence, the marginal sums of the data and the expected frequencies agree:

$$\sum_j \hat{\mu}_{ij} = x_{i+} \quad \text{and} \quad \sum_i \hat{\mu}_{ij} = x_{j+}$$

For the uniform-association model, these relationships continue to hold, along with a new constraint,

$$\sum_{i,j} ij\hat{\mu}_{ij} = \sum_{i,j} ijx_{ij}$$

By iteration over these three sets of constraints, starting from a table with all entries 1.0 and adjusting $\hat{\mu}_{ij}$, expected frequencies under the uniform-association model are found.

Expected frequencies produced by this procedure are shown at the bottom of Table 13.3. Any 2×2 section of this table has the same odds ratio, giving the estimate $\hat{\theta} = 0.636$. This single value summarizes the association in the entire table. To test the fit of this model, the observed and expected frequencies are compared with the usual X^2 or G^2 statistic. The model involves one more parameter than does the independence model, so the test has one degree of freedom fewer: the total number is $(a - 1)(b - 1) - 1 = ab - a - b$. For Table 13.1, $X^2(5) = 1.10$ and $G^2(5) = 1.07$. The uniform-association model fits these data very well.

Although the uniform-association model is developed above as a description of the association, it is also a model for the frequencies. Uniform association implies that

$$\log \mu_{ij} = \lambda + \lambda_{A(i)} + \lambda_{B(j)} + ij\tau \qquad (13.3)$$

where $\tau = \log \theta$. This is a log-linear model, albeit a more complicated one than those used before, due to the coefficient ij of τ. In this sense, it is a model of partial dependence, with $\lambda_{AB(ij)} = ij\tau$. However, this form of the model is harder to understand than the odds-ratio form (Equation 13.2), since it obscures the simple constraint on the association. So, although the models in the next two sections can be written in forms analogous to Equation 13.3, those forms are not emphasized.

If the final term of Equation 13.3 is removed, the resulting model describes independence. Thus, the uniform-association model and the independence model are hierarchically related and one can test for the presence of ordinal association with a difference test that compares them. The difference statistic tests the hypothesis that $\tau = 0$. For the data in Table 13.1, this hypothesis is rejected with $\Delta G^2(1) = 43.64 - 1.07 = 42.57$. Where the association is ordered (even if not perfectly uniform), this test is substantially more powerful than a test of the independence hypothesis $A \perp\!\!\!\perp B$. Of equal importance, a difference test can profitably be used when the sample size is far too small to support any test of overall fit (Agristi & Yang, 1987).

13.3.   ADDITIVE ASSOCIATION MODELS

Uniform association is a simple model, and although it often fits much better than does pure independence, it is quite restricted. All α_{ij} are fitted by the same parameter, suggesting that the categories are equally spaced with respect to their association. For many sets of data, this equal spacing cannot be expected to hold. As they stand, the association coefficients in Table 13.3 relating the rows with middle and high levels of training are about the same size as those relating the middle and low rows. This similarity is not inevitable, however. If more training had been given to the high group, then the difference between that group and the middle group would have been greater, that row of association coefficients would have been larger, and the table of log-odds ratios would not have been homogeneous. To accommodate effects such as this, variation in α_{ij} among the rows can be permitted. Formally, the constant association model is replaced by one in which

$$\alpha_{ij} = \theta_{A(i)} \qquad (13.4)$$

This model is known as either the *row association effects model* or the *uniform column-association model*, depending on whether one emphasizes its variable or its constant aspect. It introduces $a - 1$ parameters to the independence model (or $a - 2$ to the uniform-association model). Thus, it is tested on $(a - 1)(b - 1) - (a - 1) = (a - 1)(b - 2)$ degrees of freedom. The model is saturated when $b = 2$ and does not differ from full dependence.

The uniform column-association model also applies to data where the row factor is unordered and the column factor ordered. Suppose that the three rows of Table 13.1 represent an unordered factor—for example, they might be three types of training. Then there would be no reason to expect similar values of the association from row to row. The order of the rows could be permuted without violating the structure of their design, which would change the interrow association. However, the ordered column factor cannot be permuted, so the associations involving adjacent columns can reasonably be modeled. Uniform association along the columns, as specified by Model 13.4, is plausible. It represents an even spacing of the column categories.

A comparable *column association effect model* or *uniform row-association model* allows the association to vary across the columns:

$$\alpha_{ij} = \theta_{B(j)} \tag{13.5}$$

This model applies to tables in which the row factor is ordered and the column factor is either ordered or unordered. Its test is based on $(a-2)(b-1)$ degrees of freedom.

The row-effects and column-effects models can combined in several ways. One's first temptation is to create an additive model by writing α_{ij} as a sum of row and column terms. However, the resulting model is less useful than a log-linear model:

$$\log \alpha_{ij} = \tau + \tau_{A(i)} + \tau_{B(j)} \tag{13.6}$$

This model has a similar appearance to the log-frequency models, but applies to the association rather than to the expected frequencies. It is known as the *additive-association model* or sometimes the *R + C model* (e.g., in Goodman, 1979c). The model is not permutationally invariant and is a true ordered-category model.

The relationship between the additive-association model and the models already discussed is easiest to see by starting with a saturated log-linear association model,

$$\log \alpha_{ij} = \tau + \tau_{A(i)} + \tau_{B(j)} + \tau_{AB(ij)} \tag{13.7}$$

This model allows any pattern of association and can fit any table. There are more parameters in Model 13.7 than there are odds ratios, so their values must be restricted to obtain unique estimates. The same summation constraints that work for the λ's apply:

$$\sum_i \tau_{A(i)} = \sum_j \tau_{B(j)} = \sum_i \tau_{AB(ij)} = \sum_j \tau_{AB(ij)} = 0$$

With these restrictions, Model 13.7 contains exactly $(a-1)(b-1)$ free parameters.

Simpler models are formed from the saturated association model by eliminating parameters. Setting $\tau_{AB} = 0$ creates the additive-association model (Equation 13.6). Further fixing $\tau_A = 0$ gives uniform row effects (Equation 13.5). With the new parameterization, $\log \alpha_{ij} = \tau + \tau_{B(j)}$, so the parameter $\theta_{B(j)}$ in Equation 13.5 equals $\exp(\tau + \tau_{B(j)})$. The uniform-association model is obtained by further eliminating τ_B, and complete independence is represented when all the parameters of Equation 13.7 are zero. By deleting parameters hierarchically, six models are constructed, as shown in Table 13.4. All 6 models also include parameters λ, λ_A, and λ_B in their log-frequency form (as in Equation 13.3), which are needed to fit the marginal sums of the $\hat{\mu}_{ij}$ to their observed values. The models are log-linear in both their expected frequencies, μ_{ij}, and their association, α_{ij}.

The degrees of freedom in Table 13.4 are obtained by subtracting the number of free parameters in the model from the degrees of freedom of the independence model. In these counts, τ represents 1 parameter, τ_A represents $a - 2$ (that is, $a - 1$ values less 1 for the constraint that they sum to zero), and so forth.

The hierarchical structure of these models, shown in the bottom part of Table 13.4, means that the difference in fit between two connected models tests the necessity of the parameters by which they differ. Thus, one can test whether the row associations differ in the context of variable column effects by subtracting G^2 for the additive-effects model from that of the column-effects model.

Like the uniform-association model, the additive-association models are log-linear. As a model for log μ_{ij}, the row-and-column effects model (Equation 13.6) is

$$\log \mu_{ij} = \lambda + \lambda_{A(i)} + \lambda_{B(j)} + j\gamma_{A(i)} + i\gamma_{B(j)}$$

where $\gamma_{A(i)}$ and $\gamma_{B(j)}$ are parameters related to $\tau_{A(i)}$ and $\tau_{B(j)}$, respectively. The various uniform-effect models are generated by fixing these parameters to be equally spaced. For example, the uniform row association model is created when

TABLE 13.4
Association Models and their Hierarchical Organization

Model	Association Effects in Model	Degrees of Freedom
Independence	None	$(a - 1)(b - 1)$
Uniform association	τ	$ab - a - b$
Row effects	τ, τ_A	$(a - 1)(b - 2)$
Column effects	τ, τ_B	$(a - 2)(b - 1)$
Additive effects	τ, τ_A, τ_B	$(a - 2)(b - 2)$
Arbitrary dependence	$\tau, \tau_A, \tau_B, \tau_{AB}$	0

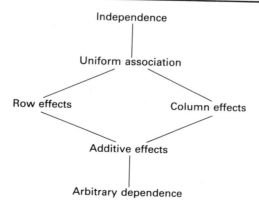

one sets $\gamma_{A(i)} = i\gamma_A$. The uniform association model in Equation 11.3 is obtained by constraining both γ_A and γ_B in this way. As noted above, this formulation of the model has less intuitive value than does the odds-ratio version. However, it is useful when one wishes to fit these models using a general log-linear model program.

The row-effects, column-effects, and uniform-association models are also special cases of the multiplicative-association model described in Section 11.3. They are obtained from this model by restricting one or both sets of parameters, $\xi_{A(i)}$ and $\xi_{B(j)}$ to equal spacing. Thus, under the multiplicative-association model, the odds ratio for adjacent columns is

$$\log \alpha_{ij} = \phi(\xi_{A(i+1)} - \xi_{A(i)})(\xi_{B(j+1)} - \xi_{B(j)})$$

(cf. Equation 11.11). If the ξ_B are set a priori so that successive terms differ by a fixed amount δ, then the model becomes

$$\log \alpha_{ij} = \phi\delta(\xi_{A(i+1)} - \xi_{A(i)})$$

This model is readily reparameterized to row-effects form. In this way the multiplicative-association model generalizes the tolerance of the association models for unordered factors: the uniform-association model requires both factors to be ordered, the uniform column-association model allows unordered rows, and the multiplicative-association model lets both rows and columns be unordered.

The general multiplicative-association model is permutationally invariant, so without further restriction, it is not an ordered-category model. It can be adapted to an ordered categorization if one constrains its parameters to have the same ordering as the categories, that is, if one requires that $\xi_{A(i)} \leq \xi_{A(k)}$ whenever $i < k$ and $\xi_{B(j)} \leq \xi_{B(l)}$ whenever $j < l$. Procedures for fitting the multiplicative-association model under these constraints have recently been developed (see Agristi, Chuang, & Kezouh, 1987; Goodman 1985, 1986, 1987).

Unless the number of empty cells is large enough to eliminate rows or columns from the table, association models of this type readily accommodate data that contain random zeros. Although the empty cells may render some of the observed cross-product ratios undefined, the iterative fitting methods mentioned briefly in the last section are based on the cell frequencies rather than the association measures. Thus, they are able to bridge the zeros and provide parameter estimates based on the table as a whole.

Tables that contain structural vacancies pose few additional difficulties. The voids are simply ignored both in fitting the model and in calculating the test statistics. As usual, the degrees of freedom for goodness-of-fit tests of these models are reduced by the number of vacant cells. If there are too many structural voids, some problems may arise from missing parameters or the constraints associated with a decomposable table. These are treated in the same manner as for unordered tests (Chapter 10).

13.4. ASSOCIATION MODELS IN MULTIWAY TABLES

The additive-association models extend to more than two factors in many ways. The saturated log-linear model for a three-factor table involves three two-way associations and one three-way association. If all three factors are ordered, each of these sets of association parameters can be described by a model similar to any of those in the last section. Moreoever, the parameters of these submodels may be the same or may differ. As with the comparable extension of the multiplicative-association model discussed in Section 11.6, there are many variations. Faced with this richness, one cannot fit models haphazardly, but must construct a model for the particular problem. This section examines one class of models for a three-factor table, known as *conditional-association models*. For other types of analysis and for the estimation algorithms, see Agresti (1984), Agresti & Kezouh (1983), and Clogg (1982).

A very powerful way to think of three-way association is as the interaction of two-way association with a third factor. Where two factors in a three-way table are ordered, the association of these factors can be described by one of the models in the last two sections and the parameters of that model examined for changes with the third factor. Suppose, for example, that the training-and-error data of Table 13.1 had been collected for a second training method, thereby adding a third factor (Table 13.5). The amount of training and the number of errors (factors A and E) are ordered; the method of training (factor M) is not. An obvious question concerning these data is whether the sensitivity of performance to the amount of training is different for the two methods. In the discussion of the first method's results in Section 13.2, the magnitude of the AE association is measured by the uniform-association parameter. In the larger design, plausible questions are (1) is the association uniform for both training methods, and (2) if it is uniform, do the association parameters depend on the method?

Consider the data at level k of factor M. Within the two-way AE table, the conditional odds ratio is

$$\alpha_{ij}^{(k)} = \frac{\pi_{ijk}\pi_{i+1,j+1,k}}{\pi_{i+1,j,k}\pi_{i,j+1,k}}$$

The superscript (k) here indicates the training method to which the conditional-association parameters apply. The most general log-linear model for the association takes the saturated two-way model (Equation 13.7) and lets its parameters vary with k:

$$\log \alpha_{ij}^{(k)} = \tau^{(k)} + \tau_{A(i)}^{(k)} + \tau_{B(j)}^{(k)} + \tau_{AB(ij)}^{(k)} \qquad (13.8)$$

In contrast, the most restrictive association model is

$$\log \alpha_{ij}^{(k)} = 0 \qquad (13.9)$$

This model asserts that there is no association within the AE table at every level

TABLE 13.5
Data from Table 13.1 and the Results of a Second Training Method

		First Method				Second Method			
		0	1	2	≥3	0	1	2	≥3
	Low	15	14	10	45	3	4	33	111
Training	Moderate	46	26	14	30	8	7	10	11
	High	42	15	7	8	108	11	11	5

of M and is equivalent to the model $A \perp\!\!\!\perp E|M$. To answer questions about the task, one examines models that fall between these.

Two restrictions of Model 13.8 answer the questions raised above. The first concerns whether the association is uniform, that is, whether the dependence of $\alpha_{ij}^{(k)}$ on i and j can be dropped to give the model

$$\log \alpha_{ij}^{(k)} = \tau^{(k)} \qquad (13.10)$$

This model is known as the *heterogeneous uniform-association model*, since it asserts uniform association between A and E but allows the magnitude of association to vary with M. Denote the number of levels of A, E, and M by a, b, and c, respectively. The heterogeneous uniform-association model introduces c free parameters—the $\tau^{(k)}$—to the conditional-independence model of Equation 13.9. Since that model has $(a - 1)(b - 1)c$ degrees of freedom, Model 13.10 has $(ab - a - b)c$ degrees of freedom. The model is comparable to fitting the two-dimensional uniform-association model separately in each population.

For the example data, the heterogeneous uniform-association model cannot be rejected ($G^2(10) = 4.19$). One concludes that the association in each set of data is adequately summarized by a single parameter. The estimated logarithmic associations are

$$\hat{\tau}^{(1)} = -0.452 \quad \text{and} \quad \hat{\tau}^{(2)} = -1.144$$

Exponentiation gives an estimate of the odds ratios:

$$\hat{\alpha}_{ij}^{(1)} = 0.636 \quad \text{and} \quad \hat{\alpha}_{ij}^{(2)} = 0.319$$

Given that the heterogeneous uniform-association model fits, the second question is whether the amount of association is the same in both tables. If so, one would conclude that the amount of training modulates the error frequency to the same extent for both methods. Specifically, one tries to replace Model 13.10 by the model

$$\log \alpha_{ij}^{(k)} = \tau \qquad (13.11)$$

This model, which differs from Model 13.10 in that τ does not vary with k, is designated the *homogeneous uniform-association model*. Since it has only a single association parameter, it is tested on $(a - 1)(b - 1)c - 1$ degrees of freedom, 1 fewer than $A \perp\!\!\!\perp E|M$. This model does not fit Table 13.5 well, being rejected with $G^2(11) = 34.63$.

Models 13.10 and 13.11 are hierarchically related, with the heterogeneous uniform-association model being the more general. The difference in their fit is a test of identical association in the context of uniform association:

Homogeneous uniform association	$G^2(11) = 34.63$
Heterogeneous uniform association	$G^2(10) = 4.19$
Identical association	$\Delta G^2(1) = 30.44$

The failure of homogeneity implies a difference in $\tau^{(k)}$. This result answers the original question about the data: the relationship of training to performance is different for the two methods. Since $\tau^{(2)}$ is farther from zero than $\tau^{(1)}$, the association is greater for the second method.

The value of the ordered-category models becomes apparent when one compares this analysis to what one has to do when using unordered models. Without using the order, the only way to show a variation in association between the methods is to reject the model of no three-way association, $[AE][AM][EM]$, in favor of the saturated model, $[AEM]$. The former model is readily rejected with $G^2(6) = 34.21$, but there is no easy way to proceed from here. The interaction is not readily characterized. In contrast, the fit of the heterogeneous uniform-association model specifies exactly what the association is and, by reducing it to a single parameter $\tau^{(k)}$ at each level of k makes the effects easy to understand and explain. The power of the single degree of freedom test of the hypothesis $\tau^{(1)} = \tau^{(2)}$ to detect differences in ordered association is much greater than that of the test of the inexact hypothesis $[AE][AM][EM]$, which has 12 degrees of freedom. The ordered-association models express dependence with a minimum of parameters and a maximum of precision.

Of course, the analysis of conditional association is not always as clean as in this artificial example. Nevertheless, the description of an interaction as the modulation of a two-way model by a third factor is a powerful approach, which extends to more complex models. Any two-way association model can be repeated over a third factor with parameters fixed or varied. For example, suppose that an additive-association model suffices to describe the two-way effects of factors A and B at each level of the third factor, C

$$\log \alpha_{ij}^{(k)} = \tau^{(k)} + \tau_{A(i)}^{(k)} + \tau_{B(j)}^{(k)} \tag{13.12}$$

Then one can ask which, if any, of the three types of parameters in this model varies with k. Each combination gives rise to a different form of model. In particular, if the row effects are constant at all levels of k and the column effects change, then a *homogeneous row- and heterogeneous column-association model* results. Many other such models can be constructed. Table 13.6 lists the 14 models created by placing hierarchical restrictions of the parameters of Equation

TABLE 13.6

Associative Variation Models for a Three-way Table
with Two Ordered Factors (A and B) and One Unordered
Factor (C) and in which the AB Association is Additive

Model	Model for log $\alpha_{ij}^{(k)}$	Degrees of Freedom
Conditional independence	0	$(a-1)(b-1)c$
Uniform association		
Homogeneous	τ	$(a-1)(b-1)c - 1$
Heterogeneous	$\tau^{(k)}$	$(ab-a-b)c$
Row association effects		
Homogeneous	$\tau + \tau_{A(i)}$	$(a-1)[(b-1)c - 1]$
Proportionally heterogeneous	$\tau^{(k)} + \tau_{A(i)}$	$(ab-a-b)c - a - 2$
Heterogeneous	$\tau^{(k)} + \tau_{A(i)}^{(k)}$	$(a-1)(b-2)c$
Column association effects		
Homogeneous	$\tau + \tau_{B(j)}$	$(b-1)[(a-1)c - 1]$
Proportionally heterogeneous	$\tau^{(k)} + \tau_{B(j)}$	$(ab-a-b)c - b - 2$
Heterogeneous	$\tau^{(k)} + \tau_{B(j)}^{(k)}$	$(a-2)(b-1)c$
Additive association effects		
Homogeneous	$\tau + \tau_{A(i)} + \tau_{B(j)}$	$(a-1)(b-1)(c-1)$ $+ (a-2)(b-2)$
Proportionally heterogeneous	$\tau^{(k)} + \tau_{A(i)} + \tau_{B(j)}$	$[(a-1)(b-1)-1](c-1)$ $+ (a-2)(b-2)$
Heterogeneous row effects	$\tau^{(k)} + \tau_{A(i)}^{(k)} + \tau_{B(j)}$	$[(a-1)c-1](b-2)$
Heterogeneous column effects	$\tau^{(k)} + \tau_{A(i)} + \tau_{B(j)}^{(k)}$	$(a-2)[(b-1)c-1]$
Both effects heterogeneous	$\tau^{(k)} + \tau_{A(i)}^{(k)} + \tau_{B(j)}^{(k)}$	$(a-2)(b-2)c$

13.12. All these models are descriptions of conditional association, in the same spirit as the more detailed discussion above. The numbers of degrees of freedom in Table 13.6 are obtained by subtracting the number of free parameters from $(a - 1)(b - 1)c$, which is the number of degrees of freedom associated with the conditional independence hypothesis $A \perp\!\!\!\perp B|C$.

The analysis described in this section does not treat the third factor as ordered. Introduction of a third ordered factor increases both the number of potential models and the precision of the hypotheses that can be tested. If there is no logical reason to select one factor over which the association of the other two factors is modulated, one must abandon the conditional-association models and look at all associations at once. There are many such *partial-association models*. Suppose that no three-way association is present (i.e., that $[AB][AC][BC]$ fits).

In this model, there are three sets of two-way odds ratios, $\alpha_{AB(ij)}$, $\alpha_{AC(ik)}$, and $\alpha_{BC(jk)}$. Each set can be described by the saturated additive model of Equation 13.8 or by some specialization of it. Then, one can ask, first, how much these two-way models can be simplified and, second, whether some of the parameters are identical in different marginal configurations. For example, one might find that the parameter $\tau_{C(k)}$ is the same in both the model for α_{AC} and the model for α_{BC}. As in the example above, the possibilities are more formidable in the abstract than they are in a real situation, since the constraints of the problem usually eliminate many of the possibilities. A full discussion of these partial-association models is longer than can be included here, so the reader is referred to the references cited above.

13.5. LATENT SCALE VALUES

When one works with an ordered factor, there is a strong temptation to place the categories on a continuum by assigning numbers to them. Such numbers can describe the categories, measure their spacing, and be used in further analysis. If there are external reasons to assign particular values, one may want to use them, but ordinarily such justification is not available. Without it, the most direct way to pick numbers is to use integers, numbering the categories 1, 2, and so on. However, in many situations equal spacing is unrealistic and is not in the spirit of an ordinal analysis. A better solution is to derive the category values from the data. They may be based on the marginal distribution, on the association between factors, or on both. The additive-association models in the last two sections and the multiplicative-association models of Section 11.3 give ways to assign scale parameters based on the association. These scale values are generated by the analysis of the association and are not substantially affected by the marginal distribution of the data. In contrast, the approach to the ordering discussed in this section uses the marginal distributions to assign values to the categories and then employs these values to examine ordinal association. Of course, using the marginal distributions in this way requires that they have meaning. Thus, the paired-question data in Table 13.2 are appropriate for this type of analysis, while the training-and-error data in Table 13.1, which involves three populations, are more questionable.

Scale values based on the marginal distributions are derived from the relative frequencies of the categories. Because the categories are ordered, their probabilities can be combined over the ordering to form a cumulative distribution. By summing the proportion of observations in the individual cells, one obtains the proportion at or below each category, the scale value of a category is a function of its position in the cumulated distribution. However, the cumulative frequency at or below a category represents the upper edge of that category. If one wants a probability to stand for a category, a better choice is one that is central to the category. Hence, one is directed to the median of the category, that is, to the cumulative probability below its probabilistic midpoint. Calculation of this number amounts to adding one-half the probability in a cell to the cumulative probability below it. If the ith category has frequency x_i and observed proportion $p_i = x_i/x_+$, then this number is

$$r_i = \frac{p_i}{2} + \sum_{j<i} p_j \qquad (13.13)$$

As an example, consider statement B from the paired-question data of Table 13.2. Of the 357 subjects, 84 strongly disagreed with the statement. This is a proportion of 0.235, and so is assigned the value $r_1 = 0.235/2 = 0.118$. The second category contains a proportion $98/357 = 0.275$, so $r_2 = 0.235 + 0.275/2 = 0.373$. These calculations are shown in the top four lines of Table 13.7 (along with several other measures that are discussed later).

A more sophisticated way to view the values of Equation 13.13 is as a reflection of an unobserved or latent continuous distribution. Let X be a continuous random variable over some range. Cut this range into as many intervals as there are categories in such a way that the probabilities in the intervals equal the category probabilities. Since the probability in an interval of a continuous distribution can be pictured as areas under a density function, as in Figure 13.1, the positions of the cutpoints are adjusted so that the areas under this distribution agree with the observed proportions in the data. Adopting this description requires an ordering of the categories; were they not ordered it would make no sense to place them along a single dimension.

TABLE 13.7
Scale Values Assigned to the Marginal Distribution
of Statement B from Table 13.2

	Response			
	Strongly Disagree	Weakly Disagree	Weakly Agree	Strongly Agree
Frequency	84	98	124	51
Probability	0.235	0.275	0.347	0.143
Uniform distribution				
Cumulative probability	0.235	0.510	0.857	1.000
Ridits	0.118	0.374	0.683	0.929
Normal distribution				
Upper cutpoints	−0.721	0.025	1.068	∞
Probits	−1.187	−0.325	0.477	1.465
Logistic distribution				
Upper cutpoints	−1.179	0.039	1.792	∞
Logits	−2.015	−0.521	0.770	2.565

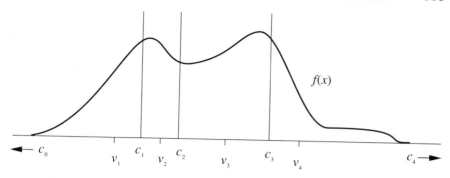

FIGURE 13.1.   Cumulative probability cutpoints placed on the density
function of an arbitrary continuous distribution

The values that represent the categories themselves, rather than the divisions
between them, are located in the middle of the intervals. The point representing
category i, denoted v_i is chosen such that the amount of the distribution below v_i
equals the probability r_i from in Equation 13.13. This procedure gives a finite
value for the rightmost category, which is a more useful value than the unspecified upper cutpoint.

More formally, let the density function of the random variable X be $f(x)$. For a
categories, assign points on the abcissa $c_0, c_1, \ldots, c_a$ such that the probability
of category a_i equals the area under $f(x)$ between c_{i-1} and c_i. The end points c_0
and c_a are placed far enough out to include the entire distribution; in effect $c_0 =
-\infty$ and $c_a = \infty$. In formal notation, the probability is the integral between the
cutpoints,

$$P(a_i) = \int_{c_{i-1}}^{c_i} f(x)\ dx \tag{13.14}$$

Similarly, the category values v_i are defined so that for r_i from Equation 13.13,

$$r_i = \int_{-\infty}^{v_i} f(x)\ dx \tag{13.15}$$

Within psychology or education, the use of a latent continuous variable to
represent a categorization is familiar. It underlies Thurstone's scaling model
(Thurstone, 1927; Thurstone, 1959) and is the basis for many models of ability in
psychological testing (e.g., Lord & Novick, 1968, Chapters 15 and 16). In the
study of perception, signal detection theory (Green & Swets, 1966/1974) is
based on latent continuous variables, and the resulting model has been used to

relate confidence ratings to continuous scores, with both detection and recognition data.

To find c_i and v_i, the distribution of X must be specified. Three distributions are commonly used, the uniform, the normal, and the logistic. These generate measures known as *ridits*, *probits*, and *logits*, respectively.

1. *The uniform distribution: ridits.* If X is uniformly distributed on the unit interval, it has the density function

$$f(x) = \begin{cases} 1 & \text{for } 0 \le x \le 1 \\ 0 & \text{otherwise} \end{cases}$$

This density function is a rectangle of unit height stretching between 0 and 1. Sections of this distribution are rectangles with a spacing along the abcissa equal to their area (Figure 13.2). In particular, the scale values are the same as the probabilities r_i. They are known as *ridits*, a name deriving from the phrase "*r*elative to an *id*entified *d*istribution" plus the particle "-it" (Bross, 1958).

Although it is simple and direct, the ridit approach is limited by this uniform distribution, which has the same spacing at the center and the extremes. For many natural situations, extreme scores are less likely than moderate ones, and small percentage changes near the ends of the distribution represent larger underlying differences than do comparable changes near the center. To represent this situation, one turns to a bell-shaped density function that falls off at the ends.

2. *The normal distribution: probits.* The natural choice for a center-weighted distribution is the normal distribution. This distribution satisfies the concerns just mentioned, being more responsive to small differences of probability in its tails. Normal distributions depend on a mean and a variance, but because the distribution here is only inferred from its probabilities, its center and scale are arbitrary. One conventionally sets the mean to 0 and the variance to 1, giving X the

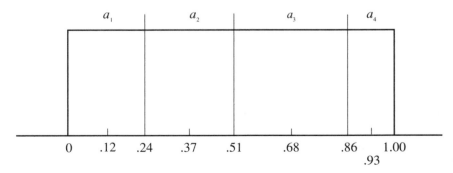

FIGURE 13.2. Cumulative probability cutpoints and category medians (ridits) placed on the density function of a uniform distribution

standard normal form. With this choice of distribution, values of the cutpoints c_i or the median interval points v_i can be looked up in a normal-distribution table. The analysis is shown in Table 13.7 and illustrated in Figure 13.3. The first category contains probability 0.235, so the first division cuts off the lower 23.5% of the distribution. Reference to the table in Appendix A.4 indicates that this abcissa is -0.722 (the value in Table 13.7 differs by 0.001 because intermediate calculations were carried to more than 3 places). Other values are obtained similarly. Again, to represent the categories themselves, values more central to the categories are useful. These scores are usually known as *probits* and are obtained by transforming the ridit scores to normal-distribution abcissas (Finney, 1971).

The probit model is widely used as a transformation of probabilities into scale values, due to the importance of the normal distribution as a theoretical and empirical construct. The examples cited above of applications of latent-distribution models largely use this distribution. The principal problem with the normal distribution is computational: there is no closed-form algebraic expression for its cumulative distribution. Hence, in calculating the probit values, one must either work from tables such as Appendix A.4 or use an approximation to the distribution. For numerical purposes, accurate approximations are available (e.g., Brophy, 1983; Press, Flannery, Teukolsky, & Vetterling, 1987; Zelen & Severo, 1964, Section 26.2), which effectively eliminate any computational problem. However, the lack of a closed expression sometimes complicates theoretical work.

3. *The logistic distribution: logits.* To avoid the algebraic difficulties of the normal distribution while keeping its general form, it is sometimes replaced by a similarly shaped but more analytically tractable distribution known as the *logistic distribution* (for properties, see Johnson & Kotz, 1970, Chapter 22). This distribution has the density function

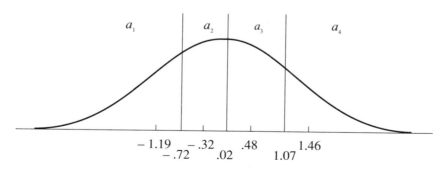

FIGURE 13.3. Cumulative probability cutpoints and category medians (probits) placed on the density function of a normal distribution

$$f(x) = \frac{e^{-(x-\alpha)/\beta}}{(1 + e^{-(x-\alpha)/\beta})^2} \tag{13.16}$$

and the cumulative distribution function

$$P(X \le x) = \frac{1}{1 + e^{-(x-\alpha)/\beta}} \tag{13.17}$$

It depends on the parameters α and β, which determine its center and its spread, respectively. One standardization of the logistic distribution sets these to 0 and 1. Then Equation 13.17 is inverted to give

$$x = \log \frac{P(X \le x)}{P(X > x)} \tag{13.18}$$

The latent values associated with the cutpoints or categories under this distribution are known as logits.

Values of the logits, for both cutpoints and category medians, are shown in Table 13.7. Although the logistic distribution is similar in shape to the normal distribution, the numbers in Table 13.7 are different. This occurs because when $\alpha = 0$ and $\beta = 1$ (as implied by Equation 13.18), the standard logistic distribution has a standard deviation of $\pi/\sqrt{3} = 1.814$, not unity. If the values of the logits are scaled down by this amount, an adequate approximation to the normal abcissas is obtained. An even better match is given by the correction $15\pi/(16\sqrt{3}) = 1.700$. The importance of this relationship is not to give an approximation for the probits, but to show that a model for the logits looks a lot like a model for the probits. If the data depend on a latent normal variable, they are well fitted by a logit model.

The logits have already played an important role in this book: in Chapter 7 the logit transformation was used as a way to convert a binary classification to a single number. Essentially, these are models for the category cutpoints in a logistic distribution. This characterization suggests one reason why the logit models are useful: they express the data relative to a distribution with attenuated tails. As referred to a latent distribution, however, the logistic model serves mainly as a substitute for the normal distribution, and with the advent of greater (and cheaper) computational power, its importance has diminished.

The three distribution-based scoring procedures can be used as the first step in analyzing multifactor data. There are several ways to do this, two of which are described here and a third in the next section. The simplest approach to a multifactor design is to replace the distribution of an ordered factor by the mean value of the scores derived from the marginal distribution. Then these means are related to the other factors of the design. For example, consider the statement-rating data in Table 13.2. From the ridits for question B in Table 13.7 calculate a mean score for each level of question A. For the 40 subjects who rated question A

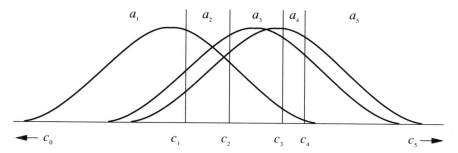

FIGURE 13.4. Normal distributions representing three subpopulations placed on a single axis

as *strongly agree*, the question B frequencies are 2, 10, 15, and 13, and the mean ridit score is

$$\left(\frac{2}{40}\right)(0.118) + \left(\frac{10}{40}\right)(0.374) + \left(\frac{15}{40}\right)(0.683) + \left(\frac{13}{40}\right)(0.929) = 0.657$$

Similar scores for the other rows are 0.616, 0.444, and 0.448. The generally declining values of these averages indicate a net negative relationship between the questions. A more extensive example using mean ridit scores, including statistical tests, appears in Section 13.7.

Another approach to the multiway table generalizes from one to several populations the division of a distribution by cutpoints. Each population is partitioned by a series of cuts, but the same dimension and the same divisions are assumed to underlie all populations. Figure 13.4 shows the picture for 3 populations (b_1, b_2, and b_3), 5 categories (a_1 to a_5), and a normal distribution. Differences among the populations are characterized by differences in the forms of their distributions. These usually have the same shape, but can differ in a few parameters, most typically only in their mean. With normal distributions, the result is Thurstone scaling. The means of these distributions can then be fitted by a model to describe interpopulation differences (Bock, 1975). Because the populations are represented by separate distributions, this approach does not require that the population factor be sampled or that it be ordered.

13.6 LATENT NORMAL DISTRIBUTIONS

Another way to extend the latent-distribution models to multiple factors is to move from univariate to multivariate distributions. This idea goes back to some of the earliest work on frequency tables by Karl Pearson (1901). He treated a 2 × 2 table of frequencies as the consequence of two orthogonal cuts in a pair of latent variables having a bivariate normal distribution. Figure 13.5 shows the contours of such a distribution, as seen from above, with two cutpoints, thus creating the four probabilities of a 2 × 2 table. The bivariate normal distribution depends on five parameters: two means, two variances, and a correlation. As with the distribution underlying the probits, this distribution is not observed directly, so its mean can be put at (0,0) and its variances set to 1, giving the density function

$$f(x,y) = \frac{1}{2\pi\sqrt{1-\rho^2}} \exp\left(-\frac{1}{2} \frac{x^2 - 2\rho xy + y^2}{1 - \rho^2}\right) \tag{13.19}$$

This distribution depends on a single parameter, the correlation ρ, which expresses the association between the categorizations. The contour ellipses in Figure 13.5 have been drawn to correspond to a positive correlation. Pearson called the estimate of ρ derived from this picture the *tetrachoric correlation coefficient*. The tetrachoric correlation model has one parameter to express the association in a 2 × 2 table, so it is saturated.

More generally, for an $a \times b$ table, $a - 1$ cuts in the underlying distribution are needed to express the rows and $b - 1$ to express the columns. A single correlation parameter still expresses the association. The estimate of this correla-

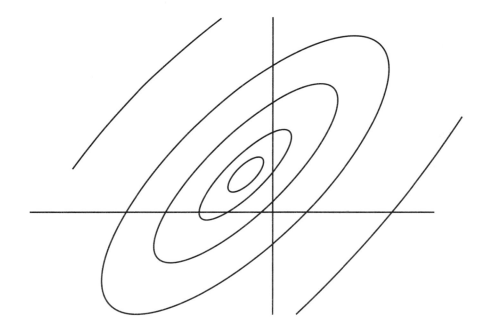

FIGURE 13.5. A bivariate normal distribution (shown in contour) cut along both axes to form a 2 × 2 categorization

tion is known as the *polychoric correlation coefficient*. The underlying correlation and its estimate are denoted by ρ_{PC} and $\hat{\rho}_{PC}$ in the discussion below, regardless of whether 2 or more categories are involved.

Before one adopts the polychoric-correlation model, its appropriateness to the situation should be considered. An underlying bivariate normal distribution is a strong assumption and does not apply to all ordered tables. It may make sense when the categories derive from a continuous variable and could in principle be measured more accurately—for example, height measured as tall or short, performance as good, average, or poor, or the error distribution in the example of Table 13.1. It is less obvious that the model applies to categories where the presence of an underlying continuum is more doubtful—for example, a measure of health (well, sick, or dying) or of opinion. It does not apply when the marginal frequencies for either category are determined by the experimenter, for example, as in the amount-of-training example. The validity of a model based on underlying continua was argued quite vehemently during the early years of statistics. Much of the discussion took the form of a comparison of the tetrachoric coefficient with the less theoretical measures of association proposed by Yule (the coefficients of association and of colligation—see Equations 9.10 and 9.11). For a sampling of these arguments, see Yule (1912) and the somewhat ill-tempered Pearson & Heron (1913). As one might expect, neither position can be accepted or rejected conclusively.

In spite of its restrictiveness, a latent normal distribution is often a reasonable model for an ordered table. The situation is probably best viewed as one of model fitting. Where the latent continua have actual significance or imply a sensible description, they can be used profitably. When the basis for the ordering is weak, where an assumption of latent normality is unreasonable (perhaps because of curvilinear association), or where some of the factors are not sampled, one should turn to other methods. Except when $a = b = 2$, the polychoric-correlation model is unsaturated, so its fit can be tested by comparing observed and predicted values with X^2 or G^2 statistics.

Estimation of ρ_{PC} has been approached in several ways. The full model depends on $a + b - 1$ parameters: $a - 1$ cutpoints for the first distribution, $b - 1$ for the second, and one correlation. Optimally, these should be estimated simultaneously, using a criterion such as likelihood maximization. It is tempting to simplify the problem by determining the cutpoints from the marginal frequencies before estimating ρ_{PC}. One locates cutpoints as if finding probits in the margins, and then determines $\hat{\rho}_{PC}$. The second part of the process is not simple, and it involves more sophisticated mathematical methods than can be covered here (Lancaster & Hamdan, 1964; see Martinson & Hamdan, 1975, and Beardwood, 1977, for a computer routine). When the polychoric-correlation model fits, this two-stage procedure is not substantially worse than simultaneous estimation (Olson, 1979).

Several of the other ordered-association models are similar to the polychoric-correlation model and often can be used in its stead. Consider the multiplicative-association model described in Section 11.3 (Goodman, 1981b, 1985). In this model the expected frequencies are

$$\log \mu_{ij} = \lambda + \lambda_{A(i)} + \lambda_{B(j)} + \phi \xi_{A(i)} \xi_{B(j)}$$

(Equation 11.5). Exponentiating this equation to get rid of the logarithms and using β_A and β_B to parameterize the marginal frequencies gives the frequency model

$$\mu_{ij} = \beta_{A(i)} \beta_{B(j)} \exp(\phi \xi_{A(i)} \xi_{B(j)}) \tag{13.20}$$

The normal density function underlying the polychoric-correlation model (Equation 13.19) at the point (x_i, y_j) can be rewritten with a bit of algebraic manipulation as

$$f(x_i, y_j) = \frac{1}{2\pi\sqrt{1-\rho^2}} \exp\left(\frac{-x_i^2}{2(1-\rho^2)}\right) \exp\left(\frac{-y_j^2}{2(1-\rho^2)}\right) \exp\left(\frac{\rho x_i y_j}{1-\rho^2}\right)$$

$$= b(x_i)b(y_j) \exp\left[\left(\frac{\rho}{1-\rho^2}\right) x_i y_j\right] \tag{13.21}$$

where

$$b(w) = \frac{1}{\sqrt{2\pi}\sqrt{1-\rho^2}} \exp\left(\frac{-w^2}{2(1-\rho^2)}\right)$$

The variables x_i and y_j interact only through the last term of Equation 13.21. The theoretical frequency in this cell is roughly proportional to this density. Equations 13.20 and 13.21 have a similar form. They are identical if

$$\beta_{A(i)} = b(x_i), \quad \beta_{B(j)} = b(y_j)$$

$$\xi_{A(i)} = x_i, \quad \xi_{B(j)} = y_j$$

and

$$\phi = \frac{\rho}{1-\rho^2} \tag{13.22}$$

This similarity implies that the multiplicative-association model should fit data that agree with the polychoric-correlation model.

Equation 13.22 gives a way to approximate the polychoric correlation with the multiplicative-association model. If one has a value of $\hat{\phi}$ from fitting the latter model, using the standardization of ξ_A and ξ_B to null means and unit variances, then Equation 13.22 can be inverted to obtain an estimate of ρ:

$$\hat{\rho}_\phi = \frac{\sqrt{1+4\hat{\phi}^2} - 1}{2\hat{\phi}} \tag{13.23}$$

This value is a reasonable approximation to the true correlation.† This transformation was mentioned in Chapter 11 (Equation 11.9) without explaining its link to the normal distribution.

Another estimate of ρ is obtained from the scale values ξ_A and ξ_B. These values indicate the spacing of the categories and under the polychoric-correlation model are comparable to abscissas of a normal distribution. One uses them with the observed proportions to calculate a Pearson correlation coefficient. Under the distribution-based standardization of ξ_A and ξ_B, the correlation is estimated by

$$\hat{\rho}_\xi = \sum_{\text{cells}} \xi_{A(i)}\xi_{B(j)}p_{ij} \qquad (13.24)$$

As an example, take the two statements in Table 13.2. Both categorizations are ordered and they are jointly sampled, so a latent bivariate model is plausible. The uniform-association model does not fit these data ($X^2(8) = 20.75$), but the multiplicative-association model is satisfactory. The estimated value of ϕ is 0.373, so Equation 13.23 gives the estimate $\hat{\rho}_\phi = -0.33$. The association parameters are $-1.71, -1.45, 0.52$, and 0.76 for the rows and $-1.36, -0.05, 0.06$, and 1.98 for the columns. These give $\hat{\rho}_\xi = -0.35$, which is nearly the same as $\hat{\rho}_\phi$. The negative values of these estimates reflect the association of low and high scores in the original table.

The multiplicative-association model is more general than the polychoric-correlation model, since $\beta_{A(i)}$ and $\beta_{B(j)}$ in Equation 13.20 are free whereas $b(x_i)$ and $b(y_j)$ in Equation 13.21 are determined by x_i, y_j, and ρ. So the polychoric-correlation model approximately implies the multiplicative-association model, but since the multiplicative-association model is more general, the reverse is not true. Of course, if the multiplicative-association model fails to fit, one can conclude that the polychoric-correlation model is almost certain to fail as well. One should also remember that both models describe the association as a univariate structure. If data have a multicomponent structure, as in the models of Section 11.5, a single association coefficient is inadequate. When this happens,

---

†Goodman (1981b) has suggested that this estimate of ρ is improved by correcting for the blocking of a continuous distribution into categories, using Sheppard's correction (see Kendall & Stewart, 1977, Section 3.18). This correction, which depends on the scale values of the extreme categories, is

$$\hat{\rho}'_\phi = \frac{12\,\hat{\rho}_\phi}{\sqrt{\left[12 - \left(\dfrac{\xi_{A(a)} - \xi_{A(1)}}{a-1}\right)^2\right]\left[12 - \left(\dfrac{\xi_{B(b)} + \xi_{B(1)}}{b-1}\right)^2\right]}}$$

Presumably $\xi_{A(a)}$ and $\xi_{B(b)}$ are the largest of their respective sets of values and $\xi_{A(1)}$ and $\xi_{B(1)}$ the smallest—otherwise there is trouble with the concept of an underlying normal distribution. This correction also applies to the estimate $\hat{\rho}_D$ defined in Equation 13.24.

the two estimates of ρ from Equations 13.23 and 13.24 may be unstable and can differ appreciably.

The polychoric-correlation model extends readily to multivariate tables. If the table has v classifications, one can infers a multivariate latent variable with v components, $\mathbf{X} = [x_1, x_2, \ldots, x_v]$. Under the assumption of normality, this variable has zero means, unit variances, and a correlation matrix $\mathbf{P}$. This correlation matrix expresses the relationships among the variables and can be estimated from the original data. Once $\mathbf{P}$ has been estimated, procedures appropriate to correlations from continuous data can be used. To take one example, one may apply the equivalent of a factor-analysis model by asserting that $\mathbf{X}$ can be written as a linear transformation of a smaller vector $\mathbf{Y}$ with fewer components,

$$\mathbf{X} = \mathbf{\Lambda Y} + \mathbf{e}$$

(Bock & Lieberman, 1970; Christoffersson, 1975; Muthén, 1978). Here $\mathbf{\Lambda}$ is an unknown matrix and $\mathbf{e}$ is a vector of errors that are uncorrelated with $\mathbf{Y}$. This equation has an implication for the form of $\mathbf{P}$, because it means that the covariance matrix of $\mathbf{X}$ is

$$\mathbf{\Sigma_X} = \mathbf{\Lambda \Sigma_Y \Lambda'} + \mathbf{\Sigma_e}$$

Details of the heavily computational algorithms that estimate the parameters of this model go well beyond this book and are found in the papers cited above. The model can be extended to accommodate multiple populations by supposing that the distributions associated with different populations are centered at different means in a multivariate extension of the picture shown in Figure 13.4 (Muthén, 1979, 1981; Muthén & Christoffersson, 1981).

13.7.   WEIGHTED LEAST-SQUARES METHODS†

The weighted least-squares procedures of Chapter 12 can be applied to ordered categories. Many of these applications give alternate ways to fit the models discussed earlier. For example, the association models described in Sections 13.2 to 13.4 are models for the odds ratio. Hence, to fit them, the function definition step of the weighted least-squares procedure is used to construct a vector containing log α_{ij}, then an appropriate linear model is fitted to this vector. The weighted least-squares approach does not change the basic model: only the method of estimation and the specific tests are different. Because no new concepts are involved, this type of application is not covered further here (see Problems 13.9 and 13.10).

Instead, consider an approach that uses of the power of the weighted least-

---

†This section depends on Chapter 12 and can be skipped if that chapter has been omitted.

squares formulation to fit a model that is not log-linear. The problem, which was mentioned briefly at the end of Section 13.5, is to fit a mean-ridit model to data from an ordered series of populations (Semenya & Koch, 1979; Semenya, Koch, Stokes, & Forthofer, 1983; Williams & Grizzle, 1972). Specifically, consider a set of a ordered populations, for each of which the frequencies of b ordered categories have been obtained. The training-and-errors data of Table 13.1 are an example: the training conditions are populations, the number of errors is a measure on those populations, and both factors are ordered. The overall scheme of the analysis uses the ordering of the factors in two ways. First, ridit (or other) scores are assigned to the within-population categories, based on the marginal distribution. Next, each population is reduced to a single score, its mean value on the ridit measure. Finally, the ordering of the populations is used to select a rational model to fit to these function values.

Before these operations are expressed in matrix form, it is helpful to step through an example, with the data in Table 13.1. The sequence of calculations is shown in Table 13.8. First, ridits are calculated that indicate the relative position of the error scores. Because the number of observations from each population has no intrinsic meaning, the three populations are given equal weight. In effect, one treats the populations as if the samples were of equal size. This is done by averaging the conditional probabilities in each row, $p_{j|i}$, over the three populations to give marginal probability scores, which are converted to ridits. These steps are shown in the top three panels of Table 13.8. Alternatively, one can calculate ridits in each row and average them to get the same result. From these scores, mean ridit scores are assigned to each of the populations,

$$y_i = \sum_j r_j p_{j|i} \qquad (13.25)$$

(Table 13.8, bottom). These scores give a single-number representation to the error frequencies in each population. As plotted in Figure 13.6, they show how the prevalence of errors changes with the amount of training. The average value of these scores is not important—the way that they were constructed forces their mean to be $\frac{1}{2}$. However, the relationships among them can be tested in any many ways. The ordering of the populations is useful here: it is helpful to divide the pattern displayed by the mean ridit scores into straight-line (linear) and curved (quadratic) components. The graph suggests that the linear component is significantly nonzero and negative (the net slope of the observations is downward) and that there is no quadratic trend (the line is essentially straight).

To complete the tests, the full weighted least-squares machinery is needed. The linear and quadratic components are functions whose values are tested. Calculation of these values is slightly different from that in Chapter 12. There the transformations were applied to each population separately. Now, because the ridits combine information across populations, they must be transformed simultaneously. The process is easiest to understand by building up the matrix opera-

TABLE 13.8
Construction of Mean Ridit Scores for the Data in Table 13.1

Original Data x_{ij}

		Number of Errors Made				
		0	1	2	≥3	
	Low	15	14	10	45	84
Training	Moderate	46	26	14	30	116
	High	42	15	7	8	72

Within-population Conditional Probabilities $p_{j|i}$

	0	1	2	≥3	
Low	0.179	0.167	0.119	0.536	1.0
Moderate	0.397	0.224	0.121	0.259	1.0
High	0.583	0.208	0.097	0.111	1.0

Calculation of Average Group Ridits

	0	1	2	≥3
Mean conditional probabilities	0.386	0.200	0.112	0.302
Cumulative mean probabilities	0.386	0.586	0.698	1.000
Ridits	0.193	0.486	0.642	0.849

Calculation of Subpopulation Scores y_i (Equation 13.25)

$$y_1 = (0.193)(0.179) + (0.486)(0.167) + (0.642)(0.119) + (0.849)(0.536)$$

$$= 0.647$$

$$y_2 = 0.482$$

$$y_3 = 0.371$$

tions in parallel with the calculation in Table 13.8. First, the conditional probabilities from the three distributions are combined into a single composite vector

$$\mathbf{p} = [0.178, \ 0.167, \ 0.119, \ 0.536, \ 0.397, \ 0.224, \ 0.121, \ 0.259, \ 0.583,$$

$$0.208, \ 0.097, \ 0.111]'$$

The mean marginal error distribution is created from this vector by the transformation $\mathbf{Ap}$, with

$$\mathbf{A} = \begin{bmatrix} \frac{1}{3} & 0 & 0 & 0 & \frac{1}{3} & 0 & 0 & 0 & \frac{1}{3} & 0 & 0 & 0 \\ 0 & \frac{1}{3} & 0 & 0 & 0 & \frac{1}{3} & 0 & 0 & 0 & \frac{1}{3} & 0 & 0 \\ 0 & 0 & \frac{1}{3} & 0 & 0 & 0 & \frac{1}{3} & 0 & 0 & 0 & \frac{1}{3} & 0 \\ 0 & 0 & 0 & \frac{1}{3} & 0 & 0 & 0 & \frac{1}{3} & 0 & 0 & 0 & \frac{1}{3} \end{bmatrix} \quad (13.26)$$

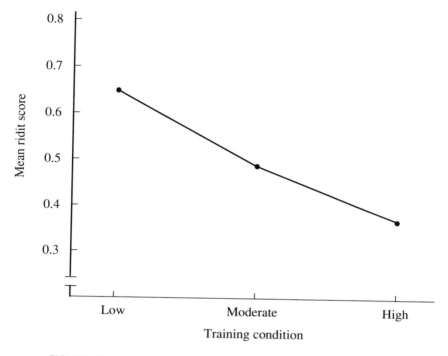

FIGURE 13.6. Error score for three training conditions of Table 13.1

The result is a 4-vector containing the average marginal proportion of the population that falls into each error category, 0.386, 0.200, 0.112, and 0.302. To produce the ridits, this vector is cumulated to the midpoint of each category by multiplication on the left by the matrix

$$\begin{bmatrix} \frac{1}{2} & 0 & 0 & 0 \\ 1 & \frac{1}{2} & 0 & 0 \\ 1 & 1 & \frac{1}{2} & 0 \\ 1 & 1 & 1 & \frac{1}{2} \end{bmatrix} \qquad (13.27)$$

(cf. Equation 13.13). This product gives the ridit vector, which for the example is $[0.193, 0.486, 0.642, 0.849]'$.

One can combine the two operations needed to get the ridits into a single transformation matrix that is the product of Matrices 13.26 and 13.27. However, this does not complete the transformation to the y_i. The functions require both the ridits v_i and the original $p_{j|i}$. To preserve these proportions, the original vector of 12 observations cannot be reduced to 4 ridits, but must be expanded into a 16-vector in which the first 12 entries reproduce the $p_{j|i}$ and the last 4 are the ridits.

The transformation that does this is $\mathbf{A}_1\mathbf{P}$, where $\mathbf{A}_1$ combines the product of Matrices 13.27 and 13.26 with a 12 × 12 identity matrix:

$$\mathbf{A}_1 = \begin{bmatrix}
1 & 0 & 0 & 0 & 0 & 0 & 0 & 0 & 0 & 0 & 0 & 0 \\
0 & 1 & 0 & 0 & 0 & 0 & 0 & 0 & 0 & 0 & 0 & 0 \\
0 & 0 & 1 & 0 & 0 & 0 & 0 & 0 & 0 & 0 & 0 & 0 \\
0 & 0 & 0 & 1 & 0 & 0 & 0 & 0 & 0 & 0 & 0 & 0 \\
0 & 0 & 0 & 0 & 1 & 0 & 0 & 0 & 0 & 0 & 0 & 0 \\
0 & 0 & 0 & 0 & 0 & 1 & 0 & 0 & 0 & 0 & 0 & 0 \\
0 & 0 & 0 & 0 & 0 & 0 & 1 & 0 & 0 & 0 & 0 & 0 \\
0 & 0 & 0 & 0 & 0 & 0 & 0 & 1 & 0 & 0 & 0 & 0 \\
0 & 0 & 0 & 0 & 0 & 0 & 0 & 0 & 1 & 0 & 0 & 0 \\
0 & 0 & 0 & 0 & 0 & 0 & 0 & 0 & 0 & 1 & 0 & 0 \\
0 & 0 & 0 & 0 & 0 & 0 & 0 & 0 & 0 & 0 & 1 & 0 \\
0 & 0 & 0 & 0 & 0 & 0 & 0 & 0 & 0 & 0 & 0 & 1 \\
\frac{1}{6} & 0 & 0 & 0 & \frac{1}{6} & 0 & 0 & 0 & \frac{1}{6} & 0 & 0 & 0 \\
\frac{1}{3} & \frac{1}{6} & 0 & 0 & \frac{1}{3} & \frac{1}{6} & 0 & 0 & \frac{1}{3} & \frac{1}{6} & 0 & 0 \\
\frac{1}{3} & \frac{1}{3} & \frac{1}{6} & 0 & \frac{1}{3} & \frac{1}{3} & \frac{1}{6} & 0 & \frac{1}{3} & \frac{1}{3} & \frac{1}{6} & 0 \\
\frac{1}{3} & \frac{1}{3} & \frac{1}{3} & \frac{1}{6} & \frac{1}{3} & \frac{1}{3} & \frac{1}{3} & \frac{1}{6} & \frac{1}{3} & \frac{1}{3} & \frac{1}{3} & \frac{1}{6}
\end{bmatrix}$$

This transformation delivers both the $p_{j|i}$ and the ridits.

Now comes Equation 13.25. This is a sum of products. The set of standard transformations defined in Section 12.2 does not include products, but these are calculated indirectly by summing logarithms (recall that $\exp[\log A + \log B] = AB$). Using this trick, the complete transformation to mean ridit scores is

$$\mathbf{y} = \mathbf{A}_3\exp[\mathbf{A}_2\log(\mathbf{A}_1\mathbf{p})] \tag{13.28}$$

where $\mathbf{A}_1$ is given above,

$$\mathbf{A}_2 = \begin{bmatrix}
1 & 0 & 0 & 0 & 0 & 0 & 0 & 0 & 0 & 0 & 0 & 0 & 1 & 0 & 0 & 0 \\
0 & 1 & 0 & 0 & 0 & 0 & 0 & 0 & 0 & 0 & 0 & 0 & 0 & 1 & 0 & 0 \\
0 & 0 & 1 & 0 & 0 & 0 & 0 & 0 & 0 & 0 & 0 & 0 & 0 & 0 & 1 & 0 \\
0 & 0 & 0 & 1 & 0 & 0 & 0 & 0 & 0 & 0 & 0 & 0 & 0 & 0 & 0 & 1 \\
0 & 0 & 0 & 0 & 1 & 0 & 0 & 0 & 0 & 0 & 0 & 0 & 1 & 0 & 0 & 0 \\
0 & 0 & 0 & 0 & 0 & 1 & 0 & 0 & 0 & 0 & 0 & 0 & 0 & 1 & 0 & 0 \\
0 & 0 & 0 & 0 & 0 & 0 & 1 & 0 & 0 & 0 & 0 & 0 & 0 & 0 & 1 & 0 \\
0 & 0 & 0 & 0 & 0 & 0 & 0 & 1 & 0 & 0 & 0 & 0 & 0 & 0 & 0 & 1 \\
0 & 0 & 0 & 0 & 0 & 0 & 0 & 0 & 1 & 0 & 0 & 0 & 1 & 0 & 0 & 0 \\
0 & 0 & 0 & 0 & 0 & 0 & 0 & 0 & 0 & 1 & 0 & 0 & 0 & 1 & 0 & 0 \\
0 & 0 & 0 & 0 & 0 & 0 & 0 & 0 & 0 & 0 & 1 & 0 & 0 & 0 & 1 & 0 \\
0 & 0 & 0 & 0 & 0 & 0 & 0 & 0 & 0 & 0 & 0 & 1 & 0 & 0 & 0 & 1
\end{bmatrix}$$

and

$$\mathbf{A}_3 = \begin{bmatrix}
1 & 1 & 1 & 1 & 0 & 0 & 0 & 0 & 0 & 0 & 0 & 0 \\
0 & 0 & 0 & 0 & 1 & 1 & 1 & 1 & 0 & 0 & 0 & 0 \\
0 & 0 & 0 & 0 & 0 & 0 & 0 & 0 & 1 & 1 & 1 & 1
\end{bmatrix}$$

The role of $\mathbf{A}_2$ in Equation 13.28 is to form the products $r_i p_{j|i}$ and $\mathbf{A}_3$ sums these products to get the mean ridit vector $[0.647, 0.482, 0.371]'$. These are the scores in Figure 13.6.

As noted in connection with Table 13.8, the average value of scores calculated in this way is always $\frac{1}{2}$. Thus, their sum is constant and their covariance matrix is singular. Only $a - 1$ of the a population scores are linearly independent. To get a workable vector of scores, $\mathbf{y}$, the three values must be reduced to two. The ordering of the training conditions makes calculation of trend components natural.† These are two (in this example) scores; *linear trend* measures the tendency for the sequence of points to ascend or descend, and *quadratic trend* measures its tendency to curve. Values of zero indicate a sequence of points that is level and straight, respectively. The two functions are

$$
\begin{aligned}
y_{\text{lin}} &= y_3 - y_1 \\
y_{\text{quad}} &= y_1 - 2y_2 + y_3
\end{aligned}
\tag{13.29}
$$

In matrix form, Equations 13.29 are calculated by multiplying the result of Equation 13.28 by

$$
\mathbf{A}_4 = \begin{bmatrix} -1 & 0 & 1 \\ 1 & -2 & 1 \end{bmatrix}
$$

Alternatively, $\mathbf{A}_3$ in Equation 12.28 can be replaced by the product

$$
\mathbf{A}_4 \mathbf{A}_3 = \begin{bmatrix} -1 & -1 & -1 & -1 & 0 & 0 & 0 & 0 & 1 & 1 & 1 & 1 \\ 1 & 1 & 1 & 1 & -2 & -2 & -2 & -2 & 1 & 1 & 1 & 1 \end{bmatrix}
$$

These transformations give the final function values and their covariance matrix:

$$
\mathbf{y} = \begin{bmatrix} -0.276 \\ 0.052 \end{bmatrix} \quad \text{and} \quad \mathbf{S}_y = \begin{bmatrix} 0.00138 & 0.00000 \\ 0.00000 & 0.00396 \end{bmatrix}
$$

As suspected from Figure 13.6, the linear coefficient is substantial and negative and the quadratic coefficient is small. The tests of Chapter 11 verify these observations. The hypothesis that both functions are zero (in the notation of Chapter 12, that $\mathbf{f}(\boldsymbol{\pi}) = \mathbf{0}$) is readily rejected ($W^2(2) = 55.72$), indicating that the populations differ in their prevalence of errors. The hypothesis of no quadratic trend cannot be rejected ($W^2(1) = 0.69$), implying that the mean ridits have an descending straight-line pattern.

---

†Most books on the analysis of variance or multiple regression contain a discussion of trend analysis. These books also include a table that gives the coefficients in Equations 13.29 and the comparable coefficients for more than 3 populations. The coefficients used here presuppose equal spacing of the populations. This assumption may not be realistic, but is a good place to start the analysis. Semenya et al. (1983) describe a way to assign positions to the populations based entirely on the data.

The condensation of the data accomplished by the definition of **y** in this example is noteworthy. By using the ordering, 12 proportions are combined into 2 functions, each of which expresses a particular aspect of the data. This pooling of information makes this procedure more robust to problems of small frequencies than are some of the direct tests based on X^2 or G^2. Because the pooling brings together several separate sources of data, central-limit properties can act to make the sampling distribution of **y** reasonably close to normal, even when the standard small-sample requirements are violated for the individual cells.

With more than two factors, either between or within populations, the analysis is similar. The ordered effects are assimilated either in the within-population definition of the functions or in the models that describe these functions. Many variants exist, depending on which factors are ordered and the way in which this ordering is to be treated. As with other multidimensional models, the simplest strategy is to work from the structure of the problem, treating higher-order effects as changes in lower-order effects over an additional variable, in the manner exemplified for the association models in Section 13.4.

13.8.   MEASURES OF ORDINAL ASSOCIATION

There are many ways to summarize the association in an ordered table as a single number, just as there are many unordered coefficients. These coefficients differ from the unordered coefficients in Chapter 9 in that they measure the association concordant with a particular ordering and ignore other aspects of the relationship. Thus, they are more specific than the unordered coefficients. This chapter, like Chapter 9, does not survey all such measures. It concentrates on general principles and describes most of the more common coefficients. The emphasis is on two-way tables.

For many sets of data, one does not really need an order-sensitive coefficient. If one factor is ordered and the other is not, an unordered coefficient adequately summarizes the association. Furthermore, there is no difference between ordered and unordered measures unless there are at least 3 levels to one of the categorizations. Excluding these conditions, the order-sensitive coefficients are those that express a connection between two ordered factors. As with the correlation coefficients, the ordered-association coefficients are most readily interpretable when they are applied to data drawn from a single population. Where data derive from several populations, the magnitude of any association coefficient is influenced by the way that these populations are established and by the frequencies with which they are sampled. A coefficient based on such data does not reflect any true population characteristic and is not likely to be useful.

Most of the ordered-association coefficients are defined to vary from -1 to $+1$, with 0 indicating no association. Typically, they behave as correlation coefficients, having negative values when the predominant frequencies are in cells that are high on one ordering and low on the other and positive values when the bulk of the observations are in cells with similarly ranked categorizations.

The most appropriate coefficient to summarize a particular table is determined by the source of the data. Different types of data permit different assumptions about the ordering. Three views are treated here, the first being the strongest, the last the weakest:

- The observations arise from the categorization of an underlying multivariate continuous distribution or a specific association model.
- The categories are ordered and observations that are separated by several category steps are more distant than observations that are fewer steps apart, but no specific scale values are present.
- The ordering is only sufficient to indicate that one observation is less than, tied with, or greater than another.

The applicability of a coefficient is limited by the strength of the model that underlies it. A measure that requires weak assumptions can always be used, although it captures less information than a stronger coefficient. Coefficients based on more stringent assumptions—for example, those that postulate a latent normal distribution—are less often applicable but are more precise when they do apply. One should not think that the strength of the assumptions make one measure better than another. The differences among them concern their precision and appropriateness in a given situation. The best choice is the measure based on the strongest model whose assumptions are reasonably well satisfied.

The first class of measures—those based on an underlying distribution—needs little further discussion. The most important is the polychoric correlation, which is based on a latent bivariate normal distribution (Section 13.6). Other models of association give different specific coefficients. Thus, in the multiplicative-association model the association is measured by the parameter ϕ and can be given an appropriate range by the transformation to ρ_ϕ (Equation 13.23). If the association is such that the parameters ξ_A and ξ_B preserve the order of the categories, then this number approximates the polychoric correlation ρ_{PC}. The coefficient ρ_ξ (Equation 13.24) gives a similar estimate. When the polychoric-correlation model is inappropriate, ρ_ϕ and ρ_ξ remain valid coefficients representing the magnitude of whatever univariate association the model detects.

Other association parameters can also be converted to effect sizemeasures by rescaling to a range from -1 to $+1$. For example, one of the transformation in Chapter 9 that was used to rescale the odds ratio (e.g., Equations 9.10 or 9.11) can be used to adjust the parameter τ of the additive-association model to this range.

13.9. CORRELATIONS BASED ON DERIVED SCORES

One can calculate a correlation coefficient as a measure of association without making the strong assumption of a latent bivariate distribution. To do so, scale values are assigned to row and column categories in any appropriate way, then the data are treated as a grouped frequency distribution and the correlation is found. One such procedure was described in Section 13.6: the coefficient $\hat{\rho}_\xi$ is a correlation based on the parameters of the multiplicative-association model (Equation 13.24). Alternatively, the ridits, probits, or logits of Section 13.5 can be used.

In general, let a_i and b_j be the values assigned to the rows and columns. Then the Pearson correlation coefficient for grouped data is

$$r = \frac{S_{AB}}{\sqrt{S_A S_B}} \tag{13.30}$$

where S_A and S_B are the sums of squares,

$$S_A = \sum_i a_i^2 x_{i+} - \frac{\left(\sum_i a_i x_{i+} \right)^2}{x_{++}} \tag{13.31}$$

$$S_B = \sum_j b_j^2 x_{+j} - \frac{\left(\sum_j b_j x_{+j} \right)^2}{x_{++}} \tag{13.32}$$

and S_{AB} is the sum of cross products,

$$S_{AB} = \sum_{i,j} a_i b_j x_{ij} - \frac{\left(\sum_i a_i x_{i+} \right)\left(\sum_j b_j x_{+j} \right)}{x_{++}} \tag{13.33}$$

Proportions can be used in these equations instead of frequencies without altering the value of r. Where the scores a_i and b_j have been standardized to mean 0 and variance 1 with respect to the marginal distributions, Equations 13.30 to 13.33 simplify to

$$r = \frac{1}{x_{++}} \sum_{i,j} a_i b_j x_{ij} = \sum_{i,j} a_i b_j p_{ij}$$

(cf. Equation 13.24).

Of the various derived scores that go into the correlation, the ridits are particularly noteworthy. Their use produces a coefficient of *rank correlation*. The size of a ridit is proportional to the number of observations below the median of the category. Hence the ridit correlation is the same as would result if the individual observations were ranked on each factor, with tied scores assigned the average of

380

their ranks, and then the correlation of the ranks were found. This calculation defines the Spearman rank correlation coefficient for a set of data where there are many ties. Thus, the ridit-based correlation coefficient can be thought of as if it were a Spearman coefficient. It is a coefficient of the second type described above: the number of steps in the categorization by which two observations differ is relevant, but no additional model or scale is assumed.

To return to the data from Table 13.2, the column ridit scores from Table 13.7 are 0.118, 0.373, 0.683, and 0.929 and the comparable row ridits are 0.056, 0.202, 0.479, and 0.833. Then Equations 13.31 to 13.33 give $S_A = 26.862$, $S_B = 27.414$, and $S_{AB} = -6.885$, and by Equation 13.30, $r = -0.25$.

If consecutive integers are assigned as scale values, the result is a coefficient of association that abandons the ordinal nature of the data in favor of equal spacing. For the example data, the poor fit of the uniform-association model gives evidence of unequal spacing, making this coefficient inadvisable. Had that model fit, the equal-spacing assumption would become tenable. Indeed, the correlation that is obtained from consecutive integer scores is the same as $\hat{\rho}_\phi$ from the uniform-association model.

Measures other than the correlation can be constructed by using derived scores. For example, Agresti (1986) uses ridits to define a variancelike measure from which a reduction-of-variability coefficient is defined.

13.10. MEASURES OF CONCORDANCE

The assignment of scale values to the categories implies an underlying continuum and suggests that an interval structure exists. Categories with a big difference in scale value are farther apart than categories whose values differ by a smaller amount. Even the ridit-based correlation puts categories farther apart that differ by several ordered steps. Association measures can be constructed that do not need these structures. If information about the size of the difference between categories is dropped, all one can say about two different categories is that one is larger than the other. Several association coefficients are based on this minimal ordering information.

When only the ordinal relationship of the categories is considered, the information in the table collapses to only 5 numbers. For any two individuals P and Q in the original sample, all one can tell about a particular ordered factor is whether P ranks above Q, below Q, or that they are tied. When two factors are considered, one of 5 things must happen:

- P and Q are ordered in the same way on both factors.
- P and Q are ordered in different ways on both factors.
- P and Q are tied on the first factor and different on the second.

- P and Q are different on the first factor and tied on the second.
- P and Q are tied on both factors.

The ordinal information in a two-way table classifying N individuals is summarized by looking (in effect) at the $\binom{N}{2}$ pairs of individuals that are formed by picking two members of the sample and classifying each pair into one of these 5 categories.

For the data in Table 13.2, there are 357 subjects, so there are $\binom{357}{2} = 63{,}546$ pairs altogether. In principle, every one of these pairs needs to be examined and classified. To make this operation practical, the cells of the contingency table (rather than the individual observations) are examined two at a time and all individuals in them classified at once. For example, the 2 people classified in cell (1,1) disagree more strongly with both statements than the 17 people in cell (2,2). These are concordant observations. There are 2 ways to choose a person from cell (1,1) and 17 ways to choose one from cell (2,2), so a total of $2 \times 17 = 34$ pairs are formed and 34 counts are added to the concordant category. Similarly, cells (1,1) and (1,2) contribute $2 \times 10 = 20$ counts to the "tied on A, different on B" classification, cells (1,3) and (2,2) contribute $15 \times 17 = 255$ counts to the discordant category, and so forth. Pairs that are tied on both factors come from the same cell: cell (1,2) contributes $\binom{10}{2} = 45$ counts to this tally. These calculations are made for every pair of cells in the table, to give

Both categorizations concordant:	11,667 pairs
Both categorizations discordant:	21,420 pairs
A tied, B different:	13,319 pairs
B tied, A different:	11,731 pairs
Both categorizations tied:	5,409 pairs
Total	63,546 pairs

These 5 frequencies summarize the full complement of ordinal information. Any measure constructed from them reflects purely the ordinal properties of the data.

Several such measures have been proposed. Fundamentally, these derive from the observation that positive association leads to concordant pairs, while negative association leads to discordant pairs. This observation suggests a measure something like

$$\tau_a = P(\text{concordant}) - P(\text{discordant})$$

This quantity is an adaptation to frequency tables of Kendall's τ coefficient for ordinal association (Kendall, 1938, 1970), in this context known as *Kendall's τ_a*. It is estimated by

$$\hat{\tau}_a = \frac{\#(\text{concordant}) - \#(\text{discordant})}{\#(\text{total pairs})} \tag{13.34}$$

For the sample data,

$$\hat{\tau}_a = \frac{11{,}667 - 21{,}420}{63{,}546} = -0.153$$

Unfortunately, Kendall's τ_a is unsatisfactory when it is applied to a contingency table, since it is does not take into account the many ties. These ties reduce the number of concordant and discordant pairs and limit the size of $\hat{\tau}_a$. Even in a table with no discordant observations, there are many ties and $\hat{\tau}_a < 1$.

The natural solution to this problem is to exclude the ties. The easiest way to do so is to restrict the calculations to untied observations by defining

$$\hat{\gamma} = P(\text{concordant} \mid \text{not tied}) - P(\text{discordant} \mid \text{not tied}) \qquad (13.35)$$

(Goodman & Kruskal, 1954). This quantity is estimated by

$$\gamma = \frac{\#(\text{concordant}) - \#(\text{discordant})}{\#(\text{concordant}) + \#(\text{discordant})} \qquad (13.36)$$

For the sample data, $\hat{\gamma} = -0.295$. As a result of the restriction to untied pairs, the absolute value of $\hat{\gamma}$ is larger than that of $\hat{\tau}_a$ and reaches ± 1 for perfect association.

Another way to account for ties is provided by *Kendall's* τ_b:

$$\hat{\tau}_b = \frac{\#(\text{concordant}) - \#(\text{discordant})}{\sqrt{\#(\text{untied}) + \#(\text{tied only on A})} \ \ \sqrt{\#(\text{untied}) + \#(\text{tied only on B})}}$$
$$(13.37)$$

(Kendall, 1945). This statistic has an attractive interpretation as the correlation of the pairwise differences (Kendall, 1970). To every pair of observations P and Q assign a score a_{PQ} of 1 if P ranks above Q on the first classification, -1 if P ranks below Q, or 0 if they are tied. A similar score b_{PQ} expresses the relationship on the second classification. Then $\hat{\tau}_b$ is the Pearson correlation of a_{PQ} and b_{PQ} over all $\binom{N}{2}$ pairs of observations. Of course, one never calculates $\hat{\tau}_b$ this way—Equation 13.37 is easier to use. For the example data,

$$\hat{\tau}_b = \frac{11{,}667 - 21{,}420}{\sqrt{(11{,}667+21{,}420) + 13{,}319} \ \ \sqrt{(11{,}667+21{,}420) + 11{,}731}}$$

$$= -0.481$$

Other methods of adjusting for ties have been proposed by Kendall (1970), Somers (1962), and Wilson (1974). These coefficients are similar to τ_a, τ_b, or γ in concept and are not covered here (see Reynolds, 1977, or Agresti, 1984, for summaries).

To test the value of statistics such as τ_a, τ_b, or γ or to construct confidence intervals for them, one needs their standard errors. The tests for the hypothesis that they equal zero are identical. The same numerator appears in all three coefficients:

$$D = \#(\text{concordant}) - \#(\text{discordant})$$

All are zero when $D = 0$. For large samples, under the hypothesis of no ordinal association in the population, the sampling variance of D is estimated by

$$\hat{\text{var}}(D) \approx \frac{\left(x^3_{++} - \sum_i x^3_{i+}\right)\left(x^3_{++} - \sum_j x^3_{+j}\right)}{9x^3_{++}} \tag{13.38}$$

(Kendall, 1970). If the sample is large enough, the ratio of D to the standard error derived from this expression can be referred to a standard normal distribution. For the example, Equation 13.38 evaluates to 4,206,181, so the hypothesis that $\tau_a = \tau_b = \gamma = 0$ is tested by

$$z = \frac{11,667 - 21,420}{\sqrt{4,206,181}} = -4.76$$

Clearly, the coefficients are nonzero.

Equation 13.38 is valid only when the concordance coefficients are zero, so it cannot be used to make confidence intervals. Interval estimates require the standard error away from zero, which is given by a more general (and more complicated) formula. In the case of $\hat{\gamma}$ and of multinomial sampling, the large-sample sampling variance is

$$\hat{\text{var}}(\gamma) \approx \frac{16 \sum_{\text{cells}} p_{ij}\left(P^{(c)}R_{ij}^{(d)} - P^{(d)}R_{ij}^{(c)}\right)^2}{x_{++}(P^{(c)} + P^{(d)})^4} \tag{13.39}$$

where $P^{(c)}$ and $P^{(d)}$ are the observed proportion of concordance and discordance,

$$P^{(c)} = 2\sum_{i<k}\sum_{j<l} p_{ij}p_{kl} \quad \text{and} \quad P^{(d)} = 2\sum_{i<k}\sum_{j>l} p_{ij}p_{kl}$$

and

$$R_{ij}^{(c)} = \sum_{i<k}\sum_{j<l} p_{kl} + \sum_{i>k}\sum_{j>l} p_{kl}$$

$$R_{ij}^{(d)} = \sum_{i<k}\sum_{j>l} p_{kl} + \sum_{i>k}\sum_{j<l} p_{kl}$$

(Goodman & Kruskal, 1963,1972; see Agresti, 1984, Chapter 10 and Appendix B). The sampling variance of $\hat{\tau}_b$ is more complicated:

$$\hat{var}(\hat{\tau}_b) = \frac{\sum_{cells} p_{ij}\phi_{ij}^2 - \left(\sum_{cells} p_{ij}\phi_{ij}\right)^2}{x_{++}\left(1 - \sum_i p_{i+}^2\right)\left(1 - \sum_j p_{+j}^2\right)} \qquad (13.40)$$

where

$$\phi_{ij} = 2(R_{ij}^{(c)} - R_{ij}^{(d)}) + (P^{(c)} - P^{(d)})\left(\frac{p_{i+}}{1 - \sum_k p_{k+}^2} + \frac{p_{+j}}{1 - \sum_l p_{k+}^2}\right)$$

When it is applied to Table 11.2, Equation 13.39 gives a standard error of 0.057, so a 95% confidence interval for γ reaches from -0.406 to -0.184. The comparable results for τ_b are 0.042 for the standard error and -0.256 to -0.131 for the confidence interval. Equations 13.39 and 13.40 are instances of the delta method for finding standard errors, mentioned briefly in connection with Equation 9.7 (see Goodman & Kruskal, 1972; see Bishop, Fienberg, & Holland, 1975, Section 14.6).

Where $|\gamma|$ is much different from 0, the distribution of $\hat{\gamma}$ for moderate samples sizes is distinctly nonnormal and inclined to be both irregular and skewed (Gans & Robertson, 1981a, b). It is difficult to characterize the safe bounds for using the normal approximation here; as rules of thumb, the normal approximation is dangerous where the sample size and cell probabilities are such as to make empty cells likely (even if not actually present) or when γ lies within a few standard deviation units of ± 1. Apparently, the distribution of τ_b is smoother and more stable than that of γ.

PROBLEMS

13.1. Which of the following models from Chapter 11 are palindromically invariant? Which are permutationally invariant?

a. The independence model
b. The off-diagonal quasi-independence model.
c. The triangles parameter model.
d. The block association model.
e. The diagonals parameter model.
f. The symmetry model.
g. The quasi-symmetry model.

386

13.2. As part of a developmental study, 50 children from each of three age groups (5, 8, and 11 years) are given a set of three problems of graded difficulty to solve. Each child is classified by the most difficult problem solved, with category p_0 indicating that no problem was solved. The data and the fit of the various association models are given in Table 13.9. Interpret these results.

13.3. What is the log-linear form of the row effects model (Equation 13.4)?

13.4. Subjects in the developmental study of problem 13.2 are also classified into males and females. Using the various three-dimensional association models, how would one answer the following questions.

a. Does the developmental rate differ for the two sexes, as expressed by the relationship to the problems?
b. Is the association between age and the problem difficulty the same for the two sexes?
c. Are there differences in the relative difficulties of the problems for the two sexes?

13.5. Construct a hierarchy diagram of the homogeneous-association models for a three-way table. Note that this diagram will contain both models of (conditional) independence and models of dependence. In particular, consider the cases where

a. Factors A and B are unordered with the frequencies of their combination fixed by design and factor C is ordered.
b. Factor A is unordered and factors B and C are ordered.

TABLE 13.9.
Data and association-model statistics for a 3×4 table.

Data

Problem solved

		p_1	p_2	p_3	p_4
	a_5	23	15	10	2
Age	a_8	8	14	16	12
	a_{11}	8	3	8	31

Fits of the association models

Model	G^2	Association parameters		
Unrelatedness	55.49			
Uniform assn.	15.10	$\hat{\tau}$ 0.628		
Row effects	14.87	$\hat{\tau}$ 0.627		
		$\hat{\tau}_A$ 0.079	-0.079	
Column effects	6.44	$\hat{\tau}$ 0.662		
		$\hat{\tau}_P$ -0.643	-0.098	0.741
Row & col effects	3.56	$\hat{\tau}$ 0.733		
		$\hat{\tau}_A$ 0.320	-0.320	
		$\hat{\tau}_P$ -0.781	-0.207	0.988

13.6. Calculate the ridit, logit, and probit scores for the following probability distributions

a. 0.58, 0.21, 0.16, and 0.05.

b. 0.06, 0.16, 0.51, 0.18, 0.09.

13.7. A two-way classification of the opinions of 403 subjects on two opinion questions is

	r_1	r_2	r_3	r_4	r_5
q_1	16	19	10	8	3
q_2	19	36	32	26	16
q_3	9	22	34	37	27
q_4	6	9	20	27	27

The multiplicative-association model fits these data with $G_2 = 7.88$ and estimates of the parameters under the variance-based constraints of Equations 11.8 are

$$\hat{\phi} = 0.308$$
$$\hat{\xi}_Q = -1.402, -0.789, 0.586, 1.335$$
$$\hat{\xi}_R = -1.688, -1.185, 0.265, 0.908, 0.866$$

Is the suggestion that a latent continuous bivariate normal distribution underlies these data plausible? Estimate the correlation.

13.8. Formulate a weighted least-squares version of the uniform-association model and the additive-association models for a two-way table.

13.9. Construct a weighted least-squares representation of the uniform association model, the row-effects model, the column-effects model, and the row-and-column-effects model. ℰ Fit these models to the data of Problem 13.2.

13.10. Formulate a weighted least-squares version of the heterogeneous uniform-association model for a three-way table in which the third factor is dichotomous. How is homogeneity of the association parameter tested in this context? ℰ Apply these models to the data used in the example in Section 13.4.

13.11. Find the marginal ridits for the problem factor in the developmental data of Problem 13.2. Use these values to calculate mean ridit scores for the ages.

13.12. For the data in Problem 13.7, calculate the correlation between the responses based on the ridits.

13.13. For the data in Problem 13.8, calculate the statistics τ_a, τ_b, and γ. Test whether each of these statistics is significantly different from zero.

A.1
PERCENTAGE POINTS OF THE CHI-SQUARE DISTRIBUTION

This table gives upper-tail percentage points of the chi-square distribution.* These are the points c_α for which

$$P[\chi^2(\nu) \geq c_\alpha] = \alpha$$

where $\chi^2(\nu)$ is a chi-square variable with ν degrees of freedom. Graphically,

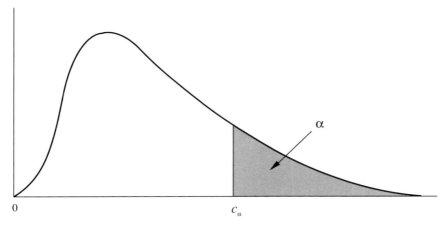

Values outside the range of the table are approximated by

$$c_\alpha \approx [\sqrt{\nu} + 2\sqrt{-\log_{10}\alpha} - 7/6]^2$$

---

*This table was calculated using a series expansion for upper-tail χ^2 probabilities (Zelen & Severo, 1964, Equations 26.4.4 and 26.4.5). Percentage points here and in Appendix A.2 were determined by numerically solving this expansion for c_α at the appropriate values of α. A reader who plans to write a program to find descriptive levels for common distributions should consult, Press, Flannery, Teukolsky, & Vetterling, (1986).

for $0.1 \leq \alpha \leq 0.0001$ and $6 \leq \nu \leq 100$ (Hoaglin, 1977). This empirically derived approximation is accurate to about 1% within this range. For larger values of ν, a standard normal approximation applies:

$$c_\alpha \approx \tfrac{1}{2}(z_\alpha \sqrt{2\nu - 1})^2$$

where z_α is the upper-tail percentage point from a normal distribution, as given in the table in Appendix A.4.

For example, a one-tailed test at the 5% level with 2 degrees of freedom has the critical value 5.99—the null hypothesis is rejected if the observed statistic exceeds this value.

Upper-tail Chi-square Probabilities

ν	\multicolumn{10}{c}{Upper-tail area, α}
	0.95	0.10	0.05	0.025	0.167	0.0125	0.01	0.005	0.001	0.0005
1	0.00	2.71	3.84	5.02	5.73	6.24	6.63	7.88	10.83	12.12
2	0.10	4.60	5.99	7.38	8.19	8.76	9.21	10.60	13.82	15.20
3	0.35	6.25	7.81	9.35	10.24	10.86	11.34	12.84	16.27	17.73
4	0.71	7.78	9.49	11.14	12.09	12.76	13.28	14.86	18.47	20.00
5	1.15	9.24	11.07	12.83	13.84	14.54	15.09	16.75	20.52	22.11
6	1.64	10.64	12.59	14.45	15.51	16.24	16.81	18.55	22.46	24.10
7	2.17	12.02	14.07	16.01	17.12	17.88	18.48	20.28	24.32	26.02
8	2.73	13.36	15.51	17.53	18.68	19.48	20.09	21.96	26.12	27.87
9	3.33	14.68	16.92	19.02	20.21	21.03	21.67	23.59	27.88	29.67
10	3.94	15.99	18.31	20.48	21.71	22.56	23.21	25.19	29.59	31.42
11	4.57	17.28	19.67	21.92	23.18	24.06	24.72	26.76	31.26	33.14
12	5.23	18.55	21.03	23.34	24.63	25.53	26.22	28.30	32.91	34.82
13	5.89	19.81	22.36	24.74	26.06	26.99	27.69	29.82	34.53	36.48
14	6.57	21.06	23.68	26.12	27.48	28.42	29.14	31.32	36.12	38.11
15	7.26	22.31	25.00	27.49	28.88	29.84	30.58	32.80	37.70	39.72
16	7.96	23.54	26.30	28.85	30.27	31.25	32.00	34.27	39.25	41.31
17	8.67	24.77	27.59	30.19	31.64	32.64	33.41	35.72	40.79	42.88
18	9.39	25.99	28.87	31.53	33.01	34.03	34.81	37.16	42.31	44.43
19	10.12	27.20	30.14	32.85	34.36	35.40	36.19	38.58	43.82	45.97
20	10.85	28.41	31.41	34.17	35.70	36.76	37.57	40.00	45.31	47.50
21	11.59	29.62	32.67	35.48	37.04	38.11	38.93	41.40	46.80	49.01
22	12.34	30.81	33.92	36.78	38.37	39.46	40.29	42.80	48.27	50.51
23	13.09	32.01	35.17	38.08	39.68	40.79	41.64	44.18	49.73	52.00
24	13.85	33.20	36.41	39.36	41.00	42.12	42.98	45.56	51.18	53.48
25	14.61	34.38	37.65	40.65	42.30	43.45	44.31	46.93	52.62	54.95
26	15.38	35.56	38.88	41.92	43.60	44.76	45.64	48.29	54.05	56.41
27	16.15	36.74	40.11	43.19	44.90	46.07	46.96	49.64	55.48	57.86
28	16.93	37.92	41.34	44.46	46.19	47.38	48.28	50.99	56.89	59.30
29	17.71	39.09	42.56	45.72	47.47	48.67	49.59	52.34	58.30	60.73
30	18.49	40.26	43.77	46.98	48.75	49.97	50.89	53.67	59.70	62.16
31	19.28	41.42	44.99	48.23	50.02	51.26	52.19	55.00	61.10	63.58
32	20.07	42.58	46.19	49.48	51.29	52.54	53.49	56.33	62.49	65.00
33	20.87	43.75	47.40	50.73	52.56	53.82	54.78	57.65	63.87	66.40
34	21.66	44.90	48.60	51.97	53.82	55.09	56.06	58.96	65.25	67.80
35	22.47	46.06	49.80	53.20	55.08	56.36	57.34	60.27	66.62	69.20
36	23.27	47.21	51.00	54.44	56.33	57.63	58.62	61.58	67.99	70.59
37	24.07	48.36	52.19	55.67	57.58	58.90	59.89	62.88	69.35	71.97
38	24.88	49.51	53.38	56.90	58.83	60.16	61.16	64.18	70.70	73.35
39	25.70	50.66	54.57	58.12	60.07	61.41	62.43	65.48	72.05	74.73
40	26.51	51.81	55.76	59.34	61.31	62.66	63.69	66.77	73.40	76.09

A.2   Bonferroni Chi-Square

This pair of tables contains upper-tail critical values for a chi-square distribution with ν degrees of freedom at the significance level

$$\alpha = \alpha_F/K$$

for familywise error rates α_F of 0.1 and 0.05. If the tabled values are used for a family of K tests for which the null hypothesis holds, the probability of one or more type I errors does not exceed α_F.

For example, to control the familywise error rate to $\alpha_F = 0.1$ over a family of 12 tests, a test with 6 degrees of freedom has a critical value of 17.27 (from the 12th row and 6th column in the first table).

Bonferroni Chi-square Probabilities at Familywise Level 0.1

Degrees of Freedom, v

K	1	2	3	4	5	6	8	9	10	12
1	2.71	4.60	6.25	7.78	9.24	10.64	13.36	14.68	15.99	18.55
2	3.84	5.99	7.81	9.49	11.07	12.59	15.51	16.92	18.31	21.03
3	4.53	6.80	8.71	10.46	12.11	13.69	16.71	18.16	19.59	22.39
4	5.02	7.38	9.35	11.14	12.83	14.45	17.53	19.02	20.48	23.34
5	5.41	7.82	9.84	11.67	13.39	15.03	18.17	19.68	21.16	24.05
6	5.73	8.19	10.24	12.09	13.84	15.51	18.68	20.21	21.71	24.63
7	6.00	8.50	10.57	12.45	14.22	15.90	19.11	20.65	22.16	25.12
8	6.24	8.76	10.86	12.76	14.54	16.24	19.48	21.03	22.56	25.53
9	6.45	9.00	11.12	13.03	14.83	16.54	19.80	21.37	22.90	25.89
10	6.63	9.21	11.34	13.28	15.09	16.81	20.09	21.67	23.21	26.22
11	6.80	9.40	11.55	13.50	15.32	17.05	20.35	21.93	23.49	26.51
12	6.96	9.58	11.74	13.70	15.53	17.27	20.59	22.18	23.74	26.77
13	7.10	9.73	11.91	13.88	15.72	17.47	20.80	22.40	23.97	27.01
14	7.24	9.88	12.07	14.05	15.90	17.66	21.00	22.61	24.18	27.24
15	7.36	10.02	12.22	14.21	16.06	17.83	21.19	22.80	24.37	27.44
16	7.48	10.15	12.36	14.35	16.22	17.99	21.36	22.98	24.56	27.64
17	7.59	10.27	12.49	14.49	16.36	18.14	21.52	23.14	24.73	27.82
18	7.69	10.39	12.61	14.62	16.50	18.29	21.67	23.30	24.89	27.99
19	7.79	10.49	12.73	14.74	16.63	18.42	21.82	23.45	25.04	28.15
20	7.88	10.60	12.84	14.86	16.75	18.55	21.96	23.59	25.19	28.30
21	7.97	10.69	12.94	14.97	16.87	18.67	22.08	23.72	25.33	28.44
22	8.05	10.79	13.04	15.08	16.98	18.78	22.21	23.85	25.46	28.58
23	8.13	10.88	13.14	15.18	17.08	18.89	22.33	23.97	25.58	28.71
24	8.21	10.96	13.23	15.27	17.18	19.00	22.44	24.09	25.70	28.84
25	8.28	11.04	13.32	15.37	17.28	19.10	22.55	24.20	25.81	28.96
26	8.35	11.12	13.40	15.45	17.37	19.20	22.65	24.30	25.92	29.07
27	8.42	11.20	13.48	15.54	17.46	19.29	22.75	24.41	26.03	29.18
28	8.49	11.27	13.56	15.62	17.55	19.38	22.84	24.50	26.13	29.29
29	8.55	11.34	13.63	15.70	17.63	19.46	22.94	24.60	26.23	29.39
30	8.62	11.41	13.71	15.78	17.71	19.55	23.02	24.69	26.32	29.49
31	8.67	11.47	13.78	15.85	17.79	19.63	23.11	24.78	26.41	29.58
32	8.73	11.54	13.84	15.92	17.86	19.70	23.19	24.86	26.50	29.67
33	8.79	11.60	13.91	15.99	17.93	19.78	23.27	24.95	26.58	29.76
34	8.84	11.66	13.97	16.06	18.00	19.85	23.35	25.03	26.67	29.85
35	8.90	11.72	14.04	16.12	18.07	19.92	23.43	25.11	26.75	29.93
36	8.95	11.77	14.10	16.19	18.14	19.99	23.50	25.18	26.82	30.02
37	9.00	11.83	14.15	16.25	18.20	20.06	23.57	25.25	26.90	30.09
38	9.05	11.88	14.21	16.31	18.27	20.12	23.64	25.33	26.97	30.17

	Degrees of Freedom, ν									
K	1	2	3	4	5	6	8	9	10	12
1	3.84	5.99	7.81	9.49	11.07	12.59	15.51	16.92	18.31	21.03
2	5.02	7.38	9.35	11.14	12.83	14.45	17.53	19.02	20.48	23.34
3	5.73	8.19	10.24	12.09	13.84	15.51	18.68	20.21	21.71	24.63
4	6.24	8.76	10.86	12.76	14.54	16.24	19.48	21.03	22.56	25.53
5	6.63	9.21	11.34	13.28	¹5.09	16.81	20.09	21.67	23.21	26.22
6	6.96	9.58	11.74	13.70	15.53	17.27	20.59	22.18	23.74	26.77
7	7.24	9.88	12.07	14.05	15.90	17.66	21.00	22.61	24.18	27.24
8	7.48	10.15	12.36	14.35	16.22	17.99	21.36	22.98	24.56	27.64
9	7.69	10.39	12.61	14.62	16.50	18.29	21.67	23.30	24.89	27.99
10	7.88	10.60	12.84	14.86	16.75	18.55	21.96	23.59	25.19	28.30
11	8.05	10.79	13.04	15.08	16.98	18.78	22.21	23.85	25.46	28.58
12	8.21	10.96	13.23	15.27	17.18	19.00	22.44	24.09	25.70	28.84
13	8.35	11.12	13.40	15.45	17.37	19.20	22.65	24.30	25.92	29.07
14	8.49	11.27	13.56	15.62	17.55	19.38	22.84	24.50	26.13	29.29
15	8.62	11.41	13.71	15.78	17.71	19.55	23.02	24.69	26.32	29.49
16	8.73	11.54	13.84	15.92	17.86	19.70	23.19	24.86	26.50	29.67
17	8.84	11.66	13.97	16.06	18.00	19.85	23.35	25.03	26.67	29.85
18	8.95	11.77	14.10	16.19	18.14	19.99	23.50	25.18	26.82	30.02
19	9.05	11.88	14.21	16.31	18.27	20.12	23.64	25.33	26.97	30.17
20	9.14	11.98	14.32	16.42	18.39	20.25	23.77	25.46	27.11	30.32
21	9.23	12.08	14.42	16.53	18.50	20.37	23.90	25.59	27.25	30.46
22	9.31	12.17	14.52	16.64	18.61	20.48	24.02	25.72	27.37	30.59
23	9.40	12.26	14.62	16.74	18.71	20.59	24.14	25.83	27.49	30.72
24	9.47	12.35	14.71	16.83	18.81	20.69	24.25	25.95	27.61	30.84
25	9.55	12.43	14.80	16.92	18.91	20.79	24.35	26.06	27.72	30.96
26	9.62	12.51	14.88	17.01	19.00	20.89	24.45	26.16	27.83	31.07
27	9.69	12.58	14.96	17.10	19.09	20.98	24.55	26.26	27.93	31.18
28	9.76	12.66	15.04	17.18	19.17	21.07	24.64	26.36	28.03	31.28
29	9.82	12.73	15.11	17.26	19.25	21.15	24.73	26.45	28.12	31.38
30	9.88	12.79	15.18	17.33	19.33	21.23	24.82	26.54	28.22	31.47
31	9.94	12.86	15.25	17.40	19.41	21.31	24.91	26.63	28.31	31.57
32	10.00	12.92	15.32	17.48	19.48	21.39	24.99	26.71	28.39	31.66
33	10.06	12.98	15.39	17.54	19.55	21.46	25.07	26.79	28.47	31.74
34	10.12	13.04	15.45	17.61	19.62	21.53	25.14	26.87	28.55	31.83
35	10.17	13.10	15.51	17.67	19.69	21.60	25.22	26.94	28.63	31.91
36	10.22	13.16	15.57	17.74	19.76	21.67	25.29	27.02	28.71	31.99
37	10.27	13.21	15.63	17.80	19.82	21.74	25.36	27.09	28.78	32.07
38	10.32	13.27	15.68	17.86	19.88	21.80	25.43	27.16	28.85	32.14

A.3   POWER CHART FOR CHI-SQUARE TESTS

This chart plots the power of a chi-square test, $1 - \beta$, as a function of $\sqrt{\omega}$, where ω is the noncentrality parameter of the chi-square distribution with ν degrees of freedom.* For example, if $\omega = 25$ for a distribution with $\nu = 10$, the power of the test is 0.955, obtained as the ordinate for the $\nu = 10$ line at the abscissa $\sqrt{\omega} = 5$. For the use of this chart, see Sections 2.9 and 5.10.

---

*Values for this chart were calculated from Equation 26.4.25 of Zelen & Severo (1964).

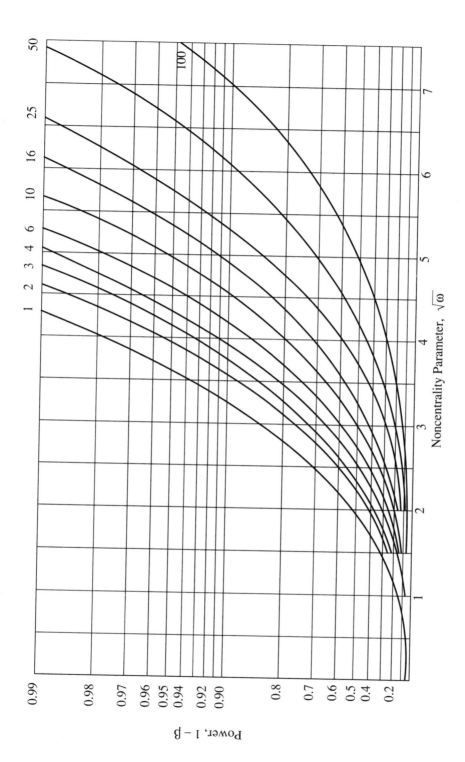

PERCENTAGE POINTS OF THE NORMAL DISTRIBUTION

This table gives upper-tail percentage points of the standard normal distribution (i.e., with mean 0 and variance 1).* These are points z_α for which $P(Z \geq z_\alpha) = \alpha$, where Z is a standard normally-distributed random variable:

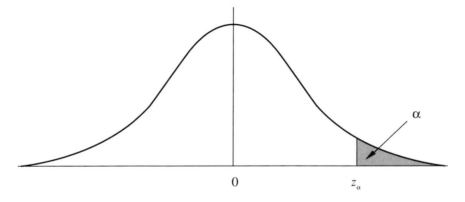

The first two digits of α are at the left of the table, the third digit is at the top. Lower-tail abcissas are the negative of the upper-tail probabilities, and two-tailed probabilities are found from the tabled entry for $\alpha/2$.

The use of this table is described in most elementary statistics texts. Specifically,

$$P(Z \geq 1.282) = 0.10$$
$$P(Z < 1.282) = 1.0 - P(Z \geq 1.282) = 0.90$$
$$P(Z \leq -0.412) = P(Z \geq 0.412) = 0.34$$
$$P(|Z| \geq 1.150) = 2P(Z \geq 1.150) = 0.25$$

---

*Value in this table were obtained by numerically solving for z_α, using the normal-curve integral algorithm of Hill & Joyce (1967; with corrections by Adams, 1969, and Holmgren, 1970).

Inverse Upper-tail Normal Distribution

p	.000	.001	.002	.003	.004	.005	.006	.007	.008	.009
0.00	—	3.090	2.878	2.748	2.652	2.576	2.512	2.457	2.409	2.366
0.01	2.326	2.290	2.257	2.226	2.197	2.170	2.144	2.120	2.097	2.075
0.02	2.054	2.034	2.014	1.995	1.977	1.960	1.943	1.927	1.911	1.896
0.03	1.881	1.866	1.852	1.838	1.825	1.812	1.799	1.787	1.774	1.762
0.04	1.751	1.739	1.728	1.717	1.706	1.695	1.685	1.675	1.665	1.655
0.05	1.645	1.635	1.626	1.616	1.607	1.598	1.589	1.580	1.572	1.563
0.06	1.555	1.546	1.538	1.530	1.522	1.514	1.506	1.499	1.491	1.483
0.07	1.476	1.468	1.461	1.454	1.447	1.440	1.433	1.426	1.419	1.412
0.08	1.405	1.398	1.392	1.385	1.379	1.372	1.366	1.359	1.353	1.347
0.09	1.341	1.335	1.329	1.323	1.317	1.311	1.305	1.299	1.293	1.287
0.10	1.282	1.276	1.270	1.265	1.259	1.254	1.248	1.243	1.237	1.232
0.11	1.227	1.221	1.216	1.211	1.206	1.200	1.195	1.190	1.185	1.180
0.12	1.175	1.170	1.165	1.160	1.155	1.150	1.146	1.141	1.136	1.131
0.13	1.126	1.122	1.117	1.112	1.108	1.103	1.098	1.094	1.089	1.085
0.14	1.080	1.076	1.071	1.067	1.063	1.058	1.054	1.049	1.045	1.041
0.15	1.036	1.032	1.028	1.024	1.019	1.015	1.011	1.007	1.003	0.999
0.16	0.994	0.990	0.986	0.982	0.978	0.974	0.970	0.966	0.962	0.958
0.17	0.954	0.950	0.946	0.942	0.938	0.935	0.931	0.927	0.923	0.919
0.18	0.915	0.912	0.908	0.904	0.900	0.896	0.893	0.889	0.885	0.882
0.19	0.878	0.874	0.871	0.867	0.863	0.860	0.856	0.852	0.849	0.845
0.20	0.842	0.838	0.834	0.831	0.827	0.824	0.820	0.817	0.813	0.810
0.21	0.806	0.803	0.800	0.796	0.793	0.789	0.786	0.782	0.779	0.776
0.22	0.772	0.769	0.765	0.762	0.759	0.755	0.752	0.749	0.745	0.742
0.23	0.739	0.736	0.732	0.729	0.726	0.722	0.719	0.716	0.713	0.710
0.24	0.706	0.703	0.700	0.697	0.693	0.690	0.687	0.684	0.681	0.678
0.25	0.674	0.671	0.668	0.665	0.662	0.659	0.656	0.653	0.650	0.646
0.26	0.643	0.640	0.637	0.634	0.631	0.628	0.625	0.622	0.619	0.616
0.27	0.613	0.610	0.607	0.604	0.601	0.598	0.595	0.592	0.589	0.586
0.28	0.583	0.580	0.577	0.574	0.571	0.568	0.565	0.562	0.559	0.556
0.29	0.553	0.550	0.548	0.545	0.542	0.539	0.536	0.533	0.530	0.527
0.30	0.524	0.522	0.519	0.516	0.513	0.510	0.507	0.504	0.502	0.499
0.31	0.496	0.493	0.490	0.487	0.485	0.482	0.479	0.476	0.473	0.470
0.32	0.468	0.465	0.462	0.459	0.457	0.454	0.451	0.448	0.445	0.443
0.33	0.440	0.437	0.434	0.432	0.429	0.426	0.423	0.421	0.418	0.415
0.34	0.412	0.410	0.407	0.404	0.402	0.399	0.396	0.393	0.391	0.388
0.35	0.385	0.383	0.380	0.377	0.375	0.372	0.369	0.366	0.364	0.361
0.36	0.358	0.356	0.353	0.350	0.348	0.345	0.342	0.340	0.337	0.335
0.37	0.332	0.329	0.327	0.324	0.321	0.319	0.316	0.313	0.311	0.308
0.38	0.305	0.303	0.300	0.298	0.295	0.292	0.290	0.287	0.285	0.282
0.39	0.279	0.277	0.274	0.272	0.269	0.266	0.264	0.261	0.259	0.256

Inverse Upper-tail Normal Distribution

p	.000	.001	.002	.003	.004	.005	.006	.007	.008	.009
0.40	0.253	0.251	0.248	0.246	0.243	0.240	0.238	0.235	0.233	0.230
0.41	0.228	0.225	0.222	0.220	0.217	0.215	0.212	0.210	0.207	0.204
0.42	0.202	0.199	0.197	0.194	0.192	0.189	0.187	0.184	0.181	0.179
0.43	0.176	0.174	0.171	0.169	0.166	0.164	0.161	0.159	0.156	0.154
0.44	0.151	0.148	0.146	0.143	0.141	0.138	0.136	0.133	0.131	0.128
0.45	0.126	0.123	0.121	0.118	0.116	0.113	0.111	0.108	0.105	0.103
0.46	0.100	0.098	0.095	0.093	0.090	0.088	0.085	0.083	0.080	0.078
0.47	0.075	0.073	0.070	0.068	0.065	0.063	0.060	0.058	0.055	0.053
0.48	0.050	0.048	0.045	0.043	0.040	0.038	0.035	0.033	0.030	0.028
0.49	0.025	0.023	0.020	0.018	0.015	0.013	0.010	0.008	0.005	0.003

A.5

PERCENTAGE POINTS OF THE LARGEST ROOT OF A WISHART MATRIX

These tables give the upper-tail percentage points of the distribution of the largest root (or eigenvalue) of a Wishart matrix at significance levels α of 0.10, 0.05, and 0.01.* These values are used to test ΔG^2 or ΔX^2 for the first association term in the multiplicative-association model and the maximum-correlation model (see Sections 11.3 to 11.5). The tables are indexed by the number of rows and columns in the frequency table and are symmetric in these arguments. No entries are given for tables in which either factor has only two levels; for such tables, critical values have the χ^2 distribution in Appendix A.1. A larger table of the Wishart root distribution is given by Pearson & Hartley, 1972 (Table 51).

For example, in a 4 × 5 table, the critical value at the 5% level is 15.24.

---

*Values in this table were computed according to the algorithm of Krishnaiah & Chang (1971; see also Clemm, Krishnaiah & Waikar, 1973). The parameters p and n of the Wishart matrix are one less than the number of rows or columns here.

Percentage Points of the Largest Root of a Wishart Matrix

					Number of Columns					
					$\alpha = 0.10$					
Number of Rows	3	4	5	6	7	8	9	10	11	12
3	7.01	9.00	10.82	12.52	14.15	15.72	17.25	18.75	20.22	21.66
4	9.00	11.25	13.26	15.14	16.92	18.64	20.30	21.92	23.50	25.06
5	10.82	13.26	15.44	17.46	19.37	21.20	22.97	24.69	26.37	28.01
6	12.52	15.14	17.46	19.60	21.62	23.55	25.42	27.22	28.98	30.70
7	14.15	16.92	19.37	21.62	23.74	25.76	27.71	29.59	31.42	33.21
8	15.72	18.64	21.20	23.55	25.76	27.87	29.89	31.84	33.74	35.59
9	17.25	20.30	22.97	25.42	27.71	29.89	31.98	34.00	35.96	37.87
10	18.75	21.92	24.69	27.22	29.59	31.84	34.00	36.08	38.10	40.06
11	20.22	23.50	26.37	28.98	31.42	33.74	35.96	38.10	40.17	42.19
12	21.66	25.06	28.01	30.70	33.21	35.59	37.87	40.06	42.19	44.26
					$\alpha = 0.05$					
3	8.59	10.74	12.68	14.49	16.21	17.88	19.49	21.07	22.61	24.12
4	10.74	13.12	15.24	17.22	19.09	20.89	22.62	24.31	25.97	27.58
5	12.68	15.24	17.52	19.63	21.62	23.53	25.37	27.16	28.90	30.60
6	14.49	17.22	19.63	21.86	23.95	25.96	27.89	29.76	31.58	33.35
7	16.21	19.09	21.62	23.95	26.15	28.24	30.24	32.19	34.08	35.92
8	17.88	20.89	23.53	25.96	28.24	30.40	32.48	34.50	36.45	38.36
9	19.49	22.62	25.37	27.89	30.24	32.48	34.63	36.71	38.73	40.69
10	21.07	24.31	27.16	29.76	32.19	34.50	36.71	38.85	40.92	42.93
11	22.61	25.97	28.90	31.58	34.08	36.45	38.73	40.92	43.04	45.11
12	24.12	27.58	30.60	33.35	35.92	38.36	40.69	42.93	45.11	47.22
					$\alpha = 0.01$					
3	12.16	14.57	16.73	18.73	20.64	22.47	24.23	25.95	27.63	29.28
4	14.57	17.18	19.50	21.66	23.69	25.64	27.52	29.34	31.12	32.86
5	16.73	19.50	21.96	24.24	26.38	28.43	30.41	32.32	34.18	36.00
6	18.73	21.66	24.24	26.62	28.86	31.00	33.05	35.04	36.98	38.86
7	20.64	23.69	26.38	28.86	31.19	33.40	35.53	37.59	39.59	41.54
8	22.47	25.64	28.43	31.00	33.40	35.69	37.89	40.01	42.07	44.08
9	24.23	27.52	30.41	33.05	35.53	37.89	40.15	42.33	44.45	46.51
10	25.95	29.34	32.32	35.04	37.59	40.01	42.33	44.57	46.74	48.85
11	27.63	31.12	34.18	36.98	39.59	42.07	44.45	46.74	48.95	51.11
12	29.28	32.86	36.00	38.86	41.54	44.08	46.51	48.85	51.11	53.32

A.6   The Greek Alphabet

Name	Lowercase	Uppercase
Alpha	α	A
Beta	β	B
Gamma	γ	Γ
Delta	δ	Δ
Epsilon	ε	E
Zeta	ζ	Z
Eta	η	H
Theta	θ	Θ
Iota	ι	I
Kappa	κ	K
Lambda	λ	Λ
Mu	μ	M
Nu	ν	N
Xi	ξ	Ξ
Omicron	o	O
Pi	π	Π
Rho	ρ	P
Sigma	σ	Σ
Tau	τ	T
Upsilon	υ	Υ
Phi	φ	Φ
Chi	χ	X
Psi	ψ	Ψ
Omega	ω	Ω

REFERENCES

The chapters in which a source is cited are given in boldface following each reference.

Abelson, R. P. & Tukey, J. W. (1963). Efficient utilization of non-numeric information in quantitative analysis: General theory and the case of simple order. *Annals of Mathematical Statistics, 34,* 1347–1369. **13**

Adams, A. G. (1969). Remark on algorithm 304: Normal curve integral. *Communications of the Association for Computing Machinery, 12,* 565–566. **A**

Agresti, A. (1983a). A survey of strategies for modeling cross-classifications having ordinal variables. *Journal of the American Statistical Association, 78,* 184–198. **13**

Agresti, A. (1983b). A simple diagonals-parameter symmetry and quasi-symmetry model. *Statistics and Probability Letters, 1,* 313–316. **11**

Agresti, A. (1984). *Analysis of ordinal categorical data.* New York: Wiley. **3, 11, 12, 13**

Agresti, A. (1986). Applying R^2-type measures to ordered categorical data. *Technometrics, 28,* 133–138. **9, 13**

Agresti, A. (1988). A model for agreement between ratings on an ordinal scale. *Biometrics, 44,* 539–548. **9**

Agristi, A., Chuang, C., & Kezouh, A. (1987). Order-restricted score parameters in association models for contingency tables. *Journal of the American Statistical Association, 82,* 619–623. **13**

Agresti, A., and Kezouh, A. (1983). Association models for multi-dimensional cross-classifications of ordinal variables. *Communications in Statistics: Theory and methods, 12,* 1261–1276. **11, 13**

Agristi, A. & Yang, M.-C. (1987). An empirical investigation of some effects of sparseness in contingency tables. *Computational Statistics and Data Analysis, 5,* 9–21. **13**

Altham, P. M. E. (1976). Discrete variable analyses for individuals grouped into families. *Biometrika, 63,* 263–269. **2**

Altham, P. M. E. (1979). Detecting relationships between categorical variables observed over time: a problem of deflating a chi-squared statistic. *Applied Statistics, 28,* 115–125. **2**

Anderson, J. A. (1984). Regression and ordered categorical variables. *Journal of the Royal Statistical Society,* Series B (Methodological), *46,* 1–30 (with discussion). **13**

Anglin, M. D., McGlothlin, W. H., and Speckart, G. (1981). The effect of parole on methadone-patient behavior. *American Journal of Drug and Alcohol Abuse, 8,* 153–170. **7**

Anscombe, F. J. (1956). On estimating binomial response relations. *Biometrika*, *43*, 461–464. **7**

Appelbaum, M. I., and Cramer, E. M. (1974). Some problems in the nonorthogonal analysis of variance. *Psychological Bulletin*, *81*, 335–343. **5**

Asmussen, S., and Edwards, D. (1983). Collapsibility and response variables in contingency tables. *Biometrika*, *70*, 567–578. **5, 7**

Atkinson, R. C., Bower, G. H., and Crothers, E. J. (1965). *An introduction to mathematical learning theory*. New York: Wiley. **10**

Barnard, G. A. (1947). Significance tests for 2 × 2 tables. *Biometrika*, *34*, 123–138. **2**

Bartlett, M. S. (1935). Contingency table interactions. *Journal of the Royal Statistical Society, Supplement* [subsequently, Series B (Methodological)], *2*, 248–251. **3**

Beardwood, J. E. (1977). A remark on algorithm AS 87: Calculation of the polychoric estimate of correlation in contingency tables. *Applied Statistics*, *26*, 121. **13**

Benedetti, J. K., and Brown, M. B. (1978). Strategies for the selection of log-linear models. *Biometrics*, *34*, 680–686. **8**

Bentler, P. M., and Bonnet, D. G. (1983). Goodness-of-fit procedures for the evaluation and selection of log-linear models. *Psychological Bulletin*, *93*, 149–166. **5**

Benzécri, J.-P. (with 33 coauthors). (1973). *L'analyse des données: Tome II: L'analyse des correspondances*. Paris: Dunod. **11**

Berkson, J. (1955). Maximum likelihood and minimum χ^2 estimates of the logistic function. *Journal of the American Statistical Association*, *50*, 130–162. **12**

Berkson, J. (1978–9). In dispraise of the exact test. *Journal of Statistical Planning and Inference*, *2*, 27–42 (with discussion in the same journal, *3*, 181–213). **2**

Berry, K. J. & Mielke, P. W., Jr. (1988). Monte Carlo comparisons of the asymptotic chi-square and likelihood-ratio tests with the nonasymptotic chi-square test for sparse $r \times c$ tables. *Psychological Bulletin*, *103*, 256–264. **2**

Beyer, W. H. (1968). *Handbook of tables for probability and statistics*, 2d ed. Cleveland, Ohio: Chemical Rubber Co. **2**

Bhapkar, V. P. (1966). A note on the equivalence of two test criteria for hypotheses in categorical data. *Journal of the American Statistical Association*, *61*, 228–235. **12**

Bhapkar, V. P. (1979). On tests of marginal symmetry and quasi-symmetry in two- and three-dimensional contingency tables. *Biometrics*, *35*, 417–426. **10, 12**

Bhapkar, V. P., and Koch, G. G. (1968). Hypothesis of 'no interaction' in multidimensional contingency tables. *Technometrics*, *10*, 107–123. **12**

Bickel, P. J., Hammel, E. A., and O'Connell, J. W. (1975). Sex bias in graduate admissions: data from Berkeley. *Science*, *187*, 398–404. **3**

Birch, M. W. (1963). Maximum likelihood in three-way contingency tables. *Journal of the Royal Statistical Society*, Series B (Methodological), *25*, 202–233. **4**

Birch, M. W. (1964). The detection of partial association, I: The 2 × 2 case. *Journal of the Royal Statistical Society*, Series B (Methodological), *26*, 313–324. **8**

Birch, M. W. (1965). The detection of partial association, II: The general case. *Journal of the Royal Statistical Society*, Series B (Methodological), *27*, 111–124. **8**

Bishop, Y. M. M., Fienberg, S. E., and Holland, P. W. (1975). *Discrete multivariate analysis: Theory and practice*. Cambridge, Mass.: MIT Press. **2, 3, 5, 6, 9, 10, 13**

Blalock, H. M., Jr. (1958). Probabilistic interpretations for the mean square contingency. *Journal of the American Statistical Association*, *53*, 102–105.

Bock, R. D. (1975). *Multivariate statistical methods in behavioral research*. New York: McGraw-Hill. **13**

Bock, R. D., and Lieberman, M. (1970). Fitting a response model for *n* dichotomously scored items. *Psychometrika*, *40*, 5–32. **13**

Bradley, D. R., Bradley, T. D., McGrath, S. G., and Cutcomb, S. D. (1979). Type I error rate of the chi-square test of independence in $R \times C$ tables that have small expected frequencies. *Psychological Bulletin*, *86*, 1290–1297. **2**

Bradley, R. A., and Terry, M. E. (1953). Rank analysis of incomplete block designs. I. The method of paired comparisons. *Biometrika, 39,* 324–345. **10**

Bresnahan, J. L. and Shapiro, M. M. (1966). A general equation and technique for the exact partitioning of chi-square contingency tables. *Psychological Bulletin, 66,* 252–262. **11**

Brier, S. S. (1980). Analysis of contingency tables under cluster sampling. *Biometrika, 67,* 591–596. **2**

Brophy, A. L. (1983). Accuracy and speed of seven approximations of the normal distribution function. *Behavior Research Methods and Instrumentation, 15,* 604–605. **13**

Bross, I. D. J. (1958). How to use ridit analysis. *Biometrics, 14,* 18–38. **13**

Brown, M. B. (1976). Screening effects in multidimensional contingency tables. *Applied Statistics, 25,* 37–46. **8**

Camilli, G., and Hopkins, K. D. (1978). Applicability of chi-square to 2 × 2 contingency tables with small expected cell frequencies. *Psychological Bulletin, 85,* 163–167. **2**

Castellian, N. J. (1965). On the partitioning of contingency tables. *Psychological Bulletin, 64,* 330–338. **11**

Caussinus, H. (1966). Contribution à l'analyse statistique des tableaux de corrélation. *Annales de la Faculté des sciences de l'Université de Toulouse pour les sciences mathematiques et les sciences physiques.* Quatrième série, Tome 29, Année 1965, 77–182. **10, 11**

Chase, G. R. (1972). On the chi-square test when the parameters are estimated independently of the sample. *Journal of the American Statistical Association, 67,* 609–611. **8**

Christoffersson, A. (1970). Factor analysis of dichotomized variables. *Psychometrika, 35,* 5–32. **13**

Cicchetti, D. V., and Fleiss, J. L. (1977). Comparison of the null distribution of weighted kappa and the C ordinal statistic. *Applied Psychological Measurement, 1,* 195–201. **9**

Clemm, D. S., Krishnaiah, P. R., and Waikar, V. B. (1973). Tables for the extreme roots of the Wishart matrix. *Journal of Statistical Computing and Simulation, 2,* 65–92. **A**

Clogg, C. C. (1982). Some models for the analysis of association in multiway cross-classifications having ordered categories. *Journal of the American Statistical Association, 77,* 803–815 (reprinted in Goodman, 1984). **13**

Cohen, J. (1960). A coefficient of agreement for nominal scales. *Educational and Psychological Measurement, 20,* 37–46. **9**

Cohen, J. (1968). Weighted kappa: Nominal scale agreement with provision for scaled disagreement of partial credit. *Psychological Bulletin, 70,* 213–220. **9**

Cohen, J. (1977). *Statistical power analysis for the behavioral sciences,* rev. ed. New York: Academic. **2**

Cohen, J., and Cohen, P. (1975). *Applied multiple regression/correlation analysis for the behavioral sciences.* Hillsdale, N. J.: Erlbaum. **1**

Cohen, J. E. (1976). The distribution of the chi-squared statistic under cluster sampling from contingency tables. *Journal of the American Statistical Association, 71,* 665–670. **2**

Conger, A. J. (1980). Integration and generalization of Kappas for multiple raters. *Psychological Bulletin, 88,* 322–328. **9**

Conover, W. J. (1974). Some reasons for not using the Yates continuity correction on 2 × 2 contingency tables. *Journal of the American Statistical Association, 69,* 374–382 (with discussion). **2**

Coombs, C. H. (1964). *A theory of data.* New York: Wiley. **11**

Coombs, C. H., Dawes, R. M., and Tversky, A. (1970). *Mathematical psychology: An elementary introduction.* Englewood Cliffs, N.J.: Prentice-Hall. **9**

Cormack, R. M. (1981). Loglinear models for capture-recapture experiment on open populations. In R. W. Hiorns and D. Cooke (eds.), *The mathematical theory of the dynamics of biological populations,* II. London: Academic. **10**

Cormack, R. M. (1985). Examples of the use of GLIM to analyze capture-recapture studies. In B. J. T. Morgan & P. M. North (eds.) *Statistics in Ornithology.* Lecture notes in statistics #29. Berlin-Heidelberg: Spring-Verlag. **10**

Cornfield, J. (1956). A statistical problem arising from retrospective studies. In J. Neyman (ed.), *Proceedings of the third Berkeley symposium on statistics and probability*: Vol. 4. *Contributions to biology and problems of health*. Berkeley: University of California Press. 3

Cox, D. R. (1970). *The analysis of binary data*. London: Methuen. 7

Cramer, F. W., and Appelbaum, M. I. (1980). Nonorthogonal analysis of variance—once again. *Psychological Bulletin, 87*, 51–57. 5

Cramèr, H. (1946). *Mathematical methods of statistics*. Princeton, N.J.: Princeton University Press. 9

Darroch, J. N. & McCloud, P. I. (1986). Category distinguishability and observer agreement. *Australian Journal of Statistics, 28*, 371–388. 9, 10

Darroch, J. N., Lauritzen, S. L., and Speed, T. P. (1980). Markov fields and log-linear interaction for contingency tables. *Annals of Statistics, 8*, 522–539. 6

Dawid, A. P. (1979). Conditional independence in statistical theory. *Journal of the Royal Statistical Society*, Series B (Methodological), *41*, 1–31. 3

Delucchi, K. L. (1983). The use and misuse of chi–square: Lewis and Burke revisited. *Psychological Bulletin, 94*, 166–176. 2

Deming, W. E., and Stephan, F. F. (1940). On the lease squares adjustment of a sampled frequency table when the expected marginal totals are known. *Annals of Mathematical Statistics, 11*, 427–444. 5

Diaconis, P., and Efron, B. (1983). Computer-intensive methods in statistics. *Scientific American, 248*:5 (May, 1983), 116–130. 8

Dixon, W. J. (ed.), (1983). *BMD P Statistical Software Manual*. Berkeley: University of California Press. 1

Draper, N. R., and Smith, H. (1981). *Applied regression analysis*, 2d edn. New York: Wiley. 12

Duncan, O. D. (1975). *Introduction to structural equation models*. New York: Academic. 6, 7

Duncan, O. D. (1979). How destination depends on origin in the occupational mobility table. *American Journal of Sociology, 84*, 793–803. 13

Edwards, D., and Havránek, T. (1985). A fast procedure for model search in multidimensional contingency tables. *Biometrika, 72*, 339–351. 8

Edwards, D., and Kreiner, S. (1983). The analysis of contingency tables by graphical methods. *Biometrika, 70*, 553–565. 3, 6, 8

Efron, B. (1978). Regression and ANOVA with zero-one data: Measures of residual variation. *Journal of the American Statistical Society, 73*, 113–121. 5

Efron, B. (1982). *The jackknife, the bootstrap and other resampling plans*. CBMS-NSF Regional Conference Series in Applied Mathematics, no. 38. Philadelphia: Society for Industrial and Applied Mathematics. 8

Efron, B., and Gong, G. (1983). A leisurely look at the bootstrap, the jackknife, and cross-validation. *American Statistician, 37*, 36–48. 8

Escofier, B. (1983). Analyse de la différence entre deux measures définies sur le produit de deux mêmes ensembles. *Cahiers de l'Anayse des Données, 8*, 325–329. 11

Fellegi, I. P. (1980). Approximate tests of independence and goodness of fit based on stratified multistage samples. *Journal of the American Statistical Association, 75*, 261–268. 2

Feller, W. (1968). *An introduction to probability theory and its applications*, Vol. 1, 3d ed. New York: Wiley. 4

Fienberg, S. E. (1972). The multiple recapture census for closed populations and incomplete 2^k contingency tables. *Biometrika, 59*, 591–603. 10

Fienberg, S. E. (1979). The use of chi-square statistics for categorical data problems. *Journal of the Royal Statistical Society*, Series B (Methodological), *41*, 54–64. 2, 8

Fienberg, S. E. (1980). *The analysis of cross-classified categorical data*, 2d ed. Cambridge, Mass.: MIT Press. 2, 3, 6, 13

Fienberg, S. E., and Larntz, K. (1976). Log linear representation for paired and multiple comparison models. *Biometrika, 63*, 245–254. 10

Finney, D. J. (1948). The Fisher-Yates test of significance in 2 × 2 contingency tables. *Biometrika*, *35*, 145–156. **2**

Finney, D. J. (1971). *Probit analysis*, 3d ed. Cambridge: Cambridge University Press. **13**

Fisher, R. A. (1935). *Statistical methods for research workers*, 5th ed. Edenburgh and London: Oliver & Boyd; more recently, 14th ed. New York: Hafner, 1973. **2**

Fleiss, J. L. (1971). Measuring nominal scale agreement among many raters. *Psychological Bulletin*, *76*, 378–382. **9**

Fleiss, J. L. (1981). *Statistical methods for rates and proportions*, 2d ed. New York: Wiley. **3, 9**

Fleiss, J. L., and Cicchetti, D. V. (1978). Inference about weighted kappa in the non-null case. *Applied Psychological Measurement*, *2*, 113–117. **9**

Fleiss, J. L., Cohen, J., and Everitt, B. S. (1969). Large sample standard errors of kappa and weighted kappa. *Psychological Bulletin*, *72*, 323–327. **9**

Freeman, G. H., and Halton, J. H. (1951). Note on an exact treatment of contingency, goodness of fit and other problems of significance. *Biometrika*, *38*, 141–149. **2**

Freeman, M. F., and Tukey, J. W. (1950). Transformations related to the angular and the square root. *Annals of Mathematical Statistics*, *21*, 607–611. **5**

Gabriel, K. R. (1966). Simultaneous test procedures for multiple comparisons on categorical data. *Journal of the American Statistical Association*, *61*, 1081–1096. **11**

Gans, L. P., and Robertson, C. A. (1981a). Distribution of Goodman and Kruskal's gamma and Spearman's rho in 2 × 2 tables for small and moderate sample sizes. *Journal of the American Statistical Association*, *76*, 942–946. **13**

Gans, L. P., and Robertson, C. A. (1981b). The behavior of estimated measures of association in small and moderate sample sizes for 2 × 3 tables. *Communications in statistics: Theory and methods*, *A10*, 1673–1686. **13**

Garner, W. R. (1962). *Uncertainty and structure as psychological concepts*. New York: Wiley. **9**

Garside, G. R., and Mack, C. (1976). Actual type 1 error probabilities for various tests in the homogeneity case of the 2 × 2 contingency table. *American Satistician*, *30*, 18–21. **2**

Gart, J. J. (1962). On the combination of relative risk. *Biometrics*, *18*, 601–610. **3**

Gart, J. J. (1970). Point and interval estimates of the common odds ratio in the combination of 2 × 2 tables with fixed marginals. *Biometrika*, *57*, 471–475. **3, 9**

Gart, J. J. (1971). The comparison of proportions: A review of significance tests, confidence intervals and adjustments for stratification. *Review of the International Statistical Institute*, *39*, 148–169. Corrigenda: *40*, 1972, 221. **9**

Gart, J. J., Pettigrew, H. M., and Thomas, D. G. (1985). The effect of bias, variance estimation, skewness and kurtosis of the empirical logit on weighted least squares analysis. *Biometrika*, *72*, 179–190. **7**

Gart, J. J., and Thomas, D. G. (1972). Numerical results on approximate confidence limits for the odds ratio. *Journal of the Royal Statistical Society*, Series B (Methodological), *34*, 441–447. **9**

Gart, J. J., and Thomas, D. G. (1982). The performance of three approximate confidence limit methods for the odds ratio. *American Journal of Epidemiology*, *115*, 453–470. **9**

Gart, J. J., and Zweifel, J. R. (1967). On the bias of various estimators of the logit and its variance with application to quantal bioassay. *Biometrika*, *54*, 181–187. **7**

Gilula, Z. (1984). On some similarities between canonical correlation models and latent class models for two-way contingency tables. *Biometrika*, *71*, 523–529. **11**

Gilula, Z., and Krieger, A. H. (1983). The decomposition and monotonicity of Pearson's chi-square for collapsed contingency tables with applications. *Journal of the American Statistical Association*, *78*, 176–180. **11**

Gilula, Z., Krieger, A. M., & Ritov, Y. (1988). Ordinal association in contingency tables: some interpretive aspects. *Journal of the American Statistical Association*, *83*, 540–545. **11**

Gokhale, D. V., and Kullback, S. (1978). *The information in contingency tables*. New York: Dekker. **5, 9**

Good, I. J. (1975). The number of hypotheses of independence for a random vector or for a multidimensional contingency table, and the Bell numbers. *Iranian Journal of Science and Technology, 4*, 77–83. **6**

Goodman, L. A. (1964a). Simultaneous confidence limits for cross-product ratios in contingency tables. *Journal of the Royal Statistical Society*, Series B (Methodological), *26*, 86–102. **9, 11**

Goodman, L. A. (1964b). Simple methods for analyzing three-factor interaction in contingency tables. *Journal of the American Statistical Association, 59*, 319–352. **9**

Goodman, L. A. (1970). The multivariate analysis of qualitative data: interactions among multiple classifications. *Journal of the American Statistical Association, 65*, 226–256 (Reprinted in Goodman, 1978). **2, 3, 5, 6**

Goodman, L. A. (1971). Partitioning of chi-square, analysis of marginal contingency tables, and estimation of expected frequencies in multidimensional contingency tables. *Journal of the American Statistical Association, 66*, 339–344. **2, 3, 6**

Goodman, L. A. (1972a). Some multiplicative models for the analysis of cross-classified data. In L. M. LeCam, J. Neyman, & E. L. Scott (eds.), *Proceedings of the sixth Berkeley symposium on mathematical statistics and probability, Vol. 1: Theory of Statistics*. Berkeley: University of California Press (reprinted in Goodman, 1984). **2, 10, 11**

Goodman, L. A. (1972b). A general model for the analysis of surveys. *American Journal of Sociology, 77*, 1035–1086 (reprinted in Goodman, 1978). **5, 6**

Goodman, L. A. (1973a). Causal analysis of data from panel studies and other kinds of surveys. *American Journal of Sociology, 78*, 1135–1191 (reprinted in Goodman, 1978). **6**

Goodman, L. A. (1973b). The analysis of multidimensional contingency tables when some variables are posterior to others: a modified path analysis approach. *Biometrika, 69*, 179–192 (reprinted in Goodman, 1978). **6, 7**

Goodman, L. A. (1978). *Analyzing qualitative/categorical data: Log-linear models and latent-structure analysis*. Cambridge, Mass.: Abt (reprinted: Lanham, Md.: University Press of America, 1985). **2, 3, 5, 6, 7**

Goodman, L. A. (1979a). Multiplicative models for square contingency tables with ordered categories. *Biometrika, 66*, 413–418 (reprinted in Goodman, 1984). **11**

Goodman, L. A. (1979b). Multiplicative models for the analysis of occupational mobility tables and other kinds of cross-classification tables. *American Journal of Sociology, 84*, 804–819 (reprinted in Goodman, 1984). **11**

Goodman, L. A. (1979c). Simple models for the analysis of association in cross-classification having ordered categories. *Journal of the American Statistical Association, 74*, 537–552 (reprinted in Goodman, 1984). **11, 13**

Goodman, L. A. (1981a). Association models and canonical correlation in the analysis of cross-classifications having ordered categories. *Journal of the American Statistical Association, 76*, 320–334 (reprinted in Goodman, 1984). **11**

Goodman, L. A. (1981b). Association models and the bivariate normal for contingency tables with ordered categories. *Biometrika, 68*, 347–355 (reprinted in Goodman, 1984). **13**

Goodman, L. A. (1984). *The analysis of cross-classified data having ordered categories*. Cambridge, Mass.: Harvard University Press. **2, 3, 10, 11, 13**

Goodman, L. A. (1985). The analysis of cross classified data having ordered and/or unordered categories: association models, correlation models, and asymmetry models for contingency tables with or without missing entries (1983 Henry L. Reitz Memorial Lecture). *Annals of Statistics, 13*, 10–69. **2, 11, 13**

Goodman, L. A. (1986). Some useful extensions of the usual correspondence analysis approach and the usual log-linear models approach in the analysis of contingency tables. *International Statistical Review, 54*, 243–309 (with discussion). **11, 13**

Goodman, L. A. (1987). New methods for analyzing the intrinsic character of qualitative variables using cross-classified data. *American Journal of Sociology, 93*, 529–583. **11, 13**

Goodman, L. A., and Kruskal, W. H. (1954). Measures of association for cross classifications. *Journal of the American Statistical Association*, *49*, 732–764 (reprinted in Goodman & Kruskal, 1979). **9, 13**

Goodman, L. A., and Kruskal, W. H. (1959). Measures of association for cross classifications, II: Further discussion and references. *Journal of the American Statistical Association*, *54*, 123–163 (reprinted in Goodman & Kruskal, 1979). **9**

Goodman, L. A., and Kruskal, W. H. (1963). Measures of association for cross classifications, III: Approximate sampling theory. *Journal of the American Statistical Association*, *58*, 310–364 (reprinted in Goodman & Kruskal, 1979). **9, 13**

Goodman, L. A., and Kruskal, W. H. (1972). Measures of association for cross classifications, IV: Simplification of asymptotic variances. *Journal of the American Statistical Association*, *67*, 415–421 (reprinted in Goodman & Kruskal, 1979). **9, 13**

Goodman, L. A., and Kruskal, W. H. (1979). *Measures of association for cross classifications*. New York: Springer Verlag. **9, 13**

Green, D. M., and Swets, J. A. (1966). *Signal detection theory and psychophysics*. New York: Wiley (reprinted: New York: Krieger, 1974). **6, 13**

Green, P. E. (1976). *Mathematical tools for applied multivariate analysis*. New York: Academic. **12**

Greenacre, M. J. (1984). *Theory and application of correspondence analysis*. London: Academic. **11**

Greenacre, M. J., and Hastie, T. (1987). The geometric interpretation of correspondence analysis. *Journal of the American Statistical Association*, *82*, 437–447. **11**

Grizzle, J. E. (1967). Continuity correction in the χ^2 test for 2×2 tables. *American Statistician*, *21*:4 (Oct, 1967), 28–32. **2**

Grizzle, J. E., Starmer, C. P., and Koch, G. G. (1969). Analysis of categorical data by linear models. *Biometrics*, *25*, 489–504. **5, 12**

Grizzle, J. E., and Williams, O. D. (1972). Log-linear models and tests of independence for contingency tables. *Biometrics*, *28*, 137–156. **12**

Guttman, L. (1941). The quantification of a class of attributes: A theory and method of scale construction. In Committee on Social Adjustment (eds.), *The prediction of personal adjustment*. New York: Social Science Research Council. **11**

Haberman, S. J. (1973). The analysis of residuals in cross-classified tables. *Biometrics*, *29*, 205–220. **5**

Haberman, S. J. (1974a). *The analysis of frequency data*. Chicago: University of Chicago Press. **5, 12**

Haberman, S. J. (1974b). Log-linear models for frequency tables with ordered classifications. *Biometrics*, *30*, 589–600. **13**

Haberman, S. J. (1977). Log-linear models and frequency tables with small expected cell counts. *Annals of Statistics*, *5*, 1148–1169. **2, 5**

Haberman, S. J. (1978). *Analysis of qualitative data*, Vol. 1: *Introductory topics*. New York: Academic. **2, 3, 5, 12**

Haberman, S. J. (1979). *Analysis of qualitative data*, Vol. 2: *New developments*. New York: Academic. **2, 3, 5, 12**

Haberman, S. J. (1981). Tests for independence in two-way contingency tables based on canonical correlation and on linear-by-linear interaction. *Annals of Statistics*, *9*, 1178–1186. **11, 13**

Haberman, S. J. (1982). Analysis of dispersion of multinomial responses. *Journal of the American Statistical Association*, *77*, 568–580. **5**

Haldane, J. B. S. (1955). The estimation and significance of the logarithm of a ratio of frequencies. *Annals of Human Genetics*, *20*, 309–311. **7**

Harris, R. J. (1985). *A primer of multivariate statistics*, (2d ed.). New York: Academic. **1, 11, 12**

Havránek, T. (1984). A procedure for model search in multidimensional contingency tables. *Biometrics*, *40*, 95–100. **8**

Haynam, G. E., Govindarajulu, Z., Leone, F. C., and Siefert, P. (1982–3). Tables of the cumulative non-central chi-square distribution. *Statistics: Mathematische Operationsforschung und Statistik (Series Statistics), 13* 413–443, 577–634; *14*, 75–139, 269–300, 457–484, 589–603. **2**

Hays, W. L. (1981). *Statistics*, 3d ed. New York: Holt, Rinehart and Winston. **1, 4, 9**

Hill, I. D., and Joyce, S. A. (1967). Algorithm 304: Normal curve integral. *Communications of the Association for Computing Machinery, 10*, 374–375. **A**

Hoaglin, D. C. (1977). Direct approximations for chi-squared percentage points. *Journal of the American Statistical Association, 72*, 508–515. **A**

Hogg, R. V., and Craig, A. T. (1978). *Introduction to mathematical statistics*, 4th ed. New York: Macmillan. **4**

Holmgren, B. (1970). Remark on algorithm 304: Normal curve integral. *Communications of the Association for Computing Machinery, 13*, 624. **A**

Hubert, L. J. (1978). A general formula for the variance of Cohen's weighted kappa. *Psychological Bulletin, 85*, 183–184. **9**

Hulchinson, T. P. (1979). The validity of the chi-square test when expected frequencies are small: A list of recent research references. *Communications in Statistics: Theory and Methods, 8*, 327–335. **2**

Ireland, C. T., and Kullback, S. (1968). Contingency tables with given marginals. *Biometrika, 55*, 179–188. **5**

Irwin, J. O. (1949). A note on the subdivision of χ^2 into components. *Biometrika, 36*, 130–134. **11**

Jewell, N. P. (1986). On the bias of commonly used measures of association in 2×2 trials. *Biometrics, 42*, 351–358. **9**

Johnson, N. L, and Kotz, S. (1969). *Distributions in statistics: Discrete distributions*. New York: Wiley. **4**

Johnson, N. L., and Kotz, S. (1970). *Distributions in statistics: Continuous univariate distributions*, vol. 2. New York: Wiley. **2, 13**

Kempthorne, O. (1979). In dispraise of the exact test: reactions. *Journal of Statistical Planning and Inference, 3*, 199–213. **2**

Kendall, M. G. (1938). A new measure of rank correlation. *Biometrika, 30*, 81–93. **13**

Kendall, M. G. (1945). The treatment of ties in rank problems. *Biometrika, 33*, 239–251. **13**

Kendall, M. G. (1970). *Rank correlation methods*, 4th edn. New York: Hafner. **13**

Kendall, M. G., and Stewart, A. (1977). *The advanced theory of statistics*, Vol. 1: *Distribution theory*, 4th ed. London: Griffin. **13**

Kendall, M. G., and Stewart, A. (1979). *The advanced theory of statistics*, Vol. 2: *Inference and relationship*, 4th ed. London: Griffin. **4**

Keppel, G. (1982). *Design and analysis: A researcher's handbook*, 2d ed. Englewood Cliffs, N.J.: Prentice-Hall. **1**

Kimball, A. W. (1954). Short-cut formulas for the exact partition of χ^2 in contingency tables. *Biometrics, 10*, 452–458. **11**

Kirk, R. E. (1982). *Experimental design*, 2d ed. Belmont, Calif.: Brooks/Cole. **1**

Koch, G. G., Landis, J. R., Freeman, J. L., Freeman, D. H., Jr., and Lehnen, R. G. (1977). A general methodology for the analysis of experiments with repeated measurement of categorical data. *Biometrics, 33*, 133–158. **12**

Koehler, K. J. (1986). Goodness-of-fit tests for log-linear models in sparse contingency tables. *Journal of the American Statistical Association, 81*, 483–493. **2**

Koehler, K. J., and Larntz, K. (1980). An empirical investigation of goodness-of-fit statistics for sparse multinomials. *Journal of the American Statistical Association, 75*, 336–344. **2**

Krippendorff, K. (1986). *Information theory: Structural models for qualitative data*. Sage University Paper Series on Quantitative Applications in the Social Sciences, No. 62. Beverly Hills, Calif.: Sage. **9**

Krishnaiah, P. R., and Chang, T. C. (1971). On the exact distribution of the extreme roots of the Wishart and MANOVA matrices. *Journal of Multivariate Analysis, 1*, 108–117. **A**

Krüger, H.-P., Lehmacher, W., and Wall, K.-D. (1981). *The fourfold table up to N* = 80/Die Vierfeldertafel bis *N* = 80. Stuttgart: Gustav Fischer. **2**

Kruskal, J. B. (1965). Analysis of factorial experiments by estimating monotone transformations of the data. *Journal of the Royal Statistical Society, Series B (Methodological)*, 27, 251–263. **13**

Kruskal, J. B., and Wish, M. (1978). *Multidimensional scaling*. Sage University Paper Series on Quantitative Applications in the Social Sciences, No. 07–011. Beverly Hills, CA: Sage. **10**

Ku, H. H., Varner, R. N., and Kullback, S. (1971). On the analysis of multidimensional contingency tables. *Journal of the American Statistical Association*, 66, 55–64. **5**

Lancaster, H. O. (1949). The derivation and partition of χ^2 in certain discrete distributions. *Biometrika*, 36, 117–129. **11**

Lancaster, H. O. (1950). The exact partition of χ^2 and its application to the problem of the pooling of small expectations. *Biometrika*, 37, 267–270. **11**

Lancaster, H. O. (1958). The structure of bivariate distributions. *Annals of Mathematical Statistics*, 29, 719–736. **11**

Lancaster, H. O., and Hamdan, M. A. (1964). Estimation of the correlation coefficient in contingency tables with possibly non-metric characters. *Psychometrika*, 29, 383–391. **13**

Larntz, K. (1978). Small-sample comparison of exact levels for chi-square goodness-of-fit statistics. *Journal of the American Statistical Association*, 73, 253–263. **2, 5**

Latscha, R. (1953). Tests of significance in a 2 × 2 contingency table: extension of Finney's table. *Biometrika*, 40, 70–86. **2**

Lebart, L., Morineau, A., and Warwick, K. M. (1984). *Multivariate descriptive statistical analysis: Correspondence analysis and related techniques for large matrices*. New York: Wiley. **11**

LeCren, E. D. (1965). A note on the history of mark-recapture population estimates. *Journal of Animal Ecology*, 34, 453–454. **10**

Lee, S. K. (1977). On the asymptotic variances of $\hat{u}$ terms in loglinear models of multidimensional contingency tables. *Journal of the American Statistical Association*, 72, 412–419. **5**

Lewis, D., and Burke, C. J. (1949). The use and misuse of the chi-square test. *Psychological Bulletin*, 46, 433–489. **2**

Liebetrau, A. M. (1983). *Measures of association*. Sage University Paper Series on Quantitative Applications in the Social Sciences, No. 32. Beverly Hills, Calif.: Sage. **9**

Light, R. L. (1971). Measures of response agreement for qualitative data: Some generalizations and alternatives. *Psychological Bulletin*, 76, 365–377. **9**

Light, R. L., and Margolin, B. H. (1971). An analysis of variance for categorical data. *Journal of the American Statistical Association*, 66, 534–544. **5**

Lord, F., and Novick, M. R. (1968). *Statistical theory of mental test scores*. Reading, Mass.: Addison-Wesley. **13**

Luce, R. D. (1959). *Individual choice behavior: A theoretical analysis*. New York: Wiley. **10**

Luce, R. D. (1960). The theory of selective information and some of its behavioral applications. In R. D. Luce (ed.), *Developments in mathematical psychology: Information, learning and tracking*. Glencoe, Ill.: Free Press. **9**

McCullagh, P. (1978). A class of parametric models for the analysis of square contingency tables with ordered categories. *Biometrika*, 65, 413–418. **13**

McCullagh, P. (1980). Regression models for ordinal data. *Journal of the Royal Statistical Society, Series B (Methodological)*. 42, 109–142 (with discussion). **13**

McCullagh, P., and Nelder, J. A. (1983). *Generalized linear models*. London: Chapman and Hall. **5, 12, 13**

McGill, W. J. (1954). Multivariate information transmission. *Psychometrika*, 19, 97–116. **9**

McNicol, D. (1971). *A primer of signal detection theory*. London: Allen & Unwin. **6**

Magidson, J. (1981). Qualitative variance, entropy, and correlation ratios for nominal dependent variables. *Social Science Research*, 10, 177–194. **5**

Mantel, N. (1977). Test and limits for the common odds ratio of several 2 × 2 contingency tables:

methods in analogy with the Mantel-Haenszel procedure. *Journal of Statistical Planning and Inference*, *1*, 179–189. 3

Mantel, N., and Greenhouse, S. W. (1968). What is the continuity correction? *American Statistician*, *22*:5 (Dec, 1968), 27–30. 2

Mantel, N., and Haenszel, W. (1959). Statistical aspects of the analysis of data from retrospective studies of disease. *Journal of the National Cancer Institute*, *22*, 719–748. 3

Margolin, B. H., and Light, R. L. (1974). An analysis of variance for categorical data, II: Small sample comparisons with chi-square and other competitors. *Journal of the American Statistical Association*, *69*, 755–764. 5

Martinson, E. O., and Hamdan, M. A. (1975). Calculation of the polychoric estimate of correlation in contingency tables. *Applied Statistics*, *24*, 272–278. 13

Mehta, C. R., and Patel, N. R. (1983). A network algorithm for performing Fisher's exact test in $r \times c$ contingency tables. *Journal of the American Statistical Association*, *78*, 427–434. 2

Miller, G. A., and Nicely, P. E. (1955). An analysis of peripheral confusions among some English consonants. *Journal of the Acoustical Society of America*, *27*, 338–352. 9

Miller, R. G., Jr. (1981). *Simultaneous statistical inference*, 2d ed. New York: Springer-Verlag. 1, 9

Milligan, G. W. (1980). Factors that affect Type I and Type II error rates in the analysis of multidimensional contingency tables. *Psychological Bulletin*, *87*, 238–244. 2

Muthén, B. (1978). Contributions to factor analysis of dichotomous variables. *Psychometrika*, *43*, 551–560. 13

Muthén, B. (1979). A structural probit model with latent variables. *Journal of the American Statistical Association*, *74*, 807–811. 13

Muthén, B. (1981). Factor analysis of dichotomous variables: American attitudes toward abortion. In E. Borgatta and D. J. Jackson (eds.), *Factor analysis and measurement in sociological research: a multidimensional perspective*. Beverly Hills, Calif.: Sage. 13

Muthén, B., and Christoffersson, A. (1981). Simultaneous factor analysis of dichotomous variables in several groups. *Psychometrika*, *46*, 407–419. 13

Myers, J. L. (1979). *Fundamentals of experimental design*, 3d ed. Boston: Allyn and Bacon. 1

Nelder, J. A., and Wedderburn, R. W. M. (1972). Generalized linear models. *Journal of the Royal Statistical Society*, Series A (General), *135*, 370–384. 12

Neyman, J. (1949). Contributions to the theory of χ^2 test. In J. Neyman (ed.), *Proceedings of the Berkeley symposium on mathematical statistics and probability*. Berkeley: University of California Press. 12

Nishisato, S. (1980). *Analysis of categorical data: Dual scaling and its applications*. Mathematical Expositions, No. 24. Toronto: University of Toronto Press. 11

Oler, J. (1985). Noncentrality parameters in chi-squared goodness-of-fit analyses with an application to log-linear procedures. *Journal of the American Statistical Association*, *80*, 181–189. 8

Olson, U. (1979). Maximum likelihood estimation of the polychoric correlation coefficient. *Psychometrika*, *44*, 443–460. 13

Olzak, L. A. (1981). Inhibition and stochastic interactions in spatial pattern perception (Doctoral dissertation, University of California, Los Angeles). *Dissertation Abstracts International*, *42*, 1651B (University Microfilms no. 8121021). 6

Olzak, L. A., and Wickens, T. D. (1983). The interpretation of detection data through direct multivariate frequency analysis. *Psychological Bulletin*, *93*, 574–585. 6

O'Neill, M. E. (1978a). Asymptotic distributions of the canonical correlation from contingency tables. *Australian Journal of Statistics*, *20*, 75–82. 11

O'Neill, M. E. (1978b). Distributional expansions for canonical correlations from contingency tables. *Journal of the Royal Statistical Society*, Series B (Methodological), *40*, 303–312. 11

O'Neill, M. E. (1981). A note on the canonical correlations from contingency tables. *Australian Journal of Statistics*, *23*, 58–66. 11

Overall, J. E. (1980). Power of chi-square tests for 2×2 contingency tables with small expected frequencies. *Psychological Bulletin*, *87*, 132–135. 2

Overall, J. E., Rhoades, H. M., and Starbuck, R. R. (1987). Small-sample tests for homogeneity of response probabilities in 2 × 2 contingency tables. *Psychological Bulletin, 102*, 307–314. **2**

Overall J. E., and Spiegel, D. K. (1969). Concerning least squares analysis of experimental data. *Psychological Bulletin, 72*, 311–322. **5**

Pagano, M., and Halvorsen, K. T. (1981). An algorithm for finding the exact significance level of $r \times c$ contingency tables. *Journal of the American Statistical Association, 76*, 931–934. **2**

Patil, G. P., and Taillie, C. (1982). Diversity as a concept and its measurement. *Journal of the American Statistical Association, 77*, 548–567 (with discussion). **5**

Pearson, E. S. (1947). The choice of statistical tests illustrated on the interpretation of data classed in a 2 × 2 table. *Biometrika, 34*, 139–167. **2**

Pearson, E. S., and Hartley, H. O. (1954). *Biometrika tables for Statisticians*, Vol. 1, 4th ed. Cambridge: Cambridge University Press. **2**

Pearson, E. S., and Hartley, H. O. (1972). *Biometrika tables for Statisticians*, Vol. 2. Cambridge: Cambridge University Press. **A**

Pearson, K. (1900). On the criterion that a given system of deviations from the probable in the case of a correlated system of variables is such that it can reasonably be supposed to have arisen from random sampling. *The London, Edinburgh, and Dublin Philosophical Magazine and Journal of Science*, Fifth Series, *50*, 157–175. **2**

Pearson, K. (1901). Mathematical contributions to the theory of evolution VII: On the correlation of characters not quantitatively measurable. *Philosophical Transactions of the Royal Society (London)*, Series A. *195A*, 1–47. **13**

Pearson K., and Heron, D. (1913). On theories of association. *Biometrika, 9*, 159–315. **13**

Pedhazur, E. J. (1982). *Multiple regression in behavioral research: explanation and prediction*, 2d ed. New York: Holt, Rinehart, & Winston. **1, 6**

Petersen, C. G. J. (1894). On the biology of our flat-fishes and on the decrease of our flat-fish fisheries with some observations showing how to remedy the latter and promote the flat fish fisheries in our seas east of the Skaw. *Report of the Danish Biological Station*, 1893–4, *IV*. **10**

Press, W. H., Flannery, B. P., Teukolsky, S. A., and Vetterling, W. T. (1986). *Numerical recipes: The art of scientific computing*. Cambridge: Cambridge University Press. **11, 13, A**

Rao, J. N. K., and Scott, A. J. (1981). The analysis of categorical data from complex sample surveys: chi-squared tests for goodness of fit and independence in two-way tables. *Journal of the American Statistical Association, 76*, 221–230. **2**

Reynolds, H. T. (1977). *The analysis of cross-classifications*. New York: Free Press. **6, 9, 13**

SAS Institute (1985). *SAS User's Guide: Statistics* (Version 5). Cary, N.C.: SAS Institute. **1, 12**

Scheffé, H. (1953). A method for judging all contrasts in the analysis of variance. *Biometrika, 40*, 87–104. **9**

Scheffé, H. (1959). *The analysis of variance*. New York: Wiley. **9**

Seber, G. A. F. (1982). *The estimation of animal abundance*, 2d edn. London: Griffin and New York: Macmillan. **10**

Seber, G. A. F. (1986). A review of estimating animal abundance. *Biometrics, 42*, 267–292. **10**

Semenya, K., and Koch, G. G. (1979). Linear models analysis for rank functions of ordinal categorical data. *Proceedings of the statistical computing section of the American Statistical Association*. Washington: American Statistical Association. **13**

Semenya, K., Koch, G. G., Stokes, M. E., and Forthofer, R. N. (1983). Linear model methods for some rank function analyses of ordinal categorical data. *Communications in Statistics: Theory and Methods, 12*, 1277–1298. **13**

Shaffer, J. P. (1973). Testing specific hypotheses in contingency tables: chi-square partitioning and other methods. *Psychological Reports, 33*, 343–348. **11**

Shannon, C. E. (1948). A mathematical theory of communication. *Bell System Technical Journal*, *27*, 379–423 and 623–656. **9**

Shannon, C. E., and Weaver, W. (1949). *The mathematical theory of communication*. Urbana: University of Illinois Press. **9**

Shapiro, S. H. (1982). Collapsing contingency tables—a geometric approach. *American Statistician*, *36*, 43–45. **5**

Simpson, E. H. (1951). The interpretation of interaction in contingency tables. *Journal of the Royal Statistical Society*, Series B (Methodological), *13*, 238–241. **3**

Smith, J. E. K. (1973). On tests of quasi-independence in psychological research. *Psychological Bulletin*, *80*, 329–333. **10**

Somers, R. H. (1962). A new asymmetric measure for ordinal variables. *American Sociological Review*, *27*, 799–811. **13**

SPSS, Inc. (1983). *SPSSˣ Users Guide*. New York: McGraw Hill. **1**

Tanner, M. A. & Young, M. A. (1985a). Modeling ordinal scale disagreement. *Psychological Bulletin*, *98*, 408–415. **9, 11**

Tanner M. A. & Young, M. A. (1985b). Modeling agreement among raters. *Journal of the American Statistical Association*, *80*, 175–180. **9**

Tatsuoka, M. M. (1971). *Multivariate analysis: Techniques for educational and psychological research*. New York: Wiley. **1, 12**

Tenenhaus, M., and Young, F. W. (1985). An analysis and synthesis of multiple correspondence analysis, optimal scaling, dual scaling, homogeneity analysis and other methods for quantifying categorical multivariate data. *Psychometrika*, *50*, 91–119. **11**

Thurstone, L. L. (1927). Psychophysical analysis. *American Journal of Psychology*, *38*, 368–389. **13**

Thurstone, L. L. (1959). *The measurement of value*. Chicago: University of Chicago Press. **13**

Upton, G. J. G. (1978). *The analysis of cross-tabulated data*. New York: Wiley. **3**

Upton, G. J. G. (1982). A comparison of alternative tests for the 2×2 comparative trial. *Journal of the Royal Statistical Society*, Series A (General), *145*, 86–105. **2**

van der Heijden, P. G. M., and De Leeuw, J. (1985). Correspondence analysis used complementary to loglinear analysis. *Psychometrika*, *50*, 429–447. **11**

Wald, A. (1943). Tests of statistical hypotheses concerning several parameters where the number of observations is large. *Transactions of the American Mathematical Society*, *54*, 426–482. **12**

Winer, B. J. (1971). *Statistical principles in experimental design*, 2d ed. New York: McGraw-Hill. **1**

Wermuth, N. (1976). Model search among multiplicative models. *Biometrics*, *32*, 253–263. **8**

Whittemore, A. S. (1978). Collapsibility of multidimensional contingency tables. *Journal of the Royal Statistical Society*, Series B (Methodological), *40*, 328–340. **5**

Wickens, T. D. (1982). *Models for behavior: Stochastic processes in psychology*. San Francisco: Freeman. **4**

Wickens, T. D., and Olzak, L. A. (1980). The statistical analysis of concurrent detection data. *Perception and Psychophysics*.

Williams, O. D., and Grizzle, J. E. (1972). Analysis of contingency tables having ordered response categories. *Journal of the American Statistical Association*, *67*, 55–63. **13**

Wilson, T. P. (1974). Measures of association for bivariate ordinal hypotheses. In H. M. Blalock, Jr. *Measurement in the social sciences*. Chicago: Aldine-Atherton. **13**

Woolson, R. F., and Brier, S. S. (1981). Equivalence of certain chi-square test statistics. *American Statistician*, *35*, 250–253. **12**

Yates, F. (1934). Contingency tables involving small numbers and the χ^2 test. *Journal of the Royal Statistical Society*, Supplement *[subsequently, Series B (Methodological)]*, *1*, 217–239. **2**

Yule, G. U. (1900). On the association of attributes in statistics: with illustrations from the material of the childhood society, &c. *Philosophical Transactions of the Royal Society of London*, Series A, *194*, 257–319. **9**

Yule, G. U. (1911). *An introduction to the theory of statistics*. London: Griffin (10th ed., 1932). **3**

Yule, G. U. (1912). On the methods of measuring association between two attributes. *Journal of the Royal Statistical Society*, *75*, 579–652 (with discussion). **9, 13**

Zelen, M., and Severo, N. C. (1964). Probability functions. In M. Abramowitz and I. A. Stegun (eds.), *Handbook of mathematical functions with formulas, graphs, and mathematical tables* (Applied Mathematics Series, No. 55). Washington: National Bureau of Standards (reprinted New York: Dover, 1972; New York: Wiley, 1972). **13, A**

Author Index

Subject Index

F

factor 52
  elimination of 140ff
familywise error rate 12
Fisher's exact test 44ff
Freeman-Tukey deviate 136

G

G^2 (likelihood-ratio statistic) 36
generalized linear model 347
Gini index 130
Goodman-Kruskal gamma 223, 383
goodness of fit statistic (Pearson X^2) 19, 22
graph 54
graphical models 156ff
  decomposition of 166ff
Greek alphabet 7, 406
"GSK model" 304ff

H

heroin users (example) 183, 192, 202ff
heterogeneous row- or column-association
    models 360
hierarchical model 70
hierarchy of models 67, 107, 159
hierarchy principle 70, 105
homogeneity, hypothesis of 23
homogeneity, marginal 263, 313
homogeneous association (3-way table) 63
homogeneous row- or column-association
    models 360
hypergeometric distribution 44
hypothesis testing 9

I

identification constraint 34, 113
independence
  complete 54
  conditional 61
  hypothesis of 23
  notation for ($\perp\!\!\!\perp$) 52, 61
  single factor 58
independent variable 178
indirect model 109
information 130, 230

conditional transmission of 235
  transmission of 230ff
interaction 72, 319
invariance, palindromic and permutational 347
iterated least squares estimation 107
iterative proportional fitting algorithm 107ff

K

kappa coefficient (agreement) 238ff, 255, 265,
    279
Kendall tau 382, 383

L

latent scale values 361ff
lattice of models 67, 107
least-squares estimate 95, 300ff, 316
  compared to maximum-likelihood 341
least-squares models 300ff
likelihood 93
likelihood ratio 100
likelihood-ratio test 36, 100
likelihood-ratio test statistic (G^2) 36, 102
linear trend 377
log-bilinear model 280
log-linear model 33
  parameter estimates under 112
log-odds ratio 221
logarithms 33, 130
logit 180, 364
logit models 181ff, 325ff
  with multilevel categories 186ff
Luce choice model 255ff, 262, 266
L^2 (likelihood-ratio statistic) 36

M

main effect 72, 319
marginal association (Brown) 211
marginal homogeneity 263, 313
maximum-correlation model 285ff
  multiterm 290ff
maximum-likelihood estimate 93, 109
  compared to least-squares 341
minimum chi-square estimate 95
minimum discrimination information estimate
    107
minimum modified chi-square statistic 308